Handbook of Research on Trends and Future Directions in Big Data and Web Intelligence

Noor Zaman
King Faisal University, Saudi Arabia

Mohamed Elhassan Seliaman
King Faisal University, Saudi Arabia

Mohd Fadzil Hassan
Universiti Teknologi PETRONAS, Malaysia

Fausto Pedro Garcia Marquez
Campus Universitario s/n ETSII of Ciudad Real, Spain

A volume in the Advances in Data Mining and
Database Management (ADMDM) Book Series

Information Science
REFERENCE
An Imprint of IGI Global

Managing Director:	Lindsay Johnston
Managing Editor:	Keith Greenberg
Director of Intellectual Property & Contracts:	Jan Travers
Acquisitions Editor:	Kayla Wolfe
Production Editor:	Christina Henning
Development Editor:	Caitlyn Martin
Cover Design:	Jason Mull

Published in the United States of America by
Information Science Reference (an imprint of IGI Global)
701 E. Chocolate Avenue
Hershey PA, USA 17033
Tel: 717-533-8845
Fax: 717-533-8661
E-mail: cust@igi-global.com
Web site: http://www.igi-global.com

Library of Congress Cataloging-in-Publication Data

Handbook of research on trends and future directions in big data and web intelligence / Noor Zaman, Mohamed Elhassan Seliaman, Mohd Fadzil Hassan, and Fausto Pedro Garcia Marquez, editors.
   pages cm
Includes bibliographical references and index.
 ISBN 978-1-4666-8505-5 (hardcover) -- ISBN 978-1-4666-8506-2 (ebook) 1. Big data. 2. Cloud computing. 3. Natural language processing. I. Zaman, Noor, 1972- editor.
 QA76.9.D32H36 2015
 005.7--dc23
                          2015010287

This book is published in the IGI Global book series Advances in Data Mining and Database Management (ADMDM) (ISSN: 2327-1981; eISSN: 2327-199X)

British Cataloguing in Publication Data
A Cataloguing in Publication record for this book is available from the British Library.

For electronic access to this publication, please contact: eresources@igi-global.com.

Advances in Data Mining and Database Management (ADMDM) Book Series

David Taniar
Monash University, Australia

ISSN: 2327-1981
EISSN: 2327-199X

MISSION

With the large amounts of information available to organizations in today's digital world, there is a need for continual research surrounding emerging methods and tools for collecting, analyzing, and storing data.

The **Advances in Data Mining & Database Management (ADMDM)** series aims to bring together research in information retrieval, data analysis, data warehousing, and related areas in order to become an ideal resource for those working and studying in these fields. IT professionals, software engineers, academicians and upper-level students will find titles within the ADMDM book series particularly useful for staying up-to-date on emerging research, theories, and applications in the fields of data mining and database management.

COVERAGE

- Decision Support Systems
- Database Testing
- Quantitative Structure–Activity Relationship
- Text Mining
- Data Analysis
- Database Security
- Information Extraction
- Profiling Practices
- Educational Data Mining
- Factor Analysis

IGI Global is currently accepting manuscripts for publication within this series. To submit a proposal for a volume in this series, please contact our Acquisition Editors at Acquisitions@igi-global.com or visit: http://www.igi-global.com/publish/.

Titles in this Series

For a list of additional titles in this series, please visit: www.igi-global.com

Improving Knowledge Discovery through the Integration of Data Mining Techniques
Muhammad Usman (Shaheed Zulfikar Ali Bhutto Institute of Science and Technology, Pakistan)
Information Science Reference • copyright 2015 • 392pp • H/C (ISBN: 9781466685130) • US $225.00 (our price)

Modern Computational Models of Semantic Discovery in Natural Language
Jan Žižka (Mendel University in Brno, Czech Republic) and František Dařena (Mendel University in Brno, Czech Republic)
Information Science Reference • copyright 2015 • 335pp • H/C (ISBN: 9781466686908) • US $215.00 (our price)

Mobile Technologies for Activity-Travel Data Collection and Analysis
Soora Rasouli (Eindhoven University of Technology, The Netherlands) and Harry Timmermans (Eindhoven University of Technology, The Netherlands)
Information Science Reference • copyright 2014 • 325pp • H/C (ISBN: 9781466661707) • US $225.00 (our price)

Biologically-Inspired Techniques for Knowledge Discovery and Data Mining
Shafiq Alam (University of Auckland, New Zealand) Gillian Dobbie (University of Auckland, New Zealand) Yun Sing Koh (University of Auckland, New Zealand) and Saeed ur Rehman (Unitec Institute of Technology, New Zealand)
Information Science Reference • copyright 2014 • 375pp • H/C (ISBN: 9781466660786) • US $265.00 (our price)

Data Mining and Analysis in the Engineering Field
Vishal Bhatnagar (Ambedkar Institute of Advanced Communication Technologies and Research, India)
Information Science Reference • copyright 2014 • 405pp • H/C (ISBN: 9781466660861) • US $225.00 (our price)

Handbook of Research on Cloud Infrastructures for Big Data Analytics
Pethuru Raj (IBM India Pvt Ltd, India) and Ganesh Chandra Deka (Ministry of Labour and Employment, India)
Information Science Reference • copyright 2014 • 570pp • H/C (ISBN: 9781466658646) • US $345.00 (our price)

Innovative Techniques and Applications of Entity Resolution
Hongzhi Wang (Harbin Institute of Technology, China)
Information Science Reference • copyright 2014 • 398pp • H/C (ISBN: 9781466651982) • US $205.00 (our price)

Innovative Document Summarization Techniques Revolutionizing Knowledge Understanding
Alessandro Fiori (IRCC, Institute for Cancer Research and Treatment, Italy)
Information Science Reference • copyright 2014 • 363pp • H/C (ISBN: 9781466650190) • US $175.00 (our price)

www.igi-global.com

701 E. Chocolate Ave., Hershey, PA 17033
Order online at www.igi-global.com or call 717-533-8845 x100
To place a standing order for titles released in this series, contact: cust@igi-global.com
Mon-Fri 8:00 am - 5:00 pm (est) or fax 24 hours a day 717-533-8661

Editorial Advisory Board

List of Contributors

Table of Contents

Section 2
Presenting Web Intelligence and Its Perspective

Section 3
Exploring the Current and Future Trends of Big Data and Web Intelligence

Detailed Table of Contents

Section 1
Presenting Big Data and Its Perspective

Chapter 1
Seema Ansari, University of Malaga, Spain & Institute of Business Management, Pakistan
Radha Mohanlal, Institute of Business Management, Pakistan
Javier Poncela, University of Malaga, Spain
Adeel Ansari, Universiti Teknologi Petronas, Malaysia
Komal Mohanlal, Institute of Business Administration, Pakistan

Combining vast amounts of heterogeneous data and increasing the processing power of existing database management tools is no doubt the emerging need of IT industry in coming years. The complexity and size of data sets that need to be acquired, analyzed, stored, sorted or transferred has spiked in the recent years. Due to the tremendously increasing volume of multiple data types, creating Big Data applications that can extract the valuable trends and relationships required for further processes or deriving useful results is quite challenging task. Companies, corporate organizations or be it government agencies, all need to analyze and execute Big Data implementation to pave new paths of productivity and innovation. This chapter discusses the emerging technology of modern era: Big Data with detailed description of the three V's (Variety, Velocity and Volume). Further chapters will enable to understand the concepts of data mining and big data analysis, Potentials of Big Data in five domains i.e. Healthcare, Public sector, Retail, Manufacturing and Personal location Data.

This chapter revises the most important aspects in how computing infrastructures should be configured and intelligently managed to fulfill the most notably security aspects required by Big Data applications. One of them is privacy. It is a pertinent aspect to be addressed because users share more and more personal data and content through their devices and computers to social networks and public clouds. So, a secure framework to social networks is a very hot topic research. This last topic is addressed in one of the two sections of the current chapter with case studies. In addition, the traditional mechanisms to support security such as firewalls and demilitarized zones are not suitable to be applied in computing systems to support Big Data. SDN is an emergent management solution that could become a convenient mechanism to implement security in Big Data systems, as we show through a second case study at the end of the chapter. This also discusses current relevant work and identifies open issues.

Chapter 3

Big data is a buzzword today, and security of big data is a big concern. Traditional security standards and technologies cannot scale up to deliver reliable and effective security solutions in the big data environment. This chapter covers big data security management from concepts to real-world issues. By identifying and laying out the major challenges, industry trends, legal and regulatory environments, security principles, security management frameworks, security maturity model, big data analytics in solving security problems, current research results, and future research issues, this chapter provides researchers and practitioners with a timely reference and guidance in securing big data processing, management, and applications.

The meteoric rise of smart devices in dominating worldwide consumer electronics market complemented with data-hungry mobile applications and widely accessible heterogeneous networks e.g. 3G, 4G LTE and Wi-Fi, have elevated Mobile Internet from a 'nice-to-have' to a mandatory feature on every mobile computing device. This has spurred serious data traffic congestion on mobile networks as a consequence. The nature of mobile network traffic today is more like little Data Tsunami, unpredictable in terms of time and location while pounding the access networks with waves of data streams. This chapter explains how Big Data analytics can be applied to understand the Device-Network-Application (DNA) dimensions in annotating mobile connectivity routine and how Simplify, a seamless network discovery solution developed at Nextwave Technology, can be extended to leverage crowd intelligence in predicting and collaboratively shaping mobile data traffic towards achieving real-time network congestion control. The chapter also presents the Big Data architecture hosted on Google Cloud Platform powering the backbone behind Simplify in realizing its intelligent traffic steering solution.

Section 2
Presenting Web Intelligence and Its Perspective

Chapter 5

Jafreezal Jaafar, Universiti Teknologi PETRONAS, Malaysia
Kamaluddeen Usman Danyaro, Universiti Teknologi PETRONAS, Malaysia
M. S. Liew, Universiti Teknologi PETRONAS, Malaysia

This chapter discusses about the veracity of data. The veracity issue is the challenge of imprecision in big data due to influx of data from diverse sources. To overcome this problem, this chapter proposes a fuzzy knowledge-based framework that will enhance the accessibility of Web data and solve the inconsistency in data model. D2RQ, protégé, and fuzzy Web Ontology Language applications were used for configuration and performance. The chapter also provides the completeness fuzzy knowledge-based algorithm, which was used to determine the robustness and adaptability of the knowledge base. The result shows that the D2RQ is more scalable with respect to performance comparison. Finally, the conclusion and future lines of the research were provided.

Chapter 6

José Moura, Instituto Universitario de Lisboa, Portugal & Instituto de Telecomunicações, Portugal
Fernando Batista, Instituto Universitario de Lisboa, Portugal
Elsa Cardoso, Instituto Universitario de Lisboa, Portugal
Luís Nunes, Instituto Universitario de Lisboa, Portugal & Instituto de Telecomunicações, Portugal

This chapter details how Big Data can be used and implemented in networking and computing infrastructures. Specifically, it addresses three main aspects: the timely extraction of relevant knowledge from heterogeneous, and very often unstructured large data sources; the enhancement on the performance of processing and networking (cloud) infrastructures that are the most important foundational pillars of Big Data applications or services; and novel ways to efficiently manage network infrastructures with high-level composed policies for supporting the transmission of large amounts of data with distinct requisites (video vs. non-video). A case study involving an intelligent management solution to route data traffic with diverse requirements in a wide area Internet Exchange Point is presented, discussed in the context of Big Data, and evaluated.

Chapter 7

The availability of a huge amount of heterogeneous data from different sources to the Internet has been termed as the problem of Big Data. Clustering is widely used as a knowledge discovery tool that separate the data into manageable parts. There is a need of clustering algorithms that scale on big databases. In this chapter we have explored various schemes that have been used to tackle the big databases. Statistical features have been extracted and most important and relevant features have been extracted from the given dataset. Reduce and irrelevant features have been eliminated and most important features have been selected by genetic algorithms (GA).Clustering with reduced feature sets requires lower computational time and resources. Experiments have been performed at standard datasets and results indicate that the proposed scheme based clustering offers high clustering accuracy. To check the clustering quality various quality measures have been computed and it has been observed that the proposed methodology results improved significantly. It has been observed that the proposed technique offers high quality clustering.

Chapter 8

Condition Monitoring (CM) is the process of determining the state of a system according to a certain number of parameters. This 'condition' is tracked over time to detect any developing fault or non desired behaviour. As the Information and Communication Technologies (ICT) continue expanding the range of possible applications and gaining industrial maturity, the appearing of new sensor technologies such as Macro Fiber Composites (MFC) has opened a new range of possibilities for addressing a CM in industrial scenarios. The huge amount of data collected by MFC could overflow most conventional monitoring systems, requiring new approaches to take true advantage of the data. Big Data approach makes it possible to take profit of tons of data, integrating in the appropriate algorithms and technologies in a unified platform. This chapter proposes a real time condition monitoring approach, in which the system is continuously monitored allowing an online analysis.

Prediction of missing associations can be viewed as one of the most fundamental problems in the machine learning. The main objective of prediction of missing associations is to determine decisions for the missing associations. In real world problems, prediction of missing associations is must because absence of associations in the attribute values may have information to predict the decision for entrepreneurs. Based on decision theory, in the past many mathematical models such as naïve Bayes structure, human composed network structure, Bayesian network modeling etc. were developed. However, these theories have certain limitations. In order to overcome the limitations, rough computing is hybridized with Bayesian classification. This chapter discusses various techniques for predicting missing associations to obtain meaningful decision from information system. A real life example is provided to show the viability of the proposed research.

The growing amount of available data generates complex problems when they need to be treated. Usually these data come from different sources and inform about different issues, however, in many occasions these data can be interrelated in order to gather strategic information that is useful for Decision Making processes in multitude of business. For a qualitatively and quantitatively analysis of a complex Decision Making process is critical to employ a correct method due to the large number of operations required. With this purpose, this chapter presents an approach employing Binary Decision Diagram applied to the Logical Decision Tree. It allows addressing a Main Problem by establishing different causes, called Basic Causes and their interrelations. The cases that have a large number of Basic Causes generate important computational costs because it is a NP-hard type problem. Moreover, this chapter presents a new approach in order to analyze big Logical Decision Trees. However, the size of the Logical Decision Trees is not the unique factor that affects to the computational cost but the procedure of resolution can widely vary this cost (ordination of Basic Causes, number of AND/OR gates, etc.) A new approach to reduce the complexity of the problem is hereby presented. It makes use of data derived from simpler problems that requires less computational costs for obtaining a good solution. An exact solution is not provided by this method but the approximations achieved have a low deviation from the exact.

Chapter 11

The arrival of E-commerce systems has contributed a lot to the economy and also played a vital role in collecting a huge amount of transactional data in the form of online orders and web enquiries, with such a huge volume of data it is getting difficult day by day to analyse business and consumer behaviour. There is a greater need for business analytical tools to help decision makers understand data properly - and understanding data will lead to amazing things such as hidden trends, effective resource utilisation, decision making ability and understanding business and its core values.

Section 3
Exploring the Current and Future Trends of Big Data and Web Intelligence

Chapter 12

The Politics of Access to Information: Exploring the Development of Software Platforms and Communications Hardware in the Digital Age 233

Shefali Virkar, University of Oxford, UK

Over the last few decades, unprecedented advances in communications technology have collapsed vast spatial and temporal differences, and made it possible for people to form connections in a manner not thought possible before. Centred chiefly on information, this revolution has transformed the way in which people around the world think, work, share, and communicate. Information and Communication Technologies (ICTs) promise a future of a highly interconnected world, wherein action is not limited by physical boundaries, and constrained physical space is replaced by a virtual 'cyberspace' not subject to traditional hierarchies and power relations. But is the promise of ICTs chimerical? To tackle these issues, central to the global policy debate over the potential development contributions of Information and Communication Technologies, and to examine whether and the extent to which disparities in access to ICTs exist, this book chapter provides a demonstration of the ways in which ICTs may be used as tools to further global economic, social, and political advancement, to shape actor behaviour, and to enhance institutional functioning; particularly in the Third World.

Chapter 13

Big Data and Data Modelling for Manufacturing Information Systems 266

Norman Gwangwava, Tshwane University of Technology, South Africa
Khumbulani Mpofu, Tshwane University of Technology, South Africa
Samson Mhlanga, National University of Science and Technology, Zimbabwe

The evolving Information and Communication Technologies (ICTs) has not spared the manufacturing industry. Modern ICT based solutions have shown a significant improvement in manufacturing industries' value stream. Paperless manufacturing, evolved due to complete automation of factories. The chapter articulates various Machine-to-Machine (M2M) technologies, big data and data modelling requirements for manufacturing information systems. Manufacturing information systems have unique requirements which distinguish them from conventional Management Information Systems. Various modelling technologies and standards exist for manufacturing information systems. The manufacturing field has unique data that require capturing and processing at various phases of product, service and factory life cycle. Authors review developments in modern ERP/CRM, PDM/PLM, SCM, and MOM/MES systems. Data modelling methods for manufacturing information systems that include STEP/STEP-NC, XML and UML are also covered in the chapter. A case study for a computer aided process planning system for a sheet metal forming company is also presented.

Chapter 14

Modeling Big Data Analytics with a Real-Time Executable Specification Language 289

Amir A. Khwaja, King Faisal University, Saudi Arabia

Big data explosion has already happened and the situation is only going to exacerbate with such a high number of data sources and high-end technology prevalent everywhere, generating data at a frantic pace. One of the most important aspects of big data is being able to capture, process, and analyze data as it is happening in real-time to allow real-time business decisions. Alternate approaches must be investigated especially consisting of highly parallel and real-time computations for big data processing. The chapter presents RealSpec real-time specification language that may be used for the modeling of big data analytics due to the inherent language features needed for real-time big data processing such as concurrent processes, multi-threading, resource modeling, timing constraints, and exception handling. The chapter provides an overview of RealSpec and applies the language to a detailed big data event recognition case study to demonstrate language applicability to big data framework and analytics modeling.

Chapter 15

In IoT, data management is a big problem due to the connectivity of billions of devices, objects, processes generating big data. Since the Things are not following any specific (common) standard, so analysis of such data becomes a big challenge. There is a need to elaborate about the characteristics of IoT based data to find out the available and applicable solutions. Such kind of study also directs to realize the need of new techniques to cope up with such challenges. Due to the heterogeneity of connected nodes, different data rates and formats it is getting a huge challenge to deal with such variety of data. As IoT is providing processing nodes in quantity in form of smart nodes, it is presenting itself a good platform for big data analysis. In this chapter, characteristics of big data and requirements for big data analysis are highlighted. Considering the big source of data generation as well as the plausible suitable platform of such huge data analysis, the associated challenges are also underlined.

Chapter 16

In this chapter, we investigate the role of influential people in an Online Social Network. We introduce a navigation approach to locate influential nodes in Online Social Networks. The purpose of quantifying influence in Online Social Networks is to determine influence within the members of an Online Social Networks and then using influence for navigation in such networks. We find out that we can take advantage of influential people in Online Social Networks to reach a target node in such networks. We utilize total number of direct friends of each node, total number of shared neighbors, the total number of common attributes, the total number of unique attributes, the distance to target node, and past visited nodes. We present an algorithm that takes advantage of influential people to reach a target in the network. Our navigation algorithm returns a path between two nodes in an average of ten percent less iterations, with a maximum of eighty percent less iterations, and only relies on public attributes of a node in the network.

With the advancement of technology we are heading towards a paperless environment. But there are still a large numbers of documents that exist in paper format in our daily lives. Thus the need to digitize these paper documents, archive them and view them at all times has arisen. The number of documents of a small organization may be in thousands, millions or even more. This chapter presents comparative analysis of different programming languages and libraries where it is intended to parallel process a huge stream of images which undergo unpredictable arrival of the images and variation in time. Since the parallelism can be implemented at different levels, different algorithms and techniques have also been discussed. It also presents the state of the art and discussion of various existing technical solutions to implement the parallelization on a hybrid platform for the real time processing of the images contained in a stream. Experimental results obtained using Apache Hadoop in combination with OpenMP have also been discussed.

In this chapter, we will discuss how "big data" is effective in "Social Networks" which will bring huge opportunities but difficulties though challenges yet ahead to the communities. Firstly, Social Media is a strategy for broadcasting, while Social Networking is a tool and a utility for connecting with others. For this perspective, we will introduce the characteristic and fundamental models of social networks and discuss the existing security & privacy for the user awareness of social networks in part I. Secondly, the technological built web based internet application of social media with Web2.0 application have transformed users to allow creation and exchange of user-generated content which play a role in big data of unstructured contents as well as structured contents. Subsequently, we will introduce the characteristic and landscaping of the big data in part II. Finally, we will discuss the algorithms for marketing and social media mining which play a role how big data fit into the social media data.

Regression testing is important activity during the maintenance phase. An important work during maintenance of the software is to find impact of change. One of the essential attributes of Software is change i.e. quality software is more vulnerable to change and provide facilitation and ease for developer to do required changes. Modification plays vital role in the software development so it is highly important to find the impact of that modification or to identify the change in the software. In software testing that issue gets more attention because after change we have to identify impact of change and have to keenly observe what has happened or what will happen after that particular change that we have made or going to make in software. After change software testing team has to modify its testing strategy and have to come across with new test cases to efficiently perform the testing activity during the software development Regression testing is performed when the software is already tested and now some change is made to it. Important thing is to adjust those tests which were generated in the previous testing processes of the software. This study will present an approach by analyzing VDM (Vienna Development Methods) to find impact of change which will describe that how we can find the change and can analyze the change in the software i.e. impact of change that has been made in software. This approach will fulfill the purpose of classifying the test cases from original test suite into three classes obsolete, re-testable, and reusable test cases. This technique will not only classify the original test cases but will also generate new test cases required for the purpose of regression testing.

The web is a rich data mining source which is dynamic and fast growing, providing great opportunities which are often not exploited. Web data represent a real challenge to traditional data mining techniques due to its huge amount and the unstructured nature. Web logs contain information about the interactions between visitors and the website. Analyzing these logs provides insights into visitors' behavior, usage patterns, and trends. Web usage mining, also known as web log mining, is the process of applying data mining techniques to discover useful information hidden in web server's logs. Web logs are primarily used by Web administrators to know how much traffic they get and to detect broken links and other types of errors. Web usage mining extracts useful information that can be beneficial to a number of application areas such as: web personalization, website restructuring, system performance improvement, and business intelligence. The Web usage mining process involves three main phases: pre-processing, pattern discovery, and pattern analysis. Various preprocessing techniques have been proposed to extract information from log files and group primitive data items into meaningful, lighter level abstractions that are suitable for mining, usually in forms of visitors' sessions. Major data mining techniques in web usage mining pattern discovery are: clustering, association analysis, classification, and sequential patterns discovery. This chapter discusses the process of web usage mining, its procedure, methods, and patterns discovery techniques. The chapter also presents a practical example using real web log data.

Foreword

Current era have higher impact on humans daily lives by linking them with internet. The vast share of that communication based on digital data and vast volumes generated from several sources including Internet documents, social media, smart mobile devices, sensory data and Big Science extra resulted in what is referred to as "Big Data". The management of such huge data in terms of common sharing and providing access timely and safely becomes one main challenge. The emerging applications providing solutions for this big data challenge along with the revolution in database technologies have transformed the way organizations manage and use their data.

Web intelligence is an emerging area of application of business intelligence, business analytics and predictive modeling on big data sources such as booming social media, sensory data and mobile devices, in order to enhance the competitive advantage of organizations. Among emerging technologies linked with big data and web intelligence are cloud computing, parallel computing, no-SQL, map-reduce, etc. Current trends and future directions are having high importance in big data and web intelligence applications such as natural language processing, personalized medicines, sentiment mining, machine translation, etc. But it still needs to be more considered, for getting more accurate and precise results by applying new trends and techniques including merging the concepts of both.

This book provides window to academic and industrial communities with recent advances in development, application and impact of new big-data platforms and technologies for exploiting floods of big data sources. In addition this book encourages more research in big data and web intelligence technologies.

Shazia Noor Zaman
Institute of Higher Education, Pakistan

Shazia Noor Zaman *is currently working as a faculty member at Institute of Higher Education in Computer Science Department, Karachi Pakistan. She received her bachelor and Masters in Computer Sciences from Karachi University, Sindh Pakistan. She further extended her achievement by achieving his PhD from Pakistan. Prior to the current appointment, she served as Assistant Professor at different Universities. She had supervised several Masters Students in her career. As a lecturer, she has taught many courses ranging from Mobile Computing, Big Data, Data Mining, Data Structures, Structured Programming, System Analysis and Design, Software Engineering, Artificial Intelligence among others. Her research interests are in the area of Software Engineering, Mobile Computing, Big Data and Service Oriented Architecture (SOA). She is actively involved in research works focusing on these areas and has secured numerous research grants, she has several publications on her credit.*

Preface

Current era have higher impact on humans daily lives by linking them with internet. The vast share of that communication based on digital data and vast volumes generated from several sources including Internet documents, social media, smart mobile devices, sensory data and Big Science extra resulted in what is referred to as "Big Data". As defined by Gartner "Big data" is extremely huge data characterized by the three (Vs): Volume, Velocity and Variety and the demand for new innovative efficient approaches of processing that support decision making. The management of such huge dynamic data in terms of common sharing and providing access timely and safely becomes one main challenge. The emerging applications providing solutions for this big data challenge along with the revolution in database technologies have transformed the way organizations manage and use their data.

Web intelligence is an emerging area application of business intelligence, business analytics and predictive modeling on big data sources such as booming social media, sensory data and mobile devices, in order to enhance the competitive advantage of organizations. Among emerging technologies linked with big data and web intelligence are cloud computing, parallel computing, no-SQL, map-reduce, etc. Current trends and future directions are having high importance in big data and web intelligence applications such as natural language processing, personalized medicines, sentiment mining, machine translation, etc. But it still needs to be more considered, for getting more accurate and precise results by applying new trends and techniques including merging the concepts of both.

The ultimate goal of this volume is to provide the academic and industrial communities with recent and up-to-date research findings, reviews and applications of Big Data and Web Intelligence in a wide spectrum of domains. This book editing has the dual objectives. The first objective is to encourage more research in big data and web intelligence technologies. The second objective is to publish the best research being conducted today. Specifically, we seek to explore how, given its current stage of development big data and web intelligence applications and innovations.

ORGANIZATION OF THE BOOK

This book consists of 21peer reviewed invited chapters authored by several international researchers around the world. Book is divided into the following three sections:

Section 1: Introducing big data and its perspectives
Section 2: Presenting web intelligence and its perspective
Section 3: Exploring the current & future trends of big data and web intelligence.

Section 1 entitled "Introducing Big Data and Its Perspectives" is to specify strictly about big data, basing on personal invitations. The second section is to specify about web intelligence and leave the third part open to general chapter submissions including merging of big data and web intelligence.

A brief description of each of the chapters follows:

SECTION 1: PRESENTING BIG DATA AND ITS PERSPECTIVE

Chapters

Chapter 1: Importance of Big Data

This chapter discusses the emerging technology of modern era: Big Data with detailed description of the three V's (Variety, Velocity and Volume). Further sections of this chapter will enable to understand the concepts of data mining and big data analysis, Potentials of Big Data in five domains i.e. Healthcare, Public sector, Retail, Manufacturing and Personal location Data and how this large amount of data is increasing rapidly as compared to the advancement in computing resources and which new technologies and architectures are needed to extract value from it by capturing and analysis processes. The chapter also discusses the privacy and security issues concerning Big Data.

Chapter 2: Security and Privacy Issues of Big Data

This chapter covers some important aspects in how computing infrastructures should be configured and intelligently managed to fulfill the most notably security aspects required by Big Data applications. These aspects include: privacy, secure framework to social networks, the traditional mechanisms to support security, SDN as an emergent management solution that could become a convenient mechanism to implement security in Big Data systems. The chapter also discusses current relevant work and identifies open issues.

Chapter 3: Big Data Security Management

This chapter covers big data security management from concepts to real-world issues. It identifies the major challenges, industry trends, legal and regulatory environments, security principles, security management frameworks, security maturity model, big data analytics in solving security problems, current research results, and future research issues.

Chapter 4: Big Data in Telecommunications: Seamless Network Discovery and Traffic Steering with Crowd Intelligence

This chapter explains how Big Data analytics can be applied to understand the Device-Network-Application (DNA) dimensions in annotating mobile connectivity routine and how Simplify, a seamless network discovery solution developed at Next wave Technology, can be extended to leverage crowd intelligence in predicting and collaboratively shaping mobile data traffic towards achieving real-time network congestion control. The chapter also presents the Big Data architecture hosted on Google Cloud Platform powering the backbone behind Simplify in realizing its intelligent traffic steering solution.

SECTION 2: PRESENTING WEB INTELLIGENCE AND ITS PERSPECTIVE

Chapters

Chapter 5: Web Intelligence: A Fuzzy Knowledge-Based Framework for the Enhancement of Querying and Accessing Web Data

This chapter discusses about the retrospective background knowledge on Web intelligence, big data and the uncertainty. It also proposes a framework that includes: the general architecture of the system and fuzzy ontology. In addition, the implementation process has been presented.

Chapter 6: Intelligent Management and Efficient Operation of Big Data

This chapter describes how Machine Learning methods and related technologies can be used to extract relevant knowledge from heterogeneous and massive amounts of data. Second, new challenges that Big Data applications and services are imposing in network infrastructures are highlighted and discussed. Third, a practical scenario concerning the efficient transmission of Big Data heterogeneous traffic through the wide area network among diverse public cloud providers is included in the chapter.

Chapter 7: Big Data Mining Based on Computational Intelligence and Fuzzy Clustering

This chapter explores various schemes that have been used to tackle the big databases. Statistical features have been extracted and most important and relevant features have been extracted from the given dataset. Reduce and irrelevant features have been eliminated and most important features have been selected by genetic algorithms (GA). Experiments have been performed at standard datasets and results indicate that the proposed scheme based clustering offers high clustering accuracy. To check the clustering quality various quality measures have been computed and it has been observed that the proposed methodology results improved significantly. It has been observed that the proposed technique offers high quality clustering.

Chapter 8: Big Data and Web Intelligence for Condition Monitoring: A Case Study on Wind Turbines

This chapter proposes a real time condition monitoring approach, in which the system is continuously monitored allowing online analysis and actions. The system is fed by data streams received from different sensors adequately located on the machine.

Chapter 9: Prediction of Missing Associations from Information System Using Intelligent Techniques

This chapter discusses various machine learning techniques that are used in extracting knowledge from an information system either qualitative or quantitative. The chapter is organized as follows: It starts with an introduction followed by information system. It also presents a model to process a real life application of predicting the decision values for the missing associations in the attribute values.

Chapter 10: Big Data and Web Intelligence: Improving the Efficiency on Decision Making Process via BDD

This paper presents a new approach in order to analyze big LDT. A new approach to reduce the complexity of the problem is hereby presented. It makes use of data derived from simpler problems that requires less computational costs for obtaining a good solution. An exact solution is not provided by this method but the approximations achieved have a low deviation from the exact.

Chapter 11: Web 2.0 Mash-Up System for Real Time Data Visualization and Analysis Using OSS

This chapter proposes an information visualization framework through data-mashups using web 2.0 technologies, which will represent highly complex data in visualized form. The framework is targeted to reduce technical requirements of system usage, as the indented system is to provide customized data representation for multiple die-missions data usage. Decision making within the system is accomplished using built-in a pre-developed logical set of rules based on the data types and their sources. The architecture design will be so versatile that each data element could be utilized in the visualization process upon request from the user for analysis and reporting.

SECTION 3: EXPLORING THE CURRENT AND FUTURE TRENDS OF BIG DATA AND WEB INTELLIGENCE

Chapters

Chapter 12: The Politics of Access to Information: Exploring the Development of Software Platforms and Communications Hardware in the Digital Age

This chapter provides a demonstration of the ways in which ICTs may be used as tools to further global economic, social, and political development, to shape actor behavior, and to enhance institutional functioning particularly in the third World.

Chapter 13: Big Data and Data Modelling for Manufacturing Information Systems

This chapter reviews recent developments in modern manufacturing information systems. This review covers: ERP/CRM, PDM/PLM, SCM, and MOM/MES systems. The chapter also covers data modelling methods for manufacturing information systems. In addition, a case study for a computer aided process planning system in the manufacturing domain is presented.

Chapter 14: Modeling Big Data Analytics with a Real-Time Executable Specification Language

The issues of capturing, processing, and analyzing in a real-time base are other challenging aspects of big data. This chapter presents highly parallel and real-time computations for big data processing using an executable real-time specification language based on the dataflow programming model.

Chapter 15: Big Data Analysis in IoT

There is a need to elaborate about the characteristics of IoT based data to find out the available and applicable solutions. Such kind of study also directs to realize the need of new techniques to cope up with such challenges. Due to the heterogeneity of connected nodes, different data rates and formats it is getting a huge challenge to deal with such variety of data. As IoT is providing processing nodes in quantity in form of smart nodes, it is presenting itself a good platform for big data analysis. In this chapter, characteristics of big data and requirements for big data analysis are highlighted. Considering the big source of data generation as well as the plausible suitable platform of such huge data analysis, the associated challenges are also underlined.

Chapter 16: Navigation in Online Social Networks

This chapter investigates the role of influential people in an Online Social Network. It introduces a navigation approach to locate influential nodes in Online Social Networks. The purpose of quantifying influence in Online Social Networks is to determine influence within the members of an Online Social Networks and then using influence for navigation in such networks.

Chapter 17: Comparative Analysis of Efficient Platforms: Scalable Algorithms and Parallel Paradigms for Large Scale Image Processing

This chapter presents comparative analysis of different programming languages and libraries where it is intended to parallel process a huge stream of images which undergo unpredictable arrival of the images and variation in time. Since the parallelism can be implemented at different levels, different algorithms and techniques have also been discussed. It also presents the state of the art and discussion of various existing technical solutions to implement the parallelization on a hybrid platform for the real time processing of the images contained in a stream. Experimental results obtained using Apache Hadoop in combination with OpenMP have also been discussed.

Chapter 18: The Effectiveness of Big Data in Social Networks

This chapter introduces Big Data as related to Social Networks. It first describes the issues of characteristic, model, security & privacy, demographic of social networks and analysis in. Second, Characteristic and landscaping of the big data in are presented. The third part of the chapter highlights fundamental concepts and algorithms for social network, big data and social media mining.

Chapter 19: Analysis of VDM++ in Regression Test Suite

In software testing that issue gets more attention because after change we have to identify impact of change and have to keenly observe what has happened or what will happen after that particular change that we have made or going to make in software. After change software testing team has to modify its testing strategy and have to come across with new test cases to efficiently perform the testing activity during the software development Regression testing is performed when the software is already tested and now some change is made to it. Important thing is to adjust those tests which were generated in the previous testing processes of the software. This study will present an approach by analyzing VDM (Vienna Development Methods) to find impact of change which will describe that how we can find the change and can analyze the change in the software i.e. impact of change that has been made in software.

Chapter 20: Web Usage Mining and the Challenge of Big Data: A Review of Emerging Tools and Techniques

The Web usage mining process involves three main phases: pre-processing, pattern discovery, and pattern analysis. Various preprocessing techniques have been proposed to extract information from log files and group primitive data items into meaningful, lighter level abstractions that are suitable for mining, usually in forms of visitors' sessions. Major data mining techniques in web usage mining pattern discovery are: clustering, association analysis, classification, and sequential patterns discovery. This chapter discusses the process of web usage mining, its procedure, methods, and patterns discovery techniques. The chapter also presents a practical example using real web log data.

Noor Zaman
King Faisal University, Saudi Arabia

Acknowledgment

I would like to acknowledge the help of all the people and close reference research friends involved in this project and, more specifically, to the authors and reviewers that took part in the review process. Without their support, this book would not have become a reality.

First, the editors would like to thank each one of the authors for their contributions. Our sincere gratitude goes to the chapter's authors who contributed their time and expertise to this book.

Second, the editors wish to acknowledge the valuable contributions of the reviewers regarding the improvement of quality, coherence, and content presentation of chapters. Most of the authors also served as referees; we highly appreciate their double task.

Noor Zaman
King Faisal University, Saudi Arabia

Section 1
Presenting Big Data and Its Perspective

Chapter 1
Importance of Big Data

Seema Ansari
University of Malaga, Spain & Institute of Business Management, Pakistan

Javier Poncela
University of Malaga, Spain

Adeel Ansari
Universiti Teknologi Petronas, Malaysia

Radha Mohanlal
Institute of Business Management, Pakistan

Komal Mohanlal
Institute of Business Administration, Pakistan

ABSTRACT

Combining vast amounts of heterogeneous data and increasing the processing power of existing database management tools is no doubt the emerging need of IT industry in coming years. The complexity and size of data sets that need to be acquired, analyzed, stored, sorted or transferred has spiked in the recent years. Due to the tremendously increasing volume of multiple data types, creating Big Data applications that can extract the valuable trends and relationships required for further processes or deriving useful results is quite challenging task. Companies, corporate organizations or be it government agencies, all need to analyze and execute Big Data implementation to pave new paths of productivity and innovation. This chapter discusses the emerging technology of modern era: Big Data with detailed description of the three V's (Variety, Velocity and Volume). Further chapters will enable to understand the concepts of data mining and big data analysis, Potentials of Big Data in five domains i.e. Healthcare, Public sector, Retail, Manufacturing and Personal location Data.

I. INTRODUCTION

Due to the advancement in sciences, engineering, and technology in recent years, the human endeavors and the social and economic activities have been generating tremendous amount of data which is referred to as Big Data. The 'Big' word in Big Data is referring to tremendous amount of data that is being generated in this modern era. Figure 1, Sources of Big Data include: online transactions, scientific experiments, research, emails, videos, audios, images, logs, events, genomic investigations, web posts, search engine queries, health records data, surveillance, geo spatial data, social networking interactions, texts and mobile phone applications, RFID scans and sensors (Eaton, Deroos, Deutsch, Lapis, & Zikopoulos, 2012), (Schneider, 2012).

DOI: 10.4018/978-1-4666-8505-5.ch001

Figure 1. A summary of various dimensions of Big Data
(Du, Z. 2013)

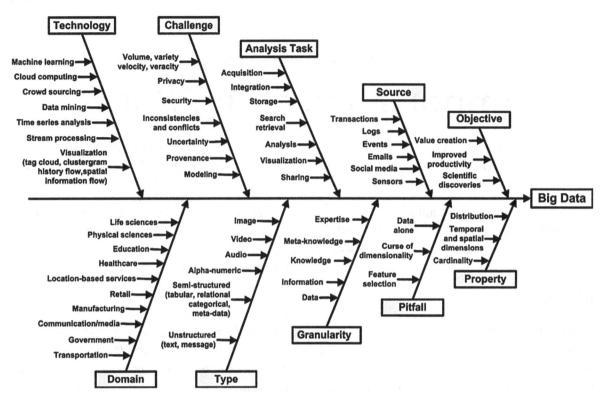

The traditional databases will not alone solve all aspects of Big data problem (Madden, 2012). We need more robust algorithms for machine learning that will be easier to apply. A data management ecosystem needs to be developed so that users can enforce consistency properties over it along with visualizing and understanding their algorithm result.

We can say that many domains and economic sectors can benefit from the big data push: life and physical sciences, medicine, education, healthcare, location-based services, manufacturing, retail, communication and media, government, transportation, banking, insurance, financial services, utilities, environment, and energy industry (Manyika, Chui, Brown, Bughin, Dobbs, Roxburgh, & Byers, 2011).

II. BACKGROUND

The phenomenon of Big Data gets more intensified and diversified with the passing years. Hence, to create Big Data applications to extract information from torrents of data becomes a challenging task for I.T. specialists and Data Analysts. Big Data Analysis has become the fertile ground for advancement of knowledge, innovation and enhanced decision-making process. In view of Dannah Boyd et.al (Du, 2013) modern society is the era of Big Data.

IBM indicates that everyday 2.5 Exabytes of data is created. Almost 90%of the existing world data has been produced in the last two years. It is interesting to know that 5 Exabytes of Data were created until 2003 but now this amount is generated merely in two days. In 2012, digital world of data was expanded to 2.72 zettabytes. It is predicted to double every two years, reaching about 8 zettabytes of data by 2015 (Intel IT Center, 2012)

Mobile subscription in the world has reached a massive figure i.e. 6 billion. Everyday 10 billion text messages are sent. With the growing technology it is predicted that by 2020 about 50 billion devices will be connected to internet. When we talk about social networking media, we encounter statistics which enable us to understand Big Data more deeply. For instance, face book has 955 million monthly active accounts using 70 different languages.140 billion friend connections, everyday 30 billion pieces of content and 2.7 billion likes and comments are posted. Twitter encounters 1 billion tweets from more than 140 million active users within 72 hours. Only Google has got more than one million servers around the world. It is predicted that within the next decade the amount of information will increase by 50 times. Though the number of data analysts and I.T. specialists will not increase with the same pace i.e. only by 1.5 times (Tankard, 2012). Many people think that Big Data is about Hadoop but in reality Hadoop is just subset of Big Data, Figure 2.

We can say that many domains and economic sectors can benefit from the values generated by big data analysis: Healthcare, administration, life and physical sciences, medicine, global personal location data, public sector, communication and media (Manyika, et al. 2011). Big Data promises its stakeholders increased productivity and innovation in diverse areas. The main objective of Big Data is to reveal secret patterns and hidden correlations-Big Data Analytics-from massive data sets having large heterogeneous and complex structures. The most challenging task is how to better utilize these data assets, including

Figure 2. Big Data is not just Hadoop
(Martin Pavlik, 2013).

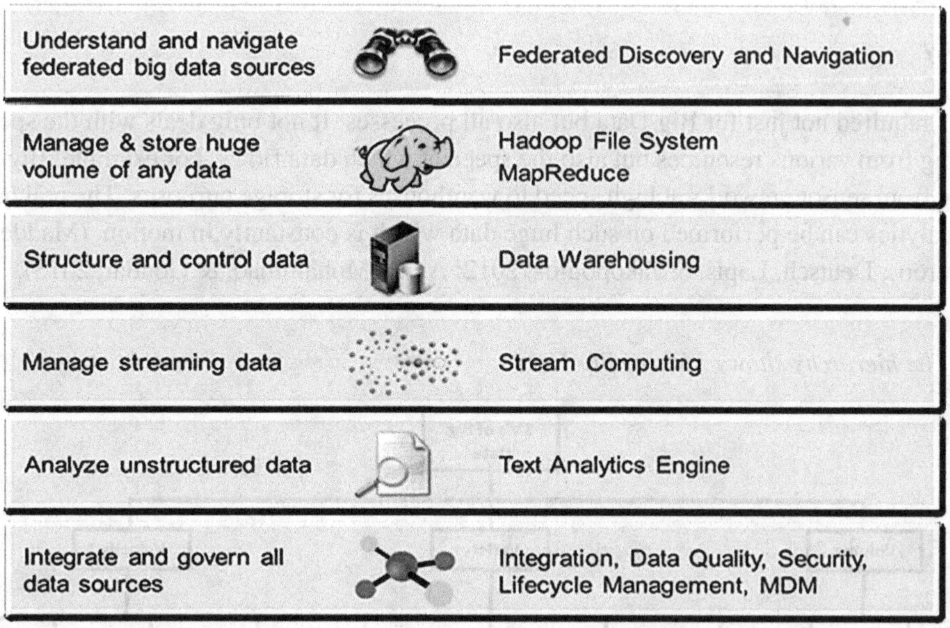

Understand and navigate federated big data sources		Federated Discovery and Navigation
Manage & store huge volume of any data		Hadoop File System MapReduce
Structure and control data		Data Warehousing
Manage streaming data		Stream Computing
Analyze unstructured data		Text Analytics Engine
Integrate and govern all data sources		Integration, Data Quality, Security, Lifecycle Management, MDM

physical and financial assets and human capital to reveal new values and insights to optimize decision making. Enterprises have realized the importance of Big Data in developing a competitive edge for business, retail, financial or service industries (Du, 2013).

III. PROPERTIES OF BIG DATA

A. The 3V's of Big Data

The data generated from biogeochemical, genomics, astronomy, medical records, private sector, military surveillance, financial services, retail, social networks, RFID, call detail records, sensor networks, click streams web logs, texts, atmospheric science and all other such sources is highly dynamic, heterogeneous and of multiple data types. Based on this, Big Data is mainly characterized by its three main components variety, velocity and its volume, as shown in Figure 3.

i. Variety

Since big data comes from various resources like social media sites, email, online transactions, sensor devices data due to which it is difficult to be handled by the existing traditional systems. Big Data is generally categorized into three types: structured, semi structured and unstructured. Structured data can be easily sorted out based on predefined tags and inserted in a data warehouse. Unstructured data is random and difficult to analyze. Semi-structured data lies between structured and unstructured data. Semi-structured data cannot be categorized into fixed fields but contains tags to separate data elements. (Seref, & Duygu, 2013)

ii. Velocity

Velocity is required not just for Big Data but also all processes. It not only deals with the speed of the data coming from various resources but also the speed at which data flows. For example: Big data may be flowing from sensor networks at high speed to warehouses for storage purposes. The real question is that the analytics can be performed on such huge data which is constantly in motion. (Madden, 2012), (Eaton, Deroos, Deutsch, Lapis, & Zikopoulos, 2012; Avita, Mohammad, & Goudar, 2013).

Figure 3. The hierarchy shows 3 V's of Big Data

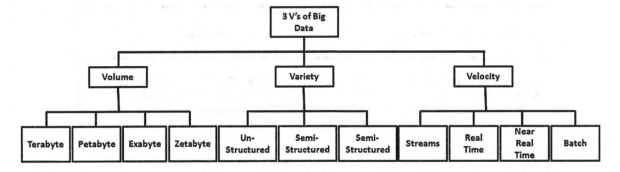

iii. Volume

As mentioned earlier, the 'Big' word in Big Data itself is used to define the volume. The size of data or volume is now larger than terabytes (1 terabyte=10^{12} Bytes) and petabytes (1 petabyte=10^{15} Bytes). It is expected to reach zettabytes (1 zettabyte= 10^{21} Bytes) in the nearby future. It is quite interesting to know that the social networking sites are producing data in order of terabytes every day.

The volume of Big Data is usually measured in Peta, Exa, Zetta or Yottabyte as given below.

- 1000 Gigabytes (GB) = 1 Terabyte (TB)
- 1000 Terabytes = 1 Petabyte (PB)
- 1000 Petabytes = 1 Exabyte (EB)
- 1000 Exabytes = 1 Zettabyte (ZB)
- 1000 Zettabytes = 1 Yottabyte (YB)

B. Value

The business leaders would be more concerned about adding more value to their business and getting more and more benefit whereas I.T professionals would have to concern with the technical issues concerning storage and processing. The need of future is to design a system which would be able to handle huge data more efficiently and effectively which appears as the first challenge. The second challenge is to filter all data that can add value to the business. This will enable the users to deduct important results and statistics from the filtered data obtained. These reports help these people to find the trends according to which they can change their business strategies and modify decisions and get more value out of their business.

C. Complexity

It is quite a challenging task to correlate and find important relationships across data coming from various sources. It is also necessary to connect and link relationships, organize into hierarchies otherwise data can quickly go out of data analyst's control.

D. Variability

Variability takes into account the inconsistencies of the data flow. Data loads become challenging to be maintained by using traditional approaches especially with the increase in usage of the social media.

E. Veracity

Detecting and correcting noisy and inconsistent data are important to conduct trustable analysis. Establishing trust in big data presents a huge challenge as the variety and number of sources grows tremendously.

IV. DATA MINING AND BIG DATA

It is generally thought that big data has a close relationship with data mining (Bughin, Chui, & Manyika, 2010; Gupta, Gupta, & Mohania, 2012). Primary goal of Big Data is extracting value from the large data sets. The data mining needs pre-processing and analytic method for finding the value (Sung-Hwan, Nam-Uk & Tai-Myoung, 2013). Indeed when we discuss about data mining the terms such as artificial intelligence, machine learning algorithms come into our mind. It is most likely that the scale of data management differs in size in Big Data to Data Mining techniques.

In (Xindong, Xingquan, Gong-Qing, & Wei, 2014), Figure 4, the concept of Big data processing network is shown using a three tier structure from inside out with considerations on data accessing and computing (Tier I), data privacy and domain knowledge (Tier II) which focuses on high level data semantics, application domain knowledge and mainly concerns with user-privacy. Tier III is based on challenges faced due to actual mining algorithms needed for Big Data processing.

Big Data is different from normally generated large volume of data in terms of its volume, variety and velocity (3 V's).These features distinguish data mining from Big Data. Relational Database management systems (RDBMS) use SQL (Structured Query Language) and focus on the ACID (Atomicity, Consistency, Integrity and Durability).Data management policy of classical DBMS is strict because RDBMS has been mainly used in the financial sector. On the other hand, big data covers many different data types. Thus, big data emphasize BASE (Basic Availability, Soft-state, and Eventual consistent) properties rather than ACID (Gupta & Mohania, 2012). In addition to this Big Data use NoSQL database. Common examples are MapReduce, Hadoop and NoSQL.

Figure 4. The three tiers of Big Data Processing Network
(Xindong, et al. 2014)

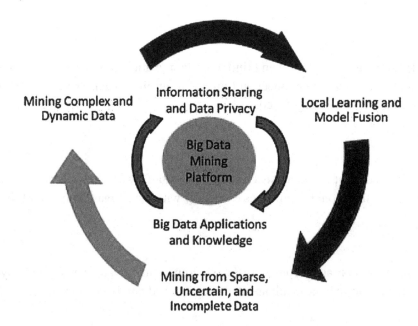

V. DATA MINING ANALYSIS

The data mining analysis Figure 5, has been classified into four major techniques (Sung-Hwan, Nam-Uk & Tai-Myoung, 2013) as listed below:

1. **Classification:** To classify is to arrange different objects according to their attributes into a set of categories. It is a two step process: Firstly, determining the data classes needed in advance using sample train of values. The next step is to classify the data set into data classes as determined by their particular attributes. (Han, Kamber, & Pei, 2006)
2. **Prediction:** Prediction and Classification are the two most common techniques used in Data mining analysis. The difference is that prediction predicts continuous values whereas classification predicts discrete value. (Han, Kamber, & Pei, 2006)
3. **Clustering:** In classification the class label of each training sample is provided i.e. supervised learning .Clustering is considered as the most important unsupervised learning i.e. it deals with finding a structure in a collection of unlabelled data.(Deepti, 2013)
4. **Association Rule Mining Techniques:** Association rule mining techniques is one of the fundamental research topics in data mining analysis. It aims at revealing interesting relationships or correlation between datasets and thereby predicts the associative and correlative behavior of new data. A number of techniques have been developed for Association Rule Mining. Frequent pattern discovery technique is one of them. (Deepti, 2013)

Figure 5. Combining Big Data and Traditional Data Mining Techniques
(Pavlik, 2013)

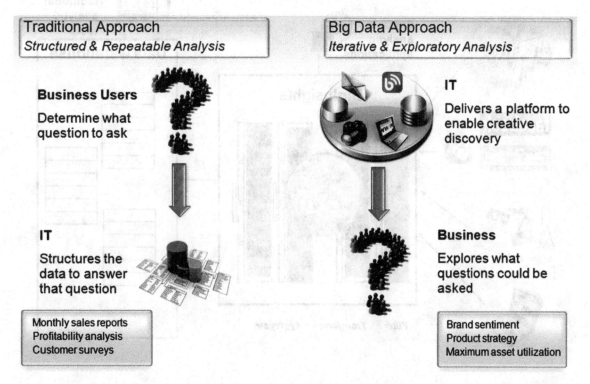

VI. BIG DATA ANALYSIS

The approach is to incorporate Big Insights as a data source to the traditional warehouse. In this implementation, Big Insights will filter relevant information which will then be combined with existing data in a warehouse.

The Figure 6 shows how BigInsights relates to the data warehouse. BigInsights and data warehouses tachnologies complement each other. BigInsights can be used as an engine to collect, sort, analyze, and draw valuable Big Data.Now, the summarized data is cached into traditional data warehouse where traditional tools can access it to answer user's queries.

VII. POTENTIALS OF BIG DATA IN FIVE DOMAINS

McKinsey Global Institute specified the potential of big data in five main domains as listed below (Manyika, et al. 2011):

1. **Healthcare:** Clinical decision support systems, analyze disease patterns, cost estimates of pharmaceutical and medical products, electronic medical record (EMR), medical images, remote patient monitoring

Figure 6. Merging Data mining analysis and Big Data Analysis
(Pavlik, 2013)

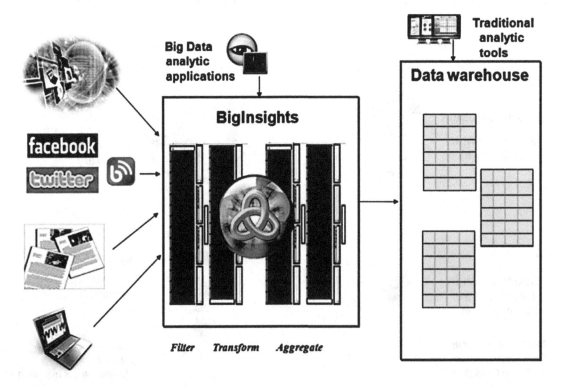

2. **Public Sector:** improve performance by uncovering variability, innovative services and products, transparency of data for accessing, discover needs and make effective choices with the information provided, automated algorithms to replace/modify human decisions

3. **Retail:** Variety and Price online comparison, enhancing the multichannel consumer experience, optimize distribution and logistics, product placement and design optimization, labor inputs optimization, effective marketing strategies.

4. **Manufacturing:** targeted products, improved design and eliminate defects prior to production, supply chain planning, web search based applications, demand forecasting, utilizing data from sensor driven operations.

5. **Personal Location Data:** GPS navigation, Geo targeted mobile advertising, Mobile phone location-based service and emergency response, urban planning, Remote personal Car safety/monitoring.

VIII. IMPORTANCE OF BIG DATA

The importance of big data lies in the fact, how the companies capture, process and analyze it efficiently and improve sales with better products and services. The importance of big data has been described in detail below (Avita, et al. 2013).

A. Big Data and Log Storage

Large amount of data is stored as Logs to analyze and solve problems. This data is stored for a limited duration normally a few weeks and keeps on changing with the software or hardware updates. The traditional warehouses are not able to handle their volume, raw and semi-structured nature. Big data analytics will enable to analyze the mountains of data while pinpointing the reasons behind systems failures. Big data also enables the logs to be stored for longer time as analyzing more data is always a better approach.

B. Big Data and Sensors

Wireless sensors are present in vending machines, home security systems, parking meters as well as healthcare equipments. If we take the example of Home security, for instance, people are using mobile devices to manage their home alarms, personal security, parking lights, and minimizing energy consumption. Managing large amount of sensor data will certainly become a Big Data issue.

C. Big Data and Risk Analysis

It is necessary for financial institutions to model and interpret data so the risk is minimized and falls in the company's accepted threshold. Generally, a large amount of data is underutilized and should be taken into consideration within the model. Big Data will enable to determine the risk patterns more accurately and predict better business strategies.

D. Big Data and Social Media

The most use of Big data is for the social media and getting customer feedback. Business organizations will get to know what the customers have to say about their products or services offered and modify decisions based on this valuable data. Big data will add value to the business.

E. Projects of Big Data

Various projects of Big Data in different domains are listed below, (Avita, et al. 2013):

1. Big Science
   a. The Large Hadron Collider (LHC) is the world's largest and highest-energy particle accelerator .It is designed with the aim of allowing researchers to test the predictions of 405 different particle physics and high energy physics theories.
   b. The Sloan Digital Sky Survey (SDSS) uses a 2.5-m wide-angle optical telescope. It is continuing to gather astronomical data at a rate of about 200 GB per night and has more than 140 terabytes of information. DSS-III will continue operating and releasing data through 2014.
2. Government
   a. The Obama administration project is making use of Big Data technology. It includes 84 different Big data programs which are a part of 6 different departments.
   b. The Community Comprehensive National Cyber Security initiated a data center, Utah Data Center, which stores data in scale of yottabytes to provide cyber security.
3. Private Sector
   a. FICO Falcon Credit Card Fraud Detection System protects 2.1 billion active accounts world-wide
   b. Wal-Mart is estimated to store about more than 2.5 petabytes of data in order to handle about more than 1 million customer transactions every hour.
   c. Amazon.com entertains millions of back-end operations on a daily basis. Every day it handles queries from more than half a million third-party sellers.
4. International Development
   a. Information and Communication Technologies for Development (ICT4D) uses the Information and Communication Technologies (ICTs) for international development.

IX. SERVICE GENERATED BIG DATA

Nowadays, there are all kinds of online services provided on the internet and daily used by millions of users. Every time when we perform a search, send an email, post a micro blog or shop on e-commerce Websites, we are gathering a trace of data to the services. (Zibin, Jieming, & Michael, 2013)

As the number of services and Users are increasing with a fast pace, the service-generated data are also increasing which is the reason behind the big data phenomenon. The service generated data includes service trace logs, Quality of Service (QoS) information, and service invocation relationship. To enhance system performance, these three types of service generated big data are exploited in this chapter for better understanding.

The following sub-sections will describe in detail how the service generated data can be processed and analyzed to enhance system performance. This chapter discusses some typical applications which will exploit the three types mentioned above. First, trace log visualization and performance problem diagnosis are investigated with the help of trace logs. Then, QoS aware fault tolerance and service QoS prediction are studied. Finally, service relationship are studied which covers service identification and service migration.

A. Service Trace Logs

Trace logs can be utilized for understanding as well as debugging the behavior of a complex, large scale distributed systems, (Wang, Zhou, Lyu, & Cai, 2013). An example of this scenario is cloud computing systems in which hundreds of machines interact with each other. In such cases, it becomes very difficult to manually diagnose the actual problem but with the help of logs we can achieve performance bottleneck localization. Real time diagnosis has become a challenging task and an important research problem due to the large volume and high velocity of trace logs. The solution is to design and implement more efficient storage, management, and analysis approaches for service generated trace logs and performance problem diagnosis as shown in Table 1.

Table 1. The trace log visualizations approaches and performance problem diagnosis adopted by companies

Companies	Approaches for Trace Log Visualization
Google, Microsoft and EBay	Use request tracing approaches that record the entering and leaving time of individual requests through the service components (Sigelman, Barroso, Burrows, Stephenson, Plakal, Beaver, Jaspan, & Shanbhag, 2010), (Han, Dang, Ge, Zhang, & Xie, 2012) & (Chen, Accardi, Kiciman, Lloyd, Patterson, Fox, & Brewer, 2004)
Stardust	Uses relational databases as repository which suffers poor query efficiency in the environment of massive data volumes (Lim, Singh, & Yajnik, 2008)
P-tracer	It is an online performance profiling tool to visualizes multi-dimensional statistical information to help administrators understand the system performance behaviors in depth
DTrace and gprof	Visualize the execution of systems as call graphs to signify where requests spend time.
Technologies and approaches for performance problem diagnosis	Description
Magpie, (Barham, Donnelly, Isaacs, & Mortier, 2004), Pip (Reynolds, Killian, Wiener, Mogul, Shah, & Vahdat, 2006) and Iron model (Thereska, & Ganger, 2008)	Application-specific approaches, which require domain knowledge to construct the performance diagnosis models.
Pinpoint (Chen, Kiciman, Fratkin, Fox, & Brewer, 2002)	Employs clustering algorithm to group failure and success logs.
Dapper (Sigelman, et al.2010)	Employs Big-table to manage the large volume of trace logs.
Principal Component Analysis (PCA)	Data mining technologies such as principal component analysis (PCA) and robust principal component analysis are also employed for identifying performance bottlenecks via modeling and mining the trace logs (Mi et al., 2013) & (Xu, Huang, Fox, Patterson, & Jordan, 2009)

i. Visualization of Trace Logs

Service log visualization becomes more challenging in the case of Big Data, the reasons being the rapid increase of log files leading to huge volume of trace logs, the unstructured and heterogeneous nature of log data, and the requirement of real-time processing of queries. Trace log visualization is used by the system designers and administrators to understand and analyze the characteristics of system performance.

ii. Performance Problem Diagnosis

Trace logs provide valuable information to find the cause of performance problems. In distributed systems such as cloud systems, it is most likely that a request will go through different hosts before it is actually served. If the user is not offered the SLA (service level agreement) by the service, it becomes a challenging task to identify the main cause of the problem.

B. Service QoS Information

Since different users may encounter quite different QoS performance such as response-time, on the same service, the volume of user-side QoS data is of much importance. This user-side service QoS information is much larger than that of server-side QoS data since data is generated from both the server as well as the user. These user-side data, which is changing from time to time, is investigated to achieve valuable information such as adaptive fault tolerance and to make personalized QoS prediction for users. (Zibin, Jieming, & Michael 2013)

i. Fault Tolerance

To design a fault tolerant service-oriented system is an even more challenging task in a distributed environment. The main reasons can be listed as:

1.   New services may be added;
2.   Original services may be disabled;
3.   QoS is changing from time to time;
4.   Highly heterogeneous and dynamic environment.

   QoS information can be considered to enhance the system performance. QoS data such as response-time, availability, throughput, etc. is recorded and monitored continuously at runtime. This large volume of QoS data can be processed effectively and efficiently to design fault tolerant systems leading to optimal performance.

ii. QoS Prediction

A number of approaches to predict personalized QoS for users are implemented For instance, user based QoS prediction approach, combination of user based and item based approaches, clustering based approach etc (Zibin, et al. 2013). By using the mentioned approaches, we can predict the missing entries in the user service matrix. As the number of users and services in the internet environment are increasing rapidly, it becomes a challenging task to process large volume of available service QoS data to predict the missing QoS values.

X. CHALLENGES AND ISSUES

Record volumes of data are being generated today due to internetworking of computers and their peripherals. Managing the growing data is a challenging task for companies and organizations. The following sections describe the challenges and issues of big data, (Avita, et al. 2013).

A. Sharing of Information and Privacy/Security

Data should be available in a reliable, complete and organized manner if decisions are to be taken based on such analysis. It will eventually lead to better decision making, accurate business models and enhance productivity and innovation. Organizations will be able to get an edge in business by analyzing such statistics. The drawback is that sharing data about the users (clients/customers/people) threatens user's privacy.

B. Storage and Processing Issues

Since analyzing Big data requires getting all the data collected and organizing it in a way to extract important information. Terabytes of data will take large amount of time to get uploaded in cloud in real time as it is changing rapidly. Capacity and Performance issues are the two major issues that are faced due to cloud distribution. One way to reduce the time from taking data from storage place to processing node is to process in the storage place only and results can be transferred for computation only. To find relevant data, whole of data set needs to be scanned which is quite cumbersome. Thus, building up indexes right in the beginning while the data is being collected and stored will reduce processing time to a great extent.

C. Challenges (Analytical/Technical)

There are certain challenges that come when analyzing Big Data such as: Do we need to store and analyze the entire data? What are the attributes of the Data which are really important to us? What if data volume and complexity increases so much that it is not known how to handle such heterogeneous and enormous data? Hence we can conclude that the type of analysis that needs to be performed on the data will depend highly on the results to be obtained e.g. Prediction of sales trends. Certain technical challenges will also be faced while dealing with Big Data (Table 2).

D. Skill Requirement

Big data is no doubt an emerging technology and data analysts with technical, research, and analytical as well as interpretive skills will play a major role in handling this future need. Organizations should held training programs to develop these skills in the individuals to produce skilled employees.

Table 2. Approaches to solve technical challenges

Challenges	Approaches Implied to Solve Technical Challenges
Fault Tolerant computing	• Divide the whole computation into tasks and assign these tasks to different nodes for computation • Apply checkpoints to keep the state of the system at certain intervals of the time so that in case of failure the process is restarted from the last checkpoint
Data Processing Speed and Scalability	• Processors are being built with more number of cores • Multiple workloads with varying performance goals are integrated into very large clusters
Relevancy of Data	• To draw more accurate conclusions, Big Data Analysts focus on quality data storage rather than storing large volumes of irrelevant data as collection and storage come at a cost. • To identify which data is relevant, how much data needs to be stored to draw conclusions from it such as decision making
Complexity of Data	• To analyze and interpret unstructured data i.e. completely raw and unorganized data. • Structured data is one which is highly manageable whereas unstructured data is cumbersome and costly. Hence to find an efficient way to manage unstructured data is required.

XI. FUTURE RESEARCH DIRECTIONS

The Human Genome Project is one project that revealed the cause behind mutation related to cancer. The Human Genome Project provides a promising example of how Big Data can lead to the discovery of cures or prevention to other diseases. Two major projects: the Human Brain Project and the US BRAIN Initiative, are aiming to construct a supercomputer so as to reveal the brain's inner working. It will enable the activity of about 100 billion neurons to be analyzed so that these simulations or patterns can thereby be utilized to help solve queries about diseases such as Alzheimer. Big Data also finds applications in Consumer industry as well as government agencies. Consumer purchasing trends can be studied and analyzed to better market products. When a shopper walks through a store while purchasing goods, their complex decision making processes can be revealed using real-time data generated from user's mobile phones or security cameras. There are a number of other domains where Big Data promises to provide benefits to us ranging from climatology to geophysics to nanotechnology (Michael, & Miller, 2013).

XII. CONCLUSION

There is no doubt in saying that Big Data will change our lives in both small and large ways. Though Big Data comes with challenges of storage, high cost, security and privacy issues as well as maintaining data, it can yield extremely useful information. We need deep understanding of opportunities and risks generated by Big Data applications. It will become an inevitable part of our lives, used in commercial, corporate organizations as well as government agencies. Since Big Data will reveal new trends and hidden patterns, our challenge will be to utilize this emerging technology for the benefits of society while minimizing the misuse of this technology.

REFERENCES

Avita, K., Mohammad, W., & Goudar, R. H. (2013). *Big Data: Issues, Challenges, Tools and Good Practices: Contemporary Computing (IC3), 2013 Sixth International Conference*. IEEE.

Barham, P., Donnelly, A., Isaacs, R., & Mortier, R. (2004). Using magpie for request extraction and workload modeling. In *Proceedings of OSDI'04: 6th Symposium on Operating Systems Design and Implementation*. USENIX Association.

Bughin, J., Chui, M., & Manyika, J. (2010). *Clouds, big data, and smart assets: Ten tech-enabled business trends to watch* (Vol. 56). McKinsley Quarterly.

Chen, M., Kiciman, E., Fratkin, E., Fox, A., & Brewer, E. (2002). Pinpoint: Problem determination in large, dynamic internet services. In *Proceedings of the International Conference on Dependable Systems and Networks (DSN'02)* (pp. 595–604). Academic Press.

Chen, M. Y., Accardi, A., Kiciman, E., Lloyd, J., Patterson, D., Fox, A., & Brewer, E. (2004). Path-based faliure and evolution management. In *Proceedings of the 1st conference on Symposium on Networked Systems Design and Implementation*. USENIX Association.

Deepti, M. (2013, December). A Review on Clustering Based Methods and Usage for Pattern Recognition. *International Journal of Engineering Research and Development, 9*(5), 23–26.

Du, Z. (2013), *Inconsistencies in big data: Cognitive Informatics & Cognitive Computing (ICCI*CC), 2013, 12th IEEE International Conference*. IEEE.

Eaton, C., Deroos, D., Deutsch, T., Lapis, G., & Zikopoulos, P. C. (2012). Understanding Big Data: Analytics for Enterprise Class Hadoop and Streaming Data. New York: McGraw-Hill Companies.

Gerhardt, B., Griffin, K., & Klemann, R. (2012). *Unlocking Value in the Fragmented World of Big Data Analytics*. Cisco Internet Business Solutions Group. Retrieved from http://www.cisco.com/web/about/ac79/docs/sp/InformationInfomediaries.pdf

Gupta, R., Gupta, H., & Mohania, M. (2012). *Cloud Computing and Big Data Analytics: What is new from Database Perspective?*. Springer-Verlag Berlin Heidelberg. doi:10.1007/978-3-642-35542-4_5

Han, J., Kamber, M., & Pei, J. (2006). *Data Mining: Concepts and Techniques* (2nd ed.). University of Illinois at Urbana-Champaign, Morgan Kaufmann Publishers.

Han, S., Dang, Y., Ge, S., Zhang, D., & Xie, T. (2012). Performance debugging in the large via mining millions of stack traces. In *Proceedings of the 34th International Conference on Software Engineering*, (pp. 145–155). Academic Press. doi:10.1109/ICSE.2012.6227198

IBM What is big data? —Bringing big data to the enterprise. (n.d.). Retrieved from www.ibm.com

Intel IT Center. (2012). *Planning Guide: Getting Started with Hadoop, Steps IT Managers Can Take to Move Forward with Big Data Analytics*. Author.

Lim, C., Singh, N., & Yajnik, S. (2008). A log mining approach to failure analysis of enterprise telephony systems. In *Proceedings of the IEEE International Conference on Dependable Systems and Networks*, (pp. 398–403). IEEE.

Madden, S. (2012). From Databases to Big Data. *IEEE Internet Computing, 16*(3), 4–6. doi:10.1109/MIC.2012.50

Manyika, J., Chui, M., Brown, B., Bughin, J., Dobbs, R., Roxburgh, C., & Byers, A. H. (2011). Big data: The next frontier for innovation, competition, and productivity. McKinsey Global Institute.

Mi, H., Wang, H., Zhou, Y., Lyu, M.R., & Cai, H. (2013). Toward Fine-Grained, Unsupervised, Scalable Performance Diagnosis for Production Cloud Computing Systems. *IEEE Transactions on Parallel and Distributed Systems, 24*(6), 1245-1255.

Michael, K., & Miller, K. W. (2013). Big Data: New Opportunities and New Challenges. IEEE Computer, 46(6), 22-24.

Pavlik, M. (2013). *Mi is az a big data.* Retrieved from http://www.scribd.com/doc/181439274/1-Mi-is-az-a-big-data-ppt

Reynolds, P., Killian, C., Wiener, J. L., Mogul, J. C., Shah, M. A., & Vahdat, A. (2006). Pip: detecting the unexpected in distributed systems. In *Proceedings of the 3rd Symposium on Networked Systems Design and Implementation (NSDI)*, (pp. 1–14). NSDI.

Schneider, R. D. (2012). *Hadoop for Dummies* (Special Edition). Canada: John Wiley&Sons.

Seref, S., & Duygu, S. (2013). *Big Data: A Review: Collaboration Technologies and Systems (CTS), 2013 International Conference.* IEEE.

Sigelman, B.H., Barroso, L.A., Burrows, M., Stephenson, P., Plakal, M., Beaver, D., Jaspan, S., & Shanbhag, C. (2010). *Dapper, a large-scale distributed systems tracing infrastructure.* Google Technical Report dapper-2010-1.

Singh, S., & Singh, N. (2012). Big Data Analytics. In *Proceedings of International Conference on Communication, Information & Computing Technology*, (pp. 1-4). Mumbai India: IEEE Conference Publications.

Sung-Hwan, K., Nam-Uk, K., & Tai-Myoung, C. (2013), *Attribute Relationship Evaluation Methodology for Big Data Security: IT Convergence and Security (ICITCS), 2013 International Conference.* ICITCS.

Tankard, C. (2012). Big Data Security. *Network Security Journal*, (7), 5–8.

Thereska, E., & Ganger, G. R. (2008). Ironmodel: Robust performance models in the wild. In *Proceedings of the 2008 ACM SIGMETRICS International Conference on Measurement and Modeling of Computer Systems*, (pp. 253–264). ACM.

Xindong, W., Xingquan, Z., Gong-Qing, W., & Wei, D. (2014). Data Mining with Big Data. *IEEE Transactions on Knowledge and Data Engineering, 26*(1), 97–107.

Xu, W., Huang, L., Fox, A., Patterson, D., & Jordan, M. I. (2009). Detecting large-scale system problems by mining console logs. In *Proceedings of the ACM 22nd Symposium on Operating Systems Principles (SOSP'09)*, (pp. 117–132). ACM. doi:10.1145/1629575.1629587

Zibin, Z., Jieming, Z., & Michael, L. (2013), *Service-generated Big Data and Big Data-as-a-Service: An Overview: Big Data (Big Data Congress), 2013 IEEE International Congress.* IEEE Conference Publications.

ADDITIONAL READING

Bakshi, K. (2012). Considerations for Big Data: Architecture and Approach, *Aerospace Conference, 2012 IEEE*, IEEE CONFERENCE PUBLICATIONS, (pp.1-7). doi:10.1109/AERO.2012.6187357

Berman, J. J. (2013). *Principles of Big Data: Preparing, Sharing, and Analyzing Complex Information* (1st ed.). Morgan Kaufmann.

Craig, T., & Ludloff, M. E. (2011). Privacy and Big Data, 1005 Gravenstein Highway North, Sebastopol, CA, 95472, ISBN: 978-1-449-30500-0, published by O'Reilly Media Inc.

Demchenko, Y., Zhao, Z., Grosso, P., Wibisono, A., & de Laat, C. (2012). Addressing Big Data challenges for Scientific Data Infrastructure, *IEEE 4th International Conference on Cloud Computing Technology and Science (CloudCom)*, IEEE CONFERENCE PUBLICATIONS, pp.(614–617).

Franks, B. (Apr 24, 2012). *Taming The Big Data Tidal Wave: Finding Opportunities in Huge Data Streams with Advanced Analytics*, ISBN: 978-1-118-20878-6, Copyright © 2000-2014 by John Wiley & Sons, Inc.

Fung, K. (2013). *Numbersense: How to Use Big Data to Your Advantage, Edition: 1*. McGraw-Hill.

Hurwitz, J., Nugent, A., Halper, F., and Kaufman, M. (Apr 15, 2013). *Big Data For Dummies*, ISBN: 978-1-118-50422-2, Copyright © 2000-2014 by John Wiley & Sons, Inc.

Kaisler, S., Armour, F., Espinosa, J. A., & Money, W. (2013). Big Data: Issues and Challenges Moving Forward, *46th Hawaii International Conference on System Sciences (HICSS)*, IEEE CONFERENCE PUBLICATIONS (pp. 995-1004) doi:10.1109/HICSS.2013.645

Kord Davis, K. (2012). Ethics of Big Data: Balancing Risk and Innovation, 1005 Gravenstein Highway North, Sebastopol, CA, 95472, USA., ISBN: 978-1-449-31179-7, published by O'Reilly Media Inc.

Krishnan, K. (2013). *Data Warehousing in the Age of Big Data (The Morgan Kaufmann Series on Business Intelligence), Edition: 1*. Morgan Kaufmann.

Liebowitz, J. (2013). *Big Data and Business Analytics, Taylor & Francis Group, 6000 Broken Sound Parkway NW, Suite 300* (pp. 33487–2742). FL: CRC Press.

Lu, T., Guo, X., Xu, B., Zhao, L., Peng, Y., & Yang, H. (2013). Next Big Thing in Big Data: The Security of the ICT Supply Chain, *2013 International Conference on Social Computing (SocialCom), IEEE CONFERENCE PUBLICATIONS*, (pp. 1066 – 1073). doi:10.1109/SocialCom.2013.172

Madden, S. (2012). *From Databases to Big Data, IEEE INTERNET COMPUTING* (pp. 4–6). Published by the IEEE Computer Society.

Mayer, V., & Cukier, K. (2013). *Big Data: A Revolution That Will Transform How We Live, Work, and Think, 215 Park Avenue South, NewYork, Newyork 10003*. USA: John Murray.

Michael, M., Chambers, M., & Dhiraj, A. (2013). Big Data, Big Analytics: Emerging Business Intelligence and Analytic Trends for Today's Businesses, ISBN: 978-1-118-20878-6, Copyright © 2000-2014 by John Wiley & Sons, Inc.

Moon, H., & Cho, S. H. (2013). Big Data and Policy design for Data Sovereignty: A Case Study on Copyright and CCL in South Korea, *2013 International Conference on Social Computing (SocialCom), IEEE CONFERENCE PUBLICATIONS*, pp. (1026 – 1029). doi:10.1109/SocialCom.2013.165

Pirenne, B., Guillemot, E. (2012),Beyond Data Management. How to foster data exploitation and better science?, *Oceans, , IEEE Xplore,* IEEE CONFERENCE PUBLICATIONS, (pp. 1-6).10.1109/OCEANS.2012.6404783

Sathi, A. Dr. (2013). Big Data Analytics: Disruptive Technologies for Changing the Game, ISBN: 978-1-58347-380-1, © 2012 IBM Corporation.

Simon, P. (2013). *Too Big to Ignore: The Business Case for Big Data,* ISBN: 978-1-118-63817-0, Copyright © 2000-2014 by John Wiley & Sons, Inc.

Singh, S., & Singh, N. (2012). Big Data analytics, *2012 International Conference on Communication, Information & Computing Technology (ICCICT)*, IEEE CONFERENCE PUBLICATIONS, pp.(1–4).

Smith, M., Szongott, C., Henne, B., & von Voigt, G. (2012). Big data privacy issues in public social media, *6th IEEE International Conference on Digital Ecosystems Technologies (DEST)*, IEEE CONFERENCE PUBLICATIONS, (pp. 1-6). doi:10.1109/DEST.2012.6227909

Smolan, R., and Erwitt, J. (Nov 20, 2012), *The Human Face of Big Data,* ISBN-10: 1454908270, ISBN-13: 978-1454908272 0, Publisher: Sterling.

Tom, W. (2012). Hadoop: The Definitive Guide, 1005 Gravenstein Highway North, Sebastopol, CA, 95472, USA., ISBN: 978-0-596-521974, published by O'Reilly Media Inc.

Xiong, W., Yu, Z., Bei, Z., Zhao, J., Zhang, F., Zou, Y., & Li, Y. et al., Xu., C. (2013). A Characterization of Big Data Benchmarks, *2013 IEEE International Conference on Big Data.* (pp. 118-225). doi:10.1109/BigData.2013.6691707

Yaser, S. A. M., Malik, M. I., & Hsuan, T. (2012). *Learning From Data.* AML Book.

Zadrozny, P., & Kodali, R. (2013). *Big Data Analytics Using Splunk: Deriving Operational Intelligence from Social Media, Machine Data, Existing Data..., Edition: 1.* Apress.

KEY TERMS AND DEFINITIONS

Big Data: Big Data may be defined as a collection of huge data that becomes challenging to process through available conventional data processing tools and applications. It involves high-volume, high-velocity and high-variety of information resources that require economical, productive and new methods of information processing for improved and enhanced decision making.

Big Data Analysis: Big Data Analysis involves seven phases: Data acquirement and record keeping, Information extraction, clean and annotate, integrate, aggregate and represent, analyze and model, and interpret the data.

Cloud Computing: Cloud computing involves a network of remote servers on the internet that facilitates storage, managing and processing data. It is a model for on demand access to a shared pool of computing resources such as networks, servers, storage, etc.

Data Mining: The sorting of huge quantities of data for useful information. It is used to discover patterns and correlations in large relational databases.

Data Warehouse: An accumulation of huge amounts of data from various sources inside a company and facilitates management in decision making. It is a relational database, intended for handling queries and analysis and not designed for transaction processing.

Database Management System (DBMS): It is a collection of software programs that enables a computer to execute database tasks such as saving & storing, retrieving, adding, removing and altering data, safety and security and reliability of data in a database.

Distributed Systems: A collection of independent machines connected by a network and equipped with software that provides the ability to machines to manage and coordinate their activities and share resources such as hardware, software and data. To the user it appears as an integrated single computer.

Hadoop: Hadoop is an open source software that has the ability to facilitate distributed data processing of huge data sets, in clusters of servers with high degree of fault tolerance. It can identify and take care of failures at the application level.

Sensors: Devices that act as a transducer to transform energy in physical environment into electrical signals. They can "sense" a physical change in the surrounding environment or other characteristics that may change due to some excitation, such as heat or force, convert that into an electrical signal and convey the information to the controlling stations.

Chapter 2
Security and Privacy Issues of Big Data

José Moura
Instituto Universitário de Lisboa, Portugal & Instituto de Telecomunicações, Portugal

Carlos Serrão
Instituto Universitário de Lisboa, Portugal & Information Sciences, Technologies and Architecture Research Center, Portugal

ABSTRACT

This chapter revises the most important aspects in how computing infrastructures should be configured and intelligently managed to fulfill the most notably security aspects required by Big Data applications. One of them is privacy. It is a pertinent aspect to be addressed because users share more and more personal data and content through their devices and computers to social networks and public clouds. So, a secure framework to social networks is a very hot topic research. This last topic is addressed in one of the two sections of the current chapter with case studies. In addition, the traditional mechanisms to support security such as firewalls and demilitarized zones are not suitable to be applied in computing systems to support Big Data. SDN is an emergent management solution that could become a convenient mechanism to implement security in Big Data systems, as we show through a second case study at the end of the chapter. This also discusses current relevant work and identifies open issues.

INTRODUCTION

The Big Data is an emerging area applied to manage datasets whose size is beyond the ability of commonly used software tools to capture, manage, and timely analyze that amount of data. The quantity of data to be analyzed is expected to double every two years (IDC, 2012). All these data are very often unstructured and from various sources such as social media, sensors, scientific applications, surveillance, video and image archives, Internet search indexing, medical records, business transactions and system logs. Big data is gaining more and more attention since the number of devices connected to the so-called "Internet of Things" (IoT) is still increasing to unforeseen levels, producing large amounts of data which needs to be transformed into valuable information. Additionally, it is very popular to buy on-demand

DOI: 10.4018/978-1-4666-8505-5.ch002

additional computing power and storage from public cloud providers to perform intensive data-parallel processing. In this way, security and privacy issues can be potentially boosted by the volume, variety, and wide area deployment of the system infrastructure to support Big Data applications.

As Big Data expands with the help of public clouds, traditional security solutions tailored to private computing infrastructures, confined to a well-defined security perimeter, such as firewalls and demilitarized zones (DMZs) are no more effective. Using Big Data, security functions are required to work over the heterogeneous composition of diverse hardware, operating systems, and network domains. In this puzzle-type computing environment, the abstraction capability of Software-Defined Networking (SDN) seems a very important characteristic that can enable the efficient deployment of Big Data secure services on-top of the heterogeneous infrastructure. SDN introduces abstraction because it separates the control (higher) plane from the underlying system infrastructure being supervised and controlled. Separating a network's control logic from the underlying physical routers and switches that forward traffic allows system administrators to write high-level control programs that specify the behavior of an entire network, in contrast to conventional networks, whereby administrators (if allowed to do it by the device manufacturers) must codify functionality in terms of low-level device configuration. Using SDN, the intelligent management of secure functions can be implemented in a logically centralized controller, simplifying the following aspects: enforcement of security policies; system (re)configuration; and system evolution. The robustness drawback of a centralized SDN solution can be mitigated using a hierarchy of controllers and/or through the usage of redundant controllers at least for the most important system functions to be controlled.

The National Institute of Standards and Technology (NIST) launched very recently a framework with a set of voluntary guidelines to help organizations make their communications and computing operations safer (NIST, 2014). This could be achieved through a systematic verification of the system infrastructure in terms of risk assessment, protection against threats, and capabilities to respond and recover from attacks. Following the last verification principles, Defense Advanced Research Projects Agency (DARPA) is creating a program called Mining and Understanding Software Enclaves (MUSE) to enhance the quality of the US military's software. This program is designed to produce more robust software that can work with big datasets without causing errors or crashing under the sheer volume of information (DARPA, 2014). In addition, security and privacy are becoming very urgent Big Data aspects that need to be tackled (Agrawal, Das, & El Abbadi, 2011). To illustrate this, the social networks have enabled people to share and distribute valuable copyrighted digital contents in a very easy way. Consequently, the copyright infringement behaviors, such as illicit copying, malicious distribution, unauthorized access and usage, and free sharing of copyright-protected digital contents, will become a much more common phenomenon. To mitigate these problems, Big Data should have solid solutions to support author's privacy and author's copyrights (Marques & Serrão, 2013a). Also, users share more and more personal data and user generated content through their mobile devices and computers to social networks and cloud services, loosing data and content control with a serious impact on their own privacy. Finally, one potentially promising approach is to create additional uncertainty for attackers by dynamically changing system properties in what is called a cyber moving target (MT) (Okhravi, Hobson, Bigelow, & Streilein, 2014). They present a summary of several types of MT techniques, consider the advantages and weaknesses of each, and make recommendations for future research in this area.

The current chapter endorses the most important aspects of Big Data security and privacy and is structured as follows. The first section discusses the most important challenges to the aspects of information security and privacy imposed by the novel requirements of Big Data applications. The second section presents and explains some interesting solutions to the problems found in the previous section. The third and fourth sections are related with two case studies in this exciting emergent area.

BIG DATA CHALLENGES TO INFORMATION SECURITY AND PRIVACY

With the proliferation of devices connected to the Internet and connected to each other, the volume of data collected, stored, and processed is increasing everyday, which also brings new challenges in terms of privacy and security. In fact, the currently used security mechanisms such as firewalls and DMZs cannot be used in the Big Data infrastructure because the security mechanisms should be stretched out of the perimeter of the organization's network to fulfill the user/data mobility requirements and the policies of BYOD (Bring Your Own Device). Considering these new scenarios, the pertinent question is what security and privacy policies and technologies are more adequate to fulfill the current top Big Data security and privacy challenges (Cloud Security Alliance, 2013). These challenges may be organized into four Big Data aspects such as infrastructure security (e.g. secure distributed computations using MapReduce), data privacy (e.g. data mining that preserves privacy/granular access), data management (e.g. secure data provenance and storage) and, integrity and reactive security (e.g. real time monitoring of anomalies and attacks).

Considering Big Data there is a set of risk areas that need to be considered. These include the information lifecycle (provenance, ownership and classification of data), the data creation and collection process, and the lack of security procedures. Ultimately, the Big Data security objectives are no different from any other data types – to preserve its confidentiality, integrity and availability.

Being Big Data such an important and complex topic, it is almost natural that immense security and privacy challenges will arise (Michael & Miller, 2013; Tankard, 2012). Big Data has specific characteristics that affect security and privacy: variety, volume, velocity, value, variability, and veracity (Figure 1). These challenges have a direct impact on the design of security solutions that are required to tackle all these characteristics and requirements (Demchenko, Ngo, Laat, Membrey, & Gordijenko, 2014). Currently, such out of the box security solution does not exist.

Cloud Secure Alliance (CSA), a non-profit organization with a mission to promote the use of best practices for providing security assurance within Cloud Computing, has created a Big Data Working Group that has focused on the Big Data security and privacy challenges (Cloud Security Alliance, 2013). CSA has categorized the different security and privacy challenges into four different aspects of the Big Data ecosystem. These aspects are Infrastructure Security, Data Privacy, Data Management and, Integrity and Reactive Security. Each of these aspects faces the following security challenges, according to CSA:

- Infrastructure Security
  - Secure Computations in Distributed Programming Frameworks
  - Security Best Practices for Non-Relational Data Stores
- Data Privacy
  - Privacy Preserving Data Mining and Analytics
  - Cryptographically Enforced Data Centric Security
  - Granular Access Control

Figure 1. The five V's of Big Data
(Adapted from ("IBM big data platform - Bringing big data to the Enterprise," 2014))

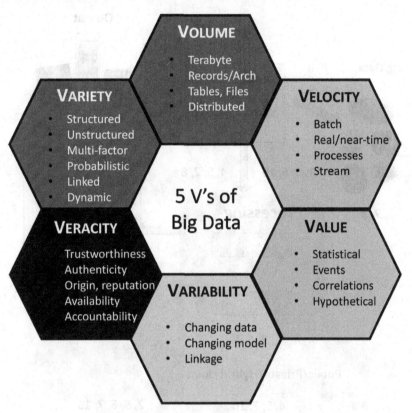

- Data Management and Integrity
  - Secure Data Storage and Transaction Logs
  - Granular Audits
  - Data Provenance
- Reactive Security
  - End-point Validation and Filtering
  - Real Time Security Monitoring.

These security and privacy challenges cover the entire spectrum of the Big Data lifecycle (Figure 2): sources of data production (devices), the data itself, data processing, data storage, data transport and data usage on different devices.

A particular aspect of Big Data security and privacy has to be related with the rise of the Internet of Things (IoT). IoT, defined by Oxford[1] as "a proposed development of the Internet in which everyday objects have network connectivity, allowing them to send and receive data", is already a reality – Gartner estimates that 26 billion of IoT devices will be installed by 2020, generating an incremental revenue of $300 billion (Rivera & van der Meulen, 2014). The immense increase in the number of connected devices (cars, lighting systems, refrigerators, telephones, glasses, traffic control systems, health monitoring devices, SCADA systems, TVs, home security systems, home automation systems, and many more)

Figure 2. Security and Privacy challenges in Big Data ecosystem
(Adapted from (Cloud Security Alliance, 2013))

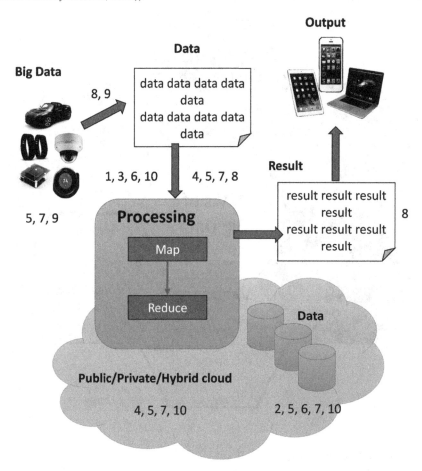

has led to manufacturers to push to the market, in a short period of time, a large set of devices, cloud systems and mobile applications to exploit this opportunity. While it presents tremendous benefits and opportunities for end-users it also is responsible for security challenges.

HP recently conducted a study on market-available IoT solutions and concluded that 70% of those contain security problems. These security problems were related with privacy issues, insufficient authorization, lack of transport encryption, insecure web interface and inadequate software protection (HP, 2014). Based on some of these findings, HP has started a project at OWASP (Open Web Application Security Project) that is entitled "OWASP Internet of Things Top Ten" (OWASP, 2014) whose objective is to help IoT suppliers to identify the top ten security IoT device problems and how to avoid them. This project, similar to the OWASP Top 10, identified the following security problems:

- **Insecure Web Interface:** Which can allow an attacker to exploit an administration web interface (through cross-site scripting, cross-site request forgery and SQL injection) and obtain unauthorized access to control the IoT device.
- **Insufficient Authentication/Authorization:** Can allow an attacker to exploit a bad password policy, break weak passwords and access to privileged modes on the IoT device.

- **Insecure Network Services:** Which can lead to an attacker exploiting unnecessary or weak services running on the device, or use those services as a jumping point to attack other devices on the IoT network.
- **Lack of Transport Encryption:** Allowing an attacker to eavesdrop data in transit between IoT devices and support systems.
- **Privacy Concerns:** Raised from the fact the most IoT devices and support systems collect personal data from users and fail to protect that data.
- **Insecure Cloud Interface:** Without proper security controls an attacker can use multiple attack vectors (insufficient authentication, lack of transport encryption, account enumeration) to access data or controls via the cloud website.
- **Insecure Mobile Interface:** Without proper security controls an attacker can use multiple attack vectors (insufficient authentication, lack of transport encryption, account enumeration) to access data or controls via the mobile interface.
- **Insufficient Security Configurability:** Due to the lack or poor configuration mechanisms an attacker can access data or controls on the device.
- **Insecure Software/Firmware:** Attackers can take advantage of unencrypted and unauthenticated connections to hijack IoT devices updates, and perform malicious update that can compromise the device, a network of devices and the data they hold.
- **Poor Physical Security:** If the IoT device is physically accessible than an attacker can use USB ports, SD cards or other storage means to access the device OS and potentially any data stored on the device.

It is clear that Big Data present interesting opportunities for users and businesses, however these opportunities are countered by enormous challenges in terms of privacy and security (Cloud Security Alliance, 2013). Traditional security mechanisms are insufficient to provide a capable answer to those challenges. In the next section, some of these solutions/proposals are going to be addressed.

SOLUTIONS/PROPOSALS TO ADDRESS BIG DATA SECURITY AND PRIVACY CHALLENGES

There is no single magical solution to solve the identified Big Data security and privacy challenges and traditional security mechanisms, which are tailored to securing small-scale static data, often fall short (Cloud Security Alliance, 2013). There is the need to understand how the collection of large amounts of complex structured and unstructured data can be protected. Non-authorized access to that data to create new relations, combine different data sources and make it available to malicious users is a serious risk for Big Data. The basic and more common solution for this includes encrypting everything to make data secure regardless where the data resides (data center, computer, mobile device, or any other). As Big Data grows and its processing gets faster, then encryption, masking and tokenization are critical elements for protecting sensitive data.

Due to its characteristics, Big Data projects need to take an holistic vision at security (Tankard, 2012). Big Data projects need to take into consideration the identification of the different data sources, the origin and creators of data, as well as who is allowed to access the data. It is also necessary to conduct a correct classification to identify critical data, and align with the organization information security policy in terms of enforcing access control and data handling policies. As a recommendation, different security mechanisms should be closer to the data sources and data itself, in order to provide security right at the origin of data, and mechanisms of control and prevention on archiving, data leakage prevention and access control should work together (Kindervag, Balaouras, Hill, & Mak, 2012).

The new Big Data security solutions should extend the secure perimeter from the enterprise to the public cloud (Juels & Oprea, 2013). In this way, a trustful data provenance mechanism should be also created across domains. In addition, similar mechanisms to the ones used in (Luo, Lin, Zhang, & Zukerman, 2013) can be used to mitigate distributed denial-of-service (DDoS) attacks launched against Big Data infrastructures. Also, a Big Data security and privacy is necessary to ensure data trustworthiness throughout the entire data lifecycle – from data collection to usage.

The personalization feature of some Big Data services and its impact on the user privacy is discussed in (Hasan, Habegger, Brunie, Bennani, & Damiani, 2013). They discuss these issues in the backdrop of EEXCESS, a concrete project aimed to both provide high level recommendations and to respect user privacy. A recent work describes proposed privacy extensions to UML to help software engineers to quickly visualize privacy requirements, and design them into Big Data applications (Jutla, Bodorik, & Ali, 2013).

While trying to take the most of Big Data, in terms of security and privacy, it becomes mandatory that mechanisms that address legal requirements about data handling, need to be met. Secure encryption technology must be employed to protect all the confidential data (Personally Identifiable Information (PII), Protected Health Information (PHI) and Intellectual Property (IP) and careful cryptographic material (keys) access management policies, need to be put in place, to ensure the correct locking and unlocking of data – this is particularly important for data stored. In order to be successful these mechanisms need to be transparent to the end-user and have low impact of the performance and scalability of data (software and hardware-based encryptions mechanisms are to be considered) (Advantech, 2013).

As previously referred, traditional encryption and anonymization of data are not adequate to solve Big Data problems. They are adequate to protect static information, but are not adequate when data computation is involved (MIT, 2014). Therefore, other techniques, allowing specific and targeted data computation while keeping the data secret, need to be used. Secure Function Evaluation (SFE) (Lindell & Pinkas, 2002), Fully Homomorphic Encryption (FHE) (Gentry, 2009) and Functional Encryption (FE) (Goldwasser et al., 2014), and partition of data on non-communicating data centers, can help solving the limitations of traditional security techniques.

Homomorphic encryption is a form of encryption which allows specific types of computations (e.g. RSA public key encryption algorithm) to be carried out on ciphertext and generate an encrypted result which, when decrypted, matches the result of operations performed on the plaintext (Gentry, 2010). Fully homomorphic encryption has numerous applications, as referred in (Van Dijk, Gentry, Halevi, & Vaikuntanathan, 2010). This allows encrypted queries on databases, which keeps secret private user information where that data is normally stored (somewhere in the cloud – in the limit an user can store its data on any untrusted server, but in encrypted form, without being worried with the data secrecy) (Ra Popa & Redfield, 2011). It also enables private queries to a search engine - the user submits an encrypted query and the search engine computes a succinct encrypted answer without ever looking at the query in the clear which could contain private user information such as the number of the national healthcare service. The homomorphic encryption also enables searching on encrypted data - a user stores encrypted files on a remote file server and can later have the server retrieve only files that (when decrypted) satisfy some boolean constraint, even though the server cannot decrypt the files on its own. More broadly, the fully homomorphic encryption improves the efficiency of secure multiparty computation.

An important security and privacy challenge for Big Data is related with the storage and processing of encrypted data. Running queries against an encrypted database is a basic security requirement for secure Big Data however it is a challenging one. This raises questions such as a) is the database encrypted with a single or multiple keys; b) does the database needs to be decrypted prior to running the query; c) do the queries need to be also encrypted; d) who as the permissions to decrypt the database; and many more. Recently a system that was developed at MIT, provides answers to some of these questions. CryptDB allows researchers to run database queries over encrypted data (Ra Popa & Redfield, 2011). Trustworthy applications that intent to query encrypted data will pass those queries to a CryptDB proxy (that sits between the application and the database) that rewrites those queries in a specific way so that they can be run against the encrypted database. The database returns the encrypted results back to the proxy, which holds a master key and will decrypt the results, sending the final answer back to the application. CryptDB supports numerous forms of encryption schemes that allow different types of operations on the data (RA Popa & Redfield, 2012). Based on CryptDB, Google has developed the Encrypted Big Query Client that will allow encrypted big queries against their BigQuery service that enables super, SQL-like queries against append-only tables, using the processing power of Google's infrastructure (Google, 2014).

Apart from more specific security recommendations, it is also important to consider the security of the IT infrastructure itself. One of the common security practices is to place security controls at the edge of the networks however, if an attacker violates this security perimeter it will have access to all the data within it. Therefore, a new approach is necessary to move those security controls near to the data (or add additional ones). Monitoring, analyzing and learning from data usage and access is also an important aspect to continuously improve security of the data holding infrastructure and leverage the already existing security solutions (Kindervag et al., 2012; Kindervag, Wang, Balaouras, & Coit, 2011).

A CASE STUDY IN A SECURE SOCIAL APPLICATION

Social networks are one of the key-applications for a large number of users. Millions and millions of persons are connected to some kind of social network – e.g. Facebook according to its own accounting has more than 829 million daily active users on average (654 million with mobile access). Social networks are quite attractive to users because they allow communication with new persons and concede users the ability to expose their own network of friends to others, creating new relations and pairings among users and between users and content (McKenzie et al., 2012). Users take advantage of this functionality to share all kinds of digital content within the social network, with other users (either they are their direct contacts or they are in other one's connections). These social network-sharing functionalities are extremely powerful and engaging of further social interaction. However, they are at the same time, the cause of serious privacy and security problems because sharing control is not on the end-user side. This represents a serious threat to the user privacy since content shared in these platforms can easily be exposed to a wider audience in just a few seconds. It is difficult, for an ordinary user, to select specific sharing properties for the content placed in social network and ensure that it stays under its control.

With the emergence of Web 2.0, users have changed from being simply information consumers to become important content producers. User generated content is content that is voluntarily developed by an individual or a consortium, and distributed through an online platform. The volume of user generated content currently produced and made available through several platforms is already immense and continues to grow in size (Kim, Jin, Kim, & Shin, 2012). For instance, Facebook stores, accesses, and analyzes more than 30 Petabytes of user generated data (100 terabytes of data are uploaded daily to Facebook) and YouTube users upload 48 hours of new video every minute of the day (McKenzie et al., 2012).

Currently, social network platforms already present a set of pre-defined but limited content privacy and security sharing controls (X. Chen & Shi, 2009). Major social network platforms offer the possibility for users to share content under specific privacy rules, which are defined by the social platform and not by the end-user. Most of the times, these rules are extremely permissive and differ from platform to platform. Also, on social networks, content is shared in a non-protected manner, making it easier for unauthorized usage and sharing. Users are also bound by subsequent privacy policies changes that threaten more and more the user right to protect its personal information and personal content.

The other problem that is most of the times associated with the security and privacy of content shared on social networks, is related to the security of the social network platform itself (Gross & Acquisti, 2005). The exploitation of the social network infrastructure can lead to security and privacy threats. On the other hand, recently on the media there have been some allegations about the cooperation of some of the most important IT suppliers (including some major social platforms) with governmental agencies to allow the unauthorized access to user's information and content. This latter fact is quite relevant, because, in theory, the social network service supplier has unlimited access to the information and content of all its customers.

This is an increasing serious problem, not only for end-users but also for organizations. More and more, organizations rely on social network services as a mean to disseminate information, create relations with and between employees and customers, knowledge capture and dissemination. The privacy and security challenges presented by these new ways of communication and interaction are very pertinent topics for both end users and organizations.

The continuous growing proliferation of mobile devices (mostly smartphones and tablets, but soon more devices will enter this scenario) with capabilities of producing content (mainly audio recordings, videos and pictures) at the palm of every user's hand, following them everywhere and anytime is also a serious threat to their content privacy and security (De Cristofaro, Soriente, Tsudik, & Williams, 2012). This user generated content creates cultural, symbolic, and affective benefit including personal satisfaction, enhanced skill or reputation, improved functionality for existing games or devices, community building or civic engagement. In more simplistic terms, user generated content creates value, economic or not.

Having all of this into consideration, it seems clear that it is necessary to have a clear separation among the social network platform providers, their social functionalities, and the user generated content that they hold. It is important to create mechanisms that transfer part of the security and sharing control to the end-user side. Having this into consideration, in this section, it is proposed and presented a paradigm shift that implies a change from the current social networks security and privacy scenario based on a social network platform centric, to another paradigm that empowers social networks users' on the control and safeguard of its privacy, passing the user generated content sharing control to the end-user side, using rights management systems (Marques & Serrão, 2013b). Also, the entity that is responsible for the storage and protection of the user generated content is independent of the social network platform itself.

This new approach creates a mechanism that protects the shared user generated content on the social network platform while it provides the content sharing and access control to the end-user.

Overall System Architecture

As referred on the previous section, the novel approach that is followed is based on open rights management systems – in particular, and for this sake, it is based on OpenSDRM (Carlos Serrão, Neves, Trevor Barker, & Massimo Balestri, 2003; Serrão, 2008). OpenSDRM is an open and distributed rights management architecture that allows the implementation of different content business models. Moreover, OpenSDRM was created having into consideration interoperability aspects (Serrão, Rodriguez, & Delgado, 2011) that permit that the different modules that compose the system to be decoupled and re-integrated to allow interoperability (Serrão, Dias, & Kudumakis, 2005; Serrão et al., 2011) with other non-OpenSDRM components, using an open and well-defined API (Figure 3). Additionally there may exist also more than one instance of each of the services on the platform, allowing the scalability and growth of the set of all possible configuration options (Serrão, Dias, & Delgado, 2005).

For the proposed scenario, the social network platform can be integrated with the rights management system, using different methods. If the social network implements a development API or if it is open-source, a much tighter integration scenario can be achieved. If not, it is possible to use other publicly available mechanisms on the platform (or out of the platform) to enable a lesser integrated scenario, but that maintains the privacy and security characteristics sought. Using mechanisms on the platform is the most common scenario and therefore is the approach that will be reflected here.

In this architecture there are some elements that cooperate in order to provide the necessary functionalities to both the end-users and the social network platform, in order to implement the necessary mechanisms to provide security and privacy to user generated content.

OpenSDRM, as an open rights management framework is composed by different services (Figure 4). Some of the services are deployed on the server-side while other are implemented on the user-side. On

Figure 3. Overview of the architecture integrated with the rights management system

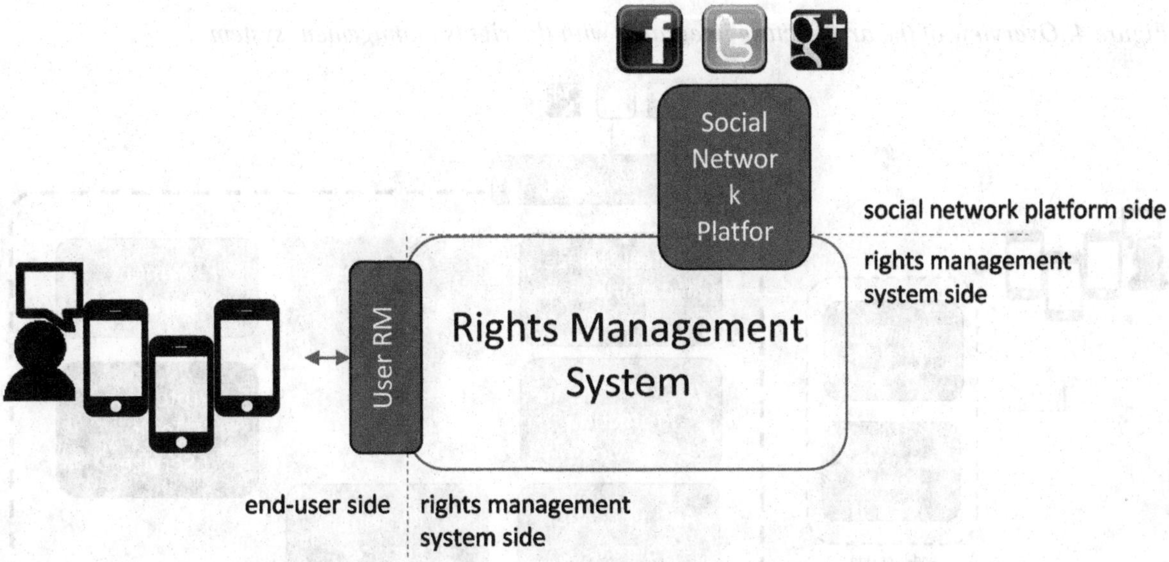

the user-side, the authorization service handles the requests to render some type of content on the user device, processing the requests and matching them to existing credentials, licenses and permissions to render the content. Also, on the end-user side the content rendering service is responsible for verifying the necessary requirements to render the content (encryption, scrambling, and others) and effectively renders the content for the end user.

On the server-side, is where a large part of the rights management responsibility lies. A set of decoupled components with a well-defined API that allows an integration between the necessary ones to implement the specific content business model. These services are the following:

- **Content Storage and Distribution Service:** This service is responsible for the storage and distribution of user generated content in a protected manner;
- **Content Protection Service:** The service is responsible for the protection of the content. The content is protected by specific protection tools and specific protection mechanisms that may change according to the content and the business model that is going to be implemented;
- **Content Registration Service:** This service is responsible for registering the content on the platform that will be used to uniquely identify the content on the system. This unique identifier is used to identify the user generated content throughout the entire content lifecycle;
- **Payment Service:** If the business model includes the possibility to trade content, this payment service is responsible to communicate with a payment gateway that implements the necessary mechanisms to process payments;
- **Protection Tools Service:** This service is responsible for the registration of content protection tools on the system and for making those tools available for the content protection service to use when implementing the content protection schemas (such as encryption, scrambling, watermarking and others);

Figure 4. Overview of the architecture integrated with the rights management system

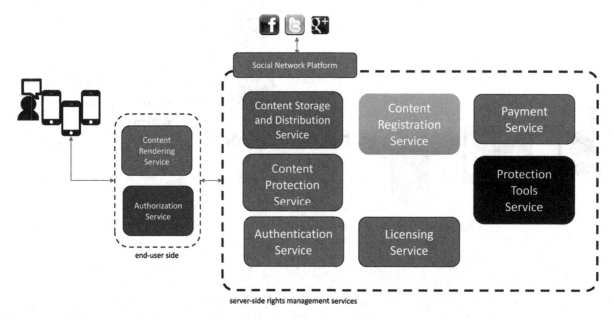

- **Authentication Service:** Handles the registration of users and services on the system as well as the requests for authenticate users on behalf of other services;
- **Licensing Service:** This is one of the most important services of the rights management framework, responsible for creating license templates, define and produce new content licenses (that represent the type of rights, permissions and/or restrictions of a given user, or group of users, over the content) and provide licenses, upon request, to specific users.

The following sections of this document will provide a description on how the user can utilize this platform to share user generated content on the social network, and how a user can access content shared by other users.

Registration on the Platform

This novel platform presupposes that all the system services are initially registered on that platform. This means that each one of the different services, either server-side or client-side have to be individually registered at the platform. This registration process assigns unique credentials to each one of the services, ensuring that they are uniquely registered and that these credentials will be used to identify and differentiate the services in future interactions (Figure 5). This registration process is conducted by the authentication service that on its turn issues credentials to all the other services and acts as a central trustworthy mechanism. Moreover, all the communication between the different services is conducted over a secure and authenticated channel, using Secure Sockets Layer/Transport Layer Security(SSL/TLS) – this ensures the authentication and security of the servers where the services are deployed and allowing the establishment of secure communication channels (Stephen A Thomas, 2000).

Figure 5. Handling the registration of new services on the platform

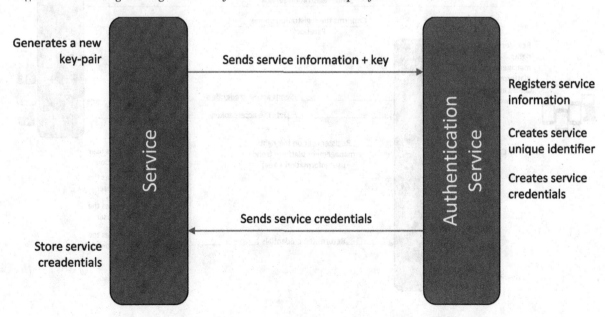

1. The authentication service (AS) has cryptographic material (K_{pub}^{AS}, K_{priv}^{AS}) and credentials that were self-issued (C^{AS}_{AS}) or issued by other trustworthy entity (C^{CA}_{AS});

2. The service that needs to be registered generates a key pair (K_{pub}^{S}, K_{priv}^{S}) and sends a registration request to the AS, passing some information about the service (S_{info}) and the public key (K_{pub}^{S}) of the service: $S_{info} + K_{pub}^{S}$;

3. AS receives this information, verifies it and then creates a unique service identifier (S_{UUID}). After this verification the AS creates the service credentials that will identify this service globally and uniquely on the platform: $C^{AS}_{S[UUID]} = K_{priv}^{AS}\{S_{UUID}, K_{pub}^{S[UUID]}, C^{AS}_{AS}\}^2$. These credentials, which are signed by AS, are then returned to the requesting service;

4. The requesting service, stores the credentials. This credential contains also the public key of the authentication service (K_{pub}^{AS}). This is used to prove this credentials to other entities that also rely on the same AS – services that trust AS, also trust on credentials issued by AS, presented by other services.

The service registration process, as described above needs to be repeated according to the number of services available within the social network platform. This enables the entire ecosystem of services to be trusted on that platform.

Another important aspect of the registration process concerns the registration of the users on the rights management platform. The registration of the user on the rights management platform can be dependent or independent of the social network platform. In the example that is presented here, it is assumed that this registration process is performed fully integrated with the social network platform.

This process performs in the following manner (Figure 6):

Figure 6. Overview of the user registration process

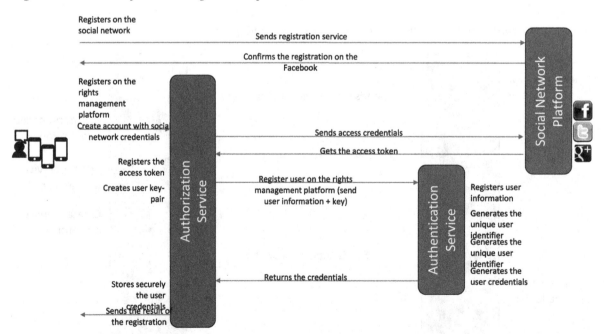

1. Assuming that the user still has no account on a social network platform, the user starts the registration process on the social network. In order to do that the user needs to supply its email address (as username) and a password;

2. The registration process on the social network platform finishes and a confirmation message is sent to the end-user;

3. Next, the user, using the client-side rights management authorization service (AUTS), initiates the registration process in the rights management platform. The AUTS presents several registration options to the end-user (integrated with some social network platforms -using either Oauth- or an independent mode). For this case, the user will use registration options by using the mode of integrated authentication;

4. The user introduces the social account credentials (email, password) on the AUTS that starts the authentication process on the social network platform. If successful, the social network returns an access token that has a specific validity and a set of permissions to conduct different operations on the social network on behalf of the user;

5. AUTS, using the user credentials (email, password) creates a secret key that is used to initialize a secure storage on the authorization service: $S_k^{SStorage} = SHA1[email+password]$;

6. The AUTS securely stores the user information, and the social network access token. Additionally, the AUTS creates a key-pair for the user (K_{pub}^U, K_{priv}^U) also storing it in a secure manner: $S_k^{SStorage}(K_{pub}^U$, K_{priv}^U, user_info, token);

7. AUTS contacts the AS to register the user on the platform. This is performed using the $C^{AS}_{S[AUTS]}$ that contains the K_{pub}^{AS}. $C^{AS}_{S[AUTS]}$ is also sent to ensure that the AUTS has been previously registered: K_{pub}^{AS} (email, K_{pub}^U, $C^{AS}_{S[AUTS]}$);

8. The AUTS receives all this information and after deciphering it, and validating the AUTS credential, registers the user information, generates a unique identifier for the user and creates credentials for the user: $C^{AS}_{UUID} = K_{priv}^{AS} \{UUID, K_{pub}^U\}$;

9. The credentials are returned to the AUTS and are securely stored: $S_k^{SStorage}(C^{AS}_{UUID})$. The user is notified about the result of the registration operation.

This is the concluding step of the service and user registration on the rights management platform. The user is now prepared to use both the rights management service and the social network platform.

Sharing Content on the Platform

The other important functionality on the system is the sharing of user generated content (UGC) on the social network. This sharing mechanism is performed through the rights management platform, and the content is stored securely on a configured location (it can be on a specific storage location, on the social platform or on the rights management platform). When the user uploads user generated content, the content is protected and the rights, permissions and restrictions about the content can be defined by the user.

This process assumes that both user that generates the content and the users willing to access the content are properly registered and authenticated on the social network platform and on the rights management platform (Figure 7).

Figure 7. Overview of the user generated content secure sharing on the social network platform

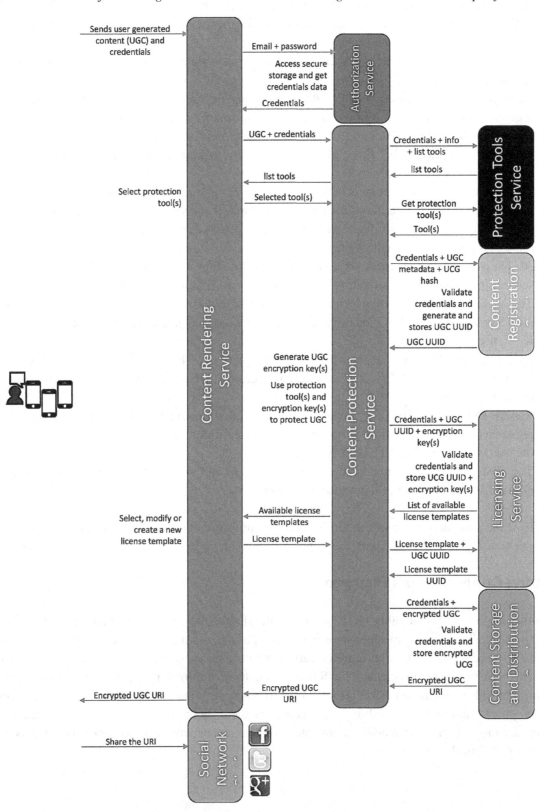

In a brief discussing way, the user generated content is uploaded to the rights management platform, the access rights and permissions are defined by the user, the content is protected, and a URI is returned to be shared on the social network platform.

The novel content sharing process, using the mechanisms described in this chapter, can be now defined in the following steps:

1. The user sends the user generated content (UGC) that it expects to share on the social network. This UGC is uploaded through the content rendering service (CRS). This service requires the user to enter its credentials (email and password), if the user is not yet authenticated. These credentials are used to access the secure storage: $S_k^{SStorage} = SHA1[email+password]$;

2. The CRS contacts the AUTS, which reads from the secure storage the user rights management system credentials: C^{AS}_{UUID};

3. The CRS uploads to the content protection service (CPS) the UGC and sends the user credentials, obtained in the previous step: UGC_{UUID}, C^{AS}_{UUID};

4. The CPS, after retrieving some metadata information about the UGC (such as the type, the format, the encoding, among others), contacts the protection tools service (PTS), requesting a list of available protection tools, that can be suitable to protect the UGC. The PTS sends its credentials and some information about the content: C^{AS}_{CPS}, UGC_info;

5. The PTS also returns a list of protection tools that match the request made by the CPS. This information is signed by PTS: $K_{priv}^{PTS}\{protection\_tools\_list\}$;

6. The CPS returns the list of protection tools to the CRS, and presents it to the user. The user selects the most appropriate protection tools, adjusting the parameters of applicability of the tools to the UGC and submits its request about the necessary protection tools;

7. The CPS requests the selected protection tools from the protection tools service. The PTS returns the requested tools to the CPS;

8. Next, the CPS requests to the content registration service for the UGC to be registered. For this, the CPS send its credentials, the UCG metadata and the content hash: C^{AS}_{CPS}, UGC_info, SHA1[UGC];

9. The content registration service (CRGS), stores the received information, and generates a unique content identifier that is returned to the content protection service: $K_{priv}^{CRS.}\{UGC_{UUID}\}$;

10. The CPS generates one or more content encryption keys (CEK[1], CEK[2] … CEK[n]) that are applied over the UGC, using the selected protection tools, in order to ensure the appropriate content protection;

11. Following this protection process, the CPS sends the content encryption keys for registration at the licensing service. Each of the content encryption keys is protected with the user key, and the entire message is protected by the CPS key: C^{AS}_{CPS}, $K_{pub}^{CPS}(K_{pub}^{U}(CEK[1], CEK[2] … CEK[n])$, UGC_{UUID});

12. The licensing service (LS) after validating all the received information, returns a list of licensing templates to the content protection service. The CPS returns the list of licensing templates to CRS, and the user can select the most appropriate license template, modify it and adapt it, or simply create a new one;

13. The license template (LIC_{TPL}) is sent to the CPS that after sends it to the licensing service and associates it with the identifier of the UGC: LIC_{TPL}, UGC_{UUID}. The licensing service returns the license template identifier (LIC_{TPL} [UUID]);

14. In the next stage, the CPS sends the protected UGC to the content storage and distribution service that stores the encrypted content: C^{AS}_{CPS}, $K_{priv}^{CPS}\{CEK[n](UGC), UGC_{UUID}\}$;

15. The content storage and distribution service returns a URI for the location of the stored encrypted UGC. This URI is returned to the user that can share it on the social network platform afterwards.

After this process is completed, the UGC shared by the user is shared on the social network platform. The user can also use the social network sharing mechanisms as a way to control how the UGC is propagated on the social network. But, in order to have a fine grained control over the UGC, the user needs to use the rights management system to produce specific licenses with the conditions under which the UGC can be used. These licenses are produced in multiple formats (either in ODRL or MPEG-21 REL). In addition, these licenses are used to support the expression of rights over the UGC. Therefore, when the user uploads user generated content to the rights management system, and after the process that was described previously, the subsequent steps are the following:

1. The CPS contacts licensing service to obtain the appropriate license template for the specific UGC, which was previously created: LIC_{TPL} [UUID]. The license template is an XML-formatted document that contains parameterized fields that can be adapted to specific rights situations;

2. A typical license template for user generated content would be composed by following elements:
   a. User unique identifier (UUID), multiple users ($UUID_1$, $UUID_2$,..., $UUID_n$) or a group identifier (G_{UUID}): these fields represent the unique identifiers of the users or groups to whom the user generated content is going to be shared;
   b. The unique identifier of the content: UGC_{UUID};
   c. List of permissions ($Permission_1$...$Permission_n$);
   d. List of restrictions ($Restriction_1$...$Restriction_n$);
   e. Validity date (validity);
   f. The different content encryption keys (CEK[1], CEK[2] ... CEK[n]). The content encryption keys are protected with user public key: $K_{pub}^{U}(CEK[1], CEK[2] ... CEK[n])$;
   g. The license signature, where the license contents are signed by the licensing service: License $= K_{priv}^{LIS} \{UUID_1.. UUID_n, G_{UUID}1, G_{UUID}n, UGC_{UUID}, Permission_1 ..Permission_n, Restriction_1 ..Restriction_n, Validity, K_{pub}^{U} (CEK[1] ... CEK[n])\}$.

3. The license is stored on the licensing service, where it can be accessed by legitimate users.

Accessing Content on the Platform

Finally the last process in this case-study is to present how the users can access user generated content that was shared by other users on the social network platform. In order to do that, the user needs to be registered on the social network platform and on the rights management system.

When navigating through the timeline of the social network platform, user generated content that was shared over the social network platform, is presented in the form of a special URI, that, when clicked, is intercepted by the rights management platform, and the access process is started.

The referred process is described in the following steps:

1. The CRS, while trying to render the content that is shared on the social network platform, detects that it is protected content, and contacts the authorization service to access the appropriate information to try rendering the content;

2. The user authenticates to the system using the authorization service, supplying its credentials (email and password) to unlock the secure storage and retrieve the user information;

3. The authorization service, using the UGC_{UUID} embedded on the URI, checks if a license for this UGC already exists on the secure storage. If a license already exists:

    a. The authorization service checks the license contents, validating the license digital signature and verifying the UGC_{UUID};

    b. If the UGC_{UUID} is the right one, the Validity is checked and the list of permissions and restrictions are evaluated;

    c. If the conditions are met, the content can be deciphered and rendered by the content rendering service. The content encryption keys can be retrieved from the license, and used to decipher the content: $K_{priv}{}^{U}(K_{pub}{}^{U}(CEK[1] \ldots CEK[n])) = CEK[1] \ldots CEK[n]$;

    d. Content is rendered by the CRS while the license conditions are fulfilled;

4. If the authorization still does not possess a valid license for the UGC_{UUID} that the content rendering service is trying to render to view, the following process should occur:

    a. The user authenticates to the system using the authorization service, supplying its credentials (email and password) to unlock the secure storage and retrieve the user information;

    b. The authorization service, after getting the appropriated user information, including the credentials, from the secure storage, allows the CRS to contact the licensing service, passing its credentials ($C^{AS}{}_{CRS}$), the user credentials ($C^{AS}{}_{UUID}$) and the user generated content identifier (UGC_{UUID}) the user is trying to render;

    c. The licensing service receives and validates the data that was sent by the CRS, and uses the user generated content unique identifier (UGC_{UUID}) and the user unique identifier (UUID) to verify the existence of a valid license. If the license exists on the system, that license is returned to the CRS, that passes it, for validation and storage, to the authorization service: License = $K_{priv}{}^{LIS} \{UUID_1 .. UUID_n, G_{UUID}1, G_{UUID}n, UGC_{UUID}, Permission_1 .. Permission_n, Restriction_1 .. Restriction_n, Validity, K_{pub}{}^{U} (CEK[1] \ldots CEK[n])\}$;

    d. The authorization service validates the license signature, verifying its contents and validity and asserting the correct UGC_{UUID};

    e. If the UGC_{UUID} is the right one, the Validity is checked and the list of permissions and restrictions are evaluated;

    f. If the conditions are met, the content can be deciphered and rendered by the CRS. The content encryption keys can be retrieved from the license, and used to decipher the content: $K_{priv}{}^{U}(K_{pub}{}^{U}(CEK[1] \ldots CEK[n])) = CEK[1] \ldots CEK[n]$;

    g. Content is rendered by the CRS while the license conditions are satisfied.

After this process is executed, the access to the CRS can be granted or not, depending on the conditions expressed on the license. For simplicity sake, there are several other processes that were not included in this description, such as, for instance, the verification of the protection mechanisms that were applied to the content, and the download of the appropriated mechanisms to allow the local temporarily unprotected version of the user generated content to be rendered.

The usage of rights management systems to offer security and privacy to shared user generated content, offers additional privacy and security mechanisms that are out of the control of the social network platform itself (Rodríguez, Rodríguez, Carreras, & Delgado, 2009). The users can take advantage of both (the rights management system and the social network platform) to offer a finer control on the content sharing privacy and security properties. This is a novel approach (Marques & Serrão, 2013b) that clearly puts the security and privacy control on the end-user side.

A CASE STUDY FOR AN INTELLIGENT INTRUSION DETECTION/ PREVENTION SYSTEM ON A SOFTWARE-DEFINED NETWORK

This section presents and discusses a case study about an intelligent Intrusion Detection/Prevention System (IDS/IPS) belonging to a software-defined network. In this case study, the IDS/IPS behavior is controlled by a Kinetic module (Feamster, 2014). The Kinetic language (Monsanto, Reich, Foster, Rexford, & Walker, 2013) is an SDN control framework where operators can define a network policy as a Finite State Machine (FSM). The transitions between states of a FSM can be triggered by different types of dynamic events in the network, (e.g. intrusion detection, host state). Based on different network events, operators can enforce different policies to the network using an intuitive FSM model. Kinetic is implemented as a Pyretic controller module written in Python. For more information about Pyretic and Python, consult respectively (Pyretic, 2014) and (Python, 2014).

"A Kinetic control program permits programmer-defined events to dynamically change forwarding behavior for an arbitrary set of flows. Such events can range from topology changes (generated by the Pyretic runtime) to security incidents (generated by an intrusion detection system). The programmer specifies an FSM description that contains set of states, each of which maps to some network behavior that are encoded using Pyretic's policy language; and a set of transitions between those states, each of which may be triggered by events that the operator defines" (Feamster, 2014). For more details on Kinetic, see (Monsanto et al., 2013).

In this case study, an implementation of an IDS/IPS security module will be developed, which should behave as follows:

- If a host is infected and is not a privileged host then it is dropped;
- If a host is infected and is a privileged (exempt) host then the traffic from that host is automatically redirected to a garden wall host, where some corrective security actions could be issued over that infected host (e.g. clean and install security patches for trying to recover it);
- If a host is not infected then the traffic from that host is forwarded towards its final destination.

Code Explanation

In Table 1, it is displayed a partial view of the Python code that implements the Kinetic control program that will be used in this section to evaluate the intelligent IDS/IPS. To become clearer, this code functionality is explained in the following paragraph.

Each time a new packet arrives to the system, the IDS/IPS initially processes that packet and defines the policy to be applied to that packet (i.e. drop | redirect | forward). This policy is then delivered to a second module that implements further MAC functionality, namely the learning algorithm of MAC

Table 1. Partial view of the code for the module IDS/IPS.

```
class gardenwall(DynamicPolicy):
 def __init__(self):
 # Garden Wall
 def redirectToGardenWall():
 client_ips = [IP('10.0.0.1'), IP('10.0.0.2')]
 rewrite_policy = rewriteDstIPAndMAC(client_ips, '10.0.0.3')
 return rewrite_policy
 ### DEFINE THE LPEC FUNCTION
 def lpec(f):
 return match(srcip=f['srcip'])
 ## SET UP TRANSITION FUNCTIONS
 @transition
 def exempt(self):
 self.case(occurred(self.event),self.event)
 @transition
 def infected(self):
 self.case(occurred(self.event),self.event)
 @transition
 def policy(self):
 # If exempt, redirect pkt to gardenwall;rewrite dstip to 10.0.0.3
 self.case(test_and_true(V('exempt'),V('infected')), C(redirectToGardenWall()))
 # If infected, drop pkt
 self.case(is_true(V('infected')),C(drop))
 # Else, identity -> forward pkt
 self.default(C(identity))
 ### SET UP THE FSM DESCRIPTION
 self.fsm_def = FSMDef(
 infected=FSMVar(type=BoolType(),
 init=False,
 trans=infected),
 exempt=FSMVar(type=BoolType(),
 init=False,
 trans=exempt),
 policy=FSMVar(type=Type(Policy,
 {drop,identity,redirectToGardenWall()}),
 init=identity,
 trans=policy))
 ### SET UP POLICY AND EVENT STREAMS
 fsm_pol = FSMPolicy(lpec,self.fsm_def)
 json_event = JSONEvent()
 json_event.register_callback(fsm_pol.event_handler)
 super(gardenwall,self).__init__(fsm_pol)
```

addresses to enhance the L2 packet forwarding. This second module is the one that effectively forwards or redirects the packet (otherwise if the packet is to be drooped, this second module will not receive any packet at all because it was already discarded by the first IDS/IPS module).

The code shown in Table 1 corresponds to the IDS/IPS module and has its code encapsulated inside a class designated by "gardenwall", which was instantiated from class "DynamicPolicy" (to support the processing of JSON events, as it will be explained below). The function "lpec" is like a packet input filter because it only selects the packets whose source IP address is specified by variable *srcip*. This aims to process the first packet of a flow exactly in the same way as all the following packets of that flow. In this example, a transition function encodes logic that indicates the new value a state variable should take when a particular event arrives at the controller. For example, the *infected* transition function encodes a single case: when an *infected* event occurs, the new value taken by the state variable *infected* is the value of that event (i.e. FALSE or TRUE). This is an example of an exogenous transition (i.e. the state variable *infected* is changed by an external event); other exogenous transition in this scenario is the one associated with the state variable *exempt*. In opposition, the transition associated to the state variable *policy* is endogenous because its state is triggered by both internal state variables of the current FSM: *infected* and *exempt*.

The Finite State Machine (FSM) (see Figure 8) used in the current scenario associates the transition functions previously defined with the appropriate state variables. The FSM definition consists of a set of state variable definitions. Each variable definition simply specifies the variable's type (i.e., set of allowable values), initial value, and associated transition functions. The infected variable is a boolean whose initial value is FALSE (representing the assumption that hosts are initially not infected), and transitions based on the infected function defined previously. Likewise, the policy variable can take the values *drop* or *identity*, initially starts in the *identity* state, and transitions based on the policy function defined previously. The FSMPolicy that Kinetic provides automatically directs each incoming external event to the appropriate *lpec* FSM, where it will be handled by the exogenous transition function specified in the FSM description (i.e. the function *self.fsm_def*). In this way, it is ensured that the FSM works as expected.

Evaluation

The network topology used in the current evaluation made with a network emulator is shown in Figure 9. All the evaluation was performed in a single Linux virtual machine (Ubuntu).

We now initiate the evaluation, opening a Linux shell, and run our Kinetic controller application with the following commands:

```
$ cd ~/pyretic
$ pyretic.py pyretic.kinetic.examples.gardenwall
```

As shown in Figure 10, the kinetic controller prints out some results from a verification of network policies using the NuSMV symbolic model checker (NuSMV, 2014). Kinetic automatically generates a NuSMV input from the program written by the programmer/operator, and verifies logic statements written in CTL (Computation Tree Logic) (CTL, 2014).

Figure 8. Finite State Machine (FSM)
(Feamster, 2014)

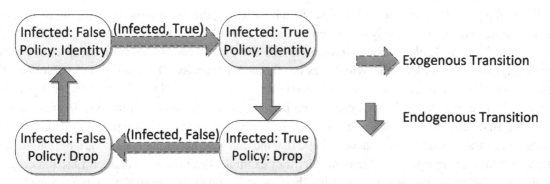

Figure 9. Network Topology under test
(Feamster, 2014)

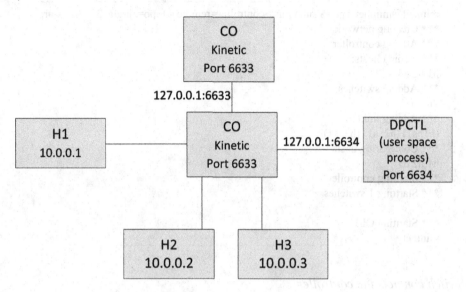

Figure 10. Kinetic controller terminal

```
*** Please report bugs to <numsv-users@fbk.eu>
*** Copyright (c) 2010, Fondazione Bruno Kessler
*** This version of NuMSV is linked to the CUDD library version 2.4.1
*** Copyright (c) 1995-2004, Regents of the University of Colorado
*** This version  of NuMSV is linked to the MiniSat  SAT solver.
*** See http://www.cs.chalmers.se/Cs/Research/FormalMethods/MiniSat
*** Copyright (c) 2003-2005, Niklas Een, Niklas Sorensson


-- specification AG ((infected & !exempt) -> AX policy = policy_1)   is true
-- specification AG (!infected -> AX policy = policy_2) is true
-- specification AG ((infected & exempt) -> AX policy = policy_3)   is true
-- specification A [ policy = policy_2  U infected ]    is true
system diameter: 3
reachable states: 12 (2^3.58496) out of 12 (2^3.58496)
========================= NuSMV Output  End ==============


POX 0.1.0 (betta)  / Copyright 2011-2013 James McCauley, et al.
Connected to pyretic frontend.
INFO:core:POX 0.1.0 (betta) is up.
```

In a second shell, we start the network emulator "mininet", performing the following command:

```
$ sudo mn --controller=remote --topo=single,3 --mac -arp
```

The obtained output result is visualized in Figure 11. In addition, the bottom line of Figure 12 shows that the Kinetic controller discovered the emulated switch.

Figure 11. Mininet terminal

```
mininet@mininet-vm:~$ sudo mn --controller=remote --topo=single, 3 --mac --arp
*** Creating network
*** Adding controller
*** Adding hosts:
h1 h2 h3
*** Adding switches:
s1
*** Adding links:
(h1, s1) (h2, s1) (h3, s1)
*** Configuring hosts
h1 h2 h3
*** Startting controller
*** Startting 1 switches
s1
*** Startting CLI:
mininet>
```

Figure 12. Switch contacts the controller

```
*** Copyright (c) 2010, Fondazione Bruno Kessler
*** This version of NuMSV is linked to the CUDD library version 2.4.1
*** Copyright (c) 1995-2004, Regents of the University of Colorado
*** This version of NuMSV is linked to the MiniSat SAT solver.
*** See http://www.cs.chalmers.se/Cs/Research/FormalMethods/MiniSat
*** Copyright (c) 2003-2005, Niklas Een, Niklas Sorensson

-- specification AG ((infected & !exempt) -> AX policy = policy_1)   is true
-- specification AG (!infected -> AX policy = policy_2) is true
-- specification AG ((infected & exempt) -> AX policy = policy_3)   is true
-- specification A [ policy = policy_2  U infected ]   is true
system diameter: 3
reachable states: 12 (2^3.58496) out of 12 (2^3.58496)
====================== NuSMV Output End ======================

POX 0.1.0 (betta)  / Copyright 2011-2013 James McCauley, et al.
Connected to pyretic frontend.
INFO:core:POX 0.1.0 (betta) is up.
INFO: openflow.of_01: [None 1] closed
INFO: openflow.of_01: [00-00-00-00-00-01 2] connected
```

Imagine now the situation that host "h1" become compromised (infected). This situation originates the transmission of an event to change the state of the FSM in a way that any traffic originated in that host should be discarded in the switch. In this network status, the traffic ICMP between hosts "h1" and "h2" becomes blocked. We issue the transmission of the "infected" event to the controller executing in a third terminal the following command:

```
$ python json_sender.py -n infected -l True --flow="{srcip=10.0.0.1}" -a
127.0.0.1 -p 50001
```

The "infected" event was sent to the controller as it is possible to be visualized in Figure 13.

After some milliseconds, the Kinetic controller received the event informing that host h1 is infected (see Figure 14). As a consequence of this, the controller changed the policy to drop the packets originated by host "h1".

After this, we have tried to send two ping messages from host "h1" to host "h2" but as it is shown in Figure 15 without any success. This occurs because the IDS/IPS installed in the switch between "h1" and "h2" a policy to drop the packets originated by host "h1".

Next, assuming that host "h1" was classified as a privileged (exempt) terminal, then the controller will be notified from this through the following event:

Figure 13. JSON event transmitted to the controller

```
mininet@mininet-vm:~/pyretic/pyretic/kinetic$ python json_sender.py -n infected -l
True --flow ="{srcip=10.0.0.1}" -a 127.0.0.1 -p 50001

Flow_Str = {srcip=10.0.0.1}

Data Payload = {'dstip': None, 'protocol': None, 'srcmac': None, 'tos': None,
'vlan_pcp': None, 'dstmac': None, 'inport': None, 'switch': None, 'ethtype': None,
'srcip': '10.0.0.1', 'dstport': None, 'srcport': None, 'vlan_id': None}


Ok
mininet@mininet-vm:~/pyretic/pyretic/kinetic$
```

Figure 14. Controller changes the policy to drop

```
-- specification A [ policy = policy_2  U infected ]    is true
system diameter: 3
reachable states: 12 (2^3.58496) out of 12 (2^3.58496)
==================== NuSMV Output  End ====================


POX 0.1.0 (betta) / Copyright 2011-2013 James McCauley, et al.
Connected to pyretic frontend.
INFO:core:POX 0.1.0 (betta) is up.
INFO: openflow.of_01: [None 1] closed
INFO: openflow.of_01: [00-00-00-00-00-01 2] connected
Received connection from ('127.0.0.1', 42143)
Received event infected is True related with flow {'srcip': 10.0.0.1}
fsm_policy:event_name= infected
fsm_policy:event_value= True
fsm_policy:event_state= {'policy': drop, 'infected': True, 'exempt': False}
fsm_policy:self.policy = if
    match:  ('srcip', 10.0.0.1)
then
    [DynamicPolicy]
    drop
else
    identity
```

Figure 15. ICMP traffic is dropped

```
s1
*** Adding links:
(h1, s1) (h2, s1) (h3, s1)
*** Configuring hosts
h1 h2 h3
*** Startting controller
*** Startting 1 switches
s1
*** Startting CLI:
mininet> h1 ping -c 2 h2
PING 10.0.0.2 (10.0.0.2) 56(84) bytes of data.

--- 10.0.0.2 ping statistics ---
2 packets transmitted, 0 received, 100% packet loss, time 1008ms

mininet>
```

```
$ python json_sender.py -n exempt -l True --flow="{srcip=10.0.0.1}" -a
127.0.0.1 -p 50001
```

Almost immediately, the Kinetic controller received the event informing that host "h1" is infected (see Figure 16). As a consequence of this, the controller changed the policy to redirect the packets originated by host "h1" to host "h3" (policy modify) for further analysis. This policy is installed in the switch.

Figure 16. Policy is changed to redirect the traffic

```
fsm_policy:event_name= infected
fsm_policy:event_value= True
fsm_policy:event_state= {'policy': drop, 'infected': True, 'exempt': False}
fsm_policy:self.policy = if
   match: ('srcip', 10.0.0.1)
then
   [DynamicPolicy]
   drop
else
   identity
Received connection from ('127.0.0.1', 42144)
Received event exempt is True related with flow {'srcip': 10.0.0.1}
fsm_policy:event_name= exempt
fsm_policy:event_value= True
fsm_policy:event_state= {'policy': modify: ('dstip', 10.0.0.3) ('dstmac',
00:00:00:00:00:03), 'infected':True, 'exempt': True}
fsm_policy:self.policy = if
   match: ('srcip', 10.0.0.1)
then
   [DynamicPolicy]
   modify: ('dstip', 10.0.0.3) ('dstmac', 00:00:00:00:00:03)
else
   identity
```

The redirection of traffic from host "h1", it is perfectly visible in Figure 17, after we repeat the ping command. One can note that the host replying to the ping is host "h3" instead of "h2". As already explained, host "h3" is responsible to recover in terms of security any privileged hosts that by some reason become compromised.

After, some corrective actions performed in host "h1" by "h3", one can assume that host "h1" has recovered. In this way, a new event is sent to the controller notifying host "h1" changed to the state of "not infected", as follows:

```
$ python json_sender.py -n infected -l False --flow="{srcip=10.0.0.1}" -a
127.0.0.1 -p 50001
```

Figure 18 illustrates some controller´s output informing that the last event was received and the forwarding policy changed to forward the traffic towards host "h2" (policy identity).

Figure 17. ICMP traffic is redirected

```
mininet> h1 ping -c 2 h2
PING 10.0.0.2 (10.0.0.2) 56(84) bytes of data.
64 bytes from 10.0.0.3 icmp_req=1 ttl=64 time=115 ms
64 bytes from 10.0.0.3 icmp_req=2 ttl=64 time=112 ms

--- 10.0.0.2 ping statistics ---
2 packets transmitted, 2 received, 0% packet loss, time 1002ms
rtt min/avg/mdev = 112.492/114.106/115.720/1.614 ms
mininet>
```

Figure 18. Policy returns back to traffic pass through (identity)

```
match: ('switch', 1) ('dstmac', 00:00:00:00:00:01)
then
   [DynamicPolicy]
   fwd 1
else
   flood on:
   --------------------------------------------------------------
   switch  |  switch edges  |  egress ports                    |
   --------------------------------------------------------------
   1       |                |  1[2]---, 1[3]---, 1[1]---        |
Received connection from ('127.0.0.1', 42145)
Received event infect is False related with flow {'srcip': 10.0.0.1}
fsm_policy:event_name= infected
fsm_policy:event_value= False
fsm_policy:event_state= {'policy': identity, 'infected': False, 'exempt': True}
fsm_policy:self.policy = if
   match: ('srcip', 10.0.0.1)
then
   [DynamicPolicy]
   identity
else
   identity
```

Security and Privacy Issues of Big Data

From Figure 19 is possible to conclude that host "h1" is now receiving response from host "h2" itself.

At this point, we finish our current evaluation of the intelligent IDS/IPS system. In the context of Big Data this is an important contribution once it facilitates the identification and solving of some attacks that a distributed Big Data architecture (in different phases of the Big Data lifecycle – from data capture to data processing and consumption) can suffer.

BIG DATA SECURITY: FUTURE DIRECTIONS

Throughout this chapter it was possible to present some of the most important security and privacy challenges that affect Big Data projects and their specificities. Although the information security practices, methodologies and tools to ensure the security and privacy of the Big Data ecosystem already exist, the particular characteristics of Big Data make them ineffective if they are not used in an integrated manner. This chapter also presents some solutions for these challenges, but it does not provide a definitive solution for the problem. It rather points to some directions and technologies that might contribute to solve some of the most relevant and challenging Big Data security and privacy issues.

Next, two different use cases were presented. Both of the use-cases present some directions that contribute to solving part of the large Big Data security and privacy puzzle. In the first use-case it was presented an approach that tries solving security and privacy issues on social network user generated content. In this approach, an open an interoperable rights management system was proposed as a way to improve the privacy of users that share content over social networks. The processes described show how the rights management system puts the end-users on the control of their own user-generated content, and how they prevent abuses from either other users or the social network platform itself. The second use-case presented the capabilities offered by SDN in increasing the ability to collect statistics data from the network and of allowing controller applications to actively program the forwarding devices, are powerful

Figure 19. ICMP traffic is reaching again host h2

```
64 bytes from 10.0.0.3 icmp_req=1 ttl=64 time=115 ms
64 bytes from 10.0.0.3 icmp_req=2 ttl=64 time=112 ms

--- 10.0.0.2 ping statistics ---
2 packets transmitted, 2 received, 0% packet loss, time 1002ms
rtt min/avg/mdev = 112.492/114.106/115.720/1.614 ms
mininet> h1 ping -c 2 h2
PING 10.0.0.2 (10.0.0.2) 56(84) bytes of data.
64 bytes from 10.0.0.2 icmp_req=1 ttl=64 time=113 ms
64 bytes from 10.0.0.2 icmp_req=2 ttl=64 time=59.5 ms

--- 10.0.0.2 ping statistics ---
2 packets transmitted, 2 received, 0% packet loss, time 1001ms
rtt min/avg/mdev = 59.529/86.713/113.897/27.184 ms
mininet>
```

46

for proactive and smart security policy enforcement techniques such as active security (Hand, Ton, & Keller, 2013). This novel security methodology proposes a novel feedback loop to improve the control of defense mechanisms of a networked infrastructure, and is centered around five core capabilities: protect, sense, adjust, collect, counter (Kreutz et al., 2014). In this perspective, active security provides a centralized programming interface that simplifies the integration of mechanisms for detecting attacks, by i) collecting data from diverse sources (to identify attacks with more assertiveness), ii) converging to a consistent policy configuration for the security appliances, and iii) enforcing countermeasures to block or minimize the effect of such attacks. Previous aspects were partially covered by our IDS/IPS case study but notably need to be further developed and are an important contribution to the security and privacy of Big Data ecosystem.

As noted throughout this chapter, although some important steps are being given towards solving Big Data security and privacy issues, there is still a long road ahead. In the conclusion of this chapter, the authors would like to refer some interesting topics where the research community could work actively to develop new Big Data security and privacy solutions.

Research challenges in this Big Data ecosystem range from the data creation (and the Big Data sources - devices), data storage and transportation, data transformation and processing, and finally data usage. To support this lifecycle, a high capacity and highly distributed architecture will be necessary, exposed to an hostile environment subject to all kinds of attacks. The SDN approach as proposed on this chapter is a possible solution to counter these threats, however further research needs to be conducted, in particular on what concerns to automatic adaptation of switching and behavior-based security policies (P. Chen, Jorgen, & Yuan, 2011; Dohi & Uemura, 2012).

There are also important research challenges on maintaining end to end data security and privacy. Ensuring that data is never revealed in clear, in particular to non-authorized parties, on any point of the Big Data lifecycle. Moving from data to programs, there are techniques for protecting privacy in browsing, searching, social interactions, and general usage through obfuscation methods. However, there is more research to be conducted on the processing of encrypted data and privacy protection in the context of both computer programs and web-based systems.

More research challenges in the Big Data area include developing techniques to perform a transparent computations over encrypted data with multiple keys, from multiple sources and multiple users. In terms of research it would be challenging to study and develop ways to delegate limited functions over encrypted data, so that third parties can analyze it. All the aspects related with key management, authorization delegation, management of rights, are topics that require further research in this field.

When considering secure and private-aware system, trust is everything. In particular, in the case of Big Data, a trustworthy environment should be established for most of the scenarios (healthcare, assisted living, SCADA systems and many others). It is particularly challenging in terms of research directions how this environment can be attained. Trusting applications that are capable of querying and processing Big Data and extract knowledge from it and, trusting devices that collect all the data from multiple sources, constitute a basic security requirement. Understand how trust can be established among the end-users, the devices (IoT) and the applications is a hot research topic for the coming years.

On what concerns Big Data, these research challenges represent only the tip of the iceberg about the problems that still need to be studied and solved on the development of secure and privacy-aware Big Data ecosystem.

REFERENCES

Advantech. (2013). *Enhancing Big Data Security*. Retrieved from http://www.advantech.com.tw/nc/newsletter/whitepaper/big_data/big_data.pdf

Agrawal, D., Das, S., & El Abbadi, A. (2011). Big data and cloud computing. In *Proceedings of the 14th International Conference on Extending Database Technology - EDBT/ICDT '11* (p. 530). New York: ACM Press. doi:10.1145/1951365.1951432

Chen, P., Jorgen, B., & Yuan, Y. (2011). Software behavior based trusted attestation. In *Proceedings - 3rd International Conference on Measuring Technology and Mechatronics Automation, ICMTMA 2011* (Vol. 3, pp. 298–301). doi:10.1109/ICMTMA.2011.645

Chen, X., & Shi, S. (2009). A literature review of privacy research on social network sites. In *Multimedia Information Networking and Security, 2009. MINES'09. International Conference on* (Vol. 1, pp. 93–97). doi:10.1109/MINES.2009.268

Cloud Security Alliance. (2013). *Expanded Top Ten Security and Privacy Challenges*. Retrieved from https://downloads.cloudsecurityalliance.org/initiatives/bdwg/Expanded_Top_Ten_Big_Data_Security_and_Privacy_Challenges.pdf

CTL. (2014). *Computation tree logic*. Retrieved July 17, 2014, from http://en.wikipedia.org/wiki/Computation_tree_logic

DARPA. (2014). *Mining and understanding software enclaves (MUSE)*. Retrieved August 03, 2014, from http://www.darpa.mil/Our_Work/I2O/Programs/Mining_and_Understanding_Software_Enclaves_(MUSE).aspx

De Cristofaro, E., Soriente, C., Tsudik, G., & Williams, A. (2012). Hummingbird: Privacy at the time of twitter. In *Security and Privacy (SP), 2012 IEEE Symposium on* (pp. 285–299). IEEE.

Demchenko, Y., Ngo, C., de Laat, C., Membrey, P., & Gordijenko, D. (2014). Big Security for Big Data: Addressing Security Challenges for the Big Data Infrastructure. In W. Jonker & M. Petković (Eds.), *Secure Data Management* (pp. 76–94). Springer International Publishing. doi:10.1007/978-3-319-06811-4_13

Dohi, T., & Uemura, T. (2012). An adaptive mode control algorithm of a scalable intrusion tolerant architecture. Journal of Computer and System Sciences, 78, 1751–1754. doi:10.1016/j.jcss.2011.10.022

Feamster, N. (2014). *Software Defined Networking*. Retrieved August 02, 2014, from https://www.coursera.org/course/sdn

Gentry, C. (2009). *A fully homomorphic encryption scheme*. Stanford University. Retrieved from http://cs.au.dk/~stm/local-cache/gentry-thesis.pdf

Gentry, C. (2010). Computing arbitrary functions of encrypted data. *Communications of the ACM, 53*(3), 97. doi:10.1145/1666420.1666444

Goldwasser, S., Gordon, S. D., Goyal, V., Jain, A., Katz, J., Liu, F.-H. ... Zhou, H.-S. (2014). Multi-input functional encryption. In Advances in Cryptology--EUROCRYPT 2014 (pp. 578–602). Springer.

Google. (2014). *Encrypted Big Query Client.* Retrieved August 03, 2014, from https://code.google.com/p/encrypted-bigquery-client/

Gross, R., & Acquisti, A. (2005). Information revelation and privacy in online social networks. In *Proceedings of the 2005 ACM workshop on Privacy in the electronic society* (pp. 71–80). doi:10.1145/1102199.1102214

Hand, R., Ton, M., & Keller, E. (2013). Active security. In *Proceedings of the Twelfth ACM Workshop on Hot Topics in Networks - HotNets-XII* (pp. 1–7). New York: ACM Press. doi:10.1145/2535771.2535794

Hasan, O., Habegger, B., Brunie, L., Bennani, N., & Damiani, E. (2013). A Discussion of Privacy Challenges in User Profiling with Big Data Techniques: The EEXCESS Use Case. In *2013 IEEE International Congress on Big Data* (pp. 25–30). IEEE. doi:10.1109/BigData.Congress.2013.13

HP. (2014). *Internet of Things Research Study.* Retrieved from http://fortifyprotect.com/HP_IoT_Research_Study.pdf

IBM big data platform - Bringing big data to the Enterprise. (2014, July). CT000.

IDC. (2012). *Big Data in 2020.* Retrieved from http://www.emc.com/leadership/digital-universe/2012iview/big-data-2020.htm

Juels, A., & Oprea, A. (2013). New approaches to security and availability for cloud data. *Communications of the ACM, 56*(2), 64. doi:10.1145/2408776.2408793

Jutla, D. N., Bodorik, P., & Ali, S. (2013). Engineering Privacy for Big Data Apps with the Unified Modeling Language. In *2013 IEEE International Congress on Big Data* (pp. 38–45). IEEE. doi:10.1109/BigData.Congress.2013.15

Kim, C., Jin, M.-H., Kim, J., & Shin, N. (2012). User perception of the quality, value, and utility of user-generated content. *Journal of Electronic Commerce Research, 13*(4), 305–319.

Kindcrvag, J., Balaouras, S., Hill, B., & Mak, K. (2012). *Control And Protect Sensitive Information In the Era of Big Data.* Academic Press.

Kindervag, J., Wang, C., Balaouras, S., & Coit, L. (2011). *Applying Zero Trust To The Extending Enterprise.* Academic Press.

Kreutz, D., Ramos, F. M. V., Verissimo, P., Rothenberg, C. E., Azodolmolky, S., & Uhlig, S. (2014). *Software-Defined Networking: A Comprehensive Survey, 49. Networking and Internet Architecture.* Retrieved from http://arxiv.org/abs/1406.0440

Lindell, Y., & Pinkas, B. (2002). Privacy Preserving Data Mining. *Journal of Cryptology, 15*(3), 177–206. doi:10.1007/s00145-001-0019-2

Luo, H., Lin, Y., Zhang, H., & Zukerman, M. (2013). Preventing DDoS attacks by identifier/locator separation. *IEEE Network, 27*(6), 60–65. doi:10.1109/MNET.2013.6678928

Marques, J., & Serrão, C. (2013a). Improving Content Privacy on Social Networks Using Open Digital Rights Management Solutions. *Procedia Technology, 9*, 405–410. doi:10.1016/j.protcy.2013.12.045

Marques, J., & Serrão, C. (2013b). Improving user content privacy on social networks using rights management systems. *Annals of Telecommunications -. Annales des Télécommunications, 69*(1-2), 37–45. doi:10.1007/s12243-013-0388-1

McKenzie, P. J., Burkell, J., Wong, L., Whippey, C., Trosow, S. E., & McNally, M. B. (2012, June 6). User-generated online content: overview, current state and context. *First Monday*. Retrieved from http://firstmonday.org/ojs/index.php/fm/article/view/3912/3266

Michael, K., & Miller, K. W. (2013). Big Data: New Opportunities and New Challenges. *Computer, 46*(6), 22–24. doi:10.1109/MC.2013.196

MIT. (2014). *Big Data Privacy Workshop, Advancing the state of the art in Technology and Practice - Workshop summary report*. Retrieved from http://web.mit.edu/bigdata-priv/images/MITBigDataPrivacyWorkshop2014_final05142014.pdf

Monsanto, C., Reich, J., Foster, N., Rexford, J., & Walker, D. (2013). Composing software-defined networks. *Proceedings of the 10th USENIX Conference on Networked Systems Design and Implementation*, 1–14. Retrieved from http://dl.acm.org/citation.cfm?id=2482626.2482629\nhttp://www.frenetic-lang.org/pyretic/

NIST. (2014). *Framework for Improving Critical Infrastructure Cybersecurity*. Retrieved from http://www.nist.gov/cyberframework/upload/cybersecurity-framework-021214-final.pdf

NuSMV. (2014). *An overview of NuSMV*. Retrieved July 23, 2014, from http://nusmv.fbk.eu/NuSMV/

Okhravi, H., Hobson, T., Bigelow, D., & Streilein, W. (2014). Finding Focus in the Blur of Moving-Target Techniques. *IEEE Security and Privacy, 12*(2), 16–26. doi:10.1109/MSP.2013.137

OWASP. (2014). *OWASP Internet of Things Top Ten Project*. Retrieved August 05, 2014, from https://www.owasp.org/index.php/OWASP_Internet_of_Things_Top_Ten_Project

Popa, R., & Redfield, C. (2011). Cryptdb: protecting confidentiality with encrypted query processing. *Proceedings of the …*, 85–100. doi:10.1145/2043556.2043566

Popa, R., & Redfield, C. (2012). CryptDB: Processing queries on an encrypted database. *Communications, 55*, 103. doi:10.1145/2330667.2330691

Pyretic. (2014). *Pyretic Language*. Retrieved August 05, 2014, from https://github.com/frenetic-lang/pyretic/wiki/Language-Basics

Python. (2014). *Python Language*. Retrieved August 03, 2014, from https://www.python.org/

Rivera, J., & van der Meulen, R. (2014). *Gartner Says the Internet of Things Will Transform the Data Center*. Retrieved August 05, 2014, from http://www.gartner.com/newsroom/id/2684915

Rodríguez, E., Rodríguez, V., Carreras, A., & Delgado, J. (2009). A Digital Rights Management approach to privacy in online social networks. In *Workshop on Privacy and Protection in Web-based Social Networks (within ICAIL'09), Barcelona*.

Serrão, C., Neves, D., Barker, T., & Balestri, M. (2003). OpenSDRM -- An Open and Secure Digital Rights Management Solution. In *Proceedings of the IADIS International Conference e-Society*.

Serrão, C. (2008). *IDRM - Interoperable Digital Rights Management: Interoperability Mechanisms for Open Rights Management Platforms*. Universitat Politècnica de Catalunya. Retrieved from http://repositorio-iul.iscte.pt/handle/10071/1156

Serrão, C., Dias, J. M. S., & Kudumakis, P. (2005). From OPIMA to MPEG IPMP-X: A standard's history across R&D projects. *Signal Processing Image Communication, 20*(9), 972–994. doi:10.1016/j.image.2005.04.005

Serrão, C., Dias, M., & Delgado, J. (2005). *Using Web-Services to Manage and Control Access to Multimedia Content*. ISWS05-The 2005 International Symposium on Web Services and Applications, Las Vegas, NV.

Serrão, C., Rodriguez, E., & Delgado, J. (2011). Approaching the rights management interoperability problem using intelligent brokerage mechanisms. *Computer Communications, 34*(2), 129–139. doi:10.1016/j.comcom.2010.04.001

Tankard, C. (2012). Big data security. *Network Security*, (7), 5–8. doi:10.1016/S1353-4858(12)70063-6

Thomas, S. A. (2000). SSL & TLS Essentials: Securing the Web (Pap/Cdr., p. 224). Wiley.

Van Dijk, M., Gentry, C., Halevi, S., & Vaikuntanathan, V. (2010). Fully homomorphic encryption over the integers. In Advances in Cryptology–EUROCRYPT '10 (pp. 24–43). doi:10.1007/978-3-642-13190-5_2

KEY TERMS AND DEFINITIONS

Big Data: The term that represents data sets that are extremely large to handle through traditional methods. Big data represents information that has such a high volume, velocity, variety, variability, veracity and complexity that require specific mechanisms in order to produce value from it.

BYOD: Abbreviation of the term for Bring Your Own Device representing the policy that allows employees to bring their own personal mobile devices to their workplace, and make use of the company information and applications.

DMZ: A Demilitarized Zone, also known as perimeter network, used to create a physical or logical separation between the organization internal and external-facing services to a public network, for instance, the Internet. An outside network device can only get access to the services on the organization DMZ.

IDS: Intrusion Detection System is a system that actively monitors networks or other systems for security policy violations or unusual activities.

IoT: The term refers to the Internet of Things, representing a network of devices that are integrated and operate with the surrounding environment, enabling the communication with other systems or with each other to improve the offered value to customers.

IPS: Intrusion Prevention Systems are a subset of IDS that besides the detection of malicious activity can also block that activity from occurring.

JSON: Although originated from Javascript, the Javascript Object Notation is a language-independent and open data format that can be used to transmit human-readable text-based object information, across domains, using an attribute-value pair's notation.

SCADA: Supervisory Control and Data Acquisition refers to systems that are used to control infrastructure processes (for instance, electrical power supply), facility-based processes (for instance, airports) or industrial processes (for instance, production).

SDN: Software Defined Networking allows network administrators to manage network services through the decoupling of the traffic sending decisions (control) system from the underlying (data) traffic forwarding systems. Some advantages of using SDN are decreasing the maintenance cost and fostering innovation on the networking infrastructure.

ENDNOTES

[1]   http://www.oxforddictionaries.com/definition/english/Internet-of-things

[2]   Some notes about the notation used: key(content) means the "content" is encrypted using "key"; key{content} represents "content" is signed using "key"; algo[content] means that "content" is hashed with the "algo" algorithm.

Chapter 3
Big Data Security Management

Zaiyong Tang
Salem State University, USA

Youqin Pan
Salem State University, USA

ABSTRACT

Big data is a buzzword today, and security of big data is a big concern. Traditional security standards and technologies cannot scale up to deliver reliable and effective security solutions in the big data environment. This chapter covers big data security management from concepts to real-world issues. By identifying and laying out the major challenges, industry trends, legal and regulatory environments, security principles, security management frameworks, security maturity model, big data analytics in solving security problems, current research results, and future research issues, this chapter provides researchers and practitioners with a timely reference and guidance in securing big data processing, management, and applications.

INTRODUCTION

Big Data has become an entrenched part of discussions of new development in information technology, businesses, governments, markets, and societies in recent years. It has inspired noteworthy excitement about the potential opportunities that may come from the study, research, analysis, and application of big data. However, accompanying those enticing opportunities and prospective rewards, there are significant challenges and substantial risks associated with big data. One of the biggest challenges for big data is increased security risk.

Security for big data is magnified by the volume, variety, and velocity of big data. With the proliferation of the Internet and the Web, pervasive computing, mobile commerce, and large scale cloud infrastructures, today's data are coming from diverse sources and formats, at a dynamic speed, and in high volume. Traditional security measures are developed for clean, structured, static, and relatively low volume of data. Undeniably, big data presents huge challenges in maintaining the integrity, confidentiality, and availability of essential data and information.

DOI: 10.4018/978-1-4666-8505-5.ch003

At the same time as big data is gaining momentum in the networked economy, security attacks are on the rise. Security perpetrators are becoming more sophisticated, wide-spread, and organized. As businesses and other organizations are moving towards a more open, user-centric, agile, and hyper connected environment that fosters intelligence, communication, innovation, and collaboration, attackers are eager to exploit the intrinsic vulnerabilities that come with open and dynamic systems. Since big data are generated by those systems, and newly developed big data infrastructures such as NoSQL databases, cloud storage, and cloud computing have not been thoroughly scrutinized for their capability of safeguarding data resources, information security presents a formidable challenge to big data adaptation and management.

By identifying and laying out the major challenges, issues, industry trends, framework, maturity model, and fundamental principles of big data security, this chapter will provide researchers and practitioners with a timely reference and guideline in securing big data processing, management, and applications.

BACKGROUND

Big Data is generally considered to have three defining characteristics: volume, variety and velocity (Zikopoulos, et al. 2012). When at least one of the dimensions is significantly high, the data is labeled big. Traditional techniques and technologies are not sufficient to handle big data. With the enormous size, speed, and/or multiplicity, big data processing requires a set of new forms of technologies and approaches to achieve effective decision support, insight discovery, and process optimization (Lancy, 2001). Although the three V's of big data definition has wide acceptance, recently, there have been attempts to expand the dimension of big data to include value and veracity (Demchenko, et al., 2013). The value dimension of big data deals with drawing inferences and testing hypothesis, and the veracity dimension is about authenticity, accountability, availability, and trustworthiness. Some researchers (e.g., Biehn, 2013) have suggested adding value and viability to the three V's.

Although big data has been discussed for over a decade since 2000, interest in big data has only experienced significant growth in the last few years. Figure 1 shows the Google search interest for the search term "Big Data" from January 2004 to June 2014. The figure does not show actual search volume. The y axis represents search interest relative to the highest point, with the highest point being scaled to 100. For more historical information about big data, the reader is referred to Press (2013), which documents the history of big data that dates back to the 1940s.

Soon after the interest in big data has gained significance, the search interest in big data security and big data privacy has also experienced remarkable growth. Figure 2 shows the Google search interest for the search term "Big Data Security" (top line) and "Big Data Privacy" (bottom line) from January 2011 to June 2014.

In order to clearly articulate, define, and build the big data ecosystem, there has been a concerted effort to develop big data architecture by both standard organizations such as National Institute of Standards and Technology (NIST) and major information technology companies such as IBM, Microsoft, and Oracle. Demchenko et al. (2013) consolidated previous models of big data architectures and proposed a Big Data Architecture Framework. This framework consists five key components of the big data ecosystem: Data Models, Big Data Management, Big Data Analytics and Tools, Big Data Infrastructure,

Figure 1. Big Data Web Search Interest, January 2004 – June 2014
Source: Google Trends

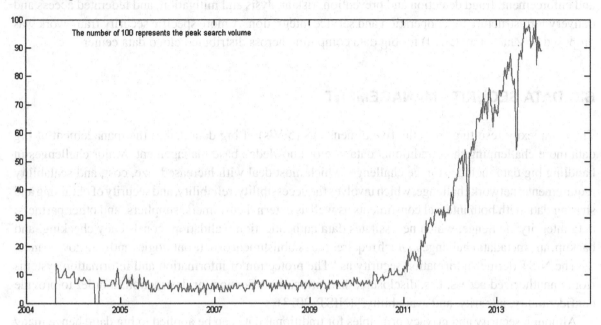

Figure 2. Big Data Security/Privacy Web Search Interest, January 2011 – June 2014
Source: Google Trends

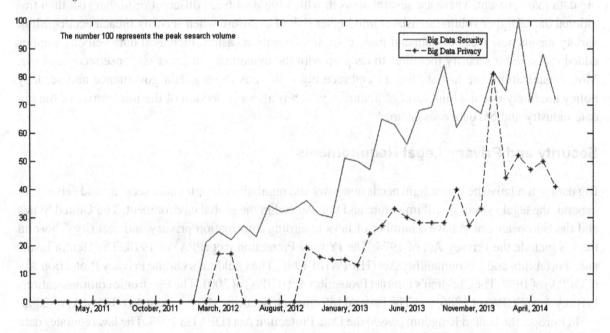

and Big Data Security. Data model defines the type and structure of data. Big data management deals with the planning, monitoring, and managing the big data life cycle. Big data infrastructure consists hardware, software, and technology services (often cloud based), including security infrastructure that establish access control, confidentiality, trust, privacy, and quality of service. Big data security goes beyond the security infrastructure to provide security lifecycle management, security governance, policy and enforcement, fraud detection and prevention, risk analysis and mitigation, and federated access and delivery infrastructure for cooperation and service integration. A more specific security framework was proposed by Zhao et al. (2014) for big data computing across distributed cloud data centers.

BIG DATA SECURITY MANAGEMENT

The complexity resulting from the five dimensions (5 V's) of big data makes the management of big data more challenging than traditional database or knowledge base management. Major challenges in handling big data include storage challenge, which must deal with increased size, cost, and scalability requirements; network challenge, which involves the accessibility, reliability, and security of obtaining and sharing data with both internal constituents as well as external customers, suppliers, and other partners; data integrity challenge, which necessitates data authentication, validation, consistency checking, and backup; and metadata challenges, which requires the establishment of data ontologies and data governance.

The NIST defines information security as "The protection of information and information systems from unauthorized access, use, disclosure, disruption, modification, or destruction in order to provide confidentiality, integrity, and availability." (NIST, 2013)

Although security and privacy principles for traditional data can be applied to big data, hence many of the existing security technologies and best practices can be extended to the big data ecosystem, the different characteristics of big data require modified approaches to meet the new challenges to effective big data management. There are several areas in which big data faces different or higher risk than traditional data. Higher volume translates into higher risk of exposure when security breach occurs. More variety means new types of data and more complex security measure. Increased data velocity implies added pressure for security measures to keep up with the dynamics and faster response/recovery time. Most organizations are just starting to embrace big data, thus the big data governance and security policy are likely not at a high level of maturity, which is also a reflection of the immaturity of the big data industry and bid data ecosystem.

Security and Privacy Legal Requirements

Big data as a relative new paradigm needs new laws and regulations to safeguard security and privacy. In general, the legal system is still immature and unbalanced in the global environment. The United States and the European Union have a number of laws regarding information privacy and security. Those in the US include the Privacy Act of 1974, The Privacy Protection Act (PPA) of 1978, The Health Insurance Portability and Accountability Act (HIPPA) of 1996, The Children's Online Privacy Protection Act (COPPA) of 1998, The Children's Internet Protection Act (CIPA) of 2001, The Electronic communications Privacy Act (ECPA) of 1986, and The Federal Information Security Management Act (FISMA) of 2002.

In Europe, the United Kingdom passed the Data Protection Act (DPA) in 1998. The law regulates data processing on personal identifiable information (PII). The European Union adopted The Data Protection Directive in 1995, which governs personal data processing within the European Union. The European Union Internet Privacy Law was ratified in 2002. A new security and privacy law, The European General Data Protection Regulation, was drafted in 2012, which supersedes the Data Protection Directive. The Federal Assembly of the Swiss Confederation passed the Federal Act on Data Protection (FADP) in 1992.

The Privacy and Data Security Law Deskbook (Sotto, 2013) provides coverage of major International laws of information security and privacy, including United States, European Union, Australia, and Singapore. The book offers practical guidance and explanation of different aspects of security and privacy issues in different legal environments, and serves as a comprehensive guide on international security and privacy topics. For new developments and general information about changes in privacy and security, the Privacy and Information Security Law Blog provides current coverage of global privacy and cybersecurity law updates and analysis.

Big Data Security Challenges

Security has become an increasing concern as more and more people are connected to the global network economy. According to the Internet Live Stats website, the number of worldwide Internet users is approaching three billions (Internet Users). There has never been a lack of security attacks, from the early days of telephone phracker to modern time cyber criminals. As the big data increases in volume, speed, and variety, the likelihood that data breach is expected to increase significantly. Recently, it is estimated that the average security breaches results in a loss of $40 million for American companies (Rowe, 2012). Symantec, an Internet security firm, estimated that the worldwide cybercrime cost is over $100 billion more than the cost of illegal drug market.

The 2014 first quarter IBM X-Force Threat Intelligence Quarterly report (IBM, 2014) states that attackers seeking for valuable data will spare no effort in looking for security vulnerability. They will devise new tools or revitalize old techniques to break the security defense system. IBM X-Force Research actively conducts security monitoring and analysis of global security issues. It has built a database of more than 76,000 computer security vulnerabilities. Cloud Security Alliance (2013a) publishes anneal top security threats in cloud computing.

Figure 3 shows the most common attack types based on data collected in 2013. Undisclosed attack involves those either using nascent tools/techniques or those were not identified by the intrusion detection

Figure 3. Most Common Attack Types in 2013
Source: IBM X-Force Threat Intelligence Quarterly (2014)

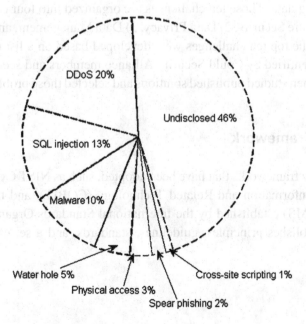

system. The most common attack among those known types is the distributed denial of service (DDoS) attack. SQL injection is a code injection technique targeting databases or data-driven applications. Watering hole is a computer attack method first described by the RSA security firm in 2012. This attack aims at a particular group of organizations and penetrates the group via infecting some group members who frequent certain targeted websites. Cross-site scripting is used by attackers to inject client-side scripts into Web pages visited by website users. Malicious activities can be carried out through the injected client-site scripts. Phishing is commonly used by attackers masquerading as a trustworthy entity to gain access to personal information such as username, passwords, and/or credit card data. A targeted phishing attack directed at specific individuals or organizations is referred to as spear phishing.

The volume of data continues to grow exponentially, the majority of big data is unstructured. Those unstructured data must be formatted and processed using big data technologies such as Hadoop. Unfortunately, Hadoop was not developed with enterprise applications and security in the blue print. It was designed to format large volume of unstructured data such as those available on publicly accessible websites. The original purpose did not include security, privacy, encryption, and risk management. Organizations using Hadoop clusters must implement additional enterprise security measures such as access control and data encryption. As Hadoop has become a widely adopted technology in the enterprise big data applications, its insufficiency in enterprise security must be recognized. A new unified security model for big data is needed.

Traditional data security technologies were developed around databases or data centers that typically have a single physical location, while big data is typically in distributed, large scale clusters. For example, a Hadoop cluster may consist of hundreds or thousands of nodes. As a result, traditional backup, recovery, and security technologies and systems are not effective in big data environment.

Big data is a new paradigm in data science and data applications. New security measures are needed to protect, access, and manage big data. Comprehensive security policies and procedures need to expend from structured data in traditional databases and data warehouses to the new big data environment. Sensitive data needs to be flagged, encrypted, and redacted in NoSQL databases, and their access needs to be granularly controlled. All access to those data by either users or applications needs to be logged and reported.

The Big Data Working Group of the Cloud Security Alliance (2013) listed the top ten security and privacy challenges for big data. Those ten challenges are organized into four categories of the big data ecosystem: 1) Infrastructure Security, 2) Data Privacy, 3) Data Management, and 4) Integrity and Reactive Security. Note that the top ten challenges were developed based on a list of high priority security and privacy problems identified by Could Security Alliance members and security trade journals. The big data working group then studied published solutions and selected those problems without established or effective solutions.

Big Data Security Framework

There are several security frameworks that have been adopted, such as NIST Cybersecurity Framework, Control Objectives for Information and Related Technology (COBIT), and the information security management system (ISMS) established by the International Standards Organization (ISO 27000). A security framework establishes principles, guidelines, standards, and a set of preferred practices for

Table 1. Top Ten Big Data Security and Privacy Challenges

Big Data Challenge	Use Case Example
Secure computations in distributed programming frameworks	Prevent untrusted mappers from snooping on requests or alter scripts/results.
Security best practices for non-relational data stores	Migrate from traditional relational databases to NoSQL databases that are more suitable to process large volume dynamic data.
Secure data storage and transactions logs	Adopt an auto-tier storage system which prioritizes data storage by putting less utilized data to a lower tier.
End-point input validation/filtering	Develop effective algorithms to validate input data from diverse and dynamic data sources
Real-time security monitoring	Implement real-time security analytics that support real-time monitoring, querying, and decision making.
Scalable and composable privacy-preserving data mining and analytics	Improve scalable privacy-preserving data mining algorithms and prevent untrusted user from accessing sensitive data.
Cryptographically enforced data centric security	Design innovative techniques to index, analyze, and process encrypted data with diverse sources. Maintain data confidentiality and integrity
Granular access control	Establish access control at a granular scale so that individual user roles and responsibilities can be set to access only authorized data, functions, or services
Granular audits	Update auditing with extended scope and granularity for real-time security and meeting compliance requirements
Data provenance	Keep track of metadata of data creation to support effective digital forensic and compliance auditing

(Adopted from Cloud Security Alliance, 2013b)

organizations to analyze, plan, design, and implement security information systems. ISO 27000 is the only framework that organizations can adopt and being certified by a third party once the set of standards such as security policy, asset management, cryptography, access control are satisfied.

The ISO 27000 consists a series of standards. Disterer (2013) discussed the ISO/IEC 27000, 27001 and 27002 for information security management, and concluded that The ISO 27000, 27001 and 27002 standards can serve as a framework to design and operate an information security management system. Those standards have been widely disseminated in Europe and Asia. It is expected that the adaptation of standards-based security framework will increase significantly in the future due the rising challenges in in information security and privacy.

The ISO 27000 standard was developed in 2009 and continues to evolve to meet the new challenges in the security industry (ISO 27000, 2009, 2012, 2014). Plan-Do-Check-Act, the classic quality management framework for the control and continuous improvement, forms the basis for security management in ISO 2700. Although the current ISO 27000 standard does not provide specific provisions for big data security, we expect that future versions will add this important coverage.

Figure 4 shows a general big data security management (BDSM) framework we adopted from the Plan-Do-Check-Act Deming cycle. The Design/Planning phase defines, identifies, and evaluates security risk, and develop appropriate policies, procedures, control, and measure according to desired security level. This phase also includes a security modeling that builds a threat model and lays out strategies for most security/privacy breach scenarios. The design blueprint will be turned into operational systems at the implementation phase. The operation phase delivers the desired functions and services with security and privacy protection and compliance to laws and regulations. The monitoring and auditing phase mea-

Figure 4. Big Data Security Management Framework

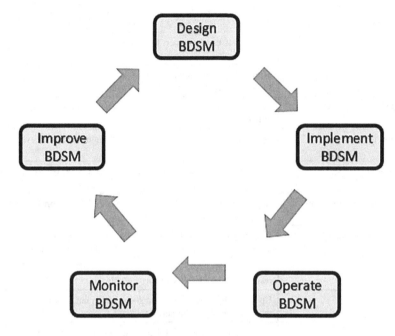

sures key performance indicators against designed objectives and provides feedback and performance reports. The deficiencies identified at the monitoring stage will be used as input for big data security system redesign, quality control, and continuous improvement.

Successful adoption of a security management framework is critical in helping organizations to identify and assess information security risks, apply suitable controls, adequately protect information assets against security breaches, and to achieve and maintain regulatory compliance. The ISO 27000 stipulates that information security management framework must deliver the following desirable outcomes (ISO/IEC 27000, 3rd Ed., 2014):

1. Meeting the security requirements of all stake holders;
2. Advancing the organization's security/privacy plans and activities;
3. Achieving the organization's information security/privacy objectives;
4. Compliance to laws, regulations, and industry mandates;
5. Facilitating continuous improvement towards achieving organizational goals.

Demchenko, Ngo, and Membrey (2013) proposed a big data security framework that focuses on data centric security. The key components in their framework consist of security lifecycle, granular access control, encryption enforced access control, trusted environment, and federated access and delivery infrastructure (FADI) for cooperation and services integration. The critical success factors to successful adaptation and implementation of the framework include security policy and procedures that are aligned with organizational security objectives, commitment from management and stakeholders, information security awareness, training and education, security incident management, business continuity plan, and monitoring and feedback.

Big Data Security Principles

Cavoukian (2013) has developed a widely recognized framework for information privacy—Privacy by Design. The central theme of Privacy by Design is that in the age of big data, privacy cannot be assured just by compliance with laws and regulations. Privacy must be ingrained in organizational design, and hence becoming the default mode of operation. The seven principles of privacy proposed by Cavoukian can be readily modified and adopted for big data security. We propose nine foundational principles for big data security:

1. Preventative and proactive security;
2. Security by default—minimal access privilege;
3. Security embedded into design and operation;
4. Defense in depth;
5. End-to-end security;
6. Visibility and transparency for trustworthiness;
7. User-centric;
8. Real-time monitoring;
9. Accountability and traceability.

Protective measures or subsystems consist of deterrence, avoidance, prevention, mitigation, detection, response, recovery, and correction should be part of the big data security management system. The big data security best practices suggested by the Association for Data-driven Marketing & Advertising (ADMA, 2013) include the following:

1. Implementation of end-to-end security measures;
2. Implementation of encryption and key management protocols and systems;
3. Implementation of layered security;
4. Assessment and implementation of vulnerability penetration testing;
5. Clear communication of security policies and the consequences for non-compliance.

Big Data Security Maturity Model

A useful approach for assessing organization's preparedness for big data security is a big data security maturity model. The idea of a maturity model is popularized by the Software Engineering Institute (SEI) at Carnegie Mellon University after they proposed the Capability Maturity Model (Paulk, et al., 1995). The classic capacity maturity model has five level: initial, repeatable, defined, managed, and optimizing. According to ESI, the software development predictability, effectiveness, and manageability improve as the organization moves up the maturity levels. The capacity maturity model has been adopted in various fields other than software development. For example, business process maturity model, risk maturity model, privacy maturity model, etc.

Figure 5 shows a bid data security management maturity model we adopted from the capacity maturity model. Along the maturity spectrum, at the very beginning, *Nonexistent*, there is no awareness of big data security risk and challenges. In the *Initial* stage, the organization has recognized the importance of big data security management in the face of big data security challenges. It is the starting point of deploying

Figure 5. Big Data Security Management Maturity Model

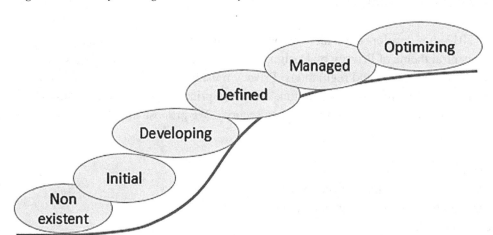

new or undocumented processes. This stage is characterized by ad hoc, or even chaotic approaches and unpredictable results. In the *Developing* stage, a broad assessment of big data security risk is carried out and certain key areas have implemented, and big data security processes documented. At the *Defined* level, the big data security processes are standardized and imbedded in routing business operations. At the *Managed* level, performance metrics are established and big data security processes are measured against the performance metrics and continuous improvement is embedded into the operations. Finally, at the *Optimizing* level, big data security processes are fine-tuned to achieve optimal results, delivering the highest level of security within the resource constraints.

Big Data for Security Industry

Although there are many challenges in big data management and applications, there are also many opportunities presented by big data that lead to new discoveries, insights, and innovative applications. In the security industry, big data analytics has helped organizations to proactively identify and predict security attacks (Hipgrave, 2013). With the advancement of big data analytics, organizations will be able to collect and analyze large volume of data from various unstructured data sources such as email, social media, e-commerce transactions, bulletin boards, surveillance video feeds, Internet traffic, etc. Forward-looking organizations are moving beyond traditional security measures to safeguard their coveted information assets. Big data security monitoring and analytical tools can be a valuable aid to security professionals and law enforcement in their fighting against cyber criminals. An example of such an application is to analyze data in confluence and in motion to detect cyber fraud/attack before serious damage occurs.

Big data security should not be an afterthought, even though the security industry is often playing catch up with the perpetrators. Those organizations that adopt big data security framework and follow big data security principles will be able to take advantage of big data analytics and be able to predict, detect, act, respond, and recover quickly from security breaches. Once the organization reaches sufficient big data security maturity level, it will be in a solid position to fight against all known security attacks. It is even possible that the organization is able to anticipate and mitigate new/unforeseen threats. Common big data analytics applications in security and public safety include crime analysis, computational criminology, terrorism informatics, open-source intelligence, and cyber security (Chen, Chiang, and Storey, 2012).

RESEARCH ISSUES AND DIRECTIONS

Big data security is of great interest to security practitioners as well as academic researchers. Many believe that we have entered the era of big data that offers enormous opportunities for transforming data science and data driven research and applications. With the advancement of big data technologies, infrastructure, data mining, business intelligence, and big data analytics, researchers and business analysts are able to gain more insights about big data security challenges, risk assessment and mitigation, and be able to develop more effective business solutions (Chang, Kauffman, and Kwon, 2014).

However, we are still at the ground level of big data paradigm shift. There are still many unsolved issues in big data security management. Most traditional security tools and technologies do not scale and perform well in big data environments. Substantial effort is needed to develop a holistic and robust big data security ecosystem. Some pioneering work has been done (Demchenko, Ngo, and Membrey, 2013; Disterer, 2013). However, there are still lingering questions such as: Is cloud computing the right infrastructure to support big data storage and processing? Is the architectural flexibility of NoSQL databases amenable to trustworthy big data security? How can we trust big data that come from a variety of untrusted input sources? Will big data "usher in a new wave of privacy incursions and invasive marketing"? (Boyd and Crawford, 2012) How do we balance the need for big data security and usability?

It is important for security professionals, regulatory bodies, law enforcement, and big data service providers as well as users to keep in mind, while we try to address those questions, big data security continues to evolve as the five V's of the big data ecosystem are constantly changing and increasing. More and more people will be involved with big data research and development, services, applications, and consumptions. No doubt that the number of people interested in exploiting the big data with malicious intent is also increasing.

As discussed in the previous section, there are many challenges in big data security and privacy. Here we list some key research issues facing big data researchers and practitioners:

1. Robust security standards designed and developed for big data from the ground up. The lack of established security standards has resulted in some vendors involved with big data systems such as NoSQL solutions to develop ad-hoc security measures.
2. Built-in security at the granular level. This has the potential to allow security control and management with surgical precision.
3. A big data security architecture that provides a security framework to integrate diverse security technologies that are available today, but do not work coherently together. Rather than piecemeal and separate solutions, we need a holistic approach to deal with current and emergent security threats.
4. Continue the development of the big data ecosystem, of which big data security is a key component. Security should be deep-rooted in all aspects of the big date lifecycle, that includes sourcing, storage, process, analysis, and delivery of results to targeted applications.
5. Reshape the cloud infrastructure for better big data security and trustworthiness, in order to alleviate the concern that big data security and privacy are cloudy in the cloud.
6. Continue the promising research in addressing information technology/system security problems using big data and big data analytics.
7. Real-time big data security analytics that integrates natural and artificial intelligence for advanced security threat analysis, prediction, detection, tracking, and response.

CONCLUSION

It is evident that big data is with us today and it is going to have a significant impact on governments, businesses, societies, and individuals in the future. As we embrace the opportunities brought by big data, we must also be keenly aware of the security challenges associated with big data infrastructure and applications. In this chapter, we explored the concepts of big data security, presented big data security management frameworks, summarized big data security challenges, identified big data security principles, and suggested a big data security maturity model. Furthermore, we discussed the application of big data analytics in solving security related problems.

Although big data security is immature today, we believe, with concerted effort from industries, governments, academicians, and practitioners, big data security will improve over time to meet those challenges discussed in this chapter. Similar to the case of Internet security, which is an afterthought when the need for security became critical and evident. The initial Internet architecture had little consideration for security and privacy. However, as Internet and the World-wide Web grew exponentially in the 1990s, multi-layer Internet security protocols were developed and those security standards helped facilitating the growth of the Internet and Internet applications. We are optimistic that big data security will follow a similar path. This chapter provides basic concepts, principles, challenges, and current issues of big data security. We hope it serves as a launching pad for advancing big data security research in the future.

REFERENCES

ADMA. (2013). *Best Practice Guideline: Big Data. A guide to maximising customer engagement opportunities through the development of responsible Big Data strategies*. Retrieved from: http://www.adma.com.au

Biehn, N. (2013). *The Missing V's in Big Data: Viability and Value*. WIRED.com Retrieved from: http://www.wired.com/insights/2013/05/the-missing-vs-in-big-data-viability-and-value/

Boyd, D., & Crawford, K. (2012). Critical Questions for Big Data: Provocations for a Cultural, Technological, and Scholarly Phenomenon. *Information Communication and Society*, *15*(5), 662–675. doi:10.1080/1369118X.2012.678878

Cavoukian, A. (2013). *Big Privacy: Bridging Big Data and the Personal Data Ecosystem Through Privacy by Design*. Retrieved from http://www.privacybydesign.ca/

Chang, R. M., Kauffman, R. J., & Kwon, Y. (2014). Understanding the paradigm shift to computational social science in the presence of big data. *Decision Support Systems*, *63*, 6780. doi:10.1016/j.dss.2013.08.008

Chen, H., Chiang, R. H., & Storey, V. C. (2012). Business Intelligence and Analytics: From Big Data to Big Impact. *Management Information Systems Quarterly*, *36*(4), 1165–1188.

Cloud Security Alliance. (2013a). *The Notorious Nine Cloud Computing Top Threats in 2013*. Retrieved from https://cloudsecurityalliance.org/download/the-notorious-nine-cloud-computing-top-threats-in-2013/

Cloud Security Alliance. (2013b). *Expanded Top Ten Big Data Security and Privacy Challenges*. Big Data Working Group. Retrieved from https://cloudsecurityalliance.org/research/big-data/

COBIT. (n.d.). Retrieved from https://cobitonline.isaca.org/

NIST Cybersecurity Framework. (n.d.). Retrieved from http://www.nist.gov/cyberframework/

Demchenko, Y., Grosso, P., de Laat, C., & Membrey, P. (2013). Addressing big data issues in Scientific Data Infrastructure. In *Proceedings of the International Conference on Collaboration Technologies and Systems (CTS)*. IEEE. doi:10.1109/CTS.2013.6567203

Demchenko, Y., Ngo, C., & Membrey, P. (2013). *Architecture Framework and Components for the Big Data Ecosystem*. Retrieved from http://www.uazone.org/demch/worksinprogress/sne-2013-02-techreport-bdaf-draft02.pdf

Disterer, G. (2013). ISO/IEC 27000, 27001 and 27002 for Information Security Management. *Journal of Information Security*, *4*(2), 92–100. doi:10.4236/jis.2013.42011

Gartner Group. (2012). *Gartner Says Big Data Creates Big Jobs: 4.4 Million IT Jobs Globally to Support Big Data By 2015*. Retrieved from http://www.gartner.com/newsroom/id/2207915

Google Trends. (n.d.). Retrieved from http://www.google.com/trends/

Hipgrave, S. (2013). Smarter fraud investigations with big data analytics. *Network Security*, *2013*(12), 7–9. doi:10.1016/S1353-4858(13)70135-1

IBM. (2014). *IBM X-Force Threat Intelligence Quarterly, IBM Security Systems*. First Quarter 2014. Retrieved from: http://www-03.ibm.com/security/xforce/

Internet Users. (n.d.). Retrieved from http://www.internetlivestats.com/internet-users/

ISO 27000. (2009, 2012, 2014). *Information Technology, Security Techniques, Information Security Management Systems, Overview and Vocabulary*. International Organization for Standardization ISO, Geneva. Retrieved from: http://www.iso27001security.com/html/27000.html

ISO 27000. (n.d.). Retrieved from http://www.27000.org/

Laney, D. (2001). *3D Data Management: Controlling Data Volume, Velocity, and Variety*. Gartner Group. Retrieved from: http://blogs.gartner.com/doug-laney/files/2012/01/ad949-3D-Data-Management-Controlling-Data-Volume-Velocity-and-Variety.pdf

Laney, D. (2012). *Deja VVVu: Others Claiming Gartner's Construct for Big Data*. Gartner Group. Retrieved from: http://blogs.gartner.com/doug-laney/deja-vvvue-others-claiming-gartners-volume-velocity-variety-construct-for-big-data/

MacDonald, N. (2012). *Information Security Is Becoming a Big Data Analytics Problem*. Gartner Report. Retrieved from https://www.gartner.com/doc/1960615/information-security-big-data-analytics

NIST. (2013). *Glossary of Key Information Security Terms, NISTIR 7298, Revision 2*. Retrieved from: http://nvlpubs.nist.gov/nistpubs/ir/2013/NIST.IR.7298r2.pdf

Paulk, M. C., Weber, C. V., Curtis, B., & Chrissis, M. B. (1995). *The Capability Maturity Model: Guidelines for Improving the Software Process. SEI series in software engineering.* Reading, MA: Addison-Wesley.

Press, G. (2013). A Very Short History of Big Data. *Forbes Magazine.* Retrieved from: http://www.forbes.com/sites/gilpress/2013/05/09/a-very-short-history-of-big-data/

Privacy and Information Security Law Blog. (n.d.). Retrieved from https://www.huntonprivacyblog.com/

Rowe, N. (2012). *The Big Data Imperative: Why Information Governance Must be Addressed.* Aberdeen Group Research Report.

Shmueli, G., & Koppius, O. R. (2011). Predictive Analytics in Information Systems Research. *Management Information Systems Quarterly, 35*(3), 553–572.

Sotto, L. J. (2013). *Privacy and Data Security Law Deskbook.* Frederick, MD: Aspen Publishers.

Zhao, J., Wang, L., Tao, J., Chen, J., Sun, W., Ranjan, R., & Georgakopoulos, D. et al. (2014). A security framework in G-Hadoop for big data computing across distributed Cloud data centres. *Journal of Computer and System Sciences, 80*(5), 994–1007. doi:10.1016/j.jcss.2014.02.006

Zikopoulos, P. C., Eaton, C., deRoos, D., Deutsch, T., & Lapis, C. (2012). *Understanding big data – Analytics for enterprise class Hadoop and streaming data.* New York, NY: McGraw Hill.

KEY TERMS AND DEFINITIONS

Big Data: Unstructured date with five characteristics: volume, velocity, variety, veracity, and value.

Big Data Security: The protection of big data from unauthorized access and ensure big data confidentiality, integrity, and availability.

Big Data Security Framework: A framework designed to help organizations to identify, assess, control, and manage big data security and maintain regulatory compliance.

Big Data Security Maturity Model: A multi-level model used to help organizations to articulate where they stand in the spectrum of big date security, from nonexistent to optimality.

Privacy: An individual's right to safeguard personal information in accordance with law and regulations.

Security: A state of preparedness against threats to the integrity of the organization and its information resources.

Security Attack: An attempt to gain unauthorized access to information resource or services, or to cause harm or damage to information systems.

Chapter 4
Big Data in Telecommunications:
Seamless Network Discovery and Traffic Steering with Crowd Intelligence

Yen Pei Tay
Quest International University Perak, Malaysia

Vasaki Ponnusamy
Quest International University Perak, Malaysia

Lam Hong Lee
Quest International University Perak, Malaysia

ABSTRACT

The meteoric rise of smart devices in dominating worldwide consumer electronics market complemented with data-hungry mobile applications and widely accessible heterogeneous networks e.g. 3G, 4G LTE and Wi-Fi, have elevated Mobile Internet from a 'nice-to-have' to a mandatory feature on every mobile computing device. This has spurred serious data traffic congestion on mobile networks as a consequence. The nature of mobile network traffic today is more like little Data Tsunami, unpredictable in terms of time and location while pounding the access networks with waves of data streams. This chapter explains how Big Data analytics can be applied to understand the Device-Network-Application (DNA) dimensions in annotating mobile connectivity routine and how Simplify, a seamless network discovery solution developed at Nextwave Technology, can be extended to leverage crowd intelligence in predicting and collaboratively shaping mobile data traffic towards achieving real-time network congestion control. The chapter also presents the Big Data architecture hosted on Google Cloud Platform powering the backbone behind Simplify in realizing its intelligent traffic steering solution.

DOI: 10.4018/978-1-4666-8505-5.ch004

INTRODUCTION

On a cold Spring day in March 2011, Japan was struck by a deadly tsunami following a strong earthquake. The aftermath was devastating, not only destruction was brought into its physical terrain, the Internet has also suffered huge *'data tsunami'* where millions of online readers roamed into major news websites, following every emergency update. With smart communication devices dominating the global consumer electronics market, posting high-resolution pictures and streaming high-definition videos over wireless networks are becoming the norms for smartphone users (Tay, 2012). Complemented with more affordable mobile broadband packages and widely accessible high-speed data networks, wireless networks today are constantly plagued by daily *'data tsunamis'*.

In suppressing mobile network congestion, mobile operators often impose data limits and fair usage policies at a costly trade-off. Not only did data capping and network throttling significantly impede user experience, implementing such mechanisms incur heavy monitoring costs on the mobile operators. While understanding network traffic trend is far beyond any straightforward mathematical equation, the sporadic nature of mobile connectivity makes network congestion complex, unpredictable and difficult to eradicate. At such, traditional radio network planning and progressive network capacity upgrades may no longer be sufficient to serve the fluctuating connectivity demand. This poses serious threats to mobile operators in need for a more effective solution for real-time congestion control.

In this chapter, we will examine *Simplify*, a mobile data solution developed at Nextwave Technology aiming to solve network congestion woes by applying Big Data technologies in forecasting, shaping and routing mobile network traffic based on analysis of real-time data collected from mobile devices. By analysing human mobility patterns and understanding their connectivity routines, *Simplify* is able to predict network behaviours and prescribe personalized network policies to each mobile device in realizing dynamic network traffic steering while improving Mobile Internet experience.

BACKGROUND

In the effort to curb mobile network congestion, the challenges facing mobile operators are far more complex than just scaling up their network infrastructure. As fluctuating mobile data demand varies from area to area, on-demand network capacity allocation is almost a mandatory requirement. Despite the advancements in software-defined radio network technologies, which allow mobile operators to flexibly configure network capacity on the fly, such deployment requires costly upgrade to existing radio base stations. Instead, the immediate priority should focus on optimizing existing mobile network traffic by reducing the cost per megabyte while maintaining good user experience.

One immediate remedy to ease mobile congestion is to employ Wi-Fi offloading solution, diverting mobile data traffic towards Wi-Fi networks. Cisco (2014) has reported that approximately 45 percent of global mobile data traffic (1.2 Exabytes per month) was offloaded onto the fixed network through Wi-Fi and Femtocell in 2013. This figure is expected to reach 51 percent (17.3 Exabytes per month) by 2018. In this section, as a prelude to our work on *Simplify*, we will first focus our evaluation on contemporary Wi-Fi offloading solutions and other related work in relieving mobile network congestion.

Access Network Discovery and Selection Function

Acknowledging the tedious task in discovering and switching in between mobile data and Wi-Fi on mobile devices, the 3rd Generation Partnership Project (3GPP), a global telecommunications standardization body that defines cellular network specifications, has proposed Access Network Discovery and Selection Function (ANDSF) as a solution to optimize mobile broadband experience in heterogeneous network environment. By introducing an ANDSF server in the Evolved Packet Core (EPC) complemented by ANDSF clients installed on mobile devices, the solution enables mobile operators to send network policies containing a list of preferred networks available for connection within the immediate vicinity of the mobile devices. Using over-the-air provisioning, Wi-Fi hotspot locations and security credentials can be sent directly to mobile devices, eliminating the need to manually search and connect to Wi-Fi networks (3GPP, 2014b). In addition, mobile users traversing different locations may enjoy seamless network experience while switching in between a variety of wireless networks based on pre-determined network priority e.g. 4G LTE has a higher connection priority over Wi-Fi and 3G. To mobile operators who are in the midst of extending 4G LTE coverage, having an ANDSF system to interactively indicate possible 4G networks in an area may completely eliminate the need to constantly advertise or publish 4G network coverage map.

However, standards-based ANDSF exposes some critical limitations. Firstly, ANDSF is fundamentally designed to cater only for SIM-based mobile devices, which means device with Wi-Fi only capability cannot be supported by the system. Moreover, all ANDSF policies require pre-configuration on the server and periodic provisioning to the targeted devices, making it impractical to suppress ad-hoc network congestion scenarios.

Furthermore, the propagation of ANDSF policy is always one-way: originating from the network to mobile devices via a standard ANDSF S14 interface. This omits valuable data gathered on mobile devices to be used in network quality analysis. In compliance to 3GPP architecture deployment model, ANDSF server is deeply entrenched within the Evolved Packet Core (EPC) in which the signalling traffic traversing in between ANDSF server and mobile devices may likely to congest the operator's network even more. The deployment of ANDSF server is operator-specific, where roaming between multiple operators' networks would be difficult to achieve. In addition, it is almost impossible for an operator to provision all public and consumer Wi-Fi hotspots into the ANDSF server, limiting its capability only to include operator-deployed or partner-owned Wi-Fi.

Nevertheless, to many mobile operators, deploying Wi-Fi networks to cover mobile network blind spots is inevitable especially with the prominent evolution of Wi-Fi standards namely the IEEE 802.11u and IEEE 802.21, which are fast-transforming Wi-Fi to become a '*mission critical*' technology interoperable with cellular networks.

Network Crowdsourcing

Over the years, Wi-Fi technology has gained solid popularity through mass-market adoption and its cost-effectiveness in deployment. According to Cisco, there are 800 million new Wi-Fi devices shipped every year with more than 700 million consumers already having access to Wi-Fi out there. The public hotspots will be approaching 5.8 million globally by 2015 (Wireless Broadband Alliance, 2011).

While companies like iPass and Boingo have long being able to aggregate Wi-Fi for enterprise customers, network crowdsourcing has becoming widely popular in recent years to federate public hotspots for consumer use. WeFi, a market leader in consumer Wi-Fi aggregation, has crowdsourced over 200 million hotspots from its mobile application installed on user smartphones worldwide. In another context, a company called Fon, customizes its Wi-Fi router to broadcast both private SSID and a public FonSpot access point, granting Fon subscribers the complimentary access to Fon hotspots globally. Unlike operator-owned Wi-Fi networks, most consumer Wi-Fi offers short-range coverage and lacks carrier-grade quality. Intermittent network performance causes variation in quality-of-service. On the other hand, the heterogeneity of Wi-Fi security authentication methods further complicates seamless access experience. To make matter worse, the existence of rogue Wi-Fi that gives free Internet access to the public in disguise to hijack user traffic, pose serious security concerns.

As for public hotspots, like those found at Starbucks and McDonald's, have literally no integration to mobile networks at all. Access to these complimentary networks usually requires a separate user identity. With such limitation, it is tedious for mobile operators and Wi-Fi service providers to correlate the multiple identities used to access their networks in realizing seamless Wi-Fi offloading experience. The effort to choreograph network load-balancing and real-time network traffic routing between cellular and Wi-Fi prove extremely challenging. With more and more Wi-Fi service providers and aggregators trying to safeguard their market shares, the choice of proprietary technologies and business models make the entire ecosystem complex and highly fragmented. As a consequence, consumers will have to install different mobile applications to access different Wi-Fi services.

Human Mobility Patterns

In a human mobility study, Gonzales et al. (2008) found that cell-tower location information can be used to characterize human mobility and that humans follow simple reproducible mobility patterns. In another study led by Massachusetts Institute of Technology, Schneider et al. (2013) concluded that 90 percent of the 40,000 sample population used only 17 trip configurations out of a million possible commuting chains in their daily travels. Such premise holds true across the board for commuters resided in two megacities namely Chicago and Paris. These findings reiterate that user mobility behaviour is largely influenced by their daily routine. Further to this, there is a positive correlation between user routines to the intra-city travel patterns and network usage behaviour by analysing the mobile phone data. As such, it is absolutely possible to construct simple predictive models to describe user connectivity behaviour.

It is also worth to note that there is a distinguished mobility patterns for native and non-native inhabitants in a city with high accuracy of location prediction, even in the absence of demographic information (Yang et al., 2014). Not only that, by employing clustering techniques e.g. *k*-means and Markov models (Liu, 2009), user health risk profile or pandemic exposure could be predicted by correlating network connectivity patterns with their social network ties. For instance, people who frequently use free Wi-Fi at fast food chains (it is also possible to identify which fast food outlet by looking at the Wi-Fi SSID) are more prone to obesity and diabetes as compared to people who only connect to the Internet at home.

NETWORK TRAFFIC STEERING WITH CROWD INTELLIGENCE

Issues, Controversies and Problems

Battling mobile network congestion definitely falls beyond the responsibility of a network department. Without a concerted strategy and ecosystem support, it is very difficult to cover all key challenges spreading across the networks, devices, services and ultimately the subscribers, in need to render the best Mobile Internet experience. While solving mobile congestion puzzle requires complex data science in crunching high-volume network data collected at real-time, the measurement on quality-of-experience from end-user perspective cannot be ignored. Understanding the correlation between users' mobile connectivity routines to network quality shall provide absolute precursors and a more holistic approach in dynamic network traffic management.

Solutions and Recommendations

Visualizing Mobile Connectivity Routine with Big Data

Leveraging on crowd intelligence to bring social good is not entirely a new concept. *Waze*, a community-based road traffic and navigation mobile application, relies on real-time traffic information posted by drivers to bypass congestion and optimize travel routes. Similarly, this concept can be applied in mobile network context.

Simplify, the world's first community ANDSF solution designed to leverage mobile consumer intelligence in collaboratively discover, access and steer network traffic for online community benefits. The solution comprises a centralized *Simplify on Cloud* server and *Simplify* mobile applications installed on mobile devices in automating network discovery, selection and switching in the heterogeneous network environment. Built-in with network crowdsourcing capability, good networks e.g. Wi-Fi, 3G and 4G LTE, are automatically discovered, tagged and uploaded to *Simplify on Cloud*. In reciprocal, the cloud-based server sends ANDSF policy containing a list of best available networks nearby with the encrypted security credentials to facilitate seamless access to these networks. In other words, *Simplify* users may no longer require to manually scan for good networks or keying-in creepy Wi-Fi passwords, such tedious tasks are handled automatically in the background enabling a total handsfree connectivity experience.

Eco Surf – the fundamental principle guiding *Simplify*'s solution design, is envisioned to reduce our carbon footprints while surfing on the Mobile Internet. The key idea is simply to leverage collective intelligence to report and avoid poor quality networks, reducing unnecessary network scans, minimizing wastage of device battery and network resources in the process. Inspired by such eco-friendly principle, product teams at Nextwave Technology made several enhancements to ANDSF standards (3GPP, 2014a) in facilitating real-time data collection on mobile connectivity. This includes the introduction of (i) *location-tagging* feature on *Simplify* application, (ii) a proprietary *ANDSF S14 Post* interface to *Simplify on Cloud*, (iii) a *Network Analytics Engine*, and (iv) a *Network Traffic Controller* powering *Simplify*'s Big Data architecture backbone.

Location Tagging

With location-tagging enabled, *Simplify* tags every connected network to its nearby cell tower identifiers and geo-locations to form network location triplet i.e. SSID, Cell-ID, GPS. These location datasets enable *Simplify* to remember the frequented network locations including home, workplace, café and campus, auto-connecting to previously tagged networks when the device comes into proximity. The mobile application intelligently manages device wireless radios based on user location and connectivity preference. Unlike most conventional smartphones that leave Wi-Fi radio on low-powered passive scanning mode, *Simplify* automatically turns Wi-Fi off completely when user leaves the frequented location, optimizing network connection while minimizing energy use. On the other hand, by associating the location information with the types of network connected in a chronological order, we are able to capture user mobility patterns and chart their mobile connectivity routines in a time series map.

ANDSF S14 Post Interface

Having *Simplify* hosted on the cloud provides two key advantages: Firstly, it prevents ANDSF data and signalling traffic from overloading mobile operator's core network. This means the data exchange between *Simplify* applications and the server can bypass mobile packet core with local IP breakout mechanism e.g. Local IP Access (LIPA), for all Internet-bound traffic to *Simplify on Cloud*. Secondly, by putting the platform on the cloud, the ANDSF solution is no longer operator-specific. This opens up the entire infrastructure for global Mobile Internet traffic steering. Essentially, smaller operators are now able to provide international data and Wi-Fi roaming with other service providers leveraging on a common platform.

Unlike 3GPP-based ANDSF server that only allows mobile devices to pull network policies over the standard ANDSF S14 Pull interface, *Simplify* mobile application captures and sends device information, data usage patterns and network quality data to the server using Nextwave-proprietary ANDSF S14 Post interface (Tay, 2013). With this enhancement, a complete feedback loop is formed enabling two-way information exchange between the server and the mobile applications sparsely deployed on the field in providing a dynamic view of real-time network conditions. With *Simplify on Cloud* server subscribing to continuous streams of data sent from thousands of mobile devices, these invaluable datasets can help network service providers to gain greater insight into every mobile consumer's connectivity pattern.

Network Analytics Engine

On *Simplify on Cloud* server, the *Network Analytics Engine* implements the descriptive analytics feature that is capable of gathering, filtering, storing and analysing the collected information. As such, every single user contributes data to formulate Device-Network-Application (DNA) dimensions (see Figure 1) in illustrating their own connectivity routine. Subsequently, a collection of these user routines using the same network can be extrapolated to derive network congestion patterns and predict network behaviours in the densely populated areas.

Network Traffic Controller

However, deciphering network and user behaviours would be meaningless without any pre-emptive measure to optimize the rapid growing network traffic. Like deploying a traffic police at the middle of crossroads diverting road traffic at peak hours, the *Network Traffic Controller* provides prescriptive

Figure 1. The Device-Network-Application (DNA) dimensions of Internet Connectivity Behaviour

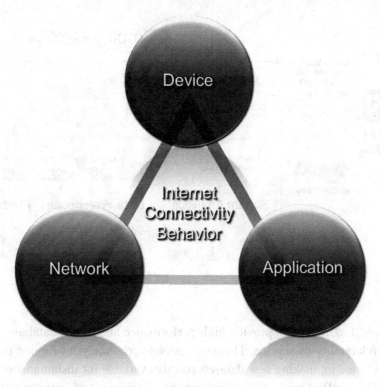

analytics to proactively shape, optimize and divert traffic flows toward alternative and less congested networks. With thousands of devices sending data simultaneously, *Simplify on Cloud* is gaining greater insight not only on mobile connectivity patterns and network behaviours, but the effectiveness of its prescriptions on steering Mobile Internet traffic.

Inside Simplify: The Big Data Architecture

With the aim to realize network traffic steering to ease network congestion, the massive volume and high-velocity of probe data received from *Simplify* applications require almost zero latency in processing. Powered by Google App Engine, both *Network Analytics Engine* and *Network Traffic Controller* constitute the core of *Simplify on Cloud's* Big Data architecture (see Figure 2). The system exposes ANDSF S14 Post web service interface using Google Cloud Endpoints in receiving real-time data streams sent from mobile devices. The data collected can be broadly classified into: (i) *Device Location* (ii) *Network Discovery Information* (iii) *Network Quality-of-Service (QoS)*, and (iv) *User Data Usage*. The corroboration of these data further describes when, where and how users connect to the networks, what devices they carry, their connectivity patterns and the present network conditions.

Unlike traditional business intelligence that follows a store, process then analyse approach, with massive raw data flooding in at high-speed, *Network Analytics Engine* uses Google Cloud Datastore,

Figure 2. Simplify Big Data Architecture

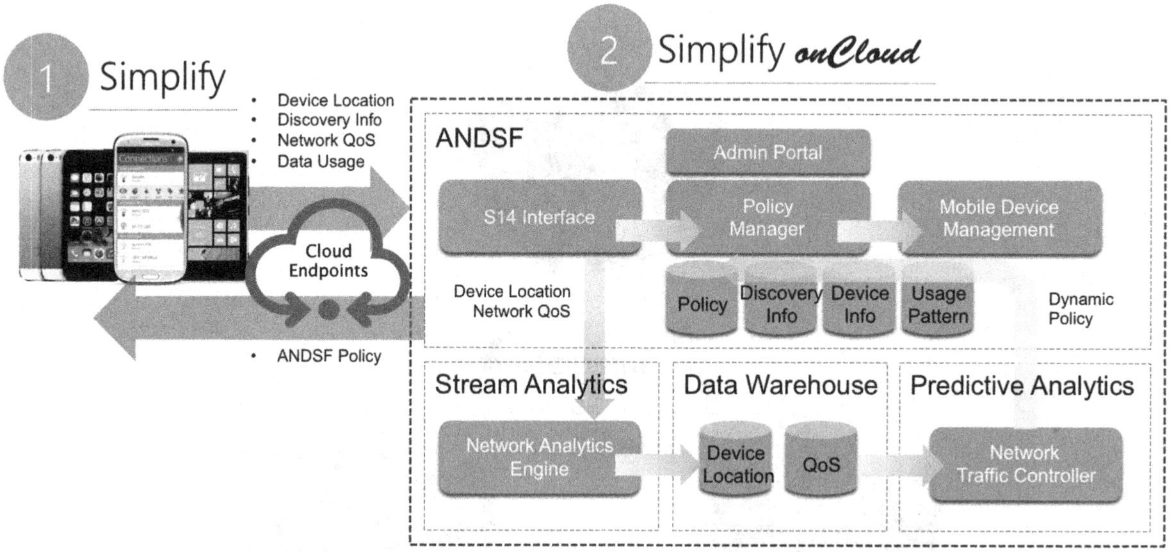

an auto-scalable NoSQL database, to provide high-performance and robust database storage for device locations and network quality-of-service. This enables Network Analytics Engine to store continuous flow of data as they come in, making new datasets readily available for instantaneous processing.

Coupling with Google BigQuery, a tool that can query terabytes of datasets within seconds, this Google-fast advantage serves as a critical edge for *Network Traffic Controller* to handle time sensitive use cases such as instant network quality analysis and near real-time network traffic steering. For example, upon detecting poor quality networks, alerts are triggered to ANDSF Policy Manager to blacklist those affected networks in its policy database. As a result, only good quality networks are propagated via ANDSF policy sent to mobile devices, delighting mobile consumers with excellent online experience. Besides, the *Network Traffic Controller* can focus on a subset of network data based on different contexts such as location and time e.g. analysing past hour data or querying network conditions at specific locations. Such flexibility allows *Simplify on Cloud* to create timely network snapshots and identify the key drivers behind certain network behaviour during peak and off-peak hours (see Figure 3).

While it is not difficult to find a linear correlation between consumer data demand and network behaviours, what is interesting to note from our analysis is that there is also positive correlation found between the type of devices used and the network data consumption. Generally, iPhone users consume 34 percent more data than any other smartphone users. What is more insightful to us is, even for a same user, the usage behaviour on Wi-Fi and mobile data network varies considerably. Many users tend to be more abusive on Wi-Fi, streaming heavy-duty multimedia content, while staying conservative on 3G data network, perhaps due to data capping policy imposed by mobile operators. When we found the type of network reacts predictably to such mobile consumer behaviour, statistical model can be built to predict network behaviours.

Using Google Prediction API, *Network Traffic Controller* learns and predicts network behaviours based on device types and locations as well as the generalized user routines. Not only does the occurrence of frequent congested networks can be known in advance, by factoring in these variables, effective

Figure 3. Discovery Map on Simplify mobile application color-coded with network quality indicators

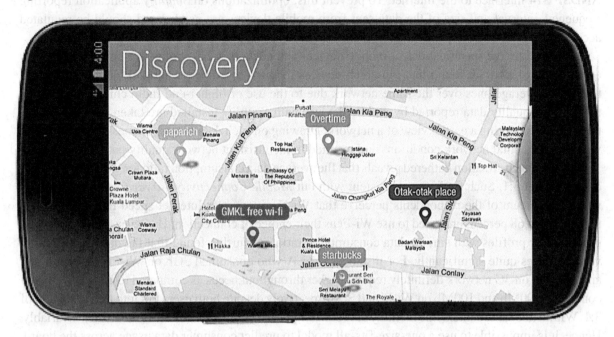

ANDSF policies can be crafted to shape, optimize and divert mobile network traffic towards alternative networks. In addition, personalized connection profiles can be prescribed to enhance Mobile Internet experience, tailoring specifically to individual routine.

Like a live traffic control centre, the *Network Analytics Dashboard* is built with Google Charts API to display real-time network conditions. Highly congested networks are plotted on a heat map, indicating the number of devices attached to them, and the list of nearby networks available for diversion. The power of combining descriptive and predictive analytics gives mobile operators a holistic view and more control over mobile network congestion while improving user experience at real time. This was never before a possibility without Big Data technologies. Today, *Simplify* is setting another technology frontier, opening up its platform to steer mobile network traffic worldwide.

Emulating the honeybee colony, *Simplify* applications are mimicking the role of worker bees in discovering good access networks on the field, sending precious information back to *Simplify on Cloud* server ("the hive") to share with the colony. The aim of employing such architecture is more than just allowing massive data to flow into the system rapidly, but it is also used to form the basis of collaborative network discovery and collective decision-making. These mechanisms are critical in realizing what Pentland (2014) coined as the 'Idea Machines', enabling diverse exploration of new networks and facilitating high-quality dense engagement within each cluster of networks to increase social intelligence.

Findings, Issues, and Limitations

While real-time network quality data critically captures instant snapshots of actual network conditions, the deployment of *Simplify* at such large scale has contributed significant network signalling traffic along

ANDSF S14 interface to the Internet. To prevent this, optimizations on *Simplify* application reporting frequency, interval and size of the data sent from mobile devices are needed and should be regulated according to peak and off-peak hours in ensuring optimum network performance.

Furthermore, the specifications of mobile devices and network access points are not homogenously equal. For instance, we found that top-notch devices tend to record better network quality-of-service than those average ones over the same network due to the use of higher-end radio chipset. Also, only the network quality data reported by mobile devices with *Simplify* installed are taken into our prediction model, rendering a partial view of a network. Drawing on such data incompleteness may distort the views on the actual network conditions and resulted in inconsistent network quality patterns observed.

The device information gathered reveals that the average data consumption ratio for Wi-Fi over mobile data stands at 3:1. Such finding is consistent with our *Mobile Connectivity Survey* (Nextwave, 2013b) where 76 percent of the respondents perceive that Wi-Fi gives faster Internet speed than mobile data network with 68 percent preferred to use Wi-Fi as their choice of connection. However, as we zoom into specific user profiles with similar data consumption ratio, we further found that the data consumption volume varies quite significantly. For instance, User A who consumed 3Gb on Wi-Fi per month and another 1Gb on 3G network definitely require higher throughput needs as compared to User B who only consumed 300Mb and 100Mb on Wi-Fi and 3G respectively despite both users fall into the same ratio of 3:1. Within this same context, the monthly data consumption volume for a same user fluctuates invariably. Hence, it is impossible to use a one-size-fits-all model to predict consumer data usage across the board.

It is also important to note that the day-to-day data pattern behaves quite sporadically, especially in the urban districts where dispersion of population movements spread across some complex overlapping layers of wireless networks covering a vast area. The tediousness in tracking every single network access point lying along the customer journey map requires massive corroborative effort. Imposing street-level tracking on user locations may draw intrusive privacy concerns. Even for mobile users who strictly follow a nine-to-five routine, there are a mixture of mobile connectivity patterns observed. Within this subset of users, although we can technically decompose their routines into time-of-day, day-of-week, day-of-month and even comparing weekday versus weekend cycles, there are still many user routines that cannot be explained using the conventional calendar cycles. The data inveracity instigates instability to our prediction model. We believe such '*irregular routine*' is not an oxymoron. There could be many other contributing factors, such as user demographics and subscription profiles, which are not immediately available to *Simplify*, obscuring the entire process of deciphering individual mobile connectivity behaviour at a deeper level.

Assessing from the graph theory perspective, when multiple mobile devices contend for a same network access point which can only cater for a limited number of devices, a constricted set phenomenon occurs. Although it is possible to solve this using market clearing property technique, the matching algorithms behind pairing each device with its preferred network to maximize quality-of-experience proves extremely complex. At one hand, the optimum network load factor for each and every network has to be computed at real-time, to avoid overloading of a network with significant number of devices. On the other hand, the relationship between a network and *Simplify on Cloud* is asymmetric. Meaning to say that while *Simplify* can instruct mobile devices to connect to a good network, but when a network gets congested, there is no direct mechanism to report congestion and query for alternative offloading route via *Simplify on Cloud* server.

In order to address these challenges, data fusion technique could be used to create multiple contexts around the data. For example, we could collaborate with mobile operators to obtain subscription profiles and billing cycle to explain certain irregular data points such as the sudden surge in mobile data consumption towards the end of monthly billing cycle. Another way to manage uncertainty is through advanced mathematics that embraces it, such as mathematical modelling and optimization algorithms that can be applied to strengthen our prediction models.

FUTURE RESEARCH DIRECTIONS

The Internet of Things

One key area to advance our research is on Internet of Things where more than 50 billion devices will be connected by 2020 (Ericsson, 2011). These are beyond smartphones and tablets, but comprising household appliances, wearable devices, implantable sensors, connected vehicles, intelligent bots and machines etc. What will be interesting to highlight is that every single device that we use and wear shall produce richer parameters to annotate our daily routines and behaviours than what we have collected and analysed today.

With this new range of devices, *Simplify* would be required to handle much complex use cases such as the ability to associate multiple types of devices belonging to a same user and to optimally allocate network bandwidth to heterogeneous devices attached to the networks. Having a federated identity is also critical in learning and predicting user behaviours as to what devices they wear, when and where they use them, so that personalized network profiles could be prescribed to these personal devices based on specific context. One important aspect to this is to employ device-profiling technique, where the data consumption ratio for each device is individually measured, computed and predicted over time to better project device data demand. For example, it is highly unlikely for a cyclist to stream high-definition video but only to keep his wearable sensors active during the workout period. Understanding these behaviours would require a lot of sophistications built into our initial prediction model in reducing the overall network resource consumption, with the vision to create a sustainable model in preserving network neutrality principles.

Heuristic Device

In catering for more aggressive data demand, the 4G LTE standards namely IP Flow Mobility (IFOM) and Multi-access Packet Data Network Connectivity (MAPCON) are evolving toward enabling future mobile devices the concurrent access to multiple types of networks at any one time. Unlike any conventional smartphone today, which can only alternate between mobile data or Wi-Fi, the next generation multi-radio devices are capable to connect multiple networks simultaneously. For instance, a mobile consumer may opt to keep an on-going WhatsApp session on mobile data while at the same time streaming high-definition YouTube video over the Wi-Fi. This provides greater bandwidth and faster Internet speed by maximizing the full capacity of both networks.

As realizing such scenario would have significant impact to the networks, understanding each consumer application behaviour is critical in achieving real-time network load-balancing and traffic shaping. Revisiting our use case above, under normal circumstances, it would be logical to split WhatsApp messaging and YouTube traffics toward two different networks for ultimate bandwidth performance. But what if one of these networks suffers from quality degradation? Should the device divert the You-

Tube traffic to mobile data instead? Can the mobile network cater additional load incurred by the high-definition video streaming without compromising user experience? This shall pose a great dilemma to the logic embedded within the multi-radio device. Undeniably, without application profiling data, it is very difficult to achieve the desired result.

Every mobile application possesses its own unique data behaviour and by adding consumer usage behaviour into the equation, *Simplify* would require to profile the frequently used mobile applications installed on consumer devices, in determining the data consumption ratio at application level, device level and user level. With the heuristic feature built-in, *Simplify* can prescribe connectivity policies tailoring to specific application usage requirements on different devices and networks. Ultimately, at such, we aim to decentralize the decision making point from *Simplify on Cloud* server to individual devices, making them more intelligent with self-learning and network forecasting capabilities. Nevertheless, the optimum network assignment and effectiveness of such deployment shall require further investigation.

Social and Behavioural Sensing

Among other things, we also see a huge potential to open up *Simplify* as a social and behavioural sensing platform for academia and industry. In this highly-connected society, the digital footprints of networked consumers prove so invaluable not only to advertisers and marketers but also to researchers in the study of computational social science, urban planning, behavioural economics, social psychology, network optimization algorithms etc. Unlike traditional research methodology, empowered with Big Data technologies, the data collection and analysis could happen in parallel. In what was coined as *Reality Mining* by MIT Professor, Alex Pentland, as the platform continues to capture and analyse individual or group patterns of human connectivity behaviour, researchers may test out their hypotheses based on huge sets of live data. Despite this remarkable vision, the concern on personal data privacy has to be dealt with absolute anonymity, sensitivity and transparency (Davenport, 2014). Perhaps, the platform should evolve into a trust network, safeguarding user personal data by obtaining informed consent from users who voluntarily participate in such living lab with the power to possess, control, dispose or re-distribute what information and the granularity level of information to be shared (Pentland, 2014).

Furthermore, *Simplify* should advance into becoming a new type of geo-social network, aiding us to derive a more precise model in predicting the likelihood of friends to co-occur at the same place and at the same time (Dong, Lepri & Pentland, 2011). With such possibility, *Simplify* may adopt social network incentives to engineer co-operative behaviour and encourage more social interactions among its users to constructively address social problems. This can be applied not only at the community level but city level, with active engagements from the municipals. For instance, city councils and authorities may direct their concerted effort towards solving social issues by providing multi-level incentives to citizens who willingly participate in reporting public infrastructure glitches. With this crowdsourcing capability, instead of lodging complaints via the call centre, urbanites can tag precise locations of traffic woes, potholes, fires, bursting water pipes etc. using *Simplify* with immediate response team deployed to rectify the issues on-site. Likewise, city councils can make announcements on local information via *Simplify*, which is seemingly more personalized, non-intrusive, fast and effective.

In addition, neighbourhood watch could be another potential application area. Too often we only found out crimes in our own neighbourhood as late as days after it happened, either from word of mouth or local newspapers. With *Simplify*, neighbours can post '*shout-out*' on thefts, robberies and other crimes nearby your area. Taking the fact that there are also many unreported cases out there, police may leverage on *Simplify*'s data to beef up patrol in high crime areas. This is a whole new way of social interactions because when you join a social network like Facebook, typically you would expect to connect to the people you know, reconnect to the people you have known and discover the people you want to know. However, *Simplify* reverse this process entirely. In order to view a '*shout-out*', a user may not be required to be a friend of the person who posted it. At a glance, user may see a list of hot topics physically close to him, connecting and grouping people into multiple clusters of geographical networks, collaborating together to bring social good.

CONCLUSION

Mobile network congestion poses a series of great challenges lying along mobile operator's value chain spanning across radio coverage, network capacity, security, quality-of-service, network optimization, standards compliance, applications variety, device specifications, subscription packages, consumer connectivity behaviours, user experience and customer loyalty. The value of employing Big Data in understanding, reconciling and addressing each of these aspects is imminent for mobile operators to achieve operational excellence.

In our vision to liberate social connectivity, it is the interactive engagements among the crowd with *Simplify* platform that makes Big Data mutually reinforcing. While *Simplify* users contribute split-second network information as they move, the data scientists at the lab could collate, aggregate and propagate synthesized network information back to the community for optimum network experience. Not only does this method open up a whole new way to collectively shape Mobile Internet traffic, the potential of leveraging crowd intelligence can go further to solve more complex social issues in the future. The realization of *Simplify*'s ecosystem presented in this chapter is consistent with what Stibel (2009) represented today's Internet as a complex network of brain neurons, wired together to store memories, associate patterns and manifest intelligence.

As pieces of Big Data originate from the crowd, mimicking the natural water cycle where evaporating steam turns into rains that shower back on the valley, we strongly believe by iteratively recycling the data back to the society can nurture new perspectives in shaping collaborative and sensible behaviours that embrace the *Eco Surf* core values, bringing technology for good in cultivating a sustainable networked society.

REFERENCES

Cisco, Inc. (2014). *Cisco Visual Networking Index: Global Mobile Data Traffic Forecast Update, 2013 – 2018*.

Davenport, T. H. (2014). *Big data at work: dispelling the myths, uncovering the opportunities*. Boston: Harvard Business Review Press. doi:10.15358/9783800648153

Dong, W., Lepri, B., & Pentland, A. (2011). Modeling the Co-evolution of Behaviors and Social Relationships Using Mobile Phone Data. In *Proceedings of the 10th International Conference on Mobile and Ubiquitous Multimedia*, (pp. 134-143). doi:10.1145/2107596.2107613

Easley, D., & Kleinberg, J. (2010). *Networks, Crowds and Markets: Reasoning About Highly Connected World*. New York: Cambridge University Press. doi:10.1017/CBO9780511761942

Ericsson. (2011). *More Than 50 Billion Connected Devices*.

Gonzalez, M. C., Hidalgo, A., & Barabsi, A.-L. (2008). *Understanding individual human mobility patterns*. Nature Scientific Reports.

Liu, B. (2009). *Web Data Mining: Exploring Hyperlinks, Contents and Usage Data*. Springer.

Nextwave Technology, N. (2013). Mobile Connectivity Report 2013. Kuala Lumpur.

Pentland, A. (2014). *Social Physics: How Good Ideas Spread – The Lessons from A New Science*. New York: The Penguin Press.

3rd Generation Partnership Project. (2014, March 17). *3GPP TS 24.302 Access to the 3GPP Evolved Packet Core (EPC) via non-3GPP access networks (Release 12)*. Retrieved April 14, 2014, from http://www.3gpp.org/DynaReport/24302.htm

3rd Generation Partnership Project. (2014, March 17). *3GPP TS 24.312 Access Network Discovery and Selection Function (ANDSF) Management Object (MO) (Release 12)*. Retrieved April 14, 2014, from http://www.3gpp.org/DynaReport/24312.htm

Schneider, C. M., Belik, V., Couronne, T., Smoreda, Z., & Gonzalez, M. C. (2013). Unraveling daily human mobility motifs. *Journal of the Royal Society, 10*(84), 1742–5662.

Stibel, J. M. (2009). *Wired for Thought: How the Brain is Shaping the Future of Internet* (pp. 105–115). Boston: Harvard Business Press.

Tay, Y. P. (2012). *Getting Ready for Data Tsunami*. Kuala Lumpur: Nextwave Technology.

Tay, Y. P. (2013). *Nextwave Simplify Solution Description: Redefine the way we connect*. Kuala Lumpur: Nextwave Technology.

Wireless Broadband Alliance. (2011). *Industry Report: Global Developments in Public Wi-Fi*.

Yang, Z., Yuan, N. J., Xie, X., Lian, D., Rui, Y., & Zhou, T. (2014). Indigenization of Urban Mobility. *arXiv preprint arXiv:1405.7769*.

KEY TERMS AND DEFINITIONS

3G: A set of third generation mobile network systems standardized by Third Generation Partnership Project (3GPP) comprising of Wideband Code Division Multiple Access (W-CDMA), High Speed Packet Access (HSPA), Evolved High Speed Packet Access (HSPA+) and 4G Long Term Evolution (LTE) technologies.

4G LTE: A fourth generation wireless communication standard defined by 3GPP for high-speed mobile data communication network evolved from Global System for Mobile (GSM) communication.

ANDSF: Access Network Discovery and Selection Function (ANDSF) is an network element within Evolved Packet Core (EPC) responsible for propagating network policies containing access network discovery information and selection based on time, location, network preference and device type.

EPC: Evolved Packet Core, the core network of 4G LTE systems introduced by 3GPP in its Release 8 standard.

Femtocell: A micro cellular base station designed for use at homes and small businesses with its backbone connected to fixed broadband network.

IEEE: The Institute of Electrical and Electronics Engineers is an organization that develops global standards in a broad range of industries including power and energy, biomedical and health care, information technology, telecommunication, nanotechnology, information on assurance, etc.

IFOM: IP Flow Mobility is a mechanism for a mobile device to simultaneously connect to 3GPP cellular access and WLAN enabling exchange of different IP flows belonging to the same or different applications being moved seamlessly between a 3GPP access and WLAN belonging to the same network provider.

SSID: The name or identifier broadcast by a WLAN access point.

WLAN: Wireless Local Area Network.

Section 2
Presenting Web Intelligence and Its Perspective

Chapter 5
Web Intelligence:
A Fuzzy Knowledge-Based Framework for the Enhancement of Querying and Accessing Web Data

Jafreezal Jaafar
Universiti Teknologi PETRONAS, Malaysia

Kamaluddeen Usman Danyaro
Universiti Teknologi PETRONAS, Malaysia

M. S. Liew
Universiti Teknologi PETRONAS, Malaysia

ABSTRACT

This chapter discusses about the veracity of data. The veracity issue is the challenge of imprecision in big data due to influx of data from diverse sources. To overcome this problem, this chapter proposes a fuzzy knowledge-based framework that will enhance the accessibility of Web data and solve the inconsistency in data model. D2RQ, protégé, and fuzzy Web Ontology Language applications were used for configuration and performance. The chapter also provides the completeness fuzzy knowledge-based algorithm, which was used to determine the robustness and adaptability of the knowledge base. The result shows that the D2RQ is more scalable with respect to performance comparison. Finally, the conclusion and future lines of the research were provided.

INTRODUCTION

There is a growing number of hypes in today's world of data. The data that change the human interaction through leveraging power of accessibility. The pervasive applications and tools such as phones, computers and cars have built the knowledge base which needs large data stores and management. MapReduce, resource description framework (RDF) as well as simple protocol and RDF query language (SPARQL) are the current technologies in data science that enable Web users to access and query information in a suitable way.

DOI: 10.4018/978-1-4666-8505-5.ch005

Perhaps, due to plethora of data, the database structures need to be enhanced in a way that will ease the query for proper processing and big data exploration. This is a challenge in big data management in which the redundancy or/and unorganized information is of concerned. As schema is the backbone for every database but it is not sufficient when the data is unstructured. Similarly, the quality of data re-usability reduces as it increases everyday through Web by making it to be unstructured. This means that the presence of unstructured data reduces the integrity of data and making it to be difficult for reuse. Many distributed databases and database schemas are now connected with large information. More specifically, large amounts of information on the Web cause the problem of uncertainty and imprecision due to access and querying bunch of data. Uncertainties, imprecisions and inconsistencies in data model is one of the tactical challenges of big data (Jewell et al., 2014; Savas, Sagduyu, Deng, & Li, 2014). The uncertain or imprecise issue of data is called veracity which among the dimensions of big data. Significantly, big data tools such as MapReduce and Hadoop deal with both structured and unstructured data to simplify accessibility. Therefore, the main contribution of this chapter is to provide a fuzzy knowledge-based framework that will be used as channel of accessing and querying big data. The framework guides in providing the precise information to the user through querying multiple data sources. This process allows machine to reason intelligently. The reasoning approach of this work is specifically using fuzzy logic-based systems. The proposed work suggests the scalability of the fuzzy knowledge base (KB).

This chapter proceeds with the second section that discusses about the retrospective background knowledge on Web intelligence, big data and the uncertainty. Third section illustrates the overview about the proposed framework which includes: the general architecture of the system and fuzzy ontology. In section four, the implementation process has been presented. Subsequently, section five discusses the result of the proposed framework. Finally, section six provides the conclusion and future works.

WEB INTELLIGENCE

Web information has great impact in human life especially in the domain of world knowledge such as uncertainty and imprecision. The Web intelligence constitutes the usage of WWW as a phenomenon of retrieving information from the storage efficiently. It acts as an agent in which the machine can reason and conveys the message using Web tools. The agent goes round and integrates the resource which finally presents the information to user through a Web page. The resources or things depend on RDF that links the entire concept together through Uniform Resource Identifier (URI). Web intelligence is a well-known research area which converges subjects such as artificial intelligence, databases, Web science, Semantic Web, and information retrieval (Berners-Lee et al., 2006; Camacho et al., 2013; Shadbolt & Berners-Lee, 2008; Shroff, 2013; Williams et al., 2014). Therefore, reasoning in Web data is the first step in finding the solution of a problem in the knowledge-based system.

To work with intelligence, it is necessary to define the complex knowledge acquisition, knowledge inference, deduction and knowledge representation in order to make the conceptualization of a knowledge model suitable for reasoning (Camacho et al., 2013; G'abor, 2007; Russell et al., 2010; Zadeh, 2004). This may lead the ontology to be machine-processable and allows the precise interpretation of knowledge representation. The knowledge representation has major three flavors: concepts, relations and instances (C, R and I). Generally, the representations are being understood by humans. In this sense, if the knowledge representation is done through the concepts and relates it to humans using symbols on a particular group, then the process is referred to as conceptualization. In accordance with Grimm et al. (2007) axioms, a set of ontological statements that can be expressed in form of vocabularies. For example; "*the weather is hot*" or "*only those who are registered with MetOcean can know the wind direction at South China Sea*". Both of these consist of instances and concepts on a particular domain. Expectedly, encoding such axiomatic concepts using semantic logic notations reduce the complexity of information. While, Web Ontology Language (OWL) is the compromising tool of reasoning between human and machine that has been widely accepted by Semantic Web community (Thomas & Sheth, 2006).

The concept of information processing in big data environment with structured and unstructured data is an essential aspect in today's world of data. It is a data to human relationship through accessing, sharing, and visualizing the raw data. Nevertheless, this creates a decentralization of structural information and knowledge representation. In doing so, the implementation of fuzzy would be the challenging aspect but is the solution to data-related industries. The fuzzy knowledge representation deals with the rules that can be interpreted as:

IF a is X AND b is Y THEN c is Z

This statement describes how the logic can infer the rule base in an inference system that would finally produce the result (antecedent to consequent). Therefore, to achieve and validate the veracity of big data, such statement must be true in a knowledge base.

BIG DATA AND THE UNCERTAINTY

Uncertainties and inconsistencies in data model is one of the tactical big data challenges (Savas et al., 2014). It is because as Web is extending, the demand for precision (precise information) is also increasing which is clearly the problem of ambiguity. "*The more uncertainty in a problem, the less precise we can be in our understanding of that problem*" (Ross, 2010). Indeed, uncertainty is also the veracity issue of big data (Jewell et al., 2014). There are currently five dimensions of big data which are called 5-Vs. These include Volume, Velocity, Value, Veracity and Variety. This chapter attempts to contribute on one of these Vs that is the Veracity. Veracity is described as the quality of trustworthiness of the data (Hurwitz, Nugent, Halper, & Kaufman, 2013; Zikopoulos, Parasuraman, Deutsch, Giles, & Corrigan, 2012). In addendum, Demchenko et al. (2013) described Veracity as the certainty or consistency in the data due to its statistical reliability.

The aspect of establishing the trust or consistency in database widens the gap between the Web reasoning approach and human thinking. People retrieve information via Web browsers which leads to the incessant increase of data in the database. Therefore, the collection of large amount of datasets from different repositories and manage it in suitable way can be referred as big data. It is aimed to reduce the complexity due to the increase of massive data from different applications. However, Mohanty et al. (2013) defined the big data as the combination of these interactivities and transactions of data.

The tools that are currently been used in the big data ecosystems are the emerging technologies such as MapReduce, Hadoop Distributed File system (HDFS) and non-relational (NoSQL) database. The database engine or agent in the knowledge base transforms the data value. MapReduce is a product of an algorithm developed by Google in order to manage its large datasets. Then the Apache used this algorithm and produced an open source project called Hadoop. It becomes an Apache-managed system derived from Google Big Table and MapReduce. Therefore, Hadoop is basically contains two parts: MapReduce and Hadoop Distributed File System (HDFS) that is the programming part and the file system respectively. Hadoop also has a number of prominent infrastructures or projects that manage the big data. These include: HBase, Cassandra, Hive, Pig, Chukwa, Zookeeper, Amazon SimpleDB, Cloudata, CouchDB, AllegroGraph, MangoDB, and others. Some of these databases run on top of HDFS which is also called NoSQL database. Since this chapter deals with fuzzy concepts, it's therefore selected the Hive and HBase for better scalability in big data management (see Figure 1). Similarly, it is discovered that HBase and HDFS are fault-tolerant applications when integrating with Hadoop (Zaharia et al., 2012).

Hive

Hive is a data warehouse system layer built on Hadoop. It allows the developer to define a structure of the unstructured big data. The method simplifies analysis and queries with the SQL-like scripting language called HiveQL. Hive latency queries are high in which it process the data that keeps in HDFS. This makes it easier for the user to use the system without knowing the MapReduce. Apache Hive is one of the most effective standards for SQL queries that works over petabytes of the data in Hadoop (Connolly, 2012).

HBase

In big data management, HBase is a columnar database engine developed on Ruby query language. It uses MapReduce engine and Hadoop framework for its data processing. It is efficient to work with non-relational data (Hurwitz et al., 2013). Therefore, NoSQL would be a good database to integrate with relational data. Connolly (2012) considers Apache HBase as a NoSQL database that runs on top of HDFS. Due to this proficiency, HBase supports Web-based implementation of big data.

Figure 1. Simple Hadoop architecture

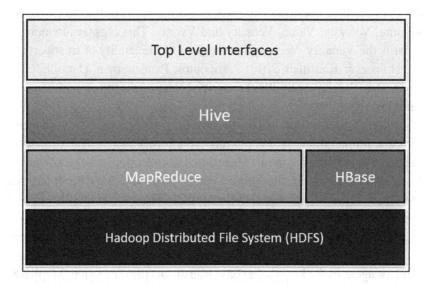

NoSQL

NoSQL, or not only SQL is an approach in big data management that operates on resources, columnar and graph database systems. It deals with relational and non-relational databases and map with the architecture for better scalability.

FRAMEWORK OVERVIEW

This part discusses an overview of the process and functionality of the processed fuzzy knowledge-based framework for the enhancement of querying and accessing Web data. Figure 2 describes the overall architecture as well as the process taken for integration of fuzzy ontology in big data.

Fuzzy Ontology

The Web ontology language (OWL) is a compromising tool of reasoning between human and machine that has widely been accepted by Semantic Web community. Ontology is an explicit specification and representation of a particular domain of interest which allows understanding a domain based on specific concepts (Gruber, 1993). The current standard of OWL is OWL 2[1] that standardized by World Wide Web Consortium (W3C) in 2009. This mechanize the interpretability of information on Web. The standard is perfect for use by applications that require and process the content of Web data rather than presenting information to humans. Unarguably, several literatures have revealed that OWL is more related to the expressiveness and computational nature of Web knowledge base (Bobillo, Delgado, Gómez-Romero, & Straccia, 2009; Lukasiewicz & Straccia, 2009; Sugumaran & Gulla, 2012; Thomas & Sheth, 2006; Yu, 2011). Therefore, this notion has become the philosophical basis of knowledge representation.

To design the knowledge base, the concepts TBox (terminological part) and ABox (assertional part) must be defined with respect to vocabularies of the datasets. Fuzzy TBox provides the general rules for data retrieval in database. The triples (S, P, O) are instances in the database. The space in the database contains the terminological files where the instances are the input of the system. On the other hand, fuzzy ABox starts from the basic facts or axioms that are used for syntactic decomposition of the rules for the instances in the database. The fuzzy here is used to describe each triple and unify with single or multiple atoms rule body (see Figure 3).

Available Resource

The resources available in the knowledge base such as the time series data is envisioned to have carried their task through integrating with the relevant concepts. The data will allocate the distributed files with the aid of APIs. For instance, the resources generated from Malaysia time series data. This may include all the connections between people, companies as well as the variables (wind speed, wind direction, etc.).

Figure 2. The framework architecture

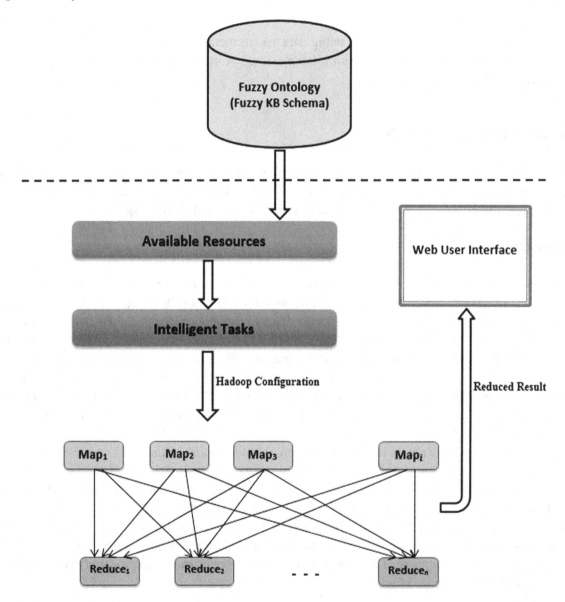

Intelligent Tasks

The available resources are processed by human and then the applications generate the tasks. Tasks are configured by Hadoop systems. The optimality is based on the human and machine from the knowledge base which allows reliability due to the automated processing power of Hadoop.

Map

The automation process taking care by the Hadoop from the intelligent tasks, mapping follows the automated tasks and specified and map each concept to the available reduce.

Figure 3. Ontology representation based on the domain ontology

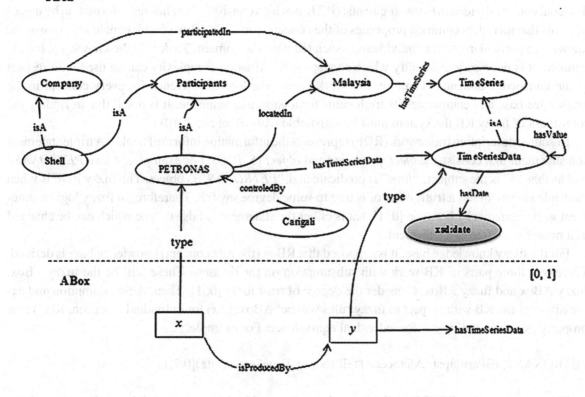

Reduce

In this part, the Hadoop performs major contribution. It processed the nodes from the available distributed files.

Web User Interface

The Web user interface for this framework is a Simple Protocol and RDF Query Language (SPARQL) endpoint. The purpose for using SPARQL is to ease the data accessibility through pulling the data from available resources in the HBase level. This means that SPARQL will enable the data expressions or queries across different sources. It is also standardized by W3C with the current version as SPARQL 1.1[2]. The data can be viewed as raw RDF or as optional graph pattern.

Querying non-RDF data of MetOcean using D2R server with SPARQL endpoint allows the database to be accessed as graph. The data is dumped and accessed using the general API. Considering the case study of meteorological and oceanographic data (MetOcean), the database with corresponding entities and properties connect the entities together, which finally enable it to have complete interlinked data of the MetOcean knowledge base.

Fuzzy Knowledge Base

The concepts are divided in to two segments: (i) TBox which consists of intentional information by means of terms that identifies common properties of the concepts; and (ii) ABox of which includes extensional knowledge particularly to the individuals associated with the domain. To decide the knowledge base is entailed, it is necessary to identify which concept of information complexity can be used with respect to the knowledge domain. Therefore, this work checks the logical inference for every concept in the knowledge base and enumerates its truth value for a particular sentence. It is noted that in finding the robustness of fuzzy KB the system must be satisfiable (Russell et al., 2010).

Resource description framework (RDF) represents the information inform of triples. A triple statement is a statement that consists: *subject, predicate* and *object (S, P, O)*. For example, *"I love PETRONAS"* means that *"I"* is the subject, *"love"* is predicate and *"PETRONAS"* is object. The fuzzy RDF is when the triple statement has a truth value or is true to some degree say 0.8. Therefore, in fuzzy logic a statement is mathematically between [0, 1] that is either the statement is false or true which can be changed as a matter of degree of a statement.

For the fuzzy knowledge base, it is supposed that RBox (the role concept) knowledge base is defined. Therefore, three parts of KB work with subsumption on the datasets. These will be the fuzzy TBox, fuzzy ABox and fuzzy RBox. Consider the degree of trust for is [0, 1]. Then, the subsumption and expressivity of the KB with respect to fuzzy rules will be: ABox: $C(x)$ for individual assertion, $R(x, y)$ for property assertion and $x = y$ for individual equivalence. For example:

PETRONAS $\sqsubseteq$ ($\exists$Participate.Metocean $\sqcap$ $\exists$Produce.TimeSeriesData)[0.7,1]

This means that the PETRONAS concept has subsumed by MetOcean participant (Participate MetOcean) and produce time series data with at least 0.7 as truth degree. Therefore, with respect to the general concept inclusion (GCI) axiom as defined by (Horrocks et al., 2006). It is when two concepts C and D are of the form $C \sqsubseteq D$ which implies:

$$\left(C \sqsubseteq D \right)' X = \inf_{x \in \Delta^I} C'\left(x\right) \to D'\left(x\right)$$

from the form $\forall x \cdot C\left(x\right) \to D\left(x\right)$

Similarly, with respect to the definition of fuzzy interpretation, $\forall x \in \Delta', |\in \left[0,1\right]$, since $0 \leq \inf_{y \in \Delta'}$ then $0 \leq \inf_{x \in \Delta^I} C'\left(x\right) \to D'\left(x\right)$ but using first order logic the

$$\inf_{x \in \Delta'}, \neg C'\left(x\right) \sqcap \inf_{x \in \Delta'} D'\left(x\right) \leq 1.$$

This means that for all the fuzzy interpretation I of the KB will be:

$0.7 \leq (x\neg$PETRONAS, $x(\exists$Participates.Metocean $\sqcap$ $\exists$Produce.TimeSeriesData)) ≤ 1

since $0 \leq \inf_{x \in \Delta'}$ *and* $1 \geq \sup_{x \in \Delta'}$.

Now, taking the semantics of equivalent classes $C \equiv D$ and the fuzzy interpretation as $C' = D'$ yield $C(x) \in [0,1]$ and $R(x,y) \in [0,1]$ in which $C(x)$ and $R(x,y)$ are the fuzzy ABox and RBox respectively. Therefore, $x \neq y \forall$ fuzzy individuals. Hence, the fuzzy interpretation concept $0 \leq C'(x) \leq 1$ is satisfied. Since, $R(x,y)[0,1] \in |$ satisfied iff $\inf_{x \in \Delta'} \leq R'(x,y) \leq \sup_{x \in \Delta'}$ and $x \neq y$ satisfied iff $x \neq y \in |$.

The Query Concept

With respect to the above knowledge base, for example; to find the MetOcean participants that produce time series data.

Query (?x, ?y): Participant (?y) $\bigwedge$ has time series data (?y, 1) $\bigwedge$ PETRONAS (?x) $\bigwedge$ produce (?x, ?y).

Therefore, Figure 4 represents the query for MetOcean participant that follows the algorithm using the SPARQL query.

The above query result has achieved with the aid of fuzzy reasoning algorithm. When the data satisfies the line 2 (ABox) and line 5 it will compute and determine whether the knowledge is entailed or not (line 7). Thus, query shows that the MetOcean participant has a time series data which is true (since it satisfies the "1" condition). This gives the user precise information of the time series data with the given dates in RDF formats.

Implementation

An interactive installation of SAP BusinessObjects Business Intelligence Platform was ran on Windows 7 Home Premium Service Park 1 with a 32-bit operating system. A 4.00 GB RAM, i5-intel® and CPU

Figure 4. Query for MetOcean participant

```
PREFIX metocean: <http://localhost:2020/metocean/>
PREFIX dcterms: <http://purl.org/dc/terms/>
PREFIX xsd: <http://www.w3.org/2001/XMLSchema#>
PREFIX rdfs: <http://www.w3.org/2000/01/rdf-schema#>
PREFIX rdf: <http://www.w3.org/1999/02/22-rdf-syntax-ns#>

SELECT ?x ?y
    WHERE {
            ?y rdf:type metocean:particpants ;
            ?y metocean:hasTimeSeries "1"^^xsd:date ;
            ?x rdf:type metocean:PETRONAS ;
            ?x metocean:produce ?y ;
        }
```

Fuzzy Reasoning Algorithm

```
1. Classify the variables: individual axioms        /* Fuzzy ABox = A */
2. Input Assertional body
```

3. QueryList $\leftarrow Q\big(x\big) \in A$

```
4. while QueryList ≠ { } do
```

5.   **for all** $h \subseteq A, h \in \big[0,1\big]$ **do**

6.   **if** $0 \leq \inf_{x \in \Delta^I}$ not found **then**

7.   Compute Interpretation $|, \forall a' \in \Delta'$.

```
8.                  for all K ≠ { }
9.                    if A(x, y), y for concept C chosen then
```

10. $\sup\big(K, x : \exists R.C\big) = \text{glb}$

```
11.                    end if
12.                  else
```

13.   **if** $\exists Q\big(x\big) s.t. \nu \in Body$

14.   **if** $\nu \notin$ in the query **then**

```
15.                          generateA(x, y)
```

16.   **for all** $Q\big(x\big) s.t. Body\big(A\big(x\big)\big) \subseteq ABox \in ABox \cdot \nu$ **do**

17. $Q\big(x\big) \leftarrow$ generateQueryElement$\big(KB, A\big(x\big)\big)$

```
18.                            end for
19.                          end if
20.                      end if
21.            end if
22.        end for
```

23. $R\big(x,y\big)\big[0,1\big] \in |$

```
24. end while
```

of 3.20GHz are the hardware systems that have been set. The software includes: XAMPP[3] package, D2RQ, Jena[4] and AllegroGraph 4.10[5] were installed. VMware[6] (VMware player) was also installed in the same machine.

The D2RQ and XAMPP were installed to create the localhost and for accessing the relational data to RDF, mapping processes as well as some supporting URIs. Similarly, for ontologies and reasoning, protégé 4.1 and other extensions were installed. Earlier, JAVA 7.2, JDK, eclipse 4.3 and JDBC were also installed. Finally, the meteorological datasets were loaded on the same machine.

EVALUATION

This part discusses the result of querying the knowledge base using SPARQL endpoint. The goal of this work was to present a framework for accessing and querying the data from the KB. Therefore, the evaluation of this chapter focuses on the performance of the KB framework and compares the system using D2RQ, Jena ARQ and AllegroGraph. At the end of this section, an evaluation of the fuzzy knowledge base has been discussed in order to provide a comprehensive discussion about the reasoning results.

Performance

As discussed about the experimental settings and applications used for this work, the testing was conducted on the same machine via SPARQL endpoint. There are many methods for evaluating the SPARQL query. Since the target of this SPARQL is retrieving data from database based on the user's decision, F-measure is suitable for this. Accordingly, it was found that the precision and recall method is the most suited method in evaluating user's decision (Auer, et al., 2013; Makhoul et al., 1999).

Performance Metrics

Triplestore and the date concepts are the two major concepts considered for these metrics. The loading time was measured as in Table 1. F-measure was used for evaluating the accuracy of the concepts (see Table 2). The F-measure (F-score) is a well-known method used in information retrieval for weighing the accuracy of the variables (Ehrig & Staab, 2004; Makhoul et al., 1999; Sasaki, 2007; Truong, Duong, & Nguyen, 2013). It consists of precision and recall as the two metrics, with non-negative value, α. Consider $N_{correct}$ to be the number of correct or relevant ratio and $N_{incorrect}$ to be the number of incorrect or irrelevant ratio. Then F-measure, F_α will be:

$$F_\alpha = \frac{(1+\alpha) \cdot precision \cdot recall}{\alpha \cdot precision + recall}$$

with

$$Precision = \frac{N_{correct}}{N_{correct} + N_{incorrect}}$$

and

Table 1. Loading time in millisecond of triples and date concepts

Dataset Limit	Triples	Date
10	825	350
100	1037	721
1000	3041	1130
10000	6022	1551

Table 2. Concept retrieval optimization

Concept Name	Precision	Recall	F-Measure
Triples	0.73977	0.59976	0.66244
URI distinct resource	0.86707	0.54692	0.33538
MetOcean foaf:document	0.88472	0.63956	0.37121

$$Recall = \frac{N_{correct}}{N_{total}}.$$

Results

When a user queries from SPARQL interface, the result appears based on his selection. For instance, if a MetOcean user wants to query with the non-information resource available to MetOcean information resource. The result of query 1 (Appendix) presents the MetOcean URIs distinct representation (see Figure 5).

Similarly, suppose the user wants to find the *date* concept of Malaysian State time series. The domain user may say: "*show me the dates used in Malaysian time series (and limited to only 10 triples)*". The result of this statement appears in Figure 6, which shows the approach is sufficient for querying the data in form of triples. Furthermore, in respect to performance metrics of these concepts, they attained the general optimization method of precision and recall, (Figure 7). Consider 1 at *x*-axis (metrics), the precision is 0.74(F_α) while recall is 0.60(F_α). Also, at precision 0.87(F_α) the recall is 0.55(F_α). Similarly, when precision is 0.89(F_α) the recall is 0.64(F_α). Apparently, this is the required optimization in both the points of precisions and recalls. They show promising result, which are the optimized retrieved and relevant for the users query.

Figure 5. The number of distinct representation

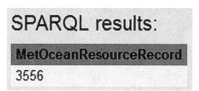

Figure 6. Triple result limited with only 10 queries

SPARQL results:

Subject	MalaysianStateTimeSeriesName	TimeSeriesYear
<http://localhost:2020/resource/johortimeseriesdata/1>	"1957 Johor Bahru Time Series data"@en	"1957"^^xsd:gYear
<http://localhost:2020/resource/johortimeseriesdata/2>	"1958 Johor Bahru Time Series data"@en	"1958"^^xsd:gYear
<http://localhost:2020/resource/johortimeseriesdata/3>	"1959 Johor Bahru Time Series data"@en	"1959"^^xsd:gYear
<http://localhost:2020/resource/johortimeseriesdata/4>	"1960 Johor Bahru Time Series data"@en	"1960"^^xsd:gYear
<http://localhost:2020/resource/johortimeseriesdata/5>	"1961 Johor Bahru Time Series data"@en	"1961"^^xsd:gYear
<http://localhost:2020/resource/johortimeseriesdata/6>	"1962 Johor Bahru Time Series data"@en	"1962"^^xsd:gYear
<http://localhost:2020/resource/johortimeseriesdata/7>	"1963 Johor Bahru Time Series data"@en	"1963"^^xsd:gYear
<http://localhost:2020/resource/johortimeseriesdata/8>	"1964 Johor Bahru Time Series data"@en	"1964"^^xsd:gYear
<http://localhost:2020/resource/johortimeseriesdata/9>	"1965 Johor Bahru Time Series data"@en	"1965"^^xsd:gYear
<http://localhost:2020/resource/johortimeseriesdata/10>	"1966 Johor Bahru Time Series data"@en	"1966"^^xsd:gYear

Figure 7. Concept optimization graph

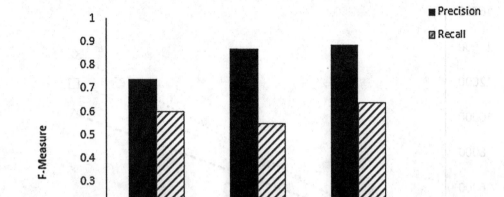

Furthermore, consider the loading time of the MetOceanSemWeb concepts on date, the triples appear in Table 1 based on the execution limit. This revealed that the MetOcean data can be mapped and create rich pathways by means of querying the resources. Thus, the concepts allow smooth connections between datasets. Nonetheless, Table 3 provided the evaluation of the system without limit using codes in the Appendix.

In continuation, Figure 8 (Query 5) indicates the scalability of Jena ARQ. It goes to the level of Q3 when the triples is about 6000. However, the presence of dip in the graph response appeared up to the end of the datasets. AllegroGraph started with the good response but immediately changed when the number of triples were closed to 4000 and get the response below the others. Interestingly, D2RQ become more scalable as the datasets passed 6000. Thus, this shows that the D2RQ had best performance among the other compared APIs.

In contrast, the system is very scalable when querying directly from SPARQL database. This is very essential as found in Hassanzadeh et al. (2009) and Samwald et al. (2011) where the D2R server was automatically queried 158 countries Clinical data trials with 7,011,000 triples. On the other hand, the D2RQ annotation facets of the relational data found to be more scalable than Vavliakis et al. (2011) as they used Jena and Sesame for their benchmarks. Correspondingly, Vandervalk et al. (2009, 2013) tested their Bio2RDF SPARQL query from relational data but with no seamless visualization which this framework provides the more interesting visualization. Thus, the method employed in this work can apparently be called scalable with respect to the existing approaches.

Fuzzy Knowledge Base Evaluation

Since SPARQL does not perform reasoning by itself, the query language needs inference. This part evaluates the results by using fuzzy KB reasoning and the proof of algorithm. Notably, managing the

Figure 8. Performance comparisons of MetOcean Semantic APIs

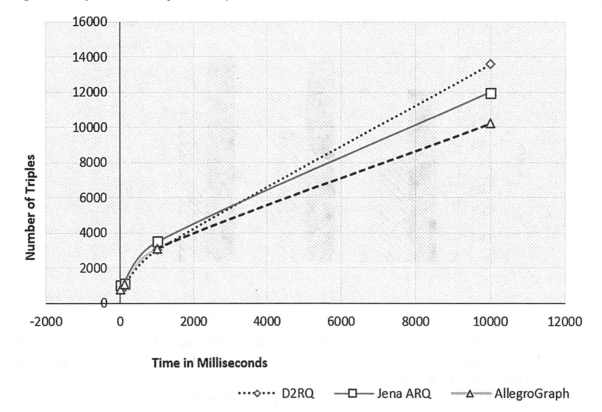

Time in Milliseconds

⋯◇⋯ D2RQ   —□— Jena ARQ   —△— AllegroGraph

Table 3. Performance comparisons in milliseconds

	D2RQ	Jena ARQ	AllegroGraph
10	825	1002	772
100	1037	1150	1098
1000	3041	3503	3117
10000	13606	12001	10200

Table 4. Evaluation query result

Query	AllegroGraph	D2RQ	Jena ARQ
Q1	19707	19057	20340
Q2	25980	21110	24050
Q3	10200	12001	13606
Q4	15010	16900	15220
Q5	1220	1170	1387

database, instance creation and knowledge annotation are the right instruments for knowledge assessment (Stuckenschmidt & Van Harmelen, 2004). Therefore, the benchmark here follows Gödel's method for evaluation of the algorithm (Bobillo et al., 2009; Kleene, 1976; Van Heijenoort, 1977). Three cretaria were evaluated. These are: expressivity, consistancy and satisfiability.

Completeness of the Reasoning Procedure for Fuzzy ALC

This section uses completeness method to evaluate the performance of the algorithm. There are four methods for solving the algorithm's performance. These include: completeness, optimality, time complexity, and space complexity (Ertel, 2011; Russell et al., 2010). However, the chapter considers completeness theorem in order to support the processes given above. Some parts of this has been discussed in (Danyaro et al., 2012). The target is to show the consistency and satisfiability level of the given knowledge base. The reader should be noted that the fuzzy ALC (Attributive Language with Complements) expressed here depend on fuzzy subsumption of fuzzy concepts knowledge base that generalizes modeling of uncertain knowledge.

Proposition 1: Complete fuzzy ALC is satisfiable iff it is a model.
Proof:

Taking the only-if direction;

Suppose the knowledge base, KB is satisfiable, then it is clear that fuzzy interpretation $I = \left\{ \Delta^I . ^I \right\}$.
Let C be the constraint in the $\varphi : Var(C) \to [0,1]$. Suppose A = ABox and I defined in ABox, then A:

1. Δ^I consist of all individual element in the domain A
2. $A^{I(x)} = \varphi\left(a_A(x)\right)$ consist of all atomic classes in A, with $\varphi\left(a_A(x)\right)$ be the truth degree of variables in $a_{R(x,y)}$
3. $R_0^I(x,y) = \varphi\left(a_{R_0(x,y)}\right)$, where R_o consist of all atomic roles, x, y individual elements in A and $\varphi\left(a_{R_0(x,y)}\right)$ represent the degree of variable of $a_{R_0(x,y)}$.
4. $x,y \in \Delta^I, R^I(x,y) = h_1 > h_2 = S^I(x,y)$.

Now, using inductive technique, it shows that all concepts and roles that can be interpreted by I is a model (Klir & Yuan, 1995).

Given C as an atomic concept, then by definition it implies C^I. Then $C = \neg A$ which indicates that A contains $\left\{\neg A(x)\lambda\right\}$. But since A is complete and C has $x_{A(x)} = \neg\lambda$ and $x_{\neg A(x)} = \neg\lambda$. So $A(x) = \neg\lambda$ contains the interpretation $A^I(x) = \neg\lambda$. Therefore, applying concept negation, it becomes $\left(\neg A\right)^I(x) = \neg\left(\neg\lambda\right) = \lambda$ which implies the concept is obvious.

Next, it is to show I is satisfiable. Assume I is not satisfiable, then without loss of generality

$$I = R \sqsubseteq S \ iff \ I^I = I \cup \left\{x : \exists R.(\exists R.B)\right\} \geq n, (x : \exists R.B) < n\right\}$$

is unsatisfiable $\forall n \in (0,1]$. But,

$$\forall x,y \in \Delta^I R(x,y) \geq \sup_z t\left(R^I(x,z), R^I(z,y)\right).$$

For t-norms it is monotonically applied that

$$t\Big(R^{I}\big(x,z\big),B^{I}\big(y\big)\Big) \geq \sup{}_{z}\, t\Big(R^{I}\big(x,z\big),t\big(R^{I}\big(z,y\big),B^{I}\big(y\big)\big)\Big)\forall x,y \in \Delta^{I}\,.$$

This implies the supremum of *y*. Assume the supremum or infimum does not exist then the value is undefined. Therefore,

$$\sup{}_{y}\, t\Big(R^{I}\big(x,y\big),B^{I}\big(y\big)\Big) \geq \sup{}_{z}\, t\Big(R^{I}\big(x,\ z\big),\sup{}_{y}\, t\big(R^{I}\big(z,y\big),B^{I}\big(y\big)\big)\Big)$$

$$\big(\exists R.B\big)^{I}\big(x\big) \geq \sup{}_{z}\, t\Big(R^{I}\big(x,z\big)(\exists R.B)^{I}\big(z\big)\Big) = \exists\Big(R.\big(\exists R.B\big)\Big)^{I}\big(x\big),$$

I holds for model of the KB, hence is unsatisfiable.

Since the given KB is unsatisfiable by contradiction it is therefore, I is satisfiable. This proof indicates that logic is decidable under Gödel's semantics. The approach supported the interpretation of different types of imprecise knowledge that has relation to the real world applications. However, it differs from (Józefowska et. al., 2008, 2010), where their proof is valid in query trie for skolem substitution only. Also, there completeness was proved by induction on a length of a query, which assumed that the query of length ≥ 1 with an equivalent query exists in trie. Similarly, Zhao and Boley (2010) proved the completeness but it was restricted to constraints sets. Hence, the chapter approach shows the desirability of the completeness property that can drive any entailed statement. This could minimize the imprecision in the database and improve the trustworthiness.

CONCLUSION

This chapter analyses the benchmark of the database query approach using precision and recall. The result shows that the smooth connections enable the transformation of data to be a good path for utilizing the MetOcean data (as a case study) and benefit its users. It also shows that D2RQ is the most scalable API among the compared ones. Therefore, the approach can contribute in solving the problem of determining relevant information in big data. Moreover, the chapter shows the application of fuzzy as a knowledge instrument for managing the database. The fuzzy KB was constructed using rule-based approach and finally achieved the satisfiability, consistence and decidability of the knowledge base.

In summary, execution this framework as a decision making will reduce the cost and improve the big data performance – effective intelligence. On the other hand, the framework provides the essential steps toward reducing the problem of imprecision. The basics for big data and architectures of fuzzy knowledge base have been elucidated with the system built on TBox and ABox. It is found that the algorithm is sufficient for a kind knowledge base that will help in querying the Web data. The method satisfied the operations in dealing with the fuzzy knowledge base. Thus, this serves as a way of enhancing the query of big data. In future, the analysis of big data evaluation will extensively be discussed. High calculations will be conducted such as statistical analysis as well as Extract, Transform and Load (ETL) processing.

REFERENCE

Auer, S., Lehmann, J., Ngonga Ngomo, A. C., & Zaveri, A. (2013). Introduction to Linked Data and Its Lifecycle on the Web. In S. Rudolph, G. Gottlob, I. Horrocks, & F. Harmelen (Eds.), *Reasoning Web. Semantic Technologies for Intelligent Data Access* (Vol. 8067, pp. 1–90). New York, NY: Springer Berlin Heidelberg. doi:10.1007/978-3-642-39784-4_1

Berners-Lee, T., Hall, W., & Hendler, J. A. (2006). A framework for web science. *Foundations and Trends in Web Science, 1*(1), 1–130. doi:10.1561/1800000001

Bobillo, F., Delgado, M., Gómez-Romero, J., & Straccia, U. (2009). Fuzzy description logics under Gödel semantics. *International Journal of Approximate Reasoning, 50*(3), 494–514. doi:10.1016/j.ijar.2008.10.003

Bobillo, F., & Straccia, U. (2011). Fuzzy ontology representation using OWL 2. *International Journal of Approximate Reasoning, 52*(7), 1073–1094. doi:10.1016/j.ijar.2011.05.003

Bobillo, F., & Straccia, U. (2013). Aggregation operators for fuzzy ontologies. *Applied Soft Computing, 13*(9), 3816–3830. doi:10.1016/j.asoc.2013.05.008

Camacho, D., Moreno, M. D., & Akerkar, R. (2013). *Challenges and issues of web intelligence research.* Paper presented at the 3rd International Conference on Web Intelligence, Mining and Semantics, Madrid, Spain. doi:10.1145/2479787.2479868

Connolly, S. (2012, May 16). *Big Data Refinery Fuels Next-Generation Data Architecture.* Retrieved from http://hortonworks.com/blog/big-data-refinery-fuels-next-generation-data-architecture

Danyaro, K., Jaafar, J., & Liew, M. (2012). Completeness Knowledge Representation in Fuzzy Description Logics. In D. Lukose, A. Ahmad, & A. Suliman (Eds.), *Knowledge Technology* (Vol. 295, pp. 164–173). New York: Springer Berlin Heidelberg. doi:10.1007/978-3-642-32826-8_17

Demchenko, Y., Grosso, P., de Laat, C., & Membrey, P. (2013). *Addressing big data issues in scientific data infrastructure.* Paper presented at the 2013 International Conference on Collaboration Technologies and Systems (CTS), San Diego, CA. doi:10.1109/CTS.2013.6567203

Ehrig, M., & Staab, S. (2004). QOM – Quick Ontology Mapping. In S. McIlraith, D. Plexousakis, & F. Harmelen (Eds.), *The Semantic Web – ISWC 2004* (Vol. 3298, pp. 683–697). New York: Springer Berlin Heidelberg. doi:10.1007/978-3-540-30475-3_47

Ertel, W. (2011). *Introduction to artificial intelligence.* New York: Springer. doi:10.1007/978-0-85729-299-5

G'abor, N. a. (2007). Ontology Development. In R. Studer, S. Grimm, & A. Abecker (Eds.), *Semantic Web Services* (pp. 107–134). New York: Springer Berlin Heidelberg. doi:10.1007/3-540-70894-4_4

Grimm, S., Hitzler, P., & Abecker, A. (2007). Knowledge Representation and Ontologies Logic, Ontologies and Semantic Web Languages. In R. Studer, S. Grimm, & A. Abecker (Eds.), *Semantic Web Services* (pp. 51–105). New York: Springer.

Gruber, T. R. (1993). A translation approach to portable ontology specifications. *Knowledge Acquisition*, 5(2), 199–220. doi:10.1006/knac.1993.1008

Hassanzadeh, O., Kementsietsidis, A., Lim, L., Miller, R. J., & Wang, M. (2009). Linkedct: A linked data space for clinical trials. *arXiv preprint arXiv:0908.0567.*

Hassanzadeh, O., Xin, R., Miller, E. J., Kementsietsidis, A., & Wang, M. (2009). Linkage Query Writer. *Proc. VLDB Endow., 2*(2), 1590-1593. doi:10.14778/1687553.1687599

Hurwitz, J., Nugent, A., Halper, F., & Kaufman, M. (2013). *Big Data For Dummies*. Hoboken, NJ: John Wiley & Sons.

Jewell, D., Barros, R. D., Diederichs, S., Duijvestijn, L. M., Hammersley, M., Hazra, A., & Plach, A. (2014). *Performance and Capacity Implications for Big Data*. IBM Redbooks.

Józefowska, J., Ławrynowicz, A., & Łukaszewski, T. (2008). On Reducing Redundancy in Mining Relational Association Rules from the Semantic Web. In D. Calvanese & G. Lausen (Eds.), *Web Reasoning and Rule Systems* (Vol. 5341, pp. 205–213). New York: Springer Berlin Heidelberg. doi:10.1007/978-3-540-88737-9_16

Józefowska, J., Ławrynowicz, A., & Łukaszewski, T. (2010). The role of semantics in mining frequent patterns from knowledge bases in description logics with rules. *Theory and Practice of Logic Programming, 10*(3), 251–289. doi:10.1017/S1471068410000098

Kleene, S. C. (1976). The work of Kurt Gödel. *Journal of Symbolic Logic*, 761-778.

Klir, G. J., & Yuan, B. (Eds.). (1995). *Fuzzy sets and fuzzy logic: theory and applications*. New Jersey: Prentice Hall.

Lukasiewicz, T., & Straccia, U. (2009). Description logic programs under probabilistic uncertainty and fuzzy vagueness. *International Journal of Approximate Reasoning, 50*(6), 837–853. doi:10.1016/j.ijar.2009.03.004

Makhoul, J., Kubala, F., Schwartz, R., & Weischedel, R. (1999). *Performance measures for information extraction*. Paper presented at the DARPA Broadcast News Workshop.

Mohanty, S., Jagadeesh, M., & Srivatsa, H. (2013). *Big Data Imperatives: Enterprise 'Big Data' Warehouse, 'BI' Implementations and Analytics*. Apress. doi:10.1007/978-1-4302-4873-6

Ross, T. J. (2010). *Fuzzy Logic with Engineering Applications*. John Wiley & Sons, Ltd. doi:10.1002/9781119994374.index

Russell, S. J., Norvig, P., & Davis, E. (2010). *Artificial intelligence: a modern approach* (Vol. 2). Prentice Hall.

Samwald, M., Jentzsch, A., Bouton, C., Kallesøe, C. S., Willighagen, E., Hajagos, J., . . . Pichler, E. (2011). Linked open drug data for pharmaceutical research and development. *Journal of Cheminformatics, 3*(1), 19.

Sasaki, Y. (2007). *The truth of the F-measure*. Teach Tutor mater. Retrieved from http://www.flowdx.com/F-measure-YS-26Oct07.pdf

Savas, O., Sagduyu, Y., Deng, J., & Li, J. (2014). Tactical big data analytics: Challenges, use cases, and solutions. *Performance Evaluation Review*, *41*(4), 86–89. doi:10.1145/2627534.2627561

Shadbolt, N., & Berners-Lee, T. (2008). Web Science Emerges. *Scientific American*, *299*(4), 76–81. doi:10.1038/scientificamerican1008-76 PMID:18847088

Shroff, G. (2013). *The intelligent web: search, smart algorithms, and big data*. Oxford, UK: Oxford University Press.

Stuckenschmidt, H., & Van Harmelen, F. (2004). *Information sharing on the semantic web*. Springer.

Sugumaran, V., & Gulla, J. A. (2012). *Applied semantic web technologies*. CRC Press.

Thomas, C., & Sheth, A. (2006). On the expressiveness of the languages for the semantic web — Making a case for 'a little more'. In S. Elie (Ed.), Capturing Intelligence (Vol. 1, pp. 3-20). Netherlands: Elsevier.

Truong, H. B., Duong, T. H., & Nguyen, N. T. (2013). A Hybrid Method For Fuzzy Ontology Integration. *Cybernetics and Systems*, *44*(2-3), 133–154. doi:10.1080/01969722.2013.762237

Van Heijenoort, J. (1977). *From Frege to Gödel: a source book in mathematical logic, 1879-1931* (Vol. 9). Harvard University Press.

Vandervalk, B., McCarthy, E. L., & Wilkinson, M. (2009). SHARE: A Semantic Web Query Engine for Bioinformatics. In A. Gómez-Pérez, Y. Yu, & Y. Ding (Eds.), *The Semantic Web* (Vol. 5926, pp. 367–369). New York, NY: Springer Berlin Heidelberg. doi:10.1007/978-3-642-10871-6_27

Vandervalk, B. P., McCarthy, E. L., & Wilkinson, M. D. (2013). *SHARE: A Web Service Based Framework for Distributed Querying and Reasoning on the Semantic Web*. Retrieved from http://arxiv.org/abs/1305.4455

Vavliakis, K. N., Symeonidis, A. L., Karagiannis, G. T., & Mitkas, P. A. (2011). An integrated framework for enhancing the semantic transformation, editing and querying of relational databases. *Expert Systems with Applications*, *38*(4), 3844–3856. doi:10.1016/j.eswa.2010.09.045

Williams, K., Li, L., Khabsa, M., Wu, J., Shih, P., & Giles, C. L. (2014). *A web service for scholarly big data information extraction*. In *Proceeding of the 2014 IEEE International Conference on Web Services (ICWS)*, (pp. 105 – 112). Anchorage, AK: IEEE. doi:10.1109/ICWS.2014.27

Yu, L. (2011). *A Developer's Guide to the Semantic Web*. New York, NY: Springer. doi:10.1007/978-3-642-15970-1

Zadeh, L. A. (2004). A Note on Web Intelligence, World Knowledge and Fuzzy Logic. *Data & Knowledge Engineering*, *50*(3), 291–304. doi:10.1016/j.datak.2004.04.001

Zaharia, M., Chowdhury, M., Das, T., Dave, A., Ma, J., McCauley, M., . . . Stoica, I. (2012). *Resilient distributed datasets: a fault-tolerant abstraction for in-memory cluster computing*. Paper presented at the 9th USENIX conference on Networked Systems Design and Implementation, San Jose, CA.

Zhao, J., & Boley, H. (2010). Knowledge Representation and Reasoning in Norm-Parameterized Fuzzy Description Logics. In *Canadian Semantic Web* (pp. 27–53). Springer. doi:10.1007/978-1-4419-7335-1_2

Zikopoulos, P., Parasuraman, K., Deutsch, T., Giles, J., & Corrigan, D. (2012). *Harness the Power of Big Data The IBM Big Data Platform*. McGraw Hill Professional.

KEY TERMS AND DEFINITIONS

Big Data Management: This is the process of managing, administering or organizing large volumes of both structured and unstructured data.

Completeness: In Artificial Intelligence (AI), completeness theorem is among the methods used for checking the validity of axioms and logical inference in the knowlegde base. However, a knowledge base is said to be complete if no formular can be added in the knowledge base.

Fuzzy Knowledge Base: In fuzzy logic systems, the fuzzy knowledge base represents the facts of the rules and linguistic variables based on the fuzzy set theory so that the knowledge base sytems will allow approximate reasoning.

Gödel's Semantics: In mathematical logic, Gödel's completeness theorem is a fundamental theorem that relies on the semantic completeness of first order logic. In the proof of algorithm, when I is satisfiable, it shows the logic is decidable under Gödel's semantics.

Satisfiablility: In this chapter, satisfiablity is the ability of the Web data concepts that are be able to test the value of the semantic query of atomic concepts. Similarly, satisfiability determines the variables of the given boolean.

Veracity: Veracity can be described as the quality of trustworthiness of the data. In other wards, veracity is the consistency in data due to its statistical reliability. It is also among the five dimentions of big data which are volume, velocity, value, variety and veracity.

Web Data: In this chapter, the Web data is the data that comes from large or diverse number of sources. Web data are developed with the help of Semantic Web tools such as RDF, OWL, and SPARQL. Also, the web data allows sharing of information through HTTP protocol or SPARQL endpoint.

Web Intelligence: The Web intelligence constitutes the usage of world wide web (WWW) as a phenomenon of retrieving information from data storage in an intelligent efficient manner. Web intelligence is a well-known research area which converges subjects such as artificial intelligence, databases, Web science, Semantic Web, and information retrieval.

ENDNOTES

[1]   http://www.w3.org/TR/owl2-overview/

[2]   http://www.w3.org/TR/sparql11-query/

[3]   XAMPP is an open source package that contains an Apache HTTP Server, a MySQL database, PHP interpreters and a Perl programming languages. It can be found at: http://www.apachefriends.org/index.html

[4]   https://jena.apache.org/

[5]   http://franz.com/agraph/allegrograph/

[6]   VMware is Virtual Machine image that allow user to run Linux in a virtual environment. Available at: http://www.vmware.com/

APPENDIX: EVALUATION QUERIES

Table 5.

Q1	PREFIX rdf: <http://www.w3.org/1999/02/22-rdf-syntax-ns#>
	PREFIX rdfs: <http://www.w3.org/2000/01/rdf-schema#>
	PREFIX foaf: <http://xmlns.com/foaf/0.1/>
	SELECT
	(COUNT(DISTINCT ?s) AS ?MetOceanResourceRecord) {
	        { ?s ?p ?o } UNION { ?o ?p ?s }
	        FILTER(!isBlank(?s) && !isLiteral(?s))
	}

Table 6.

Q2	PREFIX rdf: <http://www.w3.org/1999/02/22-rdf-syntax-ns#>
	PREFIX rdfs: <http://www.w3.org/2000/01/rdf-schema#>
	PREFIX foaf: <http://xmlns.com/foaf/0.1/>
	PREFIX metocean: <http://annotation.metocean.org/metocean/metocean.daml#>
	PREFIX dc: http://purl.org/dc/elements/1.1/
	PREFIX xsd: <http://www.w3.org/2001/XMLSchema#>
	SELECT *
	WHERE {
	        ?Subject dc:title ?MalaysianStateTimeSeriesName ;
	        dc:date ?TimeSeriesYear
	        }

Table 7.

Q3	PREFIX rdf: <http://www.w3.org/1999/02/22-rdf-syntax-ns#>
	PREFIX rdfs: <http://www.w3.org/2000/01/rdf-schema#>
	PREFIX foaf: <http://xmlns.com/foaf/0.1/>
	PREFIX metocean: <http://annotation.metocean.org/metocean/metocean.daml#>
	PREFIX vocab: http://localhost:2020/resource/vocab/]
	PREFIX xsd: <http://www.w3.org/2001/XMLSchema#>
	SELECT ?class (COUNT(?s) AS ?count) {
	?s a ?class
	}
	GROUP BY ?class ORDER BY ?count

Table 8.

Q4	PREFIX rdf: <http://www.w3.org/1999/02/22-rdf-syntax-ns#>
	PREFIX rdfs: <http://www.w3.org/2000/01/rdf-schema#>
	PREFIX foaf: <http://xmlns.com/foaf/0.1/>
	PREFIX metocean: <http://annotation.metocean.org/metocean/metocean.daml#>
	PREFIX vocab: http://localhost:2020/resource/vocab/]
	PREFIX xsd: <http://www.w3.org/2001/XMLSchema#>
	SELECT DISTINCT ?property ?hasValue
	WHERE {
	{ <http://localhost:2020/resource/johortimeseriesdata/1> ?property ?hasValue }
	UNION
	{ ?isValueOf ?property <http://localhost:2020/resource/johortimeseriesdata/1> }
	}
	ORDER BY (!BOUND(?hasValue)) ?property ?hasValue

Table 9.

| Q5 | PREFIX rdf: <http://www.w3.org/1999/02/22-rdf-syntax-ns#>
PREFIX rdfs: <http://www.w3.org/2000/01/rdf-schema#>
PREFIX foaf: <http://xmlns.com/foaf/0.1/>
PREFIX metocean: <http://annotation.metocean.org/metocean/metocean.daml#>
PREFIX vocab: http://localhost:2020/resource/vocab/]
PREFIX xsd: <http://www.w3.org/2001/XMLSchema#>
SELECT ?Participant ?Location ?Address
WHERE {
DOCUMENT http://annotation.metocean.org/metocean/metocean.daml#Document
?Address rdf:type http://localhost:2020/Address
?Address foaf:person ?particpant
}
OPTIONAL {
DOCUMENT http://annotation.metocean.org/metocean/metocean.daml#Company {
?Address metocean:atCarigali ?Location
}
FILTER (?Date "1976"^^xsd:gYear) |

Chapter 6
Intelligent Management and Efficient Operation of Big Data

José Moura
Instituto Universitario de Lisboa, Portugal &
Instituto de Telecomunicações, Portugal

Elsa Cardoso
Instituto Universitario de Lisboa, Portugal

Fernando Batista
Instituto Universitario de Lisboa, Portugal

Luís Nunes
Instituto Universitario de Lisboa, Portugal &
Instituto de Telecomunicações, Portugal

ABSTRACT

This chapter details how Big Data can be used and implemented in networking and computing infra-structures. Specifically, it addresses three main aspects: the timely extraction of relevant knowledge from heterogeneous, and very often unstructured large data sources; the enhancement on the performance of processing and networking (cloud) infrastructures that are the most important foundational pillars of Big Data applications or services; and novel ways to efficiently manage network infrastructures with high-level composed policies for supporting the transmission of large amounts of data with distinct requisites (video vs. non-video). A case study involving an intelligent management solution to route data traffic with diverse requirements in a wide area Internet Exchange Point is presented, discussed in the context of Big Data, and evaluated.

1. INTRODUCTION

Big Data is a relatively new concept. When someone is asked to define it, the tale of the blind man and the elephant immediately comes to mind. As in the tale, each person that talks about Big Data seems to have his/her own view, according to the person's background or the intended use of the data (Ward & Barker, 2013; McAfee & Brynjolfsson, 2012; Cox & Ellsworth, 1997; Diebold, 2012; Press, 2013). Big Data is closely related to the area of analytics (Davenport et al., 2010), as it also seeks to gather intel-ligence from data generating value to the business or the organization. However, a Big Data application differs in terms of the volume (referring to large data volumes), velocity (i.e., multi-structured data types) and variety (related to the change rate and time-sensitive usage to maximize the business value) of the data involved. These aspects are usually known as the 3V's. These large and diverse data streams require

DOI: 10.4018/978-1-4666-8505-5.ch006

"ever-increasing processing speeds, yet must be stored economically and fed back into business-process life cycles in a timely manner," (Michael & Miller, 2013, pp. 22). Big Data applications offer new opportunities of information processing for enhanced insight and decision-making in different disciplines such as business, finance, healthcare, transportation, research, and politics.

The successful deployment of a Big Data infrastructure requires the extraction of relevant knowledge from original heterogeneous (Parise et al, 2012), highly complex (Nature, 2008) and massive amount of data. To this end, several tools from different areas can be applied: Business Intelligence (BI) and Online Analytical Processing (OLAP), Cluster Analysis, Crowdsourcing, Network Analysis, Text Mining, and Natural Language Processing (NLP). As an example, massive amounts of textual information are constantly being produced and can be accessed from online sources, including social networks, blogs, and numerous websites. Such unstructured texts represent potentially valuable knowledge for companies, organizations, and governments. The process of extracting useful information from such unstructured texts, known as Text Mining, is now becoming a relevant research area. It draws from different fields of computer science, such as Web Mining, Information Retrieval (IR), NLP, Machine Learning (ML), and Data Mining. Today's text mining research and technology enables high-performance analytics from web's textual data, allowing to: cluster documents and web pages according to their content, find associations among entities (people, places and/or organizations), and reasoning about important data trends.

The data sets in Big Data are becoming increasingly complex (Nature, 2008). For example, the biology field is urging for robust data computing (The Apache Software Foundation, 2014a) and distributed storage solutions (The Apache Software Foundation, 2014c); machine learning algorithms for data mining tasks (Hall et al., 2009); online community collaborations need wiki-style information cooperative tools (Waldrop, 2008); sophisticated visualization techniques of intracellular signaling pathways require tools like GenMAPP (Waldrop, 2008); and innovative ways to control the Big Data infrastructure such as software-design networking (SDN). To conclude, Lawrence Hunter, a biological researcher, wrote: "Getting the most from the data requires interpreting them in light of all the relevant prior knowledge," (Marx, 2013). Clearly, satisfying this requisite also demands for new scalable Big Data solutions. In this way, the Big Data is a very challenging and exciting research area to be further explored and investigated.

An important aspect to guarantee the success of Big Data solutions is to manage with more intelligence the supporting computing/networking infrastructure. Currently, both data and collaborative applications are increasingly being moved towards Data Centers aggregated inside the cloud. Consequently, to obtain a good performance in Big Data applications it is mandatory to achieve a proper performance in Data Centers. To achieve this, some management enhancements are needed to operate more intelligently the available resources, such as: virtual machines (Dai et al., 2013), memory (Zhou & Li, 2013), CPU scheduling (Bae et al., 2012), cache (Koller et al., 2011), I/O (Ram et al., 2013), and network (Marx, 2013; Lange et al., 2011; Saleem, Hassan, & Asirvadam, 2011).

This chapter details how Big Data can be deployed and used, focusing on the following important aspects: i) timely extraction of relevant knowledge from heterogeneous, and often unstructured data sources; i) enhancement of the performance of processing and networking (cloud) infrastructures for Big Data, using more intelligent management solutions/algorithms; and iii) SDN as an intelligent and very interesting solution to conveniently manage the network infrastructures to transmit Big Data with diverse functional requisites. At the end of this chapter, a SDN application is discussed in a wide area network (WAN) environment, more specifically at an Internet exchange point (IXP). This case study shows that using high-level and intuitive management policies is possible to easily route data traffic with diverse requirements among network infrastructures owned by several entities, which is a very realistic scenario to deploy Big Data services through diverse public cloud providers, supporting the following three Big Data aspects: dynamic, diversity and distributed.

2. FROM BIG DATA TO USABLE KNOWLEDGE

The heuristics "There is no Data Like More Data" is famous in NLP and was made back in 1985, even before the web (Jelinek, 2005). A few years later, the web and the increasingly amounts of available content supported this heuristic even further. Suddenly, all the investment went to data and statistical methods research, supported by the widely spread idea that data would be the only important thing. This feeling was reflected precisely on the famous quote "Every time I fire a linguist, the performance of the speech recognizer goes up" attributed to Frederick Jelinek and also on the title "Every time I fire a linguist, my performance goes up" used by Hirschberg (1998) for one of her talks. In more recent years, the most revelant challenges in terms of data annotation have been on: how to produce annotated data with a minimal supervision; on the use of co-training, a semi-supervised learning approach based on two different aspects of the data; and on the use of bootstrapping, which consists of calculating the initial parameters from related information sources.

The challenge of big data is not, as in previous decades, to gather it, but to find a way to make use of it. In the last decades hundreds of machine learning algorithms were developed, but testing them was often difficult. Data was scarce and the algorithms that promised good scaling qualities always had a difficult time proving it. Today several companies give away huge data sets to run tests (Netflix, Amazon, Kaggle) and others (Twitter) make public data-streams available. Many efforts have been made during this last decade in finding the best methodology to tackle the increasingly amounts of available data. As a result, the incredible advances in ML methods and related technologies make it possible to continue strengthening the focus on the data. The main issue is what to do with all that data? From a Machine Learning point of view, more data usually means more reliable models and results, but also more processing time. Some ML methods may become unusable due to the amount of data, others may require large numbers of parameters, but some may even become simpler, due to the clear definition of the desired patterns and the outliers. In terms of tools, many are now surfacing, but also all major ML and Data Mining tools are upgrading to deal with the new problems. In the next sections we will review some of the most important Big Data problems (e.g. scale, speed, and data types), the ML methods used and the new role of data scientist.

Big Challenges

Big challenges differ from others mainly in scale, speed and types of data used. Nevertheless, the underlying learning mechanisms are still similar, mainly because researchers in the ML field have been dealing with large amounts of data, continuous data series, unstructured data, and focusing on scalability problems, for quite some time. Speech processing for example has always been a Big Data problem, although some years ago the problem started when trying to gather data and store it and label it. Now, most of these difficulties are solved for the most common languages with the large, publicly available, corpora and large data-storage devices. Following, we discuss how to apply ML to Big Data analysis.

On one hand, from a ML point of view, there are three main types of learning systems: Supervised, Unsupervised and Reinforced. The first type requires examples of the correct behavior or classification, the second requires only examples and (often) a distance function between examples, and the third a function to evaluate the system state. It is also possible to join search algorithms to these three broad categories.

On the other hand, the main types of analysis problems addressed by Big Data tools are the following ones:

- Clustering;
- Classification;
- Recommending systems;
- Frequent item set mining.

We now briefly describe each type of Big Data analysis problem, using the more suitable set of ML solutions, and giving a corresponding illustrative application example. Clustering is a type of unsupervised learning where the goal is to divide the data into associated groups (clusters). A typical example is learning social circles, and patterns of how information is spread.

Classification is a supervised learning problem, which consists on learning a model of a system that performs a given classification based on correct (labeled) classification examples. An example is credit card fraud analysis. It is possible to train a model with information of good and bad transactions and require that the system, given an unseen situation, provide the correct classification (with a given error margin).

Recommending systems are labeled as collaborative filtering and can also be seen as a form of supervised learning, although unsupervised learning methods are often used to compose a solution for problems of this type. The problem consists on figuring what is the best product to recommend to a user, given its own history and the histories of all other users. Amazon has been using recommending systems since the 90's to suggest products to returning costumers (Linden, Smith, & York, 2003).

Frequent item-set mining is also a form of Association Rule Learning and Unsupervised Learning. The typical problem is market basket analysis that tries to detect shopping patterns by looking for sets of items that repeat frequently.

Often, the problem is not only that the sets themselves are huge is that data is an endless continuous stream (Twitter, Facebook, Netflix), or comes in long multivariate sequences (data produced by a Kinect device during a game). Processing these sequences / streams in time for using the information is also a major issue.

To deal with this there are several strategies, depending on the problem and on the learning algorithm used:

- **Don't Use All the Data at Once:** The idea of having a training-set and a test-set running based on your PC may need to be revised and your applications may need to pull data chunks from a data-set server and throw them away when used. Works best with stochastic or one-time algorithms that require less (or no) pattern replay.

- Use incremental algorithms that continue to learn as data comes in but do not require all previous examples to be stored.
- Pre-process to simplify data and use "the interesting bits". Several algorithms are known to discover highly correlated data and related attributes; the use of these can reduce the amount of information that actually needs to be processed. Don't underestimate human ability to find patterns, especially if equipped with a good visualization tool.
- **Distribute the Data and Processing:** The use of distributed file systems seems to be one where tools are making the most difference. Currently, tools that let you distribute your data in the cloud are the basis of the main Big Data approaches.

From the clutter of "Big Data tools" that are appearing by the dozens, both from upstarts as well as from established companies one name pops up, Hadoop Distributed File System (HDFS). Hadoop is a distributed computing platform based on its own file system HDFS. This seems to be the standard that most tools aim at supporting. The Apache Mahout Project (The Apache Software Foundation, 2014b) is a leading effort for open-source, scalable machine learning algorithms. Although still in its early years it already gathered some attention and a growing community. There are a multitude of tools, either adding scalable components, or being built from scratch for this new paradigm. However, contrary to most other revolutions in the area, tools do not seem to be the only thing changing. To cope with these "big data" problems organizations are now forced to value the knowledge that can be gained by good practitioners. Professionals with these skills are becoming highly valued and a new discipline is emerging, that was labeled Data Science.

Data Science: A New Way of Looking at Information Extraction from Data

Organizations now begin to perceive the added value of having a team dedicated to data analysis supporting the decision making process. Analysts can be defined "as workers who use statistics, rigorous quantitative or qualitative analysis, and information modeling techniques to shape and make business decisions," (Davenport, Harris, & Morison, 2010). An effective analysis should impact the decision-making process. To do so, an analysis must be driven by a business need and be relevant to that business, i.e., providing insight to solving a relevant problem of the organization.

Currently, more than data analysts, organizations are seeking for data scientists to process, interpret and, mainly, find new ways of using the available data, regardless if it is internal or external, structured or un-structured, big or small. This emergent role can be characterized by a solid foundation in math, statistics, probability, and computer science, combined with strong social skills. Apart from the ability to write code and to communicate to all stakeholders (e.g., using data storytelling techniques), data scientists need to have an intense curiosity, leading him/her to dive into the root of a problem and derive a set of hypothesis that can be tested (Davenport & Patil, 2012). Given the nature of this skill set, the role of data scientist is still scarce in the marketplace.

Data Science is then an emerging discipline that encompasses data analysis, data mining, statistics, visualization, machine learning, and sometimes even business and marketing-related subjects.

Text Mining

Text Mining is the non-trivial process of extracting relevant knowledge from large collections of unstructured text documents. In this information age we are living, a relevant part of the information is available as unstructured texts, very difficult to access and to process, but still a potential source of useful knowledge.

Text mining is a recent interdisciplinary field of computer science that combines techniques from Natural Language Processing, Computational Linguistics, Data mining, Web mining, Information Retrieval and Statistics, and Machine Learning. Text Mining is about finding patterns on large unstructured text databases, contrarily to Data Mining that deals normally with large structured databases. Text Mining is also much different than traditional web search, where the user is typically looking for something that is already known and has been produced by someone else. While Text Mining focuses on extracting new information from text, traditional web search relies on filtering the material that is not currently relevant to the user's needs. Text Mining is also different from traditional Information Extraction, a major component of Text Mining that can be used to extract other high level information.

Today's text mining research and technology enables high-performance analytics from web's textual data, allowing to: cluster documents and web pages according to their content, find associations among entities (people, places and/or organizations), and reasoning about important data trends. General examples of existing Text Mining applications include: 1) classification of news stories, web pages, etc., according to their content; 2) email and news filtering; 3) organizing repositories of document-related meta-information for search and retrieval (search engines); 4) clustering documents or web pages; 5) gain insights about trends, relations between people, places and/or organizations. Text Mining applications are particularly relevant for different business aspects, including decision support in Customer Relationship Management, Marketing, and Industry. Nowadays companies are relying on text mining to discover and analyze customer's typical complaints, trends of satisfied and unsatisfied customers, and distinct groups of potential buyers, groups of competitors.

Despite the undeniable advances in the scope of Text Mining, a wide range of challenges still pose difficulties for Text Mining applications. One of the challenges relates to the fact that the number of possible words and phrase types in language cause a very high number of possible dimensions, apart from being sparse. Another important issue concerns the documents being sometimes structurally different and not statistically independent. Aspects related with the language complexity, subtle ways of establishing relations between concepts in a text, word ambiguity, and context sensitivity also pose considerable challenges. Finally, noisy data, such as spelling mistakes, and specific phenomena that is often found in microblogs, such as Twitter also pose considerable challenges to Text Mining applications.

Text Classification is a particularly important type of Text Mining tasks that consist of assigning a predefined set of classes (subject categories, topics, genres, sentiment, etc.) to a document. Examples of classification tasks include: Spam detection, Language Identification, Age/gender identification, Sentiment Analysis, Topic detection, and other tasks that are illustrated in Figure 1. Each one of the referred tasks makes use of NLP, statistics, and machine learning techniques to extract potentially relevant knowledge from the content.

Figure 1. Text classification tasks

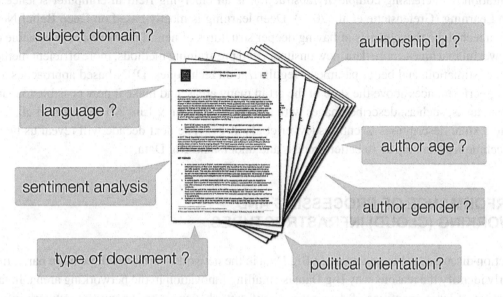

Sentiment Analysis is a relevant and well-known task that consists of extracting sentiments and emotions expressed in texts. Being the first step towards the online reputation analysis, it is now gaining particular relevance because of the rise of social media, such as blogs and social networks. The increasing amount of user-generated contents in the form of reviews, recommendations, ratings and any other form of opinion constitute huge volumes of opinionated texts all over the web that are precious sources of information, especially for decision support. Sentiment Analysis can be used to know what people think about a product, a company, an event, or a political candidate. Agencies can make use of it to check how the public sentiment is, predict election outcomes, and even to predict market trends (Bollen, Mao, & Zeng, 2011).

Open Issues

The challenges in this area are now beginning to be tapped. Most tools to analyze data are already available. Strategies to disperse data and processing in the cloud, while maintaining data privacy are also available and more are being developed.

The Data Science teams are starting to be considered a necessary asset for some companies, mainly for those whose business relies mainly on data. Applications seem to be everywhere, some are problems that have been around for a while and joined the Big Data stream; others appeared to be unsolvable until recently and are now being tackled for the first time; and others still have jumped to a new scale.

The incredible advances in Machine Learning methods, computational frameworks, and related technologies make it now possible to tackle immense quantities of data. However, learning with such data remains still a serious challenge. Most of the existing machine learning techniques works well because the process relies just on optimizing weights, based of human-designed representations and input-features, to make the best prediction. Automatically learning relevant features and multilevel representation of increasing complexity/abstraction is an emerging field in computer science known as Deep Learning (Grefenstette et al., 2014). Deep learning is mostly based on Deep Belief Networks (DBNs), a technique that consists of having deeper structures of neural networks, now possible due to: more powerful machines, more data, new unsupervised pre-training methods, more efficient methods for parameter estimation, and better parameter regularization techniques. DBN-based approaches are now achieving performances above the state of the art in many areas, and make it now possible to learn how to perform tasks, such as: describe images with sentences (Socher & Lin, 2011; Socher et al., 2014) or associate textual descriptions to entities (Iyyer et al., 2014). The next decade will reveal us how these recent techniques can help us to better process and understand Big Data.

3. PERFORMANCE OF PROCESSING AND NETWORKING (CLOUD) INFRASTRUCTURES

This section discusses the huge impact of Big Data in the networks and it has three main parts. Initially, we clearly identify the reasons why Big Data is entailing innovation in the networking arena. In fact, the transmission of large quantities of data poses significant challenges to the current network infrastructures. Additionally, networks that have been around but neither recognized nor well understood, using Big Data analysis, are becoming visible and have been clearly identified as "new networks" (e.g. social networks organized by high-level predicates of keywords). These discovered networks are normally very difficult to manage in a successful way because they have both different features and interrelations among the nodes/agents forming those networks. Then, in this section, we proceed to the second part where are identified some typical scenarios where new network requirements could potentially emerge as a consequence of Big Data exploitation. Finally, we point out some future directions in how to successfully manage the most relevant challenges imposed by Big Data applications on the networking and computing infrastructures.

Why Big Data Is Entailing Innovation in Networks

With the help of Big Data, it is now possible to envisage networks anywhere with strong interrelationships and interactions among them: from the macroscopic to the microscopic worlds; from the global finance to the social human behavior; from species evolution to DNA-level protein interaction; from legacy network infrastructures to others completely different formed by embedded devices, sensors, and very intelligent "self-x" algorithms which can evolve (learn and adjust) as, for example, humans normally do. Nevertheless, these novel network requirements should be managed in much more complex ways than the legacy networks due to some challenging features such as: ubiquitous network access, scalability of network resources (i.e. capacity, delay), abstraction/detail (i.e., what is the more convenient layer to manage the network?), heterogeneity, self-organized network infrastructures, and awareness of the context surrounding each network. Additional novel network requirements are choosing the most suitable set of management policies (e.g. reactive, predictive) to operate the emergent networks with a good performance, and learning new skills from the obtained feedback after a policy has been applied to a network infrastructure, helping to evolve the management policies.

Whichever ways the networks will evolve, the future networks will mainly involve nodes and connecting arcs (Hurlburt & Voas, 2014). Hence, future networks can be discretely measured, traversed, and described using graph theory. Also, a very important aspect to guarantee the success of Big Data is to control with more intelligence and efficiency its computing and networking infrastructures. In parallel, a very recent area to manage networks, which has a huge growth in popularity, is Software Defined Networking (Kreutz & Ramos, 2014; Lara, Kolasani, & Ramamurthy, 2014; Jarraya, 2014; Nunes et al., 2014; Feamster, Rexford, & Zegura, 2013). Using SDN it is possible to decouple the data plane from the control plane, as shown in Figure 2. In this way, the intelligent algorithms to forward/routing traffic are removed from the network devices (e.g. switches, routers) and installed in diverse controllers, potentially in a hierarchical design to satisfy both requirements of scalability and robustness to failures. These controllers can receive from higher levels some management policies via North bound interfaces. These policies are translated by the controllers to low-level pairs of <match, action> that are installed at the network devices through South bound interfaces, using a protocol like either Openflow or Ovsdb, among others. The controllers can also remotely manage the diverse network devices in a coordinated way using West/East bound interfaces. In case of any failure on network nodes or links, the SDN controllers can find alternative data paths traversing the network infrastructure in a more quick and orderly way than legacy networks because the latter rely uniquely in distributed algorithms (which spends more time to converge after a failure to a new network configuration). The next four subsections discusses usage

Figure 2. OpenFlow-enabled SDN device

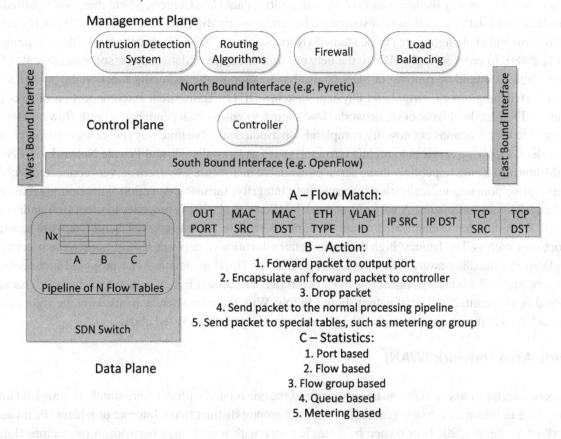

scenarios where SDN can be useful to prepare networks to satisfy novel requirements namely in data centers, Internet interdomain routing, mobile communications, and home networks. A final subsection highlights future SDN developments.

Data Centers

Ultimately data-intensive and collaborative applications are increasingly being moved towards Data Centers aggregated inside the cloud. Here, using Big Data analytics is possible to process data from multiple sources and on-the-fly extract relevant knowledge to drive the strategy or business of either enterprises or other organizations. Consequently to obtain a good performance in the supporting infrastructure for processing big quantities of data, such as low latency and high throughput, some management enhancements are needed to operate more intelligently the available computing resources in each data center, such as virtual machines (Dai et al., 2013), memory (Zhou & Li, 2013), CPU scheduling (Bae et al., 2012), and cache (Koller et al., 2011), I/O (Ram et al., 2013). Other very important functional aspect to be aware in data centers is to enhance the network performance (Marx, 2013; Lange et al., 2011; Saleem, Hassan, & Asirvadam, 2011). To enhance this performance in a more flexible way, the network resources should become virtualized. In this way, we need a "virtualized hypervisor", similar to the one used by virtual machines, to manage the virtual network functions. A SDN controller can support this network hypervisor. That is why the integration of SDN in multi-tenant Data Centers, where there is a significant proliferation of data from all sorts of sources to be processed by Big Data tools (Juniper, 2013), is a very interesting and challenging area to be studied (Koponen et al., 2014; Greenberg et al., 2009; Niranjan et al., 2009). In order to apply SDN to the network infrastructure of data centers, some intelligent software routines should be running in SDN controllers to support the following functionalities: efficient layer 2 switching among virtual and physical switches (IETF, Transparent Interconnection of Lots of Links - TRILL); load balancing; network flow slicing to ensure independence among flows; enforce legacy security functions but now in a completely distributed and dynamic way (i.e. across distinct cloud providers, supplying services to mobile terminals) such as firewalls, Virtual Private Networks (VPNs), DeMilitarized Zones to publicly make services available in a secure way from servers connected within a enterprise domain; authentication; privacy; data integrity; intrusion detection; intrusion prevention; and attack countermeasures. A very recent work by (Perry et al., 2014) proposes to use a similar design to a SDN system but implemented inside the Linux Kernel to provide at a datacenter network several properties such as, low latency, high throughput, fair allocation of network resources between users and applications, deadline-aware scheduling, and congestion (loss) avoidance. The proposed architecture has a centralized arbiter equivalent to a SDN controller. The arbiter basically decides when each packet should be transmitted and what path it should follow. With these two decisions made in the right away for each packet the authors argue that they can satisfy the properties listed above.

Wide Area Network (WAN)

A second scenario where SDN can be very useful is the one related with the more suitable control of flow switching in Internet exchange points (IXPs) either among distinct tier-x Internet providers (Feamster, Rexford, & Zegura, 2013) or owned by a single entity with a very large network infrastructure (Jain, Kumar, & Mandal, 2013). An IXP is a location where normally multiple Internet service providers connect theirs networks to exchange routes, often through a common layer-2 switching fabric. The current

Internet has globally around 300 IXPs. The commonly used routing protocol to exchange traffic in these IXPs is Border Gateway Protocol (BGP) (Cisco, 2008). However, BGP shows a significant limitation: it was conceived mainly to announce route paths to Internet destination prefixes, and as such it lacks more fine-grained decisions to route wide area traffic. For example, the routing of traffic based on the application type which originated that traffic should have an enormous interest to the efficient transmission of Big Data heterogeneous traffic. In this way, the current BGP needs to be enhanced by high-level policies at the IXP to implement distinct routing policies according the traffic characteristics (e.g. video vs. non-video). SDN exchange point (SDX) (Feamster, Rexford, & Zegura, 2013) could be used for this goal and much more. At the time of this writing, the broadest implementation of SDN in the Internet that is successfully working is described in (Jain, Kumar, & Mandal, 2013). In this work, SDN was used to control the traffic exchange among data centers owned by a single entity with mainly well-specified traffic patterns. So, an interesting question that remains to be answered is if the same SDN solution could be also successfully used in scenarios where the IXPs are traversed by traffic with much more dynamic behavior and from diverse providers. Finally, SDN could be applied at core transport (optical) networks (Azodolmolky et al., 2012) and optical multiplexing to interconnect data centers (Cyan, 2013). For further information, the reader could consult some documentation about version 1.4 of Openflow, which provides support for transactional rule changes, management of switch table space, and supports optical fiber ports (The Open Networking Foundation, 2013; Ren & Xu, 2014).

Mobile Networks

A third scenario where SDN can be very useful is the one related with mobile networks (Costa-Requena, 2014). The major challenge in future mobile networks is how to improve throughput to support the increased demand in data traffic and the decrease demand on the Average Revenue Per User (ARPU), using the current network capabilities in innovative and efficient ways. SDN could help on these issues, redesigning and/or using the current network architectures in novel ways as we discuss in the following text through several relevant examples extracted from the literature.

The first example to enhance mobile networks is to split the network edge from the core (Casado et al., 2012), with the latter forming the fabric that transports packets as defined by an intelligent edge, to software-defined IXPs (Feamster, Rexford, & Zegura, 2013). The second example is to gradually move most of the current LTE network core elements (e.g. middleboxes) to the cloud (Costa-Requena, 2014) in a dynamic way accordingly the load behavior (e.g. data pattern mobility associated to commuters along the day) and traffic characteristics (e.g. security, video transcoding). A third example illustrates how to achieve an efficient access to Big Data infrastructures through mobile devices (Wang, Liu, & Soyata, 2014; Soyata et al., 2014) potentially adjusted to network limitations on the network edge (e.g. terminals, radio access) A fourth example describes how to support an efficient flow forwarding (Pentikousis, Wang, & Hu, 2013) guaranteeing a complete isolation among them in the data path (i.e. using FlowVisor (Sherwood et al., 2010)). A fifth and last example discusses how new techno-economic models can decrease exploitation cost (Naudts et al., 2012) or eventually giving peering (collaboration) incentives to operators to enhance resources usage (e.g. offloading data traffic from a busy access technology to a less-busy one).

Home Networks

A fourth scenario is the one related with home networks (Sundaresan et al., 2011; Kumar, Gharakheili, & Sivaraman, 2013; Yiakoumis et al., 2011). An SDN-based broadband home connection can simplify the addition of new functions in measurement systems such as BISmark (Sundaresan et al., 2011), allowing the system to react to changing conditions in the home network (Kumar, Gharakheili, & Sivaraman, 2013). As an example, a home gateway can perform reactive traffic shaping, considering the current measurement results of the home network. Recent work has proposed slicing control of home networks, to allow different third-party service providers (e.g., smart grid operators) to deploy services on the network without having to install their own infrastructure (Yiakoumis et al., 2011).

Future Directions

To complement the considered usage scenarios some future directions are now discussed regarding the network evolution to successfully satisfy via SDN the challenging requirements raised by Big Data applications, supported by distributed and parallel data processing tools, such as MapReduce (Dean & Ghemawat, 2008), Hadoop (The Apache Software Foundation, 2014a), and visualization tools of large sets of data (GenMAPP (Gladstone Institute University of California at San Francisco, 2014), DIVE (Rysavy, Bromley, & Daggettet, 2014)). In this chapter we advocate that the incorporation of SDN in the networks will be a gradual evolutionary process by two main reasons. The first one is related to the existence of diverse network players. As an example, in the current Internet, there are at least three major ones, the Content Network providers, the core Autonomous Systems (ASs), and the edge operators. In this way, it seems natural that each one of these three entities could adopt SDN at different times and using diverse deployment strategies, depending on each one particular needs and already deployed solutions. This vision is also discussed in (Vissicchio, Vanbever, & Bonaventure, 2014). They discuss a gradual global strategy adoption of SDN based on which network layer and whose entity is responsible to control via SDN the Forwarding Information Base (FIB), i.e. forwarding tables, at distinct node locations of the network infrastructure. Obviously the final step of this evolutionary process is the full integration of SDN among all the existing entities. The second reason why SDN deployment should be a gradual process is concerned with system reliability after the adoption of a new SDN solution. By this, we mean that a new adopted SDN solution operating in a real network infrastructure should operate like it was initially planned for and it should not degrade the network performance when compared with previous solutions. To avoid this, each new SDN solution can be currently troubleshooted and verified in each one of the following distinct SDN aspects: static analysis verification of network configuration – Router Configuration Checker (Feamster & Balakrishnan, 2005) to avoid routing partitions and loops, static data plane verification by performing symbolic execution on packets to check flow isolation - Header Space Analysis (Kazemian, Change, & Zheng, 2013), and dynamic verification of control plane sequential composition of Finite State Machines triggered by JSON events – Kinetic (Monsanto et al., 2013). Nevertheless, after all these verifications have been successfully made, we are not always completely sure that after the deployment of a new SDN solution the network will be working completely out of problems due to two important limitations such as: each verification (e.g. data plane vs. control plane) has been made in a completely isolated way from the others; some unexpected interactions could arise from the dynamic interaction among several controllers with distinct purposes when they are in operation. In this way, an interesting area of research is to study how to perform a single-step robust troubleshooting and verification of a complete (i.e., configuration, data plane, control plane) SDN system in a similar way as proposed in (Nelson et al., 2014), including the verification of fully dynamic interactions among controllers with potential distinct goals (e.g., load balancing, security, forwarding) and fulfilling very complex policies formed by the composition (i.e., applying diverse operators such as parallel, sequential, conditional if) of other policies at high-level layers of abstraction (Foster et al., 2013).

Finally, another open issue for research is how to collect in real-time a huge amount of forensic data from the network operation, through, for example, packet inspection, traffic captures, log files, and report files, to find the root causes of different problems. All this may enable a more efficient and intelligent way to control the global network, such as the solutions given by SDN. Using this work direction, we assume the network infrastructure as a valuable producer of Big Data information to be analyzed and explored in unpredictable directions.

4. A CASE STUDY FOR AN INTELLIGENT INTERNET EXCHANGE POINT

This section discusses and evaluates an intelligent solution to manage an Internet Exchange Point (IXP). An IXP is a location on the network where normally different operator networks (also designated by Autonomous Systems – ASs) exchange traffic with each other. As discussed before there is a growing interest in applying SDN to make some aspects of wide-area network management easier and more flexible by giving operators direct control over packet-processing rules that match on multiple header fields and perform a variety of potentially very interesting management actions.

In this section, we evaluate an implementation of a software-defined IXP (SDX) (Feamster, Rexford, & Zegura, 2013). This implementation provides new programming abstractions allowing BGP (Cisco, 2008) participants to create and rule new wide area traffic delivery applications (e.g., differentiate video from other traffic), avoiding distinct applications to interfere with each other and routing their traffic with distinct high-level management policies (Feamster, 2014). This implementation acts like a controller that uses policies specified in Pyretic (Contributors, 2013b).

In this case study, we aim to implement an intelligent and efficient IXP controller module, which should have the following behavior in an IXP-BGP scenario (see Figure 3) with three peering ASs (i.e., A, B, and C):

- Each AS establishes a single BGP/TCP connection with only the route server of the SDX controller and not with any other neighbor AS; this is to guarantee that the route server is the only entity in the network that can populate the routing tables of the AS's edge routers but doing so the routing rules should satisfy both pyretic policies specified in the controller and the announced networks (to the route server) by each AS;
- AS A's policy forwards web traffic (destined to TCP port 80) to peer B;
- AS A's policy forwards traffic destined to ports 443 (HTTPS) and 8080 to peer C;
- AS B has no defined pyretic policy, so its forwarding proceeds to default BGP forwarding;
- AS C has two input ports at the SDX. Consequently, the controller has a first policy that forwards HTTPS traffic to the AS C's input port [0] for c1, a second policy that forwards traffic destined to port 80 to the AS C's input port [1] for c2, and a third policy that drops any traffic for port 8080;

Figure 3. BGP scenario
(Feamster, 2014).

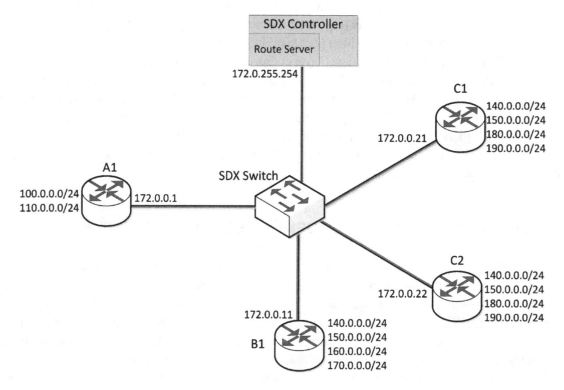

- When the route server associated to the SDX controller learns more than one BGP route to the same destination prefix, the route server decides the best path that was announced by a BGP participant applying a pre-defined criterion (e.g., choose the one with the smallest router-id).

Understanding the SDX Setup

The network topology visualized in Figure 3 will be evaluated using the network emulator mininext (Schlinker, 2014), Quagga router (Contributors, 2013a) to deploy routing with BGP (Cisco, 2008), and the SDX framework (Feamster, Rexford, & Zegura, 2013) to implement the already discussed management policies on top of BGP. Table 1 shows a partial view of the mininext setup file where each host interface is configured. Each host is configured in such a way it is within a specific AS domain.

Table 2 illustrates the BGP routing configuration for participant A (file bgpd.conf). We briefly explain some configuration details: the BGP id of AS A is 100; the A edge router-id is 172.0.0.0.1; the BGP's only neighbor is the SDX router, so the networks within A's domain are only announced to that router; the networks belonging to A's domain are 100.0.0.0/24 and 110.0.0.0/24.

The SDX presents to each participant (A, B, C) a virtual SDX switch. Each participant specifies pyretic policies for its virtual switch independently of other participants' policies. This limited view of the network ensures that the participants are not allowed to write rules for other network's traffic. For more details consult (Feamster, Rexford, & Zegura, 2013). Table 3 shows the outbound SDX management policies specified (in pyretic) for participant A. These policies were already discussed. By outbound

Table 1. Configuring host interface in mininext setup file

```
print "Configuring host interface; each host belongs to a
specific AS domain"
for host in hosts:
print "Host name: ", host.name
if host.name=='a1':
host.cmd('sudo ifconfig lo:1 100.0.0.1 netmask 255.255.255.0
up')
...
if host.name=='b1':
host.cmd('sudo ifconfig lo:140 140.0.0.1 netmask
255.255.255.0 up')
...
```

Table 2. BGP routing configuration for participant A

```
router bgp 100
bgp router-id 172.0.0.1
neighbor 172.0.255.254 remote-as 65000
network 100.0.0.0/24
network 110.0.0.0/24
redistribute static
```

policy we mean a policy to be applied to traffic entering a virtual switch on a physical port from the participant's own border router.

Table 4 shows inbound SDX management policies specified (in pyretic) for participant C. These policies were already discussed. By inbound policy we mean a policy to be applied to the traffic entering a virtual switch on a virtual port from another SDX participant. Note also that it is not necessary to specify explicitly a drop policy to traffic destined to port 8080 because the default SDX policy is drop a packet if that packet does not have a positive match with any present pyretic policy.

Evaluation

The network topology used in the current evaluation made with a network emulator is shown in Figure 3. All the evaluation was performed in a single Linux virtual machine (Ubuntu).

After the configuration process has been finalized, we can now initiate the evaluation. For that, one should open a Linux shell, and run the pyretic SDX controller with the following command:

```
./sdx-setup.sh pyretic
```

In a separate console, launch the Mininext (Schlinker, 2014) topology as follows:

```
./sdx-setup.sh mininet app_specific_peering_inboundTE
```

In a separate console, launch the SDX route server as follows:

```
./sdx-setup.sh exabgp
```

Table 3. Outbound SDX management policies specified (in pyretic) for participant A

```
final_policy = ((match(dstport=80) >> sdx.fwd(participant.
peers['B'])) +
(match(dstport=443) >> sdx.fwd(participant.peers['C'])) +
(match(dstport=8080)>> sdx.fwd(participant.peers['C'])))
```

Table 4. Inbound SDX management policies specified (in pyretic) for participant C

```
final_policy = ((match(dstport=443) >> sdx.fwd(participant.
phys_ports[0])) +
(match(dstport=80) >> sdx.fwd(participant.phys_ports[1])))
```

At this step one can check whether the participants received the routes from the SDX route server. For example, to verify the available routes on host a1, in the console running mininext, one can perform the following command:

```
mininext> a1 route -n
```

The output of previous command should be similar to the one visualized in Figure 4.

At this point, it is necessary to clarify the ip addresses that appear as the next-hop (gateway) address in each one of the routing table lines of Figure 4. To avoid flow table become too large for the SDX's switch, the SDX controller introduces the concept of Virtual Next Hops (VNHs). SDX platform assigns one (virtual) next hop for each set of IP prefixes with similar forwarding behavior. For example, in this example IP prefix pair (160.0.0.0/24, 170.0.0.0/24) have similar forwarding behavior. Thus the controller assigns a single VNH for that pair. You can verify this behavior from the output messages from Pyretic's console shown in Table 5, from where we have selected the following information:

```
Virtual Next Hop --> IP Prefix: {'VNH2': set([u'160.0.0.0/24',
u'170.0.0.0/24']), ...
Virtual Next Hop --> Next Hop IP Address (Virtual): {'VNH2': '172.0.1.2', ...
```

Figure 4. Routing table for node a1 (edge router of AS A)

```
/bgpd --daemon -A 127.0.0.1
root        36  0.0  0.2  18692  1312 pts/7    R+    07:51    0:00 ps aux
**Adding Network Interfaces for SDX Setup
Configuring participating ASs


Host name:  a1
Host name:  b1
Host name:  c1
Host name:  c2
Host name:  exabgp
** Running CLI
*** Starting CLI:
mininext> a1 route -n
Kernel IP routing table
Destination     Gateway         Genmask         Flags Metric Ref    Use Iface
140.0.0.0       172.0.1.3       255.255.255.0   UG    0      0        0 a1-eth0
150.0.0.0       172.0.1.3       255.255.255.0   UG    0      0        0 a1-eth0
160.0.0.0       172.0.1.2       255.255.255.0   UG    0      0        0 a1-eth0
170.0.0.0       172.0.1.2       255.255.255.0   UG    0      0        0 a1-eth0
172.0.0.0       0.0.0.0         255.255.0.0     U     0      0        0 a1-eth0
180.0.0.0       172.0.1.4       255.255.255.0   UG    0      0        0 a1-eth0
190.0.0.0       172.0.1.4       255.255.255.0   UG    0      0        0 a1-eth0
mininext>
```

Table 5. Output messages from Pyretic's console related with VNH configuration

```
Parsing participant's policies
Starting VNH Assignment
After new assignment
Virtual Next Hop --> IP Prefix:
{'VNH1': set([u'110.0.0.0/24', u'100.0.0.0/24']),
'VNH2': set(['160.0.0.0/24', '170.0.0.0/24']),
'VNH3': set(['140.0.0.0/24', '150.0.0.0/24']),
'VNH4': set(['190.0.0.0/24', '180.0.0.0/24'])}
Virtual Next Hop --> Next Hop IP Address (Virtual):
{'VNH1': '172.0.1.1', 'VNH2 ': '172.0.1.2', 'VNH3': '172.0.1.3', 'VNH4': '172.0.1.4',
'VNH': [IPAddress('172 .0.1.0'), IPAddress('172.0.1.1'), IPAddress('172.0.1.2'),
IPAddress('172.0.1.3'), IPAddress('172.0.1.4'), IPAddress('172.0.1.5'),
IPAddress('172.0.1.6'), IPAddress('172.0.1.7'), IPAddress('172.0.1.8'),
IPAddress('172.0.1.9'), IPAddress('172 .0.1.10'), IPAddress('172.0.1.11'),
IPAddress('172.0.1.12'), IPAddress('172.0.1. 13'), IPAddress('172.0.1.14'),
IPAddress('172.0.1.15')]}
Virtual Next Hop --> Next Hop Mac Address (Virtual)
{'VNH1': aa:00:00:00:00:01, 'VNH2': aa:00:00:00:00:02, 'VNH3': aa:00:00:00:00:03,
'VNH4': aa:00:00:00:00:04, 'VNH': 'aa:00:00:00:00:00'}
Completed VNH Assignment
```

The previous selected information shows that the SDX controller assigns (160.0.0.0/24, 170.0.0.0/24) to VNH2, which has the next-hop address such as 172.0.1.2. Refer to (Feamster, Rexford, & Zegura, 2013) for more details on Virtual Next Hops.

The next evaluation step is to check if the pyretic policies specified before can be correctly applied in our system. For this, the iperf tool can be used in the mininext console. The diverse issued commands and corresponding results are visualized and discussed as follows. From Figure 5 one can conclude that port 80 traffic for routes advertised by AS B is received by node b1.

From Figure 6, one can verify that port 80 traffic from AS A for routes advertised only by AS C is forwarded to node c2.

Finally, from Figure 7, one can also verify that the port 8080 traffic forwarded to AS C is dropped as the last client iperf message elucidates: "Connection time out". In this way, we finalize our case study.

The current case study clearly illustrates that using high-level and intuitive management policies is possible to easily route data traffic with diverse requirements (e.g. video vs. non-video) among network infrastructures owned by several entities, which is a very realistic scenario to deploy Big Data heterogeneous services in the wide area network through diverse public cloud providers. In this way, it is possible to optimize the global network performance, reduce the network costs and proactively managing customer experience.

5. CONCLUSION

This chapter discusses two important aspects related to a successful deployment of a Big Data infrastructure. The first aspect concerns the extraction of relevant knowledge from heterogeneous and massive amounts of data. The second aspect relates to new challenges that Big Data applications and services are imposing in network infrastructures.

Figure 5. Test routing path to AS B (server destination port is 80)

```
/bgpd --daemon -A 127.0.0.1
root         33  0.0  0.2  18692  1312 pts/7    R+    11:28   0:00 ps aux
**Adding Network Interfaces for SDX Setup
Configuring participating ASs


Host name:  a1
Host name:  b1
Host name:  c1
Host name:  c2
Host name:  exabgp
** Running CLI
*** Starting CLI:
mininext> b1 iperf -s -B 140.0.0.1 -p 80 &
mininext> a1 iperf -c 140.0.0.1 -B 100.0.0.1 -p 80 -t 2
------------------------------------------------------------
Client connection to 140.0.0.1, TCP port 80
Binding to local address 100.0.0.1
TCP window size: 85.3 KByte (default)
------------------------------------------------------------
[  3] local 100.0.0.1 port 80 connected with 140.0.0.1 port 80
[ ID] Interval       Transfer     Bandwidth
[  3]  0.0- 2.0 sec  78.5 MBytes   329 Mbits/sec
mininext>
```

Figure 6. Test routing path to AS C (server destination port is 80)

```
Host name:  exabgp
** Running CLI
*** Starting CLI:
mininext> b1 iperf -s -B 140.0.0.1 -p 80 &
mininext> a1 iperf -c 140.0.0.1 -B 100.0.0.1 -p 80 -t 2
------------------------------------------------------------
Client connecting to 140.0.0.1, TCP port 80
Binding to local address 100.0.0.1
TCP window size: 85.3 KByte (default)
------------------------------------------------------------
[  3] local 100.0.0.1 port 80 connected with 140.0.0.1 port 80
[ ID] Interval       Transfer     Bandwidth
[  3]  0.0- 2.0 sec  78.5 MBytes   329 Mbits/sec
mininext> c2 iperf -s -B 180.0.0.1 -p 80 &
mininext> a1 iperf -c 180.0.0.1 -B 100.0.0.2 -p 80 -t 2
------------------------------------------------------------
Client connecting to 180.0.0.1, TCP port 80
Binding to local address 100.0.0.2
TCP window size: 85.3 KByte (default)
------------------------------------------------------------
[  3] local 100.0.0.2 port 80 connected with 180.0.0.1 port 80
[ TD] Interval       Transfer     Bandwidth
[  3]  0.0- 2.0 sec  78.2 MBytes   327 Mbits/sec
mininext>
```

Figure 7. Test routing path to AS C (server destination port is 8080)

```
mininext> b1 iperf -s -B 140.0.0.1 -p 80 &
mininext> a1 iperf -c 140.0.0.1 -B 100.0.0.1 -p 80 -t 2
------------------------------------------------------------
Client connecting to 140.0.0.1, TCP port 80
Binding to local address 100.0.0.1
TCP window size: 85.3 KByte (default)
------------------------------------------------------------
[  3] local 100.0.0.1 port 80 connected with 140.0.0.1 port 80
[ ID] Interval        Transfer      Bandwidth
[  3] 0.0- 2.0 sec  78.5 MBytes   329 Mbits/sec
mininext> c2 iperf -s -B 180.0.0.1 -p 80 &
mininext> a1 iperf -c 180.0.0.1 -B 100.0.0.2 -p 80 -t 2
------------------------------------------------------------
Client connecting to 180.0.0.1, TCP port 80
Binding to local address 100.0.0.2
TCP window size: 85.3 KByte (default)
------------------------------------------------------------
[  3] local 100.0.0.2 port 80 connected with 180.0.0.1 port 80
[ ID] Interval        Transfer      Bandwidth
[  3] 0.0- 2.0 sec  78.2 MBytes   327 Mbits/sec
mininext> c1 iperf -s -B 180.0.0.1 -p 8080 &
mininext> a1 iperf -c 180.0.0.1 -B 100.0.0.1 -p 8080 -t 2
connect failed: Connection timed out
mininext>
```

Machine Learning methods and related technologies can be used to extract relevant knowledge from the large and diverse datasets currently available. From a Machine Learning point of view, we have seen that usually more data means more reliable models and results. The chapter focused on the massive amounts of unstructured textual information that are constantly being produced, and that can be accessed from online sources, which constitute a potential valuable source of knowledge for companies, organizations, and governments. Text Mining is described as a recent research area that is responsible for extracting useful information from such unstructured texts, drawing knowledge and techniques from different fields of computer science. Today's text mining research and technology enables high-performance analytics from web's textual data, allowing to: cluster documents and web pages according to their content, find associations among entities (people, places and/or organizations), and reasoning about important data trends.

The challenges being imposed in the network infrastructure to efficiently transmit Big Data, which is typically heterogeneous and distributed, were also discussed as follows: decide about the best deployment strategy for new network management solutions; choose the most correct method to fully troubleshoot and verify, in an automatic way, each new network management solution before its real implementation; and collect real-time forensic data from the network operation to supervise and control the network infrastructure in both novel and efficient ways.

Finally, a practical scenario concerning the efficient transmission of Big Data heterogeneous traffic through the wide area network among diverse public cloud providers was presented. In this way, we have studied a solution that enhances the current Internet inter-AS routing protocol (i.e. BGP) with high-level management policies at the IXP to implement distinct routing policies according the traffic characteristics (e.g. video vs. non-video). This solution has been also validated and, from the obtained results, we can conclude that the default BGP routing, only based in the destination IP prefixes, can be complemented with further information (e.g. destination port). This last characteristic enables traffic routing also based in application details, which can enhance the customer experienced quality.

REFERENCES

Asuncion, A., & Newman, D. J. (2007). *UCI Machine Learning Repository*. University of California Irvine School of Information. Retrieved May 15, 2015, from http://www.ics.uci.edu/~mlearn/MLRepository.html

Azodolmolky, S., Nejabati, R., Peng, S., Hammad, A., Channegowda, M. P., Efstathiou, N. … Simeonidou, D. (2012). Optical FlowVisor: An OpenFlow-based Optical Network Virtualization Approach. In *National Fiber Optic Engineers Conference* (p. JTh2A.41). Optical Society of America. Retrieved May 15, 2015, from http://www.opticsinfobase.org/abstract.cfm?URI=NFOEC-2012-JTh2A.41

Bae, C., Xia, L., Dinda, P., & Lange, J. (2012). Dynamic Adaptive Virtual Core Mapping to Improve Power, Energy, and Performance in Multi-socket Multicores. In *Proceedings of the 21st International Symposium on Applied Computing* (pp. 247–258). doi:10.1145/2287076.2287114

Bollen, J., Mao, H., & Zeng, X. (2011). Twitter mood predicts the stock market. *Journal of Computational Science*, 2(1), 1–8. doi:10.1016/j.jocs.2010.12.007

Casado, M., Koponen, T., Shenker, S., & Tootoonchian, A. (2012). Fabric: a retrospective on evolving SDN. *Hot Topics in Software Defined Networking (HotSDN)*, (pp. 85–89). Retrieved May 15, 2015, from http://dl.acm.org/citation.cfm?id=2342459

Cisco. (2008). Border Gateway Protocol. *Update*. Retrieved April 2, 2014, from http://docwiki.cisco.com/wiki/Border_Gateway_Protocol

Contributors. (2013a). Quagga Routing Suite. *Online*. Retrieved May 15, 2015, from http://www.nongnu.org/quagga/

Contributors. (2013b). *The Policy: Pyretic's Foundation*. Retrieved April 18, 2014, from https://github.com/frenetic-lang/pyretic/wiki/Language-Basics

Costa-Requena, J. (2014). SDN integration in LTE mobile backhaul networks. In *International Conference on Information Networking* (pp. 264–269). doi:10.1109/ICOIN.2014.6799479

Cox, M., & Ellsworth, D. (1997). Application-controlled demand paging for out-of-core visualization. *Proceedings. Visualization '97 (Cat. No. 97CB36155)*.

Cyan. (2015). Z-Series. *Cyan*. Retrieved May 13, 2015, from http://www.cyaninc.com/products/z-series-packet-optical

Dai, Y., Qi, Y., Ren, J., Shi, Y., Wang, X., & Yu, X. (2013). A lightweight VMM on many core for high performance computing. *ACM SIGPLAN Notices*, 48(7), 111-120. Retrieved May 15, 2015, from http://dl.acm.org/citation.cfm?doid=2517326.2451535

Davenport, T. H., Harris, J. G., & Morison, R. (2010). *Analytics at Work: Smarter Decisions, Better Results*. Harvard Business School Press Books. Retrieved May 15, 2015, from http://www.amazon.com/dp/1422177696

Davenport, T. H., & Patil, D. J. (2012). Data scientist: The sexiest job of the 21st century. *Harvard Business Review, 90*(10), 70–76. PMID:23074866

Dean, J., & Ghemawat, S. (2008). MapReduce : Simplified Data Processing on Large Clusters. *Communications of the ACM, 51*(1), 1–13. doi:10.1145/1327452.1327492

Diebold, F. X. (2012). A Personal Perspective on the Origin(s) and Development of "Big Data": The Phenomenon, the Term, and the Discipline, Second Version. *SSRN Electronic Journal*. Retrieved May 15, 2015, from http://econpapers.repec.org/RePEc:pen:papers:13-003

Feamster, N. (2014). *Software Defined Networking*. Retrieved July 15, 2014, from Available from https://www.coursera.org/course/sdn

Feamster, N., & Balakrishnan, H. (2005). Detecting BGP configuration faults with static analysis. In *Proc. Networked Systems Design and Implementation*, (pp. 49–56). Retrieved May 15, 2015, from http://www.usenix.org/event/nsdi05/tech/feamster/feamster_html/

Feamster, N., Rexford, J., Shenker, S., Clark, R., Hutchins, R., Levin, D., & Bailey, J. (1986). SDX: A Software-Defined Internet Exchange. *Proceedings IETF 86*. Retrieved May 13, 2015, from http://www.ietf.org/proceedings/86/slides/slides-86-sdnrg-6

Feamster, N., Rexford, J., & Zegura, E. (2013). The Road to SDN. *Queue, 11*(12), 20–40. Retrieved May 15, 2015, from http://dl.acm.org/citation.cfm?doid=2559899.2560327

Foster, N., Guha, A., Reitblatt, M., Story, A., Freedman, M. J., Katta, N. P., & Harrison, R. et al. (2013). Languages for software-defined networks. *IEEE Communications Magazine, 51*(2), 128–134. doi:10.1109/MCOM.2013.6461197

Gladstone Institute University of California at San Francisco. (2014). GenMAPP. *GenMAPP*. Retrieved May 13, 2015, from http://www.genmapp.org/about.html

Greenberg, B. A., Hamilton, J. R., Kandula, S., Kim, C., Lahiri, P., & Maltz, A. … Maltz, D. A. (2009). VL2: a scalable and flexible data center network. In *Proceedings of the ACM SIGCOMM 2009 Conference on Data Communication* (Vol. 9, pp. 51–62). ACM. Retrieved May 15, 2015, from http://doi.acm.org/10.1145/1592568.1592576

Grefenstette, E., Blunsom, P., De Freitas, N., & Hermann, K. M. (2014). A Deep Architecture for Semantic Parsing. In *ACL Workshop on Semantic Parsing* (pp. 22–27). doi:10.3115/v1/W14-2405

Hall, M., National, H., Frank, E., Holmes, G., Pfahringer, B., Reutemann, P., & Witten, I. H. (2009). The WEKA Data Mining Software : An Update. *SIGKDD Explorations, 11*(1), 10–18. doi:10.1145/1656274.1656278

Hirschberg, J. (1998). *"Every time I fire a linguist, my performance goes up", and other myths of the statistical natural language processing revolution*. Paper presented at the 15th National Conference on Artificial Intelligence, Madison, WI.

Hurlburt, G. F., & Voas, J. (2014). Big data, networked worlds. *Computer, 47*(4), 84–87. doi:10.1109/MC.2014.82

Iyyer, M., Boyd-Graber, J., Claudino, L., Socher, R., & Daumé, H. III. (2014). A Multi-Sentence Neural Network for Connecting Textual Descriptions to Entities. In *Conference on Empirical Methods in Natural Language Processing (EMNLP 2014).*

Jain, S., Kumar, A., & Mandal, S. (2013). B4: Experience with a globally-deployed software defined WAN. *Sigcomm*, 3–14. Retrieved May 15, 2015, from http://dl.acm.org/citation.cfm?id=2486019

Jarraya, Y., Madi, T., & Debbabi, M. (2014). A Survey and a Layered Taxonomy of Software-Defined Networking. *IEEE Communications Surveys and Tutorials, 16*(4), 1955–1980. doi:10.1109/COMST.2014.2320094

Jelinek, F. (2005). Some of my best friends are linguists. *Language Resources and Evaluation, 39*(1), 25–34. doi:10.1007/s10579-005-2693-4

Juniper. (2013). *Integrating SDN into the Data Center.* White Paper. Retrieved May 15, 2015, from http://www.juniper.net/us/en/local/pdf/whitepapers/2000542-en.pdf

Kazemian, P., Change, M., & Zheng, H. (2013). Real Time Network Policy Checking Using Header Space Analysis. *USENIX Symposium on Networked Systems Design and Implementation.* Retrieved May 15, 2015, from http://yuba.stanford.edu/~peyman/docs/net_plumber-nsdi13.pdf

Koller, R., Verma, A., & Rangaswami, R. (2011). Estimating application cache requirement for provisioning caches in virtualized systems. In *IEEE International Workshop on Modeling, Analysis, and Simulation of Computer and Telecommunication Systems - Proceedings* (pp. 55–62). doi:10.1109/MASCOTS.2011.67

Koponen, T., Amidon, K., Balland, P., Casado, M., Chanda, A., & Fulton, B. … Zhang, R. (2014). Network Virtualization in Multi-tenant Datacenters. In *Proceedings of the 11th USENIX Symposium on Networked Systems Design and Implementation (NSDI 14)* (pp. 203–216). USENIX. Retrieved May 15, 2015, from http://blogs.usenix.org/conference/nsdi14/technical-sessions/presentation/koponen

Kreutz, D., & Ramos, F. (2014). Software-Defined Networking: A Comprehensive Survey. *arXiv Preprint arXiv:* …, 49. Retrieved May 15, 2015, from http://arxiv.org/abs/1406.0440

Kumar, H., Gharakheili, H. H., & Sivaraman, V. (2013). User control of quality of experience in home networks using SDN. In *Advanced Networks and Telecommunications Systems (ANTS), 2013 IEEE International Conference on* (pp. 1–6). doi:10.1109/ANTS.2013.6802847

Lange, J. R., Pedretti, K., Dinda, P., Bridges, P. G., Bae, C., Soltero, P., & Merritt, A. (2011). *Minimal-overhead virtualization of a large scale supercomputer.* ACM SIGPLAN Notices. doi:10.1145/1952682.1952705

Lara, A., Kolasani, A., & Ramamurthy, B. (2013). Network Innovation using OpenFlow: A Survey. *IEEE Communications Surveys & Tutorials*, (99), 1–20. Retrieved May 15, 2015, from http://ieeexplore.ieee.org/lpdocs/epic03/wrapper.htm?arnumber=6587999

Linden, G., Smith, B., & York, J. (2003). Amazon.com recommendations: Item-to-item collaborative filtering. *IEEE Internet Computing, 7*(1), 76–80. doi:10.1109/MIC.2003.1167344

Marx, V. (2013). Biology: The big challenges of big data. *Nature*, *498*(7453), 255–260. doi:10.1038/498255a PMID:23765498

McAfee, A., & Brynjolfsson, E. (2012). Big Data. The management revolution. *Harvard Business Review, 90*(10), 61–68. Retrieved May 15, 2015, from http://www.buyukverienstitusu.com/s/1870/i/Big_Data_2.pdf

Michael, K., & Miller, K. W. (2013). Big Data: New Opportunities and New Challenges. *Computer*, *46*(6), 22–24. doi:10.1109/MC.2013.196

Miller, K. W., & St, M. (2013). Big Data : New Opportunities and New Challenges. *Computer*, *46*(6), 22–24. doi:10.1109/MC.2013.196

Monsanto, C., Reich, J., Foster, N., Rexford, J., & Walker, D. (2013). Composing software-defined networks. In *Proceedings of the 10th USENIX Conference on Networked Systems Design and Implementation*. Retrieved May 15, 2015, from http://dl.acm.org/citation.cfm?id=2482626.2482629

Nature. (2008). Community cleverness required. *Nature, 455*(7209), 1.

Naudts, B., Kind, M., Westphal, F. J., Verbrugge, S., Colle, D., & Pickavet, M. (2012). Techno-economic analysis of software defined networking as architecture for the virtualization of a mobile network. In *Proceedings - European Workshop on Software Defined Networks, EWSDN 2012* (pp. 67–72). doi:10.1109/EWSDN.2012.27

Nelson, T., Ferguson, A. D., Scheer, M. J. G., & Krishnamurthi, S. (2014). Tierless Programming and Reasoning for Software-Defined Networks. In *Proceedings of the 11th USENIX Symposium on Networked Systems Design and Implementation (NSDI 14)* (pp. 519–531). USENIX. Retrieved May 15, 2015, from http://blogs.usenix.org/conference/nsdi14/technical-sessions/presentation/nelson

Niranjan Mysore, R., Pamboris, A., Farrington, N., Huang, N., Miri, P., & Radhakrishnan, S. … Mysore, R. N. (2009). PortLand: a scalable fault-tolerant layer 2 data center network fabric. In *SIGCOMM '09 Proceedings of the ACM SIGCOMM 2009 Conference on Data Communication* (pp. 39–50). ACM. Retrieved May 15, 2015, from http://doi.acm.org/10.1145/1592568.1592575

Nunes, B. A. A., Mendonca, M., Nguyen, X. N., Obraczka, K., & Turletti, T. (2014). A Survey of Software-Defined Networking: Past, Present, and Future of Programmable Networks. *IEEE Communications Surveys and Tutorials*, *16*(3), 1617–1634. doi:10.1109/SURV.2014.012214.00180

Parise, S., Iyer, B., & Vesset, D. (2012). Four Strategies to Capture and Create Value from Big Data. *Ivey Business Journal, 76*(4), 1–5. Retrieved May 15, 2015, from http://search.ebscohost.com/login.aspx?direct=true&db=bth&AN=78946504&site=bsi-live

Pentikousis, K., Wang, Y., & Hu, W. (2013). Mobileflow: Toward software-defined mobile networks. *IEEE Communications Magazine*, *51*(7), 44–53. doi:10.1109/MCOM.2013.6553677

Perry, J., Ousterhout, A., Balakrishnan, H., Shah, D., & Fugal, H. (2014). Fastpass: A Centralized "Zero-Queue" Datacenter Network. In Sigcomm (pp. 307-318). doi:10.1145/2619239.2626309

Press, G. (2013). A Very Short History Of Big Data. *Forbes*. Retrieved April 2, 2014, from http://www.forbes.com/sites/gilpress/2013/05/09/a-very-short-history-of-big-data/

Ram, K., Cox, A., Chadha, M., & Rixner, S. (2013). Hyper-Switch: A Scalable Software Virtual Switching Architecture. In USENIX ATC 2013 (pp. 13–24).

Ren, T., & Xu, Y. (2014). Analysis of the New Features of OpenFlow 1.4. In *2nd International Conference on Information, Electronics and Computer* (pp. 73-77). doi:10.2991/icieac-14.2014.17

Rysavy, S. J., Bromley, D., & Daggett, V. (2014). DIVE: A graph-based visual-analytics framework for big data. *IEEE Computer Graphics and Applications*, *34*(2), 26–37. doi:10.1109/MCG.2014.27 PMID:24808197

Saleem, H. M., Hassan, M. F., & Asirvadam, V. S. (2011). P2P service discovery in clouds with message level intelligence. In *2011 National Postgraduate Conference - Energy and Sustainability: Exploring the Innovative Minds, NPC 2011*.

Schlinker, B. (2014). *Mininext*. Retrieved May 13, 2015, from https://github.com/USC-NSL/miniNeXT

Sherwood, R., Gibb, G., Yap, K. K.-K. K., Appenzeller, G., Casado, M., McKeown, N., & Parulkar, G. M. (2010). Can the Production Network Be the Testbed? In R. H. Arpaci-Dusseau & B. Chen (Eds.), *9th USENIX Symposium on Operating Systems Design and Implementation, OSDI 2010, October 4-6, 2010, Vancouver, BC, Canada, Proceedings* (Vol. M, pp. 365–378). USENIX Association. Retrieved May 15, 2015, from http://static.usenix.org/legacy/events/osdi10/tech/full_papers/Sherwood.pdf

Socher, R., Karpathy, A., Le, Q. V., Manning, C. D., & Ng, A. Y. (2014). Grounded Compositional Semantics for Finding and Describing Images with Sentences. *Transactions of the Association for Computational Linguistics*, *2*(April), 207–218.

Socher, R., & Lin, C. (2011). Parsing natural scenes and natural language with recursive neural networks. *Proceedings of the 28th International Conference on Machine Learning (ICML 2011)*, (pp. 129–136). http://nlp.stanford.edu/pubs/SocherLinNgManning_ICML2011.pdf

Soyata, T., Ba, H., Heinzelman, W., Kwon, M., & Shi, J. (2014). Accelerating Mobile-Cloud Computing. In Communication Infrastructures for Cloud Computing (pp. 175–197). doi:10.4018/978-1-4666-4522-6.ch008

Sundaresan, S., Teixeira, R., Tech, G., Feamster, N., Pescapè, A., & Crawford, S. (2011). Broadband Internet Performance : A View From the Gateway. *Computer Communication Review*, *41*(4), 134–145. doi:10.1145/2043164.2018452

The Apache Software Foundation. (2014a). Apache Hadoop Project. *Hadoop*. Retrieved February 18, 2014, from http://hadoop.apache.org

The Apache Software Foundation. (2014b). Apache Mahout Project. *Mahout*. Retrieved July 18, 2014, from https://mahout.apache.org

The Apache Software Foundation. (2014c). Apache Cassandra Database. *Cassandra*. Retrieved February 18, 2014, from http://cassandra.apache.org/

The Open Networking Foundation. (2013). *OpenFlow Switch Specification, Version 1.4.0*. Retrieved April 10, 2014, from https://www.opennetworking.org/images/stories/downloads/sdn-resources/onf-specifications/openflow/openflow-spec-v1.4.0.pdf

Vissicchio, S., Vanbever, L., & Bonaventure, O. (2014). Opportunities and research challenges of hybrid software defined networks. *Computer Communication Review, 44*(2), 70–75. doi:10.1145/2602204.2602216

Waldrop, M. (2008). Big data: Wikiomics. *Nature, 455*(7209), 22–25. doi:10.1038/455022a PMID:18769412

Wang, H., Liu, W., & Soyata, T. (2014). Accessing Big Data in the Cloud Using Mobile Devices. In P. I. S. R. Hershey (Ed.), *Handbook of Research on Cloud Infrastructures for Big Data Analytics* (pp. 444–470). doi:10.4018/978-1-4666-5864-6.ch018

Ward, J. S., & Barker, A. (2013). *Undefined By Data: A Survey of Big Data Definitions*. Retrieved May 15, 2015, from http://arxiv.org/abs/1309.5821

Yiakoumis, Y., Yap, K.-K., Katti, S., Parulkar, G., & McKeown, N. (2011). Slicing home networks. In *Proceedings of the 2nd ACM SIGCOMM workshop on Home networks - HomeNets '11* (pp. 1-6). doi:10.1145/2018567.2018569

Zhou, R., & Li, T. (2013). Leveraging Phase Change Memory to Achieve Efficient Virtual Machine Execution. In *International Conference on Virtual Execution Environments (VEE)* (pp. 179-190). doi:10.1145/2451512.2451547

KEY TERMS AND DEFINITIONS

Big Data: The term that represents data sets that are extremely large to handle through traditional methods. Big data represents information that has such a high volume, velocity, variety, variability, veracity and complexity that require specific mechanisms to produce real value from it in a timely way.

Intelligent Data Management: A set of solutions to help organizations reduce cost, complexity, and time when they aim to analyze their data in order to extract some well identified usefulness.

IXP: It is an Internet location where normally multiple Internet service providers connect theirs networks to exchange traffic messages. This exchange is made possible by a routing path vector protocol, i.e. BGP.

JSON: The Javascript Object Notation (JSON) is a language-independent and open data format that can be used to transmit human-readable text-based object information, across domains, using an attribute-value pair's notation and easy-to-access manner.

Machine Learning: It is a type of Artificial Intelligence (AI) that provides computers with the ability to learn without being explicitly programmed. Machine learning explores the construction and study of algorithms that can learn from and make predictions on data.

SDN: Software Defined Networking (SDN) allows logically centralized controllers to manage network services through the decoupling of system control from the underlying traffic exchange. Some advantages of using SDN are decreasing the maintenance cost and fostering innovation on networking infrastructures.

Text Mining: A process of extracting relevant knowledge from large collections of unstructured text documents. In this way, text mining usually involves the process of structuring the input text, deriving patterns within the structured data, and finally evaluation and interpretation of the output.

Chapter 7
Big Data Mining Based on Computational Intelligence and Fuzzy Clustering

Usman Akhtar
Air University – Multan, Pakistan

Mehdi Hassan
Air University – Multan, Pakistan

ABSTRACT

The availability of a huge amount of heterogeneous data from different sources to the Internet has been termed as the problem of Big Data. Clustering is widely used as a knowledge discovery tool that separate the data into manageable parts. There is a need of clustering algorithms that scale on big databases. In this chapter we have explored various schemes that have been used to tackle the big databases. Statistical features have been extracted and most important and relevant features have been extracted from the given dataset. Reduce and irrelevant features have been eliminated and most important features have been selected by genetic algorithms (GA).Clustering with reduced feature sets requires lower computational time and resources. Experiments have been performed at standard datasets and results indicate that the proposed scheme based clustering offers high clustering accuracy. To check the clustering quality various quality measures have been computed and it has been observed that the proposed methodology results improved significantly. It has been observed that the proposed technique offers high quality clustering.

1. INTRODUCTION

The era of petabyte (10^{15}) has almost gone, leaving us to confront of zettabytes (10^{21}) era. Technology uprising has been facilitating millions of people all around the globe to generate tremendous amount of data via ever-increased used of variety of digital technology that generate continuous streams of data. A recent survey by New Vantage Partner (Davenport, 2013) reports that "It is about variety, not volume", but many people still believe that the issue with big data is either scale or volume. Big data involves

DOI: 10.4018/978-1-4666-8505-5.ch007

variety of data forms like text, images, videos, and sounds etc. It is estimated that nearly twenty percent of data available to enterprises is structured in nature and other eighty percent is unstructured data. (Judith Hurwitz, April 2013).

From the data mining perspective, big data has opened many new challenges and opportunities. Even big data involves hidden knowledge and insights; it brings many new issues to extract these hidden insight patterns. The traditional processes of knowledge discovery processes are not well suited for big data. In general, the existing data mining techniques encounter difficulties when they are require handling heterogeneity, volume, privacy, and accuracy. KDD is a knowledge discovery data process of unveiling hidden knowledge and insights from a large volume of data (Fayyad, Piatetsky-Shapiro, & Smyth, 1996), when it comes to extract useful information from big data then it became a most interesting and challenging step. Another problem that arises in the data mining algorithms is to inadequate scalability of the algorithms that do not matches the 3-Vs (variety, velocity, and volume) of the emerging big data. Big data not only brings new challenges, but it also brings new opportunities. Big data would become a useless monster if we don't have the right tools to harness its "wildness"(Che, Safran, & Peng, 2013). Current data mining techniques are not ready to meet new challenges of big data.

In data mining, the conventional data mining algorithms have difficulties in handling the challenges drawn by the unstructured data which is often vague and uncertain. For the pattern recognition and data mining, clustering is mostly used to search in very large databases. So, there is a need of clustering algorithms that used to search large datasets (Havens, Bezdek, Leckie, Hall, & Palaniswami, 2012).In clustering each group share some similarity and clustering is a form of data analysis.

2. BIG DATA CHARACTERISTICS

Big Data involves large datasets which are complex and cannot easily analyzed, interprets, and processed further (Sagiroglu & Sinanc, 2013). Big Data concern large-volume, complex growing datasets with multiple, autonomous sources of data generation (Xindong, Xingquan, Gong-Qing, & Wei, 2014). Big Data is usually in large volume and heterogeneous characteristics of Big Data that is extremely challenging for discovering useful information. The main attributes of Big Data are volume, velocity, and variety. Volume is one of the main features of Big Data that are massive in scale and usually generated in every second. It is a scale characteristic. Another attributes are velocity or speed such as social media data. Variety is one of the main attribute of big data that is heterogeneous in nature. It includes different types such as text data, images and multi-dimensional arrays data.

3. DATA MINING CHALLENGES WITH BIG DATA

The goals of the data mining techniques go beyond extracting requested information or even hidden patterns and it must deal with heterogeneity, scalability, and accuracy. There is a need for designing and implementing large scale machine learning and data mining algorithms which accomplish the processing of very large scale data. There are two main challenging areas for big data mining. These areas are computing platform problem, and big data mining algorithms problem.

Big Data mining platform is a major challenge on data accessing and processing. Big Data often stored at different locations and volume of data is continuously growing. An effective computing platform is highly desirable. Typical data mining algorithms load all the data into the main memory, this however a clear technical barrier for Big Data even you have a very massive amount of main memory to grasp all data for computing. Single processor is enough for the small scale data mining tasks to fulfill data mining goals. For the medium scale data mining tasks, data is typical large cannot be fit into the main memory. Common solutions are parallel computing or collective mining to sample and then aggregate data from different sources. For big data mining, data scale is beyond the capability of a single processor to handle so typical solution relies on cluster computing with high performance computing platform. Data mining tasks deploy some parallel programming tools such as MapReduce or large number of computing nodes.

Current data mining algorithms are not ready to meet the new challenges of big data. Sparse, uncertain, and incomplete data are the main attributes when dealing with big data applications. High-dimensional space issues deteriorate the reliability of the models. Common approaches are to sample the data and then extract features and then apply approaches to achieve high accuracy. Uncertain is a special type of data in which data fields are not easily deterministic. For Example data produced from GPS (Global Positioning System) equipment are inherently uncertain in nature.

4. BACKGROUND AND RELATED WORK

Currently the Big Data processing depend on the parallel programming model like MapReduce(Dean & Ghemawat, 2008). MapReduce is batch-oriented parallel computing models and it is widely applied in machine learning and data mining algorithms. Cheng-Tao Chu(Cheng T. Chu, 2006)proposed a programming model for machine learning which is based on MapReduce programming model. For the very large data several algorithms have been proposed LFCM (literal fuzzy c-means)and generalized extensible fast FCM (geFFCM)(Hathaway & Bezdek, 2006). Literal scheme simply cluster the entire dataset. The geFFCM algorithm is based on progressive sampling technique that reduce the dataset and then cluster the reduce dataset. However, geFFCM is another sampling method that can be inefficient and it is not sufficient for Big Data. Single-pass algorithm(Hore, Hall, & Goldgof, 2007)consists of small amount of data and then cluster these data set into manageable sizes and then finally combine all the chunks. P.Hore proposed online fuzzy c-mean (oFCM)(Hore, Hall, Goldgof, & Cheng, 2008)which is incremental algorithm to compute an approximate fuzzy c-mean solution. Moreover, data transformation algorithms have been proposed efficiently accessed it uses bin strategy for data reduction. Many kernel-based strategy has been applied which is called approximate kernel fuzzy c-mean(akFCM)(Havens, Chitta, Jain, & Rong, 2011) which uses sample rows to kernel matrix to determine the c-means problem and it successfully reduces the computational complexity of c-means algorithms(Chaudhry, Hassan, Khan, & Kim, 2013; Chaudhry, Hassan, Khan, Kim, & Tuan, 2013).

5. CLUSTER ANALYSIS

Cluster analysis is used to group similar objects and then organize these data into specified number of groups. Clustering techniques are usually among the unsupervised methods that do not have any previous identifiers.

1. **Cluster Partition:** Cluster can normally consider as subsets of the data set. One possible partitioning is according to the whether the subsets of the data are fuzzy or crisp. Some of the partitioning types are crisp, fuzzy (or probabilistic), and Possiblistic.
2. **Crisp Clustering of Unlabeled Objects:** Is non-empty subsets of mutually disjoint subsets. In crisp clustering the union of the subset is equal to zero.
3. **Fuzzy Clustering:** Are more flexible then crisp methods. In fuzzy clustering there is concept of degree of membership objects belong to several clusters with different degree of membership. Each column of the fuzzy portioning sum must equal to 1.
4. **Possiblistic Partition:** Relaxes the condition that do not allow partition columns necessary sum to 1.

6. CLUSTERING METHODS

Partitioning is one of the most fundamental versions of cluster analysis in which several objects are organizes *(Han, 2005)*. In partitioning method number of clusters is already given. Formally, D is the given set of n objects and k is the number of clusters and then partitioning algorithms manage the objects into k a partition which are given as (k ≤ n), in this each partition represent a cluster.

a) K-Means Clustering Algorithm

K-means is hard clustering algorithms. Suppose D is a dataset in Euclidean space and n is the number of objects. The objects are distributed into k clusters with partitioning methods. To check the quality of the cluster objective function is assessed in which similar objects belong to a cluster and these objects are not belongs to other cluster. High intra-cluster and low inter-cluster similarity is the objective function aims.

$$E = \sum_{i=1}^{k} \sum_{p \in C} D\left(p, c_i\right)^2 \tag{1}$$

In Equation 1, E represents the sum of squared error and c are the centroids of clusters and p represents the point in space. D shows that the datasets and k is the number of clusters (Algorithm 1).

Algorithm 1. K-means

```
Input: K, D_i
Output: A set of K cluster
Initialize: V
1. Arbitrary choose k objects from D as the initial cluster centers;
2. Repeat
3. (Re)assign each object to the cluster to which the object is the most simi-
lar, based on the mean value of the objects in the cluster
4. Update the cluster means; that is, calculate the mean value of the objects
for each cluster
5. Until no change.
```

b) Fuzzy C-Means Algorithm

For clustering and feature analysis fuzzy C-means clustering is normally applied. Fuzzy C-means is soft clustering algorithm in which object belongs to one or more cluster with different degree of membership and regions are also overlapped.(Chaudhry, Hassan, Khan, Kim, & Tuan, 2012).

For the big data there are three different implementation techniques aims to extend the Fuzzy C-means (FCM) clustering to very large (VL) data(Hassan, Chaudhry, Khan, & Iftikhar, 2014). These techniques are based on the following:

1. Sampling Followed by Non-iterative Extensions (Havens, et al., 2012).
2. Incremental Techniques with sequence pass.
3. Kernelized version of Fuzzy C-means (FCM).

In Fuzzy C-means object got the different degree of membership and object belongs to two or more clusters. The FCM method was developed by Dunn (Dunn, 1973) and the improved version of this algorithm is proposed by Bezdek (Bezdek, 1981). Fuzzy C-means (FCM) (Hassan, Chaudhry, Khan, Iftikhar, & Kim, 2013) is based on following objective function (See Algorithm 2):

$$J_m(U,V) = \sum_{i=1}^{c}\sum_{j=1}^{n} u_{ij}^m \parallel X_j - v_i \parallel_A^2 \tag{2}$$

where U is the (c x n) partition matrix, $V = \left\{v_1,\ldots,v_c\right\}$ is the set of c cluster center in $R_d, m > 1$ is the fuzzification constant, and $\parallel . \parallel_A$ is any inner product A-induced norm. μ_{ij} and v_i are iterated until algorithms terminates, where termination is declared when there are only negligible changes in the cluster locations: $\max_1 \leq k \leq \left\{\parallel v_k, new - v_k, old \parallel^2\right\} > \in$, where $\in$ is predetermined constant. We use $\in = 10^{-3}$ in our experimentation.

Algorithm 2. Fuzzy c-means

```
Input: X, c, m
Output: U,V
Initialize: V
```
$While: \max_1 \leq \left\{\parallel v_{k,new} - v_{k,old} \parallel^2\right\} > \in do$

$$\mu_{ij} = \left[\sum_{k=1}^{c}\left(\frac{\parallel x_j - v_i \parallel}{\parallel x_j - v_k \parallel}\right)^{\frac{2}{m-1}}\right]^{-1}, \forall i,j$$

$$v_i = \frac{\sum_{j=1}^{n}\left(\mu_{ij}\right)^m x_j}{\sum_{j=1}^{n}\left(\mu_{ij}\right)^m}, \forall i$$

c) Kernel Versions of K-Mean and Fuzzy C-Means

But there are some disadvantages associated with the kernel based clustering when the data dimensionality increase then the computational complexity is the major problem. Most of the existing methods for large scale clustering are based on the Euclidean distance, and are therefore, unable to deal with the data sets that are not linearly separable. Kernel based clustering techniques address this limitation by introducing a kernel distance function to capture the nonlinear structure in data. Various kernel based clustering algorithms have been developed, including kernel K-means. A key challenge faced by all the kernel-based algorithms is scalability as they require computing the full kernel matrix whose size is quadratic in the number of data points.

The kernel and the fuzzy algorithm can be representing by adjusting the parameter in objective function. We can also donate the center of the cluster using $d_k(v_j, \mathbf{X}_i)$ as $d_k(j, i)$.

i. Kernel K-Means

Let $X = \{x1, x2, ..., xn\}$ be the input data set consisting of n data points, where $x_i \in \Re^d$, C be the number of clusters and $K \in \Re^{n \times n}$ be the kernel matrix with $K_{ij} = \kappa(xi, xj)$ where $\kappa(\cdot, \cdot)$ is the kernel function. Let H_k belongs to Reproducing Kernel Hilbert Space (RKHS) and it uses kernel function $\kappa(\cdot, \cdot)$, and $\left| \cdot \right|_{Hk}$ be the functional norm for H_k. Kernel k-means objective is to reduce the clustering errors. Table 1 shows the hard and fuzzy variations to solve the c-means optimization. In hard partition m is equal to 1, as object only belong to one cluster. For the soft clustering algorithm the fuzzification constant is greater than 1 as object may belong to more than one clusters.

Hard clustering membership function:

$$u_{ij} = \{_{0,}^{1,} d_k(j, i) = \min_1 \le k \le d_k(k, i), \forall j, i \tag{3}$$

Fuzzy c-means membership update:

$$\mu_{ij} = \left[\sum_{k=1}^{c} \left(\frac{d_k(j, i)}{d_k(k, i)} \right)^{\frac{2}{m-1}} \right]^{-1}, \forall i, j \tag{4}$$

Table 1. Hard and Fuzzy variation to solve c-means optimization

Algorithm	m	H	U
Hard (crisp)	m = 1	$v_j = 0, \forall_j$	Using eq. 3
Fuzzy	m > 1	$v_j = 0, \forall_j$	Using eq. 4

Kernel Distance between an object and a cluster:

$$d_k\left(j,i\right) = u_j^T K u_j + K_{ii} - 2\left(u_j^T K\right)_i.$$ (5)

Although this technique handles the memory complexity, it still requires the computation of the full kernel matrix. The objective of our work is to reduce both the computational complexity and the memory requirements of kernel *K*-means (See Algorithm 3).

ii. Kernel Fuzzy C-Means

Consider a non-linear mapping function, in this function D_K is defined as transformed feature vector x. In kernel clustering feature vector x is not explicitly transform, we usually need to simplify the dot product $\Phi\left(x\right).\Phi\left(x\right) = k\left(x,x\right)$. There are many forms of kernel function some are polynomial and radial basis function (RBF) $k\left(x,y\right) = \exp\left(\left\|x-y\right\|^2\right)/\sigma$. Construct the kernel matrix of n objects $K = \left[K_{ij} = k\left(x_i,x_j\right)\right]^{n\times n}$. This kernel matrix usually represents all pairwise dot products. These dot products are associated with the feature vectors in the high dimensional space called Reproducing Kernel Hilbert Space (RKHS).

Algorithm 3. Kernel K-means

```
Input:  K − n × n  kernel matrix
Data:  m = 1, U ∈ {0,1}^{c×n}  cluster membership matrix
Initialize:  U
While:  max{|U − U'|} > 0  do
U' = U
Compare  d_k(j,i), ∀i,j,  using Eq. (5)
Update  U using Eq. (3)
```

Algorithm 4. Kernel Fuzzy C-Means

```
Input:  K − n × n  kernel matrix m - fuzzifier
Data:  U ∈ [0,1]^{c×n}  cluster membership matrix
Initialize:  U
While:  max{|U − U'|} > 0  do
U' = U
Compare  d_k(j,i), ∀i,j,  using Eq. (5)
Update  U using Eq. (4)
```

7. METHODOLOGY

Our aim is to cluster the data using fuzzy approaches along with dimensionality reduction algorithms by employing computational intelligence techniques. Dimensionality reduction can be achieved by using the genetic algorithms (GA); it allows a flexible representation of modeling criteria, tradeoffs amongst multiple objectives. We have proposed two different schemes these are feature extraction and the other scheme is feature selection. For the effectiveness of the proposed scheme, we have used different clustering quality measure indices. Our proposed techniques outperform the other techniques at all quality measures.

a) Feature Extraction

In order to increase classification/clustering accuracy, feature extraction is a process of deriving new features from the original data. Feature extraction increases the clustering accuracy (Raymer, Punch, Goodman, Kuhn, & Jain, 2000). In our proposed scheme we have exploited the statistical feature extraction strategy. After the feature extraction, GA has been utilized for selection of most relevant and important features.

Statistical moments are frequently used for texture analysis. The nth order moment about mean is calculated by the following expression:

$$u_n = \sum_{i=0}^{L-1} \left(z_i - m \right)^n . p\left(z_i \right) \tag{6}$$

Figure 1. Workflow of the proposed technique

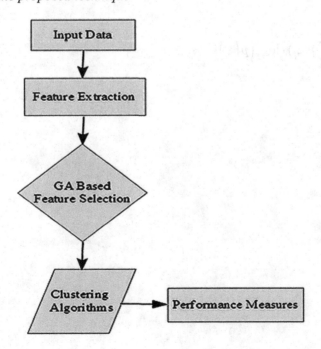

where z indicates the change in intensity and $p\left(z_i\right)$ represent the histogram intensity in this region. L is the number of possible intensity levels, and m is the mean intensity. To calculate the moment of histogram we have the following formulas:

$$\text{Mean} = \text{FM1} = \sum_{i=0}^{L-1} z_i . p\left(z_i\right) \tag{7}$$

$$\text{Standard Deviation} = \text{FM2} = \sqrt{u_2} \tag{8}$$

$$\text{Smoothness} = \text{FM3} = 1 + \frac{1}{1+\sigma} \tag{9}$$

$$\text{Third Moment} = \text{FM4} = \sum_{i=0}^{L-1}\left(z_i - m\right)^3 . p\left(z_i\right) \tag{10}$$

$$\text{Uniformity} = \text{FM5} = \sum_{i=0}^{L-1} p^2\left(z_i\right) \tag{11}$$

$$\text{Entropy} = \text{FM6} = -\sum_{i=0}^{L-1} p(z_i) \cdot \log_2\left(p\left(z_i\right)\right) \tag{12}$$

$$\text{FM7} = \sum_{i=0}^{L-1} p^3\left(z_i\right) \tag{13}$$

$$\text{FM8} = \sum_{i=0}^{L-1} p^4\left(z_i\right) \tag{14}$$

$$\text{FM9} = \sum_{i=0}^{L-1} p^5\left(z_i\right) \tag{15}$$

The above mentioned Moment of Gray Level Histogram (MGH) is extracted from the data and is used for clustering. Some of the moments like FM7, FM8, and FM9 are taken from another research paper related to statistical features (Hassan, et al., 2012; Sheshadri & Kandaswamy, 2007).

b) Genetic Algorithm in Feature Selection

Genetic Algorithm has been successfully applied successfully too many problems and also applied in pattern recognition and classification. The problem of dimensionality reduction is well suitable to handle with Genetic Algorithm. Feature optimization is being used to reduce the feature space which increases the computational time. Feature selection is normally achieved by eliminating irrelevant, redundant, and noisy features. Higher dimensional data need more computational time. To achieve better performance and reduces the computational cost then select those features that are most significant and eliminate the redundant features. Many search methods are available to select the most important features. In our research we have extracted nine features. Genetic search approach is mostly used to optimize the features and then given these features to the algorithms for clustering. WEKA (Holmes, Donkin, & Witten, 1994) is a machine learning tool this is uses genetic search method. We have shortlisted five features using GA these are given in Table 2.

We have used the following parameters of GA, population selected as 100. Mutation and the Crossover are given as 0.033 and 0.7, respectively.

8. EVALUATION CRITERIA

In our research work following are the performance measures indices.

i. Partition Coefficient (PC)

The validity measure partition Coefficient developed by J.C. Bezdek (Bezdek†, 1973)and normally measures the overlapping between clusters. We can calculate the partition coefficient with following equation:

$$PC = \frac{\sum_j^N \sum_i^c \mu_{ij}^2}{N} \tag{16}$$

where μ_{ij} represents the fuzzy membership function in cluster i. best clustering is achieved when partition coefficient value becomes maximum.

Table 2. Feature Selected for Clustering by WEKA using Genetic Search Method

Feature Type	Statistical Features
Total Features	09
Number of Selected Feature	05
Name of selected features	Average, relative smoothness, uniformity, measure of randomness, FM8.

ii. Classification Entropy (CE)

Classification entropy is another index that is applied to measure the fuzziness of the cluster lower the value of CE show the best clustering. Classification entropy (CE) is proposed by J.C. Bezdek.

$$CE = -\frac{1}{N}\sum_{i=1}^{c}\sum_{j=1}^{N}\mu_{ij}\log_2\left(\mu_{ij}\right) \qquad (17)$$

where μ_{ij} represents the fuzzy membership of data point j to cluster i. Minimal classification entropy shows the best clustering.

iii. Dunn Index (DI)

Dunn Index is applied on compact and separated clusters and it is calculated by:

$$DI\left(c\right) = \min_{i\in c}\left\{\min_{j\in c,i\neq j}\left\{\frac{\min_{X\in C_i,y\in C_j}d(x,y)}{\max_{k\in c}\left\{\max_{X,yC}d\left(x,y\right)\right\}}\right\}\right\} \qquad (18)$$

Computational time is the only drawback when uses Dunn Index (DI) as the cluster and the number of object increase then it becomes computationally very expensive. A higher Dunn index indicates better clustering.

iv. Davis Bouldin Index (DBI)

Davis Bouldin Index (DBI) is normally applied when there is a need to evaluate clusters internally as it is an internal evaluation scheme. To calculate the Davis Bouldin Index (DBI):

$$DBI = \frac{1}{n}\sum_{i=1}^{n}\max\left\{\frac{S_n\left(Q_i\right)+s_n\left(Q_j\right)}{S\left(Q_i,Q_j\right)}\right\} \qquad (19)$$

where n represents number of cluster s, S_n is a centroid distance. For compact cluster the ratio is small as compared to the well-separated clusters.

9. EXPERIMENTAL RESULTS AND DISCUSSION

We have performed the experiments on three different schemes. Firstly, the experiments performed without the features extraction and feature selection. Secondly, the experiment performed with the feature extraction, uses statistical features with total of nine features extracted from the datasets. In the third experiment we have selected the most important features using GA. All the computations have been performed on Intel core i5 with Matlab version (R2010a).

Datasets:

2DI5: (n = 7500, c = 15, d = 2) It contains 7500 2-D vectors, with a grouping of 15 clusters. Synthetic 2-d data with 7500 vectors and 15 Gaussian clusters with different degree of cluster overlapping (I.Sidoroff).

A-Sets: (n = 3000 vectors, c = 20, d =2) It contains Synthetic two dimensional data with varying number of clusters and vectors(I.Sidoroff).

Scenario I

In Scenario I the proposed scheme has been applied on 2DI5 dataset. The obtained dataset have been given as input to the clustering algorithm without employing any feature extraction strategy. Various clustering quality measures have been computed from clustered data. It has been observed from experiments that all extracted features are not equally important. Some of those have less contribution or some may be redundant. To overcome this problem, important and most relevant features are selected by using GA.

Table 3 shows the clustering quality measures without feature extraction scheme. We have extracted statistical features from given dataset and feed as input to the algorithm.

Clustering has been performed based on the extracted features and various clustering quality measures are computed and shown in Table 4. It is clearly evident that the feature extraction strategy gives outstanding clustering results when measures with performance indices.

Table 3. Performance Measures without Features Extraction on 2DI5

Algorithm	Partition Coefficient (PC)	Classification Entropy (CE)	Dunn Index (DI)	Davis Bouldin Index (DBI)
k-means	-	-	0.2712	0.7957
FCM	0.7117	0.5728	0.1061	0.8955
kernel k-means	-	-	0.0321	0.5538
kernel FCM	0.7055	0.5283	0.2671	0.9447

Table 4. Performance Measures with Features Extraction on 2DI5

Algorithm	Partition Coefficient (PC)	Classification Entropy (CE)	Dunn Index (DI)	Davis Bouldin Index (DBI)
k-means	-	-	0.2936	0.5814
FCM	0.9717	0.0606	0.1671	0.5879
kernel k-means	-	-	0.0434	0.2538
kernel FCM	0.8061	0.3496	0.3271	0.0425

Clustering based on the selected features has been performed and computed clustering quality measures are shown in Table 5, it can be observed that all clustering algorithms yields outstanding results as compared to without feature extraction strategy.

We also shows the graphical representation of our results in Figure 2 and Figure 3. We have utilized the values of Dunn Index and it has been noticed that our scheme outperforms the other schemes as shown in Figure 2.

In Figure 3, we have plotted a comparison based on Davies Bouldin Index (DBI) value. The results indicate that our scheme based on feature selection perform very well on the 2DI5 dataset.

Table 5. Performance Measures with selected features on 2DI5.

Algorithm	Partition Coefficient (PC)	Classification Entropy (CE)	Dunn Index (DI)	Davis Bouldin Index (DBI)
k-means	-	-	0.4184	0.3067
FCM	0.9977	0.0084	0.2771	0.0265
kernel k-means	-	-	0.2114	0.0473
kernel FCM	0.7455	0.4606	0.3621	0.0235

Figure 2. Performance Measures results of Dunn Index (DI) on 2DI5 dataset

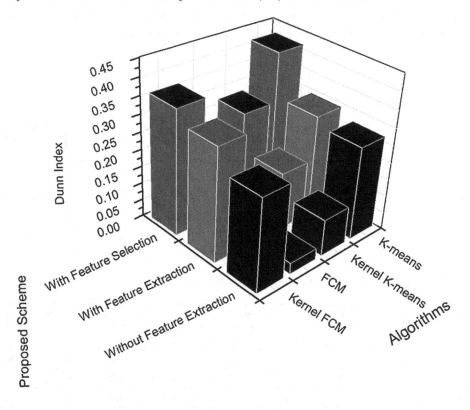

Figure 3. Performance Measure results with Davis Bouldin Index (DBI) on 2DI5 dataset

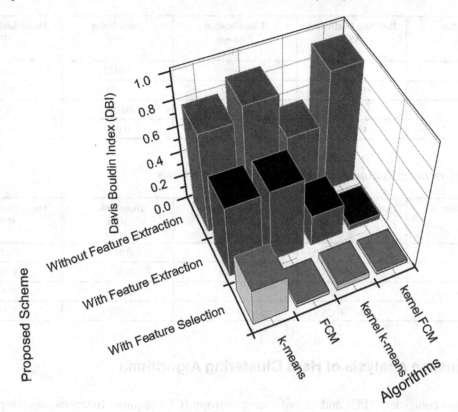

Scenario II

We also performed the computations on another datasets that is taken from machine learning repository. Results are being displayed in tabular form without feature extraction in Table 6, with feature extraction in Table 7 and with feature selection in Table 8. Again the improvements of clustering results have been noticed and our proposed scheme outperform the other scheme.

Table 6. Performance Measures without Features Extraction on A-sets

Algorithm	Partition Coefficient (PC)	Classification Entropy (CE)	Dunn Index (DI)	Davis Bouldin Index (DBI)
k-means	-	-	0.7074	0.7091
FCM	0.6083	1.0371	0.0128	0.6865
kernel k-means	-	-	0.6836	0.0317
kernel FCM	0.5580	1.1462	0.2530	0.9715

Table 7. Performance Measures with Features Extraction on A-sets

Algorithm	Partition Coefficient (PC)	Classification Entropy (CE)	Dunn Index (DI)	Davis Bouldin Index (DBI)
k-means	-	-	0.0127	0.6858
FCM	0.8982	0.2317	0.073	0.5228
kernel k-means	-	-	0.0011	0.0115
kernel FCM	0.8701	0.2820	0.077	0.5450

Table 8. Performance Measures with Feature Selection on A-sets

Algorithm	Partition Coefficient (PC)	Classification Entropy (CE)	Dunn Index (DI)	Davis Bouldin Index (DBI)
k-means	-	-	0.0138	0.6093
FCM	0.8778	0.2787	0.0158	0.5014
kernel k-means	-	-	0.0086	0.0092
kernel FCM	0.8776	0.2802	0.0110	0.4446

a) Performance Analysis of Hard Clustering Algorithms

Both partition coefficient (PC) and classification entropy (CE) requires fuzzy membership function. Dunn's Index (DI) is a matrix for evaluating clustering algorithms and it is usually used for internal evaluation scheme. The aim of the DI is to identify cluster that are compact enough and are well separated. Higher DI indicates better clustering. One of the drawbacks of using the DI is related to the computational cost as the number of cluster and dimensionality of data increases. We have performed three different experiments and measures the DI on two datasets. Our Proposed scheme gives the higher DI value as compared to without feature extraction and selection as shown in Fig 1. Both the k-means and kernel FCM gives the higher DI as compared to the other algorithms. These two algorithms run directly on the datasets without feature extraction techniques. Our proposed scheme also outclasses the results when it measures with the DBI. All the algorithms performed well on the proposed scheme as shown in Fig 2.We are also measures the hard clustering performance on A-sets of datasets this confirms that our proposed scheme gives outstanding results then the other scheme.

b) Performance Analysis of Fuzzy Clustering Algorithms

The purpose of the clustering quality measures is to estimate the goodness of the algorithms or it can be useful to find the optimal number of clusters for datasets in which the number of clusters are not priory known. These quality measures can also be used to compare the performance of different clustering algorithms. FCM must consider both the functionality like compactness and the separation of a fuzzy c-partition (Ramze Rezaee, Lelieveldt, & Reiber, 1998). For the fuzzy clustering PC and CE is used. PC is used to measure the amount of overlapping between clusters. Better Clustering results are obtained when PC becomes maximal. On the other hand, CE measures the fuzziness of the cluster minimum value of CE shows the better clustering. The performance analysis of FCM and Kernel FCM is calculated on 2DI5 and A-sets datasets, without using feature extraction techniques. PC indicates that FCM is better clustering algorithm as compared to Kernel FCM. On the other hand, values of CE are noted on both the datasets 2DI5 and A-sets. The kernel FCM shows the best clustering as compared to FCM as the value of CE is minimal as compared to the FCM. The results of performance analysis with feature extraction scheme are calculated. The PC gives the best results of FCM and Kernel FCM as compared to without feature selection and extraction. On the other hand, CE gives the minimal results when tested on 2DI5 and A-sets. Based on the results of four quality measures our proposed scheme outperforms the other scheme the visual results are shown in Figures 2 and 3 respectively.

10. FUTURE RESEARCH DIRECTION

In future we will continue to investigate the suitable scheme for big data mining based on computational intelligence techniques. We also interested in examine the best use of fuzzy and kernel algorithms for big data. Our aim is to examine the other cluster validity indices for large datasets. As many cluster validity measures are not suitable for the big data as these require the full access of the objects. Hence we are interested to extend some well-known clustering validity measures. These objectives are the main focus of our ongoing research work.

11. CONCLUSION

In this chapter we have proposed a scheme for clustering the big data. In proposed scheme, nine statistical features are extracted in which five most important features are selected using genetic algorithm. Clustering in high dimensional feature space requires more computational time and resources. Some features are less contributing in clustering which negatively affect the clustering quality. In order to get the optimized features WEKA using genetic algorithm is used for feature selection. In our research work five most important features are selected and then given as the input to the algorithm. Four algorithm k-means, kernel k-means, fuzzy c-means and kernel fuzzy c-means are used to cluster the dataset. Both the hard and fuzzy clustering algorithms outperform based on proposed scheme as compared to the without feature extraction and selection scheme respectively. Our proposed scheme has shown the outstanding results when measures the four cluster indices *PC, CE, DI and DBI*.

REFERENCES

Bezdek, J. C. (1981). *Pattern Recognition with Fuzzy Objective Function Algorithms*. Kluwer Academic Publishers.

Bezdek†, J. C. (1973). Cluster Validity with Fuzzy Sets. Journal of Cybernetics, 3(3), 58–73.

Chaudhry, A., Hassan, M., Khan, A., & Kim, J. Y. (2013). Automatic active contour-based segmentation and classification of carotid artery ultrasound images. *Journal of Digital Imaging*, 26(6), 1071–1081. doi:10.1007/s10278-012-9566-3 PMID:23417308

Chaudhry, A., Hassan, M., Khan, A., Kim, J. Y., & Tuan, T. A. (2012). *Image clustering using improved spatial fuzzy C-means*. Paper presented at the 6th International Conference on Ubiquitous Information Management and Communication. doi:10.1145/2184751.2184853

Chaudhry, A., Hassan, M., Khan, A., Kim, J. Y., & Tuan, T. A. (2013). *Automatic segmentation and decision making of carotid artery ultrasound images. In Intelligent Autonomous Systems 12* (pp. 185–196). Springer Berlin Heidelberg.

Chaudhry, A., Khan, A., Mirza, A. M., Ali, A., Hassan, M., & Kim, J. Y. (2013). Neuro fuzzy and punctual kriging based filter for image restoration. *Applied Soft Computing, 13*(2), 817–832. doi:10.1016/j. asoc.2012.10.017

Che, D., Safran, M., & Peng, Z. (2013). From Big Data to Big Data Mining: Challenges, Issues, and Opportunities. In B. Hong, X. Meng, L. Chen, W. Winiwarter & W. Song (Eds.), Database Systems for Advanced Applications (Vol. 7827, pp. 1-15). Springer Berlin Heidelberg.

Cheng, T., Chu, S. K. K., Yi, A. L., Yu, Y., Bradski, G. R., Ng, A. Y., & Olukotun, K. (2006). Map-Reduce for machine learning on multicore. MIT Press.

Davenport, T. H. (2013). Big Data Executive Survey 2013: The State of Big Data in the Large Corporate World. Academic Press.

Dean, J., & Ghemawat, S. (2008). MapReduce: Simplified data processing on large clusters. *Communications of the ACM, 51*(1), 107–113. doi:10.1145/1327452.1327492

Dunn, J. C. (1973). A Fuzzy Relative of the ISODATA Process and Its Use in Detecting Compact Well-Separated Clusters. *Journal of Cybernetics, 3*(3), 32–57. doi:10.1080/01969727308546046

Fayyad, U. M., Piatetsky-Shapiro, G., & Smyth, P. (1996). From data mining to knowledge discovery: an overview. In M. F. Usama, P.-S. Gregory, S. Padhraic, & U. Ramasamy (Eds.), *Advances in knowledge discovery and data mining* (pp. 1–34). American Association for Artificial Intelligence.

Han, J. (2005). *Data Mining: Concepts and Techniques*. Morgan Kaufmann Publishers Inc.

Hassan, M., Chaudhry, A., Khan, A., & Iftikhar, M. A. (2014). Robust information gain based fuzzy c-means clustering and classification of carotid artery ultrasound images. *Computer Methods and Programs in Biomedicine, 113*(2), 593–609. doi:10.1016/j.cmpb.2013.10.012 PMID:24239296

Hassan, M., Chaudhry, A., Khan, A., Iftikhar, M. A., & Kim, J. Y. (2013). *Medical image segmentation employing information gain and fuzzy c-means algorithm*. Paper presented at the Open Source Systems and Technologies (ICOSST), 2013 International Conference on. doi:10.1109/ICOSST.2013.6720602

Hassan, M., Chaudhry, A., Khan, A., & Kim, J. Y. (2012). Carotid artery image segmentation using modified spatial fuzzy c-means and ensemble clustering. *Computer Methods and Programs in Biomedicine, 108*(3), 1261–1276. doi:10.1016/j.cmpb.2012.08.011 PMID:22981822

Hathaway, R. J., & Bezdek, J. C. (2006). Extending fuzzy and probabilistic clustering to very large data sets. *Computational Statistics & Data Analysis, 51*(1), 215–234. doi:10.1016/j.csda.2006.02.008

Havens, T. C., Bezdek, J. C., Leckie, C., Hall, L. O., & Palaniswami, M. (2012). Fuzzy c-Means Algorithms for Very Large Data. *Fuzzy Systems. IEEE Transactions on, 20*(6), 1130–1146.

Havens, T. C., Chitta, R., Jain, A. K., & Rong, J. (2011). *Speedup of fuzzy and possibilistic kernel c-means for large-scale clustering.* Paper presented at the Fuzzy Systems (FUZZ), 2011 IEEE International Conference on.

Holmes, G., Donkin, A., & Witten, I. H. (1994). *WEKA: a machine learning workbench.* Paper presented at the Intelligent Information Systems, the 1994 Second Australian and New Zealand Conference.

Hore, P., Hall, L. O., & Goldgof, D. B. (2007). *Single Pass Fuzzy C Means.* Paper presented at the Fuzzy Systems Conference.

Hore, P., Hall, L. O., Goldgof, D. B., & Cheng, W. (2008). *Online fuzzy c means.* Paper presented at the Fuzzy Information Processing Society. Retrieved from http://cs.joensuu.fi/~isido/clustering/

Hurwitz, J., Halper, F., & Kaufman, M. (2013). *Big Data For Dummies.* Wiley.

Ramze Rezaee, M., Lelieveldt, B. P. F., & Reiber, J. H. C. (1998). A new cluster validity index for the fuzzy c-mean. *Pattern Recognition Letters, 19*(3–4), 237–246. doi:10.1016/S0167-8655(97)00168-2

Raymer, M. L., Punch, W. F., Goodman, E. D., Kuhn, L. A., & Jain, A. K. (2000). Dimensionality reduction using genetic algorithms. *Evolutionary Computation. IEEE Transactions on, 4*(2), 164–171.

Sagiroglu, S., & Sinanc, D. (2013). *Big data: A review.* Paper presented at the Collaboration Technologies and Systems (CTS), 2013 International Conference on.

Sheshadri, H. S., & Kandaswamy, A. (2007). Experimental investigation on breast tissue classification based on statistical feature extraction of mammograms. *Computerized Medical Imaging and Graphics: The Official Journal of the Computerized Medical Imaging Society, 31*(1), 46-48.

Xindong, W., Xingquan, Z., Gong-Qing, W., & Wei, D. (2014). Data mining with big data. *Knowledge and Data Engineering. IEEE Transactions on, 26*(1), 97–107.

KEY TERMS AND DEFINITIONS

Big Data: Big data is term for massive datasets having large, more varied complex structure with the difficulties of storing, analyzing and visualizing for further processes or results.

Cluster Analysis: Cluster analysis aims at identifying groups of similar objects and, therefore helps to discover distribution.

Crisp Clustering: Hard clustering of unlabeled objects which is non-empty mutually disjoints subsets so that the union of the subset is equal to zero.

Feature Extraction: It is a process of deriving new features from the original features in order to reduce the cost of feature measurement, increase classifier efficiency, and allow higher classification accuracy.

Fuzzy Clustering: It is more flexible then crisp methods. Fuzzy clustering allows objects belong to several clusters with different degree of membership. Each column of the fuzzy portioning sum must equal to 1.

Variety: The rise of information coming from new sources both inside and outside the walls of the enterprise or organization creates integration, management, governance, and architectural pressures in IT.

Velocity: How fast data is being produced, changed and the speed with which data must be received, understood and processed.

Volume: The large amount of data generated in every second or data intensity that must be ingested, analyzed, and managed to make decisions based on complete data analysis.

Chapter 8
Big Data and Web Intelligence for Condition Monitoring:
A Case Study on Wind Turbines

Carlos Q. Gómez
University of Castilla-La Mancha, Spain

Fausto P. García
University of Castilla-La Mancha, Spain

Marco A. Villegas
University of Castilla-La Mancha, Spain

Diego J. Pedregal
University of Castilla-La Mancha, Spain

ABSTRACT

Condition Monitoring (CM) is the process of determining the state of a system according to a certain number of parameters. This 'condition' is tracked over time to detect any developing fault or non desired behaviour. As the Information and Communication Technologies (ICT) continue expanding the range of possible applications and gaining industrial maturity, the appearing of new sensor technologies such as Macro Fiber Composites (MFC) has opened a new range of possibilities for addressing a CM in industrial scenarios. The huge amount of data collected by MFC could overflow most conventional monitoring systems, requiring new approaches to take true advantage of the data. Big Data approach makes it possible to take profit of tons of data, integrating in the appropriate algorithms and technologies in a unified platform. This chapter proposes a real time condition monitoring approach, in which the system is continuously monitored allowing an online analysis.

INTRODUCTION

Condition monitoring (CM) is defined as the process of determining the state of system according to a parameter of the system. The main propose of CM in this chapter is to identify a significant change of this condition of the system which is indicative of a developing fault. It is usually considered as part of a predictive maintenance strategy, in which maintenance actions, and therefore preventive maintenance tasks, are scheduled to prevent failure and avoid its consequences. The objective is to extend the life cycle of the system analysed, and to avoid major failures, resulting in considerable cost and associated downtime reduction.

DOI: 10.4018/978-1-4666-8505-5.ch008

The so called Information and Communication Technologies (ICT) have grown up with no precedents, and all aspects of human life have been transformed under this new scenario. All industrial sectors have rapidly incorporated the new technologies, and some of them have become de facto standards like supervisory control and data acquisition (SCADA) systems. Large amounts of data started to be created, processed and saved, allowing an automatic control of complex industrial systems. In spite of this progress, there are some challenges not well addressed yet. Some of them are: the analysis of tons of data, as well as continuous data streams; the integration of data in different formats coming from different sources; making sense of data to support decision making; and getting results in short periods of time. These all are characteristics of a problem that should be addressed through a big data approach.

This chapter proposes a real time condition monitoring approach, in which the system is continuously monitored allowing online analysis and actions. The system is fed by data streams received from different sensors adequately located on the machine.

The proposed methodology is applied to the industry of wind energy, in particular to the detection of failures in the blades like surface cracking, scuffing, pitting, etc.

Other interesting application is the detection of ice on wind turbine blades. It is known that icing causes a variety of problems for wind turbines, increased fatigue of components due to imbalance in the load or power reduction due to disrupted aerodynamics (Homola, Nicklasson, & Sundsbø, 2006).

All the information analysed by the system is obtained through non-destructive techniques using transducers, which are being used in wind power industry with great success. However, it is worth to mention that wind power is just as an illustrative example of application, while the methodology is applicable in many different scenarios across several industries.

BACKGROUND

Wind energy is inexhaustible, ecologically and environmentally friendly. It is becoming one of the most widespread and productive methods for generating electrical energy (see Figure 1). Today, it is a mature technology and this energy source is applied to both large scale and small installations. It certainly has become a mainstay within the energy systems of many countries, and is recognized as a reliable and affordable source of electricity (Beattie & Pitteloud, 2012).

In 2013, wind energy represented 3.5% of total energy demand. And by 2016 is expected to be the global installed capacity of 500,000 MW. In addition to onshore wind farms, wind farms are built in the sea (offshore), several kilometres from the coast, to take advantage of the best wind conditions to overcome the negative relief effects. In these installations it is common to find much more powerful machines than which are installed onshore. The diameter of the turbine is a crucial parameter: longer blades, more swept area and more energy produced.

This trend to building ever larger blades carries out certain problems. The blades have to bear more and more weight and strength due to its greater sweep area. This means an increased fatigue in the blade structure, and therefore any blade failure entails very high costs. It has been estimated that the time between failures in wind turbine blades is 5 years. The time spent in repairing one of these blades is 2 days on average in onshore wind turbines. However, in the case of offshore wind turbines the downtime could increase up to a month.

The repair costs of a wind turbine blade may vary between 20000€ to 50000€ depending on the required operations, e.g. if it is necessary to take it down and if it can be repaired in the field or it has

Figure 1. Wind turbine research center in Ohio.

to be carried back to the factory. These costs can be multiplied by 10 if the turbine is located offshore due to the associated costs of transporting the new blade and difficult working conditions for replacement (Söker, Berg-Pollack, & Kensche, 2007). In addition to these costs, is necessary to add lost profits caused by the downtime.

To deal with these problems companies have invested great resources to develop reliable preventive maintenance. This was responsible of ensuring the adequate working of wind turbines by means of periodic reviews, which consisted on oil changes on the gearbox, visual inspections of blades, retighten screws, etc. Nowadays has emerged a new form of maintenance, called predictive maintenance, in order to avoid the defects as far as possible, whose function is to try to detect a potential failure before it occurs, to avoid triggering a fatal error. For this reason, this approach requires a system capable of providing real-time status of the machine, independently, safely and accurately (Figure 2).

BIG DATA IN STRUCTURAL HEALTH MONITORING

The non-destructive inspection tests are used with the purpose of detecting superficial or even internal discontinuities of a certain material, as well as assessing its properties. The Structural Health Monitoring (SHM) is the process of implementing a damage detection strategy in a given structure. By SHM is possible to detect structural changes. It is commonly used for checking welding points and components, or for assessing the density of a material. Most of the times, the obtained data on these tests are not directly understandable, and may require the analysis of qualified professionals.

Figure 2. Wind turbine condition monitoring for blade and tower

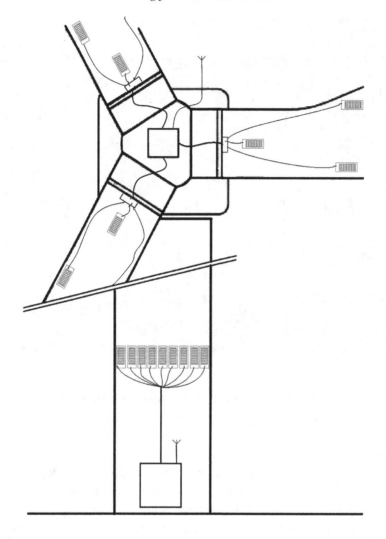

The implementation of such a system for predictive maintenance purposes represents a big challenge, and many factors contribute to make it harder. Some of them are related with the nature of the data, as they primarily consist on time-domain signals while data mining techniques have traditionally focused on cross-section data (with no time dimension). Another concerning fact is the problem of integrating the result of multiple signal analysis in a unified and consistent framework. But probably the most challenging fact is the problem of dealing with huge amounts of data, as the traditional algorithms are not specially designed for being scalable over terabytes or even petabytes of data.

The problem this large amount of data to analyse is mainly due to the development of new types of sensors at a low cost, and the possibility of transmitting tons of data everywhere. These factors let to build a 'digital projection' of the machines' life, consisting on all the data that have been collected about them, including their surrounding working conditions. for example, the health monitoring of a machine should focus on the more critical components, not only on those that will cause a larger failure rates, but also those that would produce longer down-time failures. In wind turbines it is known that the highest failure rates of structural components are caused by the blades, especially the pitch system, and the drive system (Pinar, García, Tobias, & Papaelias, 2013). At this light, it would be reasonable to have a number of at least 16 sensors on each blade and 48 sensors on the tower. These sensors are commonly Macro Fiber Composites (MFC) devices that work at ultrasonic frequencies, in the range of MHz. A typical signal sampled at 4MHz during one second will represent 9.72MB of data. Having 96 sensors in a single turbine, it would represent the amount of 933 MB of data in just a matter of a second. These dimensions get even bigger when we consider the tracking of multiple wind turbines, e.g. a wind farm with 80 turbines would generate 72.9 GB of data each second. In addition, it must to be add all the information about environmental working conditions, which usually come from SCADA systems.

Even though Big Data has become one of the most popular buzzword, the industry has evolved towards a definition around this term on the base of three dimensions: volume, variety and velocity (Zikopoulos & Eaton, 2011).

Data volume is normally measured by the quantity of raw transactions, events or amount of history that creates the data volume. Typically, data analysis algorithms have used smaller data sets called training sets to create predictive models. Most of the times, the business use predictive insight that are severely gross since the data volume has purposely been reduced according to storage and computational processing constraints. By removing the data volume constraint and using larger data sets, it is possible to discover subtle patterns that can lead to targeted actionable decisions, or they can enable further analysis that increase the accuracy of the predictive models.

Data variety came into existence over the past couple of decades, when data has increasingly become unstructured as the sources of data have proliferated beyond operational applications. In industrial applications, such variety emerged from the proliferation of multiple types of sensors, which enable the tracking of multiple variables in almost every domain in the world. Most technical factors include sampling rate of data and their relative range of values.

Data velocity is about the speed at which data is created, accumulated, ingested, and processed. An increasing number of applications are required to process information in real-time or with near real-time responses. This may imply that data is processed on the fly, as it is ingested, to make real-time decisions, or schedule the appropriate tasks.

PROPOSED METHODOLOGY

The approach proposed in this chapter is based on the use of three sources of information. These sources are not independent, because they provide information about the same physical event. The signals picked up by the transducers will be processed in the very first step by three parallel filters. They will be responsible of extracting the useful information to be used in the condition monitoring. The results are three set of signals: vibrations, acoustic emission and ultrasonic signals, each of them analysed by an independent 'line' of the system (Figure 3).

Vibrations

The first approach analyses only low frequencies that are characteristics of vibrations. It is possible to get valuable information related with the integrity of a blade structure analysing the vibrations in dynamic conditions (Abouhnik & Albarbar, 2012). The extracted information shows the natural frequencies of a

Figure 3. Functional Schema of Signal Analysis

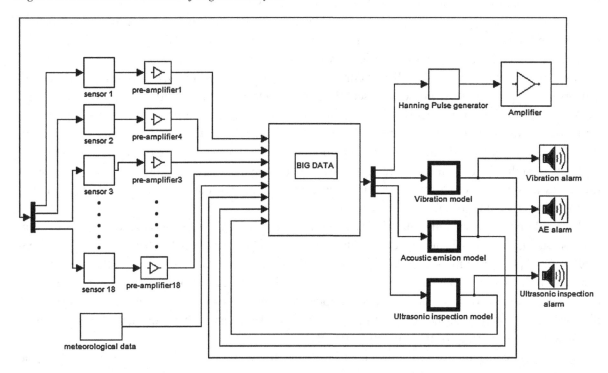

blade, and their respective harmonics. These vibrations are registered on a model that analyses the amplitude and frequency. Because the manufacturing of the blade is manual, and blades are not identical, the system will create a unique model for each blade. The model will learn from these two parameters over a period of time, and these parameters will be associated to a free fault model. Therefore these signals are processed online in the time domain and in the frequency domain. In the time domain is applied an upper and lower limit amplitude for signals, based on what it has learned in the previous period, which correspond to very strong vibrations that can trigger broken fibres due to the fatigue of these large vibrations, then trigger an alarm. Same data are analysed in the frequency domain, and the natural frequencies and their harmonics are compared with the learned in the model. If there is a new energy peak in the frequency domain, which may be due to a failure in its structure has altered the natural frequency of the blade, and then an alarm should be triggered.

Employing the Big Data approach is possible to analyse large amounts of information, even coming from different sensors and places. In this sense, the information obtained from meteorological sensors on the turbine becomes highly profitable and valuable. These data are usually extracted from SCADA systems, and should include wind speed and direction which definitely determine the blade vibrations in its natural frequencies. That information is also taken into account in the design of the trained model, thus making possible to predict the blade vibration for different wind directions and speeds.

Acoustical Emissions

The second approach is focused on the detection of acoustic emission. When repetitive loads are applied on a certain material, it is known that they produce micro-breaks which liberate energy out of the material

(Beattie, 1997). This energy takes the form of elastic wave which produce sound. With the help of sensors properly disposed it is possible to capture and record this sound. These sensors translate that mechanical energy in small electrical signals, which usually are pre-amplified in order to obtain a clearer signal. During the installation of the system is important to adequately locate the sensors, and to fix them to the material by good coupling. The signals are captured, amplified and recorded in a computer for posterior analysis. The frequency of the signal produced by the micro-breaks depends on several factors, e.g. the nature of the material, the type of discontinuity and the source of the emission. On this base it is possible to characterize the source of the emission by isolating certain frequencies with the help of appropriate filters. In many works it is common to use three sensors, which are properly located to determine the source of the emission with high accuracy, usually with the help of triangulation algorithms.

In wind turbine blades domain, the acoustic emission is a major way to detect micro-breaks between the glass fibers of a blade in real time.

The method proposed in this chapter consists on the use of 16 MFCs on each blade (Figure 4). Most of the sensors are located in the first third of the blade, where breaks commonly occur.

These sensors are constantly recording data. When a fiber break occurs, the elastic waves reach the MFC and the signal is recorded (Figure 5). Knowing the distance between the MFCs, and measuring the time delay between the activation of every sensor, it is possible to accurately compute the location of the break and its characteristics, depending on the type of wave issued, (amplitude, frequency ...).

The large amount of data generated by all the sensors, as well as the meteorological data, are processed by the Big Data system, and a specific model for each blade is generated. It is important to note that when meteorological data predict rain or hail, acoustic emission detection should be disabled, because each impact of each raindrop produces similar sound waves, which can be confused with those issued by a fault. The system will create a proper model for each blade, will record the detected acoustic-emission source locations and the most probable types of defect. In parallel, when an acoustic emission is detected, the ultrasonic inspection is activated in order to corroborate the possible damage.

The last approach is an active search for defects using the technique of pulse-echo ultrasound. In this case the transducer is excited with a short pulse with frequencies above 20 kHz. These signals are applied to the material, and the received echoes are studied. In order to strengthen the ultrasound analysis, the signals will be emitted in the form of white noise. This line could be subdivided into two parts. The first one would perform a general periodic monitoring: when a failure event is detected; the second part is initiated to perform a more exhaustive analysis which verifies the actual existence of a break and its location.

Figure 4. Sensor location in the Wind Turbine Blade

Figure 5. Crack delay signal simulations. The source is located by triangulation algorithms.

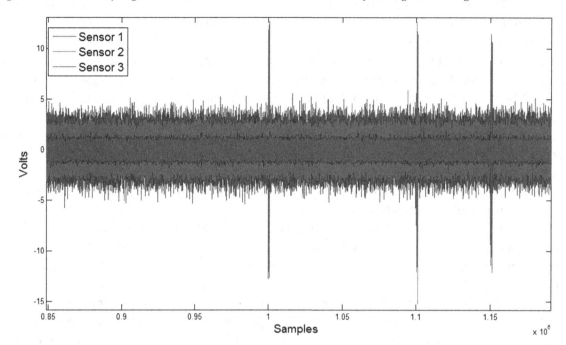

Ultrasound Inspection

This approach is an active search for defects using ultrasonic inspections and ice detection. For fault detection, in contrast to acoustical emissions, ultrasonic short pulses are applied on the material to be examined. A combination of the pulse-echo and pitch-catch techniques is used. The ultrasonic short pulses produce waves that travel through the material, and these waves are reflected when reach the interface or a discontinuity (Su, Ye, & Lu, 2006). These echoes give information such as the break location by measuring the arrival time of the echo, as well as the type of defect (Figure 6).

For ice detection on blades, meteorological data from SCADA systems are also used. It is known that the ice on the blade changes the properties of wave propagation, especially the velocity. If the me-

Figure 6. Crack source location by triangulation algorithms

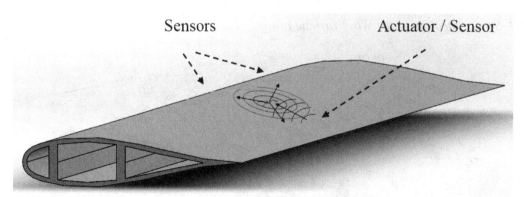

teorological information predicts the presence of frost, and ice build-up on the blades, the ultrasonic transducer will emit the short pulses and the system will compare the collected signals with the ones coming from normal (previous) conditions.

BIG DATA AND CLOUD COMPUTING

The large amount of data generated by sensors will require a powerful computing architecture that can manager this volumes of data with no problems of saturation neither response delays. Nowadays, the concept of Cloud Computing has got popularity in the industry as well as in the academic community. It introduces the idea of 'elastic resources' that expand and contract according to the system load dynamics (Taniar, 2009). In this way, computational resources can be shared across applications, resulting in great reduction of costs and latency (Minelli, Chambers, & Dhiraj, 2012). Even though this is a novel trend in industry, it is well founded in rather known concepts like parallel computing, concurrent computing and operating system architecture. They all have more than four decades in academic and research community, and have been raised now under the name of Cloud Computing. There are various reasons for this resurgence, e.g. the penetration of Internet in any sector and industry of economy, the increasing power of computers at a lower prices, the advent of embedded systems and definitely the evolution of software industry. This new paradigm has offered a solution to an immense quantity business models. Some of them are included in one of the following service models (see Figure 7).

Figure 7. Hierarchy of Service Models in Cloud Computing Industry

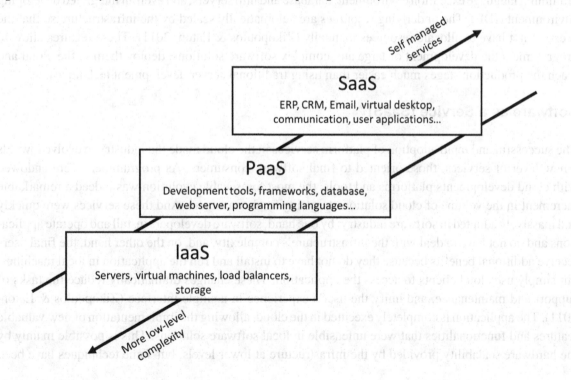

Infrastructure as a Service (IaaS)

They are the most architectural layer of a computing system. The services that users can access include storage, load balancers, firewalls, virtual private networks (VPN) and virtual local area networks (VLAN), but the most generally consumed service at this level is computing power: the user is provided with network access to an operating system, which can be executed either by a real machine or by an emulator. The latter has crystalized in the industry with the name of virtual machine (VM), and many products have extended these techniques not only for infrastructural services, but also for final users. Some of them are VMware, VirtualBox, Xen, Hyper-V. Most of the tools provided by a IaaS cloud are focused on managing such virtual machines in software containers called pools. VM pools are able to run large numbers of virtual machines, and scale up and down the resources according to the whole charge in the system (Zikopoulos & Eaton, 2011). From the customer point of view, the services provided in this layer will require considerable technical knowledge and expertise because they involve installing, patching and maintaining operating system images as well as the actual final application software and its dependencies.

Platform as a Service (PaaS)

The technical complexity involved in IaaS products became a barrier for their adoption in many domains. For that reason, the cloud providers started to build up a new layer of services, which will be closer to the customer requirements. The users will not have to worry about infrastructure issues, they should be able to focus on the concrete business requirements. PaaS is conceived to make it possible: the user is provided with a computing platform that ideally fits all his requirements: an operating system, a programming language execution environment, database and http servers, and even an integrated developing environment (IDE). The underlying resources are automatically scaled by the infrastructure so that the users do not have to allocate resources manually (Zikopoulos & Eaton, 2011). These features allow to programmers the development of large and complex software solutions, deploy them in the cloud and reach the production stages much easier than using traditional server development techniques.

Software as a Service (SaaS)

The successful and rapid adoption of platform services in the cloud made the industry to evolve towards a new layer of services, those oriented to final software consumers. As programmers were endowed with cloud developments platforms and tools, the most foreseeable evolution was indeed a remarkable increment in the volume of cloud solutions targeting final consumers. And these services were quickly and massively adopted in software industry: by one hand, software developers install and operate applications and do not have to deal with the infrastructure's complexity, and, on the other hand, the final users receive additional benefits because they do not have to install and run the application in local machines, but simply use cloud clients to access the application. These changes dramatically reduce the tasks of support and maintenance, and unify the user's experience in a single interface (Zikopoulos & Eaton, 2011). The application is completely executed in the cloud, allowing the implementation of new valuable features and functionalities that were unfeasible in local software solutions. This is possible mainly by the hardware scalability provided by the infrastructure at lower levels, but some techniques have been designed to optimize time and resources also at the software layer. A software optimization technique that has become very popular among SaaS providers is multitenancy, which consists on grouping several logic instances of an application in a single bunch which is served by a single shared resource.

Other big sub product in this trend is the so called Internet of Things (IoT) which is becoming more and more popular these days. It is a natural consequence of the previous developments, since it consists on the interconnection of uniquely identifiable embedded computing like devices with the existing Internet infrastructure. Companies like Xively, AT&T, Axeda, Cisco and others are offering solutions specifically targeted to this new growing market.

PROPOSED INFRASTRUCTURE

The sensors are controlled by a node (in some domains it is called wasp-mote), which is a device capable of receive streams of data from sensors, split them in packages, and send them through the network with the appropriate metadata. Several considerations should be done in this point. With respect to the volume of data generated, it is important to make the accurate estimations in order to acquire the correct hardware which supports it. For example, if it is need to install forty MFC sensor on a wind turbine, and capture data at 25 kHz, it would mean approximately 360MB of data every second. Would the node support this? Is its data bus enough for ingesting such a stream? These all are factors that should be considered when hardware options are being evaluated.

Once the data has been properly collected by the node, it is time to transmit them to the computing centre. This process is usually done by mean of REST web services, which work over the HTTP requests and responses layer; nevertheless, some alternative technologies have recently emerged, like WebSockets and other streaming solutions. Some of these efforts have crystallized in the HTML5 standard that web browser must accomplish. Even these all alternatives, it is important to select the most appropriate data transmission technology. Some criteria will help for this:

- **Granularity:** The granularity of the requests (bunches of data send) from the node to the server has to allow the latter to scale their resources as needed. In other words, it is necessary to balance the trade-off between small and big queries. Small queries will let the server scale smoother, but at the price of a higher number of queries. As certain amount of protocols related bytes is attached to each query, the total efficiency of the system could decrease when the size of the queries is arbitrarily reduced.

- **Responsiveness:** One of the strongest requirements in industrial applications is the responsiveness of the whole system. It is true also for monitoring systems, where no real time decision is made, but streams of data has to be continuously processed to guarantee safe working conditions. This is the case of wind turbines condition monitoring. In the next sections we are going to present how it could be achieved in a cloud computing environment.

Task Queues

Regardless the cloud provider selected, the system should be designed to scale and balance the resources as needed, otherwise the system much probably will collapse at demand picks. The most common approach for doing so consists on splitting the load in a proper way: by doing so, some tasks are processed 'in the background' by some worker threads, and some other tasks are directly dispatched in the "main thread". The correct separation depends on several factors, like the quantity of expected requests, the volume of the received data and the computing cost of processing each request. In all cases, the incoming requests are organized in small and discrete units of work, called 'tasks', and are pushed into a queue, at the time that some 'worker' processes dispatch them as soon as possible. The scalability of the system comes when the 'workers' are replicated to timely consume the processes in the queue, and this is done dynamically and according to the current system load.

In today's cloud industry this approach is widely used, though using different names according to the specific provider. For example, in Google Cloud Platform it is called 'Task Queues', while in Amazon Web Services (AWS) it is named 'Simple Queue Service'. In Windows Azure Cloud Platform it is a bit trickier to match this functionality. It will be a combination of the 'Service Bus' and 'Scheduler' functionalities both provided in Azure platform. The Scheduler provides a mechanism for multiple process orchestration, integrating them all in a single logical base, but it needs the help of the Service Bus, which provide the messaging and buffering tools for making possible such integration.

Processing Algorithms

The algorithms executed by these tasks depend on the concrete application to build. In wind turbine condition monitoring with MFC sensors, task processing will probably consist on analysing the received raw signal, first making a sort of feature extraction. Feature extraction is a form of dimensionality reduction where the data is transformed into a reduced representation set of features. The objective of this step is twofold: reduce the redundancy in the data, and spotlight the relevant information contained in the data.

Once this information is computed, the following common step is to compare them with the previously stored data. The most elegant and efficient way of doing it is by means of statistical modelling techniques. A statistical model is an abstract formalization of the relationships between the principal variables in a certain phenomenon. By using a model, it is possible to condense huge amounts of data in just few values. These values usually correspond to the parameters of the model. The process of optimizing the value of the parameters is called model training, because the model is fitted to the data according certain restrictions (Sheikh, 2013). There are lots of different approaches to modelling data. For signal analysis it is very common the use of the Fast Fourier Transform (FFT) and Wavelet Transform (WT).

Using the appropriate modelling technique, and having a set of well-trained models, it is possible to detect novelties in the data by just testing the new data against the models. Depending on the case, the appropriate system message has to be triggered (warning, error, fault...).

Data Logging

The following step consists on storing the relevant data in a proper way. For the case when the stream of received data is extremely big, it would be good to consider the possibility to design a feature extraction process targeted to reduce dimensionality in data for storing purposes. In these cases, instead of storing the full set of data receive, it will store only a representation. Part of this process would imply re-training the stored models, in order to update them according to the newest system's state.

Conventional relational databases are not well suitable for this kind of applications, firstly because of the huge volume of the data gathered, and secondly, due to the nature of the data itself: relational databases were designed mainly for enterprise applications, where the data is definitely transactional and relational. In the big data applications it is very common to work with unstructured data, even with dynamic formats and relationships. For that reason, many efforts were devoted to build schema-less databases which are better suited for these new kind of applications. MongoDB is probably the most popular product in this sector, which usually is referred with the general name of 'NoSQL' databases. They were rapidly adopted by cloud providers as one of the key infrastructure components. Some examples are 'Cloud Datastorage' from Google and Amazon S3 from AWS.

FUTURE RESEARCH DIRECTIONS

Even though Big Data technologies are opening new exciting horizons in the ICT industry, some authors point out the necessity of approaching the data exploitation from another more semantic and holistic perspective (Barone et al., 2010), due to the overwhelming volume of data coming from different sources, and even in different formats. The idea behind this new approach is to make sense of data at the light of a conceptual model that encapsulates the semantic of the raw data in a unified framework. In the context of industrial applications, it would entail a tighter integration between the theoretical and experimental (data-based) model of a machinery performance, with wide consequences in the whole product life-cicle, from operation and maintenance management, to the earlier stages of product developing and design.

CONCLUSION

The proposed model is used to cover the most important requirements of the structural health monitoring and vibration monitoring in a wind turbine blade. The system analyses the received signals online and acts depending on different events. After the signal processing stages, the system records the status of each wind turbine to predict future failures and to get failure patterns between different wind turbines. The advantages of the proposed methodology include the exploitation of large volumes of data online, as well as the integration of continuous parallel analysis in an unified framework. Additional advantages come from the fact that the system uses the same transducers for three different purposes, which implies that the whole system is simplified and costs are reduced.

ACKNOWLEDGMENT

The work reported herewith has been financially supported by the Spanish Ministerio de Economía y Competitividad, under Research Grant IPT-2012-0563-120000 (IcingBlades).

REFERENCES

Abouhnik, A., & Albarbar, A. (2012). Wind turbine blades condition assessment based on vibration measurements and the level of an empirically decomposed feature. *Energy Conversion and Management*, *64*, 606–613. doi:10.1016/j.enconman.2012.06.008

Barone, D., Yu, E., Won, J., Jiang, L., & Mylopoulos, J. (2010). Enterprise modeling for business intelligence. In *The practice of enterprise modelling (PoEM'10)* (Vol. 68, pp. 31–45). Berlin: Springer. doi:10.1007/978-3-642-16782-9_3

Beattie, A. G. (Ed.). (1997). Acoustic emission monitoring of a wind turbine blade during a fatigue test. In *AIAA Aerospace Sciences Meeting (AIAA/ASME '97)*. American Institute of Aeronautics and Astronautics. doi:10.2514/6.1997-958

Berson, A., & Smith, S. J. (1997). *Data warehousing, data mining, and OLAP*. New York: McGraw-Hill.

Homola, M. C., Nicklasson, P. J., & Sundsbø, P. A. (2006). Ice sensors for wind turbines. *Cold Regions Science and Technology, 46*(2), 125–131. doi:10.1016/j.coldregions.2006.06.005

Lehmann, M., Büter, A., Frankenstein, B., Schubert, F., & Brunner, B. (2006). Monitoring System for Delamination Detection–Qualification of Structural Health Monitoring (SHM) Systems. In *Proceedings of the Conference on Damage in Composite Material (CDCM '06)*. Stuttgart.

Minelli, M., Chambers, M., & Dhiraj, A. (2012). *Big data, big analytics: emerging business intelligence and analytic trends for today's businesses*. Hoboken, NJ: John Wiley & Sons.

Pinar Pérez, J. M., García Márquez, F. P., Tobias, A., & Papaelias, M. (2013). Wind turbine reliability analysis. *Renewable & Sustainable Energy Reviews, 23*, 463–472. doi:10.1016/j.rser.2013.03.018

Sheikh, N. (2013). *Implementing Analytics: A Blueprint for Design, Development, and Adoption*. Morgan Kaufmann.

Söker, H., Berg-Pollack, A., & Kensche, C. (2007). Rotor Blade Monitoring – The Technical Essentials. In *Proceedings of the German Wind Energy Conference (DEWEK '07)*. Bremen.

Su, Z., Ye, L., & Lu, Y. (2006). Guided Lamb waves for identification of damage in composite structures: A review. *Journal of Sound and Vibration, 295*(3), 753–780. doi:10.1016/j.jsv.2006.01.020

Taniar, D. (2009). *Progressive Methods in Data Warehousing and Business Intelligence: Concepts and Competitive Analytics*. Hershey, PA: IGI Global. doi:10.4018/978-1-60566-232-9

World Wind Energy Association. (2012). *World wind energy report*. Bonn: WWEA.

Zikopoulos, P., & Eaton, C. (2011). *Understanding big data: Analytics for enterprise class hadoop and streaming data*. New York: McGraw-Hill.

KEY TERMS AND DEFINITIONS

Acoustical Emission: Non-destructive technique used for detecting elastic waves produced by a material as repetitive loads are applied on it.

Big Data: The set of methodologies and technologies that allow the capture, management and exploitation of considerable amounts of data within a tolerable period of time.

Cloud Computing: A set of internet-based computing services, resources, technologies and infrastructures that are remotely available for end-users.

Data Mining: A subfield of computer science focused on patterns discovery in large data sets involving methods at the intersection of artificial intelligence, machine learning, statistics, and database systems.

Filter: A signal processing technique used for partial or complete suppression of some components of a given signal.

Macro Fiber Composite (MFC): A kind of low profile actuator and sensor consisting of a rectangular piezo-ceramic rods stacked between layers of adhesive, electrodes and polyimide film.

Parallel Computing: A computation technique consisting on the concurrent execution of subtasks for the accomplishment of a bigger task.

Chapter 9

Prediction of Missing Associations from Information System Using Intelligent Techniques

Debi Prasanna Acharjya
VIT University, India

V. Santhi
VIT University, India

ABSTRACT

Prediction of missing associations can be viewed as one of the most fundamental problems in the machine learning. The main objective of prediction of missing associations is to determine decisions for the missing associations. In real world problems, prediction of missing associations is must because absence of associations in the attribute values may have information to predict the decision for entrepreneurs. Based on decision theory, in the past many mathematical models such as naïve Bayes structure, human composed network structure, Bayesian network modeling etc. were developed. However, these theories have certain limitations. In order to overcome the limitations, rough computing is hybridized with Bayesian classification. This chapter discusses various techniques for predicting missing associations to obtain meaningful decision from information system. A real life example is provided to show the viability of the proposed research.

INTRODUCTION

Huge repository of data is accumulated across various domains at the present age of Internet. It is due to the wide spread of distributed computing which involves dispersion of data geographically. In addition, these data are neither crisp nor deterministic due to presence of uncertainty and vagueness. Obtaining meaningful information by analyzing these data is a great challenge for humans. Therefore, it is very difficult to extract expert knowledge from the universal dataset without any automated techniques.

DOI: 10.4018/978-1-4666-8505-5.ch009

Also, there is much information hidden in these data. Most of our traditional tools for machine learning and knowledge extraction are crisp, deterministic and precise in character. So, it is essential for a new generation of computational theories and tools to assist human in extracting knowledge from the rapidly growing digital data. Knowledge discovery in databases (KDD) is the field that has evolved into an important and active area of research because of theoretical challenges associated with the problem of discovering intelligent solutions for huge data. Knowledge discovery and data mining is the rapidly growing interdisciplinary field which merges database management, statistics, computational intelligence and related areas. The basic aim of all these is knowledge extraction from voluminous data.

The processes of knowledge discovery in databases and machine learning appear deceptively simple when viewed from the perspective of terminological definition (Fayaad, 1996). The nontrivial process of identifying valid, novel, potentially useful, and ultimately understandable patterns in data is known as knowledge discovery in databases. It consists of several stages such as data selection, cleaning of data, enrichment of data, coding, data mining and reporting. The different stages are shown in the following Figure 1. In addition, closely related process of information retrieval is defined by Rocha (2001) as "the methods and processes for searching relevant information out of information systems that contain extremely large numbers of documents". However in execution, these processes are not simple at all, especially when executed to satisfy specific personal or organizational knowledge management require-

Figure 1. The KDD Process

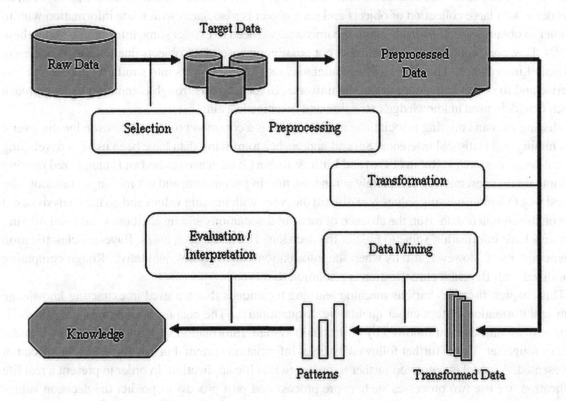

ments. It is also observed that, usefulness of an individual data element or pattern of data elements change dramatically from individual to individual, organization to organization, or task to task. It is because of the acquisition of knowledge and reasoning that involve in vagueness and incompleteness. In addition, knowledge extraction or description of data patterns generally understandable is also highly problematic. Therefore, there is much need for dealing with the incomplete and vague information in classification, concept formulation, and data analysis.

The data collected through wide variety of fields is not free from uncertainties and vagueness. Handling such uncertainties and vagueness was a great challenge for humans. However, the problem has been tackled for a long time by logicians, mathematicians and computer scientists, particularly in the area of machine learning, and artificial intelligence. The earliest and most successful one is being the notion of fuzzy sets by L. A. Zadeh (1965) that captures impreciseness in information. Though it is wide spread today, but it has certain limitations in designing membership functions. An expertise is required to design membership function in order to obtain meaningful knowledge. On the other hand rough set of Z. Pawlak (1982) is another attempt that captures indiscernibility among objects to model imperfect knowledge (Pawlak & Skowron, (2007a, 2007b, 2007c)) with the help of equivalence relation. In addition, many other advanced methods such as rough set with similarity (Slowinski & Vanderpooten, 2000), rough fuzzy sets and fuzzy rough set (Dubois & Prade, 1990), rough set on fuzzy approximation spaces (Acharjya & Tripathy, 2008), rough set on intuitionistic fuzzy approximation spaces (Acharjya & Tripathy, 2009), dynamic rough set (Li & Hu, 2007), covering based rough set (Zhu & Wang, 2007) were discussed by different authors to extract knowledge from the huge amount of data. Universe can be considered as a large collection of objects and each object is associated with some information with it. In order to obtain some knowledge about the universe, we need to extract some information about these objects. However, uniquely identification is not possible in case of all objects due to lack of sufficient amount of information. Therefore, it is essential to classify these objects into similarity classes to charaterize and to obtain knowledge about the universe. In recent years, rough computing is an approach which is widely used in knowledge extraction and machine learning.

Missing data and missing associations in data values is a common problem in knowledge discovery, data mining and statistical inference. Several approaches to missing data have been used in developing trained decision systems. Rubin (1976) and Little & Rubin (2002) have studied and categorized missing data into three types: missing completely at random, missing at random, and not missing at random. The easiest way to handle missing values is to discard the cases with missing values and do the analysis based only on the complete data. But, the absence of missing associations among attribute values and missing data may have information value to predict the decision. To handle such cases, Bayesian classification is generally used. However, it fails when the information system is not qualitative. Rough computing hybridized with Bayesian classification is a solution to this end.

This chapter discusses various machine learning techniques that are used in extracting knowledge from an information system either qualitative or quantitative. The chapter is organized as follows: It starts with an introduction followed by information system. Information system is followed by foundations of rough set. This is further followed by order information system. Further Bayesian classification is presented. A model is presented further to process a real life application. In order to present a real life application, we use two processes such as pre process and post process to predict the decision values for the missing associations in the attribute values. In pre process we use rough set on intuitionistic fuzzy approximation spaces with ordering rules to find the suitable classification of data set, whereas in post process we use Bayesian classification to explore decision values for the missing associations in the attribute values. Real life application is followed by a conclusion. Finally, a complete reference is provided at the end of the chapter.

INFORMATION SYSTEM

The fundamental objective of inductive learning and data mining is classification. But, we may not face with a simply classification while dealing real world problems. Ordering of objects is one such problem. Before we discuss machine learning techniques, one must know about an information system. An information system contains a finite set of objects typically represented by their values on a finite set of attributes. Such information system may be conveniently described in a tabular form in which each row represents an object whereas each column represents an attribute. Each cell of the information system contains an attribute value. Now, we define formally an information system as below.

An information system is a table that provides a convenient way to describe a finite set of objects called the universe by a finite set of attributes thereby representing all available information and knowledge. The attribute sets along with the objects in an information system consists of the set of condition attributes and decision attributes. Therefore it is also named as decision table (Pawlak, 1981). Let us denote the information system as $I = (U, A, V, f)$, where U is a finite non-empty set of objects called the universe and A is a non-empty finite set of attributes. For every $a \in A$, V_a is the set of values that attribute a may take. Also $V = \underset{a \in A}{\cup} V_a$. In addition, for every $a \in A, f_a : U \to V_a$ is the information function (Tripathy, Acharjya & Cynthya, 2011).

For example, a sample information system is presented in Table 1 in which $U = \{x_1, x_2, x_3, x_4, x_5, x_6, x_7\}$ represents a nonempty finite set of objects; and A = {Cough, Vomiting, Cold, Temperature, Delirium,

Table 1. Qualitative information system

Objects	Cough	Vomiting	Cold	Temperature	Delirium	Fever
x_1	Always	Seldom	Seldom	High	Never	Yes
x_2	Seldom	Never	Always	Normal	Never	No
x_3	Never	Always	Seldom	Very high	Never	Yes
x_4	Always	Seldom	Seldom	Normal	Never	No
x_5	Never	Always	Seldom	High	Never	No
x_6	Seldom	Never	Always	Very high	Never	Yes
x_7	Always	Always	Never	High	Never	Yes

Fever} be a finite set of attributes. In particular, object x_1 is characterized in the table by the attribute value set (cough, always), (vomiting, seldom), (cold, seldom), (temperature, high), (delirium, never) and (fever, yes) which form the information about the object. The information system presented in Table 1 is a qualitative system, where all the attribute values are discrete and categorical (qualitative).

In the information system shown in Table 2, $U = \left\{x_1, x_2, x_3, x_4, x_5\right\}$ represents a set of patients and A = {Temperature, Blood Pressure, Cholesterol} represents a finite set of attributes. In particular, object x_1 is characterized in the table by the attribute value set (temperature, 98.7), (blood pressure, 112), and (cholesterol, 180) which form the information about the object. This information system is a quantitative system, since all the attribute values are non categorical (Acharjya & Geetha 2014).

FOUNDATIONS OF ROUGH SET

Invent of computers, communication technologies, and database systems have created a new space for machine learning. Therefore, data analysis is of prime importance in recent years. In the hierarchy of data processing, data is the root which transforms into information and further refined to avail it in the form of knowledge. It is observed that, certain hidden information also lies in information system in spite of data analysis. Identifying such hidden information helps in taking right decision at right time and it provides an advantage to any organization. The real challenge arises when larger volume of inconsistent data is presented for extraction of knowledge and decision making. The major issue lies in converting large volume of data into knowledge and to use that knowledge to make a proper decision. Though present technologies help in creating large databases, but most of the information may not be relevant. Therefore, attribute reduction becomes an important aspect for handling such voluminous database by eliminating superfluous data. Rough set theory developed by Z. Pawlak (1982, 1991) used to process uncertain and incomplete information is a tool to the above mentioned problem. In addition, it has many applications in all the fields of science and engineering. One of its strength is the attribute dependencies, their significance among inconsistent data. At the same time, it does not need any preliminary or additional information about the data. Therefore, it classifies imprecise, uncertain or incomplete information expressed in terms of data.

Table 2. Quantitative information system

Object	Temperature (F)	Blood Pressure	Cholesterol
x_1	98.7	112	180
x_2	102.3	143	184
x_3	99	125	197
x_4	98.9	106	193
x_5	100.3	134	205

Rough Set

Every object of the universe of discourse, has some information (data, knowledge) associated in it. Objects characterized by same information are indiscernible in view of the available information about them. This is the basic philosophy behind rough set theory and the indiscernibility relation obtained in this way is the mathematical foundation of rough set theory. In this section we give some definitions and notations as developed by Z. Pawlak (1982), which shall be referred in the rest of the paper.

Let U be a finite nonempty set called the universe. Suppose $R \subseteq U \times U$ is an equivalence relation on U. The equivalence relation R partitions the set U into disjoint subsets. Elements of same equivalence class are said to be indistinguishable. Equivalence classes induced by R are called elementary concepts. Every union of elementary concepts is called a definable set. The empty set is considered to be a definable set, thus all the definable sets form a Boolean algebra and (U, R) is called an approximation space. Given a target set X, we can characterize X by a pair of lower and upper approximations. We associate two subsets $\underline{R}X$ and $\overline{R}X$ called the R–lower and R–upper approximations of X respectively and are given by

$$\underline{R}X = \cup \left\{ Y \in U \, / \, R : Y \subseteq X \right\} \tag{1}$$

and

$$\overline{R}X = \cup \left\{ Y \in U \, / \, R : Y \cap X \neq \phi \right\} \tag{2}$$

The R–boundary of X, $BN_R\left(X\right)$ is given by $BN_R(X) = \overline{R}X - \underline{R}X$. We say X is rough with respect to R if and only if $\overline{R}X \neq \underline{R}X$, equivalently $BN_R(X) \neq \phi$. X is said to be R–definable if and only if $\overline{R}X = \underline{R}X$ or $BN_R(X) - \phi$. So, a set is rough with respect to R if and only if it is not R–definable.

Indiscernibility Relation

Each object of the universe is associated with some information (data, knowledge) within it. These attribute values are processed to obtain some knowledge about the universe. Therefore, sufficient amount of information is required to uniquely identify, classify these objects into similar classes and to extract knowledge about the universe. The classification of the objects of the universe is done based on indiscernibility (equivalence) relation among these objects. It indicates that objects of a class cannot discern from one another based on available set of attributes of the objects (Pawlak, 1982; Tripathy & Acharjya, 2011). The indiscernibility relation generated in this way is the fundamental concept of rough set theory. Any set of all indiscernible objects is called an elementary concept, and form a basic granule (atom) of knowledge about the universe. Any union of the elementary sets is referred to be either crisp (precise) set or rough (imprecise) set. Let $B \subseteq A$ and $x_i, x_j \in U$. Then we say x_i and x_j are indiscernible by the set of attributes B in A if and only if the following (3) holds.

$$f\left(x_i, a\right) = f\left(x_j, a\right), \forall a \in B \tag{3}$$

For example, given the attributes cough, and vomiting objects $\{x_1, x_4\}$ are indiscernible. Similarly, the other indiscernible classes obtained are $\{x_2, x_6\}, \{x_3, x_5\}$ and $\{x_7\}$. In general each object $x_i, i = 1, 2,$ $\cdots, 7$ is compared with each other cell wise to find the indiscernibility. From the data set Table-1, on considering the decision attributes $d = \{fever\}$, we get the family of equivalence classes of d, i.e., the partition determined by the decision attribute d, denoted by U / d. Therefore,

$$U / d = \left\{\left\{x_1, x_3, x_6, x_7\right\}, \left\{x_2, x_4, x_5\right\}\right\}$$

On considering the target set $X = \left\{x_2, x_4, x_5, x_7\right\}$; objects x_1, x_3, x_6 and x_7 are the boundary-line objects, where the lower and upper approximations are given as below:

$$\underline{d}X = \cup\left\{Y \in U / d : Y \subseteq X\right\} = \left\{x_2, x_4, x_5\right\} and$$
$$\overline{d}X = \cup\left\{Y \in U / d : Y \cap X \neq \phi\right\} = \left\{x_1, x_2, x_3, x_4, x_5, x_6, x_7\right\}$$

Furthermore, considering the attributes $B \subseteq A$, we can associate an index (i.e. $\alpha_A(X)$) called the accuracy of approximation for any set $X \subseteq U$ as follows:

$$\alpha_A\left(X\right) = \frac{cardinality\ of\ \underline{A}X}{cardinality\ of\ \overline{A}X} = \frac{\left|\underline{A}X\right|}{\left|\overline{A}X\right|} \tag{4}$$

For example, $\alpha_D(X) = \frac{3}{7}$, where $X = \left\{x_2, x_4, x_5, x_7\right\}$ and $D = \{fever\}$. From the information system given in Table 1, it is clear that object x_7 has fever, whereas objects x_1, x_3, x_6 and x_7 have no fever.

Almost Indiscernibility Relation

Every object of the universe has certain attributes and the attribute values portray some information about that particular object. Objects that belong to same category of information are indiscernible (Pawlak (1981, 1991)). This is the fundamental basis of Pawlak's Rough set theory. But in many real life applications it has been observed that two different objects x_i and x_j may have attribute values that are not exactly identical but are almost identical. In information system (Table 2), temperature of the objects x_1, x_3 and x_4 are almost identical rather exactly identical. Keeping in view this context Acharjya and Tripathy (2008, 2010) generalized Pawlak's approach of indiscernibility to almost indiscernibility relation with the introduction of fuzzy proximity relation. This has further generalized to with the help of intuitionistic fuzzy proximity relation (Acharjya & Tripathy, 2009). Any set of almost indiscernible objects is called an elementary concept, and forms a granule (atom) of knowledge about the universe. To decide amount of identity between two attribute values, intuitionistic fuzzy proximity relation is employed on each domain of attributes. This domain of attributes helps the universal set to create an intuitionistic fuzzy approximation space on the universe.

The motivation behind this chapter is that the notion of almost indiscernibility relation is a generalization of indiscernibility relation with the use of intuitionistic fuzzy proximity relation and is mainly applicable on information systems where the attribute values are not qualitative having vague or imprecise meaning rather than qualitative. Also, the notion of intuitionistic fuzzy approximation space defined with the help of intuitionistic fuzzy proximity relation is a generalization of Pawlak's (1982) approximation space. Therefore, the rough set on intuitionistic fuzzy approximation space (Acharjya & Tripathy, 2009) generalizes the Pawlak's rough set and provides better result in real life situations under study. Now, in the succeeding part of the chapter the basic foundations of rough set on intuitionistic fuzzy approximation space is provided.

Rough Set on Intuitionistic Fuzzy Approximation Spaces

We accumulate lot of information which may be insufficient and not necessarily important to us during data analysis phase. As mentioned earlier, Zadeh (1965) introduced the concept of fuzzy set to process such vagueness and uncertainties. But it has certain limitations in choosing membership functions though it has wide acceptability today. Many researchers proposed many methods to this end such as "twofold fuzzy sets" by Dubosis and Prade (1987); "L-fuzzy set" by Gougen (1967); "Toll sets" by Dubosis and Prade (1993) and "Intuitionistic fuzzy sets" by Atanasov (1986). However, intuitionistic fuzzy set theory introduced by Atanasov is quite useful and applicable in many real life problems. It is because, till this date there is no unique method which can determine the membership values of an element in a fuzzy set. These problems are situation dependent. In addition, the membership value for an object cannot be determined for a particular situation due to less significant information about the object. Similar kind of problem arises when non membership values are getting determined. This estimation can be stated as in-deterministic. In fuzzy set theory we do not consider this in-deterministic part and we already assumed that membership values of all objects exists. But, it is not true in many real life problems. In fuzzy set theory, if μ be the degree of membership of an element x, then the degree of non membership of x is calculated using mathematical formula with the assumption that full part of the degree of membership is determinism and in-deterministic part is zero. At the same time, intuitionistic fuzzy set theory reduces to fuzzy set theory if in-deterministic part is zero. Therefore, intuitionistic fuzzy set model is a generalized and better model over fuzzy set model. Thus, rough sets on intuitionistic fuzzy approximation spaces is a generalized and better model then rough set on fuzzy approximation space (Acharjya, 2009). For completeness of the chapter, the definitions, notations and results on rough sets on IF-approximation space as studied by Acharjya and Tripathy (2009) is presented. The basic concepts of rough sets on intuitionistic fuzzy approximation space use the standard notation μ for membership and ν for non-membership.

Let U be an universal set of objects. An intuitionistic fuzzy relation R on a universal set U is an intuitionistic fuzzy set defined on $U \times U$. An intuitionistic fuzzy relation R on U is said to be an intuitionistic fuzzy proximity relation if the following properties hold.

$$\mu_R(x,x) = 1 \; and \; \nu_R(x,x) = 0 \; \forall \; x \in U$$

$$\mu_R(x,y) = \mu_R(y,x), \nu_R(x,y) = \nu_R(y,x) \; \forall \; x,y \in U$$

Let R be an intuitionistic fuzzy (IF) proximity relation on U. Then for any $(\alpha, \beta) \in J$, where

$$J = \left\{ (\alpha, \beta) \middle| \alpha, \beta \in [0,1] \right.$$

and $0 \leq \alpha + \beta \leq 1 \}$, the (α, β)-cut ' $R_{\alpha, \beta}$ ' of R is given by

$$R_{\alpha, \beta} = \left\{ (x,y) \middle| \mu_R(x,y) \geq \alpha \text{ and } \nu_R(x,y) \leq \beta \right\}$$

Let R be a IF-proximity relation on U. Two elements x and y are (α, β)-similar with respect to R if $(x,y) \in R_{\alpha, \beta}$ and we write $xR_{\alpha, \beta}y$. Two elements x and y are (α, β)-identical with respect to R for $(\alpha, \beta) \in J$, written as $xR(\alpha, \beta)y$ if and only if $xR_{\alpha, \beta}y$ or there exists a sequence of elements $u_1, u_2, u_3, \cdots, u_n$ in U such that

$$xR_{\alpha, \beta}u_1, u_1R_{\alpha, \beta}u_2, u_2R_{\alpha, \beta}u_3, \cdots, u_nR_{\alpha, \beta}y.$$

In the last case, we say that x is transitively (α, β)-similar to y with respect to R.

It is also easy to see that for any $(\alpha, \beta) \in J$, $R(\alpha, \beta)$ is an equivalence relation on U. Let $R_{\alpha, \beta}^*$ be the set of equivalence classes generated by the equivalence relation $R(\alpha, \beta)$ for each fixed $(\alpha, \beta) \in J$. The pair (U, R) is an intuitionistic fuzzy approximation space (IF-approximation space). An IF-approximation space (U, R) generates usual approximation space $(U, R(\alpha, \beta))$ of Pawlak for every $(\alpha, \beta) \in J$. The rough set on X in the generalized approximation space $(U, R(\alpha, \beta))$ is denoted by $\left(\underline{X}_{\alpha, \beta}, \overline{X}_{\alpha, \beta} \right)$ where

$$\underline{X}_{\alpha, \beta} = \cup \left\{ Y \middle| Y \in R_{\alpha, \beta}^* \text{ and } Y \subseteq X \right\} \tag{5}$$

and

$$\overline{X}_{\alpha, \beta} = \cup \left\{ Y \middle| Y \in R_{\alpha, \beta}^* \text{ and } Y \cap X \neq \phi \right\} \tag{6}$$

Let X be a rough set in the generalized approximation space $(U, R(\alpha, \beta))$. Then the (α, β)-boundary of X with respect to R denoted by $BNR_{\alpha, \beta}(X)$ as $BNR_{\alpha, \beta}(X) = \overline{X}_{\alpha, \beta} - \underline{X}_{\alpha, \beta}$. Then X is (α, β)-discernible with respect to R if and only if $\overline{X}_{\alpha, \beta} = \underline{X}_{\alpha, \beta}$ and X is (α, β)-rough with respect to R if and only if $\overline{X}_{\alpha, \beta} \neq \underline{X}_{\alpha, \beta}$.

ORDERED INFORMATION SYSTEM

All available information and knowledge about the objects under consideration are generally represented in an information system. These objects are measured by finite number of properties without considering any semantic relationships between the attribute values of a particular attribute (Yao, 2000). Different values of the same attribute are considered as distinct symbols without any connections, and therefore horizontal analyses to a large extent are considered on simple pattern matching. Hence, in general one uses the trivial equality relation on values of an attribute as discussed in standard rough set theory (Pawlak, 1982). However, it is observed in many real life applications that the attribute values are not exactly identical rather almost identical. It is because objects characterized by the almost same information are almost indiscernible in the view of available information as discussed in Table 2. Generalized information system may be viewed as information system with added semantics. For the problem of machine learning, order relations on attribute values are introduced (Yao & Ying, 2001). An order relation is a relation, which is reflexive, transitive and anti-symmetric. However, it is not appropriate in case of attribute values that are almost indiscernible.

An ordered information system (OIS) is defined as $OIS = \left\{I, \left\{\prec_a : a \in A\right\}\right\}$ where, I is a standard information system and $\prec_a$ is an order relation on attribute a. An ordering of values of a particular attribute a naturally induces an ordering of objects:

$$x \prec_{\{a\}} y \Leftrightarrow f_a(x) \prec_a f_a(y)$$

where, $\prec_{\{a\}}$ denotes an order relation on U induced by the attribute a. An object x is ranked ahead of object y if and only if the value of x on the attribute a is ranked ahead of the value of y on the attribute a. For example, the information system presented in Table 1 becomes an ordered information system on introducing the following ordering relations.

$\prec_{Cough}$: $Always \prec Seldom \prec Never$

$\prec_{Vomiting}$: $Always \prec Seldom \prec Never$

$\prec_{Cold}$: $Always \prec Seldom \prec Never$

$\prec_{Temperature}$: $Very\ high \prec High \prec Normal$

$\prec_{Delirium}$: $Never$

$\prec_{Fever}$: $Yes \prec No$

For a subset of attributes $B \subseteq A$, we define:

$$x \prec_B y \Leftrightarrow f_a(x) \prec_a f_a(y) \ \forall \ a \in B$$

$$\Leftrightarrow \bigwedge_{a \in P} f_a(x) \prec_a f_a(y) \Leftrightarrow \bigcap_{a \in P} \prec_{\{a\}}$$

Therefore, an object x is ranked ahead of y if and only if x is ranked ahead of y according to all attributes in P. It is a straightforward generalization of the standard definition of equivalence relations in rough set theory (Pawlak, (1982, 1991)), where the equality relation is used. Knowledge extraction based on order relations is a concrete example of applications on generalized rough set model with almost indiscernibility relations. This is because exactly ordering is not possible when the attribute values are almost identical. For $\alpha = 1$, and $\beta = 0$ the almost indiscernibility relation, reduces to the indiscernibility relation and thus it generalizes the Pawlak's indiscernibility relation.

BAYESIAN CLASSIFICATION

Databases are rich with hidden information that can be used for intelligent decision making. Classification and prediction are two forms of data analysis that can help provide us with a better understanding of the high dimensional data. In general, classification is used to predict future data trends. However, classification also predicts categorical labels (Han & Kamber, 2006). In this section, we discuss the fundamental concepts of Bayesian classification that can predict class membership probabilities. Bayesian classification is derived from Bayes' theorem. Lin & Haug, (2008) studied various classification algorithms for predicting medical problems.

Let T be a data tuple. In Bayesian terms, T is considered as evidence. As usual, it is described by measurements made on a set of q-attributes. Let H be some hypothesis, such that the data tuple T belongs to some specified class C. For classification, we determine $P(H \mid T)$, the probability that the hypothesis H holds given the evidence T. We define according to Bayes' theorem as:

$$P(H \mid T) = \frac{P(T \mid H)P(H)}{P(T)} \tag{7}$$

Now, we present the definitions, notations and results on Bayesian classification. Let D be a training set of tuples, where each tuple T is represented by q- dimensional attribute vector $T = \left(t_1, t_2, t_3, \cdots, t_q\right)$, with $t_i = x\left(a_i\right) i = 1, 2, 3, \ldots, q$; depicting q measurements made on the tuple from q attributes, respectively, $a_1, a_2, a_3, \cdots, a_q$.

Suppose that the decision attribute d has m classes $C_1, C_2, C_3, \cdots, C_m$. Therefore, $V_d = \left\{C_1, C_2, C_3, \cdots, C_m\right\}$. Given a tuple T, the classifier will predict that T belongs to class having the highest posterior probability, conditioned on T. That is, the naive Bayesian classifier predicts that tuple T belongs to class C_i if and only if $P\left(C_i \mid T\right) > P\left(C_j \mid T\right)$ for $j \neq i; 1 \leq i, j \leq m$. The class C_i for which $P(C_i \mid T)$ is maximum is called the maximum posteriori hypothesis. By Bayes theorem

$$P\left(C_i \mid T\right) = \frac{P\left(T \mid C_i\right)P\left(C_i\right)}{P(T)} \tag{8}$$

As $P(T)$ is constant for all classes, only $P(T \mid C_i) P(C_i)$ need to be maximized. If the class prior probabilities are not known, then it is assumed that the classes are equally likely, that is, $P(C_1) = P(C_2) = \ldots = P(C_m)$. Therefore, we would maximize $P(T \mid C_i)$. Otherwise the class prior probability $P(C_i) = |C_i| / |D|$ is to be estimated, where $|C_i|$ is the cardinality of the C_i and $P(T \mid C_i) P(C_i)$ is to be maximized. Given dataset with many attributes it is observed that computing $P(T \mid C_i)$ is computationally expensive. Thus the naïve assumption of class conditional independence is made to reduce computations. This presumes that the values of the attributes are conditionally independent of one another, given the class label of the tuple. Therefore,

$$P(T \mid C_i) = \prod_{k=1}^{q} P(t_k \mid C_i) \tag{9}$$

where t_k refers to the value of attribute a_K for tuple T. We define $P(t_k \mid C_i) = n_c / n$, where n_c, n is defined as the number of times that the attribute value t_k was seen with the label C_i and the number of times C_i is seen in the decision attribute d respectively. It is also observed that sometimes we might not see a particular value t_k with a particular label C_i. This results in zero probability as $n_c = 0$. Again this zero probability will dominate the classification of future instances as Baye's classifier multiplies the $P(t_k \mid C_i)$ together. In order to overcome this problem we need to hallucinate some counts to generalize beyond our training material by using m-estimate as discussed by Mitchell (1997) in machine learning. Therefore, we define $P(t_k \mid C_i)$ as

$$P(t_k \mid C_i) = \frac{n_c + mp}{n + m} \tag{10}$$

where p is the prior estimate of the probability and m is the equivalent sample size (constant). In the absence of other information, assume a uniform prior $p = \frac{1}{k}$, where $k = \left| V_{a_k} \right|$.

PROPOSED PREDICTION MODEL

This section proposes an association rule prediction model that consists of pre process and post process as shown in Figure 2. In pre process, we process the data after data cleaning by using rough set on intuitionistic fuzzy approximation space and ordering rules. Based on the classification obtained in pre process, Bayesian classification is used in post process to predict the decision of missing associations of attribute values. The main advantage of this model is that, it works for both qualitative and quantitative data.

Identification of right problem is the fundamental step of any model. Incorporation of prior knowledge is always associated with the problem definition. The potential validity or usefulness of an individual data element or pattern of data element may change dramatically from organization to organization because of the acquisition of knowledge and reasoning that may be involved in vagueness and incompleteness.

Figure 2. Proposed prediction model

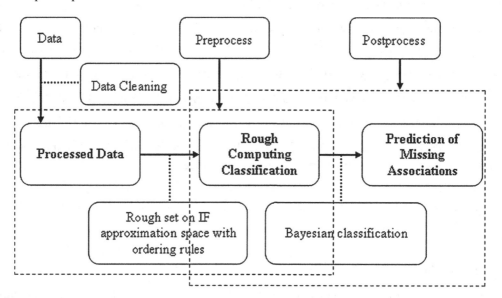

It is very difficult for humans to predict missing associations that is hidden in the voluminous data. Therefore, the most important challenge is to predict data pattern and unseen associations from the accumulated voluminous data. Thus, it is essential to deal with the incomplete and vague information in classification, data analysis, and concept formulation. To this end we use rough set on intuitionistic fuzzy approximation space with ordering rules in preprocess to mine suitable classification. In preprocess as shown in Figure 3 we use rough set on intuitionistic fuzzy approximation spaces with ordering rules for processing data, and classification after removal of noise and missing data. Based on the classification obtained in preprocess, we use Bayesian classification to predict decision for missing or unseen associations of data values.

Preprocessing Architecture Design

This section presents preprocess architecture design that consists of problem undergone, target data, data cleaning, intuitionistic fuzzy proximity relation, data classification, and ordering rules as shown in Figure 3. Problem definition and incorporation of prior knowledge are the fundamental steps of any model. Then structuring the objectives and the associated attributes a target dataset is created on which data mining is to be performed. Before further analysis a sequence of data cleaning tasks such as removing noise, consistency check, and data completeness is done to ensure that the data are as accurate as possible. Finally for each attribute, the (α, β)-equivalence classes based on intuitionistic fuzzy proximity relation is computed. The intuitionistic fuzzy proximity relation identifies the almost indiscernibility among the objects. This result induces the (α, β)-equivalence classes. On imposing order relation on this classification the categorical classes are obtained.

Figure 3. Preprocessing architecture design

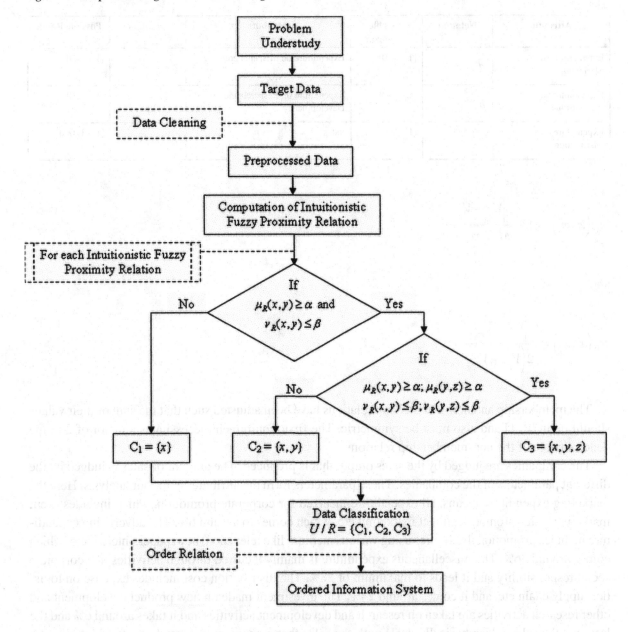

AN APPLICATION ON MARKETING STRATEGIES

This section demonstrates the proposed model by considering a real life problem for extracting information. To demonstrate the model, a case study on different cosmetic company's business strategies in a country is considered. In Table 3, few parameters for business strategies to get maximum sales; their possible range of values and intuitionistic fuzzy proximity relation which characterizes the relationship between parameters is considered. The intuitionistic fuzzy proximity relation $R\left(x_i, x_j\right)$ which identifies the almost indiscernibility among the institutions x_i and x_j is defined as below:

Table 3. Attribute descriptions table

Attribute	Notation	Possible Range	Attribute	Notation	Possible Range
Expenditure on Marketing	a_1	[1 – 150]	Expenditure on Miscellaneous	a_4	[1 – 700]
Expenditure on Advertisement	a_2	[1 – 900]	Expenditure on Research and Development	a_5	[1 – 150]
Expenditure on Distribution	a_3	[1 – 600]	Sales	a_6	[1 – 12000]

$$\mu_R\left(x_i, x_j\right) = 1 - \frac{\left|V_{x_i} - V_{x_j}\right|}{Max\ range}$$

and

$$\nu_R\left(x_i, x_j\right) = \frac{\left|V_{x_i} - V_{x_j}\right|}{2\left(V_{x_i} + V_{x_j}\right)}$$

The membership and non-membership relations have been adjusted such that the sum of their values should lie in [0, 1] and also must be symmetric. The first requirement necessitates a major of 2 in the denominators of the non-membership relations.

The companies are judged by the sales output that is produced. The amount of sales is judged by the different parameters of the companies. These parameters form the attribute set for our analysis. Here the marketing expenditure means, all expenditure incurred for corporate promotion, which includes event marketing, sales promotion, direct marketing etc. which comes to around 6%. The advertising expenditure includes promotional activities using various medium like television, newspaper, internet etc. which comes around 36%. The miscellaneous expenditure is mainly incurred through activities like corporate social responsibility and it leads to maximum of 28%. The distribution cost includes expense on logistic, supply chain etc. and it comes around 24%. The investment made on new product development and other research activities are taken on research and development activities and it takes around 6% and the last one, the sales which basically deals with the sales that a company can produce after investing the expenditure in different fields mentioned above. The company can observe the profit by subtracting the value of the total expenditure from the value of the total sales. But it may not be possible for a company to excel in all the above fields. However, some of the parameters considered above may have higher influence on the sales than other parameters. The importance of parameters depends upon the control parameters and so varies along with the values of these parameters. In fact, it has been observed that if we increase the values of α and decrease the value of β more and more parameters become indispensable.

The companies having high expenditure in marketing, advertisement, distribution, miscellaneous, and research and development is the ideal case. But such a blend of cases is rare in practice. So, a company may not excel in all the parameters in order to get maximum sales. However, out of these parameters, some parameters may have greater influence on others. But, the attribute values on these parameters obtained are almost indiscernible and hence can be classified by using rough set on intuitionistic fuzzy approximation space and ordering rules.

In view of the length of the paper and to make our analysis simple, a small universe of 10 institutions and the information pertaining to them are presented in the Table 4. The identities of the companies are kept confidential as they do not affect our analysis. The data collected is considered to be the representative figure and tabulated below in Table 4. Intuitionistic fuzzy proximity relations R_i; $i = 1, 2, 3, \cdots, 6$ corresponding to attributes a_1, a_2, a_3, a_4, a_5 and a_6 are given in Table 5, Table 6, Table 7, Table 8, Table 9 and Table 10 respectively.

On considering the almost similarity of 98% and dissimilarity of 1% i.e., $\alpha \geq 0.98$, $\beta < 0.01$ for membership and non-membership values respectively, it is observed from Table 5 that $\mu_{R_1}(x_1, x_1) = 1$,

$\nu_{R_1}(x_1, x_1) = 0$; $\mu_{R_1}(x_2, x_2) = 1$; $\nu_{R_1}(x_2, x_2) = 0$; $\mu_{R_1}(x_2, x_3) = 0.981$; $\nu_{R_1}(x_2, x_3) = 0.009$; $\mu_{R_1}(x_2, x_5) = 0.995$; $\nu_{R_1}(x_2, x_5) = 0.002$; $\mu_{R_1}(x_4, x_4) = 1$; $\nu_{R_1}(x_4, x_4) = 0$; $\mu_{R_1}(x_4, x_8) = 0.985$; $\nu_{R_1}(x_4, x_8) = 0.007$; $\mu_{R_1}(x_8, x_7) = 0.982$; $\nu_{R_1}(x_8, x_7) = 0.009$; $\mu_{R_1}(x_7, x_9) = 0.983$; $\nu_{R_1}(x_7, x_9) = 0.008$;

Table 4. Small universe of information system

Comp.	Mkt. (a_1)	Advt. (a_2)	Dist. (a_3)	Misc. (a_4)	R&D (a_5)	Sales (a_6)
x_1	18.276	162.236	30.236	72.146	9.156	1220.586
x_2	37.321	163.72	82.568	68.257	1.513	623.538
x_3	34.531	37.773	25.237	79.237	8.769	11232.76
x_4	2.076	5.393	6.793	8.290	0.383	42.767
x_5	36.621	36.772	492.534	25.343	35.967	1352.264
x_6	27.333	38.660	16.496	24.343	1.523	561.697
x_7	7.033	866.916	508.676	637.530	38.963	11449.56
x_8	4.323	4.173	1.753	3.176	0.003	60.89
x_9	9.563	872.57	80.768	632.535	1.453	1197.725
x_{10}	26.678	161.268	26.593	9.269	33.928	558.395

Table 5. Intuitionistic fuzzy proximity relation for attribute Marketing $\left(a_1\right)$

R_1	x_1	x_2	x_3	x_4	x_5	x_6	x_7	x_8	x_9	x_{10}
x_1	1 0	0.873 0.063	0.892 0.054	0.892 0.054	0.878 0.061	0.94 0.03	0.925 0.037	0.907 0.047	0.942 0.029	0.944 0.028
x_2	0.873 0.063	1 0	0.981 0.009	0.765 0.117	0.995 0.002	0.933 0.033	0.798 0.101	0.78 0.11	0.815 0.093	0.929 0.035
x_3	0.892 0.054	0.981 0.009	1 0	0.784 0.108	0.986 0.007	0.952 0.024	0.817 0.092	0.799 0.101	0.834 0.083	0.948 0.026
x_4	0.892 0.054	0.765 0.117	0.784 0.108	1 0	0.77 0.115	0.832 0.084	0.967 0.017	0.985 0.007	0.95 0.025	0.836 0.082
x_5	0.878 0.061	0.995 0.002	0.986 0.007	0.77 0.115	1 0	0.938 0.031	0.803 0.099	0.785 0.108	0.82 0.09	0.934 0.033
x_6	0.94 0.03	0.933 0.033	0.952 0.024	0.832 0.084	0.938 0.031	1 0	0.865 0.068	0.847 0.077	0.882 0.059	0.996 0.002
x_7	0.925 0.037	0.798 0.101	0.817 0.092	0.967 0.017	0.803 0.099	0.865 0.068	1 0	0.982 0.009	0.983 0.008	0.869 0.065
x_8	0.907 0.047	0.78 0.11	0.799 0.101	0.985 0.007	0.785 0.108	0.847 0.077	0.982 0.009	1 0	0.965 0.017	0.851 0.075
x_9	0.942 0.029	0.815 0.093	0.834 0.083	0.95 0.025	0.82 0.09	0.882 0.059	0.983 0.008	0.965 0.017	1 0	0.886 0.057
x_{10}	0.944 0.028	0.929 0.035	0.948 0.026	0.836 0.082	0.934 0.033	0.996 0.002	0.869 0.065	0.851 0.075	0.886 0.057	1 0

$\mu_{R_1}\left(x_6,x_6\right)=1$; $\nu_{R_1}\left(x_6,x_6\right)=0$; $\mu_{R_1}\left(x_6,x_{10}\right)=0.996$; and $\nu_{R_1}\left(x_6,x_{10}\right)=0.002$. Therefore, the companies x_2, x_3 and x_5 are $\left(\alpha,\beta\right)$-identical. Similarly, x_4, x_7, x_8 and x_9 are $\left(\alpha,\beta\right)$-identical; x_6 and x_{10} are $\left(\alpha,\beta\right)$-identical. Therefore, we get

$$U / R_1^{\alpha,\beta} = \left\{\left\{x_1\right\}, \left\{x_2, x_3, x_5\right\}, \left\{x_4, x_7, x_8, x_9\right\}, \left\{x_6, x_{10}\right\}\right\}$$

It indicates that, the values of the attribute expenditure on marketing are classified into four categories namely low, average, high and very high and hence can be ordered. Similarly, the different equivalence classes obtained from Table 6, 7, 8, 9 and 10 corresponding to the attributes expenditure on advertisement, distribution, miscellaneous, R&D and total sales are given below.

$$U / R_2^{\alpha,\beta} = \left\{\left\{x_1, x_2, x_{10}\right\}, \left\{x_3, x_5, x_6\right\}, \left\{x_4, x_8\right\}, \left\{x_7, x_9\right\}\right\}$$

$$U / R_3^{\alpha,\beta} = \left\{\left\{x_1, x_3, x_4, x_6, x_8, x_{10}\right\}, \left\{x_2, x_9\right\}, \left\{x_5\right\}, \left\{x_7\right\}\right\}$$

Table 6. Intuitionistic fuzzy proximity relation for attribute Advt. $\left(a_2\right)$

R_2	x_1	x_2	x_3	x_4	x_5	x_6	x_7	x_8	x_9	x_{10}
x_1	1 0	0.998 0.001	0.862 0.069	0.826 0.087	0.861 0.07	0.863 0.069	0.217 0.391	0.824 0.088	0.211 0.395	0.999 0.001
x_2	0.998 0.001	1 0	0.86 0.07	0.824 0.088	0.859 0.071	0.861 0.069	0.219 0.391	0.823 0.089	0.212 0.394	0.997 0.001
x_3	0.862 0.069	0.86 0.07	1 0	0.964 0.018	0.999 0.001	0.999 0	0.079 0.461	0.963 0.019	0.072 0.464	0.863 0.069
x_4	0.826 0.087	0.824 0.088	0.964 0.018	1 0	0.965 0.017	0.963 0.018	0.043 0.479	0.999 0.001	0.036 0.482	0.827 0.087
x_5	0.861 0.07	0.859 0.071	0.999 0.001	0.965 0.017	1 0	0.998 0.001	0.078 0.461	0.964 0.018	0.071 0.464	0.862 0.069
x_6	0.863 0.069	0.861 0.069	0.999 0	0.963 0.018	0.998 0.001	1 0	0.08 0.46	0.962 0.019	0.073 0.463	0.864 0.068
x_7	0.217 0.391	0.219 0.391	0.079 0.461	0.043 0.479	0.078 0.461	0.08 0.46	1 0	0.041 0.479	0.994 0.003	0.216 0.392
x_8	0.824 0.088	0.823 0.089	0.963 0.019	0.999 0.001	0.964 0.018	0.962 0.019	0.041 0.479	1 0	0.035 0.482	0.825 0.087
x_9	0.211 0.395	0.212 0.394	0.072 0.464	0.036 0.482	0.071 0.464	0.073 0.463	0.994 0.003	0.035 0.482	1 0	0.21 0.395
x_{10}	0.999 0.001	0.997 0.001	0.863 0.069	0.827 0.087	0.862 0.069	0.864 0.068	0.216 0.392	0.825 0.087	0.21 0.395	1 0

$$U / R_4^{\alpha,\beta} = \left\{\{x_1, x_2, x_3\}, \{x_4, x_8, x_{10}\}, \{x_5, x_6\}, \{x_7, x_9\}\right\}$$

$$U / R_5^{\alpha,\beta} = \left\{\{x_1, x_3\}, \{x_2, x_4, x_6, x_8, x_9\}, \{x_5, x_7, x_{10}\}\right\}$$

$$U / R_6^{\alpha,\beta} = \left\{\{x_1, x_5, x_9\}, \{x_2, x_6, x_{10}\}, \{x_3, x_7\}, \{x_4, x_8\}\right\}$$

From the above analysis, it is clear that the attribute expenditure on advertisement and expenditure on distribution classify the universe into four categories. Let it be low, average, high, and very high and thus can be ordered. Similarly, the attributes expenditure on miscellaneous and total sales classify the universe into four categories such as medium, average, high and very high and hence can be ordered. The attribute expenditure on R&D classifies the universe into three categories namely low, average and very high. Therefore, the ordered information system of the small universe Table 4 is given in Table 11.

Table 7. Intuitionistic fuzzy proximity relation for attribute Dist. $\left(a_3 \right)$

R_3	x_1	x_2	x_3	x_4	x_5	x_6	x_7	x_8	x_9	x_{10}
x_1	1 0	0.913 0.044	0.992 0.004	0.961 0.02	0.23 0.385	0.977 0.011	0.203 0.399	0.953 0.024	0.916 0.042	0.994 0.003
x_2	0.913 0.044	1 0	0.904 0.048	0.874 0.063	0.317 0.342	0.89 0.055	0.29 0.355	0.865 0.067	0.997 0.002	0.907 0.047
x_3	0.992 0.004	0.904 0.048	1 0	0.969 0.015	0.221 0.389	0.985 0.007	0.194 0.403	0.961 0.02	0.907 0.046	0.998 0.001
x_4	0.961 0.02	0.874 0.063	0.969 0.015	1 0	0.19 0.405	0.984 0.008	0.164 0.418	0.992 0.004	0.877 0.062	0.967 0.017
x_5	0.23 0.385	0.317 0.342	0.221 0.389	0.19 0.405	1 0	0.207 0.397	0.973 0.013	0.182 0.409	0.314 0.343	0.223 0.388
x_6	0.977 0.011	0.89 0.055	0.985 0.007	0.984 0.008	0.207 0.397	1 0	0.18 0.41	0.975 0.012	0.893 0.054	0.983 0.008
x_7	0.203 0.399	0.29 0.355	0.194 0.403	0.164 0.418	0.973 0.013	0.18 0.41	1 0	0.155 0.422	0.287 0.357	0.197 0.402
x_8	0.953 0.024	0.865 0.067	0.961 0.02	0.992 0.004	0.182 0.409	0.975 0.012	0.155 0.422	1 0	0.868 0.066	0.959 0.021
x_9	0.916 0.042	0.997 0.002	0.907 0.046	0.877 0.062	0.314 0.343	0.893 0.054	0.287 0.357	0.868 0.066	1 0	0.91 0.045
x_{10}	0.994 0.003	0.907 0.047	0.998 0.001	0.967 0.017	0.223 0.388	0.983 0.008	0.197 0.402	0.959 0.021	0.91 0.045	1 0

Postprocess of Empirical Study

Bayesian classification analysis can do the data classification. However data are already classified in preprocess. The objective of this process is to use Bayesian classification to predict the unseen association rule from the order information system and hence to get better knowledge affecting the decision making. In order to show post processing analysis, we consider an unseen association of attribute values T = {Mkt. = High, Advt. = Average, Dist. = Low, Misc. = Average, R&D = High} to predict the decision 'sales'. Let us take $T = \left\{ t_1, t_2, t_3, t_4, t_5 \right\}$, where t_1 is Mkt. = High; t_2 is Advt. = Average; t_3 is Dist. = Low; t_4 is Misc. = Average; and t_5 is R&D = High. From the preprocessing, it is clear that the decision 'sales' has 4 classes say C_1 = Very high, C_2 = High, C_3 = Average and C_4 = Medium. But,

$P\left(t_i \mid C_1 \right) = 0$ for $i = 1, 4, 5$ and $P\left(t_i \mid C_1 \right) = \dfrac{1}{2}$ for $i = 2, 3$ with $P\left(C_1 \right) = \dfrac{2}{10}$. Thus, it dominates the classification of future instances as Bayes classifier multiplies $P\left(t_i \mid C_1 \right)$ together. Therefore, by using *m*-estimate we get:

Table 8. Intuitionistic fuzzy proximity relation for attribute Misc. $\left(a_4\right)$

R_4	x_1	x_2	x_3	x_4	x_5	x_6	x_7	x_8	x_9	x_{10}
x_1	1 0	0.994 0.003	0.99 0.005	0.909 0.046	0.933 0.033	0.932 0.034	0.192 0.404	0.901 0.049	0.199 0.4	0.91 0.045
x_2	0.994 0.003	1 0	0.984 0.008	0.914 0.043	0.939 0.031	0.937 0.031	0.187 0.407	0.907 0.046	0.194 0.403	0.916 0.042
x_3	0.99 0.005	0.984 0.008	1 0	0.899 0.051	0.923 0.038	0.922 0.039	0.202 0.399	0.891 0.054	0.21 0.395	0.9 0.05
x_4	0.909 0.046	0.914 0.043	0.899 0.051	1 0	0.976 0.012	0.977 0.011	0.101 0.449	0.993 0.004	0.108 0.446	0.999 0.001
x_5	0.933 0.033	0.939 0.031	0.923 0.038	0.976 0.012	1 0	0.999 0.001	0.125 0.437	0.968 0.016	0.133 0.434	0.977 0.011
x_6	0.932 0.034	0.937 0.031	0.922 0.039	0.977 0.011	0.999 0.001	1 0	0.124 0.438	0.97 0.015	0.131 0.434	0.978 0.011
x_7	0.192 0.404	0.187 0.407	0.202 0.399	0.101 0.449	0.125 0.437	0.124 0.438	1 0	0.094 0.453	0.993 0.004	0.102 0.449
x_8	0.901 0.049	0.907 0.046	0.891 0.054	0.993 0.004	0.968 0.016	0.97 0.015	0.094 0.453	1 0	0.101 0.45	0.991 0.004
x_9	0.199 0.4	0.194 0.403	0.21 0.395	0.108 0.446	0.133 0.434	0.131 0.434	0.993 0.004	0.101 0.45	1 0	0.11 0.445
x_{10}	0.91 0.045	0.916 0.042	0.9 0.05	0.999 0.001	0.977 0.011	0.978 0.011	0.102 0.449	0.991 0.004	0.11 0.445	1 0

$$P\left(t_1 \mid C_1\right) = \frac{0 + 4\left(\frac{1}{4}\right)}{2 + 4} = \frac{1}{6}$$

$$P\left(t_2 \mid C_1\right) = \frac{1 + 4\left(\frac{1}{4}\right)}{2 + 4} = \frac{2}{6}$$

$$P\left(t_3 \mid C_1\right) = \frac{1 + 4\left(\frac{1}{4}\right)}{2 + 4} = \frac{2}{6}$$

$$P\left(t_4 \mid C_1\right) = \frac{0 + 4\left(\frac{1}{4}\right)}{2 + 4} = \frac{1}{6}$$

$$P\left(t_5 \mid C_1\right) = \frac{0 + 3\left(\frac{1}{3}\right)}{2 + 3} = \frac{1}{5}$$

Table 9. Intuitionistic fuzzy proximity relation for attribute R&D $\left(a_5\right)$

R_5	x_1	x_2	x_3	x_4	x_5	x_6	x_7	x_8	x_9	x_{10}
x_1	1 0	0.949 0.025	0.997 0.001	0.942 0.029	0.821 0.089	0.949 0.025	0.801 0.099	0.939 0.031	0.949 0.026	0.835 0.083
x_2	0.949 0.025	1 0	0.952 0.024	0.992 0.004	0.77 0.115	1 0	0.75 0.125	0.99 0.005	1 0	0.784 0.108
x_3.	0.997 0.001	0.952 0.024	1 0	0.944 0.028	0.819 0.091	0.952 0.024	0.799 0.101	0.942 0.029	0.951 0.024	0.832 0.084
x_4	0.942 0.029	0.992 0.004	0.944 0.028	1 0	0.763 0.119	0.992 0.004	0.743 0.129	0.997 0.001	0.993 0.004	0.776 0.112
x_5	0.821 0.089	0.77 0.115	0.819 0.091	0.763 0.119	1 0	0.77 0.115	0.98 0.01	0.76 0.12	0.77 0.115	0.986 0.007
x_6	0.949 0.025	1 0	0.952 0.024	0.992 0.004	0.77 0.115	1 0	0.75 0.125	0.99 0.005	1 0	0.784 0.108
x_7	0.801 0.099	0.75 0.125	0.799 0.101	0.743 0.129	0.98 0.01	0.75 0.125	1 0	0.74 0.13	0.75 0.125	0.966 0.017
x_8	0.939 0.031	0.99 0.005	0.942 0.029	0.997 0.001	0.76 0.12	0.99 0.005	0.74 0.13	1 0	0.99 0.005	0.774 0.113
x_9	0.949 0.026	1 0	0.951 0.024	0.993 0.004	0.77 0.115	1 0	0.75 0.125	0.99 0.005	1 0	0.784 0.108
x_{10}	0.835 0.083	0.784 0.108	0.832 0.084	0.776 0.112	0.986 0.007	0.784 0.108	0.966 0.017	0.774 0.113	0.784 0.108	1 0

and

$$P\left(C_1\right) = \frac{2+4\left(\frac{1}{4}\right)}{10+4} = \frac{3}{14}$$

Therefore, by using Bayesian classification we get

$$P\left(C_1 \mid T\right) = \prod_{i=1}^{5} P\left(t_i \mid C_1\right) P\left(C_1\right)$$
$$= \tfrac{1}{6} \times \tfrac{2}{6} \times \tfrac{2}{6} \times \tfrac{1}{6} \times \tfrac{2}{5} \times \tfrac{3}{14} = 0.000264$$

Similarly, we get

$$P\left(C_2 \mid T\right) = 0.0000317 \, ; P\left(C_3 \mid T\right) = 0.000713 \, ; \text{ and } P\left(C_4 \mid T\right) = 0.000099 \, .$$

Table 10. Intuitionistic fuzzy proximity relation for attribute Sales $\left(a_6\right)$

R_6	x_1	x_2	x_3	x_4	x_5	x_6	x_7	x_8	x_9	x_{10}
x_1	1 0	0.95 0.025	0.166 0.417	0.902 0.049	0.989 0.005	0.945 0.027	0.148 0.426	0.903 0.048	0.998 0.001	0.945 0.028
x_2	0.95 0.025	1 0	0.116 0.442	0.952 0.024	0.939 0.03	0.995 0.003	0.098 0.451	0.953 0.023	0.952 0.024	0.995 0.003
x_3	0.166 0.417	0.116 0.442	1 0	0.068 0.466	0.177 0.412	0.111 0.445	0.982 0.009	0.069 0.465	0.164 0.418	0.11 0.445
x_4	0.902 0.049	0.952 0.024	0.068 0.466	1 0	0.891 0.055	0.957 0.022	0.049 0.475	0.998 0.001	0.904 0.048	0.957 0.021
x_5	0.989 0.005	0.939 0.03	0.177 0.412	0.891 0.055	1 0	0.934 0.033	0.159 0.421	0.892 0.054	0.987 0.006	0.934 0.033
x_6	0.945 0.027	0.995 0.003	0.111 0.445	0.957 0.022	0.934 0.033	1 0	0.093 0.454	0.958 0.021	0.947 0.027	1 0
x_7	0.148 0.426	0.098 0.451	0.982 0.009	0.049 0.475	0.159 0.421	0.093 0.454	1 0	0.051 0.475	0.146 0.427	0.092 0.454
x_8	0.903 0.048	0.953 0.023	0.069 0.465	0.998 0.001	0.892 0.054	0.958 0.021	0.051 0.475	1 0	0.905 0.047	0.959 0.021
x_9	0.998 0.001	0.952 0.024	0.164 0.418	0.904 0.048	0.987 0.006	0.947 0.027	0.146 0.427	0.905 0.047	1 0	0.947 0.027
x_{10}	0.945 0.028	0.995 0.003	0.11 0.445	0.957 0.021	0.934 0.033	1 0	0.092 0.454	0.959 0.021	0.947 0.027	1 0

From the above computations it is clear that $P\left(C_3 \mid T\right)$ is maximum. Therefore, it is clear that the above unseen association of attribute values belongs to the decision class $C_3 =$ Average. Keeping view to the length of the paper, some of the unseen association of attribute values and its corresponding decision are presented in Table 12.

FUTURE RESEARCH DIRECTIONS

This chapter extends the concept of rough set to rough set on intuitionistic fuzzy approximation spaces and integrates Bayesian classification with rough set on intuitionistic fuzzy approximation spaces to predict the decision of unseen association of attribute values. A real life application is presented to show the viability of the extended concept. Future work will be carried out in the direction of multigranulation and its integration with Bayesian classification to solve various real life applications. In addition, integration of Bayesian classification with rough set on two universal sets is also planned for future work. These results and applications are to be addressed and studied.

Table 11. Ordered information table of the small universe

Companies	Mkt. (a_1)	Advt. (a_2)	Dist. (a_3)	Misc. (a_4)	R&D (a_5)	Sales (a_6)
x_1	Average	High	Low	High	Average	High
x_2	Very high	High	Average	High	Low	Average
x_3	Very high	Average	Low	High	Average	Very high
x_4	Low	Low	Low	Medium	Low	Medium
x_5	Very high	Average	High	Average	Very high	High
x_6	High	Average	Low	Average	Low	Average
x_7	Low	Very high	Very high	Very high	Very high	Very high
x_8	Low	Low	Low	Medium	Low	Medium
x_9	Low	Very high	Average	Very high	Low	High
x_{10}	High	High	Low	Medium	Very high	Average

$\prec_{Mkt.}: Very\ high \prec High \prec Average \prec Low$

$\prec_{Advt.}: Very\ high \prec High \prec Average \prec Low$

$\prec_{Dist.}: Very\ high \prec High \prec Average \prec Low$

$\prec_{Misc.}: Very\ high \prec High \prec Average \prec Medium$

$\prec_{R\&D}: Very\ high \prec Average \prec Low$

$\prec_{Sales}: Very\ high \prec High \prec Average \prec Medium$

Table 12. Prediction of unseen associations of attribute values

Unseen Associations	Mkt.	Advt.	Dist.	Misc.	R&D	Sales
1	High	Average	Low	Average	High	Average
2	High	Very high	Average	High	Average	High
3	Low	High	High	Medium	Average	High
4	Low	Low	Average	High	Very high	High
5	Average	Very high	High	Medium	Low	High

CONCLUSION

This Chapter extends the concepts of rough set to rough set on fuzzy approximation spaces. Further rough set on fuzzy approximation space is extended to rough set on intuitionistic fuzzy approximation space. Ordering of objects is a fundamental issue in decision making and plays a vital role in the design of intelligent information systems. This chapter integrates ordering relation, rough set on intuitionistic fuzzy approximation spaces and Bayesian classification. The main objective of integration is to predict unseen or missing associations of attribute values in the study of high dimensional database. In general, Bayesian classification is used to predict the unseen association rule. However, it is not directly applicable in case of information system containing almost indiscernible attribute values. In order to overcome this problem the proposed prediction model uses both rough set on intuitionistic fuzzy approximation space with ordering relation and Bayesian classification. The model identifies the almost indiscernibility between the attribute values in the preprocess phase whereas Bayesian classification is used in the post process to predict the decision. This helps the decision maker a priori prediction of sales. In order to illustrate the model, a real life example of 10 company's database according to different attributes is taken and shown how analysis can be performed. It is believed that, rough set on intuitionistic fuzzy approximation space with ordering relation together with Bayesian classification can be used to find furthermore information regardless of the type of associations based soft computing. In addition, the proposed model is very much useful for their application in decision making, knowledge extraction and design of knowledge bases.

REFERENCES

Acharjya, D. P. (2009). Comparative study of rough sets on fuzzy approximation spaces and intuitionistic fuzzy approximation spaces. *International Journal of Computational and Applied Mathematics*, *4*(2), 95–106.

Acharjya, D. P., & Geetha, M. A. (2014). Privacy preservation in information system. IGI Global. doi:10.4018/978-1-4666-4940-8.ch003

Acharjya, D. P., & Tripathy, B. K. (2008). Rough sets on fuzzy approximation spaces and applications to distributed knowledge systems. *International Journal of Artificial Intelligence and Soft Computing*, *1*(1), 1–14. doi:10.1504/IJAISC.2008.021260

Acharjya, D. P., & Tripathy, B. K. (2009). Rough sets on intuitionistic fuzzy approximation spaces and knowledge representation. *International Journal of Artificial Intelligence and Computational Research*, *1*(1), 29–36.

Atanasov, K. T. (1986). Intuitionistic Fuzzy Sets. *Fuzzy Sets and Systems*, *20*(1), 87–96. doi:10.1016/S0165-0114(86)80034-3

Dubosis, D., & Prade, H. (1987). Twofold fuzzy sets and rough sets-some issues in knowledge representation. *Fuzzy Sets and Systems*, *23*(1), 3–18. doi:10.1016/0165-0114(87)90096-0

Dubosis, D., & Prade, H. (1993). Toll sets and toll logic. In Fuzzy Logic, (pp.169-177). Kluwer Academic Publishers.

Fayaad, U. M. (1996). Advances in knowledge discovery and data mining. *American Association for Artificial Intelligence (AAAI) Press.*

Goguen, J. A. (1967). L–fuzzy sets. *Journal of Mathematical Analysis and Applications, 18*(1), 145–174. doi:10.1016/0022-247X(67)90189-8

Han, J., & Kamber, M. (2006). *Data Mining and Concepts and Techniques.* New York: Elsevier.

Li, D. Y., & Hu, B. Q. (2007). A kind of dynamic rough sets. In *Proceedings of the Fourth International Conference on Fuzzy Systems and Knowledge Discovery (FSKD)*, (pp. 79-85). doi:10.1109/FSKD.2007.51

Lin, J. H., & Haug, P. J. (2008). Exploiting missing clinical data in Bayesian network modeling for predicting medical problems. *Journal of Biomedical Informatics, New York, 41*(1), 1–14. doi:10.1016/j.jbi.2007.06.001 PMID:17625974

Little, R. J. A., & Rubin, D. B. (2002). *Statistical analysis with missing data* (2nd ed.). Wiley-Interscience. doi:10.1002/9781119013563

Pawlak, Z. (1981). Information systems: Theoretical foundations. *Information Systems, 6*(3), 205–218. doi:10.1016/0306-4379(81)90023-5

Pawlak, Z. (1982). Rough sets. *International Journal of Computer Information Science, 11*(5), 341–356. doi:10.1007/BF01001956

Pawlak, Z. (1991). *Rough sets: Theoretical Aspects of Reasoning about Data.* The Netherlands: Kluwer Academic Publishers. doi:10.1007/978-94-011-3534-4

Pawlak, Z., & Skowron, A. (2007a). Rudiments of rough sets. *Information Sciences, 177*(1), 3–27. doi:10.1016/j.ins.2006.06.003

Pawlak, Z., & Skowron, A. (2007b). Rough sets: Some extensions. *Information Sciences, 177*(1), 28–40. doi:10.1016/j.ins.2006.06.006

Pawlak, Z., & Skowron, A. (2007c). Rough sets and Boolean reasoning. *Information Sciences, 177*(1), 41–73. doi:10.1016/j.ins.2006.06.007

Rocha, L. M. (2001). TalkMine: A soft computing approach to adaptive knowledge recommendation. In Soft Computing Agents: New Trends for Designing Autonomous Systems (pp. 89-116). Springer. doi:10.1007/978-3-7908-1815-4_4

Rubin, D. B. (1976). Inference and missing data. *Biometrika, 63*(3), 581–592. doi:10.1093/biomet/63.3.581

Slowinski, R., & Vanderpooten, D. (2000). A generalized definition of rough approximations based on similarity. *IEEE Transactions on Knowledge and Data Engineering, 12*(2), 331–336. doi:10.1109/69.842271

Tripathy, B. K., & Acharjya, D. P. (2010). Knowledge mining using ordering rules and rough sets on fuzzy approximation spaces. *International Journal of Advances in Science and Technology, 1*(3), 41–50.

Tripathy, B. K., & Acharjya, D. P. (2011). Association rule granulation using rough sets on intuitionistic fuzzy approximation spaces and granular computing. *Annals Computer Science Series, 9*(1), 125–144.

Tripathy, B. K., Acharjya, D. P., & Cynthya, V. (2011). A framework for intelligent medical diagnosis using rough set with formal concept analysis. *International Journal of Artificial Intelligence & Applications*, *2*(2), 45–66. doi:10.5121/ijaia.2011.2204

Yao, Y. Y. (2000). Information tables with neighborhood semantics. In Data Mining and Knowledge Discovery: Theory, Tools, and Technology (pp. 108-116). Society for Optical Engineering.

Yao, Y. Y., & Sai, Y. (2001). Mining ordering rules using rough set theory. *Bulletin of International Rough Set Society*, *5*, 99–106.

Zadeh, L. A. (1965). Fuzzy sets. *Information and Control*, *8*(3), 338–353. doi:10.1016/S0019-9958(65)90241-X

Zhu, W., & Wang, F. Y. (2007). On three types of covering rough sets. *IEEE Transactions on Knowledge and Data Engineering*, *19*(8), 1131–1144. doi:10.1109/TKDE.2007.1044

Chapter 10
Big Data and Web Intelligence:
Improving the Efficiency on Decision Making Process via BDD

Alberto Pliego
Escuela Técnica Superior de Ingenieros Industriales, Spain

Fausto Pedro García Márquez
Escuela Técnica Superior de Ingenieros Industriales, Spain

ABSTRACT

The growing amount of available data generates complex problems when they need to be treated. Usually these data come from different sources and inform about different issues, however, in many occasions these data can be interrelated in order to gather strategic information that is useful for Decision Making processes in multitude of business. For a qualitatively and quantitatively analysis of a complex Decision Making process is critical to employ a correct method due to the large number of operations required. With this purpose, this chapter presents an approach employing Binary Decision Diagram applied to the Logical Decision Tree. It allows addressing a Main Problem by establishing different causes, called Basic Causes and their interrelations. The cases that have a large number of Basic Causes generate important computational costs because it is a NP-hard type problem. Moreover, this chapter presents a new approach in order to analyze big Logical Decision Trees. However, the size of the Logical Decision Trees is not the unique factor that affects to the computational cost but the procedure of resolution can widely vary this cost (ordination of Basic Causes, number of AND/OR gates, etc.) A new approach to reduce the complexity of the problem is hereby presented. It makes use of data derived from simpler problems that requires less computational costs for obtaining a good solution. An exact solution is not provided by this method but the approximations achieved have a low deviation from the exact.

INTRODUCTION

The information and communication technologies (ICT) have grown up with no precedents, and all aspects of human life have been transformed under this new scenario. All industrial sectors have rapidly incorporated the new technologies, and some of them have become de facto standards like supervisory control and data acquisition (SCADA) systems. Huge large amounts of data started to be created, pro-

DOI: 10.4018/978-1-4666-8505-5.ch010

cessed and saved, allowing an automatic control of complex industrial systems. In spite of this progress, there are some challenges not well addressed yet. Some of them are: the analysis of tons of data, as well as continuous data streams; the integration of data in different formats coming from different sources; making sense of data to support decision making; and getting results in short periods of time. These all are characteristics of a problem that should be addressed through a big data approach.

Even though Big Data has become one of the most popular buzzword, the industry has evolved towards a definition around this term on the base of three dimensions: volume, variety and velocity (Zikopoulos and Eaton, 2011).

Data *volume* is normally measured by the quantity of raw transactions, events or amount of history that creates the data volume. Typically, data analysis algorithms have used smaller data sets called training sets to create predictive models. Most of the times, the business use predictive insight that are severely gross since the data volume has purposely been reduced according to storage and computational processing constraints. By removing the data volume constraint and using larger data sets, it is possible to discover subtle patterns that can lead to targeted actionable decisions, or they can enable further analysis that increase the accuracy of the predictive models.

Data *variety* came into existence over the past couple of decades, when data has increasingly become unstructured as the sources of data have proliferated beyond operational applications. In industrial applications, such variety emerged from the proliferation of multiple types of sensors, which enable the tracking of multiple variables in almost every domain in the world. Most technical factors include sampling rate of data and their relative range of values.

Data *velocity* is about the speed at which data is created, accumulated, ingested, and processed. An increasing number of applications are required to process information in real-time or with near real-time responses. This may imply that data is processed on the fly, as it is ingested, to make real-time decisions, or schedule the appropriate tasks.

However as other authors point out, Big Data could be also classified according to other dimensions such as veracity, validity and volatility.

Data *veracity* is about the certainty of data meaning. This feature express whether data reflect properly the reality or not. It depends on the way in which data are collected. It is strongly linked to the credibility of sources. For example the veracity of the data collected from sensors depends on the calibration of sensors. The data collected from surveys could be truthful if survey samples are large enough to provide a sufficient basis for analysis. In resume, the massive amounts of data collected for Big Data purposes can lead to statistical errors and misinterpretation of the collected information. Purity of the information is critical for value (Ohlhorst, 1964).

Data *validity* is about the accuracy of data. The validity of Big Data sources must be accurate if results are wanted to be used for decision making or any other reasonable purpose (Hurwitz et al, 2013)

Data *volatility* is about how long the data need to be storage. Some difficulties could appear due to the storage capacity. If storage is limited, what and how long data is needed to be kept. With some Big Data sources, it could be necessary to gather the data for a quick analysis (Hurwitz et al, 2013).

These data are often used for decision making. DM processes are done continuously by any firm in order to maximize the profits reliability, etc. or minimize costs, risks, etc. There are software to facilitate this task, but the main problem is the capability for providing a quantitative solution when the case study has a large number of BCs. The DM problem is considered as a cyclic process in which the decision maker can evaluate the consequences of a previous decision. Figure 1 shows the normal process to solve a DM problem.

Figure 1. Decision Making Process

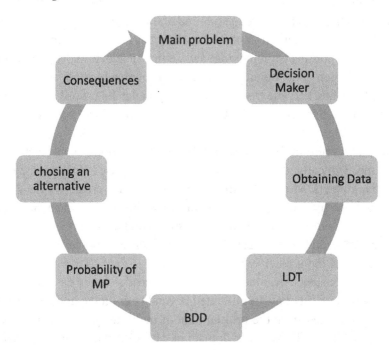

DEFINING THE MP VIA LOGICAL DECISION TREE

Decision Trees (DTs) represent one of the most commonly used tools for depicting an issue in business and encompasses all the alternatives involved.

Starting from the background given in (Lopez, 1977), the Logical Decision Tree (LDT) is introduced. It gives an alternative method to depict a DM issue including the interrelation between every single Basic Cause (BC).

Mentioned LDTs describe graphically which the roots of a certain problem are as well as its interrelation. With this purpose, and in accordance with (Mallo, 1995), both logical operators 'AND' and 'OR' are introduced in order to encompass a wider spectrum when analysing DM. Such logical operators will allow a better comprehension of the problem itself and it will fully establish the necessary background to a subsequent conversion from LDT to Binary Decision Diagram. To demonstrate that LDTs are perfectly suitable for depicting a certain condition in a DM context with a big amount of data and interrelations is sought in these lines.

LDTs are analysed as follow:

- There is a root cause, which will be known as Main Problem (MP).
- MP and its causes must be thoroughly analysed.
- Interrelation between the MP and its causes must be researched.
- The MP, as well as its roots and interrelations, must be depicted.

There are several ways to depict a particular situation/issue but LDT has been chosen in this chapter. The advantage of representing a business's issue as LDTs is that it can be seen at a glance. Thereby, a reduction in the resources needed by the business will be achieved with its consequent time and money saving.

Indeed, managers must be very careful when building the LDT because mentioned BCs must be the minimal and necessary causes which lead to a problem. Thus, for instance, BCs such as "Limited tools" or "Low tools reliability" are the minimum and necessary causes that lead to a "Wrong tools' stock".

It is important to denote that MP's causes must be mutually independent. The chance to analyse the main issues of business with a high number of BCs involved is introduced. Furthermore, companies have to deal with quite tough difficulties when having too many BCs.

To evaluate a DM problem, regardless its magnitude is carried out through LDT and its subsequent conversion to BDD.

This chapter considers a new approach based on breaking down the problem into different causes that could lead to non-desired situations. This disaggregation leads to determine the number of BCs and also identifies the manner in which all these BCs are logically interrelated. With this purpose. LDT is introduced as an alternative method to draw a DM, considering the interrelation between each BC (Lopez, 1977), that will take into account the logical operators 'AND' and 'OR' (Mallo, 1995). The Appendix shows a LDT case study composed by:

- 1 Top event or MP.
- **63 Logical Gates:** They determine the logical relation between BCs.
- **6 Levels:** It is related to the depth of each logical gate.
- **64 BCs:** Possible causes of the MP.
- There is a root cause, which will be known as Main Problem (MP).

It is showed only with OR gates because its topology will be changing in the experiments in order to analyse different scenarios that will provide different solutions.

LDT TO BDD CONVERSION

LDT conversion to BDD provides some advantages in terms of efficiency and accuracy, see (Lee CY, 1959), (Akers,1978), (Moret, 1982) and (Bryant,1986). BDD helps to show the occurrence of a serious issue in the business in a disjoint form, which indeed provides an advantage from the computational point of view.

BDD is a directed graph representation of a Boolean function, where equivalent Boolean sub-expressions are uniquely represented. A directed acyclic graph is a directed graph with no cycles, i.e. to each vertex v there is no possible directed path that starts and finishes in v. It is composed of some interconnected nodes in a way that each node has two vertices. Each can be either a terminal or non-terminal vertex. BDD is a graph-based data structure whereby the occurrence probability of a certain problem in a DM is possible to be achieved. Each single variable has two branches: 0-branch corresponds to the cases where the variable is 0; 1-branch cases are those where the event is being carried out and corresponds when the variable is 1.

The transformation from DT to BDD is achieved applying some mathematical algorithms. Ite (If-Then-Else) conditional expression is one of the BDD's cornerstones (Artigao, 2009), see Figure 2:

Figure 2 is defined as: "If BC_i variable occurs, Then f1, Else f2". The solid line always belongs to the ones as well as the dashed lines to the zeroes. Having into account the Shannon's theorem it can be obtained the following expression:

$$f = BC_i \cdot f_1 + \overline{BC}_i \cdot f_2$$

It can be also expressed as:

$$f = BC_i \cdot f_1 + \overline{BC}_i \cdot f_2 = ite\left(b_i, f_1, f_2\right)$$

Importance of a Right Variable Order

In the transformation from LDT to BDD is necessary to establish a correct ranking of BCs. A strong dependence on the variable ordering is one of the most tangible drawbacks when BDDs are used. In fact, both the BDD size as well as the CPU runtime have an awfully dependence on the variable ordering. A poor variable ordering is resulting in poor efficiency in computational terms.

BDD variable ordering has been largely treated through last decades, and there is plenty of related literature. Nevertheless, nowadays there is no method capablePrepositions act like bridges between the subject and the object of the sentence, giving the reader information about the time or space between the subject and the object. Some common prepositions are "about", "across", "after", "against", "along", "among", "around", "before", "below", "beneath", "despite", "down", "during", "for", "from", "near", "of", "off", "out", "outside", "over", "past", "since", "through", "to", "under", "until", "up", "with", and "without". Each preposition has a different meaning, though some of the differences may be slight. Seriously consider the relationship between your noun (or pronoun) and its object, and select the preposition which best describes that relationship.

Figure 2. ITE applied to BDD

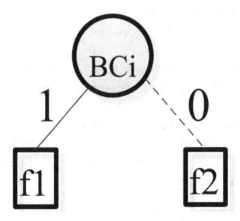

of providing an optimal solution to adapt to every BDD.

Heuristic methods have been used taking into account that the best variable ordering is desired to be achieved. The software used in herebyMake sure the adverb is not modifying a noun. Adverbs can describe verbs, adjectives, and other adverbs, but never a noun. Remember that not all adverbs end in "-ly"; check in a dictionary if you are not sure which role a word is playing.

chapter uses five different methods in order to obtain the right variables ordering. Mentioned methods are well known in the BDD environment and may be described as follow:

- **Topological Heuristic Methods:** The difference between the topological and both the Level as well as AND methods is that the topological are the easiest way to describe the tree (Artigao, 2009). Just several slight rules must be followed to rank the BCs.
    - **Top-Down-Left-Right (TDLR):** The tree is read as the method itself says i.e., from the top to the bottom and from the left to the right. That means a list of BCs will be created with the more important BCs starting up and in the right-side of the tree and follow as above mentioned.
    - **Depth-First-Search (DFS):** The tree is read from top to bottom and starting at its left. The sub-trees are identically read.
    - **Breath-First-Search (BFS):** The tree is read from left to the right and the variable ordering depends on the place they appear in the tree following that steps. It must be stated that if a repeated BC is found while reading the tree, it has to be ignored, regardless the method used.
- **Level Method:** This type of method is not so simple and direct. It makes a difference between the BCs depending on the position in the tree they are. That is, it is directly related with the number of gates there are above it. There are some important reminders to keep in mind. The repeated events will have a major importance when some BCs are in the same level. Moreover, in the cases where some BCs have the same above logic gates and are located in the same level, those that emerge the first will be given a major importance.
- **AND Method:** This method takes into account the number of AND logic gates which are in the path to the MP of a BC given. In such cases, the fewer number of AND logic gates, the major importance associated have the BC. It's fundamentally based on the idea that the BCs under an AND logic gates less important than the ones below OR logic gates (Artigao, 2009).
- **Weight ordering method:** Several considerations must be taken into account when trying to apply this method:
    - Each logic gate needs its own weighting.
    - The path followed by each BC to the MP i.e., the path defined by the different logic gates that must be crossed leading to the MP, will define the importance of each BC by multiplying them.
    - BC will be ordered in descending order.
    - The weighting assigned to each logic gate relies on two main causes:
    - The type of logic gate
    - The number of BCs underneath that logic gate.

Furthermore, recently published method has been proved to give some very good results when big-size trees are trying to be solved (García Márquez, 2012). The method associates a related weight depending on the logic gate. It considers only one of the 2n possible states will be spread whenever the logic gate found is AND.

Thus,

$$P_{AND}(n) = \frac{1}{2^n}$$

On the contrary, if the logic gate found is an OR, it considers that only one of the 2n possible states will not be spread. Therefore,

$$P_{OR}(n) = \frac{2^n - 1}{2^n}$$

Further detailed information about the conversion and variable ordering methods can be found in (García Márquez, 2012). In this chapter only AND and OR gates are used in the LDTs presented to express the interrelation between the BCs. Figure 3 shows the conversion from LDT to its corresponding BDD using the following order for BCs:

$$BC_1 > BC_2 > BC_3 > BC_4.$$

Once the conversion from DT to BDD is done, it is possible to obtain an accurate expression of the probability of occurrence of the MP Q_{MP} by assigning a probability value to each BC.

Figure 3. Conversion from LDT to BDD

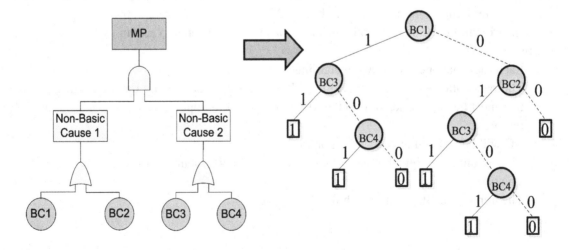

Cut-Sets and the Analytical Expression from BDD

Cut-sets (CS) turn into an important concept when referring to BDDs. They are the paths "from the top to the ones" that provide significant information due to the fact that the probability of occurrence of the MP could be achieved from them. The following CSs have been obtained from the BDD in Figure 3.

$$CS_1 = \left\{ BC_1, BC_3 \right\}$$

$$CS_2 = \left\{ BC_1, \overline{BC_3}, BC_4 \right\}$$

$$CS_3 = \left\{ \overline{BC_1}, BC_2, BC_3 \right\}$$

$$CS_4 = \left\{ \overline{BC_1}, BC_2, \overline{BC_3}, BC_4 \right\}$$

The MP probability is possible to be achieved due to the fact that the different paths (CSs) are mutually exclusive and may be expressed as the sum of probabilities of all the BDD paths, i.e. an analytic expression consisting of the sum of each analytic expression that forms the CSs. This expression will represent the utility function in the DM process.

Example

A reduced example is proposed directly in order to have a better notion of the IMs. It will base the background to the results given in the real case study. LDT in Figure 4 has been chosen toAn infinitive verb, which is a verb preceded by the word "to" (e.g. "to do", "to see"), should not have any words between the "to" and the verb. Modifiers generally should be placed before the verb.**N.B.** This is a tradition in formal writing that has always been argued about. If you are not writing a formal, academic text, you don't need to worry too much about this. Just make sure your sentence flows smoothly.

better understand the complete chapter scope.

Hence, Figure 4 is written in its abridged form.

The following mathematical expression completely defines the logical function of the LDT:

$$MP = b_1 \cdot \left(b_2 + b_3 \right) + b_4 \cdot \left(b_5 \cdot \left(b_6 + b_7 \right) \right)$$

The variable ordering generated with the BFS method produce the lower number of CSs with the following ranking:

$$b_1 > b_2 > b_3 > b_4 > b_5 > b_6 > b_7$$

Thus, the CSs produced are:

Figure 4. LDT example

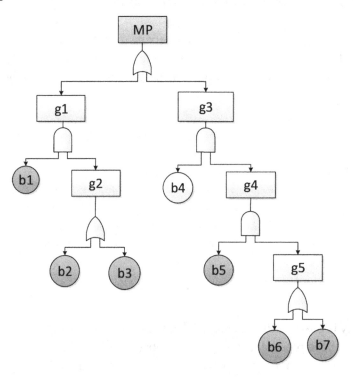

$$CS_1 = b_2 \cdot b_1$$

$$CS_2 = b_3 \cdot (1 - b_2) \cdot b_1$$

$$CS_3 = b_6 \cdot b_5 \cdot b_4 \cdot (1 - b_3) \cdot (1 - b_2) \cdot b_1$$

$$CS_4 = b_7 \cdot (1 - b_6) \cdot b_5 \cdot b_4 \cdot (1 - b_3) \cdot (1 - b_2) \cdot b_1$$

$$CS_5 = b_6 \cdot b_5 \cdot b_4 \cdot (1 - b_1)$$

$$CS_6 = b_7 \cdot (1 - b_6) \cdot b_5 \cdot b_4 \cdot (1 - b_1)$$

With all this information, once the CSs are obtained the problem is ready to achieve the MP occurrence probability by using a software simulated algorithm. For instance, the MP probability is possible to be hand-calculated in this brief example. Nonetheless, in a real case, where too many BCs are found, it has been proved that the software used is strongly needed in order to have both accuracy and low-time calculations.

Let us denote by $W = \left(w_1, w_2, \ldots w_n\right)$ a set of n probabilities associated with n BCs where $w_n \in \left[0, 1\right]$. Thus, the probability function of each BC is gathered together into a vector:

$$W = \left\{\left(w_1, w_2, \ldots w_n\right) : 0 \leq w_1, w_2, \ldots w_n \leq 1,\right\}$$

Let us start from the BCs probability vector W, where:

$$W = \left[0.4\, 0.3\, 0.65\, 0.8\, 0.2\, 0.9\, 0.7\right]$$

These equations shows that it has been given a major weight to BCs six, four and seven, respectively. Nevertheless it will be proved how this fact actually does not mean they needed to be the most significant BCs to the LDT. By using vector W it is now possible to achieve the probability of occurrence of the MP, which is as follows:

$$Q_{MP} = 41.03\,\%$$

Benefits and Drawbacks

LDT has been depicted and its following conversion to BDD has been done. Previous sections have stated the numerous advantages provided by mentioned conversion in hereby project. Besides already mentioned advantages, the equivalent BDD obtained from the LDT will provide the necessary basis to obtain a ranking of the most important BCs over the whole LDT.

When any business seeks to improve a department or inner issue in a certain department at any given time, numerous causes related with those departments involved are found. There will be several tens of BCs under the most favourable conditions which will lead to the MP. Nonetheless, and specifically when speaking about large companies, the regular scenario is to face hundreds or even tens of hundreds of BCs. In other words, this introduces a challenging scenario in computational terms due to the fact that to handle mentioned data is not straightforward.

The main reason that leads to hereby chapter to convert LDT to BDD and its subsequent BDD data handling is due to the ability to deal with hundreds or thousands of BCs using both computational time and resource management in a remarkable way. Moreover, in order to be able to simulate the Importance Measures in a reasonable computational time the CSs obtained from the BDD seems to be the feasible manner. Once the conversion from LDT to BDD is done and the CSs are achieved, it is possible to obtain the Importance Measures. In fact, the CSs as well as the probability associated to each BC provide the needed data for the Importance Measures afterward described. Exact calculations to obtain the MP probability are carried out and approximations are not needed when using BDDs. That turns out into one of the biggest advantages of the BDDs. Table 1 shows some other reasons that have influenced in the final decision to use BDDs as a formal solution to respond to the needs asked in herebyMake sure the adverb is not modifying a noun. Adverbs can describe verbs, adjectives, and other adverbs, but never a noun. Remember that not all adverbs end in "-ly"; check in a dictionary if you are not sure which role a word is playing.

Table 1. Benefits and drawbacks

LDT	BDD
Right depiction of a DM problem	Poor depiction of a DM Problem
Mathematical issues when trying to find the solution	Great efficiency finding the solution*
Poor software implementation	Well-grounded background to achieve mathematical solutions
Lack of reliable software to treat this kind of problems	Accurate software and Low Computational time*
No qualification needed by employees to depict a DM problem	Great complex associated and software is essential to obtain it

project.

The way the BDDs are able to handle all kind of trees, regardless whether they are small, medium or large size is one of the biggest advantages of using BDDs that has made them so particularly appropriate. It has been proved that when big size trees must be faced there could be some issues and there exist some different techniques. For instance, a technique successfully used is to convert the tree into small ones in a way that the software is able to simulate each single small part and then combine all the obtained results (Artigao, 2009). Pretty good results have been achieved.

$$Q_{MP} = 41.03 \%$$

BDDs makes possible to calculate the occurrence probability of a MP occurred in a business given a certain LDT. On this occasion, BDDs based algorithms do not use approximation techniques such as truncation to calculate the occurrence probability of a MP. Nonetheless, BDDs could have an incredibly high time and memory consumption, chiefly when many BCs are involved. At this point and as previously stated, a particular emphasis must be done when dealing with the variable ordering. BDD arises when a low computational time and reliable results are sought for solving LDTs problems. Thanks to BDDs is possible to achieve a good solution in an efficient and effective manner, whenever the variable ordering is tackled with special care.

NEW APPROACH TO REDUCE THE COMPUTATIONAL COST

The DM problem described is a NP-hard type problem and, therefore, for a large number of BCs, or a complex topology, it can be not recommended to find a solution. This chapter presents a novel approach for finding a good solution minimizing the computational cost. This approach is based on the logical gates, especially the AND gates, the number and the position on the tree (level), and their effects to the solution and the computational cost of the system. The reference solutions, or experimental solutions, are obtained in simple systems, where it can be extrapolated to complex systems via polynomial regression functions. These functions are setting according to the reference solutions, where it will be more precise with more reference solutions.

Table 2 shows the probabilities and CSs for different LDT cases studies. The probability of occurrence of MP and the CSs are obtained for different amounts of AND gates in each level.

Table 2. Experimental results and estimations

Probability of Occurrence of MP						Number of AND Gate	Number of Cut-Sets					
Level 1	Level 2	Level 3	Level 4	Level 5	Level 6		Level 6	Level 5	Level 4	Level 3	Level 2	Level 1
0.0756	0.291	0.3864	0.4313	0.4531	0.4638	1	63	64	72	112	288	1024
	0.0436	0.2836	0.3846	0.4308	0.453	2	63	72	144	672	4608	
		0.1637	0.3341	0.4077	0.4419	3	65	104	536	5840		
		0.027	0.2795	0.3837	0.4306	4	71	208	2528	15616		
			0.2205	0.3587	0.4191	5	85	528	7400			
			0.1578	0.3326	0.4074	6	115	1496	16432			
			0.0911	0.3036	0.3954	7	177	3673	30904			
			0.0204	0.2752	0.3832	8	303	7836	52095			
				0.2458	0.3727	9	527	14952				
				0.2154	0.3604	10	896	26177				
				0.184	0.3479	11	1463	42860				
				0.1516	0.3352	12	2294	66544				
				0.1182	0.3223	13	3462	98961				
				0.0838	0.3092	14	5048	142036				
				0.0484	0.2959	15	7144	197888				
				0.012	0.2824	16	9850	268825				
					0.2687	17	13276					
					0.2548	18	17540					
					0.2407	19	22770					
					0.2264	20	29103					
					0.2119	21	36684					
					0.1972	22	45669					
					0.1823	23	56221					
					0.1672	24	68513					
					0.1519	25	82729					
					0.1364	26	99058					
					0.1207	27	117701					
					0.1048	28	138869					
					0.0887	29	162778					
					0.0724	30	189658					
					0.0559	31	219744					
					0.0392	32	253283					

The LDT has been calculated for the cases marked in black in Table 2, and red are estimated results. The estimations have been obtained through polynomial expressions, where the polynomial degree depends on the number of experimental points obtained. The experimental solutions have been obtained using the algorithms developed by (Artigao, 2009).

Figure 5 shows the results of probabilities found exactly (E) by BDD and the predicted (P) results found by new approach. It is observed that the probability is indirectly proportional to the number of AND gates, and proportional to the level, which is expected. Moreover, the consequences of adding a new AND gate is indirectly proportional to the level. In Figure 5 is also plotted (black curve) the absolute deviation expressed as abs((E-P)/P). The deviation is proportional to the number of gates, and with values always inferior to 0,45%. It demonstrates that the accuracy of the solutions founds by the new approach is in every case very good.

The deviation has been estimated for different levels and number of AND gates and presented in Figure 6. It has been estimated through quadratic polynomial expression. It is useful in order to know approximately the accuracy of the probability estimated in Table 2.

A similar study presented in Figure 5 has been done taking into account the number of CSs, and showed in Figure 7. The number of CSs is larger in each level when the number of AND gates increase, and the number of CSs is smaller when the level is larger taking into account the same number of AND gates. The error is not as relevant for CSs than for the probabilities, because is the same independently of the number of CSs. It is relevant in order to estimate the computational cost for solving the problem. Exponential expressions have been used to evaluate the size of the CSs.

CONCLUSION

DM via LDT and the conversion to BDD is presented in this chapter. This approach often requires decision maker to obtain a complex analytic expression of the occurrence probability for a MP. The complexity of this expression depends of the number of BCs and the topology of LDT. When the LDT is formed

Figure 5. Probability Analysis

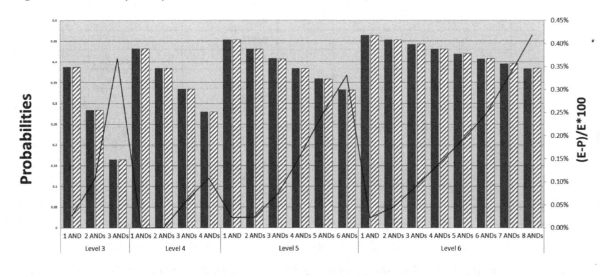

Figure 6. Deviation vs. Number of AND

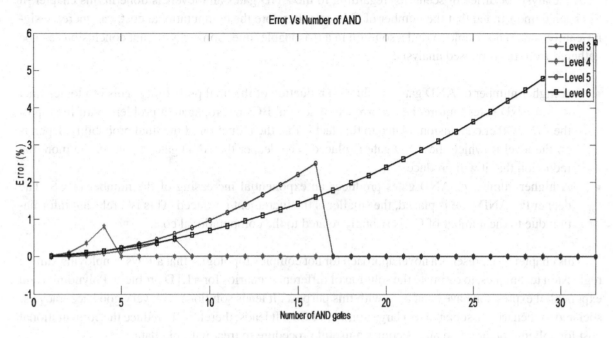

Figure 7. CS Analysis

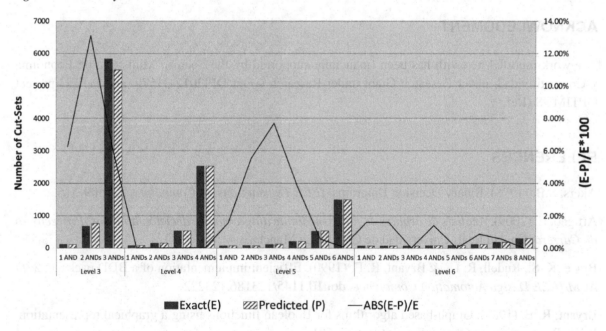

by a high number of components, the ranking of the different events is an essential factor to an efficient conversion of the logical decision tree. With this purpose, several ranking methods are presented in this chapter taking into account that there is not a method that provides the best outcomes for all the cases. Moreover a simple example is presented in order to facilitate the reader the comprehension of the followed procedure.

An analysis of different scenarios regarding to the AND gates and levels is done in this chapter. It has been demonstrated that the number of CSs, and therefore the computational cost, can increase significantly and do not viable to find a solution in a reasonable time. Some significant conclusions can be gathered from the proposed analysis:

- A higher number of AND gates produces a reduction of the final probability. This is a logical fact due to AND gates require the occurrence of several BCs to propagate a problem until the top of the LDT. Other conclusion related to this fact is that the reduction of the final probability depends on the level in which the AND gate is placed. The deeper the AND gate is placed, the more the reduction that it will produce.
- A higher number of AND gates produces an exponential increasing of the number of CS. The deeper the AND gate is placed, the smaller is the increment produced. This is a relevant information due to the number of CS is strongly related to the computational cost.

This chapter also presents a novel approach for not complex topologies that allows, employing simple regression techniques, to estimate the solution of different scenarios for a LTD problem. Polynomial and exponential expression have been used with this purpose. It leads solutions with very good accuracy associated to scenarios associated to a large number of CSs. It leads, therefore, to reduce the computational cost for solving the problem and becomes a useful procedure to treat with big data.

ACKNOWLEDGMENT

The work reported herewith has been financially supported by the Spanish Ministerio de Economía y Competitividad, under Research Grant under Research Grant DPI2012-31579, and the EU project OPTIMUS (Ref.:

REFERENCES

Akers, S.B. (1978). Binary Decision Diagrams. *IEEE Transactions on Computers*, *27*, 509-516.

Artigao, E. (2009). *Análisis de árboles de fallos mediante diagramas de decisión binarios. Proyecto fin de Carrera*. Ciudad Real: Universidad de Castilla La Mancha.

Brace, K. S., Rudell, R. L., & Bryant, R. E. (1990). Efficient implementation of a BDD package. *27th ACM/IEEE Design Automation Conference*. doi:10.1145/123186.123222

Bryant, R. E. (1986). Graph-based algorithms for Boolean functions using a graphical representation. IEEE Transactions on Computing, 35(8), 677–691.

García Márquez, F. P., & Moreno, H. (2012). *Introducción al Análisis de Árboles de Fallos: Empleo de BDDs*. Editorial Académica Española.

Hurwitz, J., Nugent, A., Halper, F., & Kaufman, M. (2013). Big Data for Dummies. Wiley & Sons, Inc.

Lee, C. Y. (1959). Representation of switching circuits by binary decision diagrams. *Bell System Technology*, *1*(38), 985–999. doi:10.1002/j.1538-7305.1959.tb01585.x

Lopez, D., & Van Slyke, W. J. (1977). Logic Tree Analysis for Decision Making. *Omega, The Int. Journal of Management Science*, *5*, 5.

Mallo, C., & Merlo, J. (1995). *Control de gestión y control presupuestario*. McGraw-Hill.

Moret, B. M. E. (1982). Decision trees and diagrams. Computing Surveys, 14(14), 593-623.

Ohlhorst, F. (2013). *Turning Big Data into Big Money*. Wiley & Sons, Inc.

Sathi, A. (2012). *Big Data Analytics. Disruptive Technologies for Changing the Game. MC Press Online*.

Zikopoulos, P., & Eaton, C. (2011). *Understanding big data: Analytics for enterprise class hadoop and streaming data. McGraw-Hill Osborne Media*.

KEY TERMS AND DEFINITIONS

Basic Events: The basic events are logical variables that adopt two possible states: 1 if the basic event occurs and 0 if it does not occur. They can be associated to a component of a system, a success, the cause of a problem, etc…

Binary Decision Diagram (BDD): A BDD is a directed acyclic graph (DAG) that simulates a logical function. The main advantage of the BDDs is the possibility of evaluating the top event using implicit formulas.

Cut-Sets (CSs): The CSs of a BDD are the paths from the root node to the terminal nodes with value 1. They represent the series of events that have to occur so that the top event occurs. The size of a BDD can be represented by the number of CSs forming it. The probability of the top event is the sum of the probabilities of the CSs.

Logical Decision Tree (LDT): It is a graphical representation of a structure function. A LDT structure consists of a root node (top event) that is broken down into various nodes located below it, where the nodes can be events, logical gates and branches. It represents the interrelations between the basics events that form a more complex event.

Non-Deterministic Polynomial-Time Hard Problem (NP-Hard): The NP-hard problems are a class of problems that are at least as hard as the hardest problem in NP. If there were a polynomial algorithm to solve any NP-Hard problem, it could be used to solve any NP problem.

Ranking Methods: The efficiency of the conversion from LDT to BDD depends strongly on the ordination of the basic events of the LDT. With this purpose there are some heuristic algorithms that try to order these events. There is not a unique method that provides the best ordination for all the cases so different methods need to be considered when a conversion is required.

Top Event: This is the event placed at the highest level of the LDT. It represents the main cause, or the success that is pretended to be studied.

APPENDIX

Figure 8. Logical Decision Tree

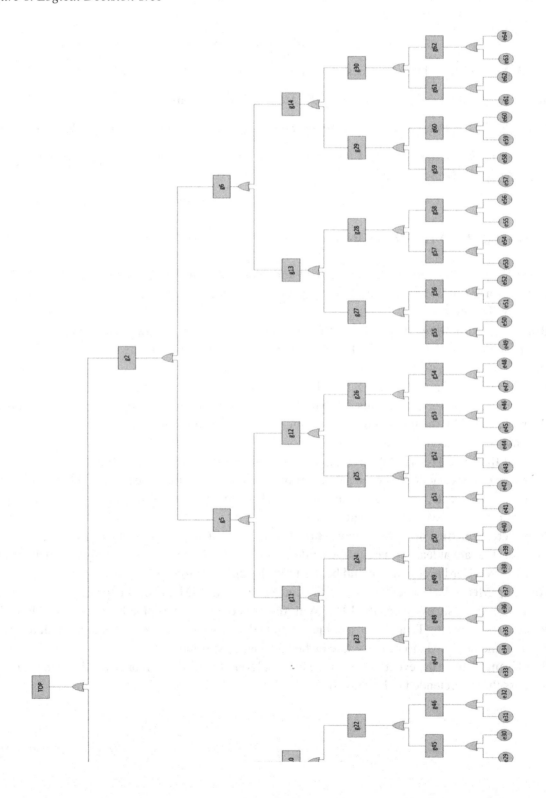

Figure 9. Logical Decision Tree, continued

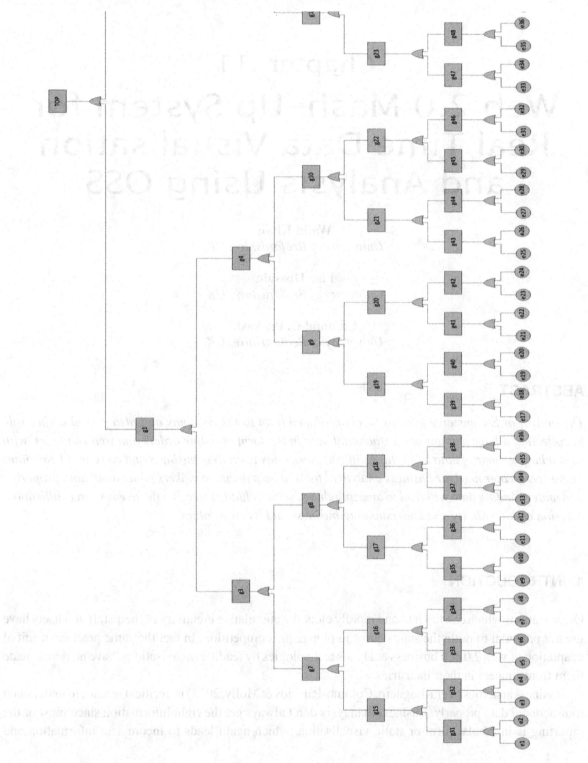

Chapter 11
Web 2.0 Mash-Up System for Real Time Data Visualisation and Analysis Using OSS

Wajid Khan
University of Bedfordshire, UK

Fiaz Hussain
University of Bedfordshire, UK

Edmond C. Prakash
University of Bedfordshire, UK

ABSTRACT

The arrival of E-commerce systems has contributed a lot to the economy and also played a vital role in collecting a huge amount of transactional data in the form of online orders and web enquiries, with such a huge volume of data it is getting difficult day by day to analyse business and consumer behaviour. There is a greater need for business analytical tools to help decision makers understand data properly - and understanding data will lead to amazing things such as hidden trends, effective resource utilisation, decision making ability and understanding business and its core values.

1. INTRODUCTION

Organizations which can tap into and rapidly clout the cumulative creativity of their staff and users have greater potential to rattle the status quo and plunge the competition. In fact the same practice of initial adaptation of web 2.0 and business analytics technologies by leading organisations, have no doubt made them front runners in their industries.

Business analytics (Vera-Baguero, Colomo-Palacios & Molly, 2013) is a critical science to understand transactional data properly. Business managers don't always get the right information since most of the reporting is in tabular form or static visualisation, which again leads to incomplete information and

DOI: 10.4018/978-1-4666-8505-5.ch011

business managers have to rely on guesses(trial and error) rather than well calculated discussion. This research is focused on analysis part of analytical process and outcome of the tools will help decision makers to execute their plans to 'win and compete' in enterprise environment.

Business analytics is comprised of solutions used to build analysis models and simulations to create scenarios, understand realities and predict future states (LaValle et al, 2013). Business analytics is the process of data execution to analyse facts and figures in more detail through information visualisation and graphical representation of data to understand and help in business execution and decision making.

1.1 Information Visualisation

Information visualisation is an act in which an individual establishes a strong connection between an internal construct and something to which access is gained through the senses. Information visualisation has addressed many of data analysis issues but the current visualisation tools either focus on one dimensional data or they are not always well coordinated with multi-attribute data or business transactions. Research like multiple coordinated visualisation (Keim et al, 2001), pixel bar charts visualisation and value- cell visualisation (Keim et al, 2007) and multi-coordinated tools (Robert, 2007) greatly contributed to understanding data in-depth and also through various aspects.

Primary focused in any business analytical tools or in information visualisation is on data. Simple visualisation models as shown in Figure 3 are basic visualisation of data included with software packages, which serves basic data analysis needs. Complex visualisation models are out-come of research mostly at Ph.D level, these models provide in-depth analysis but are very hard to practiced in enterprise and in a real time data environment.

We think that there is still a lot to be done in information visualisation, therefore we propose an easy to 'use and integrate' visualisation model - which will focus on non-aggregated, multi-attribute, multi-dimensional and multi-coordinated visualisation which is a tremendous task and very fresh approach in information visualisation, because the greatest contribution of information visualisation tools are to make it possible for the decision makers to identify the expected and discover the unexpected, which we believe could be achieved through our proposed visualisation model.

2. AIMS AND OBJECTIVES

The aim of this research is to develop an information visualisation framework through data-mashups using web 2.0 technologies, which will represent highly complex data in visualised form. The framework is targeted to reduce technical requirements of system usage, as the indented system is to provide customised data representation for multiple die-missions data usage. Decision making within the system is accomplished using built-in a pre-developed logical set of rules based on the data types and their sources. The architecture design will be so versatile that each data element could be utilised in the visualisation process upon request from the user for analysis and reporting, some of the key aims and objectives are highlighted below.

Figure 1. Visualisation through Data Mash-up

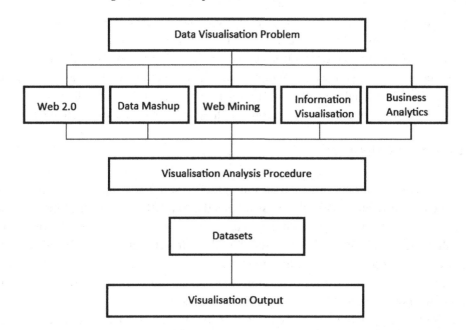

3. PROBLEM STATEMENT

Enterprise 2.0 has the resources and ability to store and create huge amounts of transactional data, as (Fry, 2004) highlighted that, data and the purpose for which it was collected could be quietly easily disassociated in such situations, and soon we ask 'if there is too much data, how could we understand it? With information retrieval system and visualisation tools, the more specific questions we ask the more specific and clear visualised results could be achieved - and off course it is a fact, but unfortunately, in an enterprise environment there are no simple questions.

For example, 'how many visits does a website receive?' To answer this simple questions we don't need information like, user IP address, screen resolution, browser and all additional information stored with website statistics, but if the question is slightly changed to 'How many visits does a website receive from the UK?' then we need additional information like IP addresses to answer such questions, so we do need to store all additional information and especially in enterprise environment because - we don't always know what factors are contributing towards a business success or failure. We understand that the solution doesn't lie with 'simple questions' or 'queries' but with analysing data in-depth and establishing relationships and links with data sources in visualised environments to understand huge volumes of data properly and easily.

4. RELATED WORK

4.1 Web 2.0

The concept of web 2.0 rejoins the new generation of web applications and it has been introduced for the first time during a conference between O'Reilly and Media Live (O'Reilly, 2007). Web 2.0 is a practice and a technology benchmark. web 2.0 is more dynamic and interactive than its predecessor, web 1.0, letting users both access content from a web site and contribute to it. web 2.0 lets users keep up with a site's latest content even without visiting the actual Web page. It also lets developers easily and quickly creates new web applications that draw on data, information, or services available on the Internet.

Web 2.0 heavily revolves around reuse and open standards based technologies with both scalability and flexibility in dynamic environments. Web 2.0 technologies helps in constructing circumstantial applications that expeditiously explore enterprise data and applications for business users and customers, Information overload is always curtailed and new dimension of modernizations are introduced to businesses and end users. Web 2.0 helps in various aspects of user friendliness, commercial impact and reusability of applications and data. Web 2.0 technologies are positioned on uncomplicated programming imitation that can help accelerate time to market by improving the usability of enterprise assets.

O'Reilly Media have given seven principles established by (Mika, Peter & Mark 2012). These principles need to be satisfied for a company or an application to be categorised as a web 2.0 application.

1. Services, not packaged software, with cost-effective scalability,
2. Control over unique, hard-to-recreate data sources that get richer as more people use them,
3. Trusting users as co-developers,
4. Harnessing collective intelligence,
5. Leveraging the long tail through customer self-service,
6. Software above the level of a single device,
7. Lightweight user interfaces, development models, AND business models.

We will scale success of our web 2.0 application on the above guideline.

4.2 Data Mash-Up

Mash-up usually refers to music or vocal editing and it is a single composition created from different songs, however data or web mash-ups, in a similar spirit, originated from the re-use of existing data sources or web applications, the emphasis being on graphical user interfaces and programming-less specifications. As described in (Jhingran, 2006), the concept of mash-ups originated from the understanding that the number of applications available on the Web and the needs to combine them to meet user requirements.

A mash-up application can be characterised as a lightweight and tactical presentation layer that uses the web platform, Web-Oriented Architecture, in order to integrate multi-sourced applications into one web-based offering. – Figure 4 highlight basic mash-up application architecture.

The mash-up data could be retrieved from several sources, i.e. from local databases or datasets or from external repositories, from a website, via crawling, or via a service oriented approach (SOA) through APIs and from other intermediate content brokers.

4.3 Mash-Up Architecture

A mash-up system could be architecturally categorised into two types.

4.3.1 Browser Based Mash-Up Application

These types of data mash-up application, usually compile and collect information on browser side using browsers compiling resources and straight-away released to client. Key advantage of this type of architecture is light-weight application and requires less resources to maintain, however there are many disadvantages if the data or mash-up application elements required to be re-used, since mash-up elements and all data is formatted and compiled at browser side therefore it is very difficult to re-use or utilise the same data for any other purpose, also this approach has security issues as most of the processing takes place at client side and therefore is considered as a less secured type of mash-up development.

4.3.2 Server Based Mash-Up Application

Server based mash-up application is widely used mash-up architecture as there are more benefits and advantages. A server based mash-up process, format and compile data at a remote site while only transmitting the output of the mash-up application. Data can be re-used and high security levels are one of the key advantages of such architecture while requires trust and proxy mash-up service resources for computation.

4.4 Mash-Up Types

Mash-up applications could be categorised into several types; these classifications vary from usage to application development - but in all these mash-up applications one thing in particular is very important, that is data, and, of course, data is the heart-beat of any mash-up application.

4.4.1 Data Mash-Up

Data mash-up applications combine similar types of media and information sources into a single representation, or output. All the mash-up applications which focus on 'similar types' of data are categorised in this type, a good example could be a news mash-up application as the application collects news, stories from different news papers eg BBC, NY Times and present collected information in one package.

Consumer mash-up applications combine different data types, also combines data from different data sources and present application in an integrated view, there are several types of application developed to serve consumers and most commonly cited is 'housingmaps.com' which combines Google maps data with Craigslist housing data in one integrated view.

4.4.2 Enterprise Mash-Up

Enterprise mash-up applications are slightly unique from data mash-up, and consumer mash-ups, as enterprise mash-ups mostly combine their own resources, applications and data with external web services which establishes a collaborative approach among business and developers likewise as explained by Hoyer and Fischer (2006).

4.4.3 Other Mash-Up Types

The above are widely used mash-up types however, this list is dynamic and more categories are introduced with time, many of them are listed in the table below. 'Client Mash-ups' are widely regarded as solving personal situational problems while enterprise mash-ups focus on collaborative and coordinated problems, consumer and business mash-ups are used as analogous terms for client mash-ups and enterprise mash-ups respectively.

Web page customisation mash-ups are more interface oriented mash-up systems which helps the presentation layout of web application development; a good example is the BBC website where we can drag content boxes to see stories that are important to us.

Process Mash-up helps in computation elements of application for example, data aggregations and sequential process automation. Front-end mash-up application helps in improving front-end by adding/deleting website widgets and gadgets; a good example of this type is iGoogle and Netvibes. Back-end mash-up applications combines web accessible data and services into more useful web services that can be accessed easily for further re-use. (Kapow and Yahoo Pipes).

Horizontal mash-up applications are dependent on execution of a previous service within the application in order to represent the information, for example on a travel website, the web application needs to execute and list all destinations and then to be displayed on a map as a kind of horizontal mash-up application.

Vertical applications depended on application output rather than execution as the next part of the application then process further information as instructions received, and the application doesn't provide information by itself.

4.5 Data Collection and Web Mining

4.5.1 Web Mining

Web mining is a technical term relating to the application of various data mining techniques to discover patterns and trends from the internet, and from a variety of enterprise datasets that are available to mash-up applications. There are typically three different forms of data mining that cover different aspects of the internet - these are web usage mining, web content mining and web structure mining. While there are many different definitions of web mining, the definition found within the Gartner Group is the most comprehensive. They define data mining as 'the process of discovering meaningful new correlations, patterns and trends by sifting through large amounts of data stored in repositories and by using pattern.'

Data mining has many different applications, most of which are based on the industry they are being utilized for. Within higher education, data mining is the process of uncovering hidden trends and patterns (that lend them towards predictive modeling) and using a combination of explicit knowledge bases, sophisticated analytical skills and academic domain knowledge. This is also known as the process of producing new observations from pre-existing observations. This has also been described as 'the process of automatically extracting useful information and relationships from immense quantities of data'. However if you were to take the purist approach, data mining does not involve looking for specific data - it simply finds patterns that are already present. This means that data mining cannot be used to unearth information in response to a question or hypothesis (Nassar & Mark, 2013).

The continued increase in growth of online information combined with the unstructured nature of web data requires the development of powerful and efficient web data mining tools. Instead web mining tools are designed to dig out useful facts and knowledge from web pages, hyperlinks, page content and usage logs. It can be used in a number of ways to enable the streamlining of business process. For example, the web mining of an e-bank service can enable the employees of a bank to support e-business, helping them to understand various marketing dynamics, new promotions or suggestions on the internet. Because of this there is now more of a tendency amongst banking companies and individuals to collect banks of information through web data mining, and to use that information for their own interests to gain business intelligence, and this helps them make enlightened business decisions.

Web mining didn't come about overnight. Web mining techniques are the result of an incredibly long process combining years of research with product development. They saw their beginnings when business data was first being stored on computers and in the internet, and their evolution continued with drastic improvements in data access, and now the developments in real-time technologies that allow internet users to navigate through data quickly. Data that is gathered from surveys, manual input or from independently networked locations to define the data collection. Semantic Web has been developed to address current web problems, and it does this by methodically structuring the content of the internet and adding semantics before extracting the maximum benefits from the power of the internet. Sir Tim Berner defined the semantic web as 'an extension of the current web in which information is given well defined meaning, better enabling computers and people to work in co-operation.' It is, in a word, a vision. The idea of having all of the data on the web systematically defined and linked together in a way that can be used and understood by machines. And not just for display purposes, but for automation, integration and the reuse of data across a whole liturgy of applications. Web mining also plays a pivotal role in achieving this, as it lets users quickly and easily find the information they need without digging for it themselves.

By definition web mining is the discovery and analysis of useful information from the internet - and is mainly used in bulk to access this data from a large number of websites. It can also be regarded as enabling the continued use of the internet - from which can draw automatically, standardizing and explaining data. But web mining doesn't come in just one form - there are various types, and these can be used to discover and enable automatic knowledge mining of user access patterns from various different web servers. This is known as web usage mining - and is subtly different from web data mining, in the sense that it is used to extract meaningful user patterns from web server access logs using data mining techniques.

Web based documents are split into three categories based on their structure: un-structured, semi-structured and fully-structured. There have been research studies into these categories, specifically on un-structured and fully-structured data, to look into their methods of extracting semantics for ontology learning. In the research that focuses on fully-structured web documents benefits from a standardized syntax such as XML. However most of the web documents in existence today are in a semi-structured format, but only a few references are made to research that specializes in this format in extracting semantics for ontology learning. In most cases the plain text has been extracted from the semi-structured pages in pre-processing, therefore neglecting embedded information within the semi-structured format. Some other researchers focus on extracting semantics from more template driven web pages, and so these methodologies are limited both in their usage and their applicability.

4.5.2 Web Usage Mining

The term 'web usage mining' was coined by (Srivastava et al, 200), and is the application of various techniques used in data mining to discover and analyze the usage patterns of web data. It analyses user interactions with web servers (including web logs or other database transactions from a group of related sites). However it has sparked privacy concerns and is currently the topic of much passionate debate. This is because the process includes mining data from the web server access logs, proxy server logs, browser logs, user profiles, registration data, user sessions or transactions, cookies, user queries, bookmark data, mouse clicks and scrolls and any other data as a result of interactions. Its aim is to discover the general patterns in web access logs, but in order to discover these patterns it is necessary to perform a few processes, including pre processing, pattern discovery and pattern analysis. Web servers automatically record and store data about all of their user interactions whenever requests for resources are received. By analyzing these web server logs, all kinds of different websites can better understand user behavior and web structure, which in turn improves the overall design of this immeasurable collection of resources. By mining web usage pattern data, we can help in the progression of internet based studies- including those based on how internet browsers are used, and how the users interaction with the browser interface changed. These patterns can be put to use in gathering business intelligence, which will in turn improve customer attraction, retention and other aspects of customer behavior.

4.5.3 Web Scraping

Web scraping is defined as the technique of automatic web data extraction, used in order to extract data from the core HTML of the website by parsing (the scouring and analysis) the web pages. It does this by using programs specially coded for manipulation of web pages. Examples of this are the converting the web page into another format such as XML, or by embedding the browsers. It can be seen as fairly close to web indexing (this indexes web content using a soft-bot mainly adopted mainly by search engines) but instead web scraping focuses on the transformation of completely unstructured web content into formally structured data, which can be stored and analyzed in a central database. It can be used for a multitude of things, including online price comparison, weather data monitoring, web research, web content mash-up and wed data integration. Not only that, but it can provide various levels of scrape like human copy and paste, text gripping (based on the UNIX command or regular expression matching facilities of programming languages like Pearl), HTTP programming (HTTP requests to the remote web server), embedding web browsers, HTML parsers and web scraping software tools. It works by allowing prolog (a language used in artificial intelligence, which has the capability to interact with web services and clients) to keep the data and extract the required information (with the help of Prolog Server Pages and some inference rules). PSP accepts the arguments generated by HTML and generates the responses from the web server so that it can interact with Prolog, therefore generating an output which is passed to the HTML. To complete the process of web scraping what you need is a web server, prolog complier and a web browser. An internet information server can be used instead of a web server to process to the scripting language instead, which in turn will produce the HTML response. By utilizing text grabbing you can use the regular expression matching technique (where you try to match a particular expression in the file) and find a match. Once a match has been found for the expression, you can then pick the values before or after it. The main limitation of scraping programs is that they are required to update frequently, which can increase the maintenance costs.

4.5.4 Web Structure Mining

Web structure mining is a field of research entirely focused on identifying more preferable documents by using the analysis of the web link structure. The idea is simple: a hyperlink from document A to document B implies that the author of document A thinks that document B contains worthwhile and useful information. Web structure mining seeks out and exploits the additional information that can be found within the structure of the hypertext. Because of this one of the most important areas of application in this area is the identification of the relevance of these linked pages - which appear equally important when analyzed, especially when you look at their content in isolation. To illustrate: a hyperlink induced topic search analyzes the hyperlink's topology by discovering authoritative information sources for broader search topics. To find this information, it goes to authority pages, which are defined in relation to hubs as their counterparts. Hubs are otherwise known as pages that link to multiple related information authorities (Haigang & Wanling, 2006). For example, Google owes its massive success to its page ranking algorithm, which states that the relevance of any page increases with the number of outbound links (hyperlinks to it from other pages) - more so if those other pages are relevant.

4.5.5 Web Content Mining

This is an automatic process of the internet which extracts patterns from web contents, data and documents (such as HTML files, images or emails). This already goes beyond simple keyword or key phrase extraction - instead it can take full advantage of the semi-structured nature of the web page text, and can use it to detect co-occurrences of terms within the texts. For example, we can also discover trends over time, which could indicate a surge or decline of interest in certain topics (such as the programming language Java). Yet another area this can be applied in is event detection - using web content mining in the identification of stories in multiple continuous news streams that correspond to new or previously unidentified events.

4.6 Enterprise 2.0: An Overview

Enterprise 2.0 was a concept first introduced by McAfee in order to showcase how Web 2.0 technologies can be used within enterprises. His focus was to explain how Web 2.0 could make work practices and the efforts of knowledge workers more visible. This is in reaction to the initial response to Web 2.0 by businesses - when introduced it fascinated almost everyone, but unfortunately it didn't seem to register with enterprises. In order for them to take these (or any) emerging technologies seriously, companies needed to see real case studies of the use of Web 2.0. Case studies in which the application had been studied and analyzed from multiple perspectives, including security, consistency or scalability. They also needed a set of best practice descriptions for its use, and specific guidelines on how they should introduce and apply Web 2.0 technologies within their organization (Tellioglu & Diesenreiter, 2013).

But how was the new technology of Enterprise 2.0 studied and discussed in other areas? While there haven't been many in depth qualitative analysis on Enterprise 2.0 within the work context and its impact, there have been multiple studies on the direction, detail, quality and format of social networking systems (particularly Facebook and Twitter). There are even qualitative studies focused on their application and real use within business. However in recent years, some managerial journals have published new results of the applied Enterprise 2.0 technology, and some books have even been published with a specific emphasis on providing explanatory guidelines for management in enterprise. While these sources were a considerable jump forward, they still did not exhaustively and qualitatively describe how and in which areas this new technology is more efficient for enterprises - or the additional value it can have to cooperative work. This is something that the research literature unfortunately still lacks - an in depth analysis and explanation of cooperation processes in very complex development environments. This is the sort of thing that needs investigating, by basing the analysis on central concepts such as awareness, trust, openness, sharing through data mash-up tools and information visualization.

However, introducing changes into any organization is a difficult subject - as resistance to change is often immediate and dramatic, without any deeper thought. Organizational culture also impacts the attitudes towards Enterprise 2.0 adoption, because the organizations general attitudes towards collaboration, open communication and information sharing hugely affect the acceptance of Enterprise 2.0 by employees and managers. The common fear that organizations have is that they will lose governance over their information, and Web 2.0 tools as perceived as a potential risk, particularly in the field of data loss. This is viewed as a direct result of employees sharing information on blogs or social networking sites. There is also a huge concern for decreased employee productivity, or the possibility that the wrong information will be posted on a network by an employee, or e.ven that employees will write questionable or offensive materials on a network. These fears are what fuels the standardization of office policies and processes when it comes to social networking and collaborative work - usually opposed. This is particularly true for organizations who operate under a command and control culture. Obviously we face a great challenge in this regard, and that is that so few people know what Enterprise 2.0 is, what it means and how it can support the organization.

Despite all of these barriers, we see some organizations not only starting to use Web 2.0 technology, but also leveraging it to change their management practices and organizational structures. Those organizations that have recognized the innovations that Web 2.0 technology represents by innovation instead of price have tapped into a priceless idea - using the knowledge (and tacit knowledge) of their workforce and therefore encouraging collaboration among their knowledge workers using the Enterprise 2.0 tools. Many more organizations are starting to scc Enterprise 2.0 technologies as an opportunity to increase their company's revenue and margins, and see its many benefits. The undeniable fact is that Enterprise 2.0 is an unavoidable technology - one which is becoming increasingly popular among enterprise specific users, and more so among knowledge workers and digital natives who have grown up with the web.

In these modern times the nature of work is constantly evolving, and being driven by the Web 2.0 technologies that enable and enhance social activities it has quickly taken on a significant role in the workplace. Enterprise 2.0 has not only become a competitive necessity, now organizations must be ready to use the technology that supports it. After all, simply adopting the technology in a process does not necessarily improve the process by itself. The technology must be fully assimilated into the organization in order to gain the full competitive advantage - and considerations about technological capabilities, willingness of adoption and organizational size must all be taken into consideration, helping in the evaluation of the organization's readiness for Enterprise 2.0.

4.7 Information Visualisation

Visualisation as a sub-field of science, statistics, and graphics has only been recognised as its own entity since the mid- to late-80s. The depth of seminal work is in line with that of a young field, but finds its strength in background drawn from years of statistics and graphic design.

Information visualisation is converting data into interactive interfaces in order to easily understand problems, hidden patterns, scope and explore data with a more rapid and intuitive approach - usually abstract data is transformed into visual images (Spence, 2001) to see the big picture at a glance.

Information Visualisations are computer based systems, it can be called a 'medium' between human-beings and data and works as a bridge to establish interactivity - between source and operator for analysis and decision making purposes. The goal of information visualisation tools is to improve data perception, correlation and exploration (Oliveira & Levkowitz, 2003).

The characteristics of a good information visualisation system are defined according to the following user tasks by Carr (1999).

- To analyse or examine entire dataset.
- Ability to see non-aggregated elements or subsets.
- Customisation and filtering to analyse data at different angles.
- Additional information available to an action performed by user.
- Relationships: the ability to relate data items with similar characteristics.
- History: the ability to undo an action and show the steps performed up to the current point.

In addressing data problems a number of techniques have been invented to explore data for trends, patterns and to analyse multidimensional data. For example, Tableau's visual spreadsheet (2006)] and SpotFire's visual data exploration interface (Ahlberg, 1996), Space-filling techniques such as squarified treemaps (Bruls, Huizing & Wijk, 2000) are particularly employed by business managers for routine data analysis.

Pixel-oriented visualisations (Keim et al 2000) are also getting popularity where large transactional data is represented by each pixel. In piexel bar charts, each pixel is arranged and coloured to indicate an item's relevance to a user query. Another well- known technique that uses pixel-level visualisation is the Seesoft software visualisation technique (Eick, Steffen & Summer, 1992) which maps each line of source code to a line of pixels. Pixel techniques have also been used to build interactive decision tree classifiers based on a visualisation of the training data, value-cell visualisation (Keim et al, 2007) was another approach toward non-aggregated data visualisation in visual bar charts. Pixel-oriented visualisations were a necessity because all other visualisation practices such as pie-charts, bar charts, x-y plots were solely focused on aggregated data, which restrict the number of data values to be visualised therefore diluting the understanding and soon the visualisations don't always give precise and accurate information to decision makers.

Pixel Bar Charts (Keim et al, 2007) and Value-cell Bar Charts; visualisations were successful to visualise non-aggregated data but there is still a lot to be done on multi-coordinated visualisation, but the multiple coordinated aspect of data visualisations are still missing. Multiple views systems use two or more distinct views to support the investigation process of a single conceptual entity. A view is considered distinct of other views if it allows the user to learn different aspects of the conceptual entity whether by presenting different data or emphasising different aspects of the same data.

Multi-coordinated visualisation practices provide good understanding of data and helps in data validation and cross examination to find hidden patterns, trends and provide critical information in decision making, however to see data source within data even multi-coordinated practices fall short, therefore we have proposed link data visualisation which provides link and relationship between different data aspects.

5. INFORMATION VISUALISATION MODEL

5.1 Seven Steps for Data Visualisation

The process of understanding data begins with a set of numbers and a goal of answering a question about the data. The steps along this path can be described as follows (Fry, 2004):

1. **Acquire:** Obtaining data from local, remote sources through web services or direct dataset access.
2. **Parse:** Organising and giving structure to collected data within in the system environment.
3. **Filter:** Removing all but the data of interest.
4. **Mine:** The application of methods from statistics or data mining, as a way to discern patterns or place the data in mathematical context.
5. **Represent:** Determination of a simple representation, whether the data takes one of many shapes such as a bar graph, list, or tree.
6. **Refine:** Improvements to the basic representation to make it clearer and more visually engaging.
7. **Interact:** The addition of methods for manipulating the data or controlling what features are visible.

We will adopt above seven steps for data visualisation which we believe is a complete data visualisation solution but will add additional sub steps to achieve link data and also multiple coordinated visualisation in a real time enterprise environment.

5.2 Proposed Framework

Principles for the information visualisation will remain the same, and all seven steps introduced by (Fry, 2004) makes perfect sense but to practice these seven steps in an enterprise environment and with data mash-up and real time data applications, we would need to alter the process and with addition of a step (history) and other visualisation sub-steps at represent layer.

In an enterprise environment, reports comparison plays a key role and to accommodate this requirement we have added 'History' to Fry (2004), seven steps for visualisation. We will store reports in XML which could be shared with internal and external application for comparison purposes. History elements of the process will also validate any changes that may have occurred to the data and could be shared with internal processing or external comparison.

5.2.1 Proposed Framework System Flow

The concept of this research revolves around information visualisation through mash-up application for enterprise practices to understand huge transactional data for resource and decision making purposes, focus is on understanding data through visualisation, interactivity of the system with end user, storage of generated results for re-use and comparisons purposes and finally light weight mash-up applications - resource friendly and economical.

Figure 2. Proposed 8 Step of Visualisation

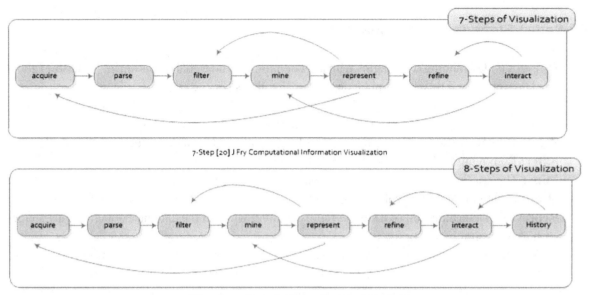

5.2.2 Acquire, Parse, Filter, Mine in Enterprise 2.0

Structuring 'data' is a focal point for any visualisation practice, in this proposed methodology, system will establish whether information visualisation request initiated from an Enterprise 2.0 environment or non-enterprise environment. In enterprise environment this proposed framework will already be aware and will have direct access to datasets through web services and APIs, mash-up application will also understand data structure and therefore can directly access information as it requires for visualisation proposes, this framework will have direct and multiple connections with data sources in an real time as if data sources changes, the framework application will be updated as the data will be acquired from the sourc.

Processing in known environments have the facility that the first four steps, acquire, parse, filter and mine could be achieved through APIs and web services. For example, if the application requires sales figures, mash-up system web intelligent agents could access 'sales figures' via APIs in XML format and the system will pass it to 'represent' layer for visualisation, any information the system requires could directly be accessed and that's a key benefit for any framework to work in 'known environments'.

5.2.3 Acquire, Parse, Filter, Mine in Non-Enterprise 2.0

If datasets are not accessible through APIs or data is in an unknown structure, mash-up application will request third party services like, (Weka 2013) is a collection of machine learning algorithms for data mining tasks, (Weka 2013) helps with pre-processing, classification, regression, clustering, association rules and even visualisation. (Rapid Miner 2014) is another open source web and data mining tool which could be accessed by mash-up application via APIs and web services. These third-party tools will help our framework to acquire, parse, filter and mine unknown datasets - once application is familiar with dataset then data could be provided to represent layer for visualization.

5.2.4 Represent

Represent layer of data visualisation will remain same for enterprise or non-enterprise environments and it is a key step in understanding transactional data effectively, therefore we have extended this layer into further elements, e-g multiple coordinated visualisation, multiple dimensional data visualisation, multi-attribute data visualisation, non-aggregated data visualisation, transactional tagging visualisation and linked data visualisation which are our contribution to information visualisation.

Multi-coordinated visualisation - is a process where data is visualised in coordinated views, which means if one visualised element updates the other updates automatically and both visualise elements displaying same data in different styles, this innovative approach will help decision makers to analyse data at different angles. Multi-attribute, multi-dimensional data is a representation of multi-attribute data which means, analysing attributes like prices, products, customers, transaction range, location and all attributes related to a transaction could be visualised.

Tagging (Ross et al, 20034) is an important feature of web 2.0, tagging is a non-hierarchical structure which is achieved by terming or assigning a keyword to a particular element. We introduce 'transactional tagging' which will help decision makers to gain insights of a particular transaction and analysed through various attributes such as units, time, space and monetary value. Transactions could be tagged manually by end users, for example a company receives online orders and a sales staff member tags those transactions such as 'corporate', 'school' or 'showbiz' our mash-up system can analyse manual tagging by visualising those tags which will serve different purposes one of them could be understanding 'markets'. Web transactions could also be automatically tagged by web intelligent agents by categorising these transactions into locations, value, different product types or analysis against resources.

5.2.5 Refine and Interact

Customisable widgets are introduced on the interactivity layer of our proposed model; at this layer we will build a user-friendly mash-up interface which will be highly customised to meet personal demands and will have options to refine results for further analysis. For example, a manager would require a company overview while a team member will only be interested to see his team performance, to accommvodate this requirement we will introduce drag and drop mash-up widgets features.

5.2.6 History

Report storage is our contribution to the theoretical visualisation model shown in Figure 6, we will store sensitive information in XML so that it could be re-used for analysis and comparison purposes, system will have the ability to allow internal and external requests.

6. PERFORMANCE ANALYSIS

6.1 Example 1

This is a basic visualisation example processed by our proposed framework in enterprise environment through mash-up application. Novelty of this framework is on data representation therefore our focus

Figure 3. Proposed Framework Flow Chart

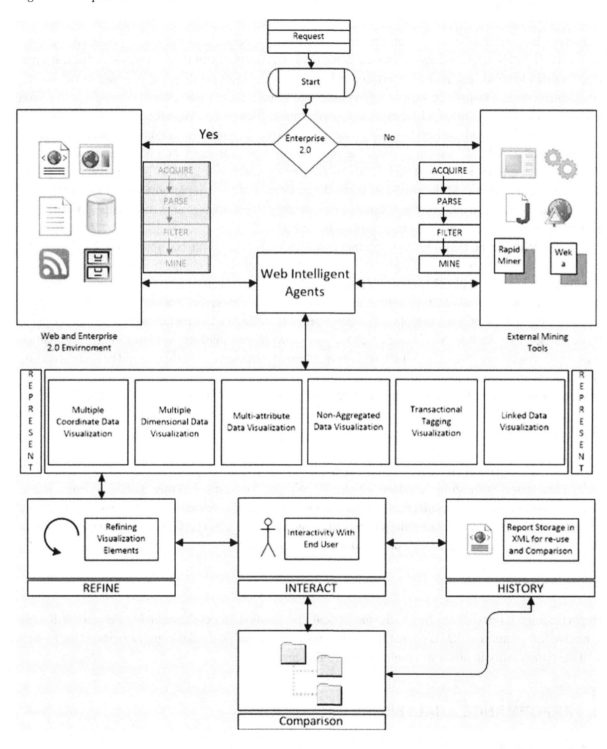

is on 'represent' layer of our proposed framework and other layers such as interact, refine and history, however we will also process unstructured dataset in our in the next example with third-party application to support the whole process.

6.1.1 Acquire, Parse, Filter, Mine

As in Figure 6. acquire, parse, filter and mine steps are handled through web intelligent & API agents as dataset is in known structure, therefore system can directly access required data for visualisation, system have collected data from various tables directly from the database and presented information in an array to represent layer, as shown below. The dataset we processed for this example consisted of over half a million rows with over five hundred attributes. Data processing step which includes acquiring, parsing, filtering and mine all done within a few seconds, system is robustly designed to process and analyse huge datasets and thus enabling business managers and end-users to select and analyse data-elements which are closely related to a specific business decision.

The process is intelligent enough that end-users or business managers can construct their own set of roles to analyse critical business or personal information through our visualisation framework. System has primarily focused on data visualisation but functions created for acquiring, parsing, filtering and mining huge volume of data enabled system has made the framework as multi-purpose framework which provide both mining and information processing and visualisation not only in one place but also with fast processing and execution of huge datasets.

6.1.2 Represent

All visualisation outputs are processed and presented to end-user at this layer, framework has adopted various types of charts such as Bar-Charts, Area-Charts, Pie-Charts; our visualisation framework also has the ability to allow end user not only to filter information and visualisation but same time provide options to visualise datasets in different styling.

6.1.2.1 Basic Visualisation

Visualistaion framework has processed a dataset which shows staff sales. The extract dataset columns are shown in data processing stage as shown above. The system has the ability to represent extracted or processed information in various formats - In this instance we have shown various staff members in a pie chart (Figure 4) which demonstrates which sales staff is contributing towards company sales figures.

Information is visualised at represent layer of our visualisation framework. Business manager looking at this graph will quite quickly understand which staff members is contributing more to company's sales thus reward them accordingly similarly staff members whose performance is below far, could be assisted

Table 1. Extracted data example.

37622	02/09/2014 21:30	01/09/2014 10:41	FIRS006	250	Emma
37638	09/09/2014 07:45	02/09/2014 11:32	SKF001	150	Anna
37724	09/09/2014 10:10	04/09/2014 09:26	SJM001	115	Paisley

Figure 4. Pie Chart for Staff Sales

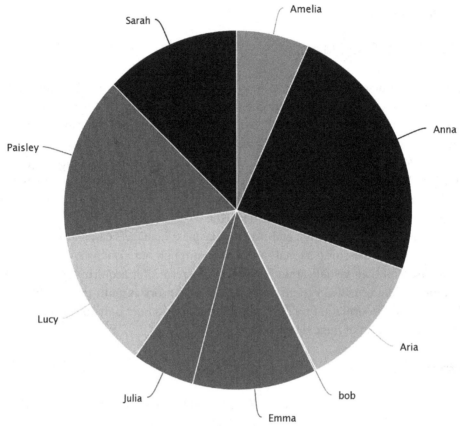

or trained further to boost efficiency. Sharing same visual data representation with all staff members will help in positive motivation in improving personal skills which will benefit company in a long run. Similarly this framework could also be used for personal purposes such home expenses or bank transactions and by education sector to process information for research or other purposes.

6.1.2.3 Advance Visualisation

Visualisation framework also allow business managers and end users to see same data in several visualised forms - this also help managers and end-users to analyse data not only in more depth but also with multi-coordinated views and multi-attribute analysis. As we have shown pie-chart which represent sales staff information, we can view some dataset with Bar-charts, Bubble-charts, Spider Web-chart and pie-chart as shown in Figure 5.

6.1.2.4 Refine and Interact

Refine and interact layers, we have developed user-friendly interfaces where end-user or business manager can quickly request and access data in visualise form - application intelligent agents will convert

Figure 5. Shows Multi-coordinated visualisation

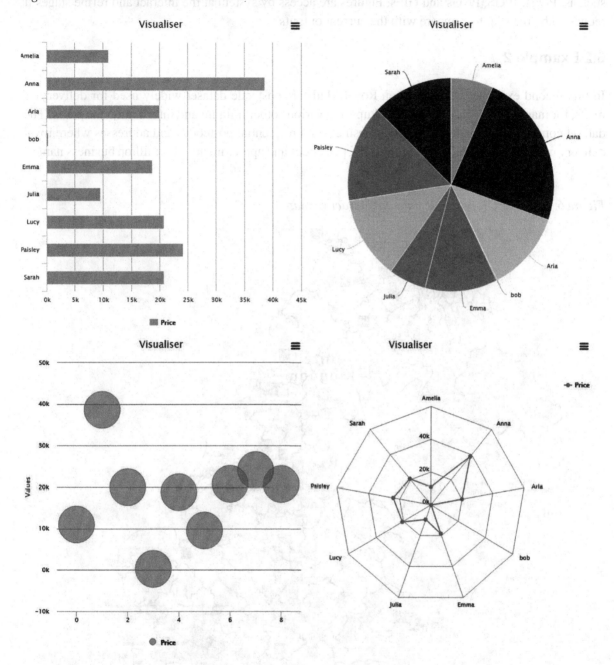

complex queries into simple task within the framework. Framework is highly optimized not only give real time outputs but delivered requested information within a couple of seconds which saves enormous time for both business managers and end-users for quick data analysis.

6.1.2.5 History

All reports generated by the framework are stored in xml format, for comparison and re-use purpose, in the above example, application also allows users to export visual information into popular file format such as, PDFs, JPGS, PNGs and GIFs. Figures are access by system at the interact and refine stages if requested by the user to compare with the current outputs.

6.2 Example 2

In this second example, we have taken Royal Mail UK postcode dataset widely used for delivery of mails, for mapping software, address lookups and various other training and information purposes. The dataset consist approximately 29 million business and residential postcodes and addresses where royal delivery mails, it also includes 1.8 million UK postcodes and approximately 1.4 million business names.

Figure 6. Showing UK postcode data on interactive map.

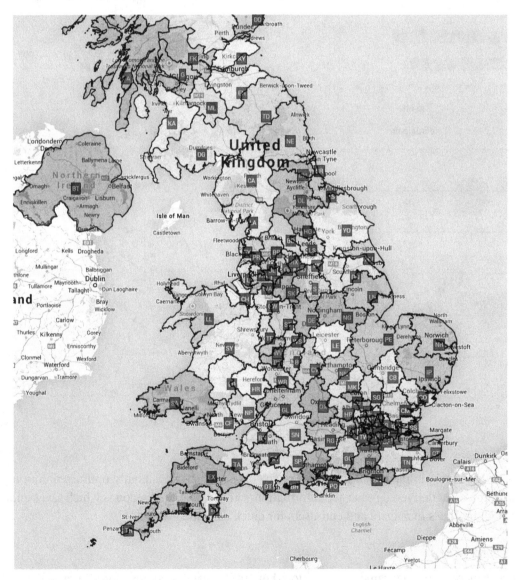

Table 2. Extracted data from dataset

AB12	393300	801100	57.101	-2.1106		Aberdeen City
AB13	385600	801900	57.10801	-2.23776	Milltimber	Aberdeen City
AB14	383600	801100	57.10076	-2.27073	Peterculter	Aberdeen City

Dataset includes tremendous amount of information from longitude to latitudes both for UK and EU, house numbers, names and address, however our visualisation framework has processed 29 million rows and extract useful and vital information for UK Postcode Project. A couple of columns and rows from the dataset are shown in Table 2.

Initially, visualisation framework highlights geographic locations of two point postcodes as shown in the image above. This visualisation gives us tremendous information about UK postcodes and its geography, this useful tool could also be used for training and information purposes both by individuals and businesses. Information visualisation more resolves around graphics and images, that's why our system have coloured each postcode into different and visible colour which helps users to distinguish postcode boundaries. Framework also enable users with an interactive layout where users can search any postcode or a particular postcode all based on user interest.

Figure 7. Showing UK postcode detailed data on interactive map.

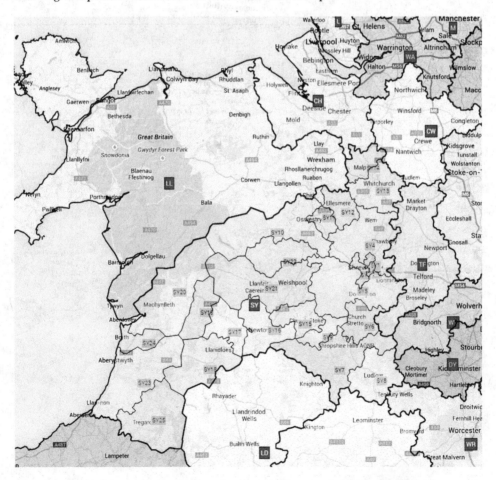

Visualisation framework also allows users to zoom-in to see further information with live maps drilling down to street names and house addresses. Users can also see sub-postcodes areas within a selected geographic location. Sub-postcodes are categorised and drilled downed into three or four digit postcodes as shown in Figure 7.

Information could be drilled downed to all postcodes within selected or searched area which gives more information to end users to see how postcodes are located in a live interactive map where people can not only learn about their locations but also it could be used for business and electoral purposes both by politicians and Governments for various purposes. In following image we demonstrate full six digit postcode visualisation with live and interactive map as shown in Figure 8.

Figure 8. Full Six-digit UK postcode interactive map

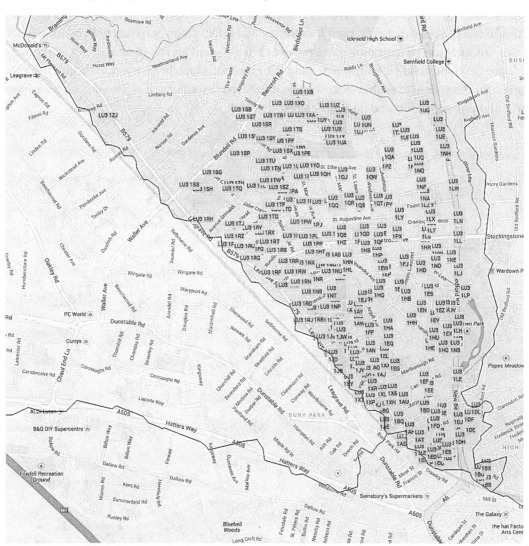

7. CONCLUSION

Our visualisation model has been tested with various type of datasets and produced some amazing visualisation trends both for educational, information and for business purposes. Our focus has always been on manipulating large datasets into meaningful information which not only saves tremendous amount of time but also helps in understanding raw and huge data which is not always easy to process and understand. In the above examples we have taken two different datasets as in example one we focused on business transactional data which uses staff performances and helps business manager with a quick glance to see how business is going whether staff members requires training or appreciation all possible with a few quick clicks.

Royal Mail postcode dataset example is simple but yet interesting; visualisation postcode data produced fascinating information about UK geography and how its divided into areas and postcodes all could be seen with live and interactive map. Information visualisation holds key in exploring hidden trends, giving more insights to managers and individuals about large data which not always give same sense as in its raw form.

REFERENCES

Ahlberg, C. (1996). Spotfire: An information exploration environment. *SIGMOD Record, 25*(4), 25–29. doi:10.1145/245882.245893

Bruls, M., Huizing, K., & Van Wijk, J. J. (2000). *Squarified treemaps*. Springer Vienna.

Carr, D. A. (1999). Guidelines for designing information visualization applications. *Proceedings of ECUE, 99,* 1–3.

De Oliveira, M. C. F., & Levkowitz, H. (2003). From visual data exploration to visual data mining: A survey. Visualization and Computer Graphics. *IEEE Transactions on, 9*(3), 378–394.

Eick, S. G., Steffen, J. L., & Sumner, E. E. Jr. (1992). Seesoft-a tool for visualizing line oriented software statistics. Software Engineering. *IEEE Transactions on, 18*(11), 957–968.

Fry, B. J. (2004). *Computational information design.* (Doctoral dissertation). Massachusetts Institute of Technology.

Haigang, L., & Wanling, Y. (2006, October). Study of Application of Web Mining Techniques in E-Business. In *Service Systems and Service Management, 2006 International Conference on* (Vol. 2, pp. 1587-1592). IEEE.

Hoyer, V., & Fischer, M. (2008). Market overview of enterprise mashup tools. In *Service-Oriented Computing–ICSOC 2008* (pp. 708–721). Springer Berlin Heidelberg. doi:10.1007/978-3-540-89652-4_62

Jhingran, A. (2006, September). Enterprise information mashups: integrating information, simply. In *Proceedings of the 32nd international conference on Very large data bases* (pp. 3-4). VLDB Endowment.

Keim, D. A., Hao, M. C., Dayal, U., & Lyons, M. (2007). Value-cell bar charts for visualizing large transaction data sets. Visualization and Computer Graphics. *IEEE Transactions on, 13*(4), 822–833.

Keim, D. A., Hao, M. C., Ladisch, J., Hsu, M., & Dayal, U. (2001). *Pixel bar charts: A new technique for visualizing large multi-attribute data sets without aggregation*. Academic Press.

LaValle, S., Lesser, E., Shockley, R., Hopkins, M. S., & Kruschwitz, N. (2013). Big data, analytics and the path from insights to value. *MIT Sloan Management Review, 21*.

Mika, P., & Greaves, M. (2012). Editorial: Semantic Web & Web 2.0. *Web Semantics: Science, Services, and Agents on the World Wide Web, 6*(1).

Minor, R. (2014). Retrieved from http://rapid-i.com/content/view/181/190/

Nassar, O. A., & Al Saiyd, N. A. (2013, March). The integrating between web usage mining and data mining techniques. In *Computer Science and Information Technology (CSIT), 2013 5th International Conference on* (pp. 243-247). IEEE. doi:10.1109/CSIT.2013.6588787

O'reilly, T. (2007). What is Web 2.0: Design patterns and business models for the next generation of software. *Communications & Stratégies*, (1), 17.

Roberts, J. C. (2007, July). State of the art: Coordinated & multiple views in exploratory visualization. In *Coordinated and Multiple Views in Exploratory Visualization, 2007. CMV'07. Fifth International Conference on* (pp. 61-71). IEEE.

Ross, P. L., Huang, Y. N., Marchese, J. N., Williamson, B., Parker, K., Hattan, S., & Pappin, D. J. et al. (2004). Multiplexed protein quantitation in Saccharomyces cerevisiae using amine-reactive isobaric tagging reagents. *Molecular & Cellular Proteomics, 3*(12), 1154–1169. doi:10.1074/mcp.M400129-MCP200 PMID:15385600

Spence, R. (2001). *Information visualization* (Vol. 1). New York: Addison-Wesley.

Srivastava, J., Cooley, R., Deshpande, M., & Tan, P. N. (2000). Web usage mining: Discovery and applications of usage patterns from web data. *ACM SIGKDD Explorations Newsletter, 1*(2), 12–23. doi:10.1145/846183.846188

Tableau Software. (2006). Retrieved from http//www.tableausoftware.com

Tellioglu, H., & Diesenreiter, S. (2013, October). Enterprise 2.0 in action: Potentials for improvement of awareness support in enterprises. In *Collaborative Computing: Networking, Applications and Worksharing (Collaboratecom), 2013 9th International Conference Conference on* (pp. 485-494). IEEE.

Vera-Baquero, A., Colomo-Palacios, R., & Molloy, O. (2013). Business process analytics using a big data approach. *IT Professional, 15*(6), 29–35. doi:10.1109/MITP.2013.60

Weka. (2013) Retrieved from http://www.cs.waikato.ac.nz/ml/weka/

KEY TERMS AND DEFINITIONS

Big Data: Big data refers to large amount of transactional data which could be computationally retrieved and analsyed to understand hidden trends, patterns and various attribute relationships.

Business Analysis: Business analysis a technique which helps business owners to bring organisational changes through analytical process achieved through data analysis.

Data Analysis: Data analysis is a process, where data is parsed and filtered through systematic procedures and methods to get useful information which helps in decision making and helping with possible conclusions.

Data Mashup Systems: Data mashup systems is combination of more than one web or computer applications to form a hybrid which helps in understanding or solution a data problem.

Information Retrieval: Information retrieval is the process of exploring stored data for connected usage.

Information Visualisation: Information visualisation is an approach where data is represented in a visual or graphical mode. It is a useful method in understanding raw or complex data elements.

Web 2.0: Web 2.0 usually refers to the second stage of World Wide Web and applications on the internet. Web 2.0 is focused on user generated and dynamic content which includes the arrival of social media.

Section 3
Exploring the Current and Future Trends of Big Data and Web Intelligence

Chapter 12
The Politics of Access to Information:
Exploring the Development of Software Platforms and Communications Hardware in the Digital Age

Shefali Virkar
University of Oxford, UK

ABSTRACT

Over the last few decades, unprecedented advances in communications technology have collapsed vast spatial and temporal differences, and made it possible for people to form connections in a manner not thought possible before. Centred chiefly on information, this revolution has transformed the way in which people around the world think, work, share, and communicate. Information and Communication Technologies (ICTs) promise a future of a highly interconnected world, wherein action is not limited by physical boundaries, and constrained physical space is replaced by a virtual 'cyberspace' not subject to traditional hierarchies and power relations. But is the promise of ICTs chimerical? To tackle these issues, central to the global policy debate over the potential development contributions of Information and Communication Technologies, and to examine whether and the extent to which disparities in access to ICTs exist, this book chapter provides a demonstration of the ways in which ICTs may be used as tools to further global economic, social, and political advancement, to shape actor behaviour, and to enhance institutional functioning; particularly in the Third World.

INTRODUCTION

The age of Information Technology – IT as we call it – has arrived. I know of no other technological advantage which has brought together so many areas of rapid and exciting development. Computers and telecommunications are converging very rapidly, huge investments are being made, and the impact of information technology will be felt at every level in our society; in industry, in commerce, in our offices and in our homes. -Kenneth Baker (1982)

DOI: 10.4018/978-1-4666-8505-5.ch012

The closing years of the 20th century were a period of turbulent change for world politics, and stood witness to two major developments that critics agree played a key role in the sculpting of the political, economic and social landscape of the 21st century. The first was the dramatic unfolding of a series of events, beginning with the symbolic dismantling of the Berlin Wall in 1989, which signalled the beginning of the end for many of the central tenets of post-World War II international relations. A plethora of forces at work in the Soviet Union and Eastern Europe over previous decades unleashed dramatic upheavals in essentially all countries of the former Eastern Bloc, culminating in the unexpected collapse of Soviet statism in 1990-91 and the subsequent demise of international communism. At the forefront of these forces were the pressures of technological change on the internal structures of the Eastern Bloc nations and on their relationships with the outside world. These led to drastic economic restructuring to compete in the high technology global environment with huge shifts in the composition of the domestic economies, a rationalisation of military forces, and a seemingly unstoppable flood of information pouring unhindered through the erstwhile Iron Curtain.

The second development was less dramatic and, beyond a handful of scientific and academic circles, was less well recognised: the invention of Hyper Text Mark-up Language (HTML) and the creation of the World Wide Web. Although network computing had been around since the 1960s, the networks themselves were rudimentary – comprising of dispersed computers linked by packet-switching technology – and remained, till the end of the 1980s, the domain of scientists, academics and a handful of graduate students (Toulouse, 1998). The invention of HTML broke this user-monopoly by simplifying network programming and, together with the launch of the graphical browser Mosaic (and its descendants Netscape Navigator and Internet Explorer), made it possible for lay computer users to access Websites and communicate with people across the globe (Norris, 2001). Whilst seemingly unrelated, the developments of the late 1980s share a remarkable thread of commonality: they are both small historical footnotes in a much larger tale. A tale in which advances in science and technology, particularly developments in information and communications technology, have moulded the evolution of international affairs, and altered the relationships within and amongst nations and the fortunes of their peoples.

The starting point of this book chapter is the recognition of an apparently new way of conceiving contemporary society, and the acknowledgement of the pivotal roles that *information*, *communication*, and *technology* play within it. Social scientists have long seen 'information' as *the* distinctive feature of the modern world, however, what makes today's age distinct from before is the growing convergence of digital computing, telecommunications, and human infrastructure; reflected in the shift in terminology from *Information Technology* or *I.T.* to *Information and Communications Technology* or *I.C.T.* (Virkar, 2014). Popular and academic literature tells us that we stand on the edge of the Information Age, where both information and technology have become 'symbol(s) of political potency and economic prosperity' (Martin, 1998: 1). We live and work in 'weightless knowledge economies' and will soon be part of a 'global information society'.

These clichés are not used without reason. The world is continuing to witness the burgeoning growth of new electronic Information and Communications Technologies (ICTs) and their associated platforms and applications: the Internet and the World Wide Web have spawned multimedia and interactive technologies, video-conferencing, virtual realities, computer-aided design, the information superhighway, and technologies for consumer profiling and surveillance; all of which enable the electronic production, transmission, processing, communication, and consumption of increasingly vast quantities of information and know-how. Like their predecessors – the printing press, the telegraph, the radio, and black-and-white television – advanced ICTs have become an intrinsic part of our everyday social, political, and economic lives. They are embedded in an array of networks and services across the spectrum of human activity: from education to politics, from the arts to sport, from medicine to music, these technologies are set to transform the way in which people work, think, act, and interact.

HYPER CONNECTIVITY: GLOBALISATION, THE INTERNET, AND THE THREAT TO NATIONAL SOVEREIGNTY

All that is solid melts into air -Marshall Berman

Information has been feared by those in authority from time immemorial. The growth of the media and the spread of information have been regarded as sources of power and change ever since the time of James I of England, when the growth in the popularity of the printing press was watched with great suspicion by both the Crown and the Church. The nascent print media gave rise to the first stirrings of parliamentary democracy in Britain and allowed, for the first time, the old political order to be challenged by new ideas (Perritt, 1998). The subsequent development of new and improved forms of communication over the next few centuries, beginning with the invention of the radio and the telegraph, and moving thence to the telephone and to television, posed new and greater threats to central power and authority (Thussu, 2000). Writing in 1894, John Stuart Mill noted that "it is hardly possible to overrate the value, in this present low state of human improvement, of placing human beings in contact with persons dissimilar to themselves, and with modes of thought and action unlike those with which they are familiar... Such communication has always been, and is peculiarly in the present age, one of the main sources of progress" (Quoted in Grace et. al., 2001:1).

Today, it may be claimed concretely that the global spread of technology and the subsequent growth of the global media have definitely impacted nation-states in ways that would be seen as 'interference' by many in positions of authority. Globalisation has collapsed spatial and temporal barriers to economic and social exchange, and its convergence with two other trends, world-wide electronic connectivity and emergent knowledge networking practices, has reinforced the importance of the role played by knowledge and information in the global political, social, and economic arenas (Virkar, 2014). An oft-quoted example of such media power is the *CNN Effect*: the impact that live, round-the-clock, global news coverage by all-news cable television channels has on public opinion and on foreign policymaking (Virkar, 2004)[1]. Many International Relations theorists and self-styled *cyberenthusiasts* alike believe that the Internet, with its seemingly limitless possibilities for information transmission and access to knowledge, poses the strongest-ever technological challenge to state sovereignty than any other communications medium in living memory. Today, we live in knowledge-driven societies poised on the threshold of an Information Age.

Theoretical Frameworks of the Information Society

It is not surprising therefore, that advances in ICTs have been, and still are, regarded by many as the impetus behind radical, if not revolutionary, socio-economic changes, and are at the centre of many fierce debates raging across the world. The concept of an 'information society' and the uses of ICTs within such a community have themselves been sources of controversy (Mansell & Silverstone, 1996). To some commentators, the extensive use of ICTs constitutes the emergence of a truly efficient, open society, whilst to others it heralds the beginning of an Orwellian police-state and the gradual demise of key civil liberties; some see the flood of information as a precursor of a highly educated public, whilst others see in it a deluge of trivia, sensationalism and propaganda (Dutton, 1999).

Amidst the divergent opinions regarding the Information Society and ICTs one thing remains undisputed: the role and importance of information, and Information Technologies, have grown in the contemporary world. Given their potential to revolutionise social, economic, political and cultural life, recent advances in ICTs have generated many theoretical perspectives on the 'Information Revolution' and its implications for society. Early discussions of computers and telecommunications reflected the concern that modern technology would become an unstoppable force, supporting increasingly centralised control in organisations and society (Skolnikoff, 1993). Theories of technological determinism were particularly popular during the 1960s, and are still subscribed to by a number of commentators today.

Concurrent to the emergence of technological determinism was the emergence of modernisation theory, and the idea that technology could be used as a tool for development. Modernisation was concerned with the development gap between the North and South, and how best to close the gap so as enable quicker and more effective growth in the Third World. The most popular variant of the theory was an adaptation of Walt Whitman Rostow's views, popularised in his 1960 volume, *The Stages of Economic Growth: A Non-communist Manifesto* (Rodda, 2004). Rostow outlined five main stages of growth: the traditional society, the preconditions for take-off, the take-off, the drive to maturity, and the age of high mass consumption. This helped define where the constituent parts of the world stood in this scheme, and how best the South could climb the ladder of development. Essentially, information technology was considered an important precondition towards achieving a reformation of politics, society, and economy, and the ultimate emergence of a modern (typically capitalist) civilization.

With the turn of the decade, however, most social scientists discarded the linear models of cause-and-effect used by technological determinism and modernisation in favour of approaches that popularised the notion that a new sort of society was emerging, and which sought to explore the underlying processes of social and technical change (Silverstone & Haddon, 1996). Possibly the best known characterisation of the Information Society is, therefore, Daniel Bell's Theory of Post-Industrialism. In his seminal work *The Coming of the Post-Industrial Society* (1973), Bell asserted that information – not raw materials or financial capital – would become the key economic resource in the coming age.

Using the United States as his benchmark, Bell identified 3 major trends in the development of an Information Society: an Increased Employment in Information- and Knowledge-Driven Job Sectors, referring to the movement of a majority of the labour-force from the *primary* (agriculture-led) and *secondary* (manufacturing-led) sectors of an economy to jobs within the *tertiary* or the service sector that involve the creation, transmission, and consumption of information; an Increased Importance of 'Knowledge' and 'Information' in Society, including its integration into the everyday working of social, political, and economic institutions; and an Increased Centrality of Decision-making by Technologists to Technologists, implying a power shift in favour of those managers and professionals skilled in the use of information and technology for planning and analysis.

Bell's information-society thesis and its subsequent applicative relevance in the modern work world has been both criticised and has tested doubtful on many counts (Virkar, 2011). Firstly, there is a constant shifting of employment subject to demand-supply patterns for agricultural goods, manufactures and services, an economic given which may be completely unconnected with an Information Revolution. In addition, ICTs can bring about job losses in every sector of the economy, including the service sector, as manual labour is replaced by advanced technology. Finally, and most importantly, the value of information as a commodity itself is highly variable; certain kinds of information are not useful, and some parts can lose value whilst others retain it depending on the circumstances.

The Politics of Access to Information: Plugging in to the Information Age

In recent times, the focus of ICT scholarship has moved away from the centrality of information *per se* to the issues and processes that shape access to information and technology, and to the notion that the ability to control this access to information and the need to acquire an understanding of the institutions and hierarchies that do so are key to functioning in a knowledge-driven economy (Robins, 1992). In this context, questions concerned with *who* is 'connected' to information technology have grown in prominence over the last few decades. They now form an important element in the burgeoning canon of 'information age' literature, and are beginning to influence the policy agenda of industrialised, technologically-advanced countries such as the USA, the UK, and those of the European Union (Selwyn, 2002). The so-called 'techno-enthusiasm' of a whole host of analysts, politicians, and other policymakers has been tempered with concerns over the potentially divisive aspects of the Information Age, in particular the development of software platforms, communications hardware, and the related global inequalities of access to ICTs. Developing countries and pressure groups within some developed nations have become increasingly alarmed at the apparent emergence of a 'digital divide', wherein those without access to the latest and, ironically, the most expensive tools and technologies will find themselves at a great disadvantage, unable to compete in an increasingly hi-tech global socio-political marketplace. Decelerating economic progress has serious implications for the social and political development of these individuals, groups, and countries, circumstances which in turn threaten overall global peace and security.

In seeking to address the overarching question of whether the developing world is being left behind in the Information Revolution with regards to Information and Communication Technology Research and Development, the discussion covered in the subsequent sections of this chapter endeavours to succinctly answer three questions: 1) is there a gap in the access to ICTs between developed and developing countries; 2) is this gap growing or closing; and finally, 3) what are the implications of this *digital divide* for the overall development and global proliferation of communications hardware and software? The central hypothesis of this book chapter being, therefore, that a digital divide exists between developed and developing nations, and that it might be bridged through the increased development and greater use of ICTs worldwide. To tackle these issues, central to the global policy debate over the potential development contributions of Information and Communication Technologies, the chapter also provides a demonstration of the ways in which ICTs may be used as tools to further global economic, social, and political development, to shape actor behaviour, and to enhance institutional functioning particularly in the Third World. The work commences with a brief conceptualisation of the Digital Divide, examining its causes and critically reviewing current debates, moving forward to an assessment of the implied consequences that such a divide has for electronic government and for policy creation. The research therein seeks to analyse, in particular, the possible positive and negative consequences of bridging the Digital Divide for the betterment of public administrative practices and for the development of a more in-depth understanding of the applicative value that such a exploration holds for the future of the communications and software industry.

THE NETWORKING REVOLUTION: ICTs AND THE DIGITAL DIVIDE

The world at large is exactly what is at stake. Geographical borders seem to be of no importance whatsoever to the new media - they simply haven't been invited to the global ICT party.- Sarai Report to The Waag [2]

One of the most urgent issues today, and one of the questions central to global policy, is how ICTs affect global development, and whether they can be used to accelerate development in the Third World. Already, the spread of ICTs, in particular the Internet and telecommunications, is becoming visible: between 1995-1998, the global telecommunications markets added 200 million telephone lines, 263 million mobile subscribers and 10 million leased lines; and Internet connections increased to 88 million from 15 million in the early nineties. It took the telephone close to 50 years to reach 50 million users, a landmark which took the Internet only 4 years to surpass (World Bank, 2002).

The main reasons behind the recent explosion in ICTs are falling operating and hardware costs. These are, in turn, largely a result of technological innovations such as the use of *fibre optic cables,* able to transmit greater quantities of information across longer distances, *new mobile wireless technologies*, allowing users to stay connected regardless of location, and the adoption of *digital packet-switching* technology, making possible real-time networking and affordable computing power (Martin, 1998). Coupled with these developments, *regulatory reform* (increased privatisation and WTO-encouraged liberalisation of the global telecom market) has had a profound impact in both developed and developing countries.

Why ICTs?

There is no doubt that Information and Communication Technologies possess many basic characteristics that would enable them to play a significant role in the development process (Virkar, 2004).

1. **Increased and Faster Access to Knowledge:** Where reduced costs of producing and transmitting information lead, atleast in theory, to the greater availability of and access to information and help reduce uncertainty and risk to the benefit of all, particularly the poor, thereby *"[m]aking inefficient markets efficient"* as the management of online auctioneers eBay put it.
2. **Increased Efficiency and Precision:** Of working and of work processes, where the adoption of new ideas and inventions results in the streamlining of business activity, from production-lines to entire organisations, which in turn leads to greater productivity, increased profits, and more innovation.
3. **Overcoming Geography:** Through the harnessing of the innate ability of ICTs to function across national boundaries, and to collapse dislocations of space and time; thereby enabling people and organisations from diverse geographical regions to pool their resources, knowledge, and expertise. The bridging of temporal and spatial barriers to trade, commerce, travel and political action is particularly favourable for developing countries that, in addition to gaining access to larger markets and global supply networks, are also able to significantly benefit from new ideas and high-quality shared information.
4. **Openness:** A singular characteristic of the digital media that results in the key organisational process of *networking*, leading to greater and more effective information-sharing, and increased accountability and transparency. In this respect ICTs are potentially extremely powerful tools of

global empowerment for, as societies across the world become more and more interconnected and as information becomes more easily and readily available in digital form, they bring days of closed-door negotiations and secret repression closer and closer to an end.

Whilst many policymakers consider ICTs to be potent tools that empower poorer communities, societies, and countries, that are able to support long term economic and social development, and that are capable of bringing about 'a closer and more productive integration of affluent and developing nations, others consider them to be detrimental overall for global political, social, and economic development (Virkar, 2011). Under such circumstances, the need to answer questions regarding the utility and functionality of ICTs in development and the kind of goals that may be best achieved through their application becomes even more pressing. The impact of ICTs may be considered under three broad headings: their impact on economic growth, their created opportunities for the poor, and the role they play in improved governance and the delivery of government services.

Impact on Economic Growth

Economic data and anecdotal evidence suggest that growth and development of the Third World are increasingly being influenced by the availability of telecommunications hardware and informatics infrastructure, and that the benefits that ICTs can bring to the developing world are manifold (Katz, 2009). Improved information exchange benefits supply chains across industry sectors globally; giving producers, suppliers, and consumers access to market data, information on regulations and standards, prices, and potential customers. ICTs and their associated digital platforms can also help to promote the transnational marketing and distribution of goods and services: *e-commerce*, for example, is expected to benefit both local producers and international businesses by opening up the global marketplace and by enabling access to virtual digital markets, whilst simultaneously streamlining the structure and functioning of local businesses and institutions. In short, ICTs level the economic playing-field, as developed country producers become less insular in losing one of their key innate privileges – an unrestricted, verging on monopolistic, access to raw materials, human resources, and rich markets worldwide.

An advanced telecommunications infrastructure is, further, central to attracting foreign direct investment, particularly when applied to enhance a country's monetary system. In this respect, the adoption of Information and Communication Technologies facilitates both the modernisation of banking and financial systems, critical to developing countries access to the highly digitised world of international finance, and the expansion of local and transnational banking services and supply chains to previously underserved groups, countries, and regions (Virkar, 2004). Finally, ICT-based virtual applications and platforms, especially electronic messaging services and the Internet, enable countries to expand their service sectors, create jobs, and comply with international business practice standards through the outsourcing of professional services from different parts of the world. This presents enhanced employment opportunities for otherwise disadvantaged professionals, and provides for better pay and higher standards of living internationally (Andrianaivo & Kpodar, 2011). An oft-quoted example is that of the Indian services sector, where software professionals write code for American companies, medical transcribers decipher prescriptions and create dental and hospital records, and call-centres cater to customers all over the so-called Western world.

Opportunities for the Poor

ICTs have the potential to create diverse opportunities for the poor, and encourage the spread of equitable development within developing countries (Virkar, 2011). A majority of the poor of the Third World live in rural areas, and for them vital information and a wide range of services are either difficult to procure or are only available at prohibitive prices. ICTs provide an affordable, versatile mechanism by which the poor might access the global storehouse of knowledge, and use the information gained therein to improve their overall standard of living (Grace, 2003). Farmers and other rural entrepreneurs, for example, may use advanced software and hardware to source information about where they can obtain the highest possible prices for their goods, by-passing exploitative intermediaries and middle-men, rather than simply selling at the nearest market for convenience.

ICTs may be further used to boost agricultural productivity and food security. Schemes piloted in villages in Southern India enable farmers and fishermen to track weather patterns, to predict wave height, and to tackle crop disease (Le Page, 2002). ICTs can also provide increased business opportunities in rural areas and create jobs for more disadvantaged sections of a population. For example in North India, a group called Technology in Action for Rural Advancement (TARA) has pioneered a scheme that involves local people (mainly women) setting up computer centres in their villages, and earning money selling computer services to villagers (Prakash, 2012). Put this way, the pay-off from Information and Communication Technologies in terms of poverty reduction, say experts, could be dramatic. Indeed, as demonstrated above, in countries such as India and Thailand results have been self-evident for the last decade (Spence & Smith, 2010).

Improved Governance and the Delivery of Government Services

Many commentators believe that networking can potentially make a great impact on the public sector, as public services are still reliant on information flows and participation in governance may be facilitated by adequate communication infrastructure (Virkar, 2013). Broadly speaking, ICTs improve governance in three ways. Firstly, they help *enhance decision-making and public administration* by reducing administrative costs, by speeding up the day-to-day processing of information, and by increasing transparency and accountability. Secondly, ICTs *improve the provision of public utilities* such as water, electricity, and sanitation, and help speed up the allocation of permits and the dispensation of complaints. The proliferation and use of ICTs in political processes can also *bring a government closer to its people*, allowing for popular access to decision-making and facilitating communication on three levels – citizen to citizen, citizen to government, and government to citizen.

Information and Communication Technologies have also long been an integral part of the education system in developed countries, and today, new forms of hardware, applications, and platforms offer powerful tools for expanding educational access and improving knowledge and skill-transfer in the Third World (Kozma, 2008). The Internet, in particular, has helped in equalising access to knowledge, has improved teacher training, and has enhanced skills in some of the poorest parts of the world. ICTs may also increase the provision and efficiency of medical services through, amongst other things, the improved storage and transmission of data, the publication and dissemination of medical findings, and the amelioration of the surveillance and monitoring of epidemics (World Bank, 2002). Similarly, such technologies may contribute to the augmentation of efforts to boost environmental protection by enabling access to accurate data relating to global climate change and pollution levels.

MIND THE GAP: EXPLORING THE CONSEQUENCES OF THE DIGITAL DIVIDE FOR DEVELOPMENT

At first glance the digital divide appears to be a simple premise.-Neil Selwyn

It would be difficult to find a more apt real-life symbol for the inequitable distribution of digital technologies than the chasm that yawns between Silicon Valley's verdant Palo Alto, home to dot.com millionaires where the average price of a house is almost $700,000, and East Palo Alto, the squalid little town on the other side of Highway 101 that not long ago gained notoriety for having America's highest murder rate (Virkar, 2004). However, whilst it is largely agreed that there are disparities in access to ICTs, a fierce debate is raging within academic and policy circles as to whether this gap is actually growing or closing.

For developing countries, the potential benefits gained from advances in ICTs are immense, and their successful adoption would imply both an acceleration of economic and social development, and greater social, economic, and political integration of isolated (usually rural) populations into mainstream community, national, and global life. The ultimate vision for many *techno-enthusiasts* is thus that of the creation of an immense Global Information Infrastructure enabling the rapid acceleration of technology assimilation into political institutions and for economic development, one that will narrow gaps in poverty and eliminate obstacles to full social integration, to equality of opportunity, and to overall worldwide prosperity (Main, 2001).

The question stands clear: with the continued prevalence of existing inequalities in current institutions and infrastructure, will Information and Communication Technologies ever become truly global? With what consequences for political, social, and economic institutional reform and policy building? Many commentators fear that countries (and the individuals, groups, and communities within them) lacking access to fundamental resources essential for them to fully benefit from advances in technological hardware and software would only be further marginalised by the ICT Revolution (World Bank, 2002). This apprehension has been encapsulated succinctly in the phrase "**digital divide**", an amorphous term that may be defined as *the gap between those individuals and communities that have, and those that do not have, access to information, ICTs, and technological know-how.*

Understanding the Concept of the Digital Divide

It is plain to see that the conditions under which ICTs are diffusing in most countries are creating deep, more complex disparities in the way in which technology is developed and propagated across the world. Equally, it is not surprising that to many, bridging this so-called *digital divide* has become the single-most pervasive development issue of the new century. Concern has been expressed in various forums – from the UN and the Group of 8 at the very top of the development ladder to university departments and local community groups at the other end of the scale – that the developing world is being, and will continue to be, left behind in the digital stakes (UNDP, 2010). Commentators consider such disparities as evidence of an ever-widening gap between the information-rich and information-poor, see this divide as continuing to manifest itself along other, multiple axes: *between countries*, hindering the economic growth of some nations whilst aiding others; and *within countries*, differentially impacting the opportunities of various individuals and groups in society *vis-à-vis* each other.

A key issue central to arriving at a more nuanced understanding of the concept is, thus, how ICTs, and the associated digital divide, relate to global development. It is a welldocumented fact that during the 1990s, the world witnessed a substantial increase in social exclusion, poverty, and income inequality; statistics showed that 50% of the world's population (more so than in previous decades) subsisted on less than $2 a day, 20% of the global population generated 80% of the world's wealth, 80% of global youth lived in the developing world and lacked access to opportunity, and more women bore a larger part of the burden of poverty, illiteracy, and malnutrition than their male counterparts (Virkar, 2004). During the latter half of the decade, coinciding with the explosive growth in Information Technology and the rise of the network economy, and despite the spectacular strides made by certain developing countries as a result of the rapid proliferation of ICTs, the gap between the developed and developing world widened in terms of technology, productivity, income, social opportunity, and living standards.

The Digital Divide Debate

A growing number of scholars and specialists feel that the digital divide is no longer a crisis; indeed, some contend that it has never been as critical an issue as it was made out to be. These commentators believe that such a paradigm of 'frenetic urgency' is the product of the 'digital delirium' of the 1990s technological and dot-com booms, and argue that, whilst in *absolute* terms the degree of access to ICTs between nations might have widened, in *relative* terms developing countries continue to show faster rates of penetration of technology than developed societies. For example, between January 1997 and August 2000, North America's share of Internet users plummeted from 62.1% of the world total to 42.6%, whilst most other regions displayed impressive gains in their relative share. Overall, the number of Internet users worldwide increased by a factor of four (Castells, 2001).

Some scholars, in consequence, hold that *the gap between rich and poor countries is closing*, with the developing world quickly catching up in terms of numbers of the users able to access, comprehend, and use effectively new technologies and their associated platforms and applications (Virkar, 2004). Many feel that the digital divide today remains a popular cause amongst politicians and interested corporates only as a means of diverting attention from more pressing issues, such as national inequalities of income, education, access to services and benefits, and labour standards, and as means of benefiting from its emotional appeal in terms of either more votes or increased sales. As one critic observed of the American government: "The current political interest in the digital divide is an attempt to reverse the damage to race-relations caused by welfare reforms and by the retreat from affirmative action" (Strover, 2003: 276).

On the surface, it must be admitted that scholars on this side of the digital divide debate appear to have a point. Measured in terms of access, it is highly likely that we will, in the coming decades, witness the fast diffusion of the Internet and other ICTs around the world, and that the bulk of the users will indeed come from developing countries despite the deeper, more lopsided power relationships prevalent. However, that is only to be expected, simply because these countries account for 80%, and growing, of the world's population, soon to be highly educated and better professionally qualified.

Illustrated in more concrete terms, the digital divide runs as follows: whilst more telephone lines have been installed in the developing world over the past 5 years relative to the developed world, in the developed world technology has moved on from fixed analogue land-lines to digital broadband, to mobile networked access, and to 3G technology that allows people to process and access more information within shorter periods of time, and to harness quantum gains in productivity and efficiency (Fink & Kenny, 2003). The ability of a user-group population to access information is yet another facet to this example, wherein the fact that the majority of the information accessible is available in English only (as documented earlier) is a substantial barrier for most people across the world.

Similarly, access to the Internet and other associated applications and platforms does not translate directly into a more *informed* use of those technologies, and people without sufficient education or skills will be unable to effectively harness informatics systems to uses that would benefit them (Virkar, 2011). Research conducted in the field by this researcher has highlighted a number of other equally pertinent social reasons behind the emergence of the digital divide. These include:

- **Socio-Economic Inequalities:** Such as not being able to afford to pay for access to computers or for associated network or connection charges.
- **Lack of Social Networks in Certain Key Areas:** Resulting in a lack of critical mass of people sharing information about the benefits of ICTs.
- **Inadequate Official Support:** Of low cost public access to technology, applications, networks, and associated infrastructure, particularly in developing countries, for want public institutions.
- **Other Social Issues:** Including gender differences involving unfavourable societal views of women accessing employment, the Internet, acquiring technical know-how, and of working outside the home.

One could therefore conclude that, whilst the digital divide measured simply in terms of the rate of penetration of ICTs is narrowing, the gap prevalent in terms of the *effectiveness* and the *ability* of ICTs to deliver on promises of increased efficiency, productivity, information processing and wealth creation continues to widen, reinforced by both technological and sociological factors, and needs to be addressed. Moreover, as Table 1 further illustrates, access to *hardware* is only one part of the digital divide; whilst the degree of density of penetration of ICTs in the Third World might remain low, there are many other factors that must be taken into consideration when judging the extent of technological differential, in particular differences in terms of networking capacity, hardware capability, and the ability of a population to access information round the clock.

Table 1. An Integrative Framework for the Digital Divide

ACCESS		USE	
Technological Access		**Technological Literacy**	
ICT Infrastructure		Technological Skills	
Hardware, Software, Bandwidth		Social and Cognitive Skills	
Social Access		**Social Use**	
Affordability		Information Seeking	
Awareness		Resource Mobilisation	
Language		Social Movements	
Content/Usability		Civic Engagement	
Location		Social Inclusion	

(Source: Moorhead, 2004)

THE POLITICS OF ACCESS TO INFORMATION: OF DIGITAL INEQUALITIES AND DIGITAL DIVIDES

While most observers extol the virtues of the information revolution, and cite its ability to "level the playing field" for all participants, it is not entirely clear that these are either realistic or likely results.- Geoffrey Kirkman

Most studies concerned with quantifying and analysing the digital divide examine inequality of access using a number of key set indicators, which can be broadly classified into two types: inter-country and intra-country.

Inter-Country Inequalities

The growth in proliferation of ICTs in the developing world over the past two decades has been impressive. From 1995-1998 alone, developing countries connected over 155 million phone lines, 4 million leased lines, and witnessed a cumulative increase of 105 million in the number mobile network subscribers. Most regions have also seen a spectacular expansion in the spread and area-coverage of the Internet and other associated technologies within the same period (Virkar, 2004). Information and Communications Technologies are reshaping the flow of investment, goods, and services in the global economy, doubling business investments and service revenues in the Third World.

However, such striking results have often masked the wide disparities prevalent between countries in terms of the degree of penetration, of investment in public and private infrastructure, of change in technological sophistication, and of differentials in content provision (see Figure 1). Consider the following: in 2004, ten years into the commercialisation of the World Wide Web, roughly two-thirds of the world's internet population resided in North America and Europe, with only 15% of the world's population constituting 88% of the world's Internet users. In contrast, South and East Asia was home to 23% of the

Figure 1. Who's Online Where?

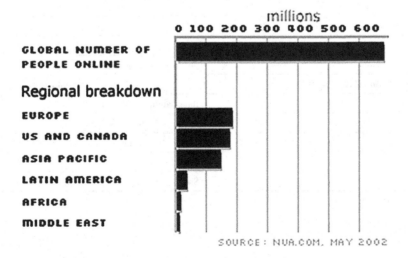

244

world's population but to only 1% of the world's internet users. 280 million people lived in the Middle East but only 1.1 million people were online, with half of those living in Israel alone. There were more telephone lines in Manhattan than in the entire geographical area of Sub-Saharan Africa (Virkar, 2004).

Internet User and Host Penetration and Density

For any technology or application to become a significant international development tool they must, first and foremost, be easily and readily accessible globally. In contrast, the diffusion of Information and Communication Technologies, particularly the Internet and its associated platforms, however rapid, has proceeded unevenly across the planet. For instance, in September 2000, of a total of 378 million Internet users or 6.2% of the world's population, North America's share of skilled technologist stood at 42.6%, Western Europe's at 23.8%, Asia's (including Japan) at 20.6%, Latin America's at 4%, the Middle East at 1.3% and Africa a meagre 0.4%. Recent data from NUA suggests that things haven't changed much since (NUA Online Surveys and Analysis, 2014).

Similarly, the level of penetration and market share of Internet broadcasters (hosts, nodes, and networks) within individual countries was much lower in the developing world – only 0.61% of India's population had access to the Internet in 2012 despite its growing software industry and increasing number of Internet users, as against over 41.5% of American households, and 30.8% of the population in the UK (Virkar, 2014). The geographical distribution of Internet hosts in 2012, illustrated by Figure 2, further demonstrates the gulf in connectivity between industrialised and developing countries.

Figure 2. Internet Hosts per 10,000 People (2012)

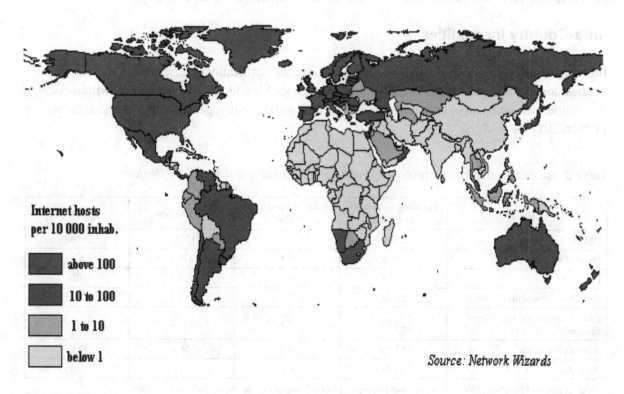

Internet hosts per 10 000 inhab.

- above 100
- 10 to 100
- 1 to 10
- below 1

Source: Network Wizards

Infrastructure Investment and Technological Inputs

Recent studies suggest that the rate of investment in information technology infrastructure is greater for the wealthy as compared to low-income countries. Countries belonging to OECD are, for instance, on average estimated to be investing over $200 *per capita* on information infrastructure, technology, and software, whilst the rest of the world is investing only an average of $20 per capita on the same (OECD, 2012). Infrastructure investments need not, however, be related directly to Information and Communication Technologies, as a want of basic infrastructure such as reliable electricity and office environments, particularly in rural areas, also hampers network connectivity and human resource efficiency (Virkar, 2011).

In addition, as indicated by Table 2, many older basal studies stress the disparity of investment in 'soft infrastructures' – human capital (i.e. scientists and technicians) and research and development – which are as essential as the 'hard' components of ICTs (World Bank, 2002).

Internet Website and Content Languages

Another indicator of the developed world's technological superiority and dominance is the apparent lack of local language content on Internet websites. As seen in Figure 3, whilst English is the native tongue of just over one-third of the global Internet community, over half the websites online are in English solely to the exclusion of other languages.

Internet content providers are still, according to numerous studies, concentrated in a few metropolitan areas of the developed world. A telling example is, for instance, the city of London that has for the last decade hosted more Internet domains than the whole of Africa (Castells, 2013).

Intra-Country Inequalities

Imbalanced access to ICTs and their associated platforms and applications is also visible within countries. Studies done in both developed and developing countries have identified several key within-country inequalities, including those of income, education, age, and disability, gender, and by geographic region (Virkar, 2011).

Table 2. Spending on Infrastructure, Investment, and Technological Inputs by Region

Region	Spending on II (US$ per Capita)	R&D as Percent of GDP	Technicians	Scientists
OECD	129.11	1.8	1326.1	2649.1
Middle East	19.93	0.4	177.8	521
East Asia	13.49	0.8	235.8	1026
Latin America and the Caribbean	28.28	0.5	205.4	656.6
Eastern Europe and Transition Economies	22.89	0.9	577.2	1841.3
Sub-Saharan Africa	11.56	0.2	76.1	324.3
South Asia	13.49	0.8	59.5	161

Source: Pyramid Research (2000) and Wilson and Rodriguez (2000). Compiled by the World Bank and infoDev.

The figure for Investment II is the average of Asia Pacific; including East Asia and South Asia.

Note: Technicians and Scientists are per 1 million persons.

Figure 3. Language and the Internet

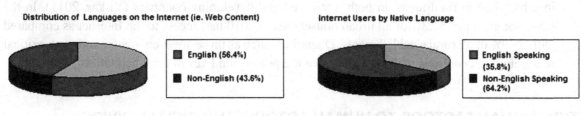

Compiled and Graphically Presented by the Author
Source: Internet World Stats, http://www.internetworldstats.com/stats7.htm

- **Income:** A recent OECD study concluded that individual or household income is an important determinant of the *presence* and of the *penetration* of Information and Communication Technologies; where higher income groups with greater purchasing power are the first to acquire and use new technology, and consequently have a head-start over persons from lower income groups who are concerned more with basic survival than with the acquisition of modern luxuries. This has been confirmed by the World Bank in stark results obtained from similar studies: in South Africa, for example, households in the wealthiest quintile are 125 times more likely to own a phone than those in the poorest quintile.

- **Gender:** In many developing countries, men have greater access to ICTs and the Internet than women do. In Latin America, for instance, *Wall Street Journal* polls targeting Internet users and technology use indicated that only 38% of the respondents polled were female. Likewise in Africa, surveys find that 86%, 83% and 64% of the Internet users in Ethiopia, Senegal, and Zambia respectively, were male. An analysis done by this author indicates that the degree to which women have access to technology seems to depend largely on societal and cultural values, particularly traditional expectations of a woman's role in the family and in society and the degree of opportunity such as the access to education to which they are exposed (Virkar, 2004). In societies where culture and/or religion places the most emphasis on a woman's reproductive and housekeeping functions, access to technology is likely to be low. By contrast, in the Western world, where there is greater emphasis on female literacy and equal of opportunity, the gender divide in access to technology is small but often highly acute. As women increasingly enter the labour force, differentials in physical and mental capabilities as a consequence of differences in race, background, and training have also led to a further polarisation in the degree of access within the female workforce.

- **Education, Age, and Disability:** Studies further indicate that the access and use of Information and Communication Technologies is related to a person's educational status and skill set. In Australia, data on average has shown that over 34% of people with a university degree were more likely to own a computer and to access the Internet than those without, whilst only 12% of those with a secondary school certificate as their highest qualification were likely to do so; a trend borne out by studies conducted in Europe and America over the last decade and a half. Access to ICTs is generally lower for older people than for persons from younger generations, the highest technological usage being prevalent in the age group 30-45 years of age. Disabled people are nearly three times less likely to have home access to the Internet than people without disabilities (Virkar, 2004).

- **Geographic Region:** Access to ICTs, again the Internet and its associated technologies, is greater in urban than in rural areas, in both developed and developing countries (Virkar, 2011). In the USA, for example, 42.3% of all urban households in 2010 had access to the Internet as compared with 38.9% of all rural establishments. Disparities such as these are even greater and more critical in developing countries, where up to 80% of the population lives in rural habitation.

FROM HUMAN FACTORS TO HUMAN ACTORS: THE DIGITAL DIVIDE AND PATTERNS OF HUMAN INTERACTION IN DEVELOPMENT

A concept of the user is fundamental to much of the research and practice of information systems design, development, and evaluation.- Roberta Lamb and Rob Kling

The design and implementation of complex computer systems requires a better understanding in practitioner circles of the users of such networks and the settings in which they work. Part of the problem resides in the implicit treatment of ordinary people as unskilled, non-specialist users of technology and their networks as comprising of elementary processes or *factors* that can be studied in isolation in a field laboratory setting (Bannon, 1991). Although psychology has a long tradition of contributing to computer systems design and implementation, it has been a neglected discipline in scholarly circles and key issues such as those relating to the underlying values of the people involved in large-scale system design and their motivation in the work setting have been missed out in recent computer science-based scholarly analysis (Salvendy, 2012).

Conceptualising and understanding people as *actors* in situations, on the other hand, with a set of skills and shared practices based on work experiences with others, requires a reorientation in the way in which the relationship between key elements of computer system design, namely people, technology, work requirements, and organisational constraints in work settings, is negotiated (Kuutti, 1996). The terms 'human factors' and 'human actors ' give a clue as to how people in system design clusters are and ought to be approached (Virkar, 2011). More particularly, the terms highlight differences in how people and their contributions are perceived, the former connotating a passive, fragmented, depersonalised, and somewhat automatic human contribution; the latter an active, controlling, involved one (Carayon et. al, 2012).

More precisely, within the *human factor* approach, the human element is more often than not reduced to being another system component with certain characteristics that need to be factored into the design equation for the overall human-machine system (Czaja & Nair, 2012). In doing so, however, the approach de-emphasises certain important elements of work design: the goals, the values, and the beliefs that technologists and system-users hold about life and about work (Jacko et. al., 2012). On the contrary,

Box 1. Winners and Losers of the Digital Age

Results of research on digital inequalities indicate that better-educated, young urban men living in developed countries are most likely to benefit from the ICT revolution; whilst less-educated, older rural women living in developing countries are most likely to be on the wrong side of the digital chasm.

(Source: Moorehead, 2004)

by using the term *human actors*, emphasis is placed on users and developers as autonomous agents possessing the capacity to control, to regulate, and to coordinate their behaviour; rather than them being on par and analysed as mere information processing automatons (Proctor & Vu, 2012).

Understanding Actor Behaviour: Winners and Losers in the Development Age

The central issue that needs to be understood whilst studying the Digital Divide, the development of ICT platforms, and the proliferation and implementation of such technologies in public sector organisations, through the additional lens of an analysis of actor interactions, is thus: *Why do people do what they do?* One approach to understanding behaviour is to look at the rationality of individual actors, rather than the system as a whole. This is largely because political actors especially are driven by a combination of organisational and institutional roles and duties and calculated self-interest, with political interaction being organised around the construction and interpretation of meaning as well as the making of choices.

Political actors, in general, have a complex set of goals including power, income, prestige, security, convenience, loyalty (to an idea, an institution or the nation), pride in work well done, and a desire to serve the public interest (as the individual actor conceives it). According to Downs (1964) actors range from being purely self-interested ('climbers' or 'conservers' motivated entirely by goals which benefit themselves and their status quo rather than their organizations or the society at large) to having mixed motives ('zealots', 'advocates' and 'statesmen' motivated by goals which combine self-interest and altruistic loyalty with larger values). An in-depth analysis of the ICT for development literature by this researcher identified five actor groups involved in games relating to the implementation of e-government projects:

1. **Politicians:** The first group identified comprises of elected representatives of various hues, guided and influenced chiefly by electoral imperatives and a need to maintain their public image, and are therefore concerned with directing both key economic policy issues as well as issues of public service delivery.

2. **Administrators / Civil Servants:** This group of actors is guided by their perceptions of existing institutional 'culture' and practices and their positive (or negative) attitudes towards internal bureaucratic reforms such as concerns about the down-sizing of administrative services to promote 'efficiency' and a sense of being policed by elected government through the introduction of ICTs.

3. **Organisations Dealing with Technical Designing of IT Systems for Tax Collection:** The approach private IT suppliers take to e-government might be considerably different to what the adopting government agency actually needs or wants from a system.

4. **Citizens:** This is another particularly interesting group of actors as one is never quite sure what their reaction to the implementation of e-government will be. Whilst in theory citizens should welcome the introduction of a system that simplifies administrative processes, in practice it is equally possible that some citizens might not be very happy if a more efficient system was put into place.

5. **International Donors:** This final actor group controls the purse-strings and oftentimes comes to the table with 'higher' ideals coloured by ideas prevalent in international politics (such as the desire to see a particular brand of 'good governance' in the developing world).

Introducing new technology and grassroots social media initiatives into political, social, and economic arenas is a tricky game to play, as computerisation alters the work-load, the work profile, and the overall level of literacy of the average public sector employee and citizen; impacting accountability, reducing the opportunities available for the exercising of discretion, making performance more visible, flattening the hierarchy, and often forcing the need for retraining and retooling and sometimes creating redundancy (Bhatnagar, 2004).

Many technology-based projects aimed at bridging digital divides often tend to face both external resistance from a general user population and internal resistance from staff recruited to run them, in particular from the middle to lower levels of a civil service, and especially when efforts are made to reengineer work-flow processes through the seamless integration of technology and to create a form of back-end computerisation that has a profound impact on the way civil servants and citizenry perform their duties and perceive their jobs. Very often in developing countries, it is the fear of the unknown that drives this resistance, especially if the introduction of new technology results in a change of procedures and the need for the acquisition of new skills and knowhow. Further, in corrupt service delivery departments, there may be pressure to slow down or delay the introduction of technology-led reforms due to the impending loss of additional incomes (Virkar, 2011).

Far from following new patterns, interactions behind efforts to bridge the current digital divide appear to reflect existing, oft-formulaic patterns of social, political, and economic inequality, and show little sign of altering drastically in the foreseeable future. Critics believe that the unequal spread of ICTs along old socio-political fault lines prompts the re-emergence of traditional set patterns of detrimental actor behaviour, engendering potentially cataclysmic consequences in terms of development prospects and policy processes in the Third World (Virkar, 2011). More particularly, such negative interactions would result in: **inhibited economic growth**, forcing poor countries into what the World Bank (2002) terms *ICT-related poverty traps*, as countries with little access get excluded from the highly digitised international trading and financial system; **increased internal tension and instability**, as poverty and increased feelings of helplessness and dependence on the West create resentment and drive people onto the streets in protest and other forms of civil unrest; **the emergence of a technologically disadvantaged workforce** that is, relative to their Western counterparts, inflexible and ill-equipped to deal with rapid external changes and, therefore, at a permanent relative disadvantage; and a **gradual erosion of global peace and security**, as countries that are unable to integrate equitably into the world trading system become increasingly poor and isolated, providing ideal breeding-grounds and hosts for extremism and terrorist networks.

BRIDGING THE DIGITAL DIVIDE: TOWARDS DEVELOPMENT OR DEPENDENCY?

ICTs represent a major opportunity for world development. However, this is an opportunity that must be promoted in full awareness of the risk that the benefits will be unevenly shared.-Robin Mansell

Today, it is widely recognised that the digital revolution holds many promises for developing countries, and that 'bridging the digital divide' has become the central developmental issue for an array of national, regional, and international organisations. Over the years, a number of governments, businesses, individuals, communities, and organisations have studied the issues at stake in the digital divide and have drafted reports ranging from statistical analyses to in-depth case studies, putting forward recommendations to address inherent problems. In general, these include specific ground-level initiatives and policy reforms, but also cover the wider issues that have had an impact on the array of digital advances and divides and that manifest themselves under the broad umbrella of the global ICT revolution, within *e-commerce*, *e-government*, *e-procurement*, and *international trade*.

Organisations and institutions, particularly those that form the political, societal, and economic core of a country, cannot afford to be left behind, as the people within those institutions are generally looked to as trendsetters and role models in addition to being responsible for societal welfare (Virkar, 2011b). Software platform and application development, therefore, needs to be able to respond swiftly and appropriately to these changes to meet need for equitable access to information and technology. The growing demand for cost-effective, high-quality programming, and the response from both the private and public sectors, has resulted in the emergence of several collaborative, cross-sectoral partnerships between software developers and government organisations globally (Virkar, 2011a). However, as illustrated in previous sections of this chapter, the underlying motivations for the individual partners and actors within these collaborations can be widely divergent, and may result in highly divisive and negative outcomes the world over.

A Summary of Current Efforts to Bridge the Digital Divide

A number of major international initiatives have been launched specifically to deal with the digital divide, such as the G-8 Summit's *Digital Opportunity Task* (DOT) *Force* and the *World Summit on the Information Society* (WSIS), which aim to bring together key leaders and policymakers from around the world for consultation, debate, and policy formulation. A variety of organisations have conducted 'e-readiness' assessments in developing countries to determine their preparedness to integrate technology and electronic work-flow best practice into the mainstream economy and into the public sector.

Elsewhere on the ground, efforts aimed at introducing new ICTs into less-developed parts of the world are concerned chiefly with putting technology to use in underserved populations through the provision of infrastructure and equipment (Main, 2001). Existing efforts range from projects that create public access centres and kiosks, where poor people can use telephones and computers, to those that incorporate ICT in healthcare and other essential public service sectors using innovative technology and small business applications to promote local entrepreneurship. Initiatives are driven by agencies that range from tiny Non-Governmental Organisations (NGOs) working in remote areas such as SchoolNet, Namibia's effort to put computers into rural schools, to multibillion-dollar multinational corporations, such as Hewlett Packard's $1 billion "e-Inclusion" scheme aimed at promoting hardware innovations especially suitable for developing country environments (Dunn & Yamashita, 2003). In order to meet connectivity needs, programmes are structured to tackle two basic issues: the need to increase developing country connectivity to international communications backbones and the need to improve internal connectivity infrastructure.

Promising technological solutions include the use of underwater cables, satellites, and Very Small Aperture Terminals or *VSATs*. Satellites, in particular, offer the cheapest form of high-speed, web-enabled connectivity to date, but their potential is still under-exploited (Graham, 2011). Another potential solution is the use of Wireless Application Protocol or WAP technologies and wireless devices, today seen as a way of digitally leapfrogging the lack of conventional telephones in developing countries. Recent years have seen an explosive growth in the number of mobile communications operators in poorer countries – Tanzania, for example, has more mobile telephone operators than the United Kingdom – and in conflict-zones such as Somalia and Rwanda, where prolonged fighting has destroyed most land-based fixed infrastructure and the number of mobile phones in circulation has exceeded the number of traditional phone lines owned by the local population (Poblet, 2011). Efforts are also being made come up with innovative schemes to expand traditional phone availability in impoverished areas, particularly by routing government funding through to successful private initiatives such as *Grameen Telecom* in Bangladesh.

A favourite solution with many international development projects involves the establishment of Internet cafés, public computer centres, kiosks, and telecentres (Virkar, 2011). Multipurpose community telecentres[3], in particular, have been set up by development agencies and national governments to counter low Internet and mobile technology penetration in a number of otherwise deprived localities such as rural Mexico and Senegal, whilst privately owned Internet cafés and gaming centres have sprung up all over the developing world. In addition, international organisations like the World Bank advocate the implementation of policy reforms in parallel to such developments and to complement improvements in infrastructure (World Bank, 2002). These reforms are generally market- and growth-oriented, and seek to create a satisfactory regulatory environment for the adoption of ICTs in developing countries. In particular, they focus on monitoring and altering the actors, the behaviours, and the interactions that encourage privatisation and competition in the telecom markets, and on providing fiscal incentives for the growth of e-commerce and its eventual mainstreaming into a country national economy (Virkar, 2011). Suggested measures deal with issues such as the management of intellectual property rights, the adoption of consumer protection policies, the development of guidelines for taxation in cyberspace, and the establishment of standards and regulatory systems for the development of technological hardware and software (Dutton, 1992).

The panoply of programmes initiated in recent years has yielded a range of benefits in the developing world (Virkar, 2014). These might be broadly summarised to include an improved standard of living for the poor through the adoption and propagation of better, automated work practices and regular access to information and connectivity with the outside world; a reduction in the vulnerabilities of the poor and a concurrent increase in their capacities and opportunities through schemes and pilot projects which promote ICT solutions for self-employment and micro-enterprises; enhanced government capacity, defined in terms of efficiency and accountability as well as enhanced political participation, leading eventually to enhanced democratisation, and the increased participation in civil society, together with the strengthening of the *body politic*, of previously disempowered groups and individuals; all resulting in the emergence of a large pool of technologically literate producers and consumers in the developing world who drive growth-led exports to the benefit of local, national, and global economies.

THE NETWORK SOCIETY: DIGITALLY EMPOWERED DEVELOPMENT

Small changes in ICTs trigger unexpectedly explosive changes in use.-John Gage

There are, however, potential downsides to being ICT-focused. Greater reliance on information technology increases the vulnerability of individuals, groups and communities within developing countries to the dangers of cyber-crime and other equally serious fraud and security risks through the reduction of manual functionality and the creation of machine-behaviour patterns of living and interaction. The transmission of viruses, worms, and spyware can seriously hamper the use of existing technological hardware and software, subvert morale, disrupt hierarchies, office-based interactions, and work-flow processes, compromise a country's e-commerce and digital government base, and potentially undermine national security in times of conflict or of diplomatic hostilities (Zin & Yunos, 2004).

There is also the danger that technology, given to self-serving governments for development purposes, may be clandestinely put to military uses or be sold by them to terrorists to further their own political agenda (Virkar, 2004). Dual-use technology particularly could, in the wrong hands, pose a serious threat to peace and security, a classic example being the supercomputer; networks of exceptionally powerful, advanced computing systems that are at once employed to predict large-scale weather patterns, to monitor seismic activity, and used in functionalities ranging from national security surveillance to genomic sequencing, but are equally capable of being behind the mass production of advanced nuclear, chemical, and biological weapons. The United States, the biggest producer of supercomputers, has imposed restrictions on its export for exactly these reasons.

Another grim reality is that the world's poorest face a variety of problems, all of them possessing broader global implications, and most of which cannot be solved through the mere provision of access to computers and technology-related infrastructure (Sklair, 2002). Key global developmental issues include people without access to clean drinking water or proper sanitation facilities, chronic food shortages, and illiterate populations. Furthermore, the HIV/AIDS pandemic is set to explode within the developing world, with the Asia-Pacific region alone predicted to account for 40% of new global infections by 2020. Prolonged armed conflicts, particularly in Africa, are devastating developing economies and resulting in massive humanitarian crises (UNDP, 2014). In the face of numerous efforts being made to combat the digital divide, therefore, the fundamental question must be asked: will simply investing in the development and dissemination of technological infrastructure in developing countries, both hard and soft, automatically lead to better lives for the people who live there?

Consequently, scholars emphasise that Information and Communication Technologies are increasingly becoming pre-requisites for rapid economic development, and are crucial in helping the South to digitally leapfrog conventional industrialisation and to catch up with the knowledge-based, knowledge-driven economies of the North (Virkar, 2004). Similarly, the competitiveness of developing countries in the international trading system will increasingly depend on their ability to exchange digital information globally. Scholarly literature contends that there is a strong positive correlation between poverty and a lack of access to ICTs, and argues that the more developed a country's infrastructure is, the greater its attractiveness to foreign investors becomes and the more probable rapid economic growth (Trujillo, 2003).

However, despite the number of reported success stories, evidence from the field indicates a high rate of information system failure in the developing world (Heeks, 2002). Whilst failures are in themselves a cause for concern, a lack of success in developing countries is even more alarming because of the large opportunity costs associated with failed projects and the inability of these countries to recover quickly from them independently. Developing countries, with their multitude of development problems, can ill afford to keep pouring scarce resources into projects that are likely fail. Some critics feel that allowing technological innovations to hog the development limelight would only further compound the problems of the Third World, diverting attention and funds away from other high-priority areas. Others maintain further that current efforts to bridge the digital divide are generally more talk than action, and are only likely to increase the dependency of poorer countries on the developed world its peoples (Virkar, 2011).

One line of critique focuses on currently popular 'trade-not-aid' policies, which many scholars feel could make the South more dependent on imports from the North, simply because Southern nations are not capable of selling enough national products and services in the global market to compete with their Northern counterparts (Stiglitz & Charlton, 2006). In the rapidly changing, winner-takes-all environment of the global economy, many feel that if left to free market forces, telecommunications and the Internet are likely to increase inequalities between advanced nations and the developing world (McChesney, 1998). Some scholars suggest that technology could become instrumental in the creation of a transnational *virtual élite*, as the benefits of market-driven development in developing countries stay limited to a small minority of highly skilled professionals, further polarising the educated élite and the less-educated poor (Uimonen, 1997). Building on this, other commentators believe that developing countries are disadvantaged both by the set-up of, and power structures found within, current global ICT régimes and the ever-increasing complexity of international knowledge networks (Wade, 2002).

Another line of argument points out that the cornerstone of the global ICT-for-development campaign rests on the assumption that ICTs possess 'some inherent quality that enables them to leapfrog institutional obstacles and skill and resource deficiencies on the ground', an idea founded on the premise that technology is an objective, rational entity, and not something that incorporates, and is affected by, politics and culture (Virkar, 2004). The neutrality of technology is reinforced by repeated emphasis on innovation in today's world, stemming from theories of modernisation or the forcible (often incongruous) application of science and Western (or Northern) rationalism to human development in the Third World (Bessant, 1987). Adherents of this school of thought believe that as technology developed in the West spreads to the Third World, poor country users are increasingly caught in a hardware-software bind from which escape is limited, and user costs grow as user dependency increases. These scholars see this phenomenon as the beginning of a new form of international digital dependency, a modern-day equivalent of the 1970s Dependency Theory which contended that the problem of underdevelopment lay in the exploitative relationship between rich and poor nations, illustrated by the now-famous *centre-periphery* analogy (Lairson & Skidmore, 2003). The more recent, technological manifestations of this dependency are summarised and discussed below:

The North/Corporate Privilege in Software

Developing countries are caught in the middle of a growing 'software-hardware arms race' in the global technology market, the chief upshot of which is increased ICT complexity– extremely attractive to the younger, better-educated, wealthier user minority but intimidating for older, less well-educated, and poorer users who are not yet comfortable with even simpler models (Virkar, 2004). This can only prove detrimental to the North-South divide in ICT-based power relations, as technological improvements will continue to be pushed by the mega-corporations that profit from them, to the benefit of those Northern producers, users, and élite Southern groups that constitute the global demand for upgrades. Poorer countries, on the other hand, will either be unable to afford to keep upgrading their computer network systems, and so fall behind in terms of overall electronic competitiveness, or to sustain a reallocation of funds to such projects from priority areas such as healthcare and education.

The Northern Privilege in Internet Access and Telephone Services

Compared to the developed world, in particular the United States of America, developing countries operate at a cost disadvantage in Internet access and penetration (Roseman, 2003). Developing country *Internet Service Providers* (ISPs), being smaller and unable to invest in large capacity networks, experience more crashes and congestion than their First World counterparts, and are at the mercy of developed country ISPs which are not only larger and able to corner most of the digital traffic, but are also able to set prohibitively monopolistic access prices and global standards. Similarly, the international payments system for *Voice Over Internet Protocol* (VoIP) traffic is again dominated by America and a handful of major global firms, players who keep down the cost of telephonic services to the advantage of First World consumers in whose countries the primary digital exchanges are located. This is, however, detrimental to those Third World organisations and companies that, unable to charge prices that reflect the real costs of providing telephone services in those countries, are unable to invest in technology upgrades to remain competitive (Li et. al., 2011).

The North's Control over Development Ideology

Information and Communication Technologies, especially those platforms and applications that are Internet-enabled, have long been touted as *the* democratising force of the current age, contributing to the emergence of a new kind of 'networked politics' or 'networked governance' wherein the mobilisation of people into interest groups across physical boundaries and borders enhances participation in democratic processes and subverts traditional hierarchies of power and privilege (Virkar, 2011). However, it is widely argued that the infrastructure of the Internet and other networked communications systems is by-and-large dominated by a number of big commercial and governmental players who can potentially enforce their intellectual and political dominance over development discourse by capturing and monitoring a majority of technology users, and presenting them with selective information that suits their own singular purpose. For example, the World Bank has long been accused of popularising, through its new multistakeholder supersite *The Development Gateway*, issues and views that fit in well with the Bank's official diplomatic line, whilst using its global monetary influence to ensure that all opinions critical of the Bank's proclamations and policies are quietly ignored and remain unpublished (Wade, 2001). Seen as the most politically troubling form of technological dependency, critics worry that developing countries could remain passive recipients dependent on received Northern knowledge, rather than taking on an active role in the sharing and in creation of know-how and expertise themselves. The fallout of such a dependency may been seen today, in the constant, often-contentious North-South bickering over requirements and standards for technology transfer, intellectual-property rights, protectionism, the 'brain-drain', and the division of technological resources (Virkar, 2004). Those commentators who are highly critical of current discourse have even associated the manner in which developmental knowledge has proliferated with ideology accompanying the global re-expansion of capitalism and the re-emergence of Western neo-colonialism in the late 1990s-early 2000s.

The Threat of Cultural Neo-Colonialism

A final critique centres around current ICT-for-development discourse and the way in which the digital divide is demonstrated and is being addressed through the lens of actor interactions and social network behaviour (Virkar, 2004). Several development commentators, particularly adherents to Amartya Sen's Capabilities Approach and other theories of the New Institutionalism, contend that technology-driven development programmes in their current embodiment are oversold as agents of higher efficiency and better governance in favour of quantifiable access to ICTs, given their tendency to overlook the importance of actor interactions, actor motivations, and actor opinions, together with other individual actor differences, capabilities, and the role that choice also plays in the use, application, and ultimate valuation of new technologies (Virkar, 2011).

The result on the ground is a gap between 'hard' rational design and 'soft' socio-political actualities (see Table 3), and numerous situations where ICTs have done more harm than good (Heeks, 2002). The remoteness of project designs and the designers from the core context of the final user in physical, economic, cultural and other ways, further implies imminent ICT project failure given that project designs and actor realities are simply not built to withstand nor suit the prevailing local environment. When framed in socio-anthropological or culturally relativist terms, this gradual deterioration in the quality of interpersonal relationships, pre-empts the eventual decline of social and political capital in the developing world should ICTs not be introduced into their proposed diverse environments in a culturally sensitive manner (Virkar, 2004).

Many social anthropologists have warned that the erosion of the family and the degradation of the cultural ties that form the basis of many developing country societies will, in turn, have extremely negative effects on the behaviour and on the interactions of actors and actor groups co-existing at different levels of the various developmental and national arenas prevalent (Alampy, 2003).

Interestingly, to conclude, some of the more extreme technological optimists maintain that the rapidly falling price of both computing power and bandwidth will eventually result in a *digital deluge*, rendering any policy aimed at giving access to the so-called *information-poor* quite unnecessary and possibly even highly counter-productive. Emerging evidence is, however, likely to prove this view wrong (Virkar, 2014).

EXPLORING THE DEVELOPMENT DIVIDE IN THE DIGITAL AGE

You can put computers in community centres, but only the literate people are likely to go use them.- Esther Dyson

Table 3. The Difference Between 'Hard' Design and 'Soft' Actuality

Dimension	'Hard' Rational Design	'Soft' Political Actuality
Information	Emphasis on standardised, formal, quantitative information	Emphasis on contingent, informal, qualitative information
Technology	A simple, enabling mechanism	A complex value-laden entity; status symbol for some, tool of empowerment for some, tool of oppression for others
Processes	Stable, straight-forward, and formal; decision outcomes as optimal solutions based on logical criteria	Flexible, complex, constrained, and often informal; decision outcomes as compromises based on power games and influenced by existing power structures
Objectives and Values	Formal, organisational objectives	Multiple, informal, personal objectives
Staffing and Skills	Staff viewed as rational beings	Staff viewed as political beings in a definite hierarchy
Management Systems and Structures	Emphasis on formal, objective processes and structures	Emphasis on informal, subjective processes and structures
Other Resources: Time and Money	Used to achieve organisational objectives	Used to achieve personal objectives

(*Source: Heeks, 2002*)

Advances in Information and Communication Technologies have been the driving force behind the economic boom and global integration of financial markets and industry ever since their first commercial appearance in the late-1990s. Computer technology has transformed commerce and industry, society and politics; making possible such things as automated inventory control and just-in-time manufacturing, facilitating the emergence of new data networks, and enabling greater efficiency and productivity in virtually every aspect of human endeavour. E-mail and instant messaging have become ubiquitous in industrialised countries, and are also becoming increasingly popular in the developing world. Voice Over Internet Protocol and other communications technologies are also advancing in leaps and bounds, with new sound-enabled infrastructure and software spreading rapidly round the globe. Mobile connectivity is expanding particularly fast, with mobile phones expected to reach over 8.5 billion subscribers worldwide by end of 2016 (ITU, 2014). In addition, the provision of multiple digital services and computing platforms is fast becoming an important, rapidly growing sector of both developed and emerging economies.

Has Opportunity Come Calling…or Do We Have Our Wires Crossed?

The speed at which these transformations have occurred, the wealth that ICTs have generated, and the economic power wielded by major players in the technology industry are truly staggering and as yet unprecedented. Yet alongside such spectacular advancements are more sobering signs, particularly amongst the 3 billion people who constitute nearly half the world and who live on less than $2 a day (Shah, 2004). Poverty still persists in many regions of the world, including large pockets of industrialised nations, and a large number of people in Asia and Africa die from malnutrition and related diseases every year. The poorest areas of the world see regular surges in urban migration and populations still grow rapidly, putting greater pressure on already scarce natural resources, and illiteracy remains another major stumbling-block to prosperity in the Third World. The impact of these problems is now globally palpable. Armed conflicts erupt frequently over scarce resources, whilst law and order in many developing countries remains decidedly fragile. An upsurge in new forms of terrorism and the unchecked spread of deadly diseases such as HIV/AIDS both threaten to upset global peace and stability. On the whole, greater economic and technological progress seems only to increase disparities between the world's *haves* and *have-nots*.

An important illustration of this global 'development divide' is the growing gap that is opening up between those who are able to participate in the Information Revolution, sharing in the wealth and benefiting from the efficiency the use of technology creates, and those who are increasingly being left out of it. ICTs may be transforming the lives of the people who use them, but they do little for the large part of humanity that lacks access to them. The digital divide is therefore a multifaceted phenomenon that is both dynamic and complex, and exists at many levels: between groups and communities, between companies, between geographical regions, and between countries. As the world moves towards increasingly digitised societies, it is generally agreed by a large number of development experts, commentators, and policymakers that closing the digital divide is becoming imperative for the economic and social progress of the Third World. Whilst there is no denying that the developing world faces a multitude of other problems, it remains equally true that, given the growing importance of ICTs today, developing countries face the dilemma of either resetting some of their priorities or facing complete global exclusion.

Recent initiatives to bridge the divide within the extended context of global development have focussed on the provision of infrastructure together with the adoption of a number of macro-economic policies and improved work practices, all aimed at promoting effective free-market liberalism. However, after a number of high-profile failures, there is growing recognition amongst members of the development community that offering the world the latest in mobile technology and Internet-enabled computers will not in itself help bridge socio-economic or political disparities, and that encouraging economic growth is only a part of the larger policy response. Current discourse has failed to recognise that the digital divide is symptomatic of a much broader, much more complex set of interrelated inequalities, and that the lack of access to technology and software is connected to a wide array of unresolved problems, both within the developing world and current international systems. In consequence, current initiatives all too often neglect the crucial interrelation of factors that altogether stymy and limit success. For example, many community access projects that introduce computers into rural areas do not become self-sustaining simply because they fail to appreciate the central authority's role in the local economy, the need for locally relevant content, and the specific requirements of the local population.

Against the backdrop of a slew of project failures, it has become apparent that ICTs are not silver bullets that can magically make development problems vanish. With attention focused on the achievement of quantitative proliferation and penetration targets, as against a more holistic set of developmental goals, many feel that the ICT-for-development campaign in its present shape and form stands to lose credibility (Virkar, 2004). Technology alone is clearly not the automatic solution to the digital divide, to poverty and to other developmental problems, but a critical factor in their ultimate resolution may lie in ensuring that underserved groups and countries can harness and use built-in latent potential. If not consciously used to improve equity, therefore, new technologies may only serve to worsen prevailing socio-political divides, benefiting only those who possess sufficient skills and adequate know-how. In this vein, scholars argue that the introduction of ICTs into an arena of interaction is of particularly limited value unless people are equipped with the necessary skills and are provided with enough opportunity to exploit them to the full.

There is a need, therefore, to alter current development paradigms and, rather than seeking to find miraculous quick-fixes in technological hardware and software to deep-rooted problems, the focus ought be on understanding the reasons behind the polarisation of behaviour, both in society and in the workplace. The sheer intricacy and variety of interactions prevalent in human societies, and their relationship with Information and Communication Technologies, requires the constant local adaptation and improvisation of technological hardware and software if programmes involving Information Technology are to achieve and sustain high rates of success. The Internet, for instance, may prove extremely useful for villagers in the Indian state of Kerala where literacy levels and levels of village electrification are high, but the form the technology takes would not probably be of much use in Rwanda, where years of political instability and civil war have destroyed much of the basic infrastructure and have resulted in massive population displacements.

In summary, international ICT policy would do well to follow guidelines based on lessons learned in the field, and chief amongst these precepts is the idea that digital and developmental problems are interrelated and complex, primarily because of the variety of social and cultural contexts within which they occur. The interplay of national policies and different regulatory environments, circumscribed by a range of international forces, the power games prevalent within the international development machinery, and the fast evolving nature of ICTs themselves all add to this complexity. Again, installing volt-gobbling machines in areas that get only an erratic supply of electricity is problematic. In this context, investment in ICT-based initiatives needs be made keeping in mind prevailing socio-economic conditions, along with the necessary institutional structures and policy priorities that create, as discussed earlier, an enabling environment within which both technical artefacts and human actors succeed and flourish; an objective generally more difficult to attain than the mere sourcing of hardware and of software.

CONCLUSION

It is not ICT or food. It is ICT for food, for health, for teaching and for social and human development.
- Vincezo Schioppa

In modern times, people and their governments have struggled to find easy, cheap, and effective ways to run and improve countries. ICT-based applications have the potential to revolutionise patterns of communication between authority and citizenry, radically restructuring politics, the economy and society at all levels by making systems more integrated, transparent, and efficient. However critics of hyperdigitisation, and more particularly of the introduction of new technologies into developing country contexts, contend that formulation of one-sided reform processes is not an important enough issue to justify exposing cash-strapped governments to the risks and opportunity costs associated with large-scale ICT projects. Today, technology can provide the world with new opportunities and potentialities. However, the way in which those opportunities are grasped is circumscribed by contextual factors: political, economic, socio-cultural, behavioural, and institutional. The current concept of a 'digital divide' has been unhelpful to understand and tackle global inequities insofar as it has diverted attention away from other high-priority divides that constitute development bottlenecks. For developing countries to benefit fully from the digital revolution, current attitudes must experience a paradigm shift away from current thinking and the appropriate policies be implemented, particularly those that promote the indigenisation of ICT-based systems and the interconnection of all ICT-related divides with other development priorities.

Although the development and application of new communications hardware and software does have some potentially harmful effects on nascent business, government and society – not all firms will survive increased competition, some traditional jobs may be lost to digital machines and work-process automation, self-serving governments could use technology to spread propaganda, and the effects of technological dependence on the industrialised world are unlikely to be mitigated for some time to come – the extreme *cyberpessimism* of many critics today is unwarranted. ICT-led reforms are often complex as they involve the amelioration of both organisations and of human behaviour, and cannot be made through legislation alone. Such reforms require a change in the way users think, act, how they view their work, and how they share information; together with a simultaneous reengineering of the working of government; its business processes within individual agencies, departments, and across different levels or strata. They work best when part of a broader reform agenda in which the *status quo* is broken down through delegation, decentralisation, and citizen empowerment. The development and adoption of the new digital technologies has thus become a large game within the greater 'meta-game' of a country's development, bringing with it not only an array of benefits but also numerous challenges and obstacles that shape and are shaped by the perceptions and motivations of a multitude of actors, groups, and organisations. When considered this way, Information and Communication Technologies, in drastically improving standards of living, can save lives; and also create new jobs, connect unemployed people to previously inaccessible work opportunities, facilitate meaningful participation in mainstream political processes, and enable the inhabitants of relatively isolated villages to leverage the outside world at the click of a button.

However, the discussion put forward in this chapter reveals that at the heart of the digital divide and in attempts to create equality of access to information lies a global power struggle, brought about through a deep-seated mistrust between different actor groups and lopsided inter-country politics. This holds particularly true for the process of software conception and design where, gaps in the quality and overall technical applicability of a technology arise because those with the power and authority to take design or implementation decisions are usually unwilling to allow any initiative to go ahead that would give other actor group(s) in the game more precedence or autonomy over the process or system. Further, certain key games with local impacts get played out in different arenas between actors influenced not only by local but also national and international factors. Problems arise if designers and top-level managers assume that localised outcomes result only from direct local, quantifiable influences, discounting the impact of other 'soft' factors external to the project at hand. Added to this, there is a tendency for power élites to lose touch with ground realities when devising projects for their organisations as well as for their citizens, especially when planners comprise the higher échelons of government and operate exclusively within a top-down command-and-control system of management. There is also a danger that high-level project planners will, in looking at macro-outcomes, ignore outliers and how these may precipitate unexpected turns of events. This holds particularly true when existing patterns of communication and information exchange are inequitable and fail to be flexible or unable to adapt to rapidly changing situations.

Whilst it is widely recognised that ICTs are strategically important to a country, it must be concluded that if the developing world is to benefit, experts must cease debating over whether countries should spend their budgets on the development and propagation of ICTs or other other basic infrastructural requirements altogether; instead they should explore as to how technology may be used effectively to solve developmental problems and to meet other policy objectives. Likewise, the applicative and practitioner focus whilst considering the ways and means to employ new hardware and software in bridging digital and developmental divides should not just be on forking out cheap computers or on connecting every home to the Internet. A single well-located and well-maintained computer with Internet connectivity in an isolated village in Southern India has proved adequate in providing its inhabitants with essential information and services – storm-warnings, crop prices, medical information, legal records and learning opportunities – and raising the standard of living for the entire the local area for a radius of 10 miles. In conclusion, if developing countries are to reap the full potential of the digital revolution, what is needed is a more holistic, multi-pronged approach when tackling the range of development issues they face, supported by the simultaneous creation of an enabling environment for the effective and sustainable integration of technology into local society. Information technology might have made '*all that is solid melt into air*', but digital bridges still require concrete foundations.

REFERENCES

Bessant, J. (1987). Information Technology and the North-South Divide. In R. Finnegan, G. Salaman, & K. Thompson (Eds.), *Information Technology: Social Issues – A Reader* (pp. 163–180). London: Hodder and Stoughton.

Castells, M. (2001). *The Internet Galaxy*. Oxford: Oxford University Press. doi:10.1007/978-3-322-89613-1

Castells, M. (2013). *Communication Power*. Oxford: Oxford University Press.

Dunn, D., & Yamashita, K. (2003). 'Microcapitalism and the Megacorporation'. *Harvard Business Review*, *81*(8), 46–54. PMID:12884667

Dutton, W. H. (1992). 'The Ecology of Games Shaping Telecommunications Policy'. *Communication Theory*, *2*(4), 303–328. doi:10.1111/j.1468-2885.1992.tb00046.x

Dutton, W. H. (1999). *Society on the Line: Information Politics in the Digital Age*. Oxford: Oxford University Press.

Fink, C., & Kenny, C. J. (2003). 'W(h)ither the Digital Divide?'. *Info: The Journal of Policy. Regulation and Strategy for Telecommunications*, *5*(6), 15–24. doi:10.1108/14636690310507180

Gage, J. (2002). Some Thoughts on How ICTs Could Really Change the World. In Global Information Technology Report 2001-2002 (pp. 4–9). Readiness for the Networked World. Retrieved from www.cid.harvard.edu/cr/pdf/gitrr2002_ch01.pdf

Grace, J., Kenny, C., Qiang, C., Liu, J., & Reynolds, T. (2001). 'Information and Communication Technologies and Broad-Based Development: A Partial Review of the Evidence. *World Bank Resource Paper (2001)*. Retrieved from: http://poverty.worldbank.org/library/view/10214/

Graham, M. (2011). 'Time Machines and Virtual Portals: The Spatialities of the Digital Divide'. *Progress in Development Studies*, *11*(3), 211–227. doi:10.1177/146499341001100303

Heeks, R. (2002). 'Information Systems and Developing Countries: Failure, Success and Local Improvisations'. *The Information Society*, *18*(2), 101–112. doi:10.1080/01972240290075039

NUA Internet Surveys. (2014). *How Many Online?* Retrieved from: http://www.nua.ie/surveys/how_many_online/

Katz, R. L. (2009). 'The Economic and Social Impact of Telecommunications Output'. *Inter Economics*, *44*(1), 41–48. doi:10.1007/s10272-009-0276-0

Kirkman, G. (1999). *Its More Than Just Being Connected: A Discussion of Some Issues of Information Technology and International Development*. Paper presented at the Development E-Commerce Workshop. Retrieved from: http://cyber.law.harvard.edu/itg/libpubs/beingconnected.pdf

Lairson, T. D., & Skidmore, D. (2003). *International Political Economy: The Struggle for Power and Wealth*. Belmont: Thompson and Wadsworth.

Lamb, R., & Kling, R. (2003). 'Reconceptualising Users as Social Actors in Information Systems Research'. *Management Information Systems Quarterly*, *27*(2), 197–235.

Le Page, M. (2002, May 4th). 'Village-Life.com'. New Scientist, 44–45.

Levis, K. (2009). Winners and Losers: Creators and Casualties of the Age of the Internet. London: Atlantic Books Ltd.

Li, B., Ma, M., & Jin, Z. (2011). 'A VoIP Traffic Identification Scheme Based On Host and Flow Behavior Analysis'. Journal of Network and Systems Management, 19(1), 111–129. doi:10.1007/s10922-010-9184-7 doi:10.1007/s10922-010-9184-7

Main, L. (2001). 'The Global Information Infrastructure: Empowerment or Imperialism?'. Third World Quarterly, 22(1), 83–97. doi:10.1080/713701143 doi:10.1080/713701143

Martin, W. J. (1988). The Information Society. London: Aslib Press.

McChesney, R. W., Wood, E. M., & Foster, J. B. (1998). Capitalism and the Information Age: The Political Economy of the Global Communication Revolution. New York: Monthly Review Press.

Norris, P. (2001). Digital Divide: Civic Engagement, Information Poverty and the Internet Worldwide. Cambridge: Cambridge University Press. doi:10.1017/CBO9781139164887 doi:10.1017/CBO9781139164887

Odendaal, N. (2002). 'ICTs in Development – Who Benefits? Use of Geographic Information Systems on the Cato Manor Development Project, South Africa'. Journal of International Development, 4(1), 89–100. doi:10.1002/jid.867 doi:10.1002/jid.867

Organisation for Economic Co-operation and Development. (2000). *Learning to Bridge the Digital Divide*. Paris: OECD Publications.

Perrit, H. H. (1998). 'The Internet as a Threat to Sovereignty? Thoughts on the Internet's Role in Strengthening National and Global Governance'. *Indiana Journal of Global Legal Studies*, 5(2), 431–444.

Poblet, M. (2011). *Mobile Technologies for Conflict Management: Online Dispute Resolution, Governance, Participation*. London: Springer Verlag. doi:10.1007/978-94-007-1384-0

Prakash, N. (2012). 'Empowering Women Using Environmentally Friendly Technology in Paper Recycling'. *Research in Political Sociology*, 20(1), 125–136. doi:10.1108/S0895-9935(2012)0000020009

Robins, K. (1992). *Understanding Information: Business, Technology and Geography*. London: Belhaven Press.

Rodda, C. (2004). *'The Five Stages of Economic Growth'*. Retrieved from: http://www.cr1.dircon.co.uk/TB/5/fivestages.htm

Roseman, D. (2003). 'The Digital Divide and the Competitive Nature of ISPs: Part 1 – Issues and Arguments'. *Info: The Journal of Policy Regulation and Strategy for Telecommunications*, 5(5), 25–37. doi:10.1108/14636690310500439

Selwyn, N. (2002). *'Defining the 'Digital Divide': Developing a Theoretical Understanding of Inequalities in the Information Age'*. Occasional Paper No. 49. Cardiff University.

Shah, A. (2004). *'Poverty Facts and Stats'*. Retrieved from: http://www.globalissues.org/TradeRelated/Facts.asp

Silverstone, R., & Haddon, L. (1996). Design and Domestication of Information and Communication Technologies: Technical Change and Everyday Life. In R. Mansell & R. Silverstone (Eds.), *Communication by Design: The Politics of Information and Communication Technologies* (pp. 16–44). Oxford: Oxford University Press.

Sklair, L. (2002). *Globalisation: Capitalism and its Alternatives*. Oxford: Oxford University Press.

Skolnikoff, E. B. (1993). *The Elusive Transformation: Science, Technology and the Evolution of International Politics*. Princeton: Princeton University Press.

Stiglitz, J. (1999). '*Scan Globally, Reinvent Locally: Knowledge Infrastructure and the Localisation of Knowledge*'. Keynote Address – First Global Development Network Conference, Bonn, Germany.

Strover, S. (2003). 'Remapping the Digital Divide'. *The Information Society*, *19*(4), 275–277. doi:10.1080/01972240309481

Toulouse, C., & Luke, T. W. (1998). *The Politics of Cyberspace*. New York, NY: Routledge.

Trujillo, M. F. (2003). '*Does the Global Digital Divide Have Anything to do with Progress in Development?*'. Research Paper on Development Gateway: ICTs for Development (April 2003). Retrieved from: http://topics.developmentgateway.org/ict/rc/filedownload.do~itemId=307577

Uimonen, P. (1997). '*The Internet as a Tool for Social Development*'. Paper presented at the Annual Conference of the Internet Society. Retrieved from: http://www.i-connect.ch/uimonen/INET97.htm

United Nations Development Programme. (2001). *Human Development Report (1996-2001)*. Retrieved from: http://hdr.undp.org/reports/view_reports.cfm?type=1

Wade, R. H. (2002). 'Bridging the Digital Divide: New Route to Development or New Form of Dependency?'. *Global Governance*, *8*(4), 443–466.

Webster, F. (2002). *Theories of the Information Society* (2nd ed.). London: Routledge Press. doi:10.4324/9780203426265

Woolgar, S. (2002). *Virtual Society? Technology, Cyberbole and Reality*. Oxford: Oxford University Press.

World Bank. (2002). '*The Networking Revolution: Opportunities and Challenges for Developing Countries*'. InfoDev Working Paper.

Zin, A. N. M., & Yunos, Z. (2004). '*Computer Viruses: Future Cyber Weapons*'. National ICT Security and Emergency Response Center (NISER) Resource Paper. Retrieved from: http://www.niser.org.my/resources/computer_virus.pdf

KEY TERMS AND DEFINITIONS

Design-Actuality Gap Model or Design-Actuality Gap Framework: Is a framework for project evaluation which contends that the major factor determining project outcome is the degree of mismatch between the current ground realities of a situation ('where are we now'), and the models, conceptions, and assumptions built into a project's design (the 'where the project wants to get us').

Development Divide (The): Refers to the divide, gap, division, or differential in overall levels of human development, measured against economic, socio-anthropological, cultural, and political variables, between the world's richest and poorest individuals, groups, regions, and countries. The broad constituent elements of the Development Divide can also be described against The Human Development Divide, The Digital Divide, and The Democratic Deficit or Divide.

Digital Divide (The): Refers to the divide, gap, division, or differential in the meaningful availability of and access to technology, in particular the new digital information and communication technologies, between individuals, groups, regions, and countries; encompassing not merely quantified variables technological and technical hardware, but also levels of physical, digital, human and socio-cultural resources.

Hard Factor(s) or Hard Element(s): Refers to the actual, true-to-life, rational design elements or constituent variables of a technology or of a similarly created, automated, and independently functioning system.

Hard-Soft Analytical Framework or Hard-Soft Gap: Refers to the difference between the *actual, rational design* of a technology or man-made system (hard) adopted within a location-based project or a national policy and the *actuality of the social context*, namely people, culture, politics, etc., within which the system operates (soft).

Human Actor Approach: Refers to the approach taken whilst describing and analysing how people operating and interacting within symbiotic technology-rich ecologies and environments and their contributions are perceived; connoting active, controlling, involved, and independent human action.

Human Factor Approach: Refers to the approach taken whilst describing and analysing how people operating and interacting within symbiotic technology-rich ecologies and environments and their contributions are perceived; connoting passive, fragmented, depersonalised, and somewhat automatic human action.

Information Economy (The): Refers to the global socio-economic paradigm prevalent from the late 1990s onward, characterised by centrality and the importance of *information*, and in particular *knowledge*, as a primary raw material or a base economic resource in the creation of economic value and of commercial productivity.

Information Poor: Refers to the descriptive term indicative of the degree of quality and quantity of content, of information, and of technological hardware and software readily accessible and directly present in circulation within a given population, geographical region, system ecology, symbiotic environment, or collaborative circumstance; in the general case, delineative of between adequate and detrimentally under par availability of and access to online resources and the latest digital Information and Communication Technologies.

Information Revolution (The): Refers to the global economic paradigm prevalent from the late 1990s onward, characterised collectively by unprecedented advancements in technological innovation and the rapid global proliferation, appropriation, application, and use of new digital Information and Communication Technologies in everyday life. The Information Revolution is further described against three constituent strands - the Computer Revolution, the Internet Revolution, and the Digital Revolution.

Information Rich: Refers to the descriptive term indicative of the degree of quality and quantity of content, of information, and of technological hardware and software readily accessible and directly present in circulation within a given population, geographical region, system ecology, symbiotic environment, or collaborative circumstance; in the general case, delineative of between adequate and excellent availability of and access to online resources and the latest digital Information and Communication Technologies.

Information Society (The Global): Refers to the global socio-economic paradigm prevalent from the late 1990s onward, characterised by the centrality and the importance of *information* and *Informa-*

tion and Communication Technologies (*ICTs*) to human interaction and endeavour; conceptualised and evaluated along several distinct axes including *the technological*, *the economic*, *the occupational*, *the spatial*, and *the cultural*.

Open Access Movement (The): Refers to a political movement dedicated to the development and promotion of free operating systems, free software applications, and to the provision of free digital content; popularised to lessen the dominance of proprietary software, and to eventually replace them.

Open Knowledge or Open-Source Knowledge, or Open Content: Refers to freely and openly distributed digitised knowledge and/or rich content; disseminated online over the Internet or through other digital information and communications media or platforms, or via new digital technological hardware.

Soft Factor(s) or Soft Element(s): Refers to the human issues or socio-political, socio-economic, socio-cultural, socio-anthropological, and psycho-sociological variables or contexts – involving people, culture, politics, economics, and society - within which a rational technological or hard system operates.

ENDNOTES

[1] The CNN Effect was first noted when the news channel CNN showed heartbreaking footage of starving children in Somalia that pressured U.S. officials to send troops there. Subsequent horrifying footage of Somalis dragging the body of a dead American soldier through the streets followed, turning US public opinion against the intervention and prompting U.S. officials to withdraw their troops.

[2] Quoted in Mark Surman and Katherine Reilly, Appropriating the Internet for Social Change: Towards the Strategic Use of Networked Technologies by Transnational Civil Society Organisations, Social Science Research Council Report, November 2003, p. 62

[3] Multipurpose Community Telecentres (MCTs) are facilities that provide public access to a variety of information and communication services including Web-enabled computing, phone and fax services.

Chapter 13
Big Data and Data Modelling for Manufacturing Information Systems

Norman Gwangwava
Tshwane University of Technology, South Africa

Khumbulani Mpofu
Tshwane University of Technology, South Africa

Samson Mhlanga
National University of Science and Technology, Zimbabwe

ABSTRACT

The evolving Information and Communication Technologies (ICTs) has not spared the manufacturing industry. Modern ICT based solutions have shown a significant improvement in manufacturing industries' value stream. Paperless manufacturing, evolved due to complete automation of factories. The chapter articulates various Machine-to-Machine (M2M) technologies, big data and data modelling requirements for manufacturing information systems. Manufacturing information systems have unique requirements which distinguish them from conventional Management Information Systems. Various modelling technologies and standards exist for manufacturing information systems. The manufacturing field has unique data that require capturing and processing at various phases of product, service and factory life cycle. Authors review developments in modern ERP/CRM, PDM/PLM, SCM, and MOM/MES systems. Data modelling methods for manufacturing information systems that include STEP/STEP-NC, XML and UML are also covered in the chapter. A case study for a computer aided process planning system for a sheet metal forming company is also presented.

INTRODUCTION

The quest to improve the quality of manufactured products, achieve higher efficiency, improve communication, and complete integration of processes has resulted in large data being collected by manufacturers. The current era for large and complex data sets has been termed big data. Big data is difficult to process using traditional data processing applications. In order to achieve better control of

DOI: 10.4018/978-1-4666-8505-5.ch013

their processes, manufacturers need to capture, store, search, share, transfer, analyse and visualise data pertaining to their products, machinery, and various stages of raw material conversion. Technologies used to achieve data processing requirements in the manufacturing field are a bit complex compared to conventional database management tools. The complete life cycle of products start as a need from the customer, progresses into CAD model of the interpreted need, raw material conversion into finished product, use by the customer and regular maintenance support and finally disposal or recycling. CAD systems used to model the product store attribute data for the various parts of the product and also use unique file exchange formats. The CAD models are analysed using computer aided engineering (CAE) systems so that optimal designs can be achieved. The manufacturing process is aided by computer aided manufacturing (CAM) systems that interpret the CAD data and generate files for manipulating the raw work-piece into the finished products using appropriate machine tools. As the world population continues to grow, production output and product varieties in many companies continue to grow generating a lot of data that should be processed often. The challenges for the manufacturer are not only centred upon the product and its life cycle but the health of the manufacturing plant (plant maintenance), supply chain integration, and in some instances tracking the product during its usage period. This led to the advent of e-based maintenance systems that track the performance of plant machinery in real time.

Whilst the talk about big data is popular in customer relationship management (CRM), supply chain management (SCM), and social media, there is significant application in in-house manufacturing processes. Some manufactures use big data to leverage their technical capabilities so that they can offer customisation to their customers. The trend has been influenced by the growing trend in mass customisation and reconfigurable manufacturing systems (RMS). The capability of RMS systems to be reconfigured or changed to meet new customer demand enables manufactures to offer customised products. However reconfiguring a manufacturing facility requires highly integrated systems if ramp-up time and optimised set-ups are to be achieved without costly investments. In this instance, big data can be viewed as measuring the finite details in manufacturing plants or factories.

Achieving tightly integrated systems in manufacturing pose challenges to manufacturing system designers and system integrators. The major aspects tackled in the chapter include data modelling, data exchange formats, and systems architecture in order to address the gap in traditional and modern practice. Cooperation with suppliers and customers require neutral data exchange formats in product modelling so that both ends can view the transmitted data across different software platforms.

BACKGROUND

Industry has evolved from traditional factories dominated by mechanical production facilities powered by steam and water, through mass production based on division of labor, to introduction of electronics and IT, and currently cyber-physical systems (CPS). Koren (2010) categorized the industrial revolution into four phases namely industry 1.0, industry 2.0, industry 3.0, and industry 4.0. Industry 4.0 is the current stage which is driven by cyber-physical production systems. Rajkumar, *et al* (2010) defined Cyber-physical systems (CPS) as physical and engineered systems, whose operations are monitored, coordinated, controlled and integrated by a computing and communication core. CPS can be considered to be a confluence of embedded systems, real-time systems, distributed sensor systems and controls. CPS is leading towards smart future factories with a network of intelligent objects linking products and assets with information from the internet, as well as capturing context information.

There are many factors that drive the manufacturing trend through its progression to the current phase (industry 4.0) and beyond. Some of them include shorter product life cycles, increasing product variation (mass customisation), volatile markets, cost reduction pressures, scarce resources, cleaner production, lack of skilled workforce and aging community. In order to cope with the pressure, the modern day factories must have big data repositories to analyse and make informed decisions. The global manufacturing village is also threatened by low-volume high-mixture factories. Competition among manufacturers is ever increasing and every player must deliver high quality goods, efficiently and at low cost. Regulatory authorities are also mounting pressure on manufacturers, demanding cleaner and sustainable manufacturing practices. This results in more data being captured so as to comply with regulations. It is difficult to quantify and control anything that is not measured, hence the need for manufacturers to keep tight track of their process data, power consumption, gaseous emissions and resource consumption.

In a bid to address issues mentioned above, manufacturing automation evolved from production management and control using material resource planning (MRPI and MRPII), and ERP systems. Due to the quest to achieve tighter integration and collaboration with suppliers and clients, CRM, SCM, PDM and PLM systems became popular. These systems partly enabled manufactures to gain competitive advantage over their counterparts who did not have similar technologies. Many companies even in this current era still do not have old technologies mentioned previously. These companies, particularly in the African continent, face stiff competition from Asian and European manufactures that are shipping low cost goods across the globe. Those companies at risk still think that they can industrialise and beat the competition but the reality is that technology is increasing fast which prompts manufactures to be very strategic and speedily adopt some modern technologies which allow them more flexibility, adaptability, scalability, and rapidly meet the customers' dynamic needs at low cost. Various alternative technologies and case studies are articulated in the chapter to provide a clear roadmap to potential adopters and the researchers to further research efforts so that better systems can be availed to modern manufacturing industries.

BIG DATA AND DATA MODELLING FOR MANUFACTURING INFORMATION SYSTEMS

The chapter narrates the trends in manufacturing systems automation. Traditional systems are tracked right through to the state-of-the-arts in manufacturing automation systems. Case studies are provided for real applications in manufacturing companies. Future research is also outlined in order to further the interests for achieving more efficient and sustainable manufacturing. Big Data can be clearly distinguished in three categories as follows (Oracle®, 2013):

- **Traditional Enterprise Data:** Includes customer information from CRM systems, transactional ERP data, and general ledger data
- **Machine-Generated/ Sensor Data:** Includes Call Detail Records ("CDR"), smart meters, manufacturing sensors, equipment logs (often referred to as digital exhaust)
- **Social Data:** Include customer feedback streams, also takes the form of micro-blogging such as Twitter and social media platforms like Facebook.

The world has adopted specific terminology and standards to suit industry-specific needs. Terminology and standards used in the manufacturing sector are elaborated in the sections that follow.

Manufacturing Operations Management (MOM) and Manufacturing Execution Systems (MES)

MOM is a holistic solution to improve manufacturing operations performance. The systems are built to consolidate the management of several production processes, such as quality management, sequencing, production capacity analysis, Work-in-Process (WIP), inventory turns, standard lead times, nonconformance management, asset management, and many other processes within one system. MOM systems expand focus from a single facility to the entire supply network, monitoring a variety of aspects of the manufacturing process. Managing different aspects of the whole manufacturing organisation is associated with various challenges in trying to automate the tasks. Different software tools are needed to collect and analyse real-time data and translate it into valuable knowledge that can be used to inform decision making. Traditionally manufacturers had their own tailor made software applications because of lack of standard platforms to integrate systems at the shop floor level. In order to resolve the challenge, software providers started to package multiple execution management components into single, integrated solutions called manufacturing execution systems (MES) (Saenz, *et al*, 2009). An MES keeps track of all manufacturing information in real time, receiving up-to-the-minute data from robots, machine monitors and employees. MES solutions now include integrated components such as Computer Aided Process Planning (CAPP), CAM, Product Data Acquisition (PDA), Machine Data Acquisition (MDA), and Personnel Time Recording, as well as Time and Attendance (PTR/T&A).

Generally MES is a process-oriented manufacturing management system which acts as the comprehensive driving force for the organization and execution of the production process. Its major tasks can be summarised as follows:

- Organisation and support of all activities related to the production process.
- Implementation of the closed loop of all actions related to the execution of the production processes (planning, initiation, managing, controlling, documentation, evaluation, and review).
- Exchange of information with other levels such as corporate management (Enterprise Resource Planning, ERP) and the manufacturing / process levels, as well as operational support systems, and Supply Chain Management (SCM).

In order to achieve integration and interoperability in MES, common standards are required in modeling manufacturing information systems from the shop floor to the business logistics level. The Instrumentation, Systems, and Automation Society (ISA) developed a standard to address the integration issues. ISA-95 is a multi-part standard that defines the interfaces between enterprise activities and control activities (Gifford, 2013). The ISA-95 standard aims to enhance the development of MES applications and integrate them to other information systems of manufacturing companies, particularly ERP systems. The overall architecture for MES and its relationship to other enterprise systems is shown in Figure 1. Another standard for MES is the IEC 62264 "Enterprise-Control System Integration" set of standards, which defines the functional hierarchy levels of an enterprise, in which decisions with differing timescales and varying levels of detail must be made (IEC®, 2007). The hierarchy of levels are as listed below whilst Figure 2 gives the pictorial view.

Level 4: Business planning and logistics
Level 3: Manufacturing operations management

Figure 1. ISA-95 Manufacturing architecture

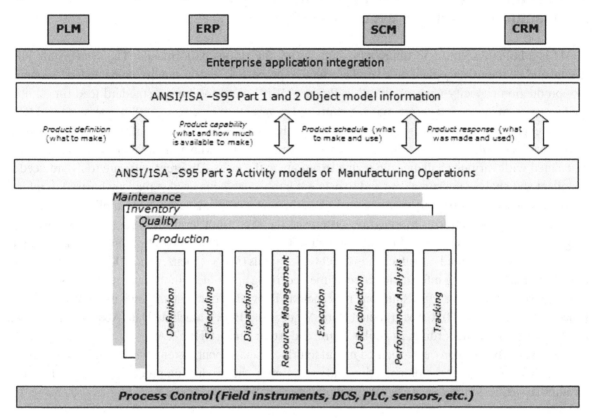

Figure 2. Functional hierarchy for the IEC 62264-3 standard

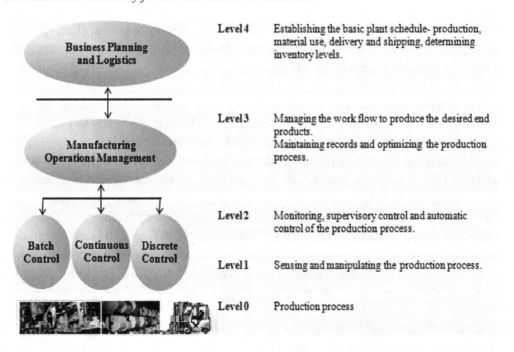

Level 2: Monitoring as well as supervisory and automated control of the production process (Batch control, Continuous control and Discrete control)

Level 1: Control of process or machinery and data acquisition

Level 0: Production process.

Figure 3 provides an overview of the divisions and the relationships among the relevant functions of manufacturing operations management activities according to the ISA-95 standards.

Enterprise Resource Planning (ERP) Systems

ERP is an organization's software management system which incorporates all facets of the business, automates and facilitates the flow of data between critical back-office functions, which may include financing, distribution, accounting, inventory management, sales, marketing, planning, human resources, manufacturing, and other operating units. The use of ERP systems in organizations allow all departments to have one source of information, streamline their business process and also access the required information almost instantly. Some degree of customisation may be necessary to enable the system users to access analytics which can aid in decision making. Plug-in business intelligence (BI) tools are also available specifically for data mining and analysis. According to Nah *et al* (2001), the most important attributes of an ERP system are its abilities to:

Figure 3. Manufacturing operations management activities according to the ISA-95 standards.

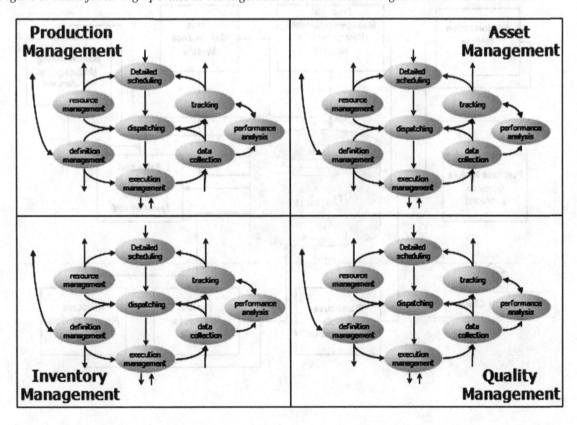

- Automate and integrate business processes across organizational functions and locations.
- Enable implementation of all variations of best business practices with a view towards enhancing productivity.
- Share common data and practices across the entire enterprise in order to reduce errors, produce and access information in a real-time environment to facilitate rapid and better decisions and cost reductions.

Manufacturing software systems evolved from material requirements planning (MRP I) systems which translated the master production schedule built for the end items into time phased net requirements for the sub-assemblies, components and raw materials planning and procurement. Since 1970s, the MRP I system has been extended from a simple MRP tool to become the standard manufacturing resource planning (MRP II).

The basic architecture of an ERP system builds upon one database, one application, and a unified interface across the entire enterprise. A generalized architecture is represented in Figure 4.

During the 2000s ERP vendors added more modules and functions as add-ons to the core modules giving birth to the extended ERPs. These ERP extensions include Advanced Planning and Scheduling (APS), e-business solutions such as Customer Relationship Management (CRM) and Supply Chain Management (SCM). To date (2014) much talk is being given to off-site based ERP solutions referred

Figure 4. General ERP Architecture

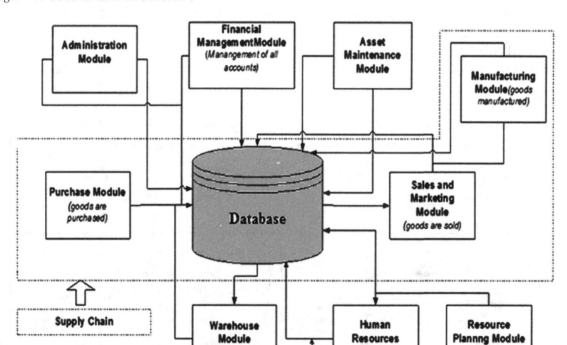

to as Cloud computing and Software as a service (SaaS) where the ERP vendors host the software on their own infrastructure and the companies only purchase the services from that package. The evolution of ERP is represented in Figure 5.

Machine-to-Machine (M2M) Technologies

M2M describes technology that enables networked devices to exchange information and perform actions without dependence on human beings (Lu. *et al,* 2011). It also means Machine-to-Machine, Man-to-Machine and Machine-to-Mobile. The technology has wide applications in remote monitoring. This technique enlightens manufacturing decisions by providing valuable production information computed from real time machine data. Typical data acquired include machine performance, engineering and quality data. The data will be conveyed to responsible authorities across the manufacturing organization, both in-house users as well as those residing in remote geographical locations. Key performance indicators (KPIs) for the operations being monitored are communicated via dashboards and customised reports. Many manufacturers are now adopting the 'software as a service' (SaaS) model in order in order to improve their efficiencies and also save themselves from the tedious task of running locally hosted systems. With SaaS, businesses leave the tasks of managing the cloud infrastructure and platform running their software applications to the cloud hosting provider. SaaS delivery mode makes it easy to enjoy the benefits of the remote monitoring cloud without having to manage complex computer network systems.

Figure 5. ERP Evolution

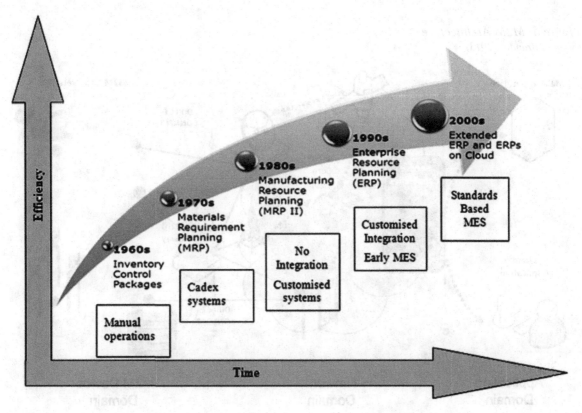

M2M is at the core of any manufacturing facility and the infrastructure builds out from there. Prior to M2M in manufacturing, industrial automation has used direct wire connections between the sensors, actuators and the controlling PCs. However due to high costs of acquiring smart production machinery, many manufacturers haven't adopted complete M2M technology rather they use manual methods of gathering and entering data into their ERP systems. Today, examples of M2M in manufacturing can be seen through the use of analog sensors to measure real-world conditions and where process control systems perform analysis and control of manufacturing processes. Another instance can be illustrated through control commands converted to analog signals to control actuators.

There are basically four components in an M2M system: 1) the intelligent device (machine or appliance) where the data originates, 2) the gateway that extracts and translates data, 3) the network which serves the data and 4) the remote client which ultimately receives the data. M2M software applications are optional but can facilitate communications, enable Web access and provide the user interface. Examples of technology used in M2M systems include sensors, RFID, Wi-Fi or cellular communications link and autonomic computing software programmed to help a networked device interpret data and make decisions.

The open connectivity (OPC) Foundation in industrial automation and the enterprise systems has become a widely accepted M2M communication standard in manufacturing (Paine, 2011). It is based on open standards and specifications to ensure that interoperability can be achieved for M2M communications in manufacturing. Other new standards created by the OPC Foundation include OPC-UA. OPC-UA is designed to be platform independent and operating system independent, supporting Windows, Linux, and a variety of Embedded Operating Systems that M2M technology vendors will be able to leverage. Figure 6 shows the typical architecture for an M2M system (Brandon, 2013).

Figure 6: M2M Architecture
(Source- Brandon, 2013)

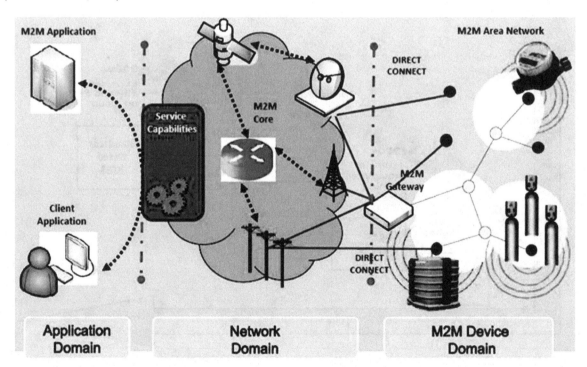

M2M communication is an important aspect of warehouse management, remote control, robotics, traffic control, logistic services, supply chain management, fleet management and telemedicine. It forms the basis for a concept known as the Internet of Things (IoT).

M2M technology improves supply chain performance in the following areas:

- **Fleet Tracking:** Monitoring fleet arrivals/departures and flagging exceptions can improve end-to-end visibility and improve planning.
- **Event-Based Monitoring of Driver Behaviour:** Documenting speed, idle time, and hard braking of delivery vehicles can reduce fuel and insurance costs, while increasing driver safety.
- **Field Force Management:** Overseeing field-force activities from a centralised location can make it possible to practice real-time routing based on traffic information.
- **Inventory-Level Monitoring:** Viewing and communicating inventory levels can help companies build automated replenishment programs and share information with suppliers.
- **Tagging High-Value Assets and Inventory:** M2M systems can help companies keep track of particularly valuable assets, such as computers, data-storage devices, consumer electronics, and ATMs.
- **Inventory-Condition Monitoring:** Involves tracking inventory longevity by monitoring parameters such as humidity, temperature, pressure, and light. Preventive maintenance: Monitoring equipment remotely and proactively improves an organization's ability to ward off failures and improve scheduled (preventive) maintenance.
- **Smart Warehouses/Supply Chain Facilities:** Through remote metering and control, companies can optimise energy use in warehouses, production facilities, and other locations, thus reducing operating costs.

Product Data Management (PDM) and Product Life-Cycle Management (PLM) Systems

Product Data Management (PDM) systems provide the tools to control access to and manage all product definition data. It does this by maintaining information (meta-data) about product information. In 3D CAD systems, product files rely heavily on each other - they have relationships and contain dependencies that drive details like feature size and placement in other models. The PDM vault allows engineers to better manage the complex interrelationships between the part, assembly and drawing files. They can share files with other team members and keep each other up to date on design modifications through a file check-in/check-out process. The product data management (PDM) tools are often integrated directly with the CAD program being used by the team for design modeling. Product Lifecycle Management can be taken as a strategic business approach that applies a consistent set of business solutions that support the collaborative creation, management, dissemination, and use of product definition information. Product Lifecycle Management (PLM) systems support the management of a portfolio of products, processes and services from initial concept, through design, launch, production and use to final disposal. The product life cycle covers the lifespan of a product from the idea through development up to disposal or recycling. The product's life cycle - period usually consists of five major steps or phases: product development, product introduction, product growth, product maturity and finally product decline. These phases exist and are applicable to all products or services. The phases can be split up into smaller ones depending on the product and must be considered when a new product is to be introduced into a market since they dictate the product's sales performance. All PLM systems use some form of PDM as the underlying data foundation on which they operate.

Many companies have migrated from 2D to 3D CAD systems for their primary product development. This has resulted in PDM becoming a virtual necessity for manufacturers. The benefits of 3D are reduced cycle time, cost savings, quality improvements, and greater innovation. However 3D CAD systems bring in challenges of data management where engineers are generating greater volumes of data. 3D files contain a variety of references, associations, and interrelationships that link them to other files, such as parts, drawings, bills of materials (BOMs), multiple configurations, assemblies, NC programming, and documentation. Product developers use 3D models to carryout various analysis and simulations so as to validate their designs. The models can also be used to demonstrate product functionality concepts to customers before committing to full production. The 3D geometric component modeling software or "kernel" modelers must reliably manage data accuracy and consistency while providing the openness and interoperability needed to facilitate the seamless exchange of 3D product data. Interoperability is crucial in product development and manufacturing where different applications for design, validation and manufacturing engineering are used at the same time requiring these systems to interoperate in upstream processes. Engineers therefore require a reliable system for managing, preserving, and safeguarding these links. Numerous product revisions are usually the norm in manufacturing firms, requiring different engineers to work within assemblies, or to collaborate on a design.

Product life is an issue for complex products with long life cycles such as plant machinery, trucks and airplanes. Plant machinery currently last longer that the products they produce. It is important to take care of life cycle data about such resources so as to maintain a healthy plant that will produce quality goods. Wear and status information can cause the machines to deviate from original settings resulting in defective products. This will also shorten the machinery life causing the investors to lose their capital investment. Examples of life cycle data for plant machinery include replaced parts, maintenance and wear indications such as capability and accuracy information. Monitoring machinery life cycle data makes it possible to carry out preventive maintenance in order to avoid unplanned maintenance and machine failures which are more costly.

PLM can be split into various disciplines as shown in Figure 7. The top four disciplines are only shown. Engineering Change Management (ECM) is a Business Process Management (BPM) discipline that spans all the phases of the product life cycle (IBM®, 2008).

Data Modeling for Manufacturing Systems

The advent of the CAD and CAM software brought about integration of designing and manufacturing processes. CAD software enables direct link between CAD and CAM. CAD enables automation of designing, while CAM enables automation of manufacturing processes. The database created by the integration of CAD/CAM is also known as manufacturing database. It includes all the data about the product generated during design like shape and dimensions, bill of materials and part lists, material specifications etc. It also includes additional data required for the manufacturing purposes. There is no time gap between the two processes and there is no duplication of efforts required on the parts of designer and the production personnel. As the integration of computer aided design and manufacturing (CAD/CAM) systems progresses, the need for management of the resulting data becomes critical. Database management systems (DBMS) have been developed to assist with this task, but currently do not satisfy

Figure 7. PLM disciplines and the product life cycle

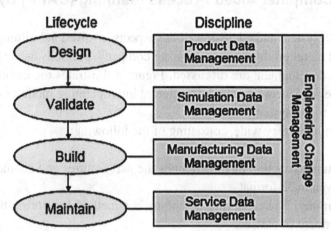

all of the needs of CAD/CAM data. CAM systems usage requires a number of catalogues, especially in process planning. Machine tools, cutting tools, inserts and tooling catalogues are sources of data which are necessary in cutting process planning.

Development of systems requires database modelling languages (DML) for the analysis stage. A DML is for specifying, visualizing, constructing, and documenting the artefacts of software systems. Common modelling languages for manufacturing systems are the unified modelling language (UML), EXPRESS/EXPRESS-G and XML.

One of the purposes of UML is to provide the development community with a stable and common design language that can be used to develop and build computer applications. The UML notation set is a language and not a methodology. This is important, because a language, as opposed to a methodology, can easily fit into any company's way of conducting business without requiring change. Since UML is not a methodology, it does not require any formal work products, yet it does provide several types of diagrams that, when used within a given methodology, increase the ease of understanding an application under development (Rumbaugh *et al*, 2005). The UML class diagram can explicitly represent the relationships between objects. Hence, the data model, even the complex one, can be well modelled by the UML manner.

EXPRESS-G Modelling Language

Express is a standard data modelling language for product data. Express is formalized in the ISO standard for the exchange of product model STEP (ISO 10303), and standardized as ISO 10303-11. EXPRESS-G is a standard graphical notation for information models. It is a useful companion to the EXPRESS language for displaying entity and type definitions, relationships and cardinality. This graphical notation supports a subset of the EXPRESS language. One of the advantages of using EXPRESS-G over EXPRESS is that the structure of a data model can be presented in a more understandable manner. A disadvantage of EXPRESS-G is that complex constraints cannot be formally specified.

Case Study for a Computer Aided Process Planning (CAPP) System

This section illustrates a system and addresses all the aspects involved in building up the process planning system for a sheet metal products manufacturing company. Methods used and the guidelines that are followed in system development are discussed. Figure 8 illustrates the architecture of the process sequencing system. The sequencing system has different interoperating modules each providing one or two essential functions to the system.

The system architecture is very wide, consisting of the following:

- **FR Module:** Feature extraction module defines the part features and geometry required from the product model given in 3d format
- **Capability Taxonomy:** The capability taxonomy is a method for storing the available tools in a hierarchical assortment of classes.
- **Database:** The system database stores the information extracted from the feature extraction module.

Figure 8. System architecture

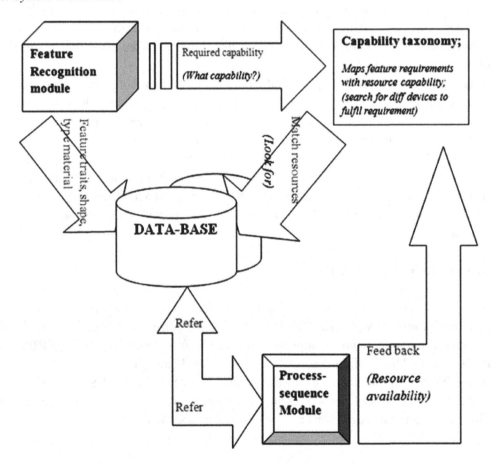

- **Process-Sequence Module:** The system module operates resembling a central operation planner being a governing module that keeps track of the potential alternatives and optimizes the operation sequence.

Figure 9 illustrates a generic procedure-design for a sheet metal part, denoted as (hurricane clip, BPH). The Figure outlines specific parameters, machine, tools and geometry in making a decision.

The database module for the process planning system is made up of repositories of data that are generated, updated, and retrieved by the FR, Taxonomy and Process sequencing modules. A unit in the database stores new sheet product geometry information extracted by the FR module, which is used as the feature input for the other modules such as the tool selection, and operation queuing. Another unit in the database stores data on cutting or punching machine configuration, available punching tools, and fixtures. It is updated by an operator. The database stores process plans (including cutting and punching plans) generated by the process planner. A process is described by the part features and stamping

Figure 9. Basic elements for the hurricane clip (BPH) product

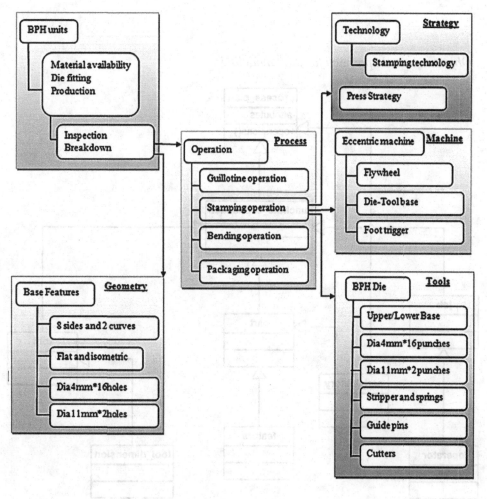

operations including task strategy, cutting conditions and tools. Database stores past processes, long-term design, planning and stamping knowledge that is used by product designers, process planners and machine operators. The UML diagram shown in Figure 10 illustrates the system model.

Each UML model consists of a number of UML class diagrams connected to each other to show the relationship between these classes. The capabilities of machinery used in the manufacturing processes, particularly the machine type, supplier, capacity (general specifications e.g. tonnage, operating speed etc), nature of jobs suitable for the machine are modelled in Figure 11. For the demonstration, Figure 12 shows the UML model of a feature. The two classes, namely peripheral features and inner-face features are sub-classes of the class feature. The class feature is a sub-class of the class part and defines two types of the part feature regions.

The inner feature class contains the properties and operations required to define the inner feature. It inherits the value of the properties from the other classes like extruded feature class, and "hole" feature class. These classes also inherit other classes to assign the values of their properties.

The typical manufacturing based system illustrated provides information that is an intermediate between the design (CAD) and the manufacturing (CAM) phases of production. The output display is in the form CAD models for the parts being manufactured (Figure 13) as well as process sequence reports (Figure 14).

Figure 10. Object-oriented approach for data modeling

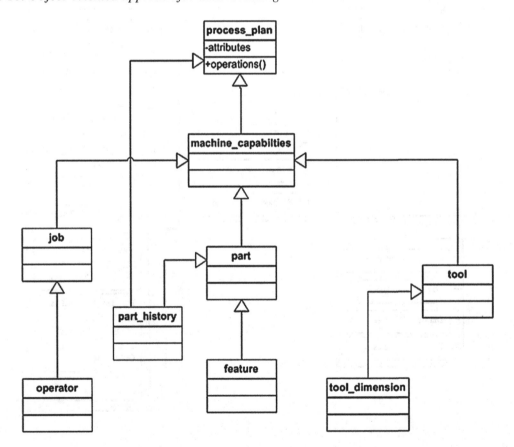

Figure 11. Capability UML model

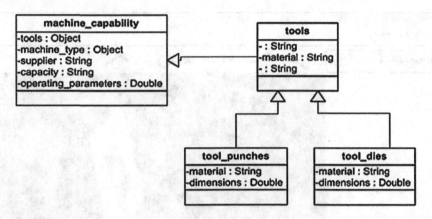

Figure 12. Feature UML model

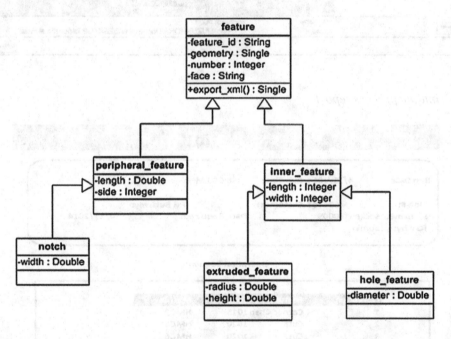

Using the Extensible Mark-up Language (XML) file format for the product/ part models is recommended since the files can be exchanged across different user platforms. The design goals of XML emphasize simplicity, generality, and usability over the internet. It is a textual data format with strong support via Unicode for the languages of the world. When other CAD applications are used as the working design environment, the interface commands may need to be changed, since different CAD developers have their own programming interface functions. In order to avoid this problem, instead of using CAD interface functions, a stand-alone feature modeller is required so that the feature-based systems become CAD software independent.

Figure 13. Part features displayed

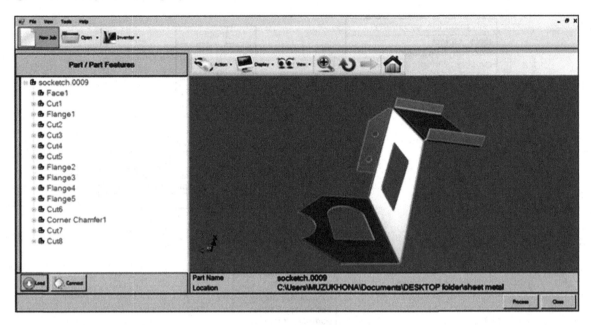

Figure 14. Printable process report

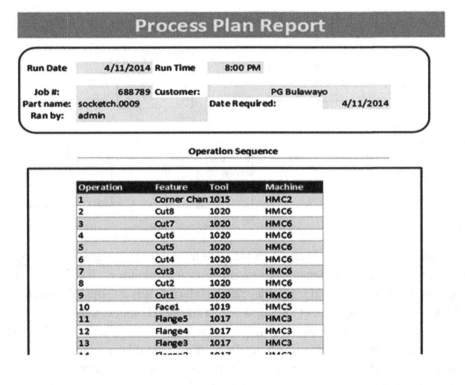

Solutions and Recommendations

There are several advantages brought to manufacturing industries by Big Data. In order to stay competitive, industries must continue to invest in modern ICT infrastructure. The more the smarter manufacturers become, the more sense they can make from Big Data. Standardisation is also at the heart of a successful ICT strategy since it brings interoperability and seamless integration across the business logistics as well as manufacturing operations on the shopfloor. Manufacturers must also adopt neutral data and file exchange formats such as XML. This enables manufacturing sites and clients in different geographical locations and also with different software applications to share their data files without experiencing compatibility problems. The whole world is increasingly becoming digitalised as witnessed by the growing number of people owning smart phones and other mobile gadgets. Whilst the social media has been in the forefront of adopting the digital trend, the manufacturing industry should also make efforts towards occupying more space in the smart gadgets platform. Building smart factories, with smart machines and systems provides a green solution to the world that is now emphasis sustainability.

Whilst there is more to gain from highly networked smart systems, there are risks associated with it. Major security areas that companies need to be worry of are 1) authorisation and authentication, 2) role-based access control, 3) data validation, session management, 4) data integrity and confidentiality, 5) auditing and monitoring and 6) the trusted environment. Technology providers have developed cyber security standards to address vulnerabilities and assessment programs to identify known vulnerabilities in their systems. Prevention, detection, response and recovery are key issues of any security strategy. Another important aspect is reliability. Unreliable sensing, processing, and transmission can cause false data reports, long delays, and data loss which could be catastrophic.

FUTURE RESEARCH DIRECTIONS

The demand for standard products with no variations or with limited variation is declining causing stocks to pile in the retail centers since customers are opting for products with their own quality specifications. Mass customization (MC), for a variety of reasons, is considered a promising approach for domestic manufacturers to maintain and grow their operation as pointed out by Buehlmann (2005). MC is always achieved through make-to-order (MTO). According to Koren (2010) mass customised production is in practice realised with flexible production systems which are able to deal with a variety of manufactured parts and adjustable assembly operations. In order to embrace MC companies must determine the depth of customisation suitable for the company's level of technology.

One of the main challenges faced by the manufacturing industries is rapid reconfiguration of manufacturing systems to handle rapid change in business environment without human intervention. An important criteria of the manufacturing factory is the flexibility characteristic of producing multiple variations of customised products. The factory must be flexible enough to support different sequences of production as well as allowing changes in the production system for new products offerings (Leitão, 2004). Reconfiguring existing manufacturing systems require detailed data about the capability of each machine and also its current state is very necessary so that an optimal solution can be achieved Alsafi and Vyatkin, (2014). In order to minimise ramp-up time during the reconfiguration process, there should be less manual involvement. Automating the whole reconfiguration process minimises the reconfiguration process overheads and also enables the manufacturer to meet demand within a short time frame.

Gwangwava *et al* (2014) proposed full-automatic reconfiguration for reconfigurable systems (FARR). The process requires an agent based approach using ontology knowledge of the manufacturing environment so as to make decisions.

In a typical research undertaken at the author's institution, customers enter their needs (customer requirements) through a web based interface. The data is fed into the company's in-house system and analysed through a quality function deployment (QFD) based system. The system can be used to generate completely new designs or to create a process plan for the customised order which will be used to reconfigure the existing system or machine tool.

CONCLUSION

Big Data is a huge fortune to manufacturing industries. The use of business analytics and intelligent tools can mine huge data repositories generated by manufacturing information systems and present reports which can be very handy in decision making. Customers in the whole globe are ever becoming cost conscious and it is only those companies that strive to provide cost effective solutions which will remain competitive. In order to make informed decisions, companies must be able to measure every detail of their processes. Cyber Physical Systems (CPS) enable companies to build smart networks that enable them to deliver green solutions which are sustainable. The smart networks enable detailed process measurement. Although this generates huge quantities of data (Big Data), the analysis of the data brings more benefits. The current advancement in technology, particularly CPS, is showing no signs of taking a downward turn hence manufactures should incorporate ICT strategies that will give them leveraged advantage over their competitors. In today's global village, collaboration across the whole supply chain is the way to go by. Interoperability and seamless integration is the only solution to gain clear visibility of all the downstream processes. Manufacturers cannot ignore security in this era of Big Data. There should always be tight security measures so as to avoid catastrophic occurrences. Investing in technology only is not enough; manufacturers should also strive to develop manpower skills with a balanced expertise in business intelligence and software development skills.

REFERENCES

Alsafi, Y., & Vyatkin, V. (2014). *Ontology-based Reconfiguration Agent for Intelligent Mechatronic Systems in Flexible Manufacturing*. Retrieved June 18, 2014, from http://homepages.engineering.auckland.ac.nz/~vyatkin/publ/RCIM-S-08-00078.pdf

Brandon, J. (2013). *M2M*. Retrieved June 20, 2014, from http://www.dot.gov.in/sites/default/files/m2m_basics.pdf

Buehlmann, U., & Bumgardnar, M. (2005). Evaluation of furniture retailer ordering decisions in the United States. Forintek Canada Corp.

Gifford, C. (2013). *The MOM Chronicles: ISA-95 Best Practices Book 3.0*. International Society of Automation.

Gwangwava, N., Mpofu, K., Tlale, N., & Yu, Y. (2014). A methodology for design and reconfiguration of reconfigurable bending press machines (RBPMs). *International Journal of Production Research*, *52*(20), 6019–6032. doi:10.1080/00207543.2014.904969

IBM®. (2008). *SOA Approach to Enterprise Integration for Product Lifecycle Management*. Retrieved August 15, 2013 from http://www.redbooks.ibm.com/redbooks/pdfs/sg247593.pdf

IEC 62264-3, Enterprise-Control System Integration – Part 3: Activity Models of Manufacturing Operations Management. (2007). Retrieved July 24, 2014, from http://www.iso.org/iso/iso_catalogue/catalogue_tc/catalogue_detail.htm?csnumber=40949

Koren, Y. (2010). *The Global Manufacturing Revolution: Product-Process-Business Integration and Reconfigurable Systems*. John Wiley & Sons Inc. doi:10.1002/9780470618813

Leitão, P. (2004). *An Agile and Adaptive Holonic Architecture for Manufacturing Control*. (PhD Thesis). University of Porto.

Lu, R., Li, X., Liang, X., Shen, X., & Lin, X. (2011). GRS: The Green, Reliability, and Security of Emerging Machine to Machine Communications. *IEEE Communications Magazine*, *49*(4), 28–35. doi:10.1109/MCOM.2011.5741143

Nah, F., Lau, J., & Kuang, J. (2001). Critical factors for successful implementation of enterprise systems. *Business Process Management Journal*, *7*(3), 285–297. doi:10.1108/14637150110392782

Oracle®. (2013). *Big Data for the Enterprise*. Retrieved August 15, 2013, from http://www.oracle.com/us/products/database/big-data-for-enterprise-519135.pdf

Paine, T. (2011). *M2M in Manufacturing*. Retrieved June 15, 2014, from http://www.kepware.com/News/M2M_in_Manufacturing-by_Tony_Paine.pdf

Rajkumar, R., Lee, I., Sha, L., & Stankovic, J. (2010). Cyber-Physical Systems: The Next Computing Revolution. In *Proceedings of the 47th Design Automation Conference* (pp. 731-736). New York: ACM Digital Library. Retrieved June 20, 2014, from http://dl.acm.org/citation.cfm?id=1837461

Rumbaugh, J., Jacobson, I., & Booch, G. (2005). *The Unified Modeling Language Reference Manual* (2nd Ed.). Pearson Education Inc. Retrieved August 10, 2013, from https://www.utdallas.edu/~chung/Fujitsu/UML_2.0/Rumbaugh--UML_2.0_Reference_CD.pdf

Saenz, B., Artiba, A., & Pellerin, R. (2009). Manufacturing Execution System- A Literature Review. *Production Planning and Control*, *20*(6), 525–539. doi:10.1080/09537280902938613

ADDITIONAL READING

Ake, K., Clemons, J., Cubine, M., & Lilly, B. (2003). *Information Technology for Manufacturing: Reducing Costs and Expanding Capabilities*. UK: CRC Press. doi:10.1201/9780203488713

Allen, R. D., Harding, J. A., & Newman, S. T. (2005). The application of STEP-NC using agent-based process planning. *International Journal of Production Research*, *43*(4), 655–670. doi:10.1080/002075 40412331314406

Application Handbook, S. T. E. P. ISO 10303 Version 3. (2006). SCRA. Retrieved August 15, 2014, from http://www.engen.org.au/index_htm_files/STEP_application_hdbk_63006_BF.pdf

Cattrysse, D., Beullens, P., Collin, P., Duflou, J., & Oudheusden, D. V. (2006). Automatic Production Planning of Press Brakes for Sheet Metal Bending. *International Journal of Production Research*, *44*(20), 4311–4327. doi:10.1080/00207540600558031

Chang, K. H. (2014). *Product Design Modeling using CAD/CAE: The Computer Aided Engineering Design Series* (1st ed.). USA: Academic Press.

Chen, M., Wan, J., & Li, F. (2012). Machine-to-Machine Communications: Architectures, Standards, and Applications. *Transactions on Internet and Information Systems (Seoul)*, *6*(2), 480–497.

Ciurana, J., Ferrer, I., & Gao, J. X. (2006). Activity model and computer aided system for defining sheet metal process planning. *Journal of Materials Processing Technology*, *173*(2), 213–222. doi:10.1016/j.jmatprotec.2005.11.031

Ebner, G., & Bechtold, J. (2012). Are Manufacturing Companies Ready to Go Digital. Retrieved June 20, 2014, from http://www.capgemini.com/resource-file-access/resource/pdf/Are_Manufacturing_Companies_Ready_to_Go_Digital_.pdf

Foundations for Innovation. (2013). Strategic R&D Opportunities for 21st Century Cyber-Physical Systems. Retrieved June 15, 2014, from http://www.nist.gov/el/upload/12-Cyber-Physical-Systems020113_final.pdf

Garcia, F., Lanz, M., Järvenpää, E., & Tuokko, R. (2011). Process planning based on feature recognition method, Proceedings of IEEE International Symposium on Assembly and Manufacturing (ISAM2011), ISBN 978-1-61284-343-8, 25-27 May, 2011, Tampere, Finland. doi:10.1109/ISAM.2011.5942296

Gifford, C. (2007). *The Hitchhiker's Guide to Operations Management: ISA-95 Best Practices Book 1.0*. USA: ISA- Instrumentation, Systems, and Automation Society.

Gonzalez, F., & Rosdop, P. (2004). General information model for representing machining features in CAPP systems. *International Journal of Production Research*, *9*(42), 1815–1842. doi:10.1080/00207 540310001647587

Heng, S. (2014). Industry 4.0: Upgrading of Germany's industrial capabilities on the horizon. "Deutsche Bank Research". Retrieved June 18, 2014, from http://www.dbresearch.com/PROD/DBR_INTER-NET_EN-PROD/PROD0000000000333571/Industry+4_0%3A+Upgrading+of+Germany%E2%80%99s+industrial+capabilities+on+the+horizon.PDF

Lemaignan, S., Siadat, A., Dantan, J.-Y., & Semenenko, A. (2006). MASON: A Proposal For An Ontology Of Manufacturing Domain Distributed Intelligent Systems. Proceedings of International IEEE Workshop on Distributed Intelligent Systems (DIS 2006), Collective Intelligence and Its Applications. 195 –200.

Lohtander, M., Lanz, M., Varis, J., & Ollikainen, M. (2007). Breaking down the manufacturing process of sheet metal products into features. ISSN 1392 - 1207. *MECHANIKA*, *2*(64), 40–48.

Meyer, H., Fuchs, F., & Thiel, K. (2009). *Manufacturing Execution Systems (MES): Optimal Design, Planning, and Deployment.* USA: McGraw-Hill Professional.

Muruganandam, S. (2011). Harnessing the Power of Big Data in Global Manufacturing. Retrieved June 24, 2014, from https://www.eiseverywhere.com/file_uploads/83cea5eaa2393225cbd34d98a249 cd74_BIAP_2011_Soma_M.pdf

Nedelcu, B. (2013). About Big Data and its Challenges and Benefits in Manufacturing. *Database Systems Journal., 4*(3), 10–19.

Pedro, N. (2013). Off-line Programming and Simulation from CAD Drawings: Robot-Assisted Sheet Metal Bending. In proceeding of: Industrial Electronics Society, IECON 2013 - 39th Annual Conference of the IEEE. Retrieved April 5, 2014, from http://export.arxiv.org/ftp/arxiv/papers/1311/1311.4573.pdf

Russom, P. (2013). Operational Intelligence: Real-Time Business Analytics from Big data. Retrieved June 24, 2014, from http://www.splunk.com/web_assets/pdfs/secure/Real-time_Business_Analytics_from_Big_Data.pdf

SAS Institute Inc. (2013). 2013 Big Data Survey Research Brief. Retrieved June 10, 2014, from http://www.sas.com/resources/whitepaper/wp_58466.pdf

Systems, D. ®. (2012). A Practical Guide to Big Data: Opportunities, Challenges & Tools. Retrieved June 24, 2014, from http://www.3ds.com/fileadmin/PRODUCTS/EXALEAD/Documents/whitepapers/Practical-Guide-to-Big-Data-EN.pdf

Wan, J., Chen, M., Xia, F., Li, D., & Zhou, K. (2013). From Machine-to-Machine Communications towards Cyber-Physical Systems. Computer Science and Information Systems, 10(3), 1105-1128. Retrieved June 5, 2014, from http://www.doiserbia.nb.rs/Article.aspx?id=1820-02141300018W&AspxA utoDetectCookieSupport=1

Wiendahl, H. P., ElMaraghy, H. A., Nyhuis, P., Zäh, M. F., Wiendahl, H. H., Duffie, N., & Brieke, M. (2007). Changeable Manufacturing - Classification, Design and Operation. *Annals of the CIRP, 56*(2), 783–809. doi:10.1016/j.cirp.2007.10.003

Xie, S. Q., & Xu, X. (2006). A STEP-compliant process planning system for sheet metal parts. *International Journal of Computer Integrated Manufacturing, 19*(6), 627–638. doi:10.1080/09511920600623708

Zhao, Y., Kramer, T., & Brown, R. And Xu, X. (2011). Information Modeling for Interoperable Dimensional Metrology. London: Springer.

KEY TERMS AND DEFINITIONS

Enterprise Resource Planning (ERP): Automation and integration of a company's core business to help them focus on effectiveness & simplified success. ERP software applications can be used to manage product planning, parts purchasing, inventories, interacting with suppliers, providing customer service, and tracking orders. ERP can also include application modules for the finance and human resources aspects of a business.

Machine-to-Machine (M2M): A term used to describe any technology that enables networked devices to exchange information and perform actions without the manual assistance of humans. M2M is considered an integral part of the Internet of Things (IoT) and brings several benefits to industry and business in general as it has a wide range of applications such as industrial automation, logistics, Smart Grid, Smart Cities, health, defence etc. mostly for monitoring but also for control purposes.

Manufacturing Execution Systems (MES): A control system for managing and monitoring work-in-process on a factory floor. An MES keeps track of all manufacturing information in real time, receiving up-to-the-minute data from robots, machine monitors and employees.

Manufacturing Information Systems: A management information system designed specifically for use in a manufacturing environment. The role of manufacturing information systems is to support manufacturing operations by providing relevant and timely information for decision making at different levels of the company hierarchy. It also automates and secures the sequencing of manufacturing and business processes.

Manufacturing Operations Management (MOM): The subsequent system to Manufacturing Execution System (MES) software which expands focus from a single facility to the entire supply network and monitors a variety of aspects of the manufacturing process, including production capacity analysis, Work-in-Process (WIP), inventory turns and standard lead times.

Product Data Management (PDM)/ Product Life-Cycle Management (PLM): PDM is a category of computer software used to control data related to products. PDM creates and manages relations between sets of data that define a product, and store those relationships in a database. It is an important tool in product lifecycle management. PLM is a strategic business approach that applies a consistent set of business solutions that support the collaborative creation, management, dissemination, and use of product definition information throughout the lifecycle of the product.

STEP/STEP-NC: STandard for the Exchange of Product model data, a comprehensive ISO standard (ISO 10303) that describes how to represent and exchange digital product information. STEP is a means by which graphical information is shared among unlike computer systems around the world. It is designed so that virtually all essential information about a product, not just CAD files, can be passed back and forth among users.

Supply Chain Management (SCM): An integrated approach to planning, implementing and controlling the flow of information, materials and services from raw material and component suppliers through the manufacturing of the finished product for ultimate distribution to the end customer. It includes the systematic integration of processes for demand planning, customer relationship collaboration, order fulfillment/delivery, product/service launch, manufacturing/operations planning and control, supplier relationship collaboration, life cycle support, and reverse logistics and their associated risks.

Unified Modelling Language (UML): UML is a standard language for specifying, visualizing, constructing, and documenting the artefacts of software systems. It is also used to model non software systems as well like process flow in a manufacturing facility.

XML: Stands for "Extensible Mark-up Language. XML is used to define documents with a standard format that can be read by any XML-compatible application. It is a file format-independent language, designed primarily to enable different types of computers to exchange text, data, and graphics by allowing files to be shared, stored and accessed under different application programs and operating systems.

Chapter 14
Modeling Big Data Analytics with a Real-Time Executable Specification Language

Amir A. Khwaja
King Faisal University, Saudi Arabia

ABSTRACT

Big data explosion has already happened and the situation is only going to exacerbate with such a high number of data sources and high-end technology prevalent everywhere, generating data at a frantic pace. One of the most important aspects of big data is being able to capture, process, and analyze data as it is happening in real-time to allow real-time business decisions. Alternate approaches must be investigated especially consisting of highly parallel and real-time computations for big data processing. The chapter presents RealSpec real-time specification language that may be used for the modeling of big data analytics due to the inherent language features needed for real-time big data processing such as concurrent processes, multi-threading, resource modeling, timing constraints, and exception handling. The chapter provides an overview of RealSpec and applies the language to a detailed big data event recognition case study to demonstrate language applicability to big data framework and analytics modeling.

INTRODUCTION

Data is growing at a significant rate in the range of exabytes and beyond. This data is structured and unstructured, text based and more richer content in the form of videos, audios, and images, and from various sources such as sensor networks, government data holdings, company databases and public profiles on social network sites (Katina, 2013). Along with other various challenges related to big data such as storage, cost, security, ethics, or management, processing big data perhaps is even more challenging (Kaisler, 2013). One way to mitigate some of the processing challenges is to build prototypes or models of big data analytics that may allow understanding the underlying complexities and verifying functional correctness before actual implementation of the solutions. The sheer volume and velocity of big data is rendering our traditional systems incapable of performing analytics on the data which is constantly in

DOI: 10.4018/978-1-4666-8505-5.ch014

motion (Katal, 2013). One of the most important aspects of big data is being able to capture, process, and analyze data as it is happening in real-time. Unlike traditional data stored in some database or data warehouse for later processing, the real-time data is handled and processed as it flows into the system along with timing constraints on the validity and business response to the flowing in data. Even though various approaches have been suggested and introduced to address the problem of analyzing big data in the cloud, it still has been a challenge achieving high performance, better parallelism and real-time efficiency due to the ubiquitous nature of big data as well as the complexity of analytic algorithms (Osman, 2013). Alternate approaches must be investigated especially consisting of highly parallel and real-time computations for big data processing. This chapter will present one such approach using an executable real-time specification language based on the dataflow programming model. The language features will be presented and the language applicability for modeling big data analytics will be demonstrated through a detailed case study.

BACKGROUND

This section provides an overview of the dataflow programming paradigm and introduces the RealSpec real-time specification language.

Dataflow Programming Model

Dataflow programming paradigm was originally motivated by the ability of exploitation of massive parallelism (Johnston, 2004). The dataflow approach has the potential to exploit large scale concurrency efficiently with maximum utilization of computer hardware and distributed networks (Herath, 1988). Dataflow paradigms can employ parallelism both at fine grain instruction level as well as at various coarse grain levels, however, fine grain parallelism has significant overhead (Ackerman, 1982). Due to the fine grain parallelism overhead and the need of big data analysis and processing, this chapter will focus on coarse grain level parallelism.

Dataflow programs are represented as directed graphs. Nodes on a dataflow graph represent logical processing blocks with no side effects and working independently that can be used to express parallelism (Sousa, 2012). Freedom from side effects is necessary for efficient parallel computation (Tesler, 1968). Directed arcs between the nodes represent data dependencies between the nodes. Arcs that flow toward a node are said to be input arcs to that node, while those that flow away are said to be output arcs from that node (Johnston, 2004). The status or intermediate results of each node is kept in a special node level memory that is capable of executing the node when all of the necessary data values have arrived (Ackerman, 1982). When a node in a dataflow network receives all required inputs, the node operation is executed. The node removes the data elements from each input, performs its operation, and places the transformed data on some or all of its output arcs. The node operation then halts and waits for the next set of input data to become executable again. This way instructions are scheduled for execution as soon as their operands are available as compared to the control flow execution model where instructions are only executed when the program counter reaches the instructions regardless of whether they are ready for execution before that. Hence, in a dataflow model, several instructions can potentially execute simultaneously providing the potential for massive instruction level parallelism. Figure 1 provides a simple dataflow graph for a set of programming statements. The boxes represent execution nodes with operations.

Figure 1. Dataflow graph example

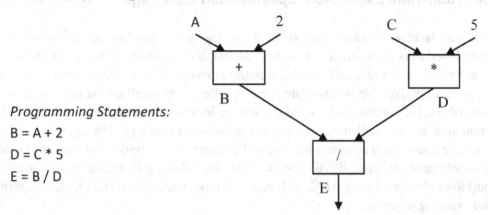

Programming Statements:

B = A + 2

D = C * 5

E = B / D

The directed arrows represent the arcs along which the data flows. The letters represent streams of data flowing in or out of the program fragment. The numbers represent constant stream at each time instant.

Considering the program fragment execution under control flow model in Figure 1, each statement is executed sequentially, i.e., first B gets the sum of A and 2, then D gets the product of C and 5, and finally E gets the quotient of B divided by D. The same program fragment under dataflow model can add A and 2 and multiply C and 5 simultaneously. Both results can then be put on their respective output arcs as B and D. As soon as both B and D are available at the inputs of the final '/' node, the operation is triggered and the result is placed as E on the output arc. The above example not only shows the instruction level parallelism of the dataflow model but also the pipelined nature of the dataflow processing. As soon as first set of B and D are available for the '/' node and it starts its execution, the next set of B and D values can simultaneously be computed by the '+' and '*' nodes. This may go on as long as stream of input values are available.

Big data processing inherently involves parallel computations and non-determinism. Sequential von Neumann machines are not oriented to such type of computations (Herath, 1988). Stream computing is critical for distributed, real-time analytics on live and dynamic big data streams (Osman, 2013). The transition from batch processing to stream processing inside the data cloud fits various time-sensitive applications and real-world use cases (Osman, 2013). Models, languages, and architectures are needed that support such parallelism. Dataflow paradigm can support such massive parallelism at various levels of granularity. With the evolution of multi-core processors and large connected processing farms, the high parallelism supported by dataflow paradigm can now be realized allowing implementation of highly parallel computations necessitated by big data analytics. Non-determinism, however, is not inherently present in dataflow streams as dataflow paradigm is functional, meaning a dataflow program will produce the same set of output for a given set of input (Johnston, 2004). Some research has been done to add non-deterministic behavior to the dataflow models (Arvind, 1977; Kosinski, 1978; Broy, 1988). The non-determinism in dataflow models will be further addressed later in the chapter.

The proposed modeling language, based on the dataflow paradigm, supports parallel computations necessary for big data processing. The next section provides an overview of the proposed language along with various features needed for modeling big data analytics. The chapter discusses language support for non-determinism as well as the use of multi-core processors on a cloud in one of the later sections.

RealSpec Real-Time Executable Specification Language

RealSpec is a declarative executable specification language for the prototyping of concurrent and real-time systems based a dataflow functional model (Khwaja, 2008a, 2008b, 2008c, 2009, 2010). RealSpec is developed on top of Lucid dataflow programming language by enhancing Lucid with features for real-time systems (Wadge, 1985). The statements in a RealSpec specification are equations defining streams and filters, not commands for updating storage locations as in the case of traditional imperative programming languages. Hence, RealSpec is a definitional language. The equations in a RealSpec specification are assertions or axioms from which other assertions can be derived using the Lucid axioms and rules of inference (Ashcroft, 1976). For example, the following RealSpec specification defines x (the output) to be the data stream <1, 2, 3, 4, 5,...> at time index <t0, t1, t2, t3, t4,...>, respectively, an infinitely varying sequence:

```
x
  where {
       x = 1 fby x+1;
    }
```

In the above specification, the where clause is an expression together with a set of definitions of variables used in the expression. These definitions are also called operator nets. The binary operator **fby** (called followed by) provides abstract iteration over sequences. The first argument of **fby** primes the pump that permits successive future values to be generated. Note that, since RealSpec is referentially transparent, the variable x denotes the same stream in all contexts. In the above example, the x on the right-hand side of the **fby** is the same as the one being defined which begins with 1. Since x is defined to be 1 at index 0, and 1 is defined to be 1 at index 0, the next value of the stream at index 1 can be produced to be 2 using x+1, ad infinitum.

User Defined Algebras and Objects in RealSpec

Lucid is based on a few fixed algebras such as integers, reals, Booleans, and strings. However, Iswim (Landin, 1966), which is the basis for Lucid does not limit any data types. In fact, Iswim is a family of languages supporting a set of primitive things consisting of data objects, a collection of operations over this set, and a collection of symbols denoting objects and operations (Wadge, 1985). In order to be able to represent processes and resources in RealSpec, Lucid's semantics were enhanced to include user defined algebras for representing complex data types and objects.

Based on the Iswim family of languages, consider if the data object is not only a collection of data elements but functions as well. In other words, data objects may have operator nets or filters in addition to a set of variables. A Lucid program then would be an operator net for this "data with operator net". Each instance of the input would be some form of this data with a specific internal state based on the values of its member data types and the output would be another form of this data with its internal state changed through the internal operator net of the data object. The internal operator net of the data object is manipulated by the operator net of the main Lucid program to produce the output data object with the changed state (Freeman-Benson, 1991). Since input/output streams contain streams of data objects which in turn contain instance variables, the "value" in these streams can be changed in two separate ways (Freeman-Benson, 1991):

- By a stream of different objects; and
- By a stream of the same object with different values in the instance variables.

Thus, the instance variables of a data object must themselves be full-fledged Lucid streams resulting in streams of data objects which contain a stream of data objects that are followed by potentially an n number of streams. For example, consider a data object d with an internal instance variable x. The stream representation for this data object may appear as:

$$
\begin{array}{cccc}
 & t' = 0 & t' = 1 & t' = 2... \\
 & d_0 & d_1 & d_2 \rightarrow \\
t'' = 0 & a_0 \downarrow & b_0 \downarrow & c_0 \downarrow \\
t'' = 1 & a_1 & b_1 & c_1 \\
t'' = 2 & a_2 & b_2 & c_2 \\
... & & &
\end{array}
$$

where t' is the time index for d stream and d_i represent object d with updated state based on its internal instance variable and manipulation functions. For each d_i, the internal instance variable x goes through a sequence of values indexed by t''. The stream values a_i, b_i, and c_i represent possibly different value streams for x for each d_i stream element.

System, Processes, and Threads

- **System:** A RealSpec specification starts with a system construct that provides a context for the rest of the specification. The system construct consists of declaration of system resources, statically defined processes, process and thread creation order, and global system level functions, if any. The system definition in RealSpec is specified using a system construct:

```
system sys {
    resources { ... }
    processes { ... }
    functions { ... }
}
```

Resources, processes, and global functions are defined within the system construct in their respective blocks. The three types of blocks can be defined in any order within the system construct. A system may or may not use any resources and globally defined functions. Hence, it is possible that a system definition does not have these two blocks defined. However, a system must have at least one process defined that will serve as the main process. For a given problem, active and passive problem components are identified and defined using the process and resource language constructs, respectively, within the system construct.

- **Process:** Processes are active components in RealSpec, i.e., processes have their own execution threads and instigate various system actions. System processes are declared within the processes block of the system construct. All statically created system processes are required to be declared in the processes block. For example, the system sys declares three processes p1, p2, and p3:

```
system sys {
 processes {
        p1;
        p2;
        p3;
    }
    ...
}
```

A process object is defined using a process construct. A process construct consists of the keyword process with process name followed by process body within curly brackets. The body of a process definition may consist of a declaration for primitive data variables, other active or passive objects, and a set of process functions. The functions in a process are declarative assertions defining operator nets of the process. All of the functions or operator nets of a process execute simultaneously and synchronously. For example, a process factorial that contains a single function calcfac(int n) to calculate factorial can be defined as follows:

```
process factorial() {
   calcfac(int n)
      where {
            calcfac(int x) = if x < 2 then 1 else x * calcfac(x-1);
      }
}
```

The same program written in an imperative language like C using recursion will look something like following:

```
#include<stdio.h>

long factorial(int);

int main()
{
    int n;
```

```
   long f;

   scanf("%d", &n);

   f = factorial(n);
   printf("%d! = %ld\n", n, f);

   return 0;
}


long factorial(int n)
{

   if (n == 0)
      return 1;
   else
      return(n * factorial(n-1));
}
```

Where there are some obvious similarities between the two programs, such as use of variables (x, n) and expressions built up from basic arithmetic operators, the two languages are quite different. In the above example, the two languages appear more similar than they really are due to the similar mathematical symbolism and conscious use of C-like notations for RealSpec. These symbols, however, are used in very different ways. In the C program, statements are commands whereas in RealSpec these are definitions. The variables in the C programs are storage locations whereas in RealSpec these are variables in the true sense of mathematics. In addition, RealSpec provides default process features such as inter-process communication, multi-threading, and process priorities by virtue of the process construct whereas these features will have to be programmatically added to the C version of the program.

Processes may be created statically or dynamically. All processes declared at the system level are statically created when system execution is started and remain active until the system is running. The processes in RealSpec are by default created and executed asynchronously. The functions or operator nets within a process, however, are executed synchronously within that process. Processes may be dynamically created by other processes by calling the **start**() function of a process. Each process has a pair of implicit functions **start**() and **end**(). Any process that is expected to be dynamically created must be declared with a dynamic qualifier which notifies a process to defer its creation until its **start**() function is called.

```
process p1() {
   process dynamic p2;

   f()
      where {
            ... p2.start() ...
      }
}
```

- **Threads:** A process has a single execution thread by default. However, a process may have as many threads as possible. Multiple threads can be defined as part of a process definition. When a process is created, all defined threads are automatically created and start simultaneous execution. The entire context of a process is duplicated for each created thread except for any shared resources. The order of thread creation and start is random unless specifically defined within the system definition using the precedence constraints. In the example below, x gets the value of x+1 if the executing thread is th1, indicated by the property pid, otherwise x gets the value of x*2. Hence, the output for thread th1 will be <1, 2, 3, 4,...> whereas for th2 that will be <1, 2, 4, 8,...>:

```
process p() threads th1, th2 {
    x
        where {
            x = 1 fby if pid == 0 then x+1 else x*2;
        }
}
```

Inter-Process Communication

The processes can also communicate with each other via message passing by using a pair of send and receive thread functions. Any two processes that are trying to communicate with each other using message passing must have matching send and receive calls. A message handshake takes place when a process or thread sends a message to another process or thread. The message handshake is based on using an implicit message buffer that is associated with each process to buffer the messages and an acknowledgement sent from the receiving process to the sending process. The message communications can either be synchronous or asynchronous. In the case of synchronous message passing, the two processes p1 and p2 are blocked or synchronized at the send and receive pair until the message transfer handshake is complete. The asynchronous message passing is indicated by specifying the **async** qualifier with both send and receive calls. The send call will put the message in p2's message buffer with p1's **pid** and will return immediately. The receive call will get the message from p2's message buffer if the message's **pid** matches p1's **pid**, otherwise it will return. In the following example of synchronous message passing with timeouts, p1 blocks for 50 microseconds and p2 blocks for 75 microseconds:

```
process p1() {
    ... p2.send(data)@tout 50 us; ...
}
process p2() {
    ... x = p1.receive() @tout 75 us; ...
}
```

Timing Constraints and Exceptions

RealSpec supports specification of both absolute and relative timing constraints for processes, messages, and data. In addition, periodic and aperiodic constraints can also be specified. The absolute timing constraints consist of minimum, maximum, and durational constraints using **@delay**, **@tout**, and **@dur** operators. In the following example, the input variable is not read until a minimum time of 25.8 us has passed:

```
process p() {
    ... x = input @delay 25.8 us; ...
}
```

In the following example, process p1 waits for a message acknowledgement from process p2 for a maximum of 5.6 ms:

```
process p1() {
    ... p2.send(data) @tout 5.6 ms; ...
}
```

In the following example, a process p1 is put to sleep by another process p2 for 10 ms:

```
process p2() {
    ... p1.sleep() @dur 10 ms ...
}
```

The events in RealSpec are by default aperiodic. Periodic events may be specified by using the **@period** operator that allows specification of the lower and upper period limit as well as period duration, e.g., x is periodically input with a lower period limit of 4.5 ms, an upper period limit of 5.5 ms and duration of 1 second:

```
x = input @period 4.5 ms 5.5 ms 1 s;
```

Relative timing constraints may be specified using a **wrt** qualifier that stands for "with respect to". The **wrt** qualifier takes as a parameter an event, process, or message name to be used as a reference for calculating a timing constraint of the associated timing operator. In the following example, the y input delay is calculated with respect to the delay of x:

```
x = input_x @delay 10 s;
y = input_y @delay 5 s wrt x;
```

In the dataflow semantics, the **wrt** qualifier is applied to the previous value of the reference event. In the above example, x will get input_x after 10 seconds delay and y will get input_y after (10 + 5) seconds delay. The dataflow stream effect of **wrt** is that the qualifier delays or pushes out the stream one time index due to the dependence on the previous time value of the reference event stream.

Constraint violations are handled using exception handlers and exceptions are raised within process functions using the keyword throw along with the exception name. Once raised, an exception must be handled by the process via a special process function called exception handler. Hence, the scope of exceptions and exception handlers in RealSpec is local to a process. Since the exception handlers are functions defined within a process scope, these handlers can access process level resources and variables. The exception handler functions are executed at the highest priority level. If multiple exceptions are raised simultaneously within a process, the order of exception raised is used for handler execution. If multiple exceptions are raised simultaneously by various processes, the priority of processes is used to determine the exception handler execution order. The following example shows an explicit throwing of an exception when x exceeds a certain threshold value limit where valueLimitException() is the name of the exception handler used to handle this particular exception:

```
z = if x > limit then throw valueLimitException(x) else normal();
...
exception valueLimitException(int y) = msg fby ...
    where {
        msg = "Error – value " ^ mkstring(y) ^ "exceeds limit!";
}
```

Abort is used in the case of fatal or hard real-time errors when recovery is not possible and is raised by using the **abort** command anywhere in the system including exception handlers. RealSpec terminates the entire system specification execution on executing the abort command.

```
exception inputTimeoutException() = printmsg fby abort
    where {
        printmsg = "Input timeout has occurred!";
    }
```

Resource Modeling

RealSpec supports modeling of system resources using data objects. In RealSpec, resources are considered as passive elements that do not have their own execution thread instead these resources passively wait for other components to require their services. Passive components are usually activated on receiving messages from other components. The predefined resources in RealSpec consist of: (a) abstract data structure resources such as semaphore, mutex, array, queue, and stack; and (b) hardware resources such as signal and analog IO. The predefined resource objects are multi-thread safe i.e., all resource objects support simultaneous access through multiple threads by using internal semaphores and a mutual exclusion mechanism. Users can also define new custom resource objects with the following resource construct template:

```
resource <name>(<parameters>) {
    <resource variables>
    <resource functions>
}
```

Once defined, resource objects must be instantiated before being used. In the following example, the system sys declares two resource objects: an input signal resource for reading a switch state and a five element queue data structure:

```
system sys {
    resources {
        signalin switch;
        queue q(5);
    }
}
```

Control System Modeling

RealSpec supports modeling of control systems using constructs to model digital and analog IO. A signal resource object is used to model a digital signal, also called discrete or quantized signal. In most applications, digital signals are represented as binary numbers so their precision of quantization is measured in bits. These signals are typically an encoding of data using 1's and 0's represented by high and low voltage levels. The signal resource may be used to model interfaces that have two states, on or off, e.g., a valve or a motor on/off button. The RealSpec signal resource has three variations: **signalin**, **signalout**, and **signalinout** to model input signals, output signals, and duplex signals, respectively. The following specification outputs **true** if the input signal is high for at least 30 seconds, otherwise it outputs **false**:

```
signalin inputSignal;
x = if inputSignal.pulsein() == 1 && inputSignal.pulseduration() >= 30 s
    then true else false;
```

RealSpec provides an analog IO resource object to model analog interfaces. The resource object **analogin** is used to model a feedback element or analog-to-digital convertor. The resource object **analogout** is used to model feed forward or digital-to-analog convertor. In the following specification snippet example, a concen **analongin** resource is declared to read methane gas concentration in the surrounding environment.

```
analogin concen(4, 20, 24);
checkGas()
    where {
        checkGas() = if gas >= GAS_THRESH_1 && gas <= GAS_THRESH_2
            then true else false
                where {
```

```
        gas = concen.sample()/20*100;
        GAS_THRESH_1 = 30;
        GAS_THRESH_2 = 45;
    }
}
```

The gas concentration is measured as current. The input current low and high reference points (4 mA and 20 mA) are passed in as parameters when declaring the resource. The digital code resolution is assumed to be 24 bits, also passed in as a parameter. The specification continuously checks for the gas concentration and if the concentration is between 30% and 45% threshold then outputs true otherwise outputs false.

RealSpec Compile Process

A prototype compiler was developed to be able build and execute RealSpec specifications. The RealSpec compiler was developed in C on a Sun Solaris system running SunOS 5.8. The target code generated was then compiled for an Intel 386 architecture based embedded platform running Embedded Configurable Operating System (eCos) 3.0 RTOS (Massa, 2003; eCos). The RealSpec compiler has a two stage compile process. A RealSpec specification is first compiled into an equivalent C code. The generated C code is then compiled for the target platform running eCos. eCos has been designed to support applications with real-time requirements, providing features such as multithreading, full preemptability, minimal interrupt latencies, all the necessary synchronization primitives, scheduling policies, and interrupt handling mechanisms needed for these type of applications. RealSpec's features and constructs are mapped to eCos features. For example, RealSpec process or thread declaration along with priority is mapped to eCos thread create function as follows:

RealSpec:

```
System sys {
 Processes {
    producer;
    consumer;
  }
}
```

eCos:

```
cyg_thread_create(1, "producer", ..., &producer_handle, ...);
cyg_thread_create(1, "consumer", ..., &consumer_handle, ...);
cyg_thread_resume(producer_handle);
cyg_thread_resume(consumer_handle);
```

where first parameter to the **cyg_thread_create** function is the default priority of both processes.

This section provided an overview of the RealSpec real-time executable specification language and its various features. The next section will provide a discussion on the application of RealSpec to Big Data analytics modeling. In doing so features and constructs of RealSpec appropriate and fitting for modeling big data as well as limitations and any potential enhancements needed to the RealSpec language for the modeling of big data will be identified.

REALSPEC FOR BIG DATA ANALYTICS

As discussed in the previous section, the RealSpec real-time specification language may have features to model handling and processing of Big Data. The big data analytic modeling can be at the workflow level or algorithm level. Since RealSpec is a functional language based on Lucid and there have been extensive examples of algorithmic programs written in Lucid (Wadge, 1985), the modeling of big data algorithms in RealSpec is a matter of using Lucid language features to write functional programs. Hence, this chapter will focus on the discussion of RealSpec appropriateness at the big data workflow or process flow level to demonstrate RealSpec can be used to model big data at the architectural level as well. Lee et al. (2013) presented a workflow framework architecture and a process flow for the big data analytics. Lee et al.'s (2013) framework and process flow will be loosely used in this section as a basis for discussing RealSpec's appropriateness for modeling big data workflow.

A Big Data Workflow Framework and Process Flow

Lee et al.'s (2013) workflow framework architecture consisted of four layers: workflow client, workflow management, compute service, and compute resource as shown in Figure 2. In the framework architecture, the workflow client layer provides the end-user environment to compose workflows with various workflow management tools. The workflow management layer provides major functions to support the workflow execution such as scheduling workflow tasks to remote applications, monitoring the status of workflow tasks and keeping track of computing resource usage, encryption and decryption of data as well as user authentication, and ensuring data required by a workflow is efficiently accessible. The compute service layer provides a collection of services to perform specific functions such as importing dataset, filtering data with criteria, classifying data with a particular algorithm, and exporting result. Finally, the compute resource layer provides computational platforms where the executable codes are hosted.

Figure 3 shows a process flow diagram proposed by Lee et al. indicating how a workflow with messages and dataset is executed in the above framework (Lee, 2013). A user composes a workflow with tasks available for data analytics which is then converted into XML. The XML commands are submitted to the backend workflow execution engine where the resource request and dataset request services are invoked to provision computing resources and to upload dataset. When the cluster is ready, the workflow planner then utilizes the scheduler to allocate tasks to the computing resources.

RealSpec Coverage of the Big Data Framework and Process Flow

Figures 2 and 3 show anticipated RealSpec coverage at the workflow architecture level with the shaded boxes. In the workflow framework in Figure 2 and the process flow in Figure 3, RealSpec can be used

Figure 2. An architecture of workflow framework

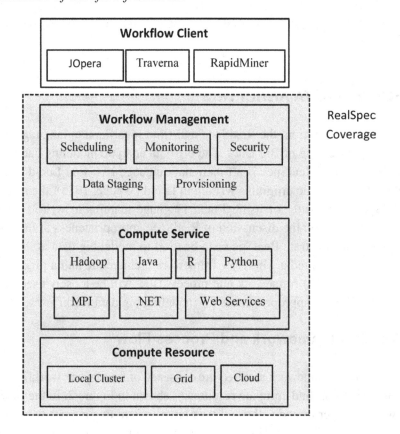

to model the Workflow Management, the Compute Service, and the Compute Resource layers. The Workflow Client layer does not need modeling in RealSpec since the workflow tasks in Lee et al.'s framework that were needed to be created in an external language like XML can be coded directly with RealSpec language constructs.

The Workflow Management layer may be modeled using RealSpec process and thread active components as this layer consists of mostly functions instigating various workflow execution activities. The inter-process communication needed between these major functions can be represented by RealSpec inter-process synchronous or asynchronous message passing mechanism.

The Compute Service layer consists of services performing various algorithmic functions to import dataset, filter data with specific criteria, and classifying data. These functions can be implemented using RealSpec basic computational operators and functions.

Finally, the Compute Resource layer has to do with actual computational platform hosts on a local cluster or a public cloud. These actual computational hosts may be modeled as a RealSpec resource data object with the acquisition and provisioning of these computational host resources being done at the Compute Service layer with a RealSpec provisioning process.

Figure 3. A Process Flow of the Workflow Framework in Figure 1

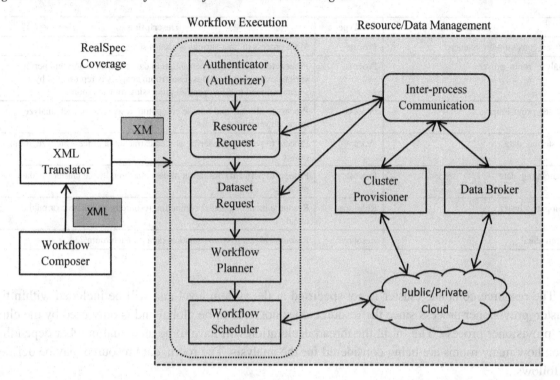

Power Consumption Data Analytics Case Study

This section builds an architectural level RealSpec specification and demonstrates RealSpec modeling of big data analytics by using a simplified version of the power consumption data analytics example from Lee et al. (2013). The example considers n number of rooms in a building with various types of power consumptions such as lighting, ventilation, low voltage devices such as printers, and high voltage devices such as servers. The power consumption workflow may consist of collection of the power consumption data at specific intervals for all rooms, extracting specific features from the data such as sum and max, clustering the data into groups based on some criteria, say, max ranges, and performing some correlation analysis on the clustered data. The power consumption data computation will also require resource provisioning on a private or public cloud.

The first step would be to identify various types of processes and resources objects required to model this example. Table 1 captures the required processes and resources needed for this example along with their descriptions. The choice of having a separate thread to perform each room analysis in the analyze_room_power process is to improve overall parallel processing. Likewise, the process cluster_provisioner has a separate provisioning thread complementing room analysis thread for ensuring each thread gets dedicate provisioning support to avoid blocking threads for computational resource allocation. The use of multi-threading in both of these cases helps in exploiting high parallel processing. In this chapter, the RealSpec keywords and language built-in features are highlighted with bold font in the specification snippets.

Table 1. RealSpec processes and resources for the power consumption analytics

Name	Type	Description
power_consumption_manager	Process	Main process to glue various analytics steps
analyze_room_power	Process	Process to collect power consumption data from all rooms and perform various extraction functions. Each room analysis is represented by a separate thread to allow parallel processing for each room.
cluster_provisioner	Process	Process to allocate and release computing resources for each analyze_room_power thread.
clustering_data	Process	Process to perform clustering of data extracted in process analyze_room_power.
coorelating_data	Process	Process to perform correlation of data clustered by the clustering_data process.
compute_cluster	Resource	Resource modeling actual computing resources on a private or public cloud.
room_data	Resource	Resource object to store statistical data for each room.

The resource compute_cluster is not specified at the system level and will be included within the cluster_provisioner process since the resource does not need to be global and is only used by the cluster_provisioner process. The 'n' in the thread declaration will have to be an actual number depending upon how many rooms are being considered for the analysis. The room_data resource may be defined as follows:

```
resource room_data {
    float sum;
    float max;
}
```

The cluster_provisioner process may be specified as follows:

```
process cluster_provision() threads cp_0, cp_1, cp_2,…, cp_n {
    compute_cluster cloud;
    provision_resource(int r_id) = if platform >= 0 then
        schedule(platform, r_id) else throw no_platform_exception(r_id)
        where {
            platform = cloud.get_platform(r_id);
        }
    release_resource(int r_id) = cloud.free_platform(r_id) fby eod;
    …
    exception no_platform_exception(int r_id) = msg fby
                            provision_resource(r_id) @delay 30 m
        where {
            msg = "Could not allocate platform for thread"
                ^ mkstring(r_id) ^… Trying again in 30 minutes!";
        }
}
```

The cluster_provision process uses compute_cluster resource to get an available platform from the cloud and to schedule the requesting thread execution on that platform. Each cluster_provision thread (cp_0 to cp_n) will be executing the same specification with their own execution context defined by thread process id, **pid**. The function provision_resource accepts the requesting thread's id and does the allocation and scheduling of the platform. In the event a platform is not available on the cloud for the requesting thread, the function throws an exception. The exception handler prints a message followed by (**fby**) a try again after 30 minutes. This will continue to happen until the thread is allocated a platform. Different handling strategies could also have been used here. For example, after n attempts a hard fail could have been implemented with a system abort. Note that currently RealSpec does not support physical scheduling of resources and that is only a suggested feature of the language that can be added to the language. At present, the actual scheduling act may be simulated by printing a message. The function release_resource frees up the allocated resource for a thread once thread execution is completed. The special keyword **eod** (end of data stream) is used to terminate the perpetual stream for the release_resource function to ensure the freeing of platform is done only once for a requesting thread. The process may define other platform provisioning and management functions as necessary.

The compute_cluster resource may be specified as follows:

```
resource compute_cluster(){
    private array int platforms(1000) = 0;
    get_platform(int r_id) = i asa (platform_is_found || i<0)
        where {
            i = platforms.size-1 fby i-1;
            platform_is_found = if i>=0 && (platforms[i]>>a) == 0
                                    then true else false;
            platforms = platforms[i]<<(r_id+1) when platform_is_found;
        }
    release_platform(int r_id) = (if platform_is_found then true
        else false) asa (platform_is_found || i<0)
        where {
            i = platforms.size-1 fby i-1;
            platform_is_found = if i>=0 && (platforms[i]>>a) == r_id+1
                                    then true else false;
            platforms = platforms[i]<<0 when platform_is_found;
        }
    available_platforms() = available asa i<0
        where {
            i = platforms.size-1 fby i-1;
            available = 0 fby available+1 whenever platforms[i]>>a == 0);
        }
    ...
}
```

The compute_cluster resource uses an internal array for keeping track of cloud platform allocations. The internal array is initialized to all zeroes indicating that all platforms are available. When the function get_platform is called by the cluster_provision process with **pid** of a thread, the function searches for an available platform and assigns the first platform found that has a corresponding zero in an array location. The function then stores the **pid** of the thread plus one to indicate this platform is now occupied by the thread **pid**. The three equations inside the where clause are all simultaneously updated for each time index. As explained previously in the chapter, the **fby** (followed by) operator allows abstract iteration or looping. So, the first and second equations are updated simultaneously for each time index. The third equation is only updated when the condition of the when operator is true. The following is a sample of the values attained by the left side of the variables in each equation at various time indexes assuming there is an empty slot at location 996:

time index	0	1	2	3	4
i	1000	999	998	997	996
platform _ is _ found	*false*	*false*	*false*	*false*	*true*
platforms	—	—	—	—	$platforms[996] = r\_id+1$

The function get_platform gets the index of the platform as a value as soon as (**asa**) a platform is found or -1 if no platform is found. At this point the equation computation is stopped for all three equations and the result is returned to the caller. The functions release_platform and available_platforms work in a similar manner.

The analyze_room_power process may be specified as follows:

```
process analyze_room_power() threads rp_0, rp_1, rp_2,…, rp_n {
    analogin power(1, 10000, 24); //low=1 KW, high=10000 KW, bits=24
    allocate_resource() = status
        where {
                status = case pid {
                        0: cp_0.provision_resource(pid);
                        1: cp_1.provision_resource(pid);
                        2: cp_2.provision_resource(pid);
                        …
                        n: cp_n.provision_resource(pid);
                }
        }
    sum() = rooms[pid].sum << ((rooms[pid].sum >> a) + consumption)
        where {
                consumption = (power.sample() @period 1 h) / 10000 * 100;
        }
```

```
max() = rooms[pid].max << consumption
            when (consumption > (room[pid].max >> a))
    where {
            consumption = (power.sample() @period 1 h) / 10000 * 100;
    }
    ...
}
```

The analyze_room_power process declares a thread for each room in the building to perform power consumption data accumulation and analysis in parallel. The order of thread creation and execution start is random unless specified at the system level declaration with precedence constraints. In this particular case, the order is not important so the default order is accepted. The process uses a predefined RealSpec resource **analogin** to sample room power at specific intervals and converts the analog data into digital based on the low and high ranges of reference input power and the number of bits used for the conversion resolution (Khwaja, 2009). In this particular example, the room power is sampled every hour.

The function allocate_resource in the analyze_room_power process uses the process id of each of the analyze_room_power threads to call the corresponding thread in the cluster_provision process which in turns tries to acquire a computing platform from the cloud and schedules the analyze_room_power thread for execution. Each case condition is executed uniquely by only the thread with the specific **pid** value on the left side of the case condition. This mechanism allows highly parallel execution of the platform provisioning and scheduling of each thread for computation on the allocated platform. This high parallel resource manipulation is possible since, in RealSpec, all predefined resources, such as array, are thread safe.

The functions sum and max in the analyze_room_power process perform the necessary statistical computation for each room power data. The running sum is maintained by reading the previous sum from the corresponding room location using the **pid** as index in the global rooms array and then updating for each subsequent power reading by the **analogin** resource at one hour intervals by adding to the previous value of the sum. The running track of peak values is also computed in similar manner. The sum and max statistical computations are used as a sample. It is possible to add more statistical related computations to the analyze_room_power process in the similar manner.

The clustering_data process may be specified as follows:

```
process clustering_data() {
    cluster_max() = status asa i==rooms.size
        where {
            i = 0 fby rooms.size+1;
            status = cond {
                    a >= RANGE_1_L && a < RANGE_1_H: write_to_cluster(i,a,1);
                    a >= RANGE_2_L && a < RANGE_2_H: write_to_cluster(i,a,2);
                    ...
                    a >= RANGE_m_L && a < RANGE_m_H: write_to_cluster(i,a,m);
            }
                where {
```

```
                    a << rooms[i].max;
                    RANGE_1_L = ...;
                    RANGE_1_H = ...;
                    RANGE_2_L = ...;
                    RANGE_2_H = ...;
                    ...
                }
        }
    cluster_size() = ...
    ...
}
```

The cluster_max function walks through the global rooms array and clusters the rooms using some predefined range rules. The example uses a simple range method here, however, any clustering algorithm may be used. The correlating_data process may be specified in a similar manner.

Finally, the power_consumption_manager may be specified as follows:

```
process power_consumption_manager() {
    analyze_max_building_consumption() = coorelating_data.correlate_max()
        asa clustering_data.cluster_max() @period 24 h;
    analyze_total_building_consumption() = coorelating_data.correlate_sum()
        asa clustering_data.cluster_sum() @period 24 h;
    ...
}
```

The power_consumption_manager process defines the workflow for the building power consumption analysis. The process correlates the respective type of data as soon as the 24 hours of data is clustered.

DISCUSSION AND FUTURE RESEARCH DIRECTIONS

The case study in the previous section demonstrated the use of RealSepc real-time specification language for modeling big data analytics. There are certain areas and features of the language that seem to be a natural fit for big data framework and analytics modeling:

- **Ubiquitous Big Data Object Modeling:** RealSpec resource construct may be used to model different types of big data objects such as video, audio, text, structured docs, and unstructured docs, with specific attributes.
- **On the Fly Processing and Analysis:** Using the processes, multi-threading, resources, and timing constraints, RealSpec provides capability to perform on the fly processing and analysis of unlimited streams of big data objects. These features make RealSpec suitable especially for time sensitive big data capture, manipulation, and analysis.
- **Parallel Streams of Big Data Objects:** Simultaneous streams of different types of related or unrelated big data objects (video, audio, structured, unstructured documents) may be inherently

supported by dataflow paradigm and hence RealSpec via multiple data streams. Dependent stream objects may be related by time indexes to reflect ordering of objects. For example, video stream object at t = 0 may be related by audio stream object at t = 0. Timing of related objects such as video and audio can be modeled by timing constraints using absolute or relative timing.

- **Parallel Processing of Big Data Streams:** Using RealSpec concurrent processes and multi-threading, any number of synchronous and/or asynchronous processes/threads along precedence constraints can be created for various types of processing as was demonstrated by the building power consumption case study in the previous section. Inter-process message passing can be used for communication between process or threads as well as synchronization.
- **Complex Event and Data Handling:** Predefined resources such as analogin/out and signalin/out provide simplified handling and manipulating of complex analog data and digital events as was demonstrated in the building power consumption case study.
- **Conciseness of the Specifications:** The above case study demonstrated that complex big data analytic scenarios may be concisely specified with RealSpec due to the declarative nature of the language.
- **Scalability.**

However, there are areas related to big data capture, processing, and analysis that seem to be lacking in the language. Adding explicit support for these feature will further enhance the applicability of the language in this domain:

- **Actual Platform Provisioning:** Currently, RealSpec does not support actual hardware platform level services. All these are soft modeled. Adding cloud level services may enhance the language executability. These services may also help in better modeling of the resource provisioning and early identification of any provisioning related issues as is usually the intent of modeling.
- **Execution Scheduling:** As with the actual hardware provisioning, the language also does not support explicit scheduling of computation on specific computing platforms. This may be another enhancement similar to the platform provisioning.
- **Data Brokage:** Similar to the above two capabilities, RealSpec does not directly support capability for best data location and/or transfer for workflow execution optimization.
- **Non-Determinism:** Non-determinism is partially supported in RealSpec. The processes, and hence the threads of these processes, in RealSpec run asynchronously to each other. Each process in RealSpec has its own internal set of data streams and hence the data streams each process work with are non-deterministic with respect to each other. This synchronicity causes the data flow between two or more processes or threads of these processes to work at different periods as the order of their executions may not be guaranteed due to decisions taken by the scheduler. In addition, the asynchronous events modeled with the analog and signal resources may also introduce non-determinism since these events may occur at different periods. However, the data streams within a process are deterministic. All data flow within a process are synchronous to each other. Most of the big data non-determinism should be addressed by the asynchronous process and events. Non-determinism at the dataflow level within a process may need to be addressed if a need arises to model non-determinism at the level. Some research in this area has been carried out (Arvind, 1977; Kosinski, 1978; Broy, 1988) and may be leveraged if needed.

CONCLUSION

RealSpec real-time specification language may be appropriate for modeling big data workflow and analytics by virtue of inherent language features needed for concurrent and real-time processing of big data streams. The building power consumption case study demonstrated applicability of various language features in this context. The language allows development of concise specification models for the big data analytics. Furthermore, the executability of the language will allow early modeling and prototyping of such complex, real-time big data analytics. The chapter also highlighted certain features that may be lacking in the language. Addition of these features to the language may further enhance the language applicability to big data analytics. Further investigation and evaluation is needed to fully understand the scope and usage of these potential features enhancements to the RealSpec language.

REFERENCES

Ackerman, W. B. (1982). Data Flow Languages. *Computer*, *15*(2), 15–25. doi:10.1109/MC.1982.1653938

Arvind, G. K. P., & Plouffe, W. (1977). Indeterminacy, monitors, and dataflow. In *Proceedings of the Sixth ACM Symposium on Operating System Principles*. West Lafayette, IN: ACM. doi:10.1145/800214.806559

Ashcroft, E. A., & Wadge, W. W. (1976). Lucid – A Formal System for Writing and Proving Programs. *SIAM Journal on Computing*, *5*(3), 336–354. doi:10.1137/0205029

Broy, M. (1988). Nondeterministic Data Flow Programs: How to Avoid the Merge Anamoly. *Science of Computer Programming*, *10*(1), 65–85. doi:10.1016/0167-6423(88)90016-0

eCos web site. (2015). Retrieved from http://ecos.sourceware.org

Freeman-Benson, B. (1991). Lobjcid: Objects in Lucid. In *Proceedings of the 4th International Symposium on Lucid and Intensional Programming*. Menlo Park, CA.

Herath, J., Yamaguchi, Y., Saito, N., & Yuba, T. (1988). Dataflow Computing Models, Languages, and Machines for Intelligence Computations. *IEEE Transactions on Software Engineering*, *14*(12), 1805–1828. doi:10.1109/32.9065

Johnston, W. M., Paul Hanna, J. R., & Millar, R. J. (2004). Advances in Dataflow Programming Languages. *ACM Computing Surveys*, *36*(1), 1–34. doi:10.1145/1013208.1013209

Kaisler, S., Armour, F., Espinosa, J. A., & Money, W. (2013). Big Data: Issues and Challenges Moving Forward. In *Proceedings of the 46th Hawaii International Conference on System Sciences*. Maui, HI: IEEE. doi:10.1109/HICSS.2013.645

Katal, A., Wazid, M., & Goudar, R. H. (2013). Big Data: Issues, Challenges, Tools and Good Practices. In *Proceedings of the Sixth International Conference on Contemporary Computing (IC3)*. Noicla, India. doi:10.1109/IC3.2013.6612229

Katina, M., & Miller, K. W. (2013). Big Data: New Opportunities and New Challenges. *Computer, 46*(6), 22-24.

Khwaja, A. A., & Urban, J. E. (2008a). RealSpec: An Executable Specification Language for Prototyping Concurrent Systems. In *Proceedings of the 19th IEEE/IFIP International Symposium on Rapid System Prototyping*. Monterey, CA: IEEE. doi:10.1109/RSP.2008.9

Khwaja, A. A., & Urban, J. E. (2008b). RealSpec: An Executable Specification Language for Modeling Resources. In *Proceedings of the 20th International Conference on Software Engineering and Knowledge Engineering (SEKE 2008)*. San Francisco Bay, CA.

Khwaja, A. A., & Urban, J. E. (2008c). Timing, Precedence, and Resource Constraints in the RealSpec Real-Time Specification Language. In *Proceedings of the 2008 IASTED International Conference on Software Engineering and Applications*. Orlando, FL: IASTED.

Khwaja, A. A., & Urban, J. E. (2009). RealSpec: an Executable Specification Language for Modeling Control Systems. In *Proceedings of the 12th IEEE International Symposium on Object/component/service-oriented Real-time Distributed Computing (ISORC 2009)*. Tokyo, Japan: IEEE. doi:10.1109/ISORC.2009.36

Khwaja, A. A., & Urban, J. E. (2010). Preciseness for Predictability with the RealSpec Real-Time Executable Specification Language. In *Proceedings of the 2010 IEEE Aerospace Conference*. Big Sky, MT: IEEE. doi:10.1109/AERO.2010.5446788

Kosinski, P. R. (1978). A Straightforward Denotational Semantics for Non-determinate Data Flow Programs. In *Proceedings of the 5th ACM SIGACT-SIGPLAN Symposium on Principles of Programming Languages*. Tucson, AZ: ACM. doi:10.1145/512760.512783

Landin, P. J. (1966). The Next 700 Programming Languages. *Communications of the ACM, 9*(3), 157–166. doi:10.1145/365230.365257

Lee, C., Chen, C., Yang, X., Zoebir, B., Chaisiri, S., & Lee, B.-S. (2013). A Workflow Framework for Big Data Analytics: Event Recognition in a Building. In *Proceedings of the IEEE 9th World Congress on Services*. Santa Clara, CA: IEEE.

Massa, A. J. (2003). *Embedded Software with eCos*. Prentice Hall.

Osman, A., El-Refaey, M., & Elnaggar, A. (2013). Towards Real-Time Analytics in the Cloud. In *Proceedings of the 2013 IEEE 9th World Congress on Services*. Santa Clara, CA: IEEE. doi:10.1109/SERVICES.2013.36

Sousa, T. B. (2012). Dataflow Programming Concept, Languages and Applications. In *Doctoral Symposium on Informatics Engineering*.

Tesler, L. G., & Enea, H. J. (1968). A Language Design for Concurrent Processes. In *Proceedings of AFIPS 1968 Spring Joint Computer Conference*. Atlantic City, NJ: AFIPS.

Wadge, W. W., & Ashcroft, E. A. (1985). *Lucid – The Dataflow Programming Language*. London: Academic Press.

KEY TERMS AND DEFINITIONS

Big Data Analytics: Process of examining large data sets containing a variety of data types for specific patterns, correlations, market trends, customer preferences and other relevant information.

Dataflow Paradigm: Programming paradigm that models programs as directed graphs of the data flowing between operations.

Declarative Language: A non-procedural language where a program specifies what needs to be done rather than how to do.

Executable Specification Language: A software specification language with operational semantics.

Parallel Computing: Computation of several sub-tasks concurrently to solve a large or complex task.

RealSpec: A functional, declarative, and dataflow executable real-time specification language.

Real-Time Specification Language: A language that allows specification of real-time software systems requirements.

Software Modeling: A high-level language used to build simplified prototypes of software systems.

Chapter 15
Big Data Analysis in IoT

Aqeel-ur-Rehman
Hamdard University, Pakistan

Rafi Ullah
Hamdard University, Pakistan

Faisal Abdullah
Hamdard University, Pakistan

ABSTRACT

In IoT, data management is a big problem due to the connectivity of billions of devices, objects, processes generating big data. Since the Things are not following any specific (common) standard, so analysis of such data becomes a big challenge. There is a need to elaborate about the characteristics of IoT based data to find out the available and applicable solutions. Such kind of study also directs to realize the need of new techniques to cope up with such challenges. Due to the heterogeneity of connected nodes, different data rates and formats it is getting a huge challenge to deal with such variety of data. As IoT is providing processing nodes in quantity in form of smart nodes, it is presenting itself a good platform for big data analysis. In this chapter, characteristics of big data and requirements for big data analysis are highlighted. Considering the big source of data generation as well as the plausible suitable platform of such huge data analysis, the associated challenges are also underlined.

INTRODUCTION

Internet of Things (IoT) is a concept of providing uniquely identifiable objects connectivity to Internet. When billions of things connect, it will be difficult to manage and analysis huge amount of data as each object will send and retrieve data. Many challenges are related with analysis of big data on IoT due to the heterogeneity, variable data formats, priorities and specifically numerous numbers of connected devices.

Big data actually refers to huge amount of data. It includes all type of data. The data is traditionally collected and then processed and move to data warehouse for analysis. When a large amount data is collected from different sources, it may not necessarily relational data. This data can be treated as big data. As data is increasingly becoming more varied, more complex and less structured, it has become

DOI: 10.4018/978-1-4666-8505-5.ch015

imperative to process it quickly. Meeting such demanding requirements poses an enormous challenge for traditional databases and scale-up infrastructures. Big Data refer to new scale-out architectures that address these needs.

In IoT, data management is a big problem due to the connectivity of billions of devices, objects, processes generating big data. Since the Things are not following any specific (common) standard, so analysis of such data becomes a big challenge. There is a need to elaborate about the characteristics of IoT based data to find out the available and applicable solutions (Shi & Liu, 2011). Such kind of study also directs to realize the need of new techniques to cope up with such challenges.

Big Data

Big data actually refers to more data or huge amount of data. It includes all type of data. The data is traditionally collected. And then processed and move to data warehouse for analysis. When a large amount data is collected from different sources, it may not necessarily relational data. This data can be treated as big data.

As data is increasingly becoming more varied, more complex and less structured, it has become imperative to process it quickly. Meeting such demanding requirements poses an enormous challenge for traditional databases and scale-up infrastructures. Big Data refer to new scale-out architectures that address these needs (O'Leary, 2013).

Big Data is characterized by its variety of attributes as follows that is often referred to as a multi-V model (Assunção, Calheiros, Bianchi, Netto, & Buyya, 2014).

- **Variety:** Data types
- **Velocity:** Data production and processing speed
- **Volume:** Data size
- **Veracity:** Data reliability and trust
- **Value:** Worth derived from exploiting Big Data

Big Data is presenting a complex range of analysis and use problems. These can include (Villars, Olofson, & Eastwood, 2011):

- Having a computing infrastructure that can ingest, validate, and analyze high volumes (size and/ or rate) of data
- Assessing mixed data (structured and unstructured) from multiple sources
- Dealing with unpredictable content with no apparent schema or structure
- Enabling real-time or near real-time collection, analysis, and answers

Internet of Things

The Internet of Things (IoT) refers to the next generation of Internet which will be comprising over large number of heterogeneous nodes from small sensors and handheld devices to large web servers and super computer clusters (Bin, Yuan, & Xiaoyi, 2010). The term internet of things was first coined by Kevin Ashton over a decade ago. IoT is actually a great revolution in the history of computing. In IoT concept everything will be connected to internet having its own identity and everything will be able to communicate with each other (refer to Figure 1). It is actually a concept which is a combination of many other concepts such as Cloud computing, Ubiquitous computing, and wireless sensors networks and technologies like IPv6, RFID technology, and wireless communication technologies. IoT is the core of Smart Planet that is proposed by IBM Corporation (Bin, Yuan, & Xiaoyi, 2010).

There are three visions of IoT (i) Things Oriented vision, (ii) Internet Oriented vision, and (iii) Semantic Oriented vision. According to a survey, in near future, billions of things will be interconnected. They will be having capability of sending and receiving data. All objects around us will communicate and respond to a phenomenon. These objects may contain our cell phones, computers, vehicles, all liv-

Figure 1. Internet of Things

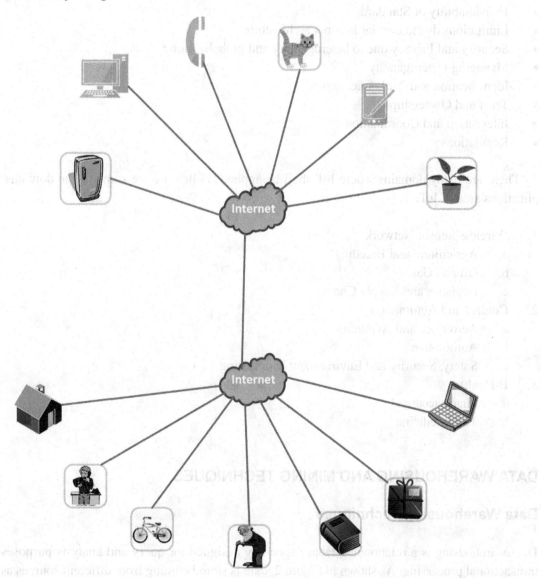

ing things, and appliances in our room and so many other things. Due to such huge connected network a huge amount of data will be produced which will require being stored, analyzed and processed. Smart connectivity with existing networks and context aware computation using network resources is an indispensable part of IoT (Gubbi, Buyya, Marusic, & Palaniswami, 2013). For technology to disappear from the consciousness of the user, the Internet of Things demands: (i) a shared understanding of the situation of its users and their appliances, (ii) software architectures and pervasive communication networks to process and convey the contextual information to where it is relevant, and (iii) the analytics tools in the Internet of Things that aim for autonomous and smart behavior. With these three fundamental grounds in place, smart connectivity and context-aware computation can be accomplished (Gubbi, Buyya, Marusic, & Palaniswami, 2013).

There are many challenges associated with the new emerging concept of IoT (Aqeel-ur-Rehman, Mehmood, & Baksh, 2013) listed as follows:

- Unavailability of Standard
- Limitations due to current Internet architecture
- Security and Privacy due to heterogeneity and globalization
- Managing Heterogeneity
- Identification and Authentication
- Trust and Ownership
- Integration and Coordination
- Regulations

There are many domains where IoT shall be applied. Following are some of the domains and applications area of IoT:

1. Wireless Sensor Network
   a. Agriculture and Breeding
   b. Oil and Gas
   c. Logistics and Supply Chain
2. Control and Automation
   a. Aerospace and Aviation
   b. Automotive
   c. Safety, Security and Environment Monitoring
3. E-Health
   a. Pharmaceutical
   b. Tele-Medicine

DATA WAREHOUSING AND MINING TECHNIQUES

Data Warehousing Techniques

Data warehousing is a relational database specially designed for query and analysis purposes not for transactional processing. As shown in Figure 2, data is stored coming from different sources as well as

Figure 2. Data Warehouse Technique

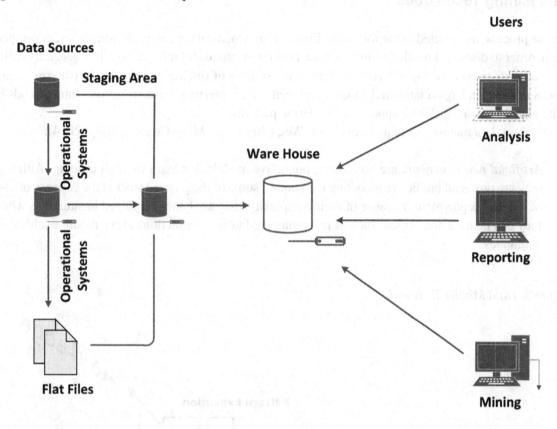

historical data i.e. data of previous transactions. Data warehousing enabled an organization to consolidate data from different sources and to separate analysis workload from transaction workload. In addition to a relational database, a data warehouse environment includes an Extraction, Transportation, transformation, and Loading (ETL) solution, an Online Analytical Processing (OLAP) engine, client analysis tools, and other applications that manage the process of gathering data and delivering it to business users. Data store in data warehouse is actually the data obtain as a result of different operational systems or transactions. For reporting purposes the data is first pass through operational data store.

The data warehouse is:

- **Subject-Oriented:** The data in the data warehouse is organized so that all the data elements relating to the same real-world event or object are linked together.
- **Non-Volatile:** Data in the data warehouse are never over-written or deleted — once committed, the data are static, read-only, and retained for future reporting.
- **Integrated:** The data warehouse contains data from most or all of an organization's operational systems and these data are made consistent.
- **Time-Variant:** For an operational system, the stored data contains the current value. The data warehouse, however, contains the history of data values.
- **No Virtualization:** A data warehouse is a physical repository.

Data Mining Techniques

It is the process, as depicted in the following Figure 3, in which data is analyzed from different perspective in order to discover knowledge and summarizing them into useful information. It is generally called knowledge discovery. Technically, data mining is the process of finding correlations or patterns among dozens of fields in large relational databases and then these patterns are used to predict future trends by using algorithms and different approaches to define patterns.

Different data mining techniques are (Chun-Wei, Chin-Feng, Ming-Chao, & Yang, 2014):

1. *Artificial neural network* are non-linear, predictive models that learn through training. Although they are powerful predictive modeling techniques, some of the power comes at the expense of ease of use and deployment. Because of their complexity, they are better employed in situations where they can be used and reused, such as reviewing credit card transactions every month to check for anomalies.

Figure 3. Data Mining Technique

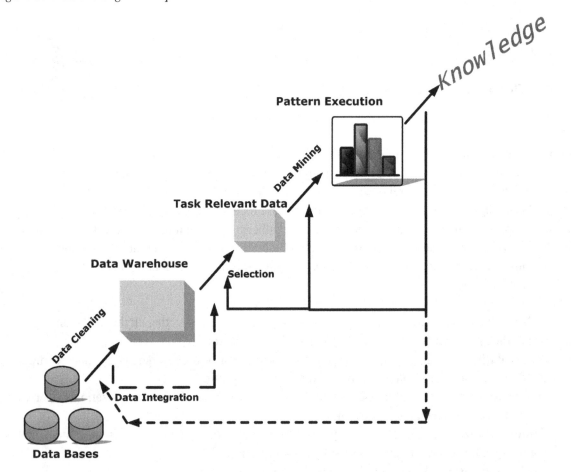

2. *Decision trees* are tree-shaped structures that represent decision sets. These decisions generate rules are used to classify data. Decision trees are the favored technique for building understandable models.

3. *The nearest-neighbor method* classifies dataset records based on similar data in a historical dataset.

SOURCES OF BIG DATA

There are two main sources of big data. One is the entirely new data sources and other is revolution in existing data generated sources. According to a survey in 2011 data growth in past five year was nearly infinite. The entirely new data sources include those industries which digitized their contents. Some of the new data sources include:

- Media/Entertainments
- Video surveillance
- Life sciences
- Health care
- Transportation, telecommunication etc.

Expanding existing sources of big data include:

- Smart instrumentation
- Banking
- Financial transactions etc.

We can infer that IoT is actually the main source of big data. As in IoT, billions of things will be having unique identification and connected with each other and each and every object will send and receive data. So this will generate huge amount of data. It can be best explained by example of library. Each book will be having its own RFID. Each book will be able to send their status to every other book and other object in library. If library have 1000 book and each book sends 2 MB of data per hour. It means that 2 GB per hour and 48 GB per day data are producing in library. The concepts of IoT will results an infinite amount of data which are to be analyzed, process and son on. There new techniques will be applied to collect, analyze and process that data.

DATA CHARACTERISTICS IN IoT

In IoT environment, collected data will be having different properties. Following are some of the important properties and requirements that we have to deal with:

Heterogeneity

In internet of things the main property of data and devices is heterogeneity. It means that different devices will be connecting for different purposes. For example a fan may be connected to your smart phone.

Also their performance is different. And each collects different type of data. Each object will be given its own ID which will differentiate one object from another. The data heterogeneity is due to difference in architecture of IoT and application model. The "big data" solutions and cloud platforms can provide infrastructure and tools for handling, processing and analyzing deluge of the IoT data. However, we still need efficient methods and solutions that can structure, annotate, share and make sense of the IoT data and facilitate transforming it to actionable knowledge and intelligence in different application domains since many of the devices and resources in IoT are highly distributed and heterogeneous (Barnaghi, Wang, Henson, & Taylor, 2012).

Polymorphism

In internet of things the huge amount of data may exist in many forms. It may be audio, video, text or image. The data is static as well as dynamic. In internet of things large amount of sensors are used for reading. Some of sensors collect text data; some will collect audio and so on. Therefore this variety of data leads to polymorphism of data. And data become difficult to analyze due to polymorphism.

Data Transmission

The data is not only collected it must be transmitted somewhere for processing. The main problem is of transmission over Wireless Sensor Network (WSN) to main source of IoT. As we have already discussed the polymorphic nature and heterogeneity of data, so some data is difficult to sense but easy to transmit like text data. And some data is easy to sense but difficult to transmit like multimedia data. The transmission of data depends on many factors such as battery power of WSN and the application running there. The secret data should be transmitted without the intervention of any one. In such WSN when data is corrupted it is difficult to find whether error is due to software failure or some other reasons because data is in polymorphic nature. This leads to difficulty in data management and analyzing in IoT.

Data in Large Quantity

Data in IoT will be in very large quantity as each object will have its own data. For example, book store having 1000 books. In RFID system each book will be having its own RFID i.e. there will be 1000 RFID's. Each will process let say 100 MB data per day. So in total 100 x 1000 MB = 100 GB of data is processing per day. Then what about billions of things when connect together in IoT. So, IoT leads to a huge amount of data. The situation becomes more critical when data in some real time system is processed.

Data Integration

As the data come from different devices or human beings itself are the source of data, so it may be in form of some physical phenomenon. This data can be integrated with existing applications data processing chain in order to support situation awareness and context awareness. In such cases it is important to integrate one kind of data with other kind of heterogeneous data. Semantic descriptions can support this integration by enabling interoperability between different sources; however, analysis and mapping between different semantic description models is still required to facilitate the IoT data integration with other existing domain knowledge (Barnaghi, Wang, Henson, & Taylor, 2012).

Data Abstraction

It is the way of representing physical world data in simpler form to the users. Different ontologies, such as W3C, SSN ontologies, are available which provide number of constructs to present and manage the data.

Data Access

Data access in IoT is one of the difficult tasks in internet of things because of heterogeneous devices and different sensor network across the networks. Data access in IoT can be implemented at low level usually at network level etc. For this purposes some low level programming and operating system is required.

Interpretation and Perception

Data is usually collected as physical phenomenon by some sensors or any collecting source. It should be interpreted correctly first. Because there will be huge amount of data collected in Internet of things. May be not all the data is useful to us. So it must be first interpreted correctly. And then must percept correctly by the receiving device. In internet of things it is a great challenge that how to interpret huge amount of data in to useful data and how to percept that data.

Security and Privacy

Big data is less structured and informal therefor it poses the problems of security and privacy. When big contains some sensitive information or something private then using normal approaches may result some serious security problem. Database managements systems have normally security for normal data but in big data software no such security involve. The sensitive data present in big data must ensure the data itself is secure. Same security should be applied to big data as they are in database of big data if data is sensitive.

NEED OF BIG DATA ANALYSIS AND AVAILABLE ANALYSIS TECHNIQUES

Why Analyze Big Data?

Big data analysis is the process in which big data is examined in order to uncover, show hidden patterns, Unknown correlation in data and much other information that can be used to take better decisions. Big data analysis is the process of figuring out which data is useful and which is not. If you don't do so a simple query can take hour or even days to process in such a huge amount of data.

When we talking about big data in internet of things. That data is data obtain by billions interconnected devices which can communicate to each other. The devices may send every sort of data, in which there may be some irrelevant data or there may be some redundant data whose redundancy is not important for us. Rather that redundant data is harmful for operation such as processing, analyzing and transaction in our data. Storing all data and then querying that data may not bring fruitful results. It must be first analyze and the hidden patterns should be uncovered. And only correlated data is then data warehoused. By doing so now you are able to get your result of query like normal relational database query. The analysis of even small databases is important and even mandatory.

Available Option for Analyzing Big Data

There are four types of Big Data analytics as mentioned in Table 1.

- **Basic Analytics for Insight:** Basic analytics for insight is just an option for data analysis. Insight Analytics is an easy-to-use tool for creating your own performance improvement dashboards. It is a type of analysis that comprises over the slicing and dicing of data, reporting, simple visualization and monitoring and anomaly detection. Insight Analytics provides a comprehensive set of visual and intuitive dashboards to focus in on key metrics. It is usually for data analysis but not so huge amount of data. It also helps in making decisions.
- **Advanced Analytics for Insight:** It is more complex analysis such as predictive modeling and other pattern-matching techniques. Here the analysis includes predictions of data. And the pattern of data also included in this type of analysis. Data is predicted using available data. And also the data analyzed using patterns of data occurred. Advance analytics help in making quick, right, bold and confident decisions.
- **Operationalized Analytics:** Analytics become part of the business process. Operational analytics also called real time business intelligence. These systems analyze huge amount of data in stream of real time operations. Mainly these systems focus on improving existing operations. These systems use various types of data mining and data aggregation tools to improve and get more transparent information about business planning. For operational analytics system must meet the following three requirements:
  - Uptime
  - Real time
  - Scalable.
- **Monetized Analytics:** Analytics are utilized to directly drive revenue. Monetized analytics is the process of converting raw data in to valuable and useful form. It helps in decision making such as predictive maintenance based on multiple insight sources.

Table 1. Types of Analysis of Big Data

Types of Analysis	Description
Basic analytics for insight	Slicing and dicing of data, reporting, simple visualizations, basic monitor.
Advanced analytics for insight	More complex analysis such as predictive modeling and other pattern-matching techniques.
Operationalized analytics	Analytics become part of the business process.
Monetized analytics	Analytics are utilized to directly drive revenue.

CHALLENGES OF BIG DATA ANALYSIS IN IoT

As big data is collection of so large and complex data set which is difficult to process using traditional data processing applications and hands on database management tools. Some of the challenges in big data analysis (Stankovic, 2014) include storages, curation, capture, search, sharing, transfer, analysis and virtualization.

Challenge 1: The first challenge is how to store such a huge amount of data i.e. petabyte data. As we know that billions of devices will be connected together which will results large amount of data. Where this large amount of data will be stored?

Challenge 2: The second challenge to big data is the searching in that data. Ordinary searching algorithms might not work efficiently on huge amount of data. There must be some new searching techniques which could be efficient on such large amount of data. Regular searching algorithms will be very slow and will not bring fruitful results.

Challenge 3: The third challenge is data curation. Data curation is the management of data so to make it able for contemporary use and available for reuse and discovery. Data which is not properly managed has no value to us. It is great challenge to IoT because large amount of data is difficult to manage.

Challenge 4: Data sharing is very important concept in IoT which is difficult task. In IoT concept large number of devices will be connected and data will be on cloud for sharing purposes. Sharing of data on clouds will require some intelligent techniques. The major challenge is that how large amount of data will be shared among different devices.

Challenge 5: In IoT data is needed to be transferred from point to point through global network. When data is so large like in petabyte transferring it is a great challenge. The pre-existing networking protocols might not work in IoT. There may be necessity of some more efficient and intelligent protocols for data transfer over network. How that data will transfer and what will be the techniques is a challenge.

Challenge 6: When we actually store data, share it and analyze it, our main goal is to process our data for getting information. Analysis of small amount of data is not a very difficult task. But in huge amount of data i.e. data generated by billions connected devices, the analysis become very tedious job and this is off course a challenge to IoT.

Challenge 7: The other challenge is data virtualization. Virtualization means data management in such a way to make it available for application to retrieve. It can be done by using some formulas and some techniques. By virtualization data will be easily retrieved by application without knowing technical skills and how physically data is stored somewhere.

Challenge 8: Another great challenge is privacy of data. For example for electronic healthcare record data should not be exposed to unauthenticated persons.

Challenge 9: Timeliness means time required for the analysis of data. This is another challenge in IoT. The challenge is how to overcome the time taken for analysis of big data.

Challenge 10: Incompleteness is also a challenge in IoT. It means that what should be the response if the information provided by some devices were not complete. For example, what if in healthcare system the patient does not give full information?

In Table 2, a comparison of the characteristics of normal data and the big data is presented.

Table 2. Normal Data vs Big Data

Characteristics	Normal Data	Big Data
Storage of data	Very Easy	Difficult
Searching	Easy	Very difficult
Data Curation	Easy	Very difficult
Sharing of data	Easy	Difficult
Transferring of data	Very easy	Difficult
Data Analysis	Easy	Very difficult
Data Virtualization	Easy	Very difficult
Data Privacy	Easy	Very difficult
Timeliness	Very easy	Very difficult
Incompleteness	Easy	Very difficult

FUTURE RESEARCH DIRECTIONS

Big data analysis is the need of future as the globally connected devices are generating variety of data with respect to deferent domains, application areas, formats, system platforms etc. As the size of the network in terms of nodes is growing, it is also becoming the source of processing. The processing power in totality will be enough to deal with the generated data for analysis and generating useful results. The domains of Agriculture, Healthcare and Smart Cities will be the most dominant among others, so there is a requirement to generate solutions for IoT and other global networks for big data Analysis.

Data Analytics is a complex problem and it requires people with expertise and support of specialize tools for data cleaning, classification, understanding and selecting specific methods. Cloud Computing can be utilized providing Analytics as a service or Big data as service to have a quick and accurate solution.

CONCLUSION

IoT is an emerging concept of global network. The challenge associated with the IoT are communication technology, heterogeneity, privacy, security and many others related issues. As the world is getting part of the global network in form of internet, cloud computing and IoT, the amount of data getting in and out of the network is getting increased manifold. Due to the heterogeneity of connected nodes, different data rates and formats it is getting a huge challenge to deal with such variety of data. As IoT is providing processing nodes in quantity in form of smart nodes, it is presenting itself a good platform for big data analysis. In this chapter, characteristics of big data and requirements for big data analysis are highlighted. Considering the big source of data generation as well as the plausible suitable platform of such huge data analysis, the associated challenges are also underlined. There is a need of various solutions to deal with the challenges associated with big data and its analysis. New advanced technologies like cloud computing and 5G technologies may provide enormous support in providing the solutions to the open challenges.

REFERENCES

Aqeel-ur-Rehman, M.K., & Baksh, A. (2013). Communication Technology That Suits IoT-A Critical Review. Wireless Sensor Networks for Developing Countries (pp. 14-25). Springer.

Assunção, M. D., Calheiros, R. N., Bianchi, S., Netto, M. A., & Buyya, R. (2014). Big Data computing and clouds: Trends and future directions. *Journal of Parallel and Distributed Computing*.

Barnaghi, P., Wang, W., Henson, C., & Taylor, K. (2012). Semantics for the Internet of Things: Early progress and back to the future. *International Journal on Semantic Web and Information Systems*, 8(1), 1–21. doi:10.4018/jswis.2012010101

Bin, S., Yuan, L., & Xiaoyi, W. (2010). *Research on data mining models for the internet of things*. Paper presented at the 2010 International Conference on Image Analysis and Signal Processing (IASP).

Chun-Wei, T., Chin-Feng, L., Ming-Chao, C., & Yang, L. T. (2014). Data Mining for Internet of Things: A Survey. *IEEE Communications Surveys and Tutorials*, 16(1), 77–97. doi:10.1109/SURV.2013.103013.00206

Gubbi, J., Buyya, R., Marusic, S., & Palaniswami, M. (2013). Internet of Things (IoT): A vision, architectural elements, and future directions. *Future Generation Computer Systems*, 29(7), 1645–1660. doi:10.1016/j.future.2013.01.010

O'Leary, D. E. (2013). 'Big data', the 'internet of things' and the 'internet of signs. *Intelligent Systems in Accounting, Finance & Management*, 20(1), 53–65. doi:10.1002/isaf.1336

Shi, W., & Liu, M. (2011). *Tactics of handling data in internet of things*. Paper presented at the 2011 IEEE International Conference on Cloud Computing and Intelligence Systems (CCIS). doi:10.1109/CCIS.2011.6045121

Stankovic, J. A. (2014). Research Directions for the Internet of Things. *Internet of Things Journal, IEEE*, 1(1), 3–9. doi:10.1109/JIOT.2014.2312291

Villars, R. L., Olofson, C. W., & Eastwood, M. (2011). *Big data: What it is and why you should care*. White Paper, IDC.

ADDITIONAL READING

Aggarwal, C. C., Ashish, N., & Sheth, A. (2013). *The internet of things: A survey from the data-centric perspective Managing and mining sensor data* (pp. 383–428). Springer.

Ahn, S.-H., Kim, N.-U., & Chung, T.-M. (2014). *Big data analysis system concept for detecting unknown attacks*. Paper presented at the 2014 16th International Conference on Advanced Communication Technology (ICACT). doi:10.1109/ICACT.2014.6778962

Aqeel-ur-Rehman, Abbasi, A. Z., Islam, N., & Shaikh, Z. A. (2014). A review of wireless sensors and networks' applications in agriculture. *Computer Standards & Interfaces*, 36(2), 263–270. doi:10.1016/j.csi.2011.03.004

Athreya, A. P., & Tague, P. (2013). *Network self-organization in the internet of things.* Paper presented at the 2013 10th Annual IEEE Communications Society Conference on Sensor, Mesh and Ad Hoc Communications and Networks (SECON).

Atzori, L., Iera, A., & Morabito, G. (2010). The internet of things: A survey. *Computer Networks, 54*(15), 2787–2805. doi:10.1016/j.comnet.2010.05.010

Bandyopadhyay, D., & Sen, J. (2011). Internet of things: Applications and challenges in technology and standardization. *Wireless Personal Communications, 58*(1), 49–69. doi:10.1007/s11277-011-0288-5

Chen, F., Deng, P., Wan, J., Zhang, D., Vasilakos, A. V., & Rong, X. (2015). Data Mining for the Internet of Things: Literature Review and Challenges. *International Journal of Distributed Sensor Networks, 501*, 431047.

Costa-Pérez, X., Festag, A., Kolbe, H.-J., Quittek, J., Schmid, S., Stiemerling, M., & Van Der Veen, H. (2013). Latest trends in telecommunication standards. *Computer Communication Review, 43*(2), 64–71. doi:10.1145/2479957.2479968

Islam, N., & Aqeel-ur-Rehman. (2013). A comparative study of major service providers for cloud computing. Proceedings of the 1st International Conference on Information and Communication Technology Trends (ICICTT'13), 228-232, Karachi, Pakistan.

Jagadish, H., Gehrke, J., Labrinidis, A., Papakonstantinou, Y., Patel, J. M., Ramakrishnan, R., & Shahabi, C. (2014). Big data and its technical challenges. *Communications of the ACM, 57*(7), 86–94. doi:10.1145/2611567

Koch, C. (2013). *Compilation and synthesis in big data analytics Big Data* (pp. 6–6). Springer.

Labrinidis, A., & Jagadish, H. (2012). Challenges and opportunities with big data. *Proceedings of the VLDB Endowment, 5*(12), 2032–2033. doi:10.14778/2367502.2367572

Larose, D. T. (2014). *Discovering knowledge in data: an introduction to data mining.* John Wiley & Sons. doi:10.1002/9781118874059

Madden, S. (2012). From databases to big data. *IEEE Internet Computing, 16*(3), 0004-0006.

Mainetti, L., Patrono, L., & Vilei, A. (2011). *Evolution of wireless sensor networks towards the internet of things: A survey.* Paper presented at the 2011 19th International Conference on Software, Telecommunications and Computer Networks (SoftCOM).

Mayer-Schönberger, V., & Cukier, K. (2013). *Big data: A revolution that will transform how we live, work, and think.* Houghton Mifflin Harcourt.

Patil, P. S., Rao, S., & Patil, S. B. (2011). *Optimization of data warehousing system: Simplification in reporting and analysis.* Paper presented at the IJCA Proceedings on International Conference and workshop on Emerging Trends in Technology (ICWET).

Sagiroglu, S., & Sinanc, D. (2013). *Big data: A review.* Paper presented at the 2013 International Conference on Collaboration Technologies and Systems (CTS). doi:10.1109/CTS.2013.6567202

Said, O., & Masud, M. (2013). Towards internet of things: Survey and future vision. *International Journal of Computer Networks*, 5(1), 1–17.

Schroeder, R., & Meyer, E. (2012). *Big data: what's new. Internet, Politics, Policy 2012: Big Data*. Big Challenges.

Suciu, G., Suciu, V., Halunga, S., & Fratu, O. (2015). *Big Data, Internet of Things and Cloud Convergence for E-Health Applications New Contributions in Information Systems and Technologies* (pp. 151–160). Springer.

Whitmore, A., Agarwal, A., & Da Xu, L. (2014). The Internet of Things—A survey of topics and trends. *Information Systems Frontiers*, 1–14.

KEY TERMS AND DEFINITIONS

Big Data: Huge Quantity of Data generated by Smart Devices.

Cloud Computing: The practice of using a network of remote servers hosted on the Internet to store, manage, and process data, rather than a local server or a personal computer.

Data Analysis: Logical Operations to Evaluate Data.

Data Characteristics: Specific Attributes of Data.

Data Curation: The Management of Data throughout its Lifecycle.

Data Intensive Computing: A class of parallel computing applications which use a data parallel approach to processing large volumes of data.

Data Mining: Knowledge Discovery Process.

Data Virtualization: Agile data integration approach organizations use to gain more insight from their data.

Data Warehousing: System for Data Reporting and Analysis.

Internet of Things: Global Network of Smart Devices.

IoT: Standard Abbreviation of Internet of Things.

Ubiquitous Computing: Computing everywhere for everyone.

Wireless Sensor Networks (WSN): Wireless network consisting of spatially distributed autonomous devices using sensors.

Chapter 16
Navigation in Online Social Networks

Mehran Asadi
Lincoln University, USA

Afrand Agah
West Chester University of Pennsylvania, USA

ABSTRACT

In this chapter, we investigate the role of influential people in an Online Social Network. We introduce a navigation approach to locate influential nodes in Online Social Networks. The purpose of quantifying influence in Online Social Networks is to determine influence within the members of an Online Social Networks and then using influence for navigation in such networks. We find out that we can take advantage of influential people in Online Social Networks to reach a target node in such networks. We utilize total number of direct friends of each node, total number of shared neighbors, the total number of common attributes, the total number of unique attributes, the distance to target node, and past visited nodes. We present an algorithm that takes advantage of influential people to reach a target in the network. Our navigation algorithm returns a path between two nodes in an average of ten percent less iterations, with a maximum of eighty percent less iterations, and only relies on public attributes of a node in the network.

1. INTRODUCTION

In a network of objects, objects can be people or computers, which we refer to them as nodes of the network. Over the course of human history, the collections of social ties among friends have grown steadily in complexity. When people live in neighborhoods or attend schools, the social environment already favors opportunities to form friendships with others like oneself. In the most basic sense, a network is any collection of objects in which some pairs of these objects are connected by links. Have the people in the network adapted their behaviors to become more like their friends, or have they sought out people who were already like them (Easley & Kleinberg, 2011)? (Milgram, 1967) Showed that real world networks are characterized by the small world phenomenon, where any two people in the world are connected through a short chain of acquaintances. The fact that makes Milgram's original result surprising is that most people tend to move in close social circles tied to a geographical location, profession, or activity.

DOI: 10.4018/978-1-4666-8505-5.ch016

Many Online Social Networks have user base in the hundreds of millions and a very important factor in navigation of data in such networks is the flow of information. So if we start from any particular node and use the Random Walk model, the information will spread in the network until the flow of information reaches to equilibrium. One of the main problems faced by many researchers is the difficulty of collecting acquaintanceship and related data from human subjects. (Ghosh & Lerman, 2008) claim that a community is composed of individuals who have more influence on individuals within the community than on those outside of it. The more paths there are, the more opportunities one node has to affect the other. They gave a mathematical formulation of influence in terms of the number of paths of any length that link two nodes, and redefined modularity in terms of the influence metric. They use this metric to show how to partition the network into communities.

Authors in (Backstrom, Huttenlocher. & Kleinberg, 2006) have considered the ways in which communities in social networks grow over time, both at the level of individuals and their decisions to join communities, and at a more global level, in which a community can evolve in both membership and content. They consider membership, growth and change in communities. They found that propensity of individuals to join communities, and of communities to grow rapidly, depend in subtle ways on the underlying network structure. To find influential people in an Online Social Network (Ghosh & Lerman, 2010) emphasize the need to distinguish between different dynamic processes occurring in complex networks based on their distinct characteristics. They categorize such processes into conservative and non-conservative, based on the nature of the flow. They classify structural models, which predict the influence standings of actors within a network into conservative and non-conservative models based on the underlying dynamic process that these models emulate. To what extent can the evolution of a social network be modeled using features intrinsic to the network itself?

Authors in (Liben-Nowell, & Kleinberg, 2007) offer a very natural basis for link prediction. They consider common neighbors, similarity and growth. By use of a random predictor, they predict connection between nodes. Authors in (Lattanzi, Panconesi, & Sivakumar, 2011) use affiliation networks and prove that in networks produced by this model, not only do short paths exit among all pairs of nodes but also natural local routing algorithms can discover them effectively. Affiliation network is a bipartite graph with people on one side and interests on the other. The affiliation network comes with an associated friendship graph in which two people are friends if they share an interest. Authors in (Dunn, Gupta, Gerber, & Spatscheck, 2012) compare where users navigate from Online Social Networks versus from search engines. They found out that not only does the outgoing traffic for a major Online Social Network compares with that of a search engine but also Online Social Networks are competing with search engines in their ability to act as conduits between users and websites.

2. RELATED WORK AND BACKGROUND

Targeted crawler algorithms (Humbert, Studer, Grossglauser, & Hubaux, 2013) allow a crawler to find a path from a source node to a target node assuming: (a) the crawler controls at least one node in the Online Social Networks, which is attainable by simply registering on most Online Social Network, and (b) the crawler knows when its target is reached, either by comparing attributes or unique ids. The targeted crawler algorithms can be seen as a frontier (Humbert, Studer, Grossglauser, & Hubaux, 2013) that is expanding toward the target node using a distance function. The distance function represents how different two nodes are: the more they have in common, the less distant they are. For each step in the algorithm, the frontier spreads toward the node that has the least remaining distance to the target. The frontier expansion can be seen in Figure 1 and Figure 2. Assume we want to find a path from node *A* to node *K*. At the first step (Figure 1), the frontier consists of all *A*'s friends. Then using the distance function, we find *G* is the closer to the target (Figure 2). Hence *G* goes to the explored set represented in white, and the frontier represented in grey is extended to *G*'s friends.

Two procedures to find key players by (a) the identification of key players for the purpose of optimally diffusing a property through the network by using the key players as seeds and (b) the identification of key players for the purpose of disrupting or fragmenting the network by removing the key nodes, are discussed in (Borgatti, 2006). Our work finds a procedure to find key players locally for a path between two nodes while (Borgatti, 2006) focuses on key players for the network as a whole.

The definition of influential nodes changes with the application and the type of commodity flowing through a network. While our work focuses on navigation paths, identifying influential nodes in Online Social Network using principal component centrality are developed in (Ilyas & Radha, 2011). Here we are interested in connectedness at the level of behavior - the fact that each individual's actions have implicit consequences on the outcomes of everyone in the system (Easley & Kleinberg, 2011). We investigate prediction of people behavior and influences in Online Social Networks. Our focus is on how different nodes can play distinct roles in information flow through an Online Social Network.

Our focus is on how different nodes can play distinct roles in information flow through an Online Social Network. If two people in an Online Social Network have a friend in common, then there is an increased likelihood that they will become friends themselves at some point in the future (Easley & Kleinberg, 2010).

Figure 1. Targeted Crawler at the first iteration

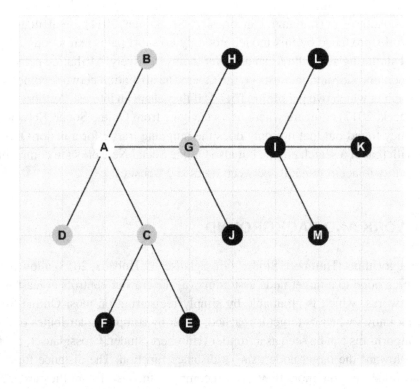

Figure 2. Targeted Crawler at the second iteration

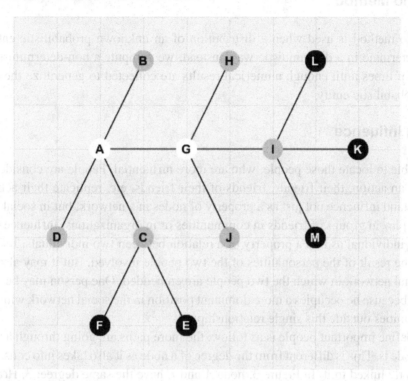

3. PREDICTION IN ONLINE SOCIAL NETWORK

The terminology of Online Social Network reflects largely similar views, through its emphasis on the connections one forms with friends, fans, followers, and so forth. An Online Social Network can be viewed as a graph $G = (V, E)$. Vertices (nodes) are representing people and edges are representing social links. Social links can be undirected (e.g. friends on Facebook) or directed (e.g. followers on Twitter). An Online Social Network allows people to have attributes that are included in the Social Network list of attributes. For each attribute, people can define a privacy policy: visible to all, visible to friends, or private.

Our work is based on the following assumption: from a graph G with privacy policies on attributes and links, we can deduce a public sub-graph G' based on public attributes and public links (Adamic & Adar, 2003), (Pedarsani, 2013). Because of the default behavior of Online Social Network is to share the most and hide the less, we can deduce G', thanks to users that do not change this default behavior. Each user that is changing the default settings contributes to shrink our graph G'.

We need a targeted crawler algorithm for our influence prediction in order to be able to navigate efficiently in an Online Social Network. This is for the following two main reasons: (a) Online Social Networks are huge (billions of users for Facebook as of today) and should not been seen as random graphs. (b) If people are connected, there is a high chance they share something in common, either a friendship, a location, a job, etc. We should not use algorithm like breadth-first search in Online Social Networks because they do not take advantage of the probability that people are connected.

a. Monte Carlo Method

The Monte Carlo method is used when a distribution of an unknown probabilistic entity is close to impossible to determine in a deterministic way. Instead, we compute a non-deterministic algorithm a certain number of times until enough numerical results are collected to generalize the distribution of the unknown probabilistic entity.

b. Predicting Influence

We want to be able to locate those people, who are more influential. People are considered influential if when they do an action, their friends, friends of their friends, etc, replicate their actions. The goal here is to understand influence not just as a property of nodes in a network, but in social interactions as the roles people play in groups of friends in communities or in organizations. Influence is not so much a property of an individual as it is a property of a relation between two individuals. Influence may be almost entirely the result of the personalities of the two people involved. But it may also be a function of the larger social network in which the two people are embedded. One person may be more powerful in a relationship because he occupies a more dominant position in the social network with greater access to social opportunities outside this single relationship.

One way to define important people is as follow: the more paths are going through a node, the more important this node is. This is different from the degree of a node as it also takes into consideration nodes that are not directly linked to it. In Figure 3, node *A* and *E* have the same degree: 3. However because *E*'s friends are more connected, there are more paths that go through E than paths that go through *A*.

Figure 3. Degree vs. Influence

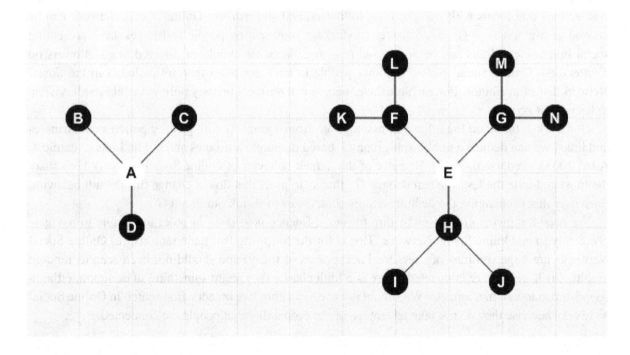

If for 100 computed paths a particular node N_1 is part of 50 paths and another node N_2 is part of 10 paths, then we say N_1 is more important than N_2 because it connects more people together. The influence of a node N in the network is defined in equation (1):

$$Influence(N_i) = \# \, of Paths Going Through(N_i) \tag{1}$$

Computing (1) is highly time consuming. Once we have the influence associated to each node, a navigation path can be defined by hoping from influent node to influent node until the target is reached.

4. PERFORMANCE EVALUATION

The dataset used for following experimentation comes from Stanford University (Stanford Large Network Dataset Collection). Data was collected from users who had manually shared their circles in the Google+ Social Network. The original dataset consisted in 107 thousands nodes and 13.7 million edges. In order to reduce running time of the experimentation, the dataset has been reduced to 700 nodes and 35 thousands edges. Moreover, bidirectional links between 2 nodes have been made unidirectional. This allows us to enlighten the different behaviors of our crawlers with a smaller data set.

Each node of our sample networks is part of at least one link, either the head or the tail of the link. Each node has between 0 and 452 friends. Nodes that have at least one friend have in average 66 friends.

a. Shortest Path

In order to gauge the effectiveness of influence navigation, we directly compared it with shortest path navigation, as depicted in Figure 4.

Figure 5 shows navigation data for graph sizes ranging from 10 to 990. Although Influence navigation is effective at really small sizes (less than 50 nodes), it's clear that the influence navigation is not as effective as the shortest path navigation as graph size increases (y-axis represents path length between two randomly selected vertices). Figure 6 illustrates a look at a larger range of graph sizes.

As we predicted, the influence navigation path increases as graph size increases, while the shortest path remains very small, as illustrated in Figure 7. When looking at time, we can also see that Influence navigation requires more time as graph size increases.

b. Simple Crawler

Assume the Online Social Network has N nodes. The first way to compute our influence is to compute all possible paths as defined in equation (1). The Targeted Crawler algorithm, which corresponds to the navigation between 2 nodes, is executed $O(N^2)$ times. If no path is found between source and targets node, the influence table is not updated. If a path is found between source and target node, for each node N_i part of the path, $Influence\ (N_i)$ is incremented by one.

Figure 4. Shortest Path Navigation

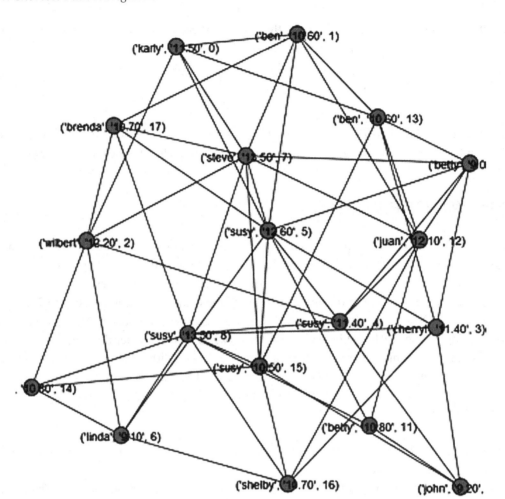

Assuming the Targeted Crawler algorithm runs in $O(1)$ time, computing the full set of paths will be done in $O\left(N^2\right)$ time. For a 1 ms computation time per iteration and 10^6 nodes (which is not unrealistic for Online Social Network, and even far from the truth for some), the computation would take approximately 10^{12} ms or 31 years. We can easily realize how this is infeasible.

c. Monte Carlo Crawler

The first approach showed that it is possible to define and influence value for each node in the network. The method described in section (b) can return very precise results, however the method is also highly time consuming and infeasible for large Online Social Network. Can we reduce the computation time and still have correct results?

Figure 5. Navigation Data for Graph size of 10 to 999

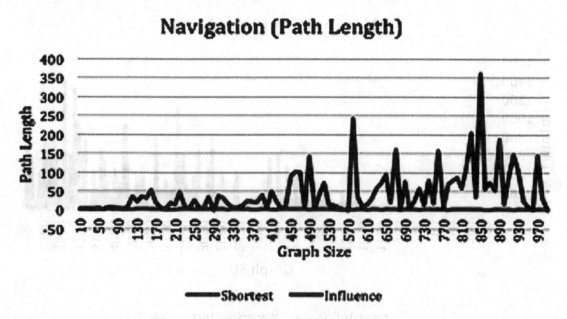

Figure 6. Navigation Data for large graph size

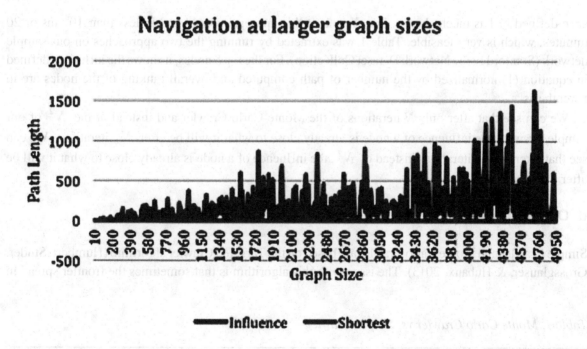

Our second approach aims to use the Monte Carlo method to approximate the influence of a node. In-stead of running the Targeted Algorithm on all possible N^2 paths, we are going to restrict the execution time of the influence calculation to $O(N)$. To do that, our second approach selects two random nodes and then runs the Targeted Algorithm N times. With this procedure, the time spent to compute our influ-

Figure 7. Navigation Time

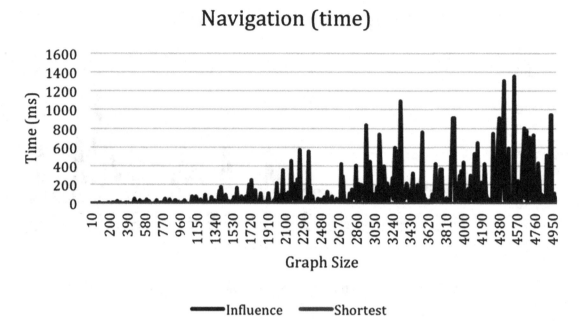

ence defined in 1 is much shorter. For $N = 10^6$, this approach would end in less than 10^6 ms or 20 minutes, which is very feasible. Table 1 was extracted by running the two approaches on our sample network (Stanford Large Network Dataset Collection). For the top 5 nodes, it shows the influence defined in equation (1) normalized by the number of path computed and overall ranking of the nodes are in parenthesis.

We can see that after only N iterations of the Monte Carlo Crawler and instead of the N^2 of our Simple Crawler, the influence of a node is already close to what it will be after N^2 iterations. We can see that after only N iterations instead of N^2, the influence of a node is already close to what it will be after N^2 iterations.

d. Our Approach

Simple Crawler and Monte Carlo Crawler are based on the Targeted Crawler algorithm (Humbert, Studer, Grossglauser, & Hubaux, 2013). The issue with this algorithm is that sometimes the frontier spread in

Table 1. Monte Carlo Crawler vs. Simple Crawler

Node Id	Simple Crawler	Monte Carlo Crawler
206	16.3(1)	17.2(1)
422	9.8(2)	7.87(4)
170	9.6(3)	8.91(2)
938	8.4(4)	4.48(5)
675	7.1(5)	8.91(2)

the wrong direction and this can lead to unnecessary time consumption to find the path from a source to a target. Simple Crawler showed that it is possible to compute an influence value for a node. Monte Carlo Crawler showed that it is possible to compute this value in a reasonable amount of time. From the two previous approaches, we can conclude the goal for our third approach should be finding a navigation algorithm that (a) should not go back or expand in the wrong direction, (b) should be computable in a reasonable amount of time and (c) should hop using influential nodes of the network. Authors in (Wang, Pedreschi, Song, Giannotti, & Barabasi) showed that mobility measures alone yield surprising predictive power, comparable to traditional network and similarity between two individuals' movements strongly correlates with their proximity in the social network. We use some quantities, which have been proven to perform reasonably well in previous studies (Wang, Pedreschi, Song, Giannotti, & Barabasi).

Computing the Influence Value (IV) of a node N_i in a path P_i from source node S to target node T is defined as a function with multiple parameters:

$$IV(N_i) = \lambda_1 a + \lambda_2 b + \lambda_3 c + \lambda_4 d + \lambda_5 e + \lambda_6 f \tag{2}$$

where each λ_i is a predefined weight parameter and (a) The number of direct friends (DF) of N_i: with V the set of vertices and E the set of edges of the network, direct friends of a node Ni are the friends that are reachable with a path of length one. They are defined by equation (3):

$$DF(N_i) = \left\{ f \mid f \in V \text{ and } (N_i, f) \in E \right\} \tag{3}$$

1. **Shared Neighbors (SN):** If Ni and T share a direct friend, then there is a path of length 2 going from N_i to T. Common neighbors are defined in equation (4):

$$SN\left(N_i, T\right) = \left\{ f \mid f \in DF(N_i) \text{ and } f \in DF(T) \right\} \tag{4}$$

2. The number of attributes in common.
3. The number of unique attributes.
4. **Distance to T:** The distance between N_i and T is computed using attributes of the nodes. The more attribute they share, the smaller their distance is. See equation 5. Here J is the set of available attributes in Online Social Network and $A_j\left(N_i\right)$ is the attribute j of node N_i. The distance function can be simplified as in equation 5:

$$dist\left(N_i, T\right) = \mid J \mid - \sum_{j \in J} bool\left(A_j\left(N_i\right) == A_j\left(T_i\right)\right) \tag{5}$$

5. The already crawled path: this is a list of nodes that have already been visited by the algorithm. Our Influence Crawler algorithm is defined in Table 2. Each time from the source node, we choose the highest influential friend and then consider this friend as the next hop until the target is reached.

Table 2. Algorithm of Influence Crawler

Algorithm 1 Influence Crawler

Input: N_i, S, T
Path: $= \varnothing$
Current: $= S$
While current $\notin$ DF (T) do
f* = friend of current with maximum influence
If IV (f*) > 0 then
Add f* to path
Current = f*
Else ◁ Dead end case
Failure
End if
End while

As our Influence Crawler is executed, multiples issues have to be resolved. In the early stage of routing, the distance between N_i and T decreases rapidly until we are in a virtual area where nodes are highly similar. People that share a lot are usually connected. As the diameter of the Facebook graph is around 6 (Ugander, Karrer, Backstrom & Marlow, 2011), we can consider that N_i has a high probability of having friends in common with T once our algorithm run for 4 to 5 iterations. At this point, we can use the set of shared neighbors between N_i and T to help our algorithm to select the next hop more efficiently. The similarity between N_i and T defined in (c) is also a measure of relative proximity. In Online Social Networks, we are generally connected to people that look like us. Hence the more similar N_i and T are, the higher chance there is a short path between them.

Our influence values (as illustrated in Table 3) should be higher for nodes that are in the direction of the target. The already crawled path is passed as an argument of our influence function defined in

Table 3. Algorithm for calculating Influence Value

Algorithm 2 Influence Value
Function IV (N_i) If $N_i \in$ path then ◁ uses (f) Influence = 0 Else if $N_i \in$ DF (T) then ◁ uses (b) Influence = K Else if $N_i \in$ DF (DF (T)) then ◁ uses (b) Influence = L Else ◁ uses (a)(c)(d)(e) Influence = M−α_Dist (N_i , T)+β *|DF (N_i)| End if Return influence End function With K > L > M

equation (2). This allows our algorithm to select those nodes that are close to the source. The crawler can now return the next hop more efficiently by knowing what are the previous hops.

The correct direction of spreading can be defined as the direction that returns one of the shortest paths between S and T, but not necessarily the shortest as it is impossible to know the shortest path without exploring the whole graph. The next hop should be chosen carefully because with our "can't go back" feature, we can't risk our algorithm to go in a dead-end direction. This can be avoided by making a compromise between two factors: (a) the next hop should be closer to the target and (b) the next hop should be as connected as possible. If we favor (a) we are at risk to go straight and found ourselves in an impasse. If we favor (b), we risk finding ourselves with an inefficient algorithm that is running in circle.

5. SIMULATION RESULTS

In Tables 4-6 we compare our Influence Crawler with the Targeted Crawler. Data have been extracted by running the two algorithms on the same random source and target nodes.

We can see that our Influence Crawler founds the target node in a less number of iterations. However it is also possible that our Influence Crawler doesn't find a path when one exists. Our Influence Crawler stops in two cases: (i) it reaches a dead-end in the graph because the algorithm made bad choices during its execution or (ii) we arbitrarily stop it because it takes too long comparing to the Targeted Crawler and our goal is to make an algorithm that is more efficient. Our Influence Crawler is constructed such as it

Table 4. Average results for 1000 iterations of the crawlers.

	Target Crawler	Influence Crawler	Difference
# Iterations	17.746	2.92	-83.5%
Path length	2.495	2.436	-2.4%
Time (ms)	1.303	0.393	-69.8%
Success rate	80.4%	51.6%	-28.8%

Table 5. Success only

	Target Crawler	Influence Crawler	Difference
# Iterations	19.327	2.754	-85.8%
Path length	3.103	2.754	-11.3%

Table 6. Average results for 1000 iterations of the Influence Crawler followed by the Targeted Crawler if failure.

	Target Crawler then Influential Crawler	Difference
# Iterations	14.243	-10.2%
Time (ms)	1.249	-4%
Success rate	80.4%	0%

adds a node to the general path at each iteration. Therefore the length of the returned path will always be equal to the number of iterations of the algorithm whereas in the Targeted Crawler, the length of the path is usually much smaller than the number of iterations.

Considering results in Table 4, we have a success rate of 50% with our Influence Crawler for 2.4 iterations in average. This means our Crawler fails 50% of the time, as depicted in Table 5. The number of iteration for a fail case is at most 8. In the case our Influence Crawler fails, we decide to run the Targeted Crawler to find a path instead. With this in mind, we can compute the average number of iteration needed to find a path between two nodes.

This means the combination of the Targeted Crawler and our Influence Crawler runs in average 10% less iterations and has 50% chance of finding a path in 83% less iterations, as indicated in Table 6.

6. CONCLUSION

The purpose of quantifying influence in Online Social Networks is to determine influence within the members of an Online Social Network. Then using influence for navigation in such networks. We find out that we can take advantage of influential people in Online Social Networks to reach a target in such network. Our navigation algorithm returns a path between two nodes in an average of 10% less iterations, with a maximum of 83% less iterations, and only relies on public attributes of a node in the network. We hope to develop a network perspective as a powerful way of looking at complex systems in general and a way of thinking about social dynamics, internal structure and feedback effects of the social networks.

ACKNOWLEDGMENT

The authors would like to acknowledge Mr. Bastien Lebayle for his contributions to this chapter.

REFERENCES

Acquisti, A. (2012). *An experiment in hiring discrimination via online social networks*. Berkeley.

Adamic, L. A., & Adar, E. (2003). *Friends and neighbors on the web*. ScienceDirect.

Albert, R. (1999). The diameter of the World Wide Web. *Nature, 401*(6749), 130–131. doi:10.1038/43601

Backstrom, L., Huttenlocher, D., & Kleinberg, J. (2006). *Group Formation in Large Social Networks: Membership, Groeth, and Evolution*. KDD. doi:10.1145/1150402.1150412

Borgatti, S. (2006). Identifying sets of key players in a social network. *Computational & Mathematical Organization Theory, 12*(1), 21–34. doi:10.1007/s10588-006-7084-x

Chaabane, A., Acs, G., & Kaafar, M. (2012). *You are what you like! Information leakage through users' interests*. NDSS.

Cho, J., & Roy, S. (2004). Impact of search engines on page popularity. *International World Wide Web Conference*. doi:10.1145/988672.988676

Dey, R., Tang, C., Ross, K., & Saxena, N. (2012). *Estimating age privacy leakage in online social networks*. INFOCOM. doi:10.1109/INFCOM.2012.6195711

Dunn, C., Gupta, M., Gerber, A., & Spatscheck, O. (2012). *Navigation Characteristics of Online Social Networks and Search Engines Users*. WOSN. doi:10.1145/2342549.2342560

Easley, D., & Kleinberg, J. (2010). *Networks Crowds and Markets*. Cambridge. doi:10.1017/CBO9780511761942

Ghosh, R., & Lerman, K. (2008). *Community Detection using a Measure of Global Influence*. KDD.

Ghosh, R., & Lerman, K. (2010). *Predicting Influential Users in Online Social Networks*. KDD.

Humbert, M., Studer, T., Grossglauser, M., & Hubaux, J. P. (2013). *Nowhere to hide: Navigation around privacy in online in social networks*. The 18th European Symposium on Research in Computer Security (ESORICS). doi:10.1007/978-3-642-40203-6_38

Ilyas, M. U., & Radha, H. (2011). Identifying influential nodes in online social networks using principal component centrality. *IEEE International Conference*. doi:10.1109/icc.2011.5963147

Lattanzi, S., Panconesi A. & Sivakumar D. (2011). *Milgram-Routing in Social Networks*. The International World Wide Web, IW3C2.

Liben-Nowell, D., & Kleinberg, J. (2007). The Link Prediction Problem for Social Networks. *Journal of the American Society for Information Science and Technology*, 58(7), 1019–1031. doi:10.1002/asi.20591

Milgram, S. (1967). The small world problem. *Psychology Today*, *1*, 61.

Pedarsani, P. (2013). *Privacy and dynamics of social networks*. Ecole Polytechnique Federale de Lausanne.

Ugander, J., Karrer, B., Backstrom, L., & Marlow, C. (2011). *The anatomy of the Facebook social graph*. Cornell University.

Wang, D., Pedreschi, D., Song, C., Giannotti, F., & Barabasi, A. (2011). Human mobility, social ties and link prediction. *KDD Conference*. doi:10.1145/2020408.2020581

KEY TERMS AND DEFINITIONS

Attributes: A predefined set of properties of a node in a network.

Influence: The ability of persuading people to do an action.

Navigation: Staring from one source node in a network and traversing different paths in order to reach to a specific destination node.

Neighboring Nodes: Nodes in a network that share a link.

Node Similarities: Common attributes among different nodes.

Online Social Networks: When people interact with each other over the Internet.

Web Crawlers: Algorithms that are being used to do navigation on a network.

Chapter 17

Comparative Analysis of Efficient Platforms:
Scalable Algorithms and Parallel Paradigms for Large Scale Image Processing

Khawaja Tehseen Ahmed
Bahauddin Zakariya Univeristy, Pakistan

Arsalaan Ahmed Shaikh
NUST School of Electrical Engineering and Computer Science, Pakistan

Mazhar Ul-Haq
NUST School of Electrical Engineering and Computer Science, Pakistan

Raihan ur Rasool
NUST School of Electrical Engineering and Computer Science, Pakistan

ABSTRACT

With the advancement of technology we are heading towards a paperless environment. But there are still a large numbers of documents that exist in paper format in our daily lives. Thus the need to digitize these paper documents, archive them and view them at all times has arisen. The number of documents of a small organization may be in thousands, millions or even more. This chapter presents comparative analysis of different programming languages and libraries where it is intended to parallel process a huge stream of images which undergo unpredictable arrival of the images and variation in time. Since the parallelism can be implemented at different levels, different algorithms and techniques have also been discussed. It also presents the state of the art and discussion of various existing technical solutions to implement the parallelization on a hybrid platform for the real time processing of the images contained in a stream. Experimental results obtained using Apache Hadoop in combination with OpenMP have also been discussed.

1. INTRODUCTION

This research is part of an ongoing project that aims to offer a service of dematerialization of documents to very small enterprises. Dematerialization is being done in order to archive documents that exist in a paper form, and efficiently retrieve them on demand from anywhere. When this service will be operational, scanners located in very small firms will be able to digitize paper documents before sending these

DOI: 10.4018/978-1-4666-8505-5.ch017

so obtained numeric images to a server. Then, this server will process the received images in order, on one hand, to improve the quality of and, on the other hand, to reduce the volume of the digitized images. This process has been described in Figure 1.

Finally, the processed images will be communicated to an archiving center which will allow the owner of an archived document, to consult its digital image. For this purpose data and task parallelism is required for High Performance Computing and the processing of every image may contain tasks which could be run in parallel on the various cores of each computational node. Image processing is widely applied in many applications such as medical image processing, non-photorealistic rendering, remote sensing, optical sorting and many more. The processing of the flow of images is difficult to characterize. Some applications require to process images that are of very large size and require that all the processing can be done in a very short interval of time. The throughput of arrival of the images may undergo great and unpredictable variations according to the time and the duration of the processing of an image can also undergo great and unpredictable variations according to the image type and size. The overall process can be divided into three portions scanning and transmitting, processing and archival. The focus of this study is towards the processing module which receives images and processes them. Our aim is to study the problems that may arise in this area and technologies that address them, and propose and test a solution. Following are some areas of concern: Processing of images that are contained in a stream. The number of images to process at any given time may vary to a great extent The processing time is dynamic and depends on each individual image Because of the varying amount of load on the processing module, a scalable platform is needed to be identified and technologies that provide parallelism have to be studied so that the system efficiently processes high number of images in a certain amount of time. This chapter describes various aspects of different technologies related to image processing on hybrid platform. The objective of this research is to analyze various technical solutions in parallel image processing, where different techniques are compared to each other, and the best suited techniques are suggested for parallel image processing on large scalable infrastructure. Section 2 analyzes different platforms and argues

Figure 1. Conversion and archival of documents

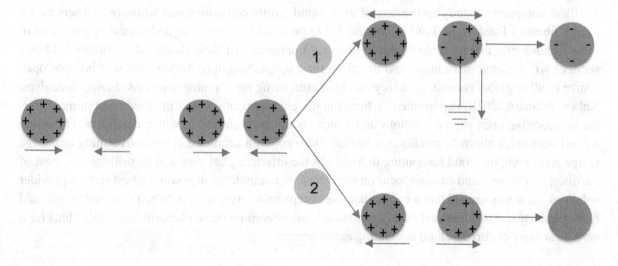

for the suitability of one of them on the basis of different measures and benefits. Section 3 presents different programming languages and libraries for parallel image processing (task parallelism), while section 4 discusses few techniques and algorithms for data parallelism. Section 5 gives the detail of the experiments conducted and test the environment. Section 6 concludes and suggests the future directions.

2. RELATED WORK

In cloud computing comparative study, surveys and analysis performed in web services, image processing, networks, distributed computing and utility computing. Purpose of these activities is to envision the future of cloud computing, highlight the strengthening and weaknesses of this interactive environment, present ideologies for its progression. Such kind of comparative study performed on distributed load balancing (Randles, Lamb, & Taleb-Bendiab, 2010) for cloud computing to achieve fault tolerance, scalability, and maximum availability by centrally focusing load balancing. Another effort made to identify the similarities and differences of the architectural approaches of cloud computing (Rimal, Choi, & Lumb, 2009). Areas for future research are also highlighted by this survey. Taxonomy introduced to describe the cloud computing architecture and existing services like Google and Amazon. A Comparative Study of the Current Cloud Computing Technologies and Offers (Mahjoub, Mdhaffar, Halima, & Jmaiel, 2011) was conducted with the aim to facilitate the users to easily choose the better competitive cloud service provider match with their need. They also presented the ways to be able to build own cloud infrastructure with available open source tools and technologies. Performance of cloud computing for scientific computing workload (Iosup, Ostermann, Yigitbasi, Prodan, Rahringer, & Epema, 2011) is focused for load scheduling. For this Many-Task Computing (MTC) in real scientific computing was quantified. In MTC, users employ loosely coupled applications comprising many tasks to achieve their scientific goals. Experimentation performed for comparative results based on commercial services including Amazon EC2. Analysis performed to enhance virtualization by presenting the performance of the Amazon EC2 platform using micro-benchmarks and kernels for evaluation of the usefulness of the current cloud computing services for scientific computing (Ostermann, Iosup, Yigitbasi, Prodan, Rahringer, & Epema, 2010). A comparative study and review of grid, cloud, utility computing and software as a service for use by libraries Patel, Syfi, Tew, & Jaradat, 2011) presented to foster the understanding and need of these technologies in applicable contexts. Practical implication of their sharing show future of library services will become more integrated based on their usage. Secondly the services will become open source to all at global context. A survey on cloud computing open source solutions (Endo, Goncalves, Kelner, & Sadok, 2010) is presented by focusing the environmental issues in cloud computing, different comparative open source solutions and which should be preferred in which condition. This gives a good startup for alternate candidate selection. Here comes a need of a comparative study of a large image processing on cloud computing to highlight the efficient platforms and algorithms. As most of the discussed surveys and analysis focus on web services, computational powers or best service provider solutions but it was needed that a comprehensive comparative analysis should be presented that should focus platforms, algorithms and experimentation results based on these platforms and algorithms for a very clear view of current cloud computing environments.

3. ANALYSIS OF PLATFORMS AND COMPUTING TECHNOLOGIES

This section discusses different options for scalable and efficient computing and discusses history of computing in brief in order to suggest a platform for this particular project. Over the period of time, scientific community has come across different computing paradigms to achieve high performance and scalability through commodity machines, which include Grid, Utility, Ubiquitous and Cloud computing. Each technique has its own benefits and limitations. In Grid computing the resources were combined from the different administrative domains to reach a common goal (Resource Sharing) and each node could get and contribute its resources to the resource pool. Grid computing intended to create a virtual super computer by connecting different remote machines. Unfortunately Grids did not make a little headway outside the academic circles and is considered to be a 'hard to implement' technology. With the passage of time technologies evolved and converged in to a service model, and it's when Utility and Ubiquitous Computing came in. Utility computing emphasized on combining computer resources and services into a package as a metered service. The idea of resource utilization is just similar to the public utility such as water, electricity, natural gas and telephone. After the introduction of utility computing, SAAS (Software as a service) model became famous which is basically all about 'Software on emand', where internet is a delivery and development platform. With the improvements in virtualization technology and the introduction of SAAS model a new kind of computing platform emerged namely Cloud, where everything can be made available in the form of service (X as a Service). Cloud computing appears to be a more compelling paradigm as it offers resources as a service (Infrastructure as a Service (IaaS)) and deliver them on IP-based connectivity providing highly scalable, reliable on-demand. Cloud computing offers a number of benefits including listed below.

- Software on Subscription,
- Reduced Software Maintenance,
- Increased Reliability,
- Increased Scalability,
- Cost Reduction,
- Portability/Accessibility,
- Efficient Use of Computer Resources,
- Versionless Software.

High performance computing can be achieved through Clusters, Grids and Supercomputers. However Cloud computing combines the benefits of all and excludes their limitations. With the help of a scalable platform like Cloud, efficient processing of image streams can be realized through the implementation of data and task parallelism.

4. COMPARATIVE ANALYSIS OF PROGRAMMING LANGUAGES AND LIBRARIES

In the Table 1 we can see the analysis of different options that we have for parallel programming and their performance in different perspectives. A. Analysis Outcomes Here are some outcomes and results observed:

Table 1. Comparison of different programming languages and libraries

Features	UPC	OpenMP	PVM	CAF	MPI	PThreads
Efficiency	Yes (Karypis & Kumar, 1998)	Yes (Chapman, Jost, & Van Der Pas, 2008)	Yes (Kasprzyk, Nawrowski, & Tomczewski, 2002)	Yes (Midkiff, 2005)	Yes (Gropp, Lusk, Doss, & Skjellum, 1996)	Yes (Dongarra, 2008)
Portability	Yes (Karypis & Kumar, 1998)	Yes (Chapman, Jost, & Van Der Pas, 2008)	Yes (Buyya, 1999)	No (Bode, 2000)	Yes (Gropp, Lusk, Doss, & Skjellum, 1996)	Yes (Dongarra, 2008)
Data Parallelism	Yes (Hierarchical parallelism) (Adiga, Almasi, Aridor, Barik, Beece, Bellofatto, & Lu, 2002)	Yes (Eigenmann & de Supinski, 2008)	Yes (Pollard, Mewhort, & Weaver, 2000)	SPDM (Single Program Multiple Data) (Li & Midkiff, 2005) (Fitch, Rayshubskiy, Eleftheriou, Ward, Giampapa, Zhestkov, & Germain, 2006)	Yes (Pacheco, 1997)	No (Blume, Doallo, Rauchwerger, Tu, Eigenmann, Grout, & Pottenger, 1996)
Task Parallelism	Yes (Hierarchical parallelism) (Adiga, Almasi, Aridor, Barik, Beece, Bellofatto, & Lu, 2002)	No (Zheng, Wang, & Wu, 2010)	Yes (Sterling, 2002)	Yes (Woerner, Wright, Profet, Bryan, & Williamson, n.d.)	Yes (Pacheco, 1997)	Yes (Bruaset & Tveito, 2006)
Reliability	Yes (Noeth, Ratn, Mueller, Schulz, & de Supinski, 2009)	Yes (Chapman, Jost, & Van Der Pas, 2008)	Yes (Kasprzyk, Nawrowski, & Tomczewski, 2002)	Yes (Grandinetti, 2005)	Yes (Dongarra, Laforenza, & Orlando, 2003)	Yes (Moderate in some cases) (Domeika, 2011)
Development Cost	Moderate (Lin & Franklin, 2004)	Low(Eigenmann & de Supinski, 2008) (Dongarra, Laforenza, & Orlando, 2003)	Less (Ropo, Westerholm, & Dongarra, 2009)	Less (Almasi, Cascaval, & Wu, 2007)	High (Dongarra, Laforenza, & Orlando, 2003)	High (Yu, Zhou, & Wu, 2002)
Hardware Cost	Less (Moderate in some cases) (Vajtersic, Zinterhof, & Trobec, 2009)	Moderate (Altintas, Birnbaum, Baldridge, Sudholt, Miller, Amoreira, & Ludaescher, 2005)	Moderate (Gropp, 2002)	High (in some cases) (Patterson, Snir, & Graham, 2005)	Moderate/ Less in some cases (Gropp, Lusk, Doss, & Skjellum, 1996)	Moderate (Laplante, 1993)
Distributed Memory	Yes (Schwiegelshohn, Badia, Bubak, Danelutto, Dustdar, Gagliardi, & Von Voigt, 2010)	No (Alexandrov, van Albada, Sloot, & Dongarra, 2006)	Yes (Hellwagner & Reinefeld, 1999)	Yes (Krause, Shokin, Resch, & Shokina, 2011)	Yes (Rose, Gelijns, Moskowitz, Heitjan, Stevenson, Dembitsky, & Meier, 2001)	No (Blume, Doallo, Rauchwerger, Tu, Eigenmann, Grout, & Pottenger, 1996)

continued on following page

Table 1. Continued

Features	UPC	OpenMP	PVM	CAF	MPI	PThreads
Shared Memory	Yes (Karypis & Kumar, 1998)	Yes (Yang & Guo, 2005)	Yes (Beguelin, Dongarra, Geist, Manchek, & Sunderam, 1991)	Yes (Krause, Shokin, Resch, & Shokina, 2011)	Yes (Karniadakis & Kirby, 2003)	Yes (Blume, Doallo, Rauchwerger, Tu, Eigenmann, Grout, & Pottenger, 1996)
Scalability	Yes (Karypis & Kumar, 1998)	Less/ Restricted (Chapman, 2005)	Yes (Ropo, Westerholm, & Dongarra, 2009)	Yes (Rus, Rauchwerger, & Hoeflinger, 2003)	Yes (Dongarra, Laforenza, & Orlando, 2003)	Yes (Gropp & Lusk, 1998)
Communicational Issues	Less (Malawski, Meizner, Bubak, & Gepner, 2011)	Less (Hanawa, Muller, Chapman, & de Supinski, 2010)	Moderate, High (in some cases) (Yeo, Park, Yang, & Hsu, 2010)	Moderate (Silva, Dutra, & Costa, 2014)	Moderate (Hager & Wellein, 2010)	High (Gropp & Lusk, 1998)
Programming Efforts	Less (Moderate is some cases) (Bischof, 2008)	More (Dongarra, Laforenza, & Orlando, 2003)	Moderate (Dongarra, Laforenza, & Orlando, 2003)	High (Bode, 2000)	More (Tveito, Langtangen, Nielsen, & Cai, 2010) (Tullsen, Eggers, & Levy, 1995)	More (Yu, Zhou, & Wu, 2002)
HPC	Yes (Anderson, Bai, Bischof, Blackford, Demmel, Dongarra, & Sorensen, 1999)	Yes (Yang & Guo, 2005)	Yes (Cerqueira, 2007)	Yes (Nakamura, Hochstein, & Basili, 2006)	Yes (Cerqueira, 2007)	No (Chandra, 2001)
Development Time	Less (Doerffer, Hirsch, Dussauge, Babinsky, & Barakos, 2010)	Less (Eigenmann & de Supinski, 2008)	Less (Adam, Jack, Weicheng, Robert, & Sunderam, n.d.)	Moderate (Stone, 1973)	Less(while using library functions) (Rego & Sunderam, 1992)	More (Yu, Zhou, & Wu, 2002)

- Global shared memory model of UPC has ability of easy access of non-localdata in parallel program using thru global pointers.
- User level shared memory is not good for in cluster usage.
- Shared memory programming leads towards poor performance on clusters.
- Hybrid programming model uses optimistically fine-grain and coarse-grain access.Results shows that programmers must careful using global pointer for remote access cost is too high while good performance is achieved in MPI on clusters.
- UPC supports fine-grain programming model and it can achieve good performance on clusters only if fine-grain remote accesses are used carefully.
- Coarse-grain parallel algorithms and bulk communications are required for good performance and it is in case of naïve implementation and absolute performance on cluster is poor that the difference will be Insignificant.
- For highest performance, message passing paradigm like MPI or SHMEM will give the best performance

- If 'Program Development Time' is major concern then choose a hybrid UPC implementation and use bulk and collective communication schemes
- On Clusters, fine-grain languages are slow so use these for small data and run on SMP otherwise use coarse-grain

A. Analysis Conclusion

In this section fine-grain, coarse-grain technologies Open (Open Multi-Processing), MPI, UPC, Java, PThread, CAF, and PVM having shared and distributed memory models were compared feature-wise in a tabular format to show a clear picture of their performance parameters. Table 1 shows that MPI and OpenMP have best Parallel computing performance parameters and work well in heavy load. A suitable option out of MPI and OpenMP will be finalized after having a comparison of shared and distributed memory model with respect to our needs.

B. Comparison between OpenMP and MPI

The Table 2 compares OpenMP with MPI. In some cases OpenMP works much better than MPI on a multi-core server for the same application. In other cases, MPI has been shown to run faster. It depends upon an application, that what type of parallelization we want to implement.

Table 2. Comparison of MPI with OpenMP

Features	OpenMP	MPI
Portability	Yes(Chapman, Jost, & Van Der Pas, 2008)	yes (Gropp, Lusk, Doss, & Skjellum, 1996)
Scalability	Less(Chapman, 2005)	more (Dongarra, Laforenza, & Orlando, 2003)
Reliability	Yes(Chapman, Jost, & Van Der Pas, 2008)	yes (Dongarra, Laforenza, & Orlando, 2003)
Distributed Memory	Does not support(Alexandrov, van Albada, Sloot, & Dongarra, 2006)	Supports shared memory systems(Rose, Gelijns, Moskowitz, Heitjan, Stevenson, Dembitsky, & Meier, 2001)
Shared memory	Support shared memory systems (Yang & Guo, 2005)	Support shared memory systems(Karniadakis & Kirby, 2003)
Data parallelism	Supports Data Parallelism(Eigenmann & de Supinski, 2008)	Supports Data Parallelism(Pacheco, 1997)
Task parallelism	Does not support Task parallelism(Zheng, Wang, & Wu, 2010)	Supports Task Parallelism(Pacheco, 1997)
Costly	Yes(Altintas, Birnbaum, Baldridge, Sudholt, Miller, Amoreira, & Ludaescher, 2005)	Less costly(Gropp, Lusk, Doss, & Skjellum, 1996)
Communication issues	Less communication Issues(Hanawa, Muller, Chapman, & de Supinski, 2010)	More communication issues(Hager & Wellein, 2010)
Debugging	Less harder to Debug(Dongarra, Laforenza, & Orlando, 2003)	Harder to Debug(Tveito, Langtangen, Nielsen, & Cai, 2010)(Tullsen, Eggers, & Levy, 1995)
Programming efforts	Relatively less Required(Dongarra, Laforenza, & Orlando, 2003)	Relatively more required(Tveito, Langtangen, Nielsen, & Cai, 2010)(Tullsen, Eggers, & Levy, 1995)
Multithreading/Multi Processing	Multithreading(Chapman, Jost, & Van Der Pas, 2008)	Multiprocessing(Dongarra, Laforenza, & Orlando, 2003)

5. COMPARISON OF TECHNIQUES AND ALGORITHMS FOR DATA PARALLELISM

This section compares features, advantages and drawbacks of solutions available for data parallelism. Table 3 compares some frameworks for processing large data sets.

It is evident that all of the presented solutions can be used in our project; however Hadoop is best suited since it works on unstructured data very efficiently. Hadoop is used to develop software for reliable, scalable, distributed computing. And for task parallelism simple concepts of process threads are being used. The two main sub projects that we are most interested in are Hadoop Distributed File System and Hadoops implementation of MapReduce. MapReduce is a framework for processing huge datasets on certain kinds of distributable problems using a large number of computers (nodes), collectively referred to as a cluster. Computational processing can occur on data stored either in a file system (unstructured) or within a database (structured). MapReduce is useful in a wide range of applications and architectures including: "distributed grep, distributed sort, web link-graph reversal, term-vector per host, web access log stats, inverted index construction, document clustering, machine learning, and statistical machine translation".

Processing Images Streams with Apache Hadoop

The HDFS (Hadoop Distributed File System) can prove to be very advantages to our project, one of the major hurdles that will be faced is the distribution of images over the data processing nodes in a bal-

Table 3. Comparison of the frameworks (Hadoop, GridGain, Hazelcast, DAC)

Feature/Framework	GridGain	Hadoop	Hazelcast	DAC
Map/Reduce paradigm	Yes (Chang, Chao, Lin, & Sloot, 2010)	Yes (Zhao, Rong, Jaatun, & Sandnes, 2010)	Yes (Telesca, Stanocvska-Slabeva, & Rakocevic, 2009)	Yes (Frachtenberg & Schwiegelshohn, 2008)
Load balancing and Scheduling	Yes (Lopez, Shon, & Taniar, n.d.)	Yes (Doulamis, Mambretti, & Tomkos, 2010)	Yes (Telesca, Stanoevska-Slabeva, & Rakocevic, 2009)	Yes (Coello, 1999)
JMX-based Management & Monitoring	Yes (Zoumas, Bakirtzis, Theocharis, & Petridis, 2004)	Yes (Venner, 2009)	Yes (Telesca, Stanoevska-Slabeva, Rakocevic, 2009)	Yes (de Castro, Gomez, Quintela, & Salgado, 2007)
Fail-safe	Yes (Chao, Obaidat, & Kim, 2011)	Yes (Alippi, Bouchon-Meunier, Greenwood, & Abbass, n.d.)	Yes (Telesca, Stanoevska-Slabeva, Rakocevic, 2009)	Yes (Fox & Zhuge, 2007)
Zero deployment Model	Yes (Chao, Obaidat, & Kim, 2011)	Yes (White, 2012)	Yes (Mak, Long, & Rubio, 2010)	Yes (Han, Tai, & Wikarski, 2002)
Hybrid Cloud	Yes (Buyya, Broberg, & Goscinski, 2010)	Yes (Buyya, Broberg, & Goscinski, 2010)	Yes (Buyya, Broberg, & Goscinski, 2010)	Yes (Das, Stephen, & Chaba, 2011)
Multiple nodes in one VM	Yes (Bellavista, Chang, & Chao, n.d.)	Yes (Olston & Najork, 2010)	Yes (Olston & Najork, 2010)	Yes (Unger, Bohme, & Mikler, 2002)
Works on unstructured Data	No (http://apache.org)	Yes (http://apache.org)	No (http://apache.org)	No (Das, Stephen, & Chaba, 2011)
JEE integration	Yes (Mak & Long, 2009)	No (Gruhn & Oquendo, 2006)	Yes (Mak, Long, & Rubio, 2010)	No (Fox & Zhuge, 2007)

anced and efficient way, HDFS provides a managed environment for this very purpose, it hides all the intricacies of managing data on different nodes and it provides a sort of virtualization to the interacting system which views the HDFS as a single file system. A file copied on the HDFS is distributed over the nodes in a balanced way. Although the distributed file system has many benefits there are also some disadvantages of using Apache Hadoop, there is a major degradation of performance if the files are smaller in size and larger in number, which is the case in this project as the size of each image is very small compared to the default block size (64 MB) of the HDFS and the number of images at peak time can exceed 18,000. The hadoop community recommends the opposite which is smaller number of files of large size. Although this issue is of grave nature as performance is critical for this project, there is a solution. Hadoop provides sequence file structure which stores binary data in key value pairs. Formally Apache Hadoop'ssequence file provides a persistent data structure for binary key-value pairs. In contrast with other key-value data structures such as B-Trees it cannot be edited, added or removed but it can be appended which suits our case perfectly. Data is placed in the sequence file in three possible ways.

- **Raw:** No compression is applied on the data.
- **Record Compression:** Each record, in our case the byte representation of each image is compressed and stored in the sequence file.
- **Block Compression:** The data of multiple records are compressed together and then placed within a sequence file.

Although a thorough analysis has not been conducted yet on the three different placement techniques, preliminary tests have given striking results. In one test 46 images with total size of 128 MB were compressed to just 4.2 MB so the potential of Apache Hadoop in terms utilizing storage resources efficiently is evident.

Figure 2 illustrates the proposed architecture using Apache Hadoop. The stream of images is received by the job scheduler and data processing server which marshals the images and appends them to a sequence file which will be processed in the next job schedule. The sequence file resides over several data and task performing nodes which collectively make the HDFS. Once the job scheduling server executes a job, Hadoop's MapReduce is utilized for the actual image processing of the streams embedded in the sequence file. Experimentation has been divided into following three phases;

A. Configuration Phase

In this phase configuration and setup of the above architecture is discussed. Currently we have configured Hadoop on Dell machines using Ubuntu 10.10 as base operating system. Following are the configurations. Cluster consists of two Dell Inspiron 1525 machines with dual core processors.

- 3 GB RAM.
- HDFS 20 GB.
- Operating System Ubuntu 10.10

Another more advanced cluster has also been setup using the following configurations, where cluster consists of two Apple IMac Desktop machines.

Figure 2. Architecture of Processing Module

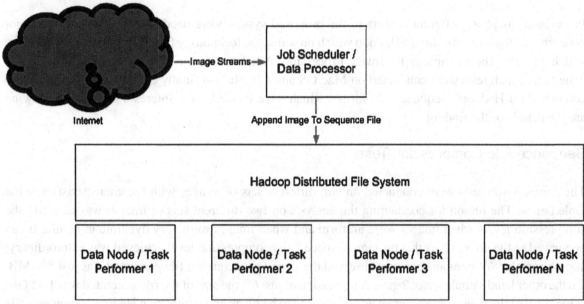

- 4GB RAM
- HDFS 1 TB
- Operating System Mac OS X Snow Leopard

Both cluster setups are ready. Another option will be considered to combine both the clusters thus introducing heterogeneity.

B. Development Phase

In the development phase a sample application for image processing was to be developed and a sample space of digital documents had to be arranged. Following are some of the main components.

- **Sequence File Generator:** The component marshals an image and appends its marshaled form into a sequence file.
- **Hadoop MapReduce Classes:** The Map class contains the code to gather images from a sequence file and forwards them to the
- **Reducer Class:** The reducer class holds the code to un-marshal the image along with the image processing logic.

Sequence File Generator and MapReduce Classes have been successfully coded and deployed. Java OCR has been used for image processing. Java OCR has been used to test some sort of image processing going on. Images of scanned text books have been used for sample space.

C. Analysis Phase

In the analysis phase different aspects of the proposed system were needed to be analyzed. A major concern was the compatibility of Hadoop which provided the technology for data parallelism, with C++ which provided the technology for Image Processing. Another area for analysis was platform heterogeneity in which tests were conducted on Mac OS and Ubuntu and finally compression analysis were conducted on Hadoop's sequence file format which have yielded some interesting results. Following are the details of the finding.

Sequence File Compression Tests

The compression tests were conducted on two different sets of images with the characteristics in the table below. The reason for conducting the analysis on two different sets of images was to verify the compression levels when images were uniform and when images were very dynamic in nature. It can be viewed in the above chart that on sample space 1 the compression level achieved was extraordinary; approximately 96% compression was observed the size of the sequence file generated was just 898 MB. On the other hand sample space 2 gave compression of just 6% the size of the file generated was 1.45 GB. If majority of the documents scanned are considered to be black and white, then Hadoop's sequence file could be deemed a success to such an extent that a change in the original architecture can be proposed. The architecture can be changed such that sequence file generation process could be embedded in the client module thus reducing huge amount of internet traffic and required bandwidth

D. Compatibility between Hadoop, C++ and Open MP

Hadoop which uses java as its primary language has provided interfaces for communication with different programming languages, for Python and Ruby it uses streams and for C++ it uses pipes. For an efficient relationship between Hadoop and C++ a highly reliable pipes interface implementation was required. Unfortunately this is not the case with Hadoop as there are some major glitches in its pipes implementation. Therefore other alternatives were studied, some suggested approaches were to remain inside the boundary of java and to provide task parallelism using java threads or Titanium which is an explicitly parallel dialect for java developed at UC Berkley to support high performance scientific computing on large scale multiprocessors. Other techniques that could be used were using Java Native Interfaces or CORBA to communicate with C/C++ thus allowing Hadoop to be compatible with it.

Table 4.

Characteristics	Sample Space 1	Sample Space 2
Number of Images	9865	2366
Total Size	20.6 GB	1.54 GB
Image Resolution	No fixed resolution but all were above 800:600	Contained images with very small and very large resolution
Color Scheme	Black & White	Images with wide variety of colors

Figure 3. Compressed Size of Images Compared with Original Size

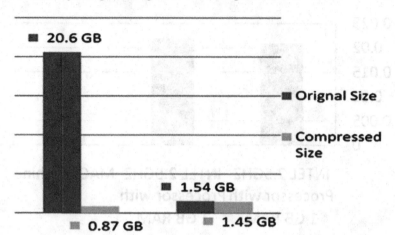

Although exploring Java only solutions was an option but it only satisfied the need of task parallelism that is why more emphasis was given to JNI through which successful compatibility was achieved. While running a job on Hadoop, C++ and OpenMP no major degradation except for overhead of JNI which was 0.01 millisecond per Image was observed therefore no optimization was gained, but it must be noted that the test program was trivial and true nature of the effects of OpenMP could yet be attained by running compute intensive tasks specially it will depend upon the algorithms which will be used. But the objective of combining Hadoop, C++ and OpenMP was successful.

6. DISCUSSION

Hadoop has no image data type therefore BytesWriteable data type is used in the test application. In the reducer the bytes are converted to Java's BufferedImage Object, for processing the application reads the red, green and blue channels of each pixel of all the images and performs mathematical computation on it. In another test application line count and character count was calculated for every image using JavaOCR open source project and the result stored in a file.

Table 5. Results of Test Conducted

Task Description	Time Taken	Machine Description	Per Image Time Taken
Batch of 500 images using Java based Mapper and Reducer	10 sec	INTEL 2.5 GHz processer with 1 GB RAM	0.021 milliseconds
Batch of 500 images using Java based Mapper and Reducer calling C++ call	11 sec	INTEL 2.5 GHz processor with 1 GB RAM	0.022 milliseconds
Batch of 15000 images using Java based Mapper and Reducer	35 sec	MAC Machine	0.0023 milliseconds

Figure 4. Time Difference per Image

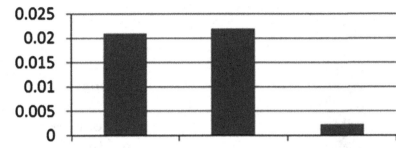

From the analysis conducted above, some changes to the original architecture can be proposed. Instead of receiving streams of images, the processing center, described in the overview of the project, will now receive a single sequence file from the client. It will result in reducing huge amount of load from the processing center. The data processor module will only merge multiple sequence files before placing it on the HDFS. Each task processor will contain three modules. Map / Reduce which will use Hadoop's MapReduce to provide data parallelism, JNI module serves as a bridge between Hadoop and C++, and the C++ / OpenMP which implements image processing techniques and task parallelism.

REFERENCES

Adam, G., Jack, B., Weicheng, D., Robert, J., & Sunderam, M. V. (n.d.). *A Users Guide and Tutorial for Networked Parallel Computing*. MIT Press.

Adiga, N. R., Almasi, G. S., Aridor, Y., Barik, R., Beece, D., Bellofatto, R., . . . Lu, M. (2002, November). An overview of the BlueGene/L supercomputer. In *Supercomputing, ACM/IEEE 2002 Conference* (pp. 60-60). IEEE.

Alexandrov, V. N., van Albada, G. D., Sloot, P. M., & Dongarra, J. (2006, May). Computational Science-ICCS 2006. In *6th International Conference, Reading, UK, May* (pp. 28-31).

Alippi, J. L. C., Bouchon-Meunier, B., Greenwood, G. W., & Abbass, H. A. (n.d.). *Advances in Computational Intelligence*.

Almási, G., Cascaval, C., & Wu, P. (2007). *Languages and Compilers for Parallel Computing: 19th International Workshop, LCPC 2006, New Orleans, LA, USA, November 2-4, 2006, Revised Papers* (*Vol. 4382*). Springer Science & Business Media.

Altintas, I., Birnbaum, A., Baldridge, K. K., Sudholt, W., Miller, M., Amoreira, C., & Ludaescher, B. (2005). A framework for the design and reuse of grid workflows. In *Scientific Applications of Grid Computing* (pp. 120–133). Springer Berlin Heidelberg. doi:10.1007/11423287_11

Anderson, E., Bai, Z., Bischof, C., Blackford, S., Demmel, J., Dongarra, J., & Sorensen, D. (1999). *LAPACK Users' guide* (Vol. 9). Siam. doi:10.1137/1.9780898719604

Andrews, G. R. (1999). *Foundations of parallel and distributed programming*. Addison-Wesley Longman Publishing Co., Inc.

Beguelin, A., Dongarra, J., Geist, A., Manchek, R., & Sunderam, V. (1991). A users' guide to PVM (parallel virtual machine). *ORNL. U. S. Atomic Energy Commission*, TM-11826.

Bellavista, Chang, & Chao. (n.d.). *Advances in Grid and Pervasive Computing*.

Bischof, C. (2008). *Parallel Computing: Architectures, Algorithms, and Applications* (Vol. 15). IOS Press.

Blelloch, G. E. (1990). *Vector models for data-parallel computing* (Vol. 356). Cambridge: MIT press.

Blume, W., Doallo, R., Rauchwerger, L., Tu, P., Eigenmann, R., Grout, J., & Pottenger, B. et al. (1996). Parallel programming with Polaris. *Computer*, *29*(12), 78–82. doi:10.1109/2.546612

Bode, A. (2000). *Euro-Par 2000 Parallel Processing: 6th International Euro-Par Conference, Munich, Germany, August 29-September 1, 2000: Proceedings* (No. 1900). Springer Science & Business Media.

Bode, A. (2000). *Euro-Par 2000 Parallel Processing: 6th International Euro-Par Conference, Munich, Germany, August 29-September 1, 2000: Proceedings* (No. 1900). Springer Science & Business Media.

Bruaset, A. M., & Tveito, A. (Eds.). (2006). *Numerical solution of partial differential equations on parallel computers* (Vol. 51). Springer Science & Business Media. doi:10.1007/3-540-31619-1

Butenhof, D. R. (1997). *Programming with POSIX threads*. Addison-Wesley Professional.

Buyya, R. (1999). *High performance cluster computing*. F'rentice.

Buyya, R., Broberg, J., & Goscinski, A. M. (Eds.). (2010). *Cloud computing: principles and paradigms* (Vol. 87). John Wiley & Sons.

Buyya, R., Yeo, C. S., & Venugopal, S. (2008, September). Market-oriented cloud computing: Vision, hype, and reality for delivering it services as computing utilities. In *High Performance Computing and Communications, 2008. HPCC'08. 10th IEEE International Conference on* (pp. 5-13). IEEE.

Cachin, C., Keidar, I., & Shraer, A. (2009). Trusting the cloud. *Acm Sigact News*, *40*(2), 81–86. doi:10.1145/1556154.1556173

Cerqueira, R. (2007). *Middleware 2007: ACM/IFIP/USENIX 8th International Middleware Conference, Newport Beach, CA, USA, November 26-30, 2007. Proceedings* (Vol. 4834). Springer.

Chandra, R. (2001). *Parallel programming in OpenMP*. Morgan Kaufmann.

Chang, R. S., Chao, H. C., Lin, S. F., & Sloot, P. M. (2010). *Advances in Grid and Pervasive Computing*. Springer-Verlag Berlin Heidelberg.

Chao, H. C., Obaidat, M. S., & Kim, J. (2011). *Computer Science and Convergence*. Springer.

Chao, H. C., Obaidat, M. S., & Kim, J. (2011). *Computer Science and Convergence*. Springer.

Chapman, B., Curtis, T., Pophale, S., Poole, S., Kuehn, J., Koelbel, C., & Smith, L. (2010, October). Introducing OpenSHMEM: SHMEM for the PGAS community. In *Proceedings of the Fourth Conference on Partitioned Global Address Space Programming Model* (p. 2). ACM. doi:10.1145/2020373.2020375

Chapman, B., Jost, G., & Van Der Pas, R. (2008). Using OpenMP: portable shared memory parallel programming (Vol. 10). MIT Press.

Chapman, B. M. (2005). *Shared Memory Parallel Programming with Open MP*. Springer-Verlag Berlin/ Heidelberg.

Coello, C. A. C. (1999). *List of references on evolutionary multiobjective optimization*. México: Laboratorio Nacional de Informática Avanzada.

Das, V. V., Stephen, J., & Chaba, Y. (Eds.). (2011). *Computer Networks and Information Technologies: Second International Conference on Advances in Communication, Network, and Computing, CNC 2011, Bangalore, India, March 10-11, 2011. Proceedings* (*Vol. 142*). Springer.

de Castro, A. B., Gómez, D., Quintela, P., & Salgado, P. (Eds.). (2007). *Numerical Mathematics and Advanced Applications: Proceedings of ENUMATH 2005 the 6th European Conference on Numerical Mathematics and Advanced Applications, Santiago de Compostela, Spain, July 2005*. Springer Science & Business Media.

Doerffer, P., Hirsch, C., Dussauge, J. P., Babinsky, H., & Barakos, G. N. (2010). *Unsteady Effects of Shock Wave Induced Separation* (Vol. 114). Springer Science & Business Media.

Domeika, M. (2011). *Software development for embedded multi-core systems: a practical guide using embedded Intel architecture*. Newnes.

Dongarra, J. (2008). *Parallel Processing and Applied Mathematics*. Berlin.

Dongarra, J., Laforenza, D., & Orlando, S. (2003). *Recent Advances in Parallel Virtual Machine and Message Passing Interface: 10th European PVM/MPI Users' Group Meeting, Venice, Italy, September 29-October 2, 2003, Proceedings* (Vol. 10). Springer Science & Business Media.

Dongarra, J., Laforenza, D., & Orlando, S. (2003). *Recent Advances in Parallel Virtual Machine and Message Passing Interface: 10th European PVM/MPI Users' Group Meeting, Venice, Italy, September 29-October 2, 2003, Proceedings* (Vol. 10). Springer Science & Business Media.

Doulamis, T., Mambretti, J., & Tomkos, I. (2010). *Networks for Grid Applications: Third International ICST Conference, GridNets 2009, Athens, Greece, September 8-9, 2009, Revised Selected Papers* (*Vol. 25*). Springer Science & Business Media.

Eigenmann, R., & de Supinski, B. R. (2008). OpenMP in a New Era of Parallelism. In *4 th International Workshop, IWOMP*. doi:10.1007/978-3-540-79561-2

Eigenmann, R., & de Supinski, B. R. (2008). OpenMP in a New Era of Parallelism. In *4 th International Workshop, IWOMP*.

Endo, P. T., Gonçalves, G. E., Kelner, J., & Sadok, D. (2010, May). A survey on open-source cloud computing solutions. In *Brazilian Symposium on Computer Networks and Distributed Systems*.

Fisher, B., Anderson, S., Bryant, J., Margolese, R. G., Deutsch, M., Fisher, E. R., & Wolmark, N. (2002). Twenty-year follow-up of a randomized trial comparing total mastectomy, lumpectomy, and lumpectomy plus irradiation for the treatment of invasive breast cancer. *The New England Journal of Medicine*, *347*(16), 1233–1241. doi:10.1056/NEJMoa022152 PMID:12393820

Fitch, B. G., Rayshubskiy, A., Eleftheriou, M., Ward, T. C., Giampapa, M., Zhestkov, Y., . . . Germain, R. S. (2006). Blue Matter: Strong scaling of molecular dynamics on Blue Gene/L. In Computational Science–ICCS 2006 (pp. 846-854). Springer Berlin Heidelberg.

Foster, I., Zhao, Y., Raicu, I., & Lu, S. (2008, November). Cloud computing and grid computing 360-degree compared. In *Grid Computing Environments Workshop, 2008. GCE'08* (pp. 1-10). IEEE. doi:10.1109/GCE.2008.4738445

Fox, G. C., & Zhuge, H. (2007). Special issue: Autonomous grid computing. *Concurrency and Computation*, *19*(7), 943–944. doi:10.1002/cpe.1087

Frachtenberg, E., & Schwiegelshohn, U. (2008, January). New challenges of parallel job scheduling. In *Job Scheduling Strategies for Parallel Processing* (pp. 1–23). Springer Berlin Heidelberg. doi:10.1007/978-3-540-78699-3_1

Garfinkel, S., & Abelson, H. (1999). *Architects of the information society: 35 years of the Laboratory for Computer Science at MIT*. MIT Press.

Ghosh, S. (2014). *Distributed systems: an algorithmic approach*. CRC press.

Grandinetti, L. (Ed.). (2005). *Grid Computing: The New Frontier of High Performance Computing: The New Frontier of High Performance Computing* (Vol. 14). Elsevier.

Gropp, W. (2002). MPICH2: A new start for MPI implementations. In Recent Advances in Parallel Virtual Machine and Message Passing Interface (pp. 7-7). Springer Berlin Heidelberg. doi:10.1007/3-540-45825-5_5

Gropp, W., & Lusk, E. (1998). *PVM and MPI are completely different*. Argonne National Lab.

Gropp, W., Lusk, E., Doss, N., & Skjellum, A. (1996). A high-performance, portable implementation of the MPI message passing interface standard. *Parallel Computing*, *22*(6), 789–828. doi:10.1016/0167-8191(96)00024-5

Gruhn, V., & Oquendo, F. (2006). Software Architecture. In *3rd European Workshop Software Architecture (EWSA 2006)*.

Hager, G., & Wellein, G. (2010). *Introduction to high performance computing for scientists and engineers*. CRC Press. doi:10.1201/EBK1439811924

Han, Y., Tai, S., & Wikarski, D. (2002). Engineering and deployment of cooperative information systems (Beijing, 17-20 September 2002). Lecture Notes in Computer Science.

Hanawa, T., Müller, M. S., Chapman, B., & de Supinski, B. R. (2010). *Beyond Loop Level Parallelism in OpenMP: Accelerators, Tasking and More*. Springer-Verlag Berlin Heidelberg.

Hellwagner, H., & Reinefeld, A. (1999). *SCI: Scalable Coherent Interface: architecture and software for high-performance compute clusters* (Vol. 1734). Springer Science & Business Media. doi:10.1007/10704208

Iosup, A., Ostermann, S., Yigitbasi, M. N., Prodan, R., Fahringer, T., & Epema, D. H. (2011). Performance analysis of cloud computing services for many-tasks scientific computing. *Parallel and Distributed Systems. IEEE Transactions on, 22*(6), 931–945.

Ivanov, N. (2012). *Real Time Big Data Processing with GridGain, 2012*.

Karniadakis, G. E., & Kirby, R. M. II. (2003). *Parallel scientific computing in C++ and MPI: a seamless approach to parallel algorithms and their implementation* (Vol. 1). Cambridge University Press. doi:10.1017/CBO9780511812583

Karypis, G., & Kumar, V. (1998). Multilevelk-way partitioning scheme for irregular graphs. *Journal of Parallel and Distributed Computing, 48*(1), 96–129. doi:10.1006/jpdc.1997.1404

Kasprzyk, L., Nawrowski, R., & Tomczewski, A. (2002). Application of a parallel virtual machine for the analysis of a luminous field. In *Recent Advances in Parallel Virtual Machine and Message Passing Interface* (pp. 122–129). Springer Berlin Heidelberg.

Krause, E., Shokin, Y. I., Resch, M., & Shokina, N. (2011). *Computational Science and High Performance Computing IV*. Springer. doi:10.1007/978-3-642-17770-5

Laplante, P. A. (1993). Real-time systems design. *Analysis*.

Li, R. E. Z., & Midkiff, S. P. (2005). *Languages and Compilers for High Performance Computing*. Academic Press.

Lind, P., & Alm, M. (2006). A database-centric virtual chemistry system. *Journal of Chemical Information and Modeling, 46*(3), 1034–1039. doi:10.1021/ci050360b PMID:16711722

Liu, D. T., & Franklin, M. J. (2004, August). GridDB: a data-centric overlay for scientific grids. In *Proceedings of the Thirtieth international conference on Very large data bases-Volume 30* (pp. 600-611). VLDB Endowment. doi:10.1016/B978-012088469-8.50054-1

Lopez, J. J. P. J., Shon, S. S. Y. T., & Taniar, D. (n.d.). *Secure and Trust Computing, Data Management, and Applications*. Academic Press.

Lynch, N. A. (1996). *Distributed algorithms*. Morgan Kaufmann.

Mahjoub, M., Mdhaffar, A., Halima, R. B., & Jmaiel, M. (2011, November). A comparative study of the current Cloud Computing technologies and offers. In *Network Cloud Computing and Applications (NCCA), 2011 First International Symposium on* (pp. 131-134). IEEE. doi:10.1109/NCCA.2011.28

Mak, G., & Long, J. (2009). *Spring Enterprise Recipes: A Problem-solution Approach*. Apress.

Mak, G., Long, J., & Rubio, D. (2010). Spring AOP and AspectJ support. In *Spring Recipes* (pp. 117–158). Apress. doi:10.1007/978-1-4302-2500-3_3

Malawski, M., Meizner, J., Bubak, M., & Gepner, P. (2011). Component approach to computational applications on clouds. *Procedia Computer Science*, *4*, 432–441. doi:10.1016/j.procs.2011.04.045

Mell, P., & Grance, T. (2009). The NIST definition of cloud computing. *National Institute of Standards and Technology*, *53*(6), 50.

Midkiff, S. P. (2005). *Languages and Compilers for High Performance Computing*. Academic Press.

Mostéfaoui, S. K., & Hirsbrunner, B. (2003, July). A context-based services discovery and composition framework for wireless environments. In *Proceedings of the IASTED International Conference on Wireless and Optical Networks (WOC'03)*, (pp. 637-642). IASTED.

Nakamura, T., Hochstein, L., & Basili, V. R. (2006, September). Identifying domain-specific defect classes using inspections and change history. In *Proceedings of the 2006 ACM/IEEE international symposium on Empirical software engineering* (pp. 346-355). ACM. doi:10.1145/1159733.1159785

Noeth, M., Ratn, P., Mueller, F., Schulz, M., & de Supinski, B. R. (2009). ScalaTrace: Scalable compression and replay of communication traces for high-performance computing. *Journal of Parallel and Distributed Computing*, *69*(8), 696–710. doi:10.1016/j.jpdc.2008.09.001

Noonan, W., & Dubrawsky, I. (2006). *Firewall fundamentals*. Pearson Education.

Olston, C., & Najork, M. (2010). Web crawling. *Foundations and Trends in Information Retrieval*, *4*(3), 175–246. doi:10.1561/1500000017

Ostermann, S., Iosup, A., Yigitbasi, N., Prodan, R., Fahringer, T., & Epema, D. (2010). A performance analysis of EC2 cloud computing services for scientific computing. In *Cloud computing* (pp. 115–131). Springer Berlin Heidelberg. doi:10.1007/978-3-642-12636-9_9

Pacheco, P. S. (1997). *Parallel programming with MPI*. Morgan Kaufmann.

Papadimitriou, C. H. (2003). *Computational complexity* (pp. 260–265). John Wiley and Sons Ltd.

Patel, A., Seyfi, A., Tew, Y., & Jaradat, A. (2011). Comparative study and review of grid, cloud, utility computing and software as a service for use by libraries. *Library Hi Tech News*, *28*(3), 25–32. doi:10.1108/07419051111145145

Patterson, C. A., Snir, M., & Graham, S. L. (Eds.). (2005). *Getting Up to Speed: The Future of Supercomputing*. National Academies Press.

Pollard, A., Mewhort, D. J., & Weaver, D. F. (2000). *High performance computing systems and applications*. Springer Science & Business Media.

Randles, M., Lamb, D., & Taleb-Bendiab, A. (2010, April). A comparative study into distributed load balancing algorithms for cloud computing. In *Advanced Information Networking and Applications Workshops (WAINA), 2010 IEEE 24th International Conference on* (pp. 551-556). IEEE. doi:10.1109/WAINA.2010.85

Rego, V. J., & Sunderam, V. S. (1992). Experiments in concurrent stochastic simulation: The EcliPSe paradigm. *Journal of Parallel and Distributed Computing*, *14*(1), 66–84. doi:10.1016/0743-7315(92)90098-8

Rimal, B. P., Choi, E., & Lumb, I. (2009, August). A taxonomy and survey of cloud computing systems. In *INC, IMS and IDC, 2009. NCM'09. Fifth International Joint Conference on* (pp. 44-51). Ieee. doi:10.1109/NCM.2009.218

Ropo, M., Westerholm, J., & Dongarra, J. (Eds.). (2009). *Recent Advances in Parallel Virtual Machine and Message Passing Interface: 16th European PVM/MPI Users' Group Meeting, Espoo, Finland, September 7-10, 2009, Proceedings* (Vol. 5759). Springer.

Rose, E. A., Gelijns, A. C., Moskowitz, A. J., Heitjan, D. F., Stevenson, L. W., Dembitsky, W., & Meier, P. (2001). Long-term use of a left ventricular assist device for end-stage heart failure. *The New England Journal of Medicine, 345*(20), 1435–1443. doi:10.1056/NEJMoa012175 PMID:11794191

Rus, S., Rauchwerger, L., & Hoeflinger, J. (2003). Hybrid analysis: Static & dynamic memory reference analysis. *International Journal of Parallel Programming, 31*(4), 251–283. doi:10.1023/A:1024597010150

Schwiegelshohn, U., Badia, R. M., Bubak, M., Danelutto, M., Dustdar, S., Gagliardi, F., & Von Voigt, G. et al. (2010). Perspectives on grid computing. *Future Generation Computer Systems, 26*(8), 1104–1115. doi:10.1016/j.future.2010.05.010

Seiler, L., Carmean, D., Sprangle, E., Forsyth, T., Abrash, M., Dubey, P., & Hanrahan, P. et al. (2008, August). Larrabee: A many-core x86 architecture for visual computing. *ACM Transactions on Graphics, 27*(3), 18. doi:10.1145/1360612.1360617

Silva, F., Dutra, I., & Costa, V. S. (Eds.). (2014). *Euro-Par 2014: Parallel Processing: 20th International Conference, Porto, Portugal, August 25-29, 2014, Proceedings* (*Vol. 8632*). Springer.

Sterling, T. L. (2002). *Beowulf cluster computing with Linux*. MIT Press.

Stone, H. S. (1973). An efficient parallel algorithm for the solution of a tridiagonal linear system of equations. *Journal of the ACM, 20*(1), 27–38. doi:10.1145/321738.321741

Telesca, L., Stanoevska-Slabeva, K., & Rakocevic, V. (2009). Digital Business. In *First International ICTS Conference, DigiBiz*.

Telesca, L., Stanoevska-Slabeva, K., & Rakocevic, V. (2009). Digital Business. In *First International ICTS Conference, DigiBiz*.

Tullsen, D. M., Eggers, S. J., & Levy, H. M. (1995, July). Simultaneous multithreading: Maximizing on-chip parallelism. In ACM SIGARCH Computer Architecture News (Vol. 23, No. 2, pp. 392-403). ACM.

Tveito, A., Langtangen, H. P., Nielsen, B. F., & Cai, X. (2010). *Elements of Scientific Computing* (Vol. 7). Springer Science & Business Media. doi:10.1007/978-3-642-11299-7

Unger, H., Böhme, T., & Mikler, A. (Eds.). (2002). *Innovative Internet Computing Systems: Second International Workshop, IICS 2002: Proceedings*. Springer-Verlag.

Vajteršic, M., Zinterhof, P., & Trobec, R. (2009). *Overview–Parallel Computing: Numerics, Applications, and Trends* (pp. 1–42). Springer London.

Venner, J. (2009). *Pro Hadoop*. Apress. doi:10.1007/978-1-4302-1943-9

Von Laszewski, G. (2002, January). Grid computing: Enabling a vision for collaborative research. In *Applied Parallel Computing* (pp. 37–52). Springer Berlin Heidelberg. doi:10.1007/3-540-48051-X_4

White, T. (2012). *Hadoop: The definitive guide*. O'Reilly Media, Inc.

Xie, Yin, Ruan, Ding, Tian, Majors, ... Qin, X. (2010, April). Improving mapreduce performance through data placement in heterogeneous hadoop clusters. In *Parallel & Distributed Processing, Workshops and Phd Forum (IPDPSW), 2010 IEEE International Symposium on* (pp. 1-9). IEEE.

Yang, L. T., & Guo, M. (2005). *High-performance computing: paradigm and infrastructure* (Vol. 44). John Wiley & Sons. doi:10.1002/0471732710

Yeo, S. S., Park, J. J. J. H., Yang, L. T., & Hsu, C. H. (Eds.). (2010). *Algorithms and Architectures for Parallel Processing: 10th International Conference, ICA3PP 2010, Busan, Korea, May 21-23, 2010. Proceedings* (Vol. 6081). Springer.

York, J., & Pendharkar, P. C. (2004). Human–computer interaction issues for mobile computing in a variable work context. *International Journal of Human-Computer Studies, 60*(5), 771–797. doi:10.1016/j.ijhcs.2003.07.004

Yu, S., Zhou, W., & Wu, Y. (2002, October). Research on network anycast. In *Algorithms and Architectures for Parallel Processing, 2002. Proceedings. Fifth International Conference on* (pp. 154-161). IEEE.

Zhao, G., Rong, C., Jaatun, M. G., & Sandnes, F. E. (2010, June). Deployment models: Towards eliminating security concerns from cloud computing. In *High Performance Computing and Simulation (HPCS), 2010 International Conference on* (pp. 189-195). IEEE.

Zheng, W., Wang, B., & Wu, Y. (2010, July). Task partition comparison between multi-core system and GPU. In *ChinaGrid Conference (ChinaGrid), 2010 Fifth Annual* (pp. 175-182). IEEE. doi:10.1109/ChinaGrid.2010.17

Zoumas, C. E., Bakirtzis, A. G., Theocharis, J. B., & Petridis, V. (2004). A genetic algorithm solution approach to the hydrothermal coordination problem. *Power Systems. IEEE Transactions on, 19*(3), 1356–1364.

Chapter 18
The Effectiveness of Big Data in Social Networks

Khine Khine Nyunt
University of Wollongong, Singapore

Noor Zaman
King Faisal University, Saudi Arabia

ABSTRACT

In this chapter, we will discuss how "big data" is effective in "Social Networks" which will bring huge opportunities but difficulties though challenges yet ahead to the communities. Firstly, Social Media is a strategy for broadcasting, while Social Networking is a tool and a utility for connecting with others. For this perspective, we will introduce the characteristic and fundamental models of social networks and discuss the existing security & privacy for the user awareness of social networks in part I. Secondly, the technological built web based internet application of social media with Web2.0 application have transformed users to allow creation and exchange of user-generated content which play a role in big data of unstructured contents as well as structured contents. Subsequently, we will introduce the characteristic and landscaping of the big data in part II. Finally, we will discuss the algorithms for marketing and social media mining which play a role how big data fit into the social media data.

PART I: SOCIAL NETWORKS ANALYSIS

Social Networks

Social Networks is a social structure which involves different subjects of any interested topics internationally whereby at least a group of two people interactively exchange. It is in an open space where it gives to post like a common forum for representatives of anthropology, sociology, history, social psychology, political science, human geography, biology, economics, communications science and other disciplines who are share with an interest in the study of the empirical structure of social relations and associations that may be expressed in network form.

DOI: 10.4018/978-1-4666-8505-5.ch018

The behind abstract concept was based on discrete mathematics using graph theory to construct the pairwise structure relation model between them comprising nodes which is starting point in social networks. Most social network services are web-based internet applications and provide users to interact over the Internet with exchanging interested information, such as including e-mail and instant messaging, chatting, mobile connectivity, photo & video sharing and blogging. Social networks allow to users to post unstructured social contents to share ideas, pictures, posts, activities, events, and interests with people in their network. In this session, we will discuss the issues of characteristic, model, security & privacy, demographic and analysis on social networks.

1.1 Characterization

Online social networks are based on users while web pages are based on contents. Users of social networking sites form a social network, which provides a powerful means of sharing, organizing, and finding content and contacts. The researchers found three main points (Mislove, Marcon, Gummadi, Druschel, & Bhattacharjee, 2007) – 1) the degree of distributions in social networks follow a power-law and the coefficients for both in-degree and out-degree are similar so that nodes with high in-degree also tend to have high out-degree. 2) Social networks appear to be composed of a large number of highly connected clusters consisting of relatively low degree nodes so that the clustering coefficient is inversely proportional to node degree. 3) The networks each contain a large, densely connected core. As a result, path lengths are short, but almost all shortest paths of sufficient length traverse the highly connected core.

Based on the research, we conclude that the "nodes" or the relation between members of the network are those users who established the number of "friends" within the online network, establishing themselves as many as friendship and as close to the "core" of that social network as possible. This means that the closer to the core of a social network that you are, the faster you're able to propagate information out to a wider segment of the network. This is exactly the kind of opportunity that most marketers look for. Furthermore, we will discuss the some core characteristics of social networks:

1. **Interactive User Based:** Unlike the websites which based on content that was updated by one user and read by Internet visitors, social networks like Facebook, Twitter, LinkedIn etc. are so interactive timely. User can create the account themselves, populate the network with conversations and content and fill with network-based online gaming application. Moreover, social media services have openness for feedback and participation. They encourage voting, comments and the sharing of information. This is what make social networks so much more exciting and dynamic for Internet users.

2. **Community:** Social media allows communities to form quickly and communicate effectively. Communities share common interests, beliefs or hobbies such as a love of photography, a political issue. Social Media allow not only to discover new friends within these within these interest based communities, but you can also reconnect with old friends that you lost contact with many years ago.

3. **Emotion:** The social networks provide not only the information but also allow the users with emotional sense that no matter what happens, can easily reach to their friends so that friends can instantly communicate over any of crises or issue and give support or suggestion on the current situation. Beyond the characteristics, Social Networks can generate social influence among the

users by changing thought and actions by actions of others. There can be the companionship by sharing information or other activities among the user. Another function is Social Support as aid and assistant exchanged through social relationship and interpersonal transactions.

1.2 Social Networks Modeling

Nowadays, there are many applications for social network analysis or graph theory comes out from many academic department like mathematics, computer science and physics for studies of online social networks such as Facebook, Twitter or Google+. By definition a network is a structure of nodes which are connected by edges. In Social Networks, the nodes as representing people and edges as representing relationships and the nodes can be assigned attributes which could be demographic information about the individual.

In this section we will discuss very fundamental networks model which are applied in Social Networks. Modeling social networks serves at least two purposes. First, it helps us understand how social networks form and evolve. Secondly, in studying network-dependent social processes by simulation, such as diffusion or retrieval of information, successful network models can be used for specifying the structure of interaction. (Toivonena, et al., 2009)

1) Erdos-Renyi Model or Bernoulli Random Graph

Erdos-Renyi model is the simplest underlying distribution model and also known as a Bernoulli Random Graph or Bernoulli Network. By Definition, the model G(n,p) assumes that it is a random graph which have n nodes and for every pair of nodes (i,j), with probability p ($0 \leq p \leq 1$) an edge exists between the two nodes.

This random graph model can find the application of Analysis of Social Network of all kinds. For example, one person who is a Facebook user u can form a graph of network of friends $N(u)$, where nodes are people and two people are connected by an edge if they are mutual friends, call this particular user's friendship neighborhood. It resembles a random graph which is the structure of small networks of friends. This says that most people in the average user's immediate friendship neighborhood are essentially the same and essentially random in their friendships among the friends of u.

2) Clustering

Even though the Erdos-Renyi model is the very fundamental of modeling network formation, there is some lacking characteristics in social and economic networks. The main issue is that the presence of link tends to be correlated. For example, we consider the triple of nodes and two of them are each connected to the third one. So the consideration is those two nodes (first and second) are linked to each other. This concept lead to be much larger in social network. For instance, social networks tend to exhibit significant clustering which is a collection of individuals with dense friendship patterns internally and sparse friendships externally. This has led to a series of richer random graph-based models of networks.

- **Markov Graphs:** (Frank & Strauss, 1986) generalized the Bernoulli random graphs and identified a class of random graphs which they called Markov graphs. Their finding was a link forms to be dependent on whether neighboring link are formed or not. It means making one link dependent on a second, and the second on the third, can imply some interdependencies between the first and third. These sorts of dependencies are difficult to analyze but statistical estimation of networks.

- **Small World Network:** Another variation on a Bernoulli network was explored by (Watts & Strogatz, 1998). The model demonstrates how to construct a tractable family of toy networks that can simultaneously have significant clustering and small geodesic distances. The famous feature of this model is possession of large range of P (0<=P<=1) that produces small-world graphs with significant clustering (Scholarpedia.org, 2012). They started with a very structured network that exhibits a high degree of clustering. Then by randomly rewiring enough links, one ends up with a network that has a small average distance between links but still has substantial clustering. This rewiring process widely used in Social Networks.

- **Exponential Random Graph Models:** Exponential random graph models (ERGMs), also called p∗ models, constitute a family of statistical models for social networks. These models take the form of a probability distribution of graphs:

$$\Pr\left(X = x\right) = (1 \,/\, k)\exp\left\{\eta' g\right\}$$

for a set of tie indicator valuables X on a network of fixed note size n, where x is a realization, with a parameter vector η and a vector of network statistics g. Each value of the parameter vector corresponds to a probability distribution on the set of all graphs with n nodes. (Robins, 2009)

There are some basic theoretical assumptions about social networks which are main reason for using ERGM. (Lusher, Koskinen & Robins, 2013)

1. Social networks are locally emergent which permits instant transmission of messages direct to followers.
2. Network ties not only self-organize but they are also influenced by actor attributes and other exogenous factors.
3. The patterns within networks can be seen as evidence for ongoing structural processes.
4. Multiple processes can operate simultaneously.
5. Social networks are structured, yet stochastic.

1.3 Security and Privacy

Popularity of social networking sites such as Facebook and Twitter have gained large user base, and large amount of information in recent year. On the other hand, many attackers exploit different way of attack on social networking sites. Many social networking sites try to prevent those exploitations, but still not overcome yet. In this section, we will discuss the more issues on Privacy, Identity theft, spam and malware which are the threats that social network users may not be aware.

1) Privacy Issues

Privacy issue is one of the main concerns, since many social network user are not careful about what they expose on their social network space. Social networking sites are a powerful and fun way to communicate with the world and they are vary in the level of security and privacy offered. The basic contents of security information is called profile which is provided by users however the large volume and accessibility of profile information are available on social networking sites which is attracted to whom are seeking to exploit the information. This becomes profile information security concern. There can be stealing the profile credentials information using some technologies that invite users to persuade malicious programs with the intention of malware activities. Social networking sites are fundamentally providing privacy concern however most of social networking site guideline are not enough for any intruders. The potential privacy breach is actually real concerned into the systematic framework of social media sites. Unfortunately, the flaws render social media system to almost indefensible. Privacy concern has been alerted over a number of profile incidents which has considered embarrassing for users. It has created a wide range of online interpersonal victimization. Sources of users' profile and personal information leakage are as below;

- **Poor Privacy Settings:** Most social network users are not aware about their privacy settings who can access online which their profile is public. Also, many social networking sites default privacy setting is still not safe, even the safest privacy setting, there are still flaws that allow attackers to access user's information.
- **Leakage of Information to Third Party Application:** These third party applications are very popular among social network users. Once users add and allow third party applications to access their information, these applications can access user's data automatically. It is also capable of posting on users' space or user's friend's space, or may access other user's information without user's knowledge (Krishnamurthy & Will, 2008).
- **Leakage of Information to Third Party Domain:** The use of third party domain in many social networking websites to track social network user's activities, or allows advertisement partner to access and aggregate social network user's data for their commercial benefit (Krishnamurthy & Will, 2008).

2) Identity Theft

The second issue is identity theft, attackers make use of social networks account to steal victim's identities. Profile cloning is one of the most famous identity theft and there are couple of different method to be clone the profile. The first method is that the attackers create a profile and sending a friend request to those who targeted. Social network user are not careful when accept friend request. This is one of the method that attackers take advantage of trust among friends. The second method is eyeing on the profile those are public online. So attackers can easily duplicate the information of the user. The third method is that attackers steal user's profile from one social networking site and use that information to register an account in another social network site. The last method is social phishing. The attackers provide a fake website which is very authentic and users are providing personal information.

3) Spam Issues

The third is the spam issue which attackers make use of social networks to increase spam click through rate, which is more effective than the traditional email spam. According to Nexgate, social media brand protection and compliance, social media spam has risen 355% on a typical social media account in the first half of 2013 (Nexgate, 2013). There are two types of spam in social network which are "Link Spam" and "Text Spam".

- **Link Spam:** It will appear as a single link with no surrounding text. If user click on the link, it route to the spammer's website which contain ads. This spamdexing process helps to increase the website rank in search result. Other method is to put a short phrase accompanying the link to attract the user that promises easy money, pills, porn, etc. Another method of remaining mysterious or vague is to shorten the link altogether without revealing where the link is pointing. This links can also automatically send similarly spammy links to all of the user's contacts.
- **Text Spam:** Spammers try to engage text through private message box or chat box to the user for telling fake story which is to distribute the message to as many people as possible or something horrible will happen. Some message can be like donation such as cancer or other needy issues to share a link. There may be the request to send money to the original sender. Some message are promise easy money like "work from home" schemes. The spammer typically extorts money from the victim by charging a fee to join the program. Text spam is more on phishing attack which allow the perpetrator to gather identification information from the victim, which may then be used to gain access to other accounts, such as bank accounts.

4) Malware Issue

The forth is the malware issue which is widely used by attackers use to spread malware very speedy through connectivity among users. Social networking sites are always facing new kind of malware and cannot determine whether URLs or embedded links are malicious or not.

There are many possible way that attackers can spread malware among the social networks. Fake Account is one of the method for attacker to easily connect with social network users to view their profile. For example, attacker can create fake profile as a celebrity that attracts victims to contact them. Second method is using APT (Application Programming Interface) third party application for leakage of user's personal information. This application seems to be good but some malicious link hide inside and takes users to malicious domain and spread malware to users. Third method is that attacker uses advertisement as a medium to spread malware across social networks. When users click on ads, it will be redirected to the malicious websites and ask user to download malicious cod such as Java or Active X content to their browser. This is the way malware will be infected user's computer. The fourth method is "Clickjacking". When user click on the item such as video, link or photo, the hidden code will be triggered to perform malicious action. Some of the worst case is, user has asked to input their particular when user click on the video or link or page. The last method to discuss here is Cross-site scripting (XSS) attacks which are type of injection. Attackers can use XSS to send a malicious script to user which can access cookies, session tokens or other sensitive information.

For example, **Koobface** is a warm that can spread social networking websites and email websites. Upon successful infection, it can gather login information for sites like Facebook, Myspace, Skype and so on. For example in Facebook, the message with video link can be spread to user who are friend of a Facebook user whose computer had already been infected. Upon receipt, it can be routed to a third party website and ask user to download the Adobe Flash player. If user download and execute the file, Koobface can easily infect user's system and attacker can easily steal the user's information.

Social networking media should aware of new age spammers and attackers in this technology age. Social networking media should truly investigate the new age spammers and their technique and empower the media security with automated detection, classification and removal of spam, malicious and inappropriate content across all major social media platforms.

1.4 Analysis

Based on the research data between 2012 and 2013 from Pew research center, 42% of online adults use multiple social networking sites, but Facebook remains the platform of choice. 71% of online user are in Facebook so that Facebook remains the dominant social networking platform. (Pewinternet, 2013) Currently, Pinterest and Instagram get popular among younger adults. Pinterest is a social bookmarking site where users collect and share photos of their favorite events, interests and hobbies. Instagram is an online mobile photo and video sharing social networking sites and allow to share digital media to other social networking sites like Facebook and Twitter. LinkedIn is business oriented social networking service and mainly use for professional networking.

In our analysis, we are indicating comparison chart for Facebook vs Twitter based on the distinct differences which gather from the variety of internet sources.

Table 1. The comparison chart for Facebook vs Twitter

Description	Facebook	Twitter
Launch date	February 4, 2004	July 6, 2006
Number of users	1.28 billion (monthly active, March 2014)	Over 500 million
Languages	Available in 70 languages	Available in 29 languages
Users express approval of content by	"Like" or "Share"	"Retweet" or "Favorite"
Privacy settings	Can use different settings for various groups	Either public or private
Post length	Unlimited	140 characters
Users express opinions of content by	"Comment" or "Reply"	"Reply"
Edit posts	Yes	No
Add friends	Yes	No
Instant messaging	Yes	No
Follow trending topics	No	Yes

Facebook and Twitter, both are basically Social Networking Services lunched in February, 2004 and July, 2006 respectively. Currently, Facebook has 1.28 billion as of March 2014 and Twitter has over 500 million users. *We can say that Facebook still remains the dominant social networking platform. Here we have couple of analysis based on the both services.*

- **Features:** Facebook features include Friends, Fans, Wall, News Feed, Fan Pages, Groups, Apps, Live Chat, Likes, Photos, Videos, Text, Polls, Links, Status, Pokes, Gifts, Games, Messaging, Classified section, upload and download options etc. while Twitter has Tweet, Retweet, Direct Messaging, Follow People & Trending Topics, Links, Photos and Videos. Based on the features, we can say that Facebook has more features to attract users. Some of the features can do both services like post updates, share links, private messages, upload photos and follow people. Some differences like language availability which is 70 languages available in Facebook and only 29 languages in Twitter. Moreover, Facebook allow unlimited length for post while twitter allow to tweet with 140 characters. Facebook allow friends to comment on the post and edit after post but twitter doesn't allow either. Facebook has a good feature to add friends but Twitter doesn't have "add friend" feature as well as no instant messaging allow.

- **Privacy:** When comes to this privacy point, Facebook has various privacy setting for user choices which allows users to set privacy settings independently. Users can be able to select their profile as public (visible everyone) or not even searchable except by acknowledged friends. Additionally, users can set any privacy setting on individual post or upload photos and other sharing link as public, friends or custom. Furthermore, users can control their timeline and tagging as individual can view whether hide or allow the post before public. Twitter has two privacy settings which are public and private. Private messages is only for the people who follow the user. User are also allow to select "Protect my Tweets" feature. And Twitter also have option to choose for photo tagging but there is no review feature like Facebook.

- **Communication:** All connection must be mutual in Facebook. Facebook allow individuals to share their interest to friends such as posting messages on the wall, upload photos and video as instant messages, share link, write long notes, send private message to friends, instant chat and even playing game together as well as friends are allow give comment on posting of their view. So from communication point of view, if many people interact with your post via likes, comments and share, it's possible for your post to have a longer news feed shelf life and if your community share your post, there's a higher probability by seeing people who aren't not in your friend list. In contrast, connection can be one way or two way in Twitter. You can make friend as much as you can by using follow features without knowing each other. It seems more active in the way of social communication. You should choose Twitter, if you have a lot of content to share and plan to be proactive in your interaction with other accounts. But the limitation is that Twitter allows users to tweet with 140 character messages and other users can follow these messages on their twitter feed. It is main feature to communicate with other individual who has similar interest. Moreover, depending on how many people you follow, a tweet can literally stay in your feed for mere seconds unless you retweets your post.Twitter is basically centered on real-time conversation, while Facebook is more of an ongoing conversation that people get to eventually.

- **Advertising:** Based on research report by resolution (Resolution, 2014), advertiser spend much more with Facebook but Twitter perform better. Of course, most advertiser would eyeing on the number of users so that Face book is the great place of social networking to advertise. But

Facebook ads is much more complex than Twitter. In the Facebook ads, you have to identify your marketing objective first. Facebook will guide you to the most appropriate type. Then you have to decide target people by location, age, gender, interest, language, education, etc. You can also target the friends of people who already like page or app. lastly, there is a budget which will allow you to space out your ads over a broader timeframe. You can either pay for specific action or per thousand impressions. Price can be varied due to the competition in the demographic you are targeting. Then you can see which ads and images are performing the best through Facebook's analytics dashboard and it is final stage to advertise.

Twitter is simple. There is two categories: Promoted tweets which you want to advertise a specific message of product. Another one is Promoted Account which is suitable who goal is new followers. You need to pay only when you add new followers. You have two kinds of targeting. The first one is by keyword which will allow you to target who search or tweet with a specific term. The second one is by interest and followers who follow the specific accounts. For example, a skin care band might want to target users who follow accounts that tweet about anti-aging advice. There is a budget too. But it is different with Facebook that you can set lifetime and daily maximum budgets for your campaign. If you set promoted tweets, you set the amount you are willing to pay every time someone retweets, replies, favorites, follows or clicks on your tweet. If you set promoted account, you pay per follower.

PART II: BIG DATA

Big Data

"Big data is the term increasingly used to describe the process of applying serious computing power – the latest in machine learning and artificial intelligence – to seriously massive and often highly complex sets of information." (Microsoft enterprise insight, 2013). Big data is accepted both the structured and the unstructured data which go beyond relational database and traditional data warehousing platforms to incorporate technologies that are suited to processing and storing non transactional forms of data.

The fundamental challenge of Big Data is not collecting data. It is about - what is the starting point; what are the computation paths to discover; what are the appropriate algorithms; and How to visualize the findings. According to statistics published by IBM in 2011, the massive adoption of Facebook, Twitter and other social media services has resulted in the generation of about 2.5 quintillion bytes each day. (International Business Machine, 2011) Conducting big data analysis has a significant role in maximizing the utility of social media.

2.1 Characteristics

In recent year, we have heard of the 3Vs' of big data characteristic, Volume, Variety and Velocity. Now IBM scientists break big data into four dimension: 4V's of big data which getting attention on most notably of Veracity. (IBM, 2014).

- **Volume:** the scale of data which determines the value and whether it can actually be considered as big data or not. Social Media has many factors to increase the data volume such as unstructured data streaming or increase of sensor and machine to machine data being collected. Referring IBM, It is estimated that 2.5 quintillion bytes (2.3 Trillion gigabyte) of data are created each day and in coming 2020 it would be 40 Zettabytes (40Trillion gigabyte), an increase of 300 times from 2005

- **Velocity:** It is the speed of generation of data or how fast the data is generated and processed to meet the demands and challenges. It is all about data streaming in social media at exceptional speed.
- **Variety:** Variety refers to the many sources and types of data both structured and unstructured. Data in social media come in all types of formats. Having reference from IBM, as of 2011, the global size of data in healthcare was estimated to be 150 Exabyte (161 billion gigabytes). By 2014, there will be 420 million wearable wireless health monitors, estimated four billions videos per hour on YouTube, 400 million tweets are sent per day and 30 billion pieces of content are shared on Facebook every month.
- **Veracity:** It is uncertainty of data. Social Media data flows can be highly unpredictable with periodic peaks. According to IBM analysis, one in three business leaders don't trust the information to make decision.

2.2 Infrastructure

Infrastructural technologies are the core of the Big Data. The main purpose is the process and store both structure and unstructured data. For many decades, enterprises relied on relational databases which are the collections of data in a form of rows and column in a table for structured data. In this technology aged, new form of unstructured data which comes from sensors, devices, video/audio, networks, log files, transactional applications, web, and social media - much of it generated in real time and in a very large scale which is meant that data capture had to move beyond merely rows and columns in tables. As a result, new infrastructural technologies emerged, capable of wrangling a vast variety of data, and making it possible to run applications on systems with thousands of nodes, potentially involving thousands of terabytes of data.

By literature review, here we are presenting some key infrastructural technology:

- **Hadoop:** Hadoop is one of the popular java open-source programming framework that support the processing of large data sets in a distributed computing environment. Hadoop implements a data-crawling strategy over massively scaled-out, share-nothing data partitions where various nodes in the system are able to perform different parts of a query on different parts of the data simultaneously (Maltby, 2011). This works very well for big data and it can run applications on systems with thousands of nodes involving thousands of terabytes. Hadoop's distributed file system facilitates rapid data transfer rates among nodes and allows the system to continue operating uninterrupted in case of a node failure. This approach lowers the risk of catastrophic system failure, even if a significant number of nodes become inoperative (Kakade & Chavan, 2014). Hadoop is used by Google, Yahoo and IBM for search engines and advertising. The preferred operating systems for Hadoop are Windows, Linux, BSD (Berkeley Software Distribution) and OS X which is Unix- based graphical interface operating systems developed and marketed by Apple Inc.
- **NoSQL Databases:** It stands for Not Only SQL, represents the new class of data management technologies which involved in processing large volume of structured, semi-structured and unstructured data. They scale very well as agile sprints, quick iteration and frequent code pushes.

Moreover, NoSQL databases are flexible and easy to use object-oriented programming. And they use efficient scale-out architecture instead of expensive monolithic architecture. But Most of the early NoSQL systems did not attempt to provide ACID which is atomicity, consistency, isolation and durability guarantees, contrary to the prevailing practice among relational database systems. NoSQL databases are typically used in big data and real time web application. Some NoSQL databases, like HBase, can work concurrently with Hadoop.

- **Massively Parallel Processing (MPP) Databases:** Data is partitioned across multiple servers or nodes and queries are processed via network interconnect on central server and running parallel. MPP databases provide ACID (Atomicity, Consistency, Isolation and Durability) compliance as well as include cost based optimizers and monitor the distribution of data within the system. In general, MPP is more efficient than Hadoop. Based on the literature review, we conclude some comparison between Hadoop and MPP. 1) Hadoop expand existing programming technology into large scale processing while MPP expand existing database technology into large scale processing. 2) Hadoop is designed to run on any hardware, cheaper cluster of commodity server while MPP run on expensive specialize software. 3) Hadoop is open source community while MPP is invented by Teradata, Netezza, GreenPlum, Vertica, ParAccel, etc. 4) Hadoop uses Java while MPP use SQL.

2.3 Analytics

Big data analytics is the process of examining large amount of data (big data), in an effort to uncover hidden patterns, unknown correlations and other useful information (Shang et.al, 2013). Major goal of big data analytics is to help data scientists and others who analyse huge volumes of transaction data and other source of data that conventional analytics and business intelligence solutions can't touch. High performance of analytics is necessary to process that much data and the result analysis can provide competitive advantages in business benefit for more effective marketing strategy and increased revenue for organization.

Big data accepted both structured and unstructured data which comes from sensors, devices, video/audio, networks, log files, transactional applications, web, and social media - much of it generated in real time and in a very large scale. Big data analytic can be done by software which commonly used an advanced analytic disciplines such as predictive analytics, data mining, text mining, forecasting and optimization. But unstructured data may not be fit in traditional data warehouses. As a result, a new paradigm shift of big data technology has emerged with traditional one in big data analytics environments. The new technology such as NoSQL database, Hadoop and Hadoop MapReduce which are the open source software framework that can process large data sets.

By literature review, there are variety of techniques has been developed and adapted to visualize, analyse, manipulate and aggregate big data. Here we are presenting some techniques for big data analytic:

- **Data Mining:** is an analytic process designed to explore data (usually large amounts of data - typically business or market related - also known as "big data") in search of consistent patterns and/or systematic relationships between variables, and then to validate the findings by applying the detected patterns to new subsets of data. The ultimate goal of data mining is prediction and predictive data mining is the most common type of data mining and one that has the most direct business applications. (Kaur & Paul, 2014)

- **Cluster Analysis:** Cluster analysis is used for classifying objects that splits a diverse group into smaller groups of similar objects.
- **Crowdsourcing:** A technique for collecting data submitted by a large group of people or community (i.e., the "crowd") through an open call, usually through networked media such as the Web. This is a type of mass collaboration and an instance of using Web 2.0.
- **Association Rule Learning:** A way of finding relationships among variables. It is often used in data mining and these techniques consists of a variety of algorithms to generate and test possible rules.
- **Machine Learning:** A subspecialty of computer science (within a field historically called "artificial intelligence") concerned with the design and development of algorithms that allow computers to evolve behaviors based on empirical data. A major focus of machine learning research is to automatically learn to recognize complex patterns and make intelligent decisions based on data. Natural language processing is an example of machine learning.
- **Visualization:** It is used for creating images, diagrams, or animations to communicate, understand, and improve the results of big data analyses.
- **Time Series Analysis:** A collection of observations of well-defined data items obtained through repeated measurements over time. Examples of time series analysis include the hourly value of a stock market index or the number of patients diagnosed with a given condition every day.

2.4 Application

Nowadays, many applications come up with big data technology in many industries. Enterprises can save money, grow revenue and achieve many other business objectives by using big data technology. Big Data allow company to build new applications, improve the effectiveness and lower cost of existing applications. Here we presented the some key type of applications and their characteristics and some example of commercial software in niche market.

- **Vertical Applications:** This type of application can define and built based on the user's specific requirements to achieve their business process and goal. Example: AutoGrid, ellucian, Knewton and etc.
- **Consumers:** This type of application uses central data warehouse for reporting, planning, trend-tracking, analysis and accounting for specific user needs. Example: Facebook, twitter, Google, Amazon, ebay, Linkedin and etc.
- **Operational Intelligence:** It is a form of real-time dynamic, business analytics that delivers visibility and insight into business operations. Example: AppDynamics, New Relic, Splunk, Sumo Logic and etc.
- **Data as a Service:** It is a cloud strategy used to facilitate the accessibility of business-critical data in a well-timed, protected and affordable manner. Example: DataSift, Factual, FICO, Gnip and etc.
- **Ad / Media Applications:** This type of application build in the digital media and fully integrated with marketing solutions. Example: DataXu, LuckySort, Media Science, MetaMarkets and etc.
- **Business Intelligence:** BI is a transformation software that from raw data to meaningful and useful information for business analysis purpose. Example: IBM Cognos, MicroStrategy, Oracle Hyperion, SAP Business Objects, and etc.

- **Analytics and Visualization:** This type of application is ability to derive actionable information to help business competition and growth. It provides data driven strategies to share, innovate and deliver very quickly and easily real-time information. Example: 1010Data, Opera, SAS, Teradata Aster, TIBCO Spotfire and etc.

PART III: ALGORITHMS AROUND SOCIAL NETWORKS

Algorithms around Social Networks

Nowadays, popular sites like Facebook, Instagram, Twitter, and Pinterest create massive quantities of data and they need a very large scale applications to process the customer's perspective in a fastest way. And the data in Social Media are both structured and unstructured. So the task of capturing, processing and managing data is beyond the traditional scale of most common software. Now, Big Data fits into this picture to manage unstructured data. It is in a trends that many Big Data applications have been introduced algorithms specifically to make sense of social media data. So we need to look into the important of social media algorithms. Among the algorithms we are presented in this paper for Marketing and Social Media Mining.

3.1 Social Media Algorithm for Marketing

As marketing becomes increasingly digitized, it is important for businesses to remain in competitive edge. So enterprise are finding new way to retain their customers. Social Media is a good platform to advertise in technology age by leveraging big data, social media sites and mobile experiences with marketing algorithms which are playing a big role in this trends.

Here we will discuss with example of giant media Facebook and Twitter.

In Facebook, the content which shows up in a user's News Feed is dictated by an algorithm which determine on post-by-post basis whether a post is qualified to pass into a user's News Feed. Facebook used an algorithm – named EdgeRank. There are three way to measure EdgeRank: Affinity Score, Edge Weight and Time decay. (EdgeRank, 2014)

- **Affinity Score:** Means how "connected" a particular user is to the Edge. For example, if I write frequently on my friend's wall and we have 100 mutual friends. So my affinity score with my friend is very high. So Facebook knows I will probably want to see his status updates.
- **Edge Weight:** Each category of edges has a different default weight. In plain English, this means that comments are worth more than likes.
- **Time Decay:** How old the story is, it loses points because it consider old news. Every time, when you log into Facebook, you will see the stories with the highest EdgeRank in your News Feed.

For marketing, how a marketer can increase EdgeRank. First, you encourage user to visit your page frequently, "like" your page and write on your page wall so that user's friends can see your brand information and your band will be promoting among the user's friends. Second, you encourage user for sharing and commenting on your post so that your brand affinity score will be high. Third, keep your post on regular schedule so that users can see your brand information whenever they log into Facebook at any time.

In Twitter, the service that enables users to send and read short 140 character text messages, called "tweets". Another feature is "Trending topics" on Twitter, it shows the most popular conversation topics to user. Trends are determined by an algorithm that looks through all tweets on Twitter. This algorithm identifies topics that are immediately popular, rather than topics that have been popular for a while or on a daily basis, to help you discover the hottest emerging topics of discussion on Twitter that matter most to you. You can see "trends" whenever you go to your stream. You can see location based trends those are trending in the same geographic region or you can activate tailored trends for those who you follow.

Form marketing point of view, this is the point that how can we create trending topics. First method is that your post should require action. Based on how many people you follow or how many follower you have, your post will get more interactions and that will become a trending topics for your post. Second method is encourage retweets. It is a strong action because it is kind of a personal endorsement who retweeting your post. If the more people retweet, the more likely it to get trend.

Based on this two example, Facebook and Twitter, each platform is different. So we can conclude that understand the basic social media algorithms will help you to develop your online marketing and attracting the right audience.

3.2 Social Media Mining

Social Media Mining is the process of representing, analyzing, and extracting actionable patterns from social media data (Zafarani, Abbasi, & Liu, 2014). Social Media Mining introduces basic concepts and principal algorithms suitable for investigating massive social media data which is different from the traditional data.

Social Media Data is unstructured and large amount of volume in real time data. So new trend of computational data analysis approaches in social media combines social theories with statistical and data mining methods. In social media mining, we collect information about individuals and entities, measure their interactions, and discover patterns to understand human behavior (Zafarani et al., 2014). The task of mining in social media data is mining content with social relation which is generated by user. In this challenges in social media data, big data is playing the role to exploit the characteristics of social media and use its multidimensional, multisource, and multisite data to aggregate information with sufficient statistics for effective mining. Social Media Mining is a new interdisciplinary field in Social Media.

1) Data Mining in Social Media

Data Mining is the search for valuable information in large volumes of data. The process of discovering useful information from a collection of raw data is Knowledge Discovery in Databases (KDD). KDD process takes raw data as input and knowledge as output. In social media mining, the raw data is the content generated by individuals, and the knowledge encompasses the interesting patterns observed in this data (Zafarani et al., 2014). The standard KDD process is based on generic 5-steps model which developed by Fayyad et al. (Fayyad, Piatetsky-Shapiro, and Smyth, 1996).

Step 1: Data Selection and Extraction. Firstly, we have to decide what raw data is needed for the project goal and extract it from the data source to create a target data set. In social media mining, the raw data is the content generated by individuals, and the knowledge encompasses the interesting patterns observed in this data. We can collect this raw data from social media sits by using APIs (Application Programming Interfaces). Data instances are represented in tabular format using features. These instances can be labeled or unlabeled. Data representation for text data can be performed using the vector space model.

Step 2: Data Preprocessing. Quality measures need to be completed before processing the data. Quality measures include removing redundancies or noisy data, detecting sources of errors and substituting missing values. Preprocessing techniques commonly performed are aggregation, discretization, feature selection, feature extraction and sampling.

Step 3: Transformation. It is about data reduction and projection. First, we have to fine useful features to represent the data depending on the goal of the task. Second, the effective number of variables under consideration can be reduced by dimensionality reduction or transformation methods.

Step 4: Data Mining. This process is to select the appropriate data mining algorithms for searching patterns. Based on our literature review, here we are presenting some data mining algorithms which are suit to social media mining which involve both structured and unstructured data. These are decision tree learning, naïve Bayes classifier (NBC), nearest neighbor classifier, classification with network information, regression and clustering algorithms.

Step 5: Evaluation or Interpretation. This step can also involve visualization of the extracted patterns and models or visualization of the data given the extracted models. After visualization, it is ready to act on the discovered knowledge and incorporate the discovered knowledge into another system for further action.

2) Community Detection

Community is formed by individuals such that those within a group interact with each other more frequently than with those outside the group (Tang & Liu, 2010). Community detection is discovering groups in a network where individuals' group memberships are not explicitly given (Tang & Liu, 2010).

In the social networking community, the issue of community detection in social media has been widely studied in the context of the structure of the underlying graphs. In community detection, data points represent actors in social media and similarity between these actors is often defined based on the interests these users share (Zafarani et al., 2014). The major difference between clustering and community detection is that in community detection, individuals are connected to others via a network of links, whereas in clustering, data points are not embedded in a network (Zafarani et al., 2014). In particular, graph based community detection techniques are used and many important extensions that handle dynamic, heterogeneous networks in social media.

Communities in social media are either explicit (groups) or implicit (individuals). The researcher introduced community detection algorithms which are member based community detection and group based detection algorithms (Zafarani et al., 2014).

- **Member Based Community Detection Method:** It is based on three general nodes characteristic: node degree (familiarity), node reachability and node similarity.

- ○ **Node Degree:** The most common subgraph searched for in networks based on node degrees is a clique. Clique is a maximum complete subgraph in which all nodes are adjacent to each other. When using node degree, cliques are considered as communities. To find communities, we have to search for the maximum clique. To find maximum clique, Brute-force clique identification algorithm can be used theoretically. In practical, due to the computational complexity of clique identification, they added some constraints such that "Relaxing cliques" which comes from sociology with k-plex concept or "using cliques as a seed of a community" which is used by a well-known algorithm, Clique Percollation Method (CPM).
- ○ **Node Reachability:** The subgraphs where nodes are reachable from other nodes via a path. There are two concern, the first concern is in theoretical way that there is a path between them (regardless of the distance). In this case any graph traversal algorithm such as **Breadth-First Search (BFS)** and **Depth-First Search (DFS)** can be used to identify connected components (communities). But researcher found that this is not a very useful in large social media networks. The second concern is practical way that they are so closed as to be immediate neighbors. In this case, finding cliques is very challenging process. Well-known method with roots in social science are three subgraphs: k-clique, k-club, and k-clan.
- ○ **Node Similarity:** It is to determine the similarity between two nodes and similar nodes are assumed to be in same community. To compute node similarity, various normalization procedures such as the Jaccard similarity or the cosine similarity can be used.
- **Group-Based Community Detection:** In this section, researchers discussed communities that are balanced, robust, modular, dense or hierarchical based on their findings.
  - ○ **Balanced Communities:** Is that one can employ spectral clustering which provides a relaxed solution to the normalized cut and ratio cut in graphs.
  - ○ **Robust Communities:** Is search for subgraphs (example: K-edge, k-vertes) that are hard to disconnect.
  - ○ **Modular Communities:** Is that modularity is a measure the community structure which is created at random. Modularity maximization method can be used to find modular communities.
  - ○ **Dense Communities:** Which is particular interest in social media where we would like to have enough interactions for analysis to make statistical sense. Quasi-cliques method can be used for finding cliques in this communities.
  - ○ **Hierarchical Communities:** Previous communities are consider a single level. In practical, it is common to have hierarchies of communities mean that each community can have sub/super communities. Hierarchical clustering is a solution to find hierarchical communities. The Girvan-Newman algorithm is specifically designed for finding communities using divisive hierarchical clustering.

4. CONCLUSION

Big Data and Social Networks have been a hot topic for research in the last few years and continues to attract attention and significant research funding around the world. With social media, Data is flowing from daily life which generates from collection of collections data that includes different format of unstructured data. Social media becomes a one unique source of Big Data. Big Data lies real-time that can only manage by Big Data Applications. In fact, Big Data revolutionary is competition by Social Media organizations that how best they can improve complexity of dynamic contents which indeed is now exploring to improved computational methods in Social Networking. Therefore, Big Data with new computational method is definitely to remain foreseeable future in computational world.

Apart from Social Network and Big Data, we introduce the new field Social media mining which is a rapidly growing interdisciplinary field deeply rooted in computer science and social sciences. Any social media, there requires active community that communicates community detection to be interactive. The interest of social media is fast growing new arena & research technologies that needs greater intensifying to harness social media data and be developing a standardized frame work for utilizing big social media data.

This paper is one of the efforts to introduce the understanding of Big Data and Social Networks. It is designed to enable students, researchers, and practitioners to acquire fundamental concepts and algorithms for social network, big data and social media mining.

REFERENCES

Big Data at the Speed of Business. (n.d.). Retrieved Apr 10, from http://www-01.ibm.com/software/data/bigdata/what-is-big-data.html

Big Data for Enterprise. (n.d.). Retrieved Aug 01, from http://www.mongodb.com/big-data-explained#big-data-enterprise

Characteristics of Social Networks. (n.d.). Retrieved Mar 03, from http://socialnetworking.lovetoknow.com/Characteristics_of_Social_Networks

Chen, H., Chiang, R. H. L., & Storey, V. C. (2012). Business Intelligence and Analytics: From Big Data to Big Impact. *Management Information Systems Quarterly*, *36*(4), 1165–1188.

Cios, K., Pedrycz, W., & Swiniarski, R. (1998). *Data Mining Methods for Knowledge Discovery*. Boston: Kluwer Academic Publishers. doi:10.1007/978-1-4615-5589-6

Definition of Big Data. (n.d.). Retrieved Apr 20, from http://www.opentracker.net/article/definitions-big-data

Easley, D., & Kleinberg, J. (2010). *Networks, Crowds, and Markets: Reasoning about a Highly Connected World*. Cambridge: Cambridge University Press. doi:10.1017/CBO9780511761942

EdgeRank. (n.d.). Retrieved Aug 04, from http://edgerank.net/

Fayyad, U. (1996). Data Mining and Knowledge Discovery: Making Sense Out of Data. *IEEE Expert*, *11*(5), 20–25. doi:10.1109/64.539013

Fayyad, U., Piatetsky-Shapiro, G., & Smyth, P. (1996). From Data Mining to Knowledge Discovery in Databases. *AI Magazine*, 37–54.

Frank, O., & Strauss, D. (1986). Markov Graphs. *Journal of the American Statistical Association, 81*(395), 832–842. doi:10.1080/01621459.1986.10478342

How the Big Data Explosion Is Changing the World. (n.d.). Retrieved Apr 20, from http://blogs.msdn. com/b/microsoftenterpriseinsight/archive/2013/04/15/the-big-bang-how-the-big-data-explosion-is-changing-the-world.aspx

Intel Corporation. (2013). *Big Data in the Cloud: Converging Technologies.* Retrieved Mar 01, from http://www.intel.com/content/www/us/en/big-data/big-data-cloud-technologies-brief.html

Kakade, K. N., & Chavan, T. A. (2014). Improving Efficiency of GEO-Distributed Data Sets using Pact. *International Journal of Current Engineering and Technology, 4*(3), 1284–1287.

Kaur, D., & Paul, A. (2014). Performance Analysis of Different Data mining Techniques over Heart Disease dataset. *International Journal of Current Engineering and Technology, 4*(1), 220–224.

Koobface. (n.d.). Retrieved May, 10 from http://en.wikipedia.org/wiki/Koobface

Krishnamurthy, B., & Wills, C. E. (2008), *Characterizing Privacy in Online Social Networks.* WOSN '08 Proceedings of the first workshop on Online social networks. Retrieved from http://www2.research. att.com/~bala/papers/posn.pdf

Learn the Latest Social Advertising Trend. (n.d.). Retrieved July 20, from http://resolutionmedia.com/ us/white-papers/resolution-media-social-trends-report

Lusher, D., Koskinen, J., & Robins, G. (2013). *Exponential Random Graphs Models for Social Networks: Theory, Methods and Application.* Cambridge: Cambridge University press.

Maltby, D. (2011). Big Data Analytics. *ASIST Conference*, New Orleans, LA.

Manyika, J., Chui, M., Brown, B., Bughin, J., Dobbs, R., Roxburgh, C., & Byers, A. H. (2011). *Big data: The next frontier for innovation, competition, and productivity.* The McKinsey Global Institute.

Map Reduce. (n.d.). Retrieved Aug 01, from http://docs.mongodb.org/manual/core/map-reduce/

McAfee, A., & Erik Brynjolfsson, E. (2012). Big Data: The Management revolution. *Harvard Business Review*, 59–68. PMID:23074865

Mislove, A., Marcon, M., Gummadi, K. P., Druschel, P., & Bhattacharjee, B. (2007). Measurement and Analysis of Online Social Networks. *5th ACM/USENIX Internet Measurement Conference, IMC'07*, San Diego, CA. doi:10.1145/1298306.1298311

Porter, M. A. (2012). *Small World Network.* Retrieved Apr 12, from http://www.scholarpedia.org/article/ Small-world_network

Research Report. (2013). *State of Social Media Span.* Retrieved July 12, from www.nexgate.com

Robins, G. (2009). Social Networks, Exponential Random Graph (P*) Models for Computational Complexity: Theory, Techniques, and Applications. New York: Springer.

Robins, G., Pattison, P., Kalish, Y., & Lusher, D. (2007). An introduction to exponential random graph (p*) models for social networks. *Social Networks*, *29*(2), 173–191. doi:10.1016/j.socnet.2006.08.002

Russom, P. (2011). *Big Data Analytic, The Data Warehouse Institute (TDWI), Best Practices Report*. Fourth Quarter.

Shang, W., Jiang, Z. M., Hemmati, H., Adams, B., Hassan, A. E., & Martin, P. (2013). Assisting Developers of Big Data Analytics Applications When Deploying on Hadoop Clouds. *35th International Conference on Software Engineering (ICSE 2013)*. doi:10.1109/ICSE.2013.6606586

Social Media Update. (2013). Retrieved July 20, from http://www.pewinternet.org/2013/12/30/social-media-update-2013

Social Networks Modeling. (n.d.). Retrieved July 07, from http://columbiadatascience.com/2012/11/02/brief-introduction-to-social-network-modeling

Tang, L., & Liu, H. (2010). *Communication Detection in Mining in Social Media for Data Mining and Knowledge Discovery*. Morgan & Claypool Publishers.

The 4V's of Big Data. (n.d.). Retrieved Apr 20, from http://www.ibmbigdatahub.com/infographic/four-vs-big-data

The Big Data Landscape for Type of Application & Examples. (n.d.). Retrieved Apr, 15, from http://www.bigdatalandscape.com

Toivonena, R., Kovanena, L., Kiveläa, M., Onnelab, J., Saramäkia, J., & Kaskia, K. (2009). A comparative study of social network models: Network evolution models and nodal attribute models. *Social Networks*, *31*(4), 240–254. doi:10.1016/j.socnet.2009.06.004

Trending Topics. (2010). Retrieved Aug 13, from https://blog.twitter.com/2010/trend-or-not-trend

Watts, D. J., & Strogatz, S. H. (1998). Collective dynamics of `small-world' networks. *Nature*, *393*(6684), 440–442. doi:10.1038/30918 PMID:9623998

Zafarani, R., Abbasi, M., & Liu, H. (2014). *Social Media Mining: An Introduction*. Cambridge: Cambridge University Press. doi:10.1017/CBO9781139088510

KEY TERMS AND DEFINITIONS

Big Data: Extremely large and highly complex data sets that can be analyzed computationally contextually which describes approximately contemporary to human interaction based on oneself emotion.

Big Data Analytics: The process of examining very large and diverse of data which can be used of advanced analytic techniques in an effort to uncover hidden patterns, unknown correlations and other useful information.

Big Data Infrastructure: The main purpose is the process and store both structure and unstructured data.

Community Detection: Discovering groups in a network where surveillance is implicitly to each individual membership.

Knowledge Discovery in Databases (KDD): The process of discovering useful information from a collection of raw data.

Social Media Mining: The computationally process of social media data which patterns can be compute analytically.

Social Networks: Social structure which involves different subjects of any interested topics internationally whereby at least a group of two people interactively exchange.

Chapter 19
Analysis of VDM++ in Regression Test Suite

Zahid Hussain Qaisar
King Faisal University, Saudi Arabia

Farooq Ahmad
COMSATS Institute of Information Technology – Lahore, Pakistan

ABSTRACT

Regression testing is important activity during the maintenance phase. An important work during maintenance of the software is to find impact of change. One of the essential attributes of Software is change i.e. quality software is more vulnerable to change and provide facilitation and ease for developer to do required changes. Modification plays vital role in the software development so it is highly important to find the impact of that modification or to identify the change in the software. In software testing that issue gets more attention because after change we have to identify impact of change and have to keenly observe what has happened or what will happen after that particular change that we have made or going to make in software. After change software testing team has to modify its testing strategy and have to come across with new test cases to efficiently perform the testing activity during the software development Regression testing is performed when the software is already tested and now some change is made to it. Important thing is to adjust those tests which were generated in the previous testing processes of the software. This study will present an approach by analyzing VDM (Vienna Development Methods) to find impact of change which will describe that how we can find the change and can analyze the change in the software i.e. impact of change that has been made in software. This approach will fulfill the purpose of classifying the test cases from original test suite into three classes obsolete, re-testable, and reusable test cases. This technique will not only classify the original test cases but will also generate new test cases required for the purpose of regression testing.

INTRODUCTION

As now a days formal specification based development is increasing. As mentioned in our literature review we know that there are many techniques for formal specification based testing. Some technique use Z specification and some use VDM or other specification languages but there a few technique for formal specification based regression testing.

DOI: 10.4018/978-1-4666-8505-5.ch019

All existing techniques for formal specification based regression testing were either for Object-Z or for other specification languages but there was no technique for formal specification based regression testing of VDM specification based testing. So our research parameters mentioned in literature review also encouraged us to develop a technique for VDM specification language. From literature review we have clearly seen that during maintenance phase of software we require regression test suite for effective testing. In case of formal specification based software during maintenance we require formal specification based regression testing technique. Hence there was need for formal specification based regression testing for VDM specification.

RELATED WORK

We have divided our literature review chapter in two different sections. First section describes about different techniques about the formal specification based testing and the second section is about formal specification based regression testing. From first section we will select an approach for getting test cases for our baseline version and from second section we will find technique for regression testing and will compare how our technique is different from them. As there is no technique for regression testing of VDM-SL so we have done literature review of formal specification based testing (Section 1) and formal specification based regression testing (Section 2). Regression testing will be based on the testing of formal specification. We will evaluate these techniques mentioned below and will propose our technique for the regression testing.

There are two basic strategies for regression testing; retest all and selective regression testing (selecting tests from previous test history) when we apply retest all strategy, as by its name it is clear that from baseline version all the test cases should be selected for the delta version i.e. all the tests generated in the testing process for the baseline version should be executed for the delta version. It will be very time consuming (Amayreh and zin, 1999).Most of the time it can be a wasteful activity, since there may be many tests which are not required to be executed. The better option is the selective regression testing approach where we select the test cases corresponding to the modified pars of the system.

Many regression testing approaches have been proposed. In these techniques some are regression test reduction techniques. Analysis of change is very important in regression testing for selecting regression test suite as well as it is important topic in software change management. Testing software after maintenance is called regression testing. A lot of techniques are developed for this purpose including model based, component based, and code based etc (most of the techniques are code based).

Formal specification based development is increasing now a days as more critical systems are formally specified before their development. So, formal specification based testing is very important to test formally specified software and systems. Despite these techniques, some techniques are classified as formal specification based since the regression testing is performed using formal specifications. Software testing is used to validate the system functionality according to the specification. Formal specification is used to formalize the system. Formal specification overcomes the weakness of the traditional software testing but its testing is important as formal proofs are not sufficient so, we require formal specification based testing to test the formal specification. The increasing use of formal methods in software industry has increased the importance of formal specification based testing techniques. Though formal methods are increasingly used in the software industry but still there is very less work done as for as the formal specification based regression testing is concerned (korel *et al.*, 2007).

In the following section we will discuss different techniques for the formal specification based testing as it will be useful for us in our technique for test cases generation for the baseline specification.

SECTION 1: FORMAL SPECIFICATION BASED TESTING

In this section we will review techniques for formal specification based testing as these techniques will be useful for the test suite generation for the baseline version of the VDM-SL specification. So, we will present review of formal specification based testing as mentioned below.

Automated Black-Box Testing with Abstract VDM Oracles

In this paper the technique is defined to automatically test the software by analyzing its specification. In this studied technique the post condition of the software specification which is written in VDM-SL acts as test oracles. A test oracle is basically an analysis of expected output with corresponding input of the software. In the studied technique the input is screened out via analyzing the pre-condition of the software specification i.e. the input is filtered by the pre-condition of the software specification.

A mapping between abstract and concrete data is required. Here an example of radio switch in which a frequency is mapped to a particular operator on a specific position. Data Reinfication concept is also introduced which is correct if abstract and refined level have homomorphism. It means post condition must hold for the concrete input and output if the pre-conditioned is satisfied. Modern tools allow the interpretation of explicit VDM-SL definitions (Aichernig, 1999).

Studied technique provides automated test evaluation. The advantage of that approach is the automation of black box testing by the usage of structural test-data. This work could be extended with test case generation techniques in order to automate the whole test process. However the automated test evaluation especially supports random testing. Code generation is been shown of test oracles. Code generation from test oracles is been demonstrated. Another approach is also mentioned in the studied paper in which interpretation of oracles with the dynamic link facility is also shown and the third method mentioned is the CORBA. The CORBA interface of the VDM-SL toolbox is defined in IDL, the interface definition language of CORBA. This approach can be applied to as many programming languages as IDL mapping have been implemented, e.g. C++ and Java. So the language gap has been bridged through CORBA (Aichernig, 1999).

A Proof Obligation Generator for VDM-SL

In this studied well-formed ness grading of VDM-SL is studied in which it is considered and distinguished that what kind of specification language is i.e. either it is well formed or definite well-formed because specification cannot be checked through static type checker in case of division that whether the denominator of division is zero or not so to make sure that divisor in case of division should be non-zero proof obligators are use which make sure at the specification level that division will not lead to non-determinism and post condition will be hold. Here central check of the type checker is to check whether the two types are compatible or not due to rich type system of VDM-SL a simple comparison is not possible in general. Furthermore the task is un-decidable in general because of disjoint unions and subtypes (Aichernig and Larsen, 1997).

Rejection and acceptance concept is introduced through which compiler of specification according to the specification decides whether to accept or reject the particular specification here well-formed-ness and definite well-formed-ness check is evaluated and specification is graded and compiler rejects the non-well-formed specification error messages are raised in case of errors.

The studied approach has also given knowledge about context generation and proof obligations for expressions and functions. Domain checking is also considered and satisfiability is defined as there must be pre-condition to be consistent, there must be a return value satisfying the post-condition when pre-condition is satisfied. This property is called the satisfiability of implicit function (Aichernig and Larsen, 1997).

Pattern matching is done as well as proof obligators for the operations are also introduced and distinguish are made between the implicit and explicit operations as well as assertions are generated somewhat similar to the context generation. in context generation type judgments is also been analyzed. So this technique has introduced the concept of automatic generation of proof obligations for VDM-SL.In this technique large subsets of specification can be formally checked according to their internal consistency secondly using a proof tool many simple proof obligations can be proved automatically. Proof obligator give error messages through which the user can detect the missing parts in a specification.

Design and Application of a Test Case Generator for VDM-SL

In this studied research paper author has designed a test case generator which automatically generates the test cases from the software specification of software. A case study of the access control system is given in which the access control system of the security system is formally specified. CSS which is basically a comprehensive security system which has been developed by ARCS a development organization is designed .In this system the security guard visits the stations in his security round (Drosch, 1999).

CSS which is comprehensive security system is modeled and example is been demonstrated in which stations are marked as black triangles which are visited by the guard during the round. SSD has number of features which support the operator and guards for example door may unlock automatically and intrusion circuits deactivated once the guard has passed that area.

Systems have different events which are triggered when the guard or operator interacts with the system. A trace is the particular sequence of events .A scenario defined as the set of all possible traces for which the system is required to behave correctly. Interface functions are made on the bases of these events.

Input of the system is restricted by the pre-condition which is applied to each condition. So the valid inputs are allowed by restricted the system by imposing the pre-condition .On the bases of sequence of events scenarios are designed .scenarios are incorporated into VDM-SL to reject the illegal sequences of events.

The test cases are generated for the access control for this purpose test case generator is been introduced to check whether specification supports all sequences of events that are drawn from the scenarios and is the refinement correct? In other words do the explicit executable parts of the functions satisfy their implicit parts? Round step, guard step and station steps of the security guard are defined.

In this paper test case generation has been considered for tests executed as part of the specification validation process of the access control system. So test cases are automated generated and executed to the system (Drosch, 1999).

Formal Testing Based on Coverage Criteria

Formal testing based on coverage criteria classification include all the techniques That uses the coverage criteria as the test parameters to test based on the formal specification. Different criteria like control flow is used. Following are the description of the technique lie in formal testing based on coverage criteria classification.

Formalization of Software Testing Criteria using the Z Notation

A control flow criterion is best for the statement coverage, condition and decision coverage, D/C coverage, multiple condition coverage and modifies condition decision coverage (MC/DC), which uses different type of conditions and decisions. Multiple conditions are stronger but it requires lots of test cases to satisfy. MC/DC criteria are used as the intermediate criteria. It requires achievement of statement coverage and condition coverage criteria combined with the requirement that each condition should affect the decision's outcome (Sergiy and Bowen, 2001).

Control flow criteria, i.e., criteria using logical expressions, which determine the branch and loop structure of the program, are considered . All coverage criteria are formalized with the formal language Z. Every coverage criteria is presented as Z schemas. Z schema use basic mathematics to ensure the correctness of the each coverage. Z schemas ensure that there will be no ambiguities and error in the specification (Sergiy and Bowen, 2001).

Test Generation by Decomposing the Specification

Specifications that are written in Z are further decomposed and different predicates are subdivided to generate the test cases. Following are the techniques that lie under defined classification.

Improving Software Tests Using Z Specification

Traditional software technique is used for the software testing but it has much weakness while comparing to the formal specification based testing. In this technique embedded control system software development for the airbus A330/340 had discussed. More realistic data is used to validate the test. In traditional testing process, testing data have its own impact. Implementation semantics are checked and manually test cases are developed. Formal methods (Z specification) do all this work that ensure that the specification is according to the requirements.

Testing of the various application areas are reduced by the Z specification. Z specifications are supported by the tool ensure to remove the problem in the specification by automatically evaluating the test results against specification (Horcher *et al.*, 1995).

Different schema are presented, each of which denotes a test case. Test oracle problem can be overcome by directly describing the schema (using different predicate), which serve as the description of the expected output, makes the basis for the evaluation. A Case study of the Airbus discuss cabin intercommunication data system (CIDS), used in the Airbus. Test cases will be derived from the Z formal specification by first generating the test classes automatically and then manually deriving the concrete input data (Horcher *et al.*, 1995).

Automated Testing From Z Specification

Automated testing from z specification is done by specifying formal heuristics for generating test cases. Sample data is verified for automated testing. Test generating procedures must be verified and validated (Burton and York, 2000). Many heuristics can be applied to a test suit. Based on the defined heuristics criteria, test set are made for Z specification language. Most common approach to generating tests from model based specifications is based on the idea of equivalence classes. Testing for each equivalence class sample test data is used. Partitioning based approach used to Z specification testing.

Based on various hypothesis and heuristics, test cases are made as operations in Z. Abstract test case are derived based on the common testing approach like boundary value analysis or disjoint partitioning. Predicate part of the schema represents abstract test case because of partitioning selected data points out many errors. Sun domain represented by constraints of schema used in Z. Partitioning heuristics can be based on either the signature or the predicate part of the specification. As an example Square Root schema is discussed. It calculates the square root which is not greater than the output defined first. Boundary value has been chosen as an input to the schema. Input constraints can be analyzed from a schema to present the different predicates upon the inputs or the output different schema can be used to represent. Boundary value analysis is best for detecting hypothesis fault (Burton and York, 2000).

Before test the heuristics they need to be describe in Z notations. Partitioning heuristics are theorem in Z, describes the relationship between original and resulting abstract test cases (Burton and York, 2000). Input space is sub divided and functions acting of input space verify all partitions. Following is an example of formalized partitioning heuristics from .Fault can be detected by selecting test data from each sub domain. Sub domain's disjoint-ness and completeness of heuristics can be formally verifies. If all area is mapped it is complete and if not overlap the areas then they are disjoint. Heuristics can be extended to fault based testing. It restricts value at the point where fault can be detected. Necessary condition and sufficient conditions can be selected.

"CADiZ is Z type checker and theorem proves that allows a user to iteratively brows, type check and performs proofs upon a Z specification". In this tool weak specifications are also tested. Last functional units are allowed to test abstract test cases. For automated testing generic tactics are used. The completeness, disjoint-ness and satisfactory properties of heuristics are also proved using the tool. Partitioned predicate are the parameters of tactics. Complete heuristic partition is added to predicate part without change the behavior of operation schema (Burton and York, 2000)

Using Test Template Framework

Techniques used in this sub section include testing the system using formal specification by using a test template framework. Following is given the details of testing using TTF.

Specification Based Testing Framework

The framework can be defined using any model based specification notation and used to derived tests from model based specification (Stocks and Carrington, 1993). Framework is the test data and their relation to the operation in a specification and other data set. Design functional test are made using formal specification. Testing consider many parameters, not just the test data. Test template framework

(TTF) is structured strategy and formal framework of specification based testing (SBT). The TTF deals with functional unit testing specification as test design language (TDL) and TTF. Z specification is as powerful as one specification language because it uses mathematics notations.

Test template is based on real data, derived from formal specification and Test Template (TT) is always definable. Sets are used data input and valid input space is derived for each function unit. Test template is defined by the Z specification. Z is based on the basic mathematical notations. Valid input space (VIS) can be derived from constraints that make sure the input cannot fail the operation. Input class is determined the domain, that partitioned the whole Input Space. Accuracy can be determined by further subdividing the partitions.

In TTF domain testing is difficult job. Through refinement of Test template, more concrete and accurate tests are made. TTF also provide maintenance through updating of TT and re-derived. In TTF Relation between input and output clearly defined that is useful for test oracle.

Testing and Evaluation by Translating Z in Prolog Specification

In this classification the techniques included use Z specification and then Z specifications are converted into prolog then further test generation and test evaluation.

Probe: A Formal Specification Base Testing System

In this research paper the author has described that Generation of test cases can be done from formal specification. PROBE is an automatic testing system. Specification are written in Z and then translated into prolog, for making it more executable. This translation is called ZP. Like Z prolog is also widely used, based on the first order predicate logic and specification is executable. Translation can be done automatically by the tool.

Z specification is used as input to the ZP translator, which translate the Z specification into prolog. Prolog is suitable for test generation because it provides the variable's domain partition automatically (Amayareh and Zin, 1999). Backtracking is one of the features of prolog. To force the back tracking a meta-interpreter, that is written in the specific language is used. Number of iteration in the interpreter is minded and specific number of iterations is done to generate the test case. These iterations count must be reasonable to generate the test cases. Bad order can generate the errors. Errors caused by calling the logic program with different level of variable instantiated. Instantiation is caused with the calling of insufficient input arguments. Some predicates of Z are not so often used in prolog, so need to be careful from them.

Test case generator in prolog need some processing, an intelligent input/output analyzer was developed. There it contains the input part; result will be compare with expected output. Data typed can be suitably applied and un-instantiated variables are replaced with the random number. Test driver is used to execute the testing of the program. It uses input generate the result with the expected output and report the conclusion to the process (Amayareh and Zin, 1999).

Z Classification Tree

Classification tree method is used with Z specification to design test cases. In this classification technique that use classification tree method with Z specification is discussed.

Test Case Design Based on Z and the Classification-Tree Method

In this paper Classification tree method with disjunctive normal form (DNF) is applied to test case design. Classification tree method is based on the testing the specification. On the basis of functional specification with relevant aspects for test input domain in classification tree method is analyzed. Classes are iteratively classified, that are presented in form of tree. By combining different classes test cases are formed. Speed and distance control system is an example. Following classification tree is presented for the SPeDi system from (Singh *et al*., 1997).

"A disjunction Normal Form of a predicate is a disjunction of the conjunctions of the different components of the predicate". DNF approach is widely used in generating test cases from formal specification because it is purely syntax based. Schema is splitted into sun schemas, each presenting a test case which may consist of number of constraints. For performing required transformation DNF chose system having set of rule like transforming Z expression not part of regular predicate logic consisting rule to distribute quantifiers with respect to logic connectors and transforming propositional logic formulas in DNF. Possible shortcoming from DNF could be inconsistent test cases, semantically in-disjoint test cases and unstructured test cases (Singh *et al*., 1997).

Concept of test case design based on Z specification is illustrated. Any operational schema in Z is considered a test object. On basis of different classes' aspects, proofs of Z schema are analyzed. Information such as class aspect formal specification and semantics are determined. On basis of formal specification tree structure could consider the order of different classification aspects and nodes in the resulting classification are attached. Structure of tree has impact on the quality and quantity of test cases. Comparing structures result in increase in the inconsistent trees. Leaf nodes are combined to generate the test case. Manual or automated approaches are there, which make sure that each class is participated. Class is the predicate of formal specification.

Test case generation need further refinement. Main steps in test case design are identifying the relevant variable, design them on the basis of their signature, class generation, class partitioning, supplementing the classification, selecting the high level test case, Conjugate the specification schema of the test object with the predicates characterizing the selected high level test case and simplify the resulting schema to get the complete schema for the selected test case and _ Transform the test case schema into (canonical) disjunctive normal form to get refined test cases which also contain information for the evaluation of test results (Singh *et al*., 1997).

Hybrid Inspection Techniques

This classification will cover up different techniques that don't lies under the above classification. Most of them are the mixture of different techniques. In this classification the techniques that assess the quality of the formal specifications are also included.

Formal Methods and Testing

In this paper author has described that Formal methods are used in various contexts for improving the software. Formal methods and testing are both complimentary approaches for the software systems, but still they are getting more confidence (Bowen *et al*., 1995). Formal method and testing are used to verify the quality. Theme presented here is to improve the software quality from formal methods. Views of different members of the FORTEST network are presented covering black box testing, fault and conformance based testing, theory versus practice, design and refinement for testing, testing in support of specification, testability transformation, using system properties and automatic generation of test using formal specification language Z.

Effective development could be done by the combination formal and informal techniques. Formal Methods does not show any miracles. They are very good at some places. There is always need to identify what work well in which environment and defend the reasons. Formal methods used in support of testing, there are typical approaches like test and check are used for testing. Engineers often not write formal description of specification. Formal language Z provides engineers feasibility to write formal specification.

Evolutionary testing is used in support of formal methods. Claims about exception freeness and other specific safety properties first might be verified via guided dynamic search and only then subject to proof. Integrated approach reduces the risk. Test data is used to validate the system state. Better formal specification testing can be better used with black box and structured testing. Consideration must be taken while making distinguishing b/w mathematics and formal methods used by the mathematician and engineers.

Testability Transformation

In this paper author has described that testing is a crucial part of software development. Programs that are hard to test are transformed into easier one to test them effectively and easily. Branch coverage is explained which requires "for each feasible branch of the program under test, at least one test case which cause execution to traverse the branch" (Bowen *et al.*, 1995). Brach coverage test data selection problem is considered here by evolutionary testing. Evolutionary testing used Genetic Algorithm based search techniques. Evolutionary testing is good but cause problem in programming style due to fitness function Problem related fitness functions are, presence of side effects in predicates, use of flag variables and unstructured control flow. Program is transformed into easier one to generate test data efficiently (Rennard, 2000).

Goal of transformation is to transport poor program into better one and original program will be discarded after that transformation of program construction. But in another technique called testability transformation, in that program is discarded after test data generation. Program transformation is to have all function and testability transformation test data is fit for original. Lot of work needed for the testability transformation but remember that semantics must be preserved.

Utilization of System Properties in the Testing

In this research paper author has described that there are many testing processes exists but they have no sound theoretical basis. Software testing is an imprecise process that is more of an art rather than a science (Bowen *et al.*, 1995). System properties are used to generate the test cases used in testing. Test hypothesis and fault model are used. A test is used to measure the correctness under some assumptions. Fault model are largely used in network terms and hardware testing. For a specification fault model is collection of some properties with the same constraints.

Many test criteria are same if they satisfy same constraints. System properties (fault model/hypothesis) are used to compare test set and criteria. Test hypothesis and fault models allow the tester to reason about test effectiveness (Bowen *et al.*, 1995). Major issues to find system properties are, that all properties must hold and are simple to formally verify and these properties must help the tester.

Test Automation

In this studied paper the author wants to describe that Problem with testing are they cause different errors either by commission or by omission. Test automation includes both test generation and execution. Strategy of test automation is getting very appreciation. There are many tools are available to test the program. Test are generated from formal specification to formal language Z by applying automatic test generation and execution are now close to the "one button testing ".There are problems. First thing is that use cases written are more abstract that don't cover the details. Second problem is that they don't cover the major/maximum aspects. Third major problem is that we are only keen to test the functional units but many problems can cause by the non-functional issues (Bowen *et al.*, 1995).

Automatic Assessment of Z Specification

Ideas presented here describe the quality of formal specification language Z. The environment chosen is the Ceilidh system, the most widely used student programming automatic assessment system used in UK (Foxley and Salam, 1997). To measure the quality of the software it must be divided or grouped into different categories like operation, revision and transition. Specification is used to express the requirements. Z based formal specifications are used to mathematically prove the specification. It is not 100% guarantee about their validation. But it provides the best as compare to the traditional approaches. Formal specifications language Z is used to validate the requirements. Better style of presenting the system either by coding, make it more readable.

Whenever designing the software it is assumed that the output is well designed and as well as the assessment is considered the marking should be flexible. Assessment criteria can be changed with time to time or course to course. Ceilidh Suggest several assessment criteria. Specification maintainability measurement can be done by the style of presentation. In specification complexity measurement "each complexity matrix is marked relative to the corresponding counts for the model specification". Static correctness can be measure by the ZP specification. Mathematically consistency and completeness can be checked. To check the equivalence in Z, schema is animated. Animated schema is made and marked according to its correctness.

Formal Specification of an Auctioning System Using VDM++ and UML an Industrial Usage Report

In this research paper an auction system is formally specified using VDM++ the object orient version of the VDM which uses the object oriented concepts for formal specification. So author applies VDM++ and real time UML very successfully which provides a facility to the client in this project to extend the auction clock system. "Ten commandments of the formal methods" are used in that system to formalize and to design it (Berg *et al.*, 2000)

Before starting to formally specifying system we have to keep balance of technical and non-technical as driving the notation choice .we have to also identify the maturity level of the organization in this paper we learn that embedded formal method of choice is way to work. This paper emphasis on testing and we has learn that we have to test, test and test again.

TESTAF: A TEST AUTOMATION FRAMEWORK FOR CLASS TESTING USING OBJECT-ORIENTED FORMAL SPECIFICATIONS

In that particular paper a framework TESTAF is defined which supports automated generation and execution of the test cases using object-oriented formal specification. Architecture of TESTAF consists of configuration matcher, predicate parser, test generator and test driver. Formal specification and its implementation along with the test specification is required for the framework to work. Configuration matcher matches the configuration of specification to the implementation so the class name and instance variable names and method signature are matched. It generates a configuration file that has the mappings between names used in the specification and the names in the implementation.

While predicate parser contains the entry as well as exit predicate for each method in the class. Entry predicate is conjunction of the method pre-condition and the class invariant predicates. Exit predicate is conjunction of exit predication and post-condition. Symbol table is generated for the boundary value analysis. This is used to generate the test data. Initially empty shells are generated which later on are filled with the test data (Nadeem and Jaffar, 2005).

Test driver executes the test cases on the implementation .configuration mapping is semi-automated as it allows user to modify the configuration filed and change the names as same names can be possible in case of overriding and overloading so it should be semi-automated and user should change the configuration file. Concrete test cases are generated to fill the empty test shells.

This studied approach is fully automatic as test cases are generated automatically and executed automatically and have also concept of test data generation from the symbol table and boundary value analysis is done. Test case implementation is done by the test drivers (Nadeem and Jaffar, 2005).

Formal Specification and Validation at Work: A Case Study Using VDM

This research paper has described about how the formal methods if applied can be useful and can benefit in the industrial context .Formal specification and validation is done by using the ISO standard VDM-SL. The case study is given to facilitate the conclusion and to elaborate the vision.

Example of metro door management system is given in which there is high risk in case of failure so the system is critical and it is shown that how this system can be formalized and can be implemented. Door management system of the train is formalized and is managed by considering the three constraints i.e. velocity, time and control buttons (Agerholm *et al.*, 1998).

Here we got the knowledge about the state and type definition in formal specification. OMT state diagrams for doors and train are shown and animation and prototyping is used in addition to animation IFAD VDM provides the dynamic link facility which supports the binary code. During testing four errors are found in four different scenarios which are viewed using the front end graphical in corresponding three views (Agerholm *et al.*, 1998).

New thing in the studied technique is the three view graphical front end of the system and we have studied the modeling in VDM and managing the change. The advantage of that technique is that it is animated and has concept of rapid prototyping and has ability of technology transfer and has large of industrial benefits.

A Framework for Automated Testing from VDM-SL Specifications

In this particular research paper a framework for automated testing is given through which we can learn how to do testing automatically from VDM Specification. The architecture of the framework consists of scanner, parser, code generator and test generator. Scanner performs the act as lexical analyzer and generates the tokens which are input to the parser. While parser takes the tokens as inputs and generates a parse tree using a context free grammar (CFG) for the VDM-SL expressions. Parser produces the symbol table too for variables in the expression this table is used by the test generator to generate test cases based on the boundary values of variables (Nadeem and Jaffar, 2004).

Code generator generates the C language code from the parse tree .code generator also optimizes the code which is free of redundant instructions. Test generator partitions the classes into equivalence classes using the symbol table generated by the parser. Equivalence classes are generated from boundary values of the variables .from each equivalence class the test generator randomly selects test values. Source modifier re-scans the source code and inserts calls to generate code for pre-condition just before each function call. Then test driver is used to execute the test cases on the implementation and evaluates the post condition expression. The test driver creates the log file for the test execution.

This studied approach gives idea how to generate code from VDM-SL and gives concepts about parsing the VDM-SL expressions. An expression is parsed from the parse tree and code generation is done from VDM-SL. Then test cases are generated.

In this studied approach source modification concepts are introduced and we can learn about results evaluation. Test technique is fully automated as test cases are automatically generated and are also executed automatically through test drivers. It introduces the parsing of VDM-SL and code generation for the testing purpose and has ability to modify the source code and then through this modified source code which has modification of insertion of pre-conditions. It is basically fully automated framework for the VDM-SL (Nadeem and Jaffar, 2004).

Analysis of Techniques

In this above mentioned section different techniques related formal specification based testing are reviewed. Some analysis of the techniques based on some parameters will be performed. From this literature review we can clearly see that there are a few techniques for the formal specification bases regression testing. In table some parameters are defined and their description is given. On the basis of these parameters different techniques for formal specification based testing are analyzed. Some research parameters are given below with description. We will evaluate techniques by considering these parameters as given in Table 1.

On the basis of the above mentioned analysis parameters we have evaluated the techniques for formal specification based testing and analyzed them as mentioned in the Table 2. We found that few techniques provide formal specification based regression testing for VDM specification as for as regression based formal specification testing for VDM there is no technique for that purpose.

Table 1. Analysis parameters

S.No.	Parameter Name	Description
1	Input specification Languages	Used formal language is VDM or any other formal language
2	Automated test cases generation	Is technique fully or partially supports test cases generation i.e. test case generation is fully automated.
3	Specification and Implementation Conformance	Does technique guarantee that test suite is as effective as for specification and implementation i.e. implementation is according to the specification and test suite is valid for implementation as well(Nadeem and Jaffer,2005)
4	Tool Support	Is there any tool support for technique
5	Refining the Test case	Are the generated test cases are refined.
6	Coverage criteria	Is technique defines some coverage criteria for testing.
7	Automated test cases Execution	Is technique fully or partially supports test cases execution i.e. test case execution is fully automated.

Table 2. Analysis of different techniques

	Input Spec. Language	Automated Test Cases Generation	Specification and Implementation Conformance	Tool Support	Refining the Test Cases	Coverage Criteria	Automated Test Cases Execution
Singh *et al.*, 1997	Z	Partially	Partially	Fully	Partially	Fully	Partially
Nadeem and Jaffar, 2005	VDM	Fully	Fully	Fully	Fully	Fully	Fully
Amayareh and Zin, 1999	Z	Partially	Partially	Fully	Fully	Fully	Partially
Drosch, 1999	VDM	Fully	Partially	Fully	Fully	Partially	Partially
Aichernig, 1999	VDM	Partially	Fully	Partially	Partially	Partially	Partially
Nadeem and Jaffar, 2004	VDM	Fully	Fully	Fully	Partially	Partially	Fully

Proposed Approach

We have proposed an approach for regression testing which is based on formal specification of VDM-SL language. Input for our proposed approach is formal specification document written in VDM (Vienna Development Methods) which is a formal specification language. We will analyze the formal specification developed in VDM. Our proposed technique will be applied to classify test suite for regression testing by analyzing VDM specification.

Our approach has classified test suite in three types of test cases by analyzing the VDM specification of baseline version as well as delta version of the software specification. Proposed technique has compared the two versions of the software i.e. the old version which was baseline version while the other version was the changed version of the specification or also called delta version of the specification. Then we have analyzed these changes syntactically as well as semantically in the specification.

As mentioned in the Figure 1 our approach has taken two versions of specification as input. Required information for the comparator was parsed and was stored in the lists i.e. class ID, class invariants, variable ID data types, operations ID and operation pre and post conditions was stored in the lists. Comparator got this information for baseline version and compared it with the delta version as information was stored separately for baseline and delta version. Comparison was done both syntactically as well as semantically Comparator identified the changes in the Delta version and then Test suite selection was done for the delta version and test cases will be selected for the Regression testing. For test suite selection test cases for the baseline version was provided as input.

We have designed regression test suite by comparing pre and post conditions of operations on the basis of baseline version of the specification. Test selection algorithm was designed for selection of test cases.

Figure 1. Overview of Proposed Approach

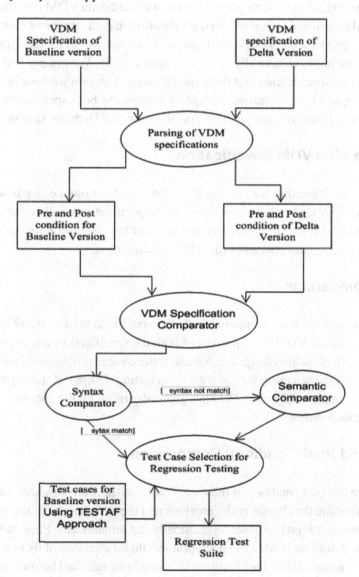

Assumptions for Proposed Technique

For our proposed technique we have assumed that a pre and post condition for the specifications should be in the DNF (Disjunctive Normal Form) and secondly we have test cases for baseline version of the specification. For delta version on the basis of baseline version we have categorized our test cases database in three different categories i.e. obsolete, re-useable and re-testable.

The basic flow for our approach has been shown in Figure 1. It states that we will be having two versions of specification baseline and delta version of the specification. We have compared these two versions to find the change or to identify the change. For that purpose we have compared operations for the class in the specification.

Parsing of VDM Specifications

In parsing of VDM specification we have parsed the baseline and delta VDM specifications. Parser have parsed both the specification and stored required information in data structures (lists). For baseline and delta version separate data structures (lists) has been used as it was useful for the comparator to compare two parsed information, both syntactically as well as semantically. We got pre and post condition and variables list for baseline specification and delta specification. Later on we have used them to compare both the specifications and have identified change by comparing both specifications. Given below is algorithm to parse the baseline version of VDM specification and Delta version specification.

Algorithm for Parsing VDM Specification

Given below in figure is algorithm for parsing of VDM specifications i.e. for baseline and for Delta version specifications. It describes how both versions of specifications will be parsed and how the required information will be stored in the as memorization of the required information is necessary for the comparison of two different versions of the VDM specification.

Specification Comparator

In our proposed approach we have compared both the specifications i.e. Baseline specification and delta version specification of VDM. Comparison of both the specification was useful to determine that whether the delta specification has changed or not and if the change is observed then what should be the mechanism for the test suite selection for the regression testing. Output of the parser mentioned above was the input of specification comparator. We have given algorithm for the comparison of specifications which has been described earlier.

Pre-Condition and Post-Condition Comparison

We have evaluated pre and post condition of the specification as these are the change identification points i.e. where we can determine the change in the previous and the new version of the specification written in VDM .This comparison was on two bases, syntactically and semantically. Pre-condition is the filter for the test input and post condition is what the operation should do after end of that operation i.e. result of the operation is post condition while the condition that should be satisfied before the entry to operation.

Table 3. Algorithm for Parsing of VDM Specifications

```
Input: Baseline VDM specification and Delta VDM specification.
Output: List of objects of baseline and delta version VDM specification classes.
///////////////////////////////////parsing of VDM ///////////////////////////////////////
Class VDMClass{
String classID
List<Operation> operations
String invariant
List variableList
}
/////////////////////////////////////Operation/////////////////////////////////////////////
Class Operation
{
String classID
String operationID
String preCondition;
String postCondition;
}
////////////////////////Description of VDM Parser class////////////////////////////////
Class Parser
{
VDMClass vdmClass
List vdmObjectsList;
```

```
///parseVDM will return a list having VDMClass objects.//////////////////////////
List<VDMClass> parseVDM(String VDMFile){
FileReader fileReader = readFile(VDMFile)
String tokens[] = fileReader.parseData()
for(i=0 i<tokens.length; i++){
If(tokens[i] == "class")
{
bool found
vdmClass = new VDMClass();
Operation operationObject;
vdmClass.setClassID(tokens[i])
int index = i;
//////////the given below while loop will parse a signle class////////
while(index<tokens.length && token[index!="class"] || token[index!="end"]))
{
index++;
if(tokens[index] == "inv")
{
vdmClass.invariant = tokens[++index];
}else if(tokens[index] == "variables")
{
vdmClass.variableList = getVariableList(tokens,index);
//this method has been defined below separately index++; //Just doing one increment other will do through while
}else if (tokens[index]== "operations")
{
```

continued on following page

Syntactical Comparison

First of our proposed approach have compared the two versions of specification syntactically and found change in the syntax of new version but even change in syntax is no guarantee of change in the test suit as there is possibility that specification might have different syntax but semantically have the same impact on the test suit.

Table 3. Continued

```
//Given below while loop will parse all operations
//Also supposed, uptill end of the class only operations will exist
while(token[index]!="end")
{
operationObject = new Operation()
if (token[index]="pre"){
operationObject.setPreCondition(token[token[index+1])
index++
}else if (token[index]=="post"){
operationObject.setPostCondition(token[token[index+1])
index++
} vdmClass.operations.add(operationObject);
} //end of while that was parsing operations
}//end if (tokens[index]== "operations")
} end if
} //here parsing of one class will be completed
//add that in list a then serach again for next class
vdmObjectsList.add(vdmClass)
} //end of for loop
return vdmObjectsList;
} //end of parseTokens()
```

```
///////////////getVariableList(String tokens[],int index)///////////////////
List<Variable> getVariableList(String tokens[],int index)
{
Variable variable;
List<Variable> variables;
while(tokens[index] != "inv" ||tokens[index] != "operations" ||tokens[index] != "end")
{
variable = new Variable();
variable.name = tokens[++index];
variable.type = tokens[++index];
variables.add(variable);
}
return variables;
}
}
//////////// End of Parser//////////////////////////////////////////////////
```

Semantically Comparison

As we have mentioned in syntax comparison only syntax comparison does not guarantee that change in syntax will lead to change in test suite. So, we have to also check specification semantically. In semantic comparison we check keeping in mind that different syntax can lead to similar semantics. As there are some operators in the VDM++ specification language that can cause change in the semantics of the specification i.e. operands position is important if we change the operands position semantics will be different. On the other hand there are also operators which do not lead to change in the semantics of the specification and eventually have no impact on regress suit if operands position is changed.

Operators that Cause Semantic Change

Here are some of operators in which operands position is important and change in operands position will lead to change in the test suit.

<, >, -,:=, subset, <=, >=, v, ^

For these operators we have to write separate function as they might lead or may not lead to change in the regression test suite.

Operators that Do Not Cause Semantic Change

Here are some of the operators which do not change the semantic of the specification if we change the position of the operands.

==,+,<>, Psubset, *,abs

Types of Possible Changes in the Specification

Following are possible changes in the specification that will lead change in the regression test suite.

Change in Class

In VDM specification the class is defined as given in figure 3. We have got this definition mentioned in the VDM tool The VDM++ language developed by CSK Corporation. We will follow this definition and analyze when we change specification from baseline to delta version that what kind of impact it can cause in term of specification based regression testing.

As we can clearly see that when we will change classes from baseline version to delta version the change can be addition of class as well as deletion of class in the delta version. Similarly identifier change will lead to change in class ID in the delta version which will be identified by syntax checker in our proposed approach. Deletion and addition of classes in the delta version specification will lead to obsolete or retest able test cases. In case of addition of new classes all test cases for that class will be considered as retest able test cases similarly in cases of deletion of class all operations of that class will be deleted which will lead obsolete test cases of all related operations and corresponding class.

Change in inheritance clause will lead to change in the other classes too in the delta version. If the changed class was super class i.e. parent class it lead to change in the child classes inherited from this parent class. In our proposed approach we are not dealing with the inheritance of classes as it will complicate our approach we will focus this for the future work.

Change in the body part of class might be due to change in the operations or functions or the data type change for the state variables. All these things we will discuss them further individually. For the synchronization and thread we are not dealing with them in the proposed approach.

Change in Operations

In VDM specification the operation is defined in the figure 4. We have got this definition mentioned in the VDM tool The VDM++ language developed by CSK Corporation.

As mentioned in the given below figure that operation definition that there are three type of operations. Implicit operation which do not have body and just have pre and post condition along with externals in standard VDM we do not have extended explicit operations as these are allowed only in VDM tool provided by CSK Corporation from which we have taken this definition. In implicit operations and functions we just have pre and post conditions and do not have operation body i.e. we do not know how to get post condition. While in case of explicit operation we have pre and post condition along which operation body which describes that how to achieve this post condition.

In case of explicit operation we have keep consideration of body of the operation along with the pre and post condition. Change in the body of operation means change in the how part i.e. how the post condition will be achieved will be changed. In delta version of specification change in body part of operation may or may not lead to change in the test cases but change in the post condition will definitely cause change in the test cases for the delta version of the specification. Externals are also important in the operations as change in the externals can change the test cases i.e. change in the data type or change in the variable will cause change in the test cases. Similarly exceptions can also play role in the regression testing as exceptions tell that what should be the behavior of system in case of that particular condition which can occur in the system so change in the exception will cause changes in the regression testing .Basically exception tells what should be the system response in case of a particular exception when it occurs if we found change in the exception our test cases will be different.

In case of change in pre and post condition the test cases for the operation will be changed and in our proposed approach we will cater them. If change is in externals it will lead also change in test cases as in externals we mention data types and variables so our approach is dealing with the change in the data type as well as change in the number of variables.

Comparison of pre and post conditions of operations has significant importance in our approach. As pre and post condition are basically entry and exit point of the operations and can play better role in change identification. In our approach we will compare pre and post conditions of operations as these are change identification points.

In semantic comparison of specification we check change in operations by comparing pre and post condition of the operation .Pre and post condition are predicates basically so change in operation's pre and post condition will be change in the operations.

Addition of operation will occur when we want to add some functionality in the new version of the specification which was not being provided in the previous baseline version of specification. For example our old specification was providing arithmetic operations like addition and subtraction to be performed on natural numbers in the new version we want to add functionality of multiplication so we have to add multiplication operation in Delta version. Addition of operations will lead to the change in regression test

Table 4. Definition for Class in VDM

```
class = 'class', identifier, [ inheritance clause ],
[ class body ],
'end', identifier ;
inheritance clause = 'is subclass of', identifier, { identifier } ;
class body = definition block, { definition block } ;
definition block = type definitions
| value definitions
| function definitions
| operation definitions
| instance variable definitions
| synchronization definitions
| thread definitions ;
```

suite by addition of new test cases while no change will lead to re-testable test cases in the specification i.e. test cases will remain same as for the previous specification and are still re-useable these test cases will be selected by the test selector.

Deletion will occur when we no longer require functionality in new version of specification that was being provided in the older version of specification i.e. for example in Table 5 we do not want functionality of subtraction in new specification so we have to delete subtraction operation. Deletion of operation will lead to obsolete test cases in regress test suite. Similarly modification in test cases will cause re-testable test cases addition in the test suit. Hence test cases for unchanged part of specification will be categorized in the re-useable test case category.

Change in Variables

In the new version of specification or in the changed version of specification either there can be addition of variable, deletion or modification of variable by data type change. Of variable or change in name of variable. In semantic checking we will ignore name of the variable i.e. variable with different name may have same functionality as in the previous version that name was different. When there is change in the variable either it is addition of variable it will be identified by pre and post condition check at the operation level .So, deletion and addition of variables in the specification will definitely lead to change in the regression test suite. Test cases selector will select test cases and for that particular change for example for deletion of variable test case selector will select or identify obsolete test cases. Test case selection will be done by the test selector.

Addition of Variable

Variable can be added when required in the delta version specification. whenever we require additional functionality of variable then this requirement will lead to addition of variable Change in variable will

Table 5. Definition of Operations in VDM

```
Operation definitions = 'operations', [ access operation definition,
{ ';', access operation definition }, [ ';' ] ] ;
access operation definition = ([ access ], [ 'static' ]) | ([ 'static' ], [ access ]),
operation definition ;
operation definition = explicit operation definition
| implicit operation definition
| extended explicit operation definition ;
explicit operation definition = identifier, ':', operation type,
identifier, parameters,
'==', operation body,
[ 'pre', expression ],
[ 'post', expression ],
;
implicit operation definition = identifier, parameter types,
[ identifier type pair list ],
implicit operation body ;
implicit operation body = [ externals ],
[ 'pre', expression ],
'post', expression,
[ exceptions ] ;
```

occur according to our requirements for example a variable will deleted when we find that it is no longer required and our specification will even provide functionality required after deletion of this variable i.e. it was additional variable not necessarily required in the older version of specification so deleted in the new version. Similarly a variable will be added when we require some values to provide functionality from specification i.e. additional variable is required to provide some required values for the Delta version of specification so variable will be added. In next section of result and discussion we have elaborated and illustrated the concept of addition and deletion of variables with the help of case study.

Change in Data Type

Change in data type will be deal as change in variable. For example if we change data type of variable from real to nat type this will be deal as variable change and will be compared syntactically and semantically by the comparator.

Deletion of Variable

Deletion of variable will cause generation of obsolete test cases while addition will cause re-testable test cases. Similarly modification will cause re-testable and re-useable test cases as mentioned above example if baseline version has variable of type real and in delta version its data type has change from real to nat then test cases for real type will become obsolete and we will require new test cases for the nat type.

Test Suite Selection

By comparing two versions of specification the baseline version and delta version by pre and post condition comparator we will select test cases for the delta version. Base for the test selection for the delta version will be the test suite of baseline version of specification. So after comparison we will select regression test suite for the delta version of the specification.

Test suite selection will be done by the test cases selector after pre and post condition evaluation of the operation. For test suite selection base will be database of test cases of baseline version. Test selector will select test cases according to the identification of change in the Delta version of VDM specification. After all test cases selector will give regression Test suite.

Obsolete Test Cases

When we have generated test suite from the baseline specification for the delta version we have to classify the test cases by comparing the two versions of the specification the old version without change and the new version which has evolved after the change. After analyzing and comparing the two versions of specification specified in VDM we came to know about some cases that were valid for old specification are no longer required for the new version of the specification i.e. test cases are now obsolete after the change in the specification.

For example there is a variable whose data type is real specified in the older version of the specification and in the new version the data type is change and new data type specified for that variable is real type so test cases that were for real data type and formed for testing this type will no longer be required for nat data type and will become obsolete for the changed version of the specification. Such test cases will be classified as obsolete test cases and will be put in the obsolete category of the test cases.

Re-Testable Test Cases

Test cases for the modified part of the specification are called re-testable test cases .these are such test cases which are specific to the modified part of the specification and are not for the previous or older version of the specification. These are designed to test the modified part of the specification or the changed part of the specification.

For example in case of change from nat data type to real. Test cases specific to test real data type will be re-testable test cases and will be categorized in the re-testable test case in testing.

Re-Useable Test Cases

Test cases those are useful for the changed version of the specification as well as for the old version of the specification. These test cases are valid for the old version of the specification as well as valid for new version of the specification after the change i.e. These test cases must be executed for both versions of the specification before and after the change.

For example if there is no change in the operation or class then all test cases for that particular operation will be still valid i.e. test cases for the baseline version will be still valid for the delta version if there is no change in the operations or classes in the delta version.

Algorithm for Comparator and Test Case Selector

For our approach operation or function's ID (identity) should be unique and in this algorithm we are assuming that original Specification of VDM before change is Baseline VDM specification (Baseline Version) and after change is Delta version VDM specification (Delta Version).

In our approach pre and post condition of operations was matched or compared with operations of Delta version syntactically as well as semantically and a list of changed and unchanged operations was maintained changed. Operations were placed in the operation changed list.

Pre and post condition of operation was extracted by the parser of VDM specifications mentioned above which was extracted and was passed it to specification comparator.

In our algorithm output of parser was the input of the comparator. Comparator compared both versions of specification and on basis of comparison change was identified in the classes and operations of the delta version. Changed operations were stored in the changed operation and unchanged operations were stored in the unchanged operations list. Comparator at the end returned list of changed unchanged and deleted operations and then these lists were used by the test selector. Test selector selected test cases for the unchanged operations i.e. selected re-useable test cases for the unchanged operations of delta version from the list of test cases for the baseline version.

For changed operations list test cases selector did not select the test cases. In fact, put corresponding test cases of the operations in the list of obsolete test cases similarly comparator also identified the deleted operation and deleted classes as well as new operations and new classes for these operations and classes test case selector will put corresponding test cases in the obsolete test cases list. Similarly for the changed operations test case selector will not select the test cases and will put them in the obsolete test cases list i.e. these are not re-useable test cases and for these kind of operation we have to make new test cases to test them i.e. re-testable test cases.

Implementation of Our Proposed Approach

As far as implementation of our proposed approach is concerned we have planned to integrate it with existing tools for the testing of VDM specification. For baseline version of specification we can get test cases by using TESTAF approach given by (Nadeem and Jaffer, 2005).After getting test cases for the

Table 6. Algorithm for Pre and Post Condition Comparator

```
Input: Output of the parser is input of comparator
Output: On the basis of comparison list of changed, unchanged, deleted and new operations and classes will be obtained output of the comparator will be
the regression test suite applicable for the delta version.
/////////////////////////Comparator//////////////////////////////////////////////
class Comparator
{
comparator()
{
parser=new parser()
}
Parse parser
List<VDMClass>baseVDMObjectslist=parser.parseVDM("C:\VDM\baseVDM.txt")
List<VDMClass>deltaVDMObjectslist=parser.ParseVDM(C:\VDM\deltaVDM.txt)
list<operation> changeoperation;
list<operation> unchangedOperation;
list<operation> deletedOperation;
list<operation> newoperation;
void findChange(List <VDMClass>baseVDMObjectslist, List <VDMClass>deltaVDMObjectslist)
{
for (each deltaVDM deltaobject)
{
for (each baseVDM baseobject)
{
String classID
bool value
If (deltaObject.classID = = baseobject.classID)
{
for(each operation of deltaObject)
{
for(each operation of baseObject)
{
If (baseObject.operation[i].Id= DeltaObject.operation[i].Id)
{
If(baseObject.operation[i].preCondition==baseObject.operation[i].preCondition)
// syntax is checking by a string comparison
Then if (isSemanticsSame(deltaObject.operation[i].preCondition,baseObject.operation[i].preCondition))
then if(baseObject.operation[i].postCondition==baseObject.operation[i].postCondition)
Then if (isSemanticsSame(deltaObject.operation[i].postCondition,baseObject.operation[i].preCondition)) unchangedOperation.add(dataObject.operation[i]);
//this is for all above ifs any any of the above four is false its means changed
else
changedOperation.add(dataObject.operation[i]);
}
}
}
}
}
}
}
```

continued on following page

Table 6. Continued

```
////////////////////////////////////////findNewClasses///////////////////////////////////////////////////
void findNewClasses(List<VDMClass> deltaObjectList, List<VDMClass> baseOjectList){
Boolean found = false;
for (each deltaObject)
{
for (each baseObject)
{
if(delta.classID=base.ClassID)
found = true;
} //end inner loop
if (!found){
changeoperation.addList(deltaObject.operations);
//when we found new class we add its all list of methods in our main list of changed
// or we can say new methods whose test cases need to be re-design
} else{ found = false }
}
}
////////////////////////////////////////findDeletedClasses///////////////////////////////////////////////
void findDeletedClasses(List<VDMClass> deltaObjectList, List<VDMClass> baseOjectList){
Boolean found = false;
for (each baseObject)
{
for (each deltaObject)
{
if(delta.classID=base.ClassID)
found = true;
} //end inner loop
if (!found){
deletedOperation.addList(baseObject.operations);
} else{ found = false; }
}
}
Boolean isSemanticSame(String deltaCondition, String baseCondition)
{
String deltaTokens[] = deltaCondition.split("< <= > >= == !=");
String baseTokens[] = baseCondition.split("< <= > >= == !=");
Condition deltaCondition = new Condition(deltaTokens);
Condition deltaCondition = new Condition(baseTokens);
if(deltaCondition.operator == "<")
{
if (baseCondition.operator == ">" &&baseCondition.firstOperator==deltaCondition.secondOperator && baseCondition.secondOperator ==
deltaCondition.firstOperator)
return true;
else
return false;
}else if(deltaCondition.operator == ">")
{
if (baseCondition.Oprand = = "<" && baseCondition.firstOprand = =deltaCondition.secondOperato && baseCondition.secondOprand = = deltaCondition.
firstOprand)
return true;
else
return false;
}else if(deltaCondition.operator == ">=")
{
if (baseCondition.operator = = "<=" &&baseCondition.firstOperator==deltaCondition.secondOperator && baseCondition.secondOprand = =
deltaCondition.firstOprand)
return true;
else
return false;
}else if(deltaCondition.operator == "<=")
{
if (baseCondition.operator = = ">=" && baseCondition.firstOprand = = deltaCondition.secondOprand && baseCondition.secondOprand ==
deltaCondition.firstOprand)
return true;
else
return false;
}else if(deltaCondition.operator == "==")
{
```

continued on following page

Table 6. Continued

```
//////////////////////since var1== var2 in sematically same we it is written as var2 == var2 so it means no change.
if (baseCondition.Oprand = = "= ="&&baseCondition.firstOprand==deltaCondition.secondOprand && baseCondition.secondOprand = = deltaCondition.
firstOprand)
return true;
else
return false;
}else if(deltaCondition.operator == "!=")
{
//////////////////////since var1 != var2 in sematically same we it is written as var2 != var2 so it means no change.
if (baseCondition.operator = = "!=" &&baseCondition.firstOprand==deltaCondition.secondOprand && baseCondition.secondOprand = = deltaCondition.
firstOprand)
return true;
else
return false;
}
}
}
class Condition
{
String firstOprand;
String operator;
String secondOprand
Condition(String []tokens)
{
this.firstOprand = token[0];
this.operator = token[1];
this.secondOprand =token[2];
}
}
```

```
///////////////////test case Selection///////////////////////////////////////////////
class TestCases
{
string ClassID;
string OperationID;
int numberofTestCases;
}
list<TestCases>BaselineVersion;
list<DeltaReuseable>
list<getObsolete>
}
Class EvaluateTestCases{
comparator comparator=new comparator()
list<VDMClass>baseVDMObjectslsit=comparator.parser.parseVDM("c:\basevdm.tx)
list<VDMClass>deltaVDMObjectslsit=comparator.parser.parseVDM("c:\deltavdm.txt")
comparator.findChange(lsit<VDMClass>baseVDMObjectslsit,lsit<VDMClass>deltaVDMObjectslsit)
list<TestCases>getReuseableTestCases(list<TestCases>baselineVersion,list<operation>unchanged)
{
list<TestCases>Reuseablelist;
list<TestCases>Obsolete;
for (each baselineVersion Testcases)
for (each operation unchanged)
if(TestCases.ClassID==unchanged.ClassID)&&(TestCases.operation.ID=unchangedoperation.operation.ID)
Deltalist.add(this.testcases);
else
Obsolete.add(this.testCases);
}
```

baseline version of the specification we have compared two specifications i.e. baseline version specification and Delta version of specification. After analyzing these changes we have selected appropriate test cases from the baseline version test suite for the regression test suite.

As we can see the association between the classes used in the algorithm for comparator and test cases selector from class diagram in the given below figure 6. In the given below diagram we have shown diagrammatically association between the classes and their association along with their operations.

Our proposed approach will hook with TESTAF approach at test case generator component of that approach for the regression test suite selection i.e. it will be sandwiched by TESTAF approach. For getting the test cases for the baseline version we can apply any existing approach but we are planning to integrate it with TESTAF approach .Our approach will be used for test selection for the Delta version of specification i.e. regression test suite. We can execute these test cases on the Delta version specification by using TESTAF approach which provides facility for test cases execution automatically through test drivers.

So; our proposed approach can easily be integrated with TESTAF approach which is basically a test automation framework for class testing using object oriented formal specification i.e. VDM++ specification based testing. Test cases will be automatically generated by using this approach and after test suite generation our proposed approach will be integrated at its test case generator component for the test selection for the Delta version of the specification. After test selection of regression test suite by our proposed approach test cases can be automatically executed by using test drivers proposed of TESTAF approach.

Analysis and Results of Technique

In the following section we have elaborated results and have discussed about these results by explaining case study which is a general computer programming example which we have taken as case study and modified it to prove our proposed approach. We have mentioned VDM based specification of that example and have modified it and then by comparing modified i.e. baseline version and delta version of specification we have generated test suite which is more effective for regress testing.

Comparison with Other Approaches

Up till now there was no approach for regression testing of VDM++ Specification. Our focus is also on pre and post condition of operations so there are maximum chances of identification of the change in the specification at operation level by comparing there pre and post conditions.

Mostly existing approaches for regression were code based a few were model based but no technique existed for the specification based regression testing for the VDM specification although techniques exist for generating test suite from specification. Our technique was for regression test suite from VDM specification in which we have given mechanism for test selection from the baseline version for the Delta version. In this technique we have introduced concept of regression testing from VDM specification rather than implementation so our approach works at the abstract level i.e. specification level.

Case Study

A case study is being presented to verify our proposed technique. It is basically a class for complex numbers which has to perform the following four arithmetic operations addition, subtraction, multiplication and division of numbers .That example is for complex numbers how to add, subtract, divide and multiply complex numbers (Nadeem and Jaffer, 2005). We will tailor it for our requirements. We have shown baseline and then delta version of our specification. Delta version of our specification contains some changes like data type changes, addition of variables, deletion and modification of operations. In this example for regression testing we have generated test cases for the baseline version and then selected test cases for the delta version of the specification i.e. Regression test suite.

Figure 2. Class Diagram of Proposed Approach

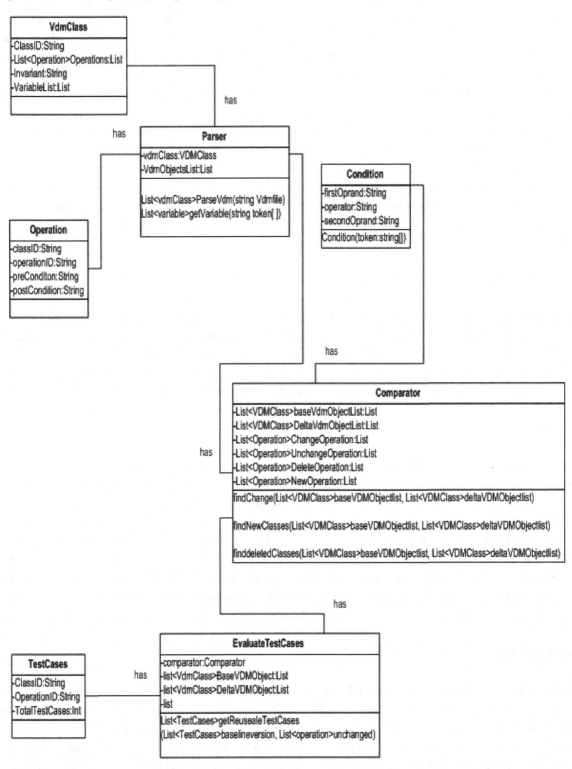

The baseline version of formal specification was the specification given below and on the basis of this specification version we have found test cases for the delta version of the specification and applied our approach on that case study. We have compared pre and post conditions of operations in both versions of the specification and have generated regression test suite for the delta version specification.

Now we already had test cases for this baseline version of specification (Table 7) and then on the basis of these test cases we have applied our approach to select test cases for the delta version of the specification.

Mentioned in Table 5 were the test cases for the baseline version VDM specification by using these test cases we have evaluated these test cases for the delta version specification. Comparator in our proposed approach will identify the change in the delta version and operation if changed will be placed in the changed operations list and unchanged operations will be placed in the unchanged operations list. For our case study we will find what kind of changes have been taken place .On basis of this change what are the test cases for the delta version specification i.e. re-useable and obsolete test cases will be defined for the delta version VDM specification.

Specification after Change (Delta Version)

Following were the changes that occurred in the modified part of the specification.

Table 7. VDM++ Specification of Baseline Version

```
Class NNcomplex
instance variables
re: real;
im: real;
inv (re>=0) & (im>=0);
operations
init: () ==> ()
init () == (re:= 0;
im:= 0;)
add: int ==> NNComplex
add(num) == (re:= re+num;
return self;)
pre num >= -re;
post re = re~+num;
subtract: int ==> NNComplex
subtract(num) == (re:= re-num;
return self;)
pre num >= re;
post re = re~-num;
multiply: int ==> NNComplex
multiply(num) == (re:= re*num;
im:= im*num;
return self;)
pre num >= 0;
post re = (re~*num) and (im = im~*num);
divide: int ==> NNComplex
divide(num) == (re:= re/num;
im:= im/num;
return self;)
pre num > 0;
post re = (re~/num) and (im = im~/num);
end NNcomplex
```

Data Type Change in Subtraction Operation

Test cases for boundary value analysis of the baseline version of the specification mentioned in Table 8 were as following.

Suppose for the Delta version of the above mentioned baseline specification of the baseline version we found following changes and we observed data type change in variable of the baseline version men-

Table 8. Test Cases for Baseline Version

Test Cases for Add Operation				Test Cases for Subtract Operation			
Test Case No.1	Input Valuesre=0im=0X=0		Expected Output0.0	Test Case No.16	Input Valuesre=0im=0x=0		Expected Output0.0
2	re=0	im=0	X=1	1.0	17	re=0	im=0	x=1	-1.0
3	re=0	im=0	X=9	9.0	18	re=0	im=0	x=9	-9.0
4	re=0	im=1	X=0	0.1	19	re=0	im=1	x=0	0.1
5	re=0	im=1	X=1	1.1	20	re=0	im=1	x=1	-0.9
6	re=0	im=1	X=9	9.1	21	re=0	im=1	x=9	-8.9
7	re=0	im=8	X=0	0.8	22	re=0	im=8	x=0	0.8
8	re=0	im=8	X=1	1.8	23	re=0	im=8	x=1	-0.2
9	re=0	im=8	X=9	9.8	24	re=0	im=8	x=9	-8.2
10	re=1	im=0	X=-1	0.0	25	re=1	im=0	X=-1	0.0
11	re=1	im=1	X=0	1.1	26	re=1	im=1	x=0	1.1
12	re=1	im=8	X=12	13.8	27	re=1	im=8	X=12	-10.2
13	re=5	im=0	X=-5	0.0	28	re=5	im=0	X=-5	10.0
14	re=5	im=1	X=-4	1.1	29	re=5	im=1	X=-4	9.1
15	re=5	im=8	X=6	11.8	30	re=5	im=8	x=6	-0.2

Test Cases for Multiply Operation				Test Cases for Divide Operation			
Test Case No.31	Input Valuesre=0im=0X=0		Expected Output0.0	Test Case No.46	Input Valuesre=0im=0x=0		Expected Outputexception
32	re=0	im=0	X=1	0.0	47	re=0	im=0	x=1	0.0
33	re=0	im=0	X=9	0.0	48	re=0	im=0	x=9	0.0
34	re=0	im=1	X=0	0.0	49	re=0	im=1	x=0	exception
35	re=0	im=1	X=1	0.1	50	re=0	im=1	x=1	0.1
36	re=0	im=1	X=9	0.9	51	re=0	im=1	x=9	0.0
37	re=0	im=8	X=0	0.0	52	re=0	im=8	x=0	exception
38	re=0	im=8	X=1	0.8	53	re=0	im=8	x=1	0.8
39	re=0	im=8	X=9	7.2	54	re=0	im=8	x=9	0.1
40	re=1	im=0	X=-1	-1.0	55	re=1	im=0	X=-1	-1.0
41	re=1	im=1	X=0	0.0	56	re=1	im=1	x=0	exception
42	re=1	im=8	X=12	21.6	57	re=1	im=8	X=12	0.2
43	re=5	im=0	X=-5	-25.0	58	re=5	im=0	X=-5	-1.0
44	re=5	im=1	X=-4	-20.4	59	re=5	im=1	X=-4	-1.3
45	re=5	im=8	X=6	34.8	60	re=5	im=8	x=6	1.0

tioned in Figure 8. So for this kind of change test cases of baseline version for this operation (starting from 15 to 30) will become Obsolete. Nat 1 data type do not include zero in valid input space so these test cases will not be valid test cases.

Secondly for the change data type we will require new test cases called re testable test cases as changed data type will change the boundary values. Our test cases for boundary value analysis will be changed and will have to test new test cases for this changed operation. Data type change in the operation in our proposed approach we will put operation in the list of changed operations. We have to test new test cases i.e. re testable test cases for the delta version of specification.

Syntactical Change with No Impact

In This example we have found change in the comparator operator of addition method which will lead in pre-condition change but this change is syntactical change which has no impact on semantic so no modification in test cases as in this case operator changed is comparator operator which has been classified in the change impacting operators i.e. which will change semantics of pre and post condition if change is in their operands positions this has been mentioned in our algorithm.

Unchanged Operation

Divide operation in the baseline version specification was observed unchanged operation in the delta version VDM specification as mentioned in Table 9. Divide operation had no change in the delta version and was same in as it was in the baseline version. There was no syntactical and semantically change so operation was added in the list of unchanged operations. For these kinds of operations test selector will select test cases which were valid for the baseline version because these are still valid for the delta version of the VDM specification.

So, all test cases of divide operation (starting from 45 to 60) mentioned in the baseline version were selected by the regression test suite selector. For that change in the specification all 15 test cases will remain valid after the change and will be categorized in the Re-useable test cases database of test cases. Change will be detected by the syntax comparator i.e. there is syntax difference of operations of baseline version and delta version of specification. After change identification of the operation syntactically our proposed approach will check it semantically that whether this change is semantically different or not.

Table 9. Data Type Change in Subtraction Operation

```
class NNcomplex
instance variables
re: nat 1 ; //nat 1 supports natural numbers greater than zero
inv (re>0); // nat 1 data type zero is not included so it will change class inv.
operations
init: ()==> ()
init () == (re:=0)
add: int ==> NNcomplex
add(num) == (re:=re-num;
return self)
pre num > re;
post re= re~ - num
end NNcomlex
```

In our case mentioned above change is syntactical which has no impact on the semantics of the operation so operation will be added to the unchanged operation list by the semantic checker in our proposed approach. All test cases of that operation will be same as for the baseline version and test cases for that operation will be selected by the regression test selector.

Syntactical Change with Impact of Change on Semantics

Given in Table 10 is example of syntactical change in the operation which has also impact on the semantics of the operation. Change in comparison operation changes the semantics of the operation.

In this case 15 test cases for the subtraction operation (starting from 31 to 45) mentioned above will become obsolete while new cases i.e. Re-testable will be added to add this changed operation as this change operation will be treated as a change in operation by our pre and post condition comparator and operation will be added to list to changed operations which will require new test cases for the testing.

If suppose there was only this change in operation of subtraction then all test cases for the other operation of the specification will still be effective for this delta version i.e. will be Re-useable test case.

Table 10. Syntactical Change in Add Operation

```
class NNcomplex
instance variables
re: real ;
im:real;
inv (re>=0) & (im>=0);
operations
init: ()==> ()
init () == (re:=0;
im:= 0)
add: int ==> NNcomplex
add(num) == (re:=re+num;
return self)
pre num < -re; //changed the comparator operator
post re= re~ + num
end NNcomlex
class NNcomplex
instance variables
re: real ;
im:real;
inv (re>=0) & (im>=0);
operations
init: ()==> ()
init () == (re:=0;
im:= 0)
add: int ==> NNcomplex
add(num) == (re:=re+num;
return self)
pre num < -re; //changed the comparator operator
post re= re~ + num
end NNcomlex
```

Results of Case Study

In above mentioned case study we have shown that our proposed approach works well for these kinds of changes observed in the delta version of the specification. For boundary value analysis of baseline version of the specification we will be having 60 no. of total test cases. Suppose there were observed mentioned above changes observed in the Delta version of the specification then overall regression test suite for the delta version are mentioned in Table 6.

So as we have shown in the above mentioned example that our proposed approach has reduced number of test cases for the regression test suite. Our proposed approach is different from retest all strategy for the regression testing as it can distinguish obsolete and re-useable test cases for the delta version. So we can claim that our approach is better approach as compare to retest all and is more effective in test suite reduction.

As we have found in our case study that our approach is working for regression test suite generation from the baseline specification by comparing pre and post condition of operations. We have seen changes like addition of variable, data type change and deletion of operation from the baseline version of the specification.

On basis of changes in the baseline version of specification of case study we have selected different kind of test cases. Obsolete test cases were found when there was deletion of variable or operation from the specification. Re-testable and re-useable test cases were observed when we modified the pre and post condition of our operations.

Advantages of Our Approach

The main advantage of our approach is that it is time saving. We can rate our approach on two parameters first is time saving as errors and bugs are found on the initial level i.e. at specification level .Testing at specification level is more useful and time saving as bugs are found and fixed at the initial level.

Second factor is cost minimization as fixing the bugs and errors at the early level will cause low cost factor as compare to fixing errors and bugs after implementation level which will cost more and will gain more time and difficulty of fixing these bugs will also increase. Complexity will increase for error

Table 11. Syntactical Change in Multiplication Operation

```
class NNcomplex
instance variables
re: real ;
im:real;
inv (re<0) & (im<0); // change in operator in class invariants
operations
init: ()==> ()
init () == (re:=0;
im:= 0)
multiply: int ==> NNcomplex
multiply(num) == (re:=re*num;
return self)
pre num < re ; //change in operator
post re= re~ * num
end NNcomlex
```

Table 12. Unchanged Divide Operation

```
class NNcomplex
instance variables
re: real ;
im:real;
inv (re>=0) & (im>=0);
operations
init: ()==> ()
init () == (re:=0;
im:= 0)
divide: int ==> NNComplex
divide(num) == (re:= re/num;
im:= im/num;
return self;)
pre num > 0;post re= re~ / num
end NNcomlex
```

fixing after the implementation .So, our approach adopted base line version of specification for selecting test cases for the delta version so it was time saving we did need to generate test cases for the delta version and we have selected test cases from baseline version.

By analyzing baseline version and using the existing test cases of baseline version of VDM specification will reduce the cost of testing the delta version specification. Cost reduction is directly proportional to the test suite reduction in our approach.

Test Suite Reduction

At the maintenance level when we require change in the software whether these changes are adoptive or corrective we have to execute test suit after the changes has been made to test the software. For that purpose we require test suit that should be minimum in number of test cases and will provide maximum result by picking and pointing more number of errors and bugs.

Hence for regression testing we cannot adopt policy of Re-test all due to cost and time factor so we require reduced set of test cases. In our case our approach provides reduced number of test cases for the regression testing.

CONCLUSION

We presented an approach for regression testing from VDM++ specification which has taken older version of specification as baseline for selection of regression test suite for the new version of specification after the change.

The baseline specification version of VDM is compared with the new version of the specification. This comparison is on the base of pre and post condition of the operations in the specification. Pre and post condition of specifications are compared both syntactically and semantically. If we found change in pre-condition or post condition it will lead in different test case selection for the regression test suite.

We have presented a case study and analyzed it and drawn test cases for that version (Baseline Version) of VDM specification. We observed change in our specification (Delta Version) and then analyzed

Table 13. Results of Case Study

Baseline Version Operations	Number of Test Cases for Baseline	Changes Identified	Number of Test Cases for Baseline
Addition Operation	15	Addition Operation Changed	Obsolete=15 Re-Useable=0 Re-Testable=15
Subtraction Operation	15	Subtraction Operation Changed	Obsolete=15 Re-Useable=0 Re-Testable=15
Multiplication Operation	15	Multiplication Operation Unchanged	Obsolete=0 Re-Useable=15 Re-Testable=0
Division Operation	15	Division Operation Unchanged	Obsolete=0 Re-Useable=15 Re-Testable=0
	Total=60		Total Obsolete=30 Total Re-Useable=30 Total Re-Testable=30

Total test cases to be executed for the Delta Version= 30 reusable +30 re testable =60 test cases

Note: we can see from the results that our approach can distinguish between re-testable and obsolete test cases so, it is better as compare to re-test all strategy. Total test cases mentioned above are to be executed on the delta version which will not include 30 obsolete test cases (mentioned above) for the execution of test cases.

specification again for the testing purpose and we found that some of the test cases became invalid for that specification and some test cases are still valid i.e. re-testable so we had identified the test cases which were obsolete and which were still re-testable after we had observed change in the specification. Change identification was done by our comparator module while test suite selection was done by the test suite selector module in our proposed approach.

REFERENCES

Agerholm, S., Lecoreur, P. J., & Reichert, E. (1998). Formal specification and validation at work: A case study using VDM-SL. *IFAD Forskerparken, 10*, DK-5230.

Aichernig, B. K. (1999). *Automated Black-Box Testing with Abstract VDM Oracles*. Technical university of Graz, Institute for Software Technology (IST), Miinzgrabenstr.11/II, A-8010 Graz, Austria.

Aichernig, B. K., & Larsen, P. G. (1997). A proof obligation generator for VDM-SL. Graz University of Technology, Institute of Software Technology (IST), Miinzgrabenstr.11/II, 8010 Graz, Austria.

Amayreh, A., & Zin, A. M. (1999). PROBE: A formal specification-based testing system. In *Proceeding of the 20th international conference on Information Systems* (pp. 400 – 404). Academic Press.

Berg, M. V., Verhoe, M., & Wigmans, M. (1999). *Formal specification of an auctioning system using VDM++ and UML, an industrial usage report*. Chess information technology.

Beydeda, S. & Gruhun, V. (2002). *Class Specification Implementation Graphs and Their Application in Regression Testing*. University of Dortmund Computer Science Department.

Bowen, J., & Clark. (2002). FORTEST: Formal methods and testing. In *Proceedings of 26th Annual International Computer Software and Applications Conference (COMPSAC 02)*, (pp. 91-101). Academic Press.

Burton, S. & York. (2000). *Automated Testing from Formal Specification*. Department of Computer Science, University of York.

Chakrabarti, S. K., & Srikant, Y. N. (2008). Test sequence computation for regression testing of reactive. In *Proceedings of the 1st conference on India software engineering conference*. Academic Press.

Chakrabarti, S. K., & Srikant, Y. N. (2006). *Specification Based Regression Testing Using Explicit Software Engineering Advances. International Conference*.

Chen, C., Chapman, R., & Chang, K. H. (1999). Test scenario and regression test suite generation from object-z formal specification for object oriented program testing. In *Proceedings of the 37th annual southeast regional conference* (CD-ROM). Academic Press.

Chen, Y., Probert, R. L., & Ural, H. (2007). Model-based regression test suite generation using dependence analysis. In *Proceedings of the 3rd international workshop on advances in model-based testing*. Academic Press.

Coporation, C. S. K. (2005). VDM++ Toolbox User Manual Revised for V6.8.1. CSK Corporation.

Droschl, G. (1999). *Design and application of a test case generator for VDM-SL.austrian research center seibersdorf and IST-Technical University of Graz.miizgrabenstr.11, 8010 Graz*. Austria: Europe.

Foxley, E., & Salam, O. (1997). *Automatic Assessment of Z specification*. Annual Joint Conference Integrating Technology in Comp. Science Education.

Fraser, G., Aichernig, B. K., & Wotawa, F. (2007). Handling Model Changes: Regression Testing and Test-Suite Update with Model-Checkers. Institute for Software Technology Graz University of Technology.

Heimdahl, M. P. E., & George, D. (2004). Test-suite reduction for model based tests: effects on test quality and implications for testing. In *Automated Software Engineering Proceedings. 19th International Conference*.

Hierons, R. M., Harman, M., & Singh, H. (2003). Automatically generating information from Z specification to support the classification tree method. In *Proceedings of the Third International Conference of Z and B Users*. doi:10.1007/3-540-44880-2_23

Horcher, H. M. (1996). Improving Software Tests using Z Specifications. In J. P. Bowen & M. G. Hinchey (Eds.), Lecture Notes in Computer Science: Vol. 967. ZUM'95: The Formal Specification Notation (pp. 152–166). Springer.

Horcher, H. M., Bowen, J. P., & Hinchey, M. G. (1995). Improving Software Tests using Z Specifications. The Formal Specification Notation. *Lecture Notes in Computer Science*, *967*, 152–166. doi:10.1007/3-540-60271-2_118

Li, Y., & Wahi, N. J. (1999). An overview of regression testing. *Software Engineering Notes*, *24*(1), 69–73. doi:10.1145/308769.308790

Liang, H. (2005). Regression testing of classes based on TCOZ specifications. In *Proceedings of the 10th IEEE International Conference on Engineering of Complex Computer Systems (ICECCS'05)* (pp. 450 – 457). IEEE. doi:10.1109/ICECCS.2005.71

Marre, B. & Blanc. (2005). *Test Selection Strategies for Lustre Descriptions in GATeL*. Laboratoire Sûreté des Logiciels, CEA/DRT/DTSI/SOL.

Martin, H., & Horcher, M. (1995). Improving software tests using Z specifications. In *Proceedings of the 9th International Conference of Z Users on The Z Formal Specification Notation* (pp. 152 – 166). Academic Press.

Meudec, C. (1999/2000). *Automatic Test Data Generation from VDM-SL Specifications. Queen's University of Belfast*. Northern Ireland.

Nadeem, A., & Jaffar, M. (2004). *A Framework for Automated Testing from VDM-SL Specifications*. Pakistan: Muhammad Ali Jinnah University Islamabad.

Nadeem, A., & Jaffar, M. (2005). *TESTAF: A Test Automation Framework for class testing using object-oriented formal specification, center for software dependability. Muhammad Ali Jinnah University Islamabad*.

Rennard, J. P. (2000). Introduction to genetic algorithms a reference book. Academic Press.

Rothermel, G., & Harrold, M. J. (1994). A framework for evaluating regression test selection techniques. In *Proceedings of the 16th international conference on Software engineering* (pp. 201 – 210). Academic Press.

Scullarrd, G. T. (1998). Test Case Selection using VDM. *Lecture Notes in Computer Science, 328*, 178 – 186.

Sergiy, A. V., & Bowen, J. P. (2001). Formalization of software testing criteria using the Z Notation. Computer Software and Applications Conference, (COMPSAC2001) 25th Annual International.

Singh, H. & Sadegh. (1997). *Test Case Design based on Z and Classification Tree Method*. First IEEE International Conference on Formal Engineering Methods System technology research Berlin Germany.

Stocks, P. A., & Carrington, D. A. (1993). A specification based testing framework. In *Proceedings of the 15th International Conference on Software Engineering*. Academic Press.

Wookcock, J. & Davies. (1998). *Using Z, specification, refinement and proof*. Academic Press.

Xu, L., Dias, M., & Richardson, D. (2004). Generating regression tests via model checking. In *Proceedings of the 28th Annual International Computer Software and Applications Conference* (COMPSAC'04) (vol. 1, pp. 336 – 341). Academic Press.

Chapter 20

Web Usage Mining and the Challenge of Big Data:
A Review of Emerging Tools and Techniques

Abubakr Gafar Abdalla
University of Khartoum, Sudan

Tarig Mohamed Ahmed
University of Khartoum, Sudan

Mohamed Elhassan Seliaman
King Faisal University, Saudi Arabia

ABSTRACT

The web is a rich data mining source which is dynamic and fast growing, providing great opportunities which are often not exploited. Web data represent a real challenge to traditional data mining techniques due to its huge amount and the unstructured nature. Web logs contain information about the interactions between visitors and the website. Analyzing these logs provides insights into visitors' behavior, usage patterns, and trends. Web usage mining, also known as web log mining, is the process of applying data mining techniques to discover useful information hidden in web server's logs. Web logs are primarily used by Web administrators to know how much traffic they get and to detect broken links and other types of errors. Web usage mining extracts useful information that can be beneficial to a number of application areas such as: web personalization, website restructuring, system performance improvement, and business intelligence. The Web usage mining process involves three main phases: pre-processing, pattern discovery, and pattern analysis. Various preprocessing techniques have been proposed to extract information from log files and group primitive data items into meaningful, lighter level abstractions that are suitable for mining, usually in forms of visitors' sessions. Major data mining techniques in web usage mining pattern discovery are: clustering, association analysis, classification, and sequential patterns discovery. This chapter discusses the process of web usage mining, its procedure, methods, and patterns discovery techniques. The chapter also presents a practical example using real web log data.

DOI: 10.4018/978-1-4666-8505-5.ch020

INTRODUCTION

The explosive growth of the internet and the substantial amount of information being generated daily has turned the web into a huge information store. The relationships between the data available online are often not exploited .Web mining analyzes web data to help create a more useful environment in which users and organizations manage information in more intelligent ways. (Srivastava, Cooley, Desphande, & Tan, 2000).

The internet has become an important medium to conduct business transactions. Therefore the application of data mining techniques in the web has become increasingly important to organizations to extract useful knowledge that can be utilized in many ways such as improving the web system performance, restructuring website design, providing personalized web pages, and deriving business intelligence. Web data mining methods have strong practical applications in E-Systems and form the basis for marketing and e-commerce activities. It can be used to provide fast and efficient services to customers as well as building intelligent web sites for businesses. Data mining in e-business is considered to be a very promising research area.

Web data mining deals with different type of data, which is semi-structured or even unstructured, called web data. Web data, can be divided into three categories: content data, structure data, and usage data. This type of data differentiates web mining from data mining.

Web data represent a new challenge to traditional data mining algorithms that work with structured data. The nature of the web data which is less structured, and the rapid growth of information being generated daily, it has become necessary for users to utilize automated tools in order to find the required information. There are several commercial web analysis tools but most of them provide explicit statistics without real knowledge. These tools are also considered slow, inflexible, and provide only limited features. While some tools are being developed that using data mining techniques, but the research still in its first stages and faces real challenges such as large storage requirements and scalability problems (Rana, 2012).

The main objectives of this chapter arc:

1. To extensively review the web usage mining methods and types;
2. To identify the mean web usage mining challenges due to the Big Data phenomena;
3. To describe the Big Data solutions for web usage mining;
4. To evaluate the different emerging methodologies and implementation tools for Big Data web usage mining.

This chapter discusses the web usage mining process, also known as web log mining, is a three-phase process: pre-processing, pattern discovery, and pattern analysis. There are many data sources for web usage mining, among all; the web server's log file is the most widely used source of information. This chapter will also cover the following major techniques in web usage mining pattern discovery in relation to Big Data:

Association Rules

It is the process of finding associations within data in the log file. This technique can be used to identify pages that are most often accessed together. Association rules can be useful for many mining purposes, such as predicting the next page and to preload it from the remote server to speed up browsing.

Clustering

In web usage mining, there are two kinds of clusters: user clusters and page clusters. User clustering can be exploited to perform market segmentation in e-commerce web sites or provide personalized web page. Clustering identifies pages with related content and can be exploited by search engines and web recommendation systems (Srivastava, Cooley, Desphande, & Tan, 2000).

Classification

Classification is the process of assigning a class to each data item based on a set of predefined classes. In web mining, classification can be used, for example, to develop a profile of users belonging to a particular class or to classify HTTP request as normal or abnormal (Srivastava, Cooley, Desphande, & Tan, 2000).

Sequential Patterns

Sequential patterns allow web-based organization to predict user visit patterns. This can help in developing strategies for advertisement targeting groups of users based on these patterns. The aim of this technique is to predict future URLs to be visited based on a time-ordered sequence of URLs followed in the past.

BACKGROUND

With emergence of Web 2.0, user's generated content, social media, wide spread of mobile internet access and above, the scale and volume of web usage data to be mined have outpaced traditional data mining processes. Unlike traditional data mining, web usage mining deals with extremely huge data sets. In addition, traditional data mining extracts patterns from databases whereas web mining usage mining extracts the patterns from web data of different formats. This makes web usage mining one the clear Big Data issues.

Web usage mining, which is one of three forms of web mining. Web mining is the use of data mining techniques to automatically extract useful knowledge from web documents and services (Rana, 2012). Web mining is not equivalent to data mining. A definition of web mining which clearly differentiates between data mining and web mining by putting an emphasis on the type of data can be given as follows: Web mining is the application of data mining techniques to extract knowledge from web data, where at least one of web data (the structure or usage data) is used in the mining process (Srivastava, Desikan, & Kumar).

Types of Web Data

Web data can be classified into four categories: Content data, structure data, usage data and user profile. (Shukla, Silakari, & Chande, 2013) (Srivastava, Cooley, Desphande, & Tan, 2000).

Content Data

Is intended for end-user, it is the data that the web page is designed to convey to users. It constitutes display of the web page in the web browser. Content data includes text data, images, videos, audios, and structured information retrieved from databases.

Structure Data

Represents how page contents are organized internally and how pages are interconnected via hyperlinks. Intra-page structure information describes how HTML or XML tags are organized within a web page. Tree structure can be used to represent the organization of a web page in which the HTML tag becomes the root of the tree. Inter-page structure information is represented by models of hyperlinks that connect web pages with each other.

Usage Data

It is generated by user's interactions with the website. Usage data includes visitor's IP address, date and time of the access, the path to requested web resource, and other attributes. This information reveals how the website is being used and can reveal users' behaviors and access patterns

User Profile

The forth type of web data is the user profile data. Profile data collects the demographic information about the website's users through registration forms.

Classification of Web Mining

Web mining can be broadly classified into three categories: web structure mining, web content mining, and web usage mining (Costa Júnior & Gong, 2005).

Web Structure Mining

In web structure mining, the hyperlink structures between web pages are analyzed so that correlations between the web pages can be discovered. The primary goal of structure mining is the discovery and retrieval of information from any type of data in the web. Web structure mining can be divided into two categories: hyperlinks structure analysis and web documents structure analysis. In the first category, hyperlinks are analyzed to construct models of hyperlinks structures in the web. In the second category, the structure of individual web pages is analyzed to describe the organization of different HTML or XML tags (Bhatia, 2011) (S, K, & J, 2011).

Web Content Mining

Web content mining refers to the process of extracting useful information from the content of web documents. Web content mining uses technologies such as Natural Language Processing (NLP) and Information Retrieval (IR) to extract useful knowledge from the web.

Content mining is different from data mining because it deals with less structured data, but similar to text mining because most of web contents are basically texts. Content data includes all sorts of text documents and multimedia documents such as images, audios, and videos (Costa Júnior & Gong, 2005) (Bhatia, 2011).

Web Usage Mining

Web usage mining is the process of discovering of new information from web servers' logs. Web usage mining involves three steps: preprocessing, patterns discovery, and patterns analysis (Rana, 2012).

Data can be collected from three different locations: web server, proxy server, and client browser (Srivastava, Cooley, Desphande, & Tan, 2000). Usage data can be collected from the web server's access logs, cookies, clients' logs, or proxy server's log files. Client side data collection is more reliable than server side the disadvantage is that collecting usage data from users' browsers requires users' cooperation. In the web usage mining research the mostly used data source is the web logs.

It is necessary to convert data in the logs into data abstractions necessary for pattern discovery. Logs files are big in size, semi-structured and contain lots of irrelevant records. Main tasks in preprocessing are: data cleaning, users identification, and sessions identification (Srivastava, Cooley, Desphande, & Tan, 2000) (Gupta & Gupta).

Techniques from several fields such as statistics, data mining, machine learning and pattern recognition can be used to extract knowledge from usage data (Srivastava, Cooley, Desphande, & Tan, 2000). Major techniques used in pattern discovery are: clustering, classification, association, and sequential patterns (Shukla, Silakari, & Chande, 2013).

Patterns are further analyzed to refine the discovered knowledge. Data can be analyzed using query language such as SQL or can be loaded into a data cube in order to perform different OLAP operations. Visualization techniques can also be used to help understand patterns and highlight trends data (Srivastava, Cooley, Desphande, & Tan, 2000) (Shukla, Silakari, & Chande, 2013).

Applications of Web Usage Mining

Different web analytics tools are available which are capable of generating statistics such as number of page views, number of hits, top referrer sites and so on. However, these tools are not designed to provide knowledge about individual users and their access patterns. Web usage mining goes steps beyond traditional web analytics by incorporating data mining techniques which are powerful.

Web data mining methods have strong practical applications in E-Systems and form the basis for marketing in e-commerce. It can be used to provide fast and efficient services to customers as well as building intelligent web sites for businesses (Mehtaa, Parekh, Modi, & Solamki, 2012). Data mining in e-business is considered to be a very promising research area. Major application areas are: website modification, site performance improvement, web personalization, and business intelligence (Srivastava, Cooley, Desphande, & Tan, 2000).

Personalization

With the massive amount of information available online, users may not have the knowledge or experience to find relevant information. Personalization tries to meet users' expectations and needs by offering customized services and content during the interaction between the users and the website. Customers prefer to visit those websites which understand their needs and provide them with customized services and fast access to relevant information. Personalization is a rapidly growing and challenging area of web content delivery which is very attractive to e-commerce applications. The goal of a personalized system is to provide users with the information they want or need without they ask for it explicitly. (Srivastava, Cooley, Desphande, & Tan, 2000) (Mehtaa, Parekh, Modi, & Solamki, 2012).

Web personalization and recommendation systems utilize data which is collected directly or indirectly form web users. This data is preprocessed and analyzed and the results are used to implement personalization. Approaches to achieve personalization include content-based filtering, rating, Collaborative filtering, rule-based filtering, and web usage mining .Web usage mining is an excellent approach to web personalization.

Examples of personalization tasks:

1. **Memorization:** Is the most widespread form of personalization, user information such as name and browsing history is stored (e.g. Using cookies) so that when the users come back this information is used to greet them and display their browsing history.
2. **Customization:** Provides a customized content and structure to users according to users' preferences.
3. **Recommendation:** Recommendation systems try to automatically recommend hyperlinks to users in order to facilitate fast and easy access to needed information. These systems utilize data that reflect users' interests and usage behavior. These data maybe captured implicitly from web server logs or explicitly through registration forms or questionnaire.

Web Site Improvement

Analysis of usage data by web usage mining provides insights into traffic behavior and how to the website is being used. This knowledge can be exploited in many forms. It can be used to develop policies for web caching, network transmission, load balancing, or data distribution. The results of usage mining can be used to enhance security by providing usage patterns the can be useful for detecting intrusion, fraud, attempted break-in, etc. These system improvements are crucial to user satisfaction from the services offered by the web system (Srivastava, Cooley, Desphande, & Tan, 2000).

Website Modification

The attractiveness of the website design is a critical aspect to the success of the web applications. This includes how the content is structure and laid out. Web usage mining provides great opportunities to web designer to understand the actual navigation behavior of the web users so that better decisions can be made about redesigning the website. For example if a pattern reveals that two pages are often accessed together, the designer can consider linking them directly with a hyperlink .

Another trend is to automatically change the structure of the website based on the usage patterns discovered from server access logs. A website that changes its design during interaction with the users is called adaptive website (Anand & Hilal, 2012) (Srivastava, Cooley, Desphande, & Tan, 2000).

Business Intelligence

Web usage mining is an excellent tool to generate business intelligence from web data. Understanding of how customers are using the website is critical from marketing and customer relationship in e-commerce. Clustering of online customers can be utilized to perform market segmentation in order to develop marketing strategies. Knowledge of user interests and behavior also help individualized marketing by targeting advertisements to interested users (Chitraa & Davamani, 2010).

Usage Characterization

Data available in the web server logs can be mined to extract interesting usage patterns. Various data mining techniques can be used for this purpose. Web users can be divided into groups based on their navigational behaviors using clustering techniques. Classification techniques can be used to find correlation between web pages or web users. In addition to clustering and classification, other techniques can be used to find interesting usage patterns (Anand & Hilal, 2012).

THE WEB USAGE MINING PROCESS (MAIN FOCUS)

Web usage mining is the process of performing data mining on web log file data. This process goes through three main phases: preprocessing, pattern discovery, and pattern analysis. Figure 1 shows the overall picture of the web usage mining. Raw logs are preprocessed with the help of site files (site topology). Then data mining techniques are applied to obtain patterns and rules. Finally, results are filtered to get "interesting" patterns and rules (Srivastava, Cooley, Desphande, & Tan, 2000).

Data Collection

Usage data can be collected from various sources such as: web servers, clients, intermediary sources between clients and servers (Srivastava, Cooley, Desphande, & Tan, 2000) (Shukla, Silakari, & Chande, 2013).

Web Server Data Collection

Server logs are considered the primary source of information for web usage mining. On each request made to the web server, an entry is recorded in the web log containing information about the request. Include the IP address, the requested URL, a timestamp, user agent and so on. The first problem with server logs is that they are not completely reliable because some of browsing information may not be registered in the log such as clients accessing a cached copy of a page in the client or proxy cache. The second problem arises when there is a proxy server between clients and the web server. In this case, clients share the same IP address and their requests are registered with same IP address in the server's

Figure 1. The Web Usage Mining Process

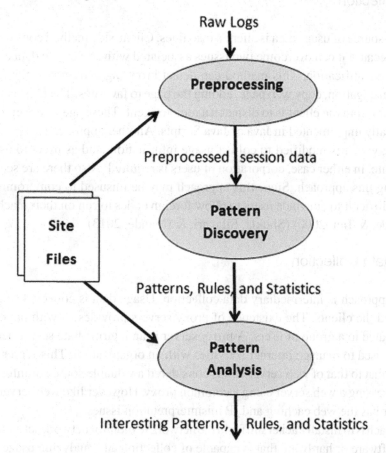

logs. It becomes difficult to identify each client uniquely. This problem is called IP misinterpretation. Another source of data which is capable of storing usage data is cookies. Cookies are piece of information generated by the web server for individual clients and stored at the client machine. The next time that client accesses the web server it send the cookie along with the request to the web server. Thus the web server can identify each user using cookie data which contains unique User ID. Cookies suffer from two major issues. They are small in size, usually less than 4KB, which limits the possible benefits. Also there will be user misinterpretation if the same browser is used by multiple users. The second problem with cookies is that user must accept them first which means cooperation from users is needed for this method to succeed. The third source of data from web server is by explicit user input through registration forms. This approach requires additional work from users and may discourage users to visit the website. Information collected through this method cannot be fully trusted because users tend to provide limited information due to privacy issues. The last source of data from the web server is by getting usage data from external sources (third party). This approach many not be appropriate due to security and privacy issues (Srivastava, Cooley, Desphande, & Tan, 2000) (Shukla, Silakari, & Chande, 2013).

Client Data Collection

The second major source of usage data is client's machines. Client-side method considered more reliable than server-side because it can overcome two issues associated with server-site data collection: caching and user sessions identification. This method can detect browsing activities at the client site such as back and forward navigation, copy web page, adding the page to favorites. The most common techniques from collecting data from the client is to dispatch a remote agent. These agents are embedded within the web page and usually implemented in Java or Java Scripts. Another approach is use a modified browser (such as Mozilla), which is modified to collect usage information, and as users to use this browser to navigate the website. In either case, corporation of users is required. Also there are security and privacy concerns regarding this approach. Since this approach may be misused to compromise user's security and privacy, it is difficult to convince users to allow foreign codes to run on their machines (Srivastava, Cooley, Desphande, & Tan, 2000) (Shukla, Silakari, & Chande, 2013).

Intermediary Data Collection

The third major approach is intermediary data collection. Usage data is collected somewhere between the web server and the clients. The existence of proxy servers provides us with opportunity to collect and study data related to a group of users. A proxy server is an intermediate server between clients and web server and is used to manage internet activities with an organization. This server maintains access logs similar in format to that of web server and is considered a valuable source of information regarding group of users accessing a web server using a common proxy. However like web servers, collecting data from proxy server has the web caching and IP misinterpretation issues.

Another approach is to install Packet sniffer in the network to monitor network activities. Packet sniffers can either be a software or hardware that is capable of collection and analyzing usage data in real time. This approach has some advantages over log files such as complete web page is captured along with the request data, cancelled requests can be captured as well. There are some disadvantages of packet sniffer. Since packet sniffers operate in real time and data is not logged, data may be lost forever. Furthermore, TCP/IP packets may be encrypted or may not arrive in sequence in the same order in which they were sent. This greatly limits the ability of useful information being extracted. Finally packet sniffers represent a serious threat to network security and may compromise users' security and privacy (Srivastava, Cooley, Desphande, & Tan, 2000) (Shukla, Silakari, & Chande, 2013).

Web Sever Logs

Web server logs are plain text (ASCII) files maintained as a normal function of the web servers to log the details of HTTP traffic. An entry is written to the logs on each HTTP request that is made to the server. Web logs take different formats depending to the server configurations (see Figure 2) (Gupta & Gupta, 2012).

Figure 2. An example of web access log.

```
196.1.197.110 - - [31/Mar/2015:16:24:37 +0200] "POST /new/index.php/en/contact HTTP/1.0"
200 10407 "http://reyada.sd/new/index.php/en/contact" "Mozilla/5.0 (Windows NT 6.1;
rv:36.0) Gecko/20100101 Firefox/36.0"

196.1.197.110 - - [31/Mar/2015:16:25:18 +0200] "POST /new/index.php/en/contact HTTP/1.0"
200 10407 "http://reyada.sd/new/index.php/en/contact" "Mozilla/5.0 (Windows NT 6.1;
rv:36.0) Gecko/20100101 Firefox/36.0"

196.1.197.110 - - [31/Mar/2015:16:25:24 +0200] "POST /new/index.php/en/contact HTTP/1.0"
200 10407 "http://reyada.sd/new/index.php/en/contact" "Mozilla/5.0 (Windows NT 6.1;
rv:36.0) Gecko/20100101 Firefox/36.0"
```

Types of Web Server Logs

Each web server may run different software with different configuration, but generally there are four types of server logs: transfer log, agent log, error log, and referrer log. Transfer and agent logs are the standard logs. The referrer and agent logs may not be turned on or may be added to the transfer log to create what is called extended log format (Jose & Lal, 2012).

Transfer Log

The server access log records all requests processed by the server. Transfer or access logs provide most of server information, such as the IP address of the client, the requested web resource, the data and time of the access. Analysing transfer log enables the web administrator to discover usage patterns such the number of visitors accessing the website from a specific domain type (.com, .edu etc), the number of unique visitors, the most popular page in the website, and the number of accesses during specific hours and days of the week.

Agent Log

The agent log provides information about the user's browser version and the operation system of the user machine. This great information for the design and the development of the website because the operating system the browser define the capabilities of the client and what the can do with the website.

Error Log

It is normal for the web user to encounter errors while browsing such as Error 404 Page Not Found. Another type of errors is when a user presses the stop button while downloading a large file. The error log also provides information about missing files and broken links. When a user encounter an error an entry will be written to the error log.

Referrer Log

This log identifies what other sites which link to the website. When a user follows the link this generate an entry in the referrer log.

Format of Access Logs

Each entry consists of a sequence of fields separated by whitespace and terminated by a CR or a CRLF. The access log can be configured to different formats that show different fields. Typical formats are Common Log Format and Combined Log Format (Sumathi, PadmajaValli, & Santhanam, 2011) (Grace, Maheswari, & Nagamalai, 2011).

Common Log Format

A typical entry of common log format might look as follows:

Host Logproprietor Username Date:Time Request Statuscode Bytes

Example:

```
   127.0.0.1 - frank [10/Oct/2000:13:55:36 -0700] "GET /product.html
HTTP/1.0" 200 2326
```

Each field of this log record is described as follows:

1. **Host:** This is the IP address of the client which made the request to the server. If there is a proxy server between the client and the server this will be the address of the proxy not the address of the client. Ex: 127.0.0.1.
2. **Log Proprietor:** The name of the owner making HTTP request. This information will not be exposed for security reasons. In this case a "hyphen" will be there.
3. **Username:** Is the HTTP authentication user ID of the user requesting the page. In the example above the username is frank.
4. **Date:Time:** This is the time that the server finished processing the request. Times are specified in GMT. The format is [day/month/year:hour:minute:second zone] where: Day = 2 digits. Month = 3 letters. Year = 4 digits. Hour = 2 digits. Minute = 2 digits. Second = 2 digits. Zone = (+/-) 4 digits. Ex: [10/Oct/2000:13:55:36 -0700].
5. **Request:** This string contains the details of the request made by the client consists of, first the method used by the client is GET, second the requested resource product.html, and third the protocol used by the client HTTP/1.0 . Ex: "GET /product.html HTTP/1.0".
6. **Status code:** This is the status code returned by the server. The status code shows whether the request resulted in a successful response or not. Generally the codes for successful requests begin in 2, a redirection codes begin in 3, codes for errors caused by the client begin in 4, and errors in the server begin 5. In the above example the status code is: 200.

7. **Bytes:** The last field indicates the size of the object returned to the client in bytes. In the above the size is 2326 bytes.

Combined Log Format

Is a commonly used log format similar to the common log format, with addition of two more fields, namely, the referrer and user agent. The format can be shown as follows:

Host Logproprietor Username Date:Time Request Statuscode Bytes Referrer User_Agent

Example:

```
    127.0.0.1 - frank [10/Oct/2000:13:55:36 -0700] "GET /product.html
HTTP/1.0" 200 2326 "http://www.example.com/start.html" "Mozilla/4.08 [en]
(Win98; I ;Nav)"
```

The additional fields are:

1. **Referrer:** Shows the page that the client was browsing before making the request. Ex: "http://www.example.com/start.html".

2. **User-Agent:** This field shows information about the client's browser and the operating system. Ex: "Mozilla/4.08 [en] (Win98; I ;Nav)".

Pre-Processing Web Logs

Data preprocessing is the most important and time consuming task in web usage mining, it takes about 80% for the total time of the mining process. The goal of preprocessing step is to clean data by removing irrelevant records and selecting essential features. The data is then is transformed into sessions file (Chitraa & Davamani).

Preprocessing consists of data cleaning, user identification, session identification, and path completion. Figure 3 shows a complete preprocessing method for web usage mining (Sheetal & Shailendra, 2012).

Data Cleaning

When a user requests a web page, a log record containing the URL of the page is written to the log, along with a log record for each file (e.g., image file, css) that constitutes the web page. Data cleaning includes the removal of records that might not be useful for mining. Following are the log records that are unnecessary and should be removed (Chitraa & Davamani):

1. Records of multimedia files and format files that have file extensions like GIF, JPEG, MPEG, and CSS and so on. These files can be identified by checking the URI field of the log entry.

Figure 3. Web log preprocessing

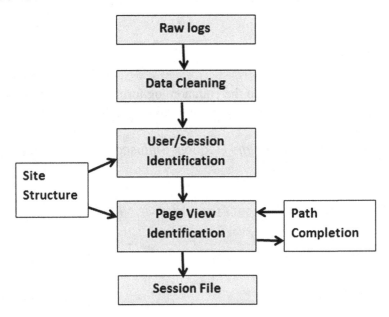

2. Failed HTTP requests should be removed. Log record with status codes that over 299 or fewer than 200 are removed. In most preprocessing methods only requests with a GET value in the method field are kept. Other records that have HEAD or POST values are removed from the log.
3. Records of search engine robot (also known as bots or spiders) are removed. These are software that visit the website and automatically search website's content.
4. At the end of the cleaning step only relevant records are kept which only show the page accesses of web users. The size of the log file should now be reduced significantly.

User Identification

In this step, individual users should be identified. A user is a single user that is accessing a web page through a browser. However, in reality, identification of users is not an easy task due to the stateless nature of the HTTP protocol. Different users may have same IP address in the log due to the use of proxy servers. The same user may access the website from different machines using different browsers. So the identification of users is the most difficult part of log preprocessing (Chitraa & Davamani).

The most used method for identifying user can be described as follows:

1. Each IP address represents a single user.
2. For the next record, if the IP address is the same as the IP address identified in the previous records, but the agent field shows a different browser or operating system, the IP address represents a different user.
3. If the same IP address, a path is constructed using the referrer field and site topology. If the page requested is not directly reachable from any previously visited page (linked with a hyperlink). A different user with the same IP address is identified.

Session Identification

The main task in this step is to divide the set of pages accessed by each user into individual sessions. A method for identifying user sessions can be adopted as follows (Chitraa & Davamani):

1. For each user, the records are sorted according to time.
2. For each record the following to tasks are repeated.
3. If the referrer website is null, appears as "-" in the log, then a new session started.
4. If the referrer site is a search engine or any other website, then it can be assumed a new session is started.

Path Completion

Some of page requests may be answered from local cache or proxy cache. These page accesses will not be recorded in the web server logs. Path completion attempts to fill in these missing page references. The referrer field and site topology are used to accomplish this task. If the requested page is not directly linked to the last page requested by the user, the referrer field can be checked to determine which page the request came from. It is assumed that the user has viewed a cached version of the page if the referrer page is in the users' recent history. Site topology can be employed instead of the referrer field to do the same task (Chitraa & Davamani).

After completing these tasks, the output file contains the log records along with two additional fields for user ID and session ID. The sessions file now contains meaningful information and is ready for the pattern discovery process.

Patterns Discovery Techniques

This section discusses various techniques that are most widely used to extract knowledge from a website log files. The following subsections classify them according to the technique used.

Association Rules

It is the process of finding associations within data items in the log file. This technique can be used to identify pages that are most often accessed together in a single user session. Association rules can be utilized, for example, as a way to guess the next page to visit so that the page can be preloaded from a remote server. These associated pages may not be linked directly via a hyperlink so this information can help web designers figure out related pages so that hyperlinks can be added between them (Srivastava, Cooley, Desphande, & Tan, 2000).

The authors in (Shastri, Patil, & Wadhai, 2010) discussed a constraint-based association rule mining approach. The goal is to make the generation of the association rules more efficient and effective. By removing useless rules and focus only on the interested rules instead of a complete set of rules. And thus eliminate the unwanted rules. In addition to the support and confidence, data and rule constraints are employed. Data constraints use SQL-like queries to focus on a subset of the transactions. For example, find items sold together on weekend days. Rule constraints specify the properties of the rules to be mined such as maximum rule length and item constraints. For example, the length of an association rule should be 3 at maximum with a specific item that should appear in every mined rule.

Maja and Tanja discussed in (Dimitrijević & Krunić, 2013) how the confidence of association rules change over time. They compared confidence levels between two time periods. They showed that interestingness measures, the confidence and the lift, along with rule pruning techniques, can be used to produce association rules that are easier to understand and allow the Webmaster to make informed decisions about improving the structure of the website. The changes in confidence levels over the two time periods have brought new information about the association rules in these two periods. If the confidence increased then the previous decision about adding a link between the pages involved in the rule has been confirmed. On the other hand, if the confidence dropped, the administrator may consider removing the link between the pages involved in the rule.

Preeti and Sanjay (Sharma & Kumar, 2011) discuss preprocessing activities that are necessary before applying data mining algorithm. Association rule mining algorithm (Apriori) is used to find most frequent associated pages. The paper discusses how association rules can be beneficial in some application areas such as business intelligence, site modification, and website restructuring.

Clustering

In web usage mining, there are two kinds of clusters: user clusters and page clusters. User clustering can be exploited to perform market segmentation in e-commerce web sites or provide personalized web. Page clustering identifies pages with related content and can be useful for search engines and web recommendation systems (Srivastava, Cooley, Desphande, & Tan, 2000).

Authors in (Langhnoja, Barot, & Mehta, 2013) described a method for performing clustering on web log file to divide web visitors into groups based on their common behaviors. The clustering technique which is based on DBSCAN algorithm helped in efficiently finding groups of users with similar interests and behavior.

The paper (M & Dixit, 2010) proposed a system for analyzing user sessions to find groups of users with similar activities. The system provides two types of clustering: clustering based on time and clustering based on IP addresses. The system allows for selection of relevant attributes and shows clustering based on either IP addresses or timestamp.

NeetuAnand and SabaHilal (Anand & Hilal, 2012) discussed a web usage mining approach for identifying user access patterns hidden in web log data. The goal is to discover unknown relationships in the data. The clustering analysis technique is applied to group similar page requests. The WEKA software is used to perform k-means clustering of URLs.

Four types of clustering approaches have been investigated in (Sujatha & Punithavalli, 2011). These represent different methods for performing clustering on web log data in order to discover hidden information about users' navigation behavior. The author discussed Ant-based clustering, fuzzy clustering, graph partitioning, and page clustering algorithm. The authors also discussed the process of web usage mining and the activities necessary for performing patterns discovery tasks.

Classification

Classification is the process of assigning a class to each data item based on a set of predefined classes. In web mining, classification can be used, for example, to develop a profile of users belonging to a particular class or to classify HTTP request as normal or abnormal (Srivastava, Cooley, Desphande, & Tan, 2000).

Priyanka and Dharmaraj (Patil & Patil, 2012) proposed an intrusion detection system based on web usage mining. Two different techniques have been used to detect intrusion: misuse detection and anomaly detection. Misuse detection employs a set of attack descriptions or "signatures". Then match the actual usage data against these descriptions, if match found, a misuse has been detected. Misuse detection works well in detecting all known attacks. However, it cannot detect new attacks. The second mode is anomaly detection. This method has the advantage of detecting all known as well as unknown attacks. This is done by comparing usage data against already constructed profiles in order to detect unexpected events or anomaly patterns of activity.

Apriori algorithm is used to learn association rules from URI lists. After that they used classification to classify each log record as either normal or a specific kind of attack. To detect anomalies they employ login and page frequencies thresholds. A model of normal behavior is constructed during the learning phase. This model is used in detection phase to compare the usage data with model. If abnormal behavior found then intrusion has been detected. Experiments have been carried out to prove that the proposed system had better or same detection rate as other similar intrusion detection systems.

The paper (Santra & Jayasudha, 2012) discussed classification of web users into "interested user" or "not interested user" based on Naïve Bayesian classification algorithm. The goal is to focus on the behavior of interested users instead of all users. An interested user is identified by checking the time spent on each page and the number of pages visited. Records of uninterested users are eliminated from the log file. Authors conducted comparative study and evaluation of Naïve Bayesian algorithm and an enhanced C4.5 decision tree. They concluded that Naïve Bayesian algorithm has an efficient implantation and a better performance than C4.5 decision tree.

Sequential Patterns

The aim of this technique is to predict future URLs to be visited based on a time-ordered sequence of URLs followed in the past. This technique finds temporal relationship among data items over ordered sequences of click-stream. Sequential patterns technique can be thought of as an extension of the association mining which is not capable of finding temporal patterns. The difference between association mining and sequential patterns is that association mining focuses on searching intra-sequence patterns, whereas sequential patterns find inter-sequence patterns (Valera & Rathod, 2013) (Sharma & Kumar, 2011).

Examples of sequential patterns can be shown as follows: If a user visits page X followed by page Y, he will visit page Z with c% confidence. 60% of clients, who placed an online order in /computer/products/webminer.html, also placed an online order /computer/products/ iis.html within 10 days.

Sequential patterns allow web-based organization to predict user visit patterns. This can help in developing strategies for advertisement targeting groups of users based on these patterns.

Patterns Analysis

The results of pattern discovery phase need to be analyzed to obtain more useful patterns. Each cluster obtained by the clustering technique needs to be analyzed to find general description of it. The association rule algorithm may generate large number of rules. We need to explore and analyze the result of association rules technique in order to focus on interesting rules. Generally, patterns are further analyzed to refine the discovered knowledge. Patterns can be analyzed using query language such as SQL or can be loaded into a data cube in order to perform different OLAP operations. Visualization techniques can also be used to help understand patterns and highlight trends data (Srivastava, Cooley, Desphande, & Tan, 2000) (Shukla, Silakari, & Chande, 2013).

Implementation Example

This section discusses the implementation of the web usage mining process. A real web log file will be utilized. Clustering and association mining will be performed to find usage patterns of the website's users.

Software Tool

Orange is a powerful and easy to use data visualization and analysis tool that supports data mining through visual programming or Python scripting. Orange can be freely downloaded from http://orange.biolab.si/ .

The Data Sets

A log file collected from the web domain of an organization. The data was collected over the period 2 Sep 2013 to 22 Oct, 2013, a total of 51 days. There were 750381 records in the log. Each record is a sequence of information about one HTTP request. A description of each filed in the log record will be presented in Table 1.

Table 1. Data description

Field	Description
IP	The IP Address of the Client
Password	HTTP authentication password. If not available a hyphen will be there instead.
Username	HTTP authentication user ID of the user requesting the page. If not available a hyphen will be there instead.
Time	The time that the server finished processing the request. Specified in GMT
The request	The request, consists of, the method used, the requested resource, and the protocol.
Status	The status code shows whether the request resulted in a successful response or not
Size	Indicates the size of the object returned to the client in bytes.
Referrer	Shows the page that the client was browsing before making the request. If not available a hyphen will be there instead.
Agent	Shows information about the client's browser and the operating system. If not available a hyphen will be there instead.

Data Pre-Processing

The following preprocessing tasks will be performed: data cleaning, user identification, and session identification. Data should be formatted and a suitable feature set should be chosen. Following are description of each task.

Data Cleaning

Irrelevant records are removed. These records do not add anay new information because they are not explicitly requested by visitors. All records are removed except the records that show the URL requested by the visitors. Data will be extracted from the log file (a text file) and stored in a relational table so that further processing would be more efficient. Following are the steps required in cleaning the log data:

1. Remove the records of multimedia and format file, file that have extension like .jpg, .mpeg, .gif, .js, .css.
2. Remove the records with status code less than 200 or greater than 299 (failed requests).
3. Remove the requests of search engines by checking the agent field for patterns like "bot", "spider".
4. Remove POST and HEAD requests.

User Identification

Since we are interested in modeling users' behaviors, it is important to identify each user uniquely. A method based on the combination of the IP address and the agent will be employed for this purpose.

1. A new IP address is considered a new user.
2. If the same IP but the agent is different, a new user is identified.

Session Identification

A session is a group of pages requested by a single user during one visit or during a specified period of time. To find users browsing patterns, it is important to group pages requested by individual users into sessions. For this purpose a navigation oriented session identification method has been adopted based on the referrer filed as the following:

1. First, sort the records of each user according to time.
2. For each record, repeat the following two tasks.
3. If the referrer is "-", then a new user session is starting.
4. If the referrer is a search engine or any other site we assume that the user is starting a new session.

Table 2 Shows the results of data cleaning, user identification, user sessions identification.

Table 2. Preprocessing results

Size of the Log File	168.3 MB
Records in the raw log file	750381
Records with failed status	161396
Multimedia & format files requests	450356
Search engines requests	106760
HEAD & POST records	6729
Number of records after cleaning	94166
Number of users	12848
Number of sessions	4966

Data Preparation

Further processing of the data is performed to extract as much useful information as possible from the log data. Following are some tasks to improve the data set.

1. Convert IP numbers to the geographical location (country) using a reverse DNS service.
2. Extract the URL from the request field.
3. Extract the browser name from the agent string.
4. Identify the top referrer sites.

Feature Set (First 3 Clicks, Last 2 Clicks)

Some user sessions contain only one or two pages, other contain more than 10 pages. Due to these differences in session's length the first three pages and the last two pages of each session will be chosen. If pages in the session are fewer than five pages there will be missing values. This is also known as First3-last2 which is one of several feature set methods presented in (Ciesielski & Lalani, 2003). The missing pages will be filled in with a hyphen. The feature set that will be used in experiments includes: the user ID, session ID, the geographic location, the first three pages in the session and the last two pages, the referrer site, and the browser name.

Pattern Discovery

In this section we will apply clustering technique on the preprocessed data. The goal is to divide user sessions into groups that share similar characteristics. The K-means clustering method with different settings will be used. The number of clusters (K) will be optimized by the software tool from 2 to 5 clusters. The tool optimizes the clustering and selects the K value that corresponds to the best clustering.

Evaluation Framework

There are different measures to assess the quality of clustering by measuring how well clusters are separated from each other, or how compact the clusters are. Following are the measure available in Orange software:

1. Clustering quality: Clusters scoring will be explored include silhouette (heuristic), Between Cluster Distance, and Distance to centroids
2. Distance measures: is used to measure the distances between examples (user sessions in our case) in the dataset. Euclidean, Manhattan, Maximal, and Hamming will be used.

Results

For each combination of scoring method and distance measure, the best score and the resulting number of clusters (best k) are shown in Table 3.

The best clustering using Silhouette (heuristic) method is achieved by the distance measure (Manhattan) which renders the highest scoring value (0.45) and resulted in two clusters. Similarly, Between-cluster-distance method achieved best clustering by using the Hamming distance measure (scoring=33982.0), this clustering resulted in two clusters. Finally, Distance-to-centroids method achieved the best clustering through the Maximal measure which gives the lowest scoring (4562.4) and resulted in five clusters.

It should be noted that the Euclidean distance measure was not able to generate best clustering (according to scoring) regardless of the scoring method used. Also, the between-cluster-distance method tends to generate two clusters except for Maximal distance measure which gives five clusters. Similarly, the distance-to-centroids method always generates five clusters regardless of the distance measure used.

It is difficult to compare different quality methods due to the differences in how they calculate the coring value. For example, according to between-cluster-distance method, biggest scoring value is better, while in distance-to-centroids method, smallest is better.

Table 3. Cluster results

Scoring Method	Distance Measures	Scoring	Best (k)
Silhouette (heuristic) *Scoring: bigger is better*	Euclidean	0.303	5
	Manhattan	**0.45**	2
	Maximal	0.0813	5
	Hamming	0.355	2
Between Cluster Distance *Scoring: bigger is better*	Euclidean	11132.4	2
	Manhattan	26855.9	2
	Maximal	4966.0	5
	Hamming	**33982.0**	2
Distance to centroids *Scoring: smaller is better*	Euclidean	6543.0	5
	Manhattan	10607.4	5
	Maximal	**4562.4**	5
	Hamming	19255.0	5

Pattern Analysis

Silhouette Combined with Manhattan Distance Measure

The best clustering by k-means algorithm and Silhouette as a scoring method was obtained by Manhattan distance measure. According to these settings, two clusters were formed.

The first cluster consists of 3517 user sessions which constitute 70.8% of the data set. 40.2% of sessions in this cluster belong to users from the United States. The next most frequent country is Sudan (17.2%). Users in this cluster tend to start their session from the homepage/ar/index.php (42.7 of the sessions). Interestingly, in 93.7% of the sessions, there is no referrer site, which means that users started browsing from the website itself and did not come from a search engine or any other site. They typed the URL or they have set the website as the homepage in their browsers. The top browser used was iPhone browser (26.6%).

The second Cluster consists of 1449 user sessions which constitute 29.2% of the total sessions. 46.7% of sessions in this cluster belong to users from Sudan. The next most frequent country is Norway (15.5%). Users in this cluster tend to start their session from page view_law.php (57.6 of the sessions). 60.5% of the sessions started by searching at Google and then arrive at the website, and usually not through the homepage but the page view_law.php. The top browser used was Opera Mini (22.7%).

Between-Cluster-Distance Combined with Hamming

The best clustering using the k-means algorithm combined with between-cluster-distance as scoring method was obtained by Hamming distance measure. According to these settings, two clusters were formed.

It should be noted that the result of this experiment is very similar to the experiment of 1 above. Clusters formed are almost identical with just minor differences.

Distance-to-Centroids Method Combined with Maximal

The best clustering using k-means algorithm with distance-centroids as scoring method was obtained by Maximal distance measure. This experiment resulted in five clusters.

The first and largest cluster contains 90.8% of the total sessions. The top countries are United States, Sudan, and India. The most entry pages were /ar/index.php and view_law.php. Most of the session had no referring site. The top browser was iPhone browser.

The second cluster consists of 3.7% of the total sessions. All users were from Sudan and started browsing from /ar/index.php and they had no referring website. All users in this cluster used Firefox browser.

The third cluster represents of 0.1% of the total sessions. All users were from Sweden and started browsing from the page dstor2005.php and they had no referring website. All users in this cluster used Firefox browser.

The fourth cluster represents of 0.6% of the total sessions. All users are from Finland and started browsing from /ar/index.php and they came from the same website. All users in this cluster used Nokia browser.

The fifth cluster represents of 4.8% of the total sessions. All users are from France and started browsing from /ar/index.php and they had no referring website. All users in this cluster used Safari browser.

General Thoughts about Clusters

The between-cluster-distance and Silhouette produced almost the same results with minor differences. These two methods assess how well the clusters are separated from each other.

The third method, the distance-to-centroids, gave very different results. The clustering consists of one large cluster, 90.8% of the total sessions, and the other four clusters share the remaining 9.2%. Each one of these four clusters is pure, meaning that the sessions are very similar, same pages visited, same browser, and same location and so on. This may raise the question whether this clustering is a really good clustering or not? After further investigation, It has been found that one cluster of them contains sessions by a single user. Another cluster consists of sessions of only two different users. Although the quality of this clustering is high and therefore interesting according to the objective measure, this clustering is might not interesting according to a subjective measure because it might not provide useful information.

Association Rules

The goal is to generate association rules from user sessions. Association rules can reveal users' behavior and navigation patterns. We will set the minimum support and minimum confidence values to 12 and 60 respectively. First we will mine association rules from the whole data set. Then we will find association rules for each country in top 10 countries in the data set.

Evaluation Framework

Whether or not a rule is interesting can be assessed either subjectively or objectively. Only the user can judge if a rule is interesting, and this judgment is subjective, it may differ from one user to another. In this project we used objective interestingness measures: support, confidence. Some rules can have high support and confidence values but still these rules are misleading. To filter out the strong but misleading rules, we will enhance the evaluation framework with the lift, which is a correlation measure based on the statistics of the data.

1. **Support:** The support of the rule A=>B is the proportion of transactions that contain both A & B.
2. **Confidence:** The confidence of the rule A=>B is the conditional probability of occurrence of B given A.
3. **Lift:** Is a simple correlation measure that used to filter out misleading association rules of the form A => B. The lift value is used identify weather A&B are positively correlated, negatively correlated, or independent.

Mining Rules from the Entire Data Set

In this experiment we selected (click1, click2, location, ref_site, and browser) from the feature set described above. The reason that we did not select the other three page of each session (click3, click4, click5) is that users did not visit more than two pages in a single session most of the time. The missing values have been filled in with a '-'. This will create problems to the association rule mining as they generate more meaningless rules, for this reason, we will remove the last three pages from each session.

After the application of the association mining technique with 14 minimum supports and 60 minimum confidences, we found 45 rules. Some rules may not be meaningful, but still, these are strong rules and represent correlations within the data set. It should be noted that even if a rule is interesting enough according to the support and confidence measures we need to check the lift column to see if antecedent and consequent of the rule are statistically correlated. This will help filter out strong but misleading rules. If the lift is less than 1, that means the antecedent and consequent of the rule are negatively correlated, if the lift is greater than 1 it means they are positively correlated, and if the lift equals 1 this means they are independent. We are interested in rules that are positively correlated. Table 4 shows the most interesting rules.

Mining Association Rules by Country

Sometimes it is desirable to divide users into groups and derive high level conclusions about these groups. In this experiment we consider each geographical location a separate group. We want to search for association rules in these groups (countries). So we will limit our search only to sessions of visitors from each location. These rules cannot be discovered from the entire data set as they may not qualify the minimum support threshold. We will consider the top countries as they represent the majority.

In this experiment we select sessions belong to the each top country and see if we can find any interesting rules specific to that location. We used minimum support and confidence as 12 and 60 respectively. Table 5 shows some of the most interesting rules.

Table 4. Most interesting rules from the data set

Rule	Supp	Conf	Lift
Location=United States => ref_site=no referrer	0.277	0.884	1.188
Click1=/ar/index.php => click2='-'	0.234	0.677	1.071
Ref_site=Google => click2=/ar/index.php	0.154	0.853	2.664
Click1=/ar/view_law.php => click2=/ar/index.php	0.155	0.610	2.129
Location=United States => ref_site=no referrer, browser=iPhone browser	0.191	0.609	3.046
Ref_site=no referrer => click2='-'	0.585	0.786	1.243

Table 5. Most interesting rules in top countries

Location	Rule	Supp	Conf	Lift
United States	click1=/ar/view_law.php, click2='-' => ref_site=no referrer	0.153	0.968	1.095
United States	click1=/ar/news.php, click2='-' => ref_site=no referrer	0.159	1.000	1.131
Sudan	click1=/ar/view_law.php => ref_site=Google	0.237	0.768	2.307
Sudan	click1=/ar/view_law.php => click2=/ar/index.php	0.259	0.838	1.563
India	click1=/ar/members.php => click2='-', ref_site=no referrer	0.939	0.951	1.011
China	click1=/en/news.php, ref_site=no referrer => click2='-'	0.157	1.000	1.245
Ukraine	click1=/ar/index.php => click2=/ar/index.php	0.946	1.000	1.057

Discussing Association Rules Results

We applied the association rule technique with minimum support and minimum confidence values set to 14 and 60 respectively. We will only discuss some of the interesting rules from the entire data set and also from each country appeared in top 10 countries.

Association Rules from Entire Data Set

According to minimum support and confidence of 14 and 60 respectively, we found 45 association rules. The results are shown in Table 4. When we check the lift column we can see that all rules represent positive correlations except for a single rule which is a negative association rule.

Following are some of the interesting rules: We will use following structure of the rules Antecedent => Consequent, (support, confidence, lift).

1. If the user from the United States, then there is no referrer. The is rule means that users from United States start their sessions directly from the website itself and did not arrive from a search engine or any other website. It also means these users are familiar with the web site, the entered the URL directly or they have set the website as the homepage in their browser. The rule is: location = United States => ref_site= no referrer, (0.277, 0.884, 1.188).
2. The second rule states that if a user accesses the homepage (/ar/index.php) then the next page is '-', mean is empty. This means the session contains a single page. The rule is: click1=/ar/index. php -> click2= -, (0.234, 0.677, 1.071).
3. If a user accesses the homepage (/ar/index.php) then he arrived from Google. The rule is: ref_ site=Google => click2=/ar/index.php, (0.154, 0.853,2.664).
4. The next rule is: click1=/ar/view_law.php => click2=/ar/index.php, (0.155, 0.610, 2.129). This rule means the two pages; view_law.php and index.php are accessed together in users sessions.
5. The next interesting rule is: Location= United States - > ref_site = no referrer, browser=iPhone browser, (0.191, 0.609, 3.046). This rule means that users from the United States open the website directly and they are mobile users.
6. If the user access the website directly by typing the web address of the website (i.e. they did not arrive from other websites via hyperlinks), then they visit a single page in their session. The rule is: ref_site=no referrer => click2='-', (0.585, 0.786, 1.243). This rule has a high support meaning that more than 50% of the sessions follow this rule.

We noticed that most of the rules related to users from the United States. This can be explained by the fact that most of the visitors are from the United States. This is why we select to search association rules in subsets of the data set so that we can find other rules.

Association Rules by Country

In this section, we will discuss the rules found that correspond to each country. The experiments were described in section 4.3.2 in the previous chapter. Following are some of the interesting rules:

1. **United States:** The rule: click1=/ar/view_law.php, click2=- => ref_site=no referrer, (0.153, 0.968, 1.095). This rule means that user from United states visit the page view_law.php directly without going through the homepage, and they only visited that page. this rule means that users are not only familiar with the website but also a specific page in the web site . This rule is consistent with the results shown in section 5.3.1 above.

2. **United States:** The second interesting rule is: click1=/ar/news.php, click2=- => ref_site=no referrer, (0.159, 1.000, 1.131). This rule means that users only visited the page news,php directly without any referrer website. This rule is new and cannot be discovered from the entire data set.

3. **Sudan:** The second interesting rule is that user from Sudan start by searching at Google and then find the page view_law.php which is not the homepage. The rule is: click1=/ar/view_law.php => ref_site=Google, (0.237, 0.768, 2.307).

4. **Sudan:** The third interesting rule is that the pages view_law.php and the home page /ar/index.php often accessed together in a single session which is consistent with results in section 5.3.1 above. The rule is: click1=/ar/activity/view_law.php -> /ar/index.php, (0.259, 0.838, 1.563).

5. **India:** One interesting rule found. Other rules basically mean the same thing. The rule is: click1=/ar/members.php => click2=-, ref_site=no referrer, (0.939, 0.951, 1.011). this means that users from Indian visited a single page in their session, members.php, and they did not arrive from a search engine or any other site. It should be note that this rule has very high support and confidence. Almost all users from India follow this rule and have very similar behavior which is a surprising result. This may raise the question why visitors from this location have high interest in this single page? We found that there sessions actually belong to a single user.

6. **China:** The new and most interesting rule is that if the first page in the sessions is /en/news.php and there is no referrer site then users will not visit more pages. The rule is: click1=/en/news.php, ref_site=no referrer => click2=-, (0.157, 1.000, 1.245). the rule is new and cannot be discovered from the entire dataset.

7. **Ukraine:** The first interesting rule. When users visit the homepage then they arrive from parliament.gov.sd. ref_site=parliament.gov.sd => click1=/ar/index.php, (0.946, 0.959, 1.014).

8. **Ukraine:** The second interesting rule states that users revisit the same page. This is a strong which is a surprising result. This may be attributed to the website design. The rule is: click1=/ar/index.php =>click2=/ar/index.php, (0.946, 1.000, 1.057). After investigating the data, we found that the sessions are actually belonging to different users. Different users have the same strange behavior of revisiting the homepage multiple times in their sessions. We suspect the homepage design might be the reason.

General Thoughts about Association Rules

The general behavior of visitors that revealed by the association rules can be described as follows: visitors are either regular visitors that familiar with website or they arrive after searching at Google. If visitors arrive from Google they usually tend to visit page view_law.php. This specific page is very popular and visitors have increased interest in its content.

After portioning the data set and searching sessions according to the geographical location, we were able to discover new association rules that could not be discovered from the entire data set because they might not qualify the minimum support threshold. Some of these new rules are quite interesting and revealed strange behaviors in user navigations

CHALLENGES AND RESEARCH ISSUES (FUTURE DIRECTIONS)

Challenges

Web data represent a new challenge to traditional data mining algorithms that work with structured data. Some web analysis tools are being developed that offer an implementation of some data mining techniques, but the research in this area still in its infancy. Using data mining in the web is faced by real challenges such as large storage requirements and scalability problems (Rana, 2012).

In the pre-processing phase, log file needs to be cleaned from irrelevant records. Records of graphics and failed HTTP requests are removed. For some domains these information should be removed while in other domains it should not be eliminated. Thus pre-processing is highly dependent on the domain and there is no standard techniques that can be applied to all domains (Srivastava, Cooley, Desphande, & Tan, 2000).

In practice; it is difficult to identify web users uniquely due to the stateless nature of the HTTP protocol and presence of proxy servers. A single user may access the website from different machines using different browser. The same machine or browser may be used by several users. In web usage mining research it is usually assumed that the same IP address and the same user agent means the same user. However, the same user may come from different IP address or use different browsers. This represents a real challenge when identifying users accessing a website.

For identification of user sessions, we assumed in our example that if a user opens the website directly by typing the web address in the browser, the user is starting a new session. Furthermore, if the user is arriving from a search engine or other website via a hyperlink, we also assumed that user is starting a new session. We need to make some assumptions when identifying users' sessions and such assumptions may affect the accuracy of the results of the usage mining.

Web caching represents another problem. Accesses to cached pages are not recorded in the server logs leaving us without information about these accesses. The existence of a proxy server represents another challenge. Clients accessing a web server through a proxy server will be assigned same IP address and will be registered in the server log. So it becomes difficult to identify each user uniquely from the web server logs (Shukla, Silakari, & Chande, 2013).

The interpretation of the knowledge extracted by data mining techniques may be limited due to the limitations of the data set. Web logs are basically used for debugging purposes and for knowing how much traffic the website is getting and not intended for studying users' behaviors and finding their interests. To improve the quality of the discovered patterns, it is important to extract as much useful information as possible from the available data in the log file.

FUTURE RESEARCH DIRECTION

Future research may explore new and different feature sets. This chapter, discussed the first three clicks and the last two clicks feature set. A feature set implies that the first three pages and the last two pages will be included in each user session. Such feature set has limitations and might not be good for other data mining goals. In addition to developing new feature sets, it might be helpful to extract more information from the raw log file, similar to extracting location information from raw IP numbers, so that the quality of the data set will be improved and as a result more interpretable and actionable patterns will be mined.

Log file data go through various kinds of transformations during the preprocessing phase. Such transformations may affect the quality of the data set. To handle this issue, future research may focus on better preprocessing techniques.

This chapter discussed association rules, clustering classification and sequential patterns analysis. Other data mining techniques that work with structured data can be incorporated into the web usage mining process. In addition to exploring different data mining techniques, more data can be combined with log file's data in many ways. Results of one kind of analysis can be used as input to other data mining techniques. For instance, results of text analytic, information extracted from web page content can be combined with web log data. This combination provides a rich data source for pattern discovery and lead to significant knowledge to be mined

Privacy Issues

It is very important to maintain users' privacy while performing web usage mining. Users may hesitate to reveal their personal information implicitly or explicitly. Some users may hesitate to visit those websites that make use of cookies or agents. Most users want to maintain strict anonymity on the web. In such environment it becomes difficult to perform usage mining (Srivastava, Cooley, Desphande, & Tan, 2000) (Mehtaa, Parekh, Modi, & Solamki, 2012). On the other hand site administrators are interested in finding out about users' demographic information and their usage patterns. This information is extremely important for improvement of the site. For tasks of personalization and improving the browsing experience, it is required that each user is identified uniquely every time they visit the website.

The main challenge is to develop rules such that administrators can perform analysis on usage data without compromising the identity of individual user. Furthermore there should be strict regulations that prevent usage data from being exchanged or sold to other sites. Every site should inform its users about the privacy policies followed by them so that users are aware when deciding to reveal personal information.

To meet the need to maintain users' privacy while browsing the website, W3C presented what is called Platform for Privacy Preferences (P3P) . (Srivastava, Cooley, Desphande, & Tan, 2000). P3P allows privacy policies followed by the website to be published in a machine readable format. When the user visits the site for the first time the browser reads the privacy policies and then compares these policies with the security settings in the browser. If the policies are satisfactory the user can continue browsing the website, otherwise a negotiation protocol is used to arrive at a setting which is acceptable to the user. Another aim of P3P is to provide guidelines for independent organizations to can ensure that sites comply with the policy statement they are publishing (Langhnoja, Barot, & Mehta, 2013).

CONCLUSION

As a result of the internet being an important medium for business transaction and the recent interest in e-commerce, the study of web usage mining has attracted much attention from the research community. Web usage mining is the process of application of data mining techniques to usage data which is available primarily in server logs. This chapter has discussed pattern discovery from web server's logs files to get insight into visitors' behavior and usage patterns.

The web usage mining process involves three main phases: preprocessing, pattern discovery, and pattern analysis. Usage data can be collected from three main locations: web server, clients, and an intermediary location such as proxy servers. Web server log files are considered the primary source of data for usage mining. However, server logs are not entirely reliable due to various kinds of clients' caches and proxy caches. The IP address misinterpretation and users' misinterpretation are example of challenges that affect the accuracy of users' identification, which is a crucial step in web usage mining. Data in server logs have to be converted into structured format by preprocessing algorithms before apply any data mining techniques.

This chapter discussed major pattern discovery techniques in web usage mining. Techniques include: association rules, clustering, classification, and sequential patterns. These techniques are basically data mining techniques adopted form web domain.

The chapter also presented a practical example that implement an approach to web usage mining. The raw log file contained 750381 records, after preprocessing, there were12848 different users, and 4966 users sessions.

In the knowledge discovery, clustering models using k-means clustering and association rules mining have been performed to find usage patterns. The study has found that, using k-means algorithm, among all combinations of quality methods and distance measures, silhouette is better combined with Manhattan distance measure, between clusters distance is better combined with Hamming distance measure, and distance to centroids is better combined with Maximal distance measure. Regarding association rules, we have found that mining rules from the entire data set resulted in rules which are dominated by visitors from the United States. After dividing the data set according to the geographical groups so that high level conclusions about these groups can be derived, we were able to find some new and interesting associations. We found that most visitors are from the United States and Sudan and the most popular pages in the web site were the homepage index.php and view_law.php. These two pages were most often accessed together in user sessions. A significant number of users visited a single page, mostly the homepage. Most users stared their sessions by search at Google, then arrive to the page view_law.php after that they move to the homepage.

Web usage mining combines to active research areas: World Wide Web and data mining. Application of usage mining show promising results in different areas such as web personalization, business intelligence, web system improvement, and enhancing security. The study of web usage mining is expected to attract more attention as the internet becoming and important medium for business, education, news, government, etc.

REFERENCES

Anand, N., & Hilal, S. (2012). Identifying the User Access Pattern in Web Log Data. *International Journal of Computer Science and Information Technologies, 3*(2), 3536–3539.

Bhatia, T. (2011). Link Analysis Algorithms For Web Mining. *International Journal of Computer Science and Technology, 2*(2), 243–246.

Chitraa, V., & Davamani, A. S. (2010). A Survey on Preprocessing Methods for Web usage Data. *International Journal of Computer Science and Information Security, 7*(3), 78–83.

Chitraa, V., & Davamani, A. S. (2010). An Efficient Path Completion Technique for web log mining. *IEEE International Conference on Computational Intelligence and Computing Research.*

Ciesielski, V., & Lalani, A. (2003). Data Mining of Web Access Logs From an Academic Web Site. *Proceedings of the Third International Conference on Hybrid Intelligent Systems (HIS'03): Design and Application of Hybrid Intelligent Systems* (pp. 1034-1043). IOS Press.

Costa Júnior, M. G., & Gong, G. d. (2005). Web Structure Mining: An Introduction. *Proceedings of the 2005 IEEE, International Conference on Information Acquisition* (p. 6). Hong Kong: IEEE. doi:10.1109/ICIA.2005.1635156

Dimitrijević, M., & Krunić, T. (2013). Association rules for improving website effectiveness: Case analysis. *Online Journal of Applied Knowledge Management, 1*(2), 56–63.

Grace, L. J., Maheswari, V., & Nagamalai, D. (2011). Analysis of Web Logs and Web User in Web Mining. *International Journal of Network Security & Its Applications, 3*(1), 99–110. doi:10.5121/ijnsa.2011.3107

Gupta, R., & Gupta, P. (2012). Application specific web log pre-processing. *Int. J.ComputerTechology &Applications, 3*(1), 160–162.

Gupta, R., & Gupta, P. Fast Processing of Web Usage Mining with Customized Web Log Pre-processing and modified Frequent Pattern Tree. *International Journal of Computer Science & Communication Networks, 1*(3), 277-279.

Jose, J., & Lal, P. S. (2012). An Indiscernibility Approach for preprocessing of Web Log Files. *International journal of Internet Computing, 1* (3), 58-61.

Langhnoja, S. G., Barot, M. P., & Mehta, D. B. (2013). Web Usage Mining to Discover Visitor Group with Common Behavior Using DBSCAN Clustering Algorithm. *International Journal of Engineering and Innovative Technology, 2*(7), 169–173.

M, K., & Dixit, D. (2010). Mining Access Patterns Using Clustering. *International Journal of Computer Applications, 4* (11), 22-26.

Mehtaa, P., Parekh, B. P., Modi, K., & Solamki, P. (2012). Web personalization Using Web Mining: Concept and Research issue. *International Journal of information and Education Technology, 2* (5), 510-512.

Patil, P. V., & Patil, D. (2012). Preprocessing Web Logs for Web Intrusion Detection. *International Journal of Applied Information Systems*, 11-15.

Rana, C. (2012). A Study of Web Usage Mining Research Tools. *Int. J. Advanced Networking and Applications, 3*(6), 1422–1429.

S, Y., K, A., & J, S. (2011). Analysis of Web Mining Applications and Benefcial Areas. *IIUM Engineering Journal, 12* (2), 185-195.

Santra, A. K., & Jayasudha, S. (2012). Classification of Web Log Data to Identify Interested UsersUsing Naïve Bayesian Classification. *International Journal of Computer Science Issues, 9*(1), 381–387.

Sharma, P., & Kumar, S. (2011). An Approach for Customer Behavior Analysis Using Web Mining. *International Journal of Internet Computing, 1*(2), 1–6.

Shastri, A., Patil, D., & Wadhai, V. (2010). Constraint-based Web Log Mining for AnalyzingCustomers' Behaviour. *International Journal of Computers and Applications, 11*(10), 7–11.

Sheetal, & Shailendra. (2012). Efficient Preprocessing technique using Web log mining. *International Journal of Advancements in Research & Technology, 1* (6), 59-63.

Shukla, R., Silakari, S., & Chande, P. K. (2013). Web Personalization Systems and Web Usage Mining: A Review. *International Journal of Computers and Applications, 72*(21), 6–13. doi:10.5120/10468-5189

Srivastava, J., Cooley, R., Desphande, M., & Tan, P.-N. (2000). Web Usage Mining: Discovery and Applications of Usage Patterns from Web Data. *ACM SIGKDD Explorations Newsletter, 1*(2), 12–23. doi:10.1145/846183.846188

Srivastava, J., Desikan, P., & Kumar, V. (2002). Web Mining Accomplishments& Future Directions. *National Science Foundation Workshop on Next Generation Data Mining (NGDM'02)*, (pp. 51-56).

Sujatha, M., & Punithavalli. (2011). A Study of Web Navigation Pattern Using Clustering Algorithm in Web Log Files. *International Journal of Scientific & Engineering Research, 2*(9), 1–5.

Sumathi, C. P., PadmajaValli, R., & Santhanam, T. (2011). An Overview of preprocessing of Web Log Files. *Journal of Theoretical and Applied Information Technology, 34*(2), 178–185.

Valera, M., & Rathod, K. (2013). A novel approach of Mining Frequent Sequential Patterns from Customized Web Log Preprocessing. *International Journal of Engineering Research and Applications, 3*(1), 369–380.

KEY TERMS AND DEFINITIONS

Big Data: Any data set that is too difficult to be handled by traditional database systems due to its size and complexity.

Privacy: Refers to users' concerns to share personal information and reveal their browsing habits. Users want that the information they share with the website will not be shared with a third-party.

Session: A time period starts from the time the user accesses the website until they leave. It also refers to a list of web pages visited during this period.

Unstructured Data: Information which is not stored in a database. Often include text and multimedia content such as e-mail message, photos, videos, and so on.

Web Analytics: It means the analysis of web data to understand web usage and to improve the effectiveness of a website. It is also a tool to derive business intelligence.

Web Cache: Is a mechanism to store web pages temporarily to improve browsing, save bandwidth, and reduce the load on the server.

Web Log File: A text file contains information about all requests made to the server.

Web Personalization: Providing users with customized services or features without expecting from them to ask for it explicitly by adapting the presentation of the website.

Web Users: Is an individual accessing a website through a web browser.

Compilation of References

3rd Generation Partnership Project. (2014, March 17). *3GPP TS 24.302 Access to the 3GPP Evolved Packet Core (EPC) via non-3GPP access networks (Release 12)*. Retrieved April 14, 2014, from http://www.3gpp.org/DynaReport/24302.htm

3rd Generation Partnership Project. (2014, March 17). *3GPP TS 24.312 Access Network Discovery and Selection Function (ANDSF) Management Object (MO) (Release 12)*. Retrieved April 14, 2014, from http://www.3gpp.org/DynaReport/24312.htm

Abouhnik, A., & Albarbar, A. (2012). Wind turbine blades condition assessment based on vibration measurements and the level of an empirically decomposed feature. *Energy Conversion and Management, 64*, 606–613. doi:10.1016/j.enconman.2012.06.008

Acharjya, D. P., & Geetha Mary, A. (2014). Privacy preservation in information system. IGI Global. doi:10.4018/978-1-4666-4940-8.ch003

Acharjya, D. P. (2009). Comparative study of rough sets on fuzzy approximation spaces and intuitionistic fuzzy approximation spaces. *International Journal of Computational and Applied Mathematics, 4*(2), 95–106.

Acharjya, D. P., & Tripathy, B. K. (2008). Rough sets on fuzzy approximation spaces and applications to distributed knowledge systems. *International Journal of Artificial Intelligence and Soft Computing, 1*(1), 1–14. doi:10.1504/IJAISC.2008.021260

Acharjya, D. P., & Tripathy, B. K. (2009). Rough sets on intuitionistic fuzzy approximation spaces and knowledge representation. *International Journal of Artificial Intelligence and Computational Research, 1*(1), 29–36.

Ackerman, W. B. (1982). Data Flow Languages. *Computer, 15*(2), 15–25. doi:10.1109/MC.1982.1653938

Acquisti, A. (2012). *An experiment in hiring discrimination via online social networks*. Berkeley.

Adam, G., Jack, B., Weicheng, D., Robert, J., & Sunderam, M. V. (n.d.). *A Users Guide and Tutorial for Networked Parallel Computing*. MIT Press.

Adamic, L. A., & Adar, E. (2003). *Friends and neighbors on the web*. ScienceDirect.

Adiga, N. R., Almasi, G. S., Aridor, Y., Barik, R., Beece, D., Bellofatto, R., . . . Lu, M. (2002, November). An overview of the BlueGene/L supercomputer. In *Supercomputing, ACM/IEEE 2002 Conference* (pp. 60-60). IEEE.

ADMA. (2013). *Best Practice Guideline: Big Data. A guide to maximising customer engagement opportunities through the development of responsible Big Data strategies*. Retrieved from: http://www.adma.com.au

Advantech. (2013). *Enhancing Big Data Security*. Retrieved from http://www.advantech.com.tw/nc/newsletter/whitepaper/big_data/big_data.pdf

Agerholm, S., Lecoreur, P. J., & Reichert, E. (1998). Formal specification and validation at work: A case study using VDM-SL. *IFAD Forskerparken, 10*, DK-5230.

Agrawal, D., Das, S., & El Abbadi, A. (2011). Big data and cloud computing. In *Proceedings of the 14th International Conference on Extending Database Technology - EDBT/ICDT '11* (p. 530). New York: ACM Press. doi:10.1145/1951365.1951432

Ahlberg, C. (1996). Spotfire: An information exploration environment. *SIGMOD Record, 25*(4), 25–29. doi:10.1145/245882.245893

Aichernig, B. K. (1999). *Automated Black-Box Testing with Abstract VDM Oracles*. Technical university of Graz, Institute for Software Technology (IST), Miinzgrabenstr.11/II, A-8010 Graz, Austria.

Aichernig, B. K., & Larsen, P. G. (1997). A proof obligation generator for VDM-SL. Graz University of Technology, Institute of Software Technology (IST), Miinzgrabenstr.11/II, 8010 Graz, Austria.

Akers, S.B. (1978). Binary Decision Diagrams. *IEEE Transactions on Computers, 27*, 509-516.

Albert, R. (1999). The diameter of the World Wide Web. *Nature, 401*(6749), 130–131. doi:10.1038/43601

Alexandrov, V. N., van Albada, G. D., Sloot, P. M., & Dongarra, J. (2006, May). Computational Science-ICCS 2006. In *6th International Conference, Reading, UK, May* (pp. 28-31).

Alippi, J. L. C., Bouchon-Meunier, B., Greenwood, G. W., & Abbass, H. A. (n.d.). *Advances in Computational Intelligence*.

Almási, G., Cascaval, C., & Wu, P. (2007). *Languages and Compilers for Parallel Computing:19th International Workshop, LCPC 2006, New Orleans, LA, USA, November 2-4, 2006, Revised Papers (Vol. 4382)*. Springer Science & Business Media.

Alsafi, Y., & Vyatkin, V. (2014). *Ontology-based Reconfiguration Agent for Intelligent Mechatronic Systems in Flexible Manufacturing*. Retrieved June 18, 2014, from http://homepages.engineering.auckland.ac.nz/~vyatkin/publ/RCIM-S-08-00078.pdf

Altintas, I., Birnbaum, A., Baldridge, K. K., Sudholt, W., Miller, M., Amoreira, C., & Ludaescher, B. (2005). A framework for the design and reuse of grid workflows. In *Scientific Applications of Grid Computing* (pp. 120 133). Springer Berlin Heidelberg. doi:10.1007/11423287_11

Amayreh, A., & Zin, A. M. (1999). PROBE: A formal specification-based testing system. In *Proceeding of the 20th international conference on Information Systems* (pp. 400 – 404). Academic Press.

Anand, N., & Hilal, S. (2012). Identifying the User Access Pattern in Web Log Data. *International Journal of Computer Science and Information Technologies, 3*(2), 3536–3539.

Anderson, E., Bai, Z., Bischof, C., Blackford, S., Demmel, J., Dongarra, J., & Sorensen, D. (1999). *LAPACK Users' guide (Vol. 9)*. Siam. doi:10.1137/1.9780898719604

Andrews, G. R. (1999). *Foundations of parallel and distributed programming*. Addison-Wesley Longman Publishing Co., Inc.

Aqeel-ur-Rehman, M.K., & Baksh, A. (2013). Communication Technology That Suits IoT-A Critical Review. Wireless Sensor Networks for Developing Countries (pp. 14-25). Springer.

Artigao, E. (2009). *Análisis de árboles de fallos mediante diagramas de decisión binarios. Proyecto fin de Carrera*. Ciudad Real: Universidad de Castilla La Mancha.

Arvind, G. K. P., & Plouffe, W. (1977). Indeterminancy, monitors, and dataflow. In *Proceedings of the Sixth ACM Symposium on Operating System Principles*. West Lafayette, IN: ACM. doi:10.1145/800214.806559

Ashcroft, E. A., & Wadge, W. W. (1976). Lucid – A Formal System for Writing and Proving Programs. *SIAM Journal on Computing, 5*(3), 336–354. doi:10.1137/0205029

Assunção, M. D., Calheiros, R. N., Bianchi, S., Netto, M. A., & Buyya, R. (2014). Big Data computing and clouds: Trends and future directions. *Journal of Parallel and Distributed Computing*.

Asuncion, A., & Newman, D. J. (2007). *UCI Machine Learning Repository*. University of California Irvine School of Information. Retrieved May 15, 2015, from http://www.ics.uci.edu/~mlearn/MLRepository.html

Atanasov, K. T. (1986). Intuitionistic Fuzzy Sets. *Fuzzy Sets and Systems, 20*(1), 87–96. doi:10.1016/S0165-0114(86)80034-3

Auer, S., Lehmann, J., Ngonga Ngomo, A. C., & Zaveri, A. (2013). Introduction to Linked Data and Its Lifecycle on the Web. In S. Rudolph, G. Gottlob, I. Horrocks, & F. Harmelen (Eds.), *Reasoning Web. Semantic Technologies for Intelligent Data Access* (Vol. 8067, pp. 1–90). New York, NY: Springer Berlin Heidelberg. doi:10.1007/978-3-642-39784-4_1

Avita, K., Mohammad, W., & Goudar, R. H. (2013). *Big Data: Issues, Challenges, Tools and Good Practices: Contemporary Computing (IC3), 2013 Sixth International Conference*. IEEE.

Azodolmolky, S., Nejabati, R., Peng, S., Hammad, A., Channegowda, M. P., Efstathiou, N. … Simeonidou, D. (2012). Optical FlowVisor: An OpenFlow-based Optical Network Virtualization Approach. In *National Fiber Optic Engineers Conference* (p. JTh2A.41). Optical Society of America. Retrieved May 15, 2015, from http://www.opticsinfobase.org/abstract.cfm?URI=NFOEC-2012-JTh2A.41

Backstrom, L., Huttenlocher, D., & Kleinberg, J. (2006). *Group Formation in Large Social Networks: Membership, Groeth, and Evolution*. KDD. doi:10.1145/1150402.1150412

Bae, C., Xia, L., Dinda, P., & Lange, J. (2012). Dynamic Adaptive Virtual Core Mapping to Improve Power, Energy, and Performance in Multi-socket Multicores. In *Proceedings of the 21st International Symposium on Applied Computing* (pp. 247–258). doi:10.1145/2287076.2287114

Barham, P., Donnelly, A., Isaacs, R., & Mortier, R. (2004). Using magpie for request extraction and workload modeling. In *Proceedings of OSDI'04: 6th Symposium on Operating Systems Design and Implementation*. USENIX Association.

Barnaghi, P., Wang, W., Henson, C., & Taylor, K. (2012). Semantics for the Internet of Things: Early progress and back to the future. *International Journal on Semantic Web and Information Systems, 8*(1), 1–21. doi:10.4018/jswis.2012010101

Barone, D., Yu, E., Won, J., Jiang, L., & Mylopoulos, J. (2010). Enterprise modeling for business intelligence. In *The practice of enterprise modelling (PoEM'10)* (Vol. 68, pp. 31–45). Berlin: Springer. doi:10.1007/978-3-642-16782-9_3

Beattie, A. G. (Ed.). (1997). Acoustic emission monitoring of a wind turbine blade during a fatigue test. In *AIAA Aerospace Sciences Meeting (AIAA/ASME '97)*. American Institute of Aeronautics and Astronautics. doi:10.2514/6.1997-958

Beguelin, A., Dongarra, J., Geist, A., Manchek, R., & Sunderam, V. (1991). A users' guide to PVM (parallel virtual machine). *ORNL. U. S. Atomic Energy Commission*, TM-11826.

Bellavista, Chang, & Chao. (n.d.). *Advances in Grid and Pervasive Computing*.

Berg, M. V., Verhoe, M., & Wigmans, M. (1999). *Formal specification of an auctioning system using VDM++ and UML, an industrial usage report*. Chess information technology.

Berners-Lee, T., Hall, W., & Hendler, J. A. (2006). A framework for web science. *Foundations and Trends in Web Science, 1*(1), 1–130. doi:10.1561/1800000001

Berson, A., & Smith, S. J. (1997). *Data warehousing, data mining, and OLAP*. New York: McGraw-Hill.

Bessant, J. (1987). Information Technology and the North-South Divide. In R. Finnegan, G. Salaman, & K. Thompson (Eds.), *Information Technology: Social Issues – A Reader* (pp. 163–180). London: Hodder and Stoughton.

Beydeda, S. & Gruhun, V. (2002). *Class Specification Implementation Graphs and Their Application in Regression Testing*. University of Dortmund Computer Science Department.

Bezdek†, J. C. (1973). Cluster Validity with Fuzzy Sets. Journal of Cybernetics, 3(3), 58–73.

Bezdek, J. C. (1981). *Pattern Recognition with Fuzzy Objective Function Algorithms*. Kluwer Academic Publishers.

Bhatia, T. (2011). Link Analysis Algorithms For Web Mining. *International Journal of Computer Science and Technology*, 2(2), 243–246.

Biehn, N. (2013). *The Missing V's in Big Data: Viability and Value*. WIRED.com Retrieved from: http://www.wired.com/insights/2013/05/the-missing-vs-in-big-data-viability-and-value/

Big Data at the Speed of Business. (n.d.). Retrieved Apr 10, from http://www-01.ibm.com/software/data/bigdata/what-is-big-data.html

Big Data for Enterprise. (n.d.). Retrieved Aug 01, from http://www.mongodb.com/big-data-explained#big-data-enterprise

Bin, S., Yuan, L., & Xiaoyi, W. (2010). *Research on data mining models for the internet of things*. Paper presented at the 2010 International Conference on Image Analysis and Signal Processing (IASP).

Bischof, C. (2008). *Parallel Computing: Architectures, Algorithms, and Applications* (Vol. 15). IOS Press.

Blelloch, G. E. (1990). *Vector models for data-parallel computing* (Vol. 356). Cambridge: MIT press.

Blume, W., Doallo, R., Rauchwerger, L., Tu, P., Eigenmann, R., Grout, J., & Pottenger, B. et al. (1996). Parallel programming with Polaris. *Computer*, 29(12), 78–82. doi:10.1109/2.546612

Bobillo, F., Delgado, M., Gómez-Romero, J., & Straccia, U. (2009). Fuzzy description logics under Gödel semantics. *International Journal of Approximate Reasoning*, 50(3), 494–514. doi:10.1016/j.ijar.2008.10.003

Bobillo, F., & Straccia, U. (2011). Fuzzy ontology representation using OWL 2. *International Journal of Approximate Reasoning*, 52(7), 1073–1094. doi:10.1016/j.ijar.2011.05.003

Bobillo, F., & Straccia, U. (2013). Aggregation operators for fuzzy ontologies. *Applied Soft Computing*, 13(9), 3816–3830. doi:10.1016/j.asoc.2013.05.008

Bode, A. (2000). *Euro-Par 2000 Parallel Processing:6th International Euro-Par Conference, Munich, Germany, August 29-September 1, 2000: Proceedings* (No. 1900). Springer Science & Business Media.

Bollen, J., Mao, H., & Zeng, X. (2011). Twitter mood predicts the stock market. *Journal of Computational Science*, 2(1), 1–8. doi:10.1016/j.jocs.2010.12.007

Borgatti, S. (2006). Identifying sets of key players in a social network. *Computational & Mathematical Organization Theory*, 12(1), 21–34. doi:10.1007/s10588-006-7084-x

Bowen, J., & Clark. (2002). FORTEST: Formal methods and testing. In *Proceedings of 26th Annual International Computer Software and Applications Conference (COMPSAC 02)*, (pp. 91-101). Academic Press.

Boyd, D., & Crawford, K. (2012). Critical Questions for Big Data: Provocations for a Cultural, Technological, and Scholarly Phenomenon. *Information Communication and Society*, 15(5), 662–675. doi:10.1080/1369118X.2012.678878

Brace, K. S., Rudell, R. L., & Bryant, R. E. (1990). Efficient implementation of a BDD package.*27th ACM/IEEE Design Automation Conference*. doi:10.1145/123186.123222

Brandon, J. (2013). *M2M*. Retrieved June 20, 2014, from http://www.dot.gov.in/sites/default/files/m2m_basics.pdf

Broy, M. (1988). Nondeterministic Data Flow Programs: How to Avoid the Merge Anamoly. *Science of Computer Programming, 10*(1), 65–85. doi:10.1016/0167-6423(88)90016-0

Bruaset, A. M., & Tveito, A. (Eds.). (2006). *Numerical solution of partial differential equations on parallel computers* (Vol. 51). Springer Science & Business Media. doi:10.1007/3-540-31619-1

Bruls, M., Huizing, K., & Van Wijk, J. J. (2000). *Squarified treemaps*. Springer Vienna.

Bryant, R. E. (1986). Graph-based algorithms for Boolean functions using a graphical representation.IEEE Transactions on Computing, 35(8), 677–691.

Buehlmann, U., & Bumgardnar, M. (2005). Evaluation of furniture retailer ordering decisions in the United States. Forintek Canada Corp.

Bughin, J., Chui, M., & Manyika, J. (2010). *Clouds, big data, and smart assets: Ten tech-enabled business trends to watch* (Vol. 56). McKinsley Quarterly.

Burton, S. & York. (2000). *Automated Testing from Formal Specification*. Department of Computer Science, University of York.

Butenhof, D. R. (1997). *Programming with POSIX threads*. Addison-Wesley Professional.

Buyya, R., Yeo, C. S., & Venugopal, S. (2008, September). Market-oriented cloud computing: Vision, hype, and reality for delivering it services as computing utilities. In *High Performance Computing and Communications, 2008. HPCC'08. 10th IEEE International Conference on* (pp. 5-13). IEEE.

Buyya, R. (1999). *High performance cluster computing*. F'rentice.

Buyya, R., Broberg, J., & Goscinski, A. M. (Eds.). (2010). *Cloud computing: principles and paradigms* (Vol. 87). John Wiley & Sons.

Cachin, C., Keidar, I., & Shraer, A. (2009). Trusting the cloud.*Acm Sigact News, 40*(2), 81–86. doi:10.1145/1556154.1556173

Camacho, D., Moreno, M. D., & Akerkar, R. (2013). *Challenges and issues of web intelligence research*. Paper presented at the 3rd International Conference on Web Intelligence, Mining and Semantics, Madrid, Spain. doi:10.1145/2479787.2479868

Carr, D. A. (1999). Guidelines for designing information visualization applications. *Proceedings of ECUE, 99*, 1–3.

Casado, M., Koponen, T., Shenker, S., & Tootoonchian, A. (2012). Fabric: a retrospective on evolving SDN. *Hot Topics in Software Defined Networking (HotSDN)*, (pp. 85–89). Retrieved May 15, 2015, from http://dl.acm.org/citation.cfm?id=2342459

Castells, M. (2001). *The Internet Galaxy*. Oxford: Oxford University Press. doi:10.1007/978-3-322-89613-1

Castells, M. (2013). *Communication Power*. Oxford: Oxford University Press.

Cavoukian, A. (2013). *Big Privacy: Bridging Big Data and the Personal Data Ecosystem Through Privacy by Design*. Retrieved from http://www.privacybydesign.ca/

Cerqueira, R. (2007). *Middleware 2007: ACM/IFIP/USENIX 8th International Middleware Conference, Newport Beach, CA, USA, November 26-30, 2007. Proceedings* (Vol. 4834). Springer.

Chaabane, A., Acs, G., & Kaafar, M. (2012). *You are what you like! Information leakage through users' interests*. NDSS.

Chakrabarti, S. K., & Srikant, Y. N. (2008). Test sequence computation for regression testing of reactive. In *Proceedings of the 1st conference on India software engineering conference*. Academic Press.

Chakrabarti, S. K., & Srikant, Y. N. (2006). *Specification Based Regression Testing Using Explicit Software Engineering Advances. International Conference.*

Chandra, R. (2001). *Parallel programming in OpenMP*. Morgan Kaufmann.

Chang, R. M., Kauffman, R. J., & Kwon, Y. (2014). Understanding the paradigm shift to computational social science in the presence of big data. *Decision Support Systems*, *63*, 6780. doi:10.1016/j.dss.2013.08.008

Chang, R. S., Chao, H. C., Lin, S. F., & Sloot, P. M. (2010). *Advances in Grid and Pervasive Computing*. Springer-Verlag Berlin Heidelberg.

Chao, H. C., Obaidat, M. S., & Kim, J. (2011). *Computer Science and Convergence*. Springer.

Chapman, B. M. (2005). *Shared Memory Parallel Programming with Open MP*. Springer-Verlag Berlin/Heidelberg.

Chapman, B., Jost, G., & Van Der Pas, R. (2008). Using OpenMP: portable shared memory parallel programming (Vol. 10). MIT Press.

Chapman, B., Curtis, T., Pophale, S., Poole, S., Kuehn, J., Koelbel, C., & Smith, L. (2010, October). Introducing Open-SHMEM: SHMEM for the PGAS community. In *Proceedings of the Fourth Conference on Partitioned Global Address Space Programming Model* (p. 2). ACM. doi:10.1145/2020373.2020375

Characteristics of Social Networks. (n.d.). Retrieved Mar 03, from http://socialnetworking.lovetoknow.com/Characteristics_of_Social_Networks

Chaudhry, A., Hassan, M., Khan, A., Kim, J. Y., & Tuan, T. A. (2012). *Image clustering using improved spatial fuzzy C-means*. Paper presented at the 6th International Conference on Ubiquitous Information Management and Communication. doi:10.1145/2184751.2184853

Chaudhry, A., Hassan, M., Khan, A., & Kim, J. Y. (2013). Automatic active contour-based segmentation and classification of carotid artery ultrasound images. *Journal of Digital Imaging*, *26*(6), 1071–1081. doi:10.1007/s10278-012-9566-3 PMID:23417308

Chaudhry, A., Hassan, M., Khan, A., Kim, J. Y., & Tuan, T. A. (2013). *Automatic segmentation and decision making of carotid artery ultrasound images. In Intelligent Autonomous Systems 12* (pp. 185–196). Springer Berlin Heidelberg.

Chaudhry, A., Khan, A., Mirza, A. M., Ali, A., Hassan, M., & Kim, J. Y. (2013). Neuro fuzzy and punctual kriging based filter for image restoration. *Applied Soft Computing*, *13*(2), 817–832. doi:10.1016/j.asoc.2012.10.017

Che, D., Safran, M., & Peng, Z. (2013). From Big Data to Big Data Mining: Challenges, Issues, and Opportunities. In B. Hong, X. Meng, L. Chen, W. Winiwarter & W. Song (Eds.), Database Systems for Advanced Applications (Vol. 7827, pp. 1-15). Springer Berlin Heidelberg.

Chen, C., Chapman, R., & Chang, K. H. (1999). Test scenario and regression test suite generation from object-z formal specification for object oriented program testing. In *Proceedings of the 37th annual southeast regional conference* (CD-ROM). Academic Press.

Chen, M., Kiciman, E., Fratkin, E., Fox, A., & Brewer, E. (2002). Pinpoint: Problem determination in large, dynamic internet services. In *Proceedings of the International Conference on Dependable Systems and Networks (DSN'02)* (pp. 595–604). Academic Press.

Chen, P., Jorgen, B., & Yuan, Y. (2011). Software behavior based trusted attestation. In *Proceedings - 3rd International Conference on Measuring Technology and Mechatronics Automation, ICMTMA 2011* (Vol. 3, pp. 298–301). doi:10.1109/ICMTMA.2011.645

Chen, X., & Shi, S. (2009). A literature review of privacy research on social network sites. In *Multimedia Information Networking and Security, 2009. MINES'09. International Conference on* (Vol. 1, pp. 93–97). doi:10.1109/MINES.2009.268

Chen, Y., Probert, R. L., & Ural, H. (2007). Model-based regression test suite generation using dependence analysis. In *Proceedings of the 3rd international workshop on advances in model-based testing*. Academic Press.

Cheng, T., Chu, S. K. K., Yi, A. L., Yu, Y., Bradski, G. R., Ng, A. Y., & Olukotun, K. (2006). Map-Reduce for machine learning on multicore. MIT Press.

Chen, H., Chiang, R. H., & Storey, V. C. (2012). Business Intelligence and Analytics: From Big Data to Big Impact. *Management Information Systems Quarterly*, *36*(4), 1165–1188.

Chen, M. Y., Accardi, A., Kiciman, E., Lloyd, J., Patterson, D., Fox, A., & Brewer, E. (2004). Path-based faliure and evolution management. In *Proceedings of the 1st conference on Symposium on Networked Systems Design and Implementation*. USENIX Association.

Chitraa, V., & Davamani, A. S. (2010). A Survey on Preprocessing Methods for Web usage Data. *International Journal of Computer Science and Information Security*, *7*(3), 78–83.

Chitraa, V., & Davamani, A. S. (2010). An Efficient Path Completion Technique for web log mining. *IEEE International Conference on Computational Intelligence and Computing Research*.

Cho, J., & Roy, S. (2004). Impact of search engines on page popularity. *International World Wide Web Conference*. doi:10.1145/988672.988676

Chun-Wei, T., Chin-Feng, L., Ming-Chao, C., & Yang, L. T. (2014). Data Mining for Internet of Things: A Survey. *IEEE Communications Surveys and Tutorials*, *16*(1), 77–97. doi:10.1109/SURV.2013.103013.00206

Ciesielski, V., & Lalani, A. (2003). Data Mining of Web Access Logs From an Academic Web Site. *Proceedings of the Third International Conference on Hybrid Intelligent Systems (HIS'03): Design and Application of Hybrid Intelligent Systems* (pp. 1034-1043). IOS Press.

Cios, K., Pedrycz, W., & Swiniarski, R. (1998). *Data Mining Methods for Knowledge Discovery*. Boston: Kluwer Academic Publishers. doi:10.1007/978-1-4615-5589-6

Cisco, Inc. (2014). *Cisco Visual Networking Index: Global Mobile Data Traffic Forecast Update, 2013 – 2018*. Author.

Cisco. (2008). Border Gateway Protocol. *Update*. Retrieved April 2, 2014, from http://docwiki.cisco.com/wiki/Border_Gateway_Protocol

Cloud Security Alliance. (2013). *Expanded Top Ten Security and Privacy Challenges*. Retrieved from https://downloads.cloudsecurityalliance.org/initiatives/bdwg/Expanded_Top_Ten_Big_Data_Security_and_Privacy_Challenges.pdf

Cloud Security Alliance. (2013a). *The Notorious Nine Cloud Computing Top Threats in 2013*. Retrieved from https://cloudsecurityalliance.org/download/the-notorious-nine-cloud-computing-top-threats-in-2013/

COBIT. (n.d.). Retrieved from https://cobitonline.isaca.org/

Coello, C. A. C. (1999). *List of references on evolutionary multiobjective optimization*. México: Laboratorio Nacional de Informática Avanzada.

Connolly, S. (2012, May 16). *Big Data Refinery Fuels Next-Generation Data Architecture.* Retrieved from http://hortonworks.com/blog/big-data-refinery-fuels-next-generation-data-architecture

Contributors. (2013a). Quagga Routing Suite. *Online.* Retrieved May 15, 2015, from http://www.nongnu.org/quagga/

Contributors. (2013b). *The Policy: Pyretic's Foundation.* Retrieved April 18, 2014, from https://github.com/frenetic-lang/pyretic/wiki/Language-Basics

Coporation, C. S. K. (2005). VDM++ Toolbox User Manual Revised for V6.8.1. CSK Corporation.

Costa Júnior, M. G., & Gong, G. d. (2005). Web Structure Mining: An Introduction.*Proceedings of the 2005 IEEE, International Conference on Information Acquisition* (p. 6). Hong Kong: IEEE. doi:10.1109/ICIA.2005.1635156

Costa-Requena, J. (2014). SDN integration in LTE mobile backhaul networks. In *International Conference on Information Networking* (pp. 264–269). doi:10.1109/ICOIN.2014.6799479

Cox, M., & Ellsworth, D. (1997). Application-controlled demand paging for out-of-core visualization. *Proceedings. Visualization '97 (Cat. No. 97CB36155).*

CTL. (2014). *Computation tree logic.* Retrieved July 17, 2014, from http://en.wikipedia.org/wiki/Computation_tree_logic

Cyan. (2015). Z-Series. *Cyan.* Retrieved May 13, 2015, from http://www.cyaninc.com/products/z-series-packet-optical

Dai, Y., Qi, Y., Ren, J., Shi, Y., Wang, X., & Yu, X. (2013). A lightweight VMM on many core for high performance computing. *ACM SIGPLAN Notices, 48*(7), 111-120. Retrieved May 15, 2015, from http://dl.acm.org/citation.cfm?doid=2517326.2451535

Danyaro, K., Jaafar, J., & Liew, M. (2012). Completeness Knowledge Representation in Fuzzy Description Logics. In D. Lukose, A. Ahmad, & A. Suliman (Eds.), *Knowledge Technology* (Vol. 295, pp. 164–173). New York: Springer Berlin Heidelberg. doi:10.1007/978-3-642-32826-8_17

DARPA. (2014). *Mining and understanding software enclaves (MUSE).* Retrieved August 03, 2014, from http://www.darpa.mil/Our_Work/I2O/Programs/Mining_and_Understanding_Software_Enclaves_(MUSE).aspx

Das, V. V., Stephen, J., & Chaba, Y. (Eds.). (2011). *Computer Networks and Information Technologies:Second International Conference on Advances in Communication, Network, and Computing, CNC 2011, Bangalore, India, March 10-11, 2011. Proceedings (Vol. 142).* Springer.

Davenport, T. H. (2013). Big Data Executive Survey 2013: The State of Big Data in the Large Corporate World. Academic Press.

Davenport, T. H., Harris, J. G., & Morison, R. (2010). *Analytics at Work: Smarter Decisions, Better Results.* Harvard Business School Press Books. Retrieved May 15, 2015, from http://www.amazon.com/dp/1422177696

Davenport, T. H. (2014). *Big data at work: dispelling the myths, uncovering the opportunities.* Boston: Harvard Business Review Press. doi:10.15358/9783800648153

Davenport, T. H., & Patil, D. J. (2012). Data scientist: The sexiest job of the 21st century. *Harvard Business Review, 90*(10), 70–76. PMID:23074866

de Castro, A. B., Gómez, D., Quintela, P., & Salgado, P. (Eds.). (2007). *Numerical Mathematics and Advanced Applications:Proceedings of ENUMATH 2005 the 6th European Conference on Numerical Mathematics and Advanced Applications, Santiago de Compostela, Spain, July 2005.* Springer Science & Business Media.

De Cristofaro, E., Soriente, C., Tsudik, G., & Williams, A. (2012). Hummingbird: Privacy at the time of twitter. In *Security and Privacy (SP), 2012 IEEE Symposium on* (pp. 285–299). IEEE.

De Oliveira, M. C. F., & Levkowitz, H. (2003). From visual data exploration to visual data mining: A survey. Visualization and Computer Graphics. *IEEE Transactions on, 9*(3), 378–394.

Dean, J., & Ghemawat, S. (2008). MapReduce : Simplified Data Processing on Large Clusters. *Communications of the ACM, 51*(1), 1–13. doi:10.1145/1327452.1327492

Deepti, M. (2013, December). A Review on Clustering Based Methods and Usage for Pattern Recognition. *International Journal of Engineering Research and Development, 9*(5), 23–26.

Definition of Big Data. (n.d.). Retrieved Apr 20, from http://www.opentracker.net/article/definitions-big-data

Demchenko, Y., Ngo, C., & Membrey, P. (2013). *Architecture Framework and Components for the Big Data Ecosystem.* Retrieved from http://www.uazone.org/demch/worksinprogress/sne-2013-02-techreport-bdaf-draft02.pdf

Demchenko, Y., Grosso, P., de Laat, C., & Membrey, P. (2013). Addressing big data issues in Scientific Data Infrastructure. In *Proceedings of the International Conference on Collaboration Technologies and Systems (CTS)*. IEEE. doi:10.1109/CTS.2013.6567203

Demchenko, Y., Ngo, C., de Laat, C., Membrey, P., & Gordijenko, D. (2014). Big Security for Big Data: Addressing Security Challenges for the Big Data Infrastructure. In W. Jonker & M. Petković (Eds.), *Secure Data Management* (pp. 76–94). Springer International Publishing. doi:10.1007/978-3-319-06811-4_13

Dey, R., Tang, C., Ross, K., & Saxena, N. (2012). *Estimating age privacy leakage in online social networks*. INFOCOM. doi:10.1109/INFCOM.2012.6195711

Diebold, F. X. (2012). A Personal Perspective on the Origin(s) and Development of "Big Data": The Phenomenon, the Term, and the Discipline, Second Version. *SSRN Electronic Journal*. Retrieved May 15, 2015, from http://econpapers. repec.org/RePEc:pen:papers:13-003

Dimitrijević, M., & Krunić, T. (2013). Association rules for improving website effectiveness: Case analysis. *Online Journal of Applied Knowledge Management, 1*(2), 56–63.

Disterer, G. (2013). ISO/IEC 27000, 27001 and 27002 for Information Security Management. *Journal of Information Security, 4*(2), 92–100. doi:10.4236/jis.2013.42011

Doerffer, P., Hirsch, C., Dussauge, J. P., Babinsky, H., & Barakos, G. N. (2010). *Unsteady Effects of Shock Wave Induced Separation* (Vol. 114). Springer Science & Business Media.

Dohi, T., & Uemura, T. (2012). An adaptive mode control algorithm of a scalable intrusion tolerant architecture. Journal of Computer and System Sciences, 78, 1751–1754. doi:10.1016/j.jcss.2011.10.022

Domeika, M. (2011). *Software development for embedded multi-core systems: a practical guide using embedded Intel architecture*. Newnes.

Dongarra, J., Laforenza, D., & Orlando, S. (2003). *Recent Advances in Parallel Virtual Machine and Message Passing Interface: 10th European PVM/MPI Users' Group Meeting, Venice, Italy, September 29-October 2, 2003, Proceedings* (Vol. 10). Springer Science & Business Media.

Dongarra, J. (2008). *Parallel Processing and Applied Mathematics*. Berlin.

Dong, W., Lepri, B., & Pentland, A. (2011). Modeling the Co-evolution of Behaviors and Social Relationships Using Mobile Phone Data. In *Proceedings of the 10th International Conference on Mobile and Ubiquitous Multimedia*, (pp. 134-143). doi:10.1145/2107596.2107613

Doulamis, T., Mambretti, J., & Tomkos, I. (2010). *Networks for Grid Applications:Third International ICST Conference, GridNets 2009, Athens, Greece, September 8-9, 2009, Revised Selected Papers* (*Vol. 25*). Springer Science & Business Media.

Droschl, G. (1999). *Design and application of a test case generator for VDM-SL.austrian research center seibersdorf and IST-Technical University of Graz.miizgrabenstr.11, 8010 Graz.* Austria: Europe.

Du, Z. (2013), *Inconsistencies in big data: Cognitive Informatics & Cognitive Computing (ICCI*CC), 2013, 12th IEEE International Conference.* IEEE.

Dubosis, D., & Prade, H. (1993). Toll sets and toll logic. In Fuzzy Logic, (pp.169-177). Kluwer Academic Publishers.

Dubosis, D., & Prade, H. (1987). Twofold fuzzy sets and rough sets-some issues in knowledge representation. *Fuzzy Sets and Systems*, *23*(1), 3–18. doi:10.1016/0165-0114(87)90096-0

Dunn, C., Gupta, M., Gerber, A., & Spatscheck, O. (2012). *Navigation Characteristics of Online Social Networks and Search Engines Users.* WOSN. doi:10.1145/2342549.2342560

Dunn, D., & Yamashita, K. (2003). 'Microcapitalism and the Megacorporation'. *Harvard Business Review*, *81*(8), 46–54. PMID:12884667

Dunn, J. C. (1973). A Fuzzy Relative of the ISODATA Process and Its Use in Detecting Compact Well-Separated Clusters. *Journal of Cybernetics*, *3*(3), 32–57. doi:10.1080/01969727308546046

Dutton, W. H. (1992). 'The Ecology of Games Shaping Telecommunications Policy'. *Communication Theory*, *2*(4), 303–328. doi:10.1111/j.1468-2885.1992.tb00046.x

Dutton, W. H. (1999). *Society on the Line: Information Politics in the Digital Age.* Oxford: Oxford University Press.

Easley, D., & Kleinberg, J. (2010). *Networks, Crowds and Markets: Reasoning About Highly Connected World.* New York: Cambridge University Press. doi:10.1017/CBO9780511761942

Eaton, C., Deroos, D., Deutsch, T., Lapis, G., & Zikopoulos, P. C. (2012). Understanding Big Data: Analytics for Enterprise Class Hadoop and Streaming Data. New York: McGraw-Hill Companies.

eCos web site. (2015). Retrieved from http://ecos.sourceware.org

EdgeRank. (n.d.). Retrieved Aug 04, from http://edgerank.net/

Ehrig, M., & Staab, S. (2004). QOM – Quick Ontology Mapping. In S. McIlraith, D. Plexousakis, & F. Harmelen (Eds.), *The Semantic Web – ISWC 2004* (Vol. 3298, pp. 683–697). New York: Springer Berlin Heidelberg. doi:10.1007/978-3-540-30475-3_47

Eick, S. G., Steffen, J. L., & Sumner, E. E. Jr. (1992). Seesoft-a tool for visualizing line oriented software statistics. Software Engineering. *IEEE Transactions on*, *18*(11), 957–968.

Eigenmann, R., & de Supinski, B. R. (2008). OpenMP in a New Era of Parallelism. In *4 th International Workshop, IWOMP*. doi:10.1007/978-3-540-79561-2

Endo, P. T., Gonçalves, G. E., Kelner, J., & Sadok, D. (2010, May). A survey on open-source cloud computing solutions. In *Brazilian Symposium on Computer Networks and Distributed Systems*.

Ericsson. (2011). *More Than 50 Billion Connected Devices.* Author.

Ertel, W. (2011). *Introduction to artificial intelligence.* New York: Springer. doi:10.1007/978-0-85729-299-5

Fayaad, U. M. (1996). Advances in knowledge discovery and data mining. *American Association for Artificial Intelligence (AAAI) Press.*

Fayyad, U. (1996). Data Mining and Knowledge Discovery: Making Sense Out of Data. *IEEE Expert, 11*(5), 20–25. doi:10.1109/64.539013

Fayyad, U., Piatetsky-Shapiro, G., & Smyth, P. (1996). From Data Mining to Knowledge Discovery in Databases. *AI Magazine,* 37–54.

Feamster, N. (2014). *Software Defined Networking.* Retrieved July 15, 2014, from Available from https://www.coursera.org/course/sdn

Feamster, N., & Balakrishnan, H. (2005). Detecting BGP configuration faults with static analysis. In *Proc. Networked Systems Design and Implementation,* (pp. 49–56). Retrieved May 15, 2015, from http://www.usenix.org/event/nsdi05/tech/feamster/feamster_html/

Feamster, N., Rexford, J., & Zegura, E. (2013). The Road to SDN. *Queue, 11*(12), 20–40. Retrieved May 15, 2015, from http://dl.acm.org/citation.cfm?doid=2559899.2560327

Feamster, N., Rexford, J., Shenker, S., Clark, R., Hutchins, R., Levin, D., & Bailey, J. (1986). SDX: A Software-Defined Internet Exchange. *Proceedings IETF 86.* Retrieved May 13, 2015, from http://www.ietf.org/proceedings/86/slides/slides-86-sdnrg-6

Fink, C., & Kenny, C. J. (2003). 'W(h)ither the Digital Divide?'. *Info: The Journal of Policy. Regulation and Strategy for Telecommunications, 5*(6), 15–24. doi:10.1108/14636690310507180

Fisher, B., Anderson, S., Bryant, J., Margolese, R. G., Deutsch, M., Fisher, E. R., & Wolmark, N. (2002). Twenty-year follow-up of a randomized trial comparing total mastectomy, lumpectomy, and lumpectomy plus irradiation for the treatment of invasive breast cancer. *The New England Journal of Medicine, 347*(16), 1233–1241. doi:10.1056/NEJMoa022152 PMID:12393820

Fitch, B. G., Rayshubskiy, A., Eleftheriou, M., Ward, T. C., Giampapa, M., Zhestkov, Y., . . . Germain, R. S. (2006). Blue Matter: Strong scaling of molecular dynamics on Blue Gene/L. In Computational Science–ICCS 2006 (pp. 846-854). Springer Berlin Heidelberg.

Foster, I., Zhao, Y., Raicu, I., & Lu, S. (2008, November). Cloud computing and grid computing 360-degree compared. In *Grid Computing Environments Workshop, 2008. GCE'08* (pp. 1-10). IEEE. doi:10.1109/GCE.2008.4738445

Foster, N., Guha, A., Reitblatt, M., Story, A., Freedman, M. J., Katta, N. P., & Harrison, R. et al. (2013). Languages for software-defined networks. *IEEE Communications Magazine, 51*(2), 128–134. doi:10.1109/MCOM.2013.6461197

Fox, G. C., & Zhuge, H. (2007). Special issue: Autonomous grid computing. *Concurrency and Computation, 19*(7), 943–944. doi:10.1002/cpe.1087

Foxley, E., & Salam, O. (1997). *Automatic Assessment of Z specification.* Annual Joint Conference Integrating Technology in Comp. Science Education.

Frachtenberg, E., & Schwiegelshohn, U. (2008, January). New challenges of parallel job scheduling. In *Job Scheduling Strategies for Parallel Processing* (pp. 1–23). Springer Berlin Heidelberg. doi:10.1007/978-3-540-78699-3_1

Frank, O., & Strauss, D. (1986). Markov Graphs. *Journal of the American Statistical Association, 81*(395), 832–842. doi:10.1080/01621459.1986.10478342

Fraser, G., Aichernig, B. K., & Wotawa, F. (2007). Handling Model Changes: Regression Testing and Test-Suite Update with Model-Checkers. Institute for Software Technology Graz University of Technology.

Freeman-Benson, B. (1991). Lobjcid: Objects in Lucid. In *Proceedings of the 4th International Symposium on Lucid and Intensional Programming.* Menlo Park, CA.

Fry, B. J. (2004). *Computational information design.* (Doctoral dissertation). Massachusetts Institute of Technology.

G'abor, N. a. (2007). Ontology Development. In R. Studer, S. Grimm, & A. Abecker (Eds.), *Semantic Web Services* (pp. 107–134). New York: Springer Berlin Heidelberg. doi:10.1007/3-540-70894-4_4

Gage, J. (2002). Some Thoughts on How ICTs Could Really Change the World. In Global Information Technology Report 2001-2002 (pp. 4–9). Readiness for the Networked World. Retrieved from www.cid.harvard.edu/cr/pdf/gitrr2002_ch01.pdf

García Márquez, F. P., & Moreno, H. (2012). *Introducción al Análisis de Árboles de Fallos: Empleo de BDDs.* Editorial Académica Española.

Garfinkel, S., & Abelson, H. (1999). *Architects of the information society: 35 years of the Laboratory for Computer Science at MIT.* MIT Press.

Gartner Group. (2012). *Gartner Says Big Data Creates Big Jobs: 4.4 Million IT Jobs Globally to Support Big Data By 2015.* Retrieved from http://www.gartner.com/newsroom/id/2207915

Gentry, C. (2009). *A fully homomorphic encryption scheme.* Stanford University. Retrieved from http://cs.au.dk/~stm/local-cache/gentry-thesis.pdf

Gentry, C. (2010). Computing arbitrary functions of encrypted data. *Communications of the ACM, 53*(3), 97. doi:10.1145/1666420.1666444

Gerhardt, B., Griffin, K., & Klemann, R. (2012). *Unlocking Value in the Fragmented World of Big Data Analytics.* Cisco Internet Business Solutions Group. Retrieved from http://www.cisco.com/web/about/ac79/docs/sp/Information-Infomediaries.pdf

Ghosh, R., & Lerman, K. (2008). *Community Detection using a Measure of Global Influence.* KDD.

Ghosh, R., & Lerman, K. (2010). *Predicting Influential Users in Online Social Networks.* KDD.

Ghosh, S. (2014). *Distributed systems: an algorithmic approach.* CRC press.

Gifford, C. (2013). *The MOM Chronicles: ISA-95 Best Practices Book 3.0.* International Society of Automation.

Gladstone Institute University of California at San Francisco. (2014). GenMAPP. *GenMAPP.* Retrieved May 13, 2015, from http://www.genmapp.org/about.html

Goguen, J. A. (1967). L–fuzzy sets. *Journal of Mathematical Analysis and Applications, 18*(1), 145–174. doi:10.1016/0022-247X(67)90189-8

Goldwasser, S., Gordon, S. D., Goyal, V., Jain, A., Katz, J., Liu, F.-H. … Zhou, H.-S. (2014). Multi-input functional encryption. In Advances in Cryptology--EUROCRYPT 2014 (pp. 578–602). Springer.

Gonzalez, M. C., Hidalgo, A., & Barabsi, A.-L. (2008). *Understanding individual human mobility patterns.* Nature Scientific Reports.

Google Trends. (n.d.). Retrieved from http://www.google.com/trends/

Google. (2014). *Encrypted Big Query Client.* Retrieved August 03, 2014, from https://code.google.com/p/encrypted-bigquery-client/

Grace, J., Kenny, C., Qiang, C., Liu, J., & Reynolds, T. (2001). 'Information and Communication Technologies and Broad-Based Development: A Partial Review of the Evidence. *World Bank Resource Paper (2001).* Retrieved from: http://poverty.worldbank.org/library/view/10214/

Grace, L. J., Maheswari, V., & Nagamalai, D. (2011). Analysis of Web Logs and Web User in Web Mining. *International Journal of Network Security & Its Applications, 3*(1), 99–110. doi:10.5121/ijnsa.2011.3107

Graham, M. (2011). 'Time Machines and Virtual Portals: The Spatialities of the Digital Divide'. *Progress in Development Studies, 11*(3), 211–227. doi:10.1177/146499341001100303

Grandinetti, L. (Ed.). (2005). *Grid Computing: The New Frontier of High Performance Computing: The New Frontier of High Performance Computing* (Vol. 14). Elsevier.

Greenberg, B. A., Hamilton, J. R., Kandula, S., Kim, C., Lahiri, P., & Maltz, A. ... Maltz, D. A. (2009). VL2: a scalable and flexible data center network. In *Proceedings of the ACM SIGCOMM 2009 Conference on Data Communication* (Vol. 9, pp. 51–62). ACM. Retrieved May 15, 2015, from http://doi.acm.org/10.1145/1592568.1592576

Grefenstette, E., Blunsom, P., De Freitas, N., & Hermann, K. M. (2014). A Deep Architecture for Semantic Parsing. In *ACL Workshop on Semantic Parsing* (pp. 22–27). doi:10.3115/v1/W14-2405

Grimm, S., Hitzler, P., & Abecker, A. (2007). Knowledge Representation and Ontologies Logic, Ontologies and Semantic Web Languages. In R. Studer, S. Grimm, & A. Abecker (Eds.), *Semantic Web Services* (pp. 51–105). New York: Springer.

Gropp, W. (2002). MPICH2: A new start for MPI implementations. In Recent Advances in Parallel Virtual Machine and Message Passing Interface (pp. 7-7). Springer Berlin Heidelberg. doi:10.1007/3-540-45825-5_5

Gropp, W., & Lusk, E. (1998). *PVM and MPI are completely different.* Argonne National Lab.

Gropp, W., Lusk, E., Doss, N., & Skjellum, A. (1996). A high-performance, portable implementation of the MPI message passing interface standard. *Parallel Computing, 22*(6), 789–828. doi:10.1016/0167-8191(96)00024-5

Gross, R., & Acquisti, A. (2005). Information revelation and privacy in online social networks. In *Proceedings of the 2005 ACM workshop on Privacy in the electronic society* (pp. 71–80). doi:10.1145/1102199.1102214

Gruber, T. R. (1993). A translation approach to portable ontology specifications. *Knowledge Acquisition, 5*(2), 199–220. doi:10.1006/knac.1993.1008

Gruhn, V., & Oquendo, F. (2006). Software Architecture. In *3rd European Workshop Software Architecture (EWSA 2006).*

Gubbi, J., Buyya, R., Marusic, S., & Palaniswami, M. (2013). Internet of Things (IoT): A vision, architectural elements, and future directions. *Future Generation Computer Systems, 29*(7), 1645–1660. doi:10.1016/j.future.2013.01.010

Gupta, R., & Gupta, P. Fast Processing of Web Usage Mining with Customized Web Log Pre-processing and modified Frequent Pattern Tree. *International Journal of Computer Science & Communication Networks, 1*(3), 277-279.

Gupta, R., Gupta, H., & Mohania, M. (2012). *Cloud Computing and Big Data Analytics: What is new from Database Perspective?.* Springer-Verlag Berlin Heidelberg. doi:10.1007/978-3-642-35542-4_5

Gupta, R., & Gupta, P. (2012). Application specific web log pre-processing. *Int. J. Computer Techology & Applications, 3*(1), 160–162.

Gwangwava, N., Mpofu, K., Tlale, N., & Yu, Y. (2014). A methodology for design and reconfiguration of reconfigurable bending press machines (RBPMs). *International Journal of Production Research, 52*(20), 6019–6032. doi:10.1080/00207543.2014.904969

Hager, G., & Wellein, G. (2010). *Introduction to high performance computing for scientists and engineers.* CRC Press. doi:10.1201/EBK1439811924

Haigang, L., & Wanling, Y. (2006, October). Study of Application of Web Mining Techniques in E-Business. In *Service Systems and Service Management, 2006 International Conference on* (Vol. 2, pp. 1587-1592). IEEE.

Hall, M., National, H., Frank, E., Holmes, G., Pfahringer, B., Reutemann, P., & Witten, I. H. (2009). The WEKA Data Mining Software : An Update. *SIGKDD Explorations, 11*(1), 10–18. doi:10.1145/1656274.1656278

Han, S., Dang, Y., Ge, S., Zhang, D., & Xie, T. (2012). Performance debugging in the large via mining millions of stack traces. In *Proceedings of the 34th International Conference on Software Engineering*, (pp. 145–155). Academic Press. doi:10.1109/ICSE.2012.6227198

Han, Y., Tai, S., & Wikarski, D. (2002). Engineering and deployment of cooperative information systems (Beijing, 17-20 September 2002). Lecture Notes in Computer Science.

Hanawa, T., Müller, M. S., Chapman, B., & de Supinski, B. R. (2010). *Beyond Loop Level Parallelism in OpenMP: Accelerators, Tasking and More.* Springer-Verlag Berlin Heidelberg.

Hand, R., Ton, M., & Keller, E. (2013). Active security. In *Proceedings of the Twelfth ACM Workshop on Hot Topics in Networks - HotNets-XII* (pp. 1–7). New York: ACM Press. doi:10.1145/2535771.2535794

Han, J., Kamber, M., & Pei, J. (2006). *Data Mining: Concepts and Techniques* (2nd ed.). University of Illinois at Urbana-Champaign, Morgan Kaufmann Publishers.

Hasan, O., Habegger, B., Brunie, L., Bennani, N., & Damiani, E. (2013). A Discussion of Privacy Challenges in User Profiling with Big Data Techniques: The EEXCESS Use Case. In *2013 IEEE International Congress on Big Data* (pp. 25–30). IEEE. doi:10.1109/BigData.Congress.2013.13

Hassan, M., Chaudhry, A., Khan, A., Iftikhar, M. A., & Kim, J. Y. (2013). *Medical image segmentation employing information gain and fuzzy c-means algorithm.* Paper presented at the Open Source Systems and Technologies (ICOSST), 2013 International Conference on. doi:10.1109/ICOSST.2013.6720602

Hassan, M., Chaudhry, A., Khan, A., & Iftikhar, M. A. (2014). Robust information gain based fuzzy c-means clustering and classification of carotid artery ultrasound images. *Computer Methods and Programs in Biomedicine, 113*(2), 593–609. doi:10.1016/j.cmpb.2013.10.012 PMID:24239296

Hassan, M., Chaudhry, A., Khan, A., & Kim, J. Y. (2012). Carotid artery image segmentation using modified spatial fuzzy c-means and ensemble clustering. *Computer Methods and Programs in Biomedicine, 108*(3), 1261–1276. doi:10.1016/j.cmpb.2012.08.011 PMID:22981822

Hassanzadeh, O., Kementsietsidis, A., Lim, L., Miller, R. J., & Wang, M. (2009). Linkedct: A linked data space for clinical trials. *arXiv preprint arXiv:0908.0567.*

Hassanzadeh, O., Xin, R., Miller, E. J., Kementsietsidis, A., & Wang, M. (2009). Linkage Query Writer. *Proc. VLDB Endow., 2*(2), 1590-1593. doi:10.14778/1687553.1687599

Hathaway, R. J., & Bezdek, J. C. (2006). Extending fuzzy and probabilistic clustering to very large data sets. *Computational Statistics & Data Analysis, 51*(1), 215–234. doi:10.1016/j.csda.2006.02.008

Havens, T. C., Chitta, R., Jain, A. K., & Rong, J. (2011). *Speedup of fuzzy and possibilistic kernel c-means for large-scale clustering.* Paper presented at the Fuzzy Systems (FUZZ), 2011 IEEE International Conference on.

Havens, T. C., Bezdek, J. C., Leckie, C., Hall, L. O., & Palaniswami, M. (2012). Fuzzy c-Means Algorithms for Very Large Data. *Fuzzy Systems. IEEE Transactions on, 20*(6), 1130–1146.

Heeks, R. (2002). 'Information Systems and Developing Countries: Failure, Success and Local Improvisations'. *The Information Society, 18*(2), 101–112. doi:10.1080/01972240290075039

Heimdahl, M. P. E., & George, D. (2004). Test-suite reduction for model based tests: effects on test quality and implications for testing. In *Automated Software Engineering Proceedings.19th International Conference.*

Hellwagner, H., & Reinefeld, A. (1999). *SCI: Scalable Coherent Interface: architecture and software for high-performance compute clusters* (Vol. 1734). Springer Science & Business Media. doi:10.1007/10704208

Herath, J., Yamaguchi, Y., Saito, N., & Yuba, T. (1988). Dataflow Computing Models, Languages, and Machines for Intelligence Computations. *IEEE Transactions on Software Engineering, 14*(12), 1805–1828. doi:10.1109/32.9065

Hierons, R. M., Harman, M., & Singh, H. (2003). Automatically generating information from Z specification to support the classification tree method. In *Proceedings of the Third International Conference of Z and B Users.* doi:10.1007/3-540-44880-2_23

Hipgrave, S. (2013). Smarter fraud investigations with big data analytics. *Network Security, 2013*(12), 7–9. doi:10.1016/S1353-4858(13)70135-1

Hirschberg, J. (1998). *"Every time I fire a linguist, my performance goes up", and other myths of the statistical natural language processing revolution.* Paper presented at the 15th National Conference on Artificial Intelligence, Madison, WI.

Holmes, G., Donkin, A., & Witten, I. H. (1994). *WEKA: a machine learning workbench.* Paper presented at the Intelligent Information Systems, the 1994 Second Australian and New Zealand Conference.

Homola, M. C., Nicklasson, P. J., & Sundsbø, P. A. (2006). Ice sensors for wind turbines. *Cold Regions Science and Technology, 46*(2), 125–131. doi:10.1016/j.coldregions.2006.06.005

Horcher, H. M. (1996). Improving Software Tests using Z Specifications. In J. P. Bowen & M. G. Hinchey (Eds.), Lecture Notes in Computer Science: Vol. 967. ZUM'95: The Formal Specification Notation (pp. 152–166). Springer.

Horcher, H. M., Bowen, J. P., & Hinchey, M. G. (1995). Improving Software Tests using Z Specifications. The Formal Specification Notation. *Lecture Notes in Computer Science, 967,* 152–166. doi:10.1007/3-540-60271-2_118

Hore, P., Hall, L. O., & Goldgof, D. B. (2007). *Single Pass Fuzzy C Means.* Paper presented at the Fuzzy Systems Conference.

Hore, P., Hall, L. O., Goldgof, D. B., & Cheng, W. (2008). *Online fuzzy c means.* Paper presented at the Fuzzy Information Processing Society. Retrieved from http://cs.joensuu.fi/~isido/clustering/

How the Big Data Explosion Is Changing the World. (n.d.). Retrieved Apr 20, from http://blogs.msdn.com/b/microsoft-enterpriseinsight/archive/2013/04/15/the-big-bang-how-the-big-data-explosion-is-changing-the-world.aspx

Hoyer, V., & Fischer, M. (2008). Market overview of enterprise mashup tools. In *Service-Oriented Computing–ICSOC 2008* (pp. 708–721). Springer Berlin Heidelberg. doi:10.1007/978-3-540-89652-4_62

HP. (2014). *Internet of Things Research Study.* Retrieved from http://fortifyprotect.com/HP_IoT_Research_Study.pdf

Humbert, M., Studer, T., Grossglauser, M., & Hubaux, J. P. (2013). *Nowhere to hide: Navigation around privacy in online in social networks*. The 18th European Symposium on Research in Computer Security (ESORICS). doi:10.1007/978-3-642-40203-6_38

Hurlburt, G. F., & Voas, J. (2014). Big data, networked worlds. *Computer, 47*(4), 84–87. doi:10.1109/MC.2014.82

Hurwitz, J., Nugent, A., Halper, F., & Kaufman, M. (2013). Big Data for Dummies. Wiley & Sons, Inc.

Hurwitz, J., Nugent, A., Halper, F., & Kaufman, M. (2013). *Big Data For Dummies*. Hoboken, NJ: John Wiley & Sons.

IBM big data platform - Bringing big data to the Enterprise. (2014, July). CT000.

IBM What is big data? —Bringing big data to the enterprise. (n.d.). Retrieved from www.ibm.com

IBM. (2014). *IBM X-Force Threat Intelligence Quarterly, IBM Security Systems.* First Quarter 2014. Retrieved from: http://www-03.ibm.com/security/xforce/

IBM®. (2008). *SOA Approach to Enterprise Integration for Product Lifecycle Management.* Retrieved August 15, 2013 from http://www.redbooks.ibm.com/redbooks/pdfs/sg247593.pdf

IDC. (2012). *Big Data in 2020.* Retrieved from http://www.emc.com/leadership/digital-universe/2012iview/big-data-2020.htm

IEC 62264-3, Enterprise-Control System Integration – Part 3: Activity Models of Manufacturing Operations Management. (2007). Retrieved July 24, 2014, from http://www.iso.org/iso/iso_catalogue/catalogue_tc/catalogue_detail.htm?csnumber=40949

Ilyas, M. U., & Radha, H. (2011). Identifying influential nodes in online social networks using principal component centrality. *IEEE International Conference.* doi:10.1109/icc.2011.5963147

Intel Corporation. (2013). *Big Data in the Cloud: Converging Technologies.* Retrieved Mar 01, from http://www.intel.com/content/www/us/en/big-data/big-data-cloud-technologies-brief.html

Intel IT Center. (2012). *Planning Guide: Getting Started with Hadoop, Steps IT Managers Can Take to Move Forward with Big Data Analytics.* Author.

Internet Users. (n.d.). Retrieved from http://www.internetlivestats.com/internet-users/

Iosup, A., Ostermann, S., Yigitbasi, M. N., Prodan, R., Fahringer, T., & Epema, D. H. (2011). Performance analysis of cloud computing services for many-tasks scientific computing. *Parallel and Distributed Systems. IEEE Transactions on, 22*(6), 931–945.

ISO 27000. (2009, 2012, 2014). *Information Technology, Security Techniques, Information Security Management Systems, Overview and Vocabulary.* International Organization for Standardization ISO, Geneva. Retrieved from: http://www.iso27001security.com/html/27000.html

ISO 27000. (n.d.). Retrieved from http://www.27000.org/

Ivanov, N. (2012). *Real Time Big Data Processing with GridGain, 2012.*

Iyyer, M., Boyd-Graber, J., Claudino, L., Socher, R., & Daumé, H. III. (2014). A Multi-Sentence Neural Network for Connecting Textual Descriptions to Entities. In *Conference on Empirical Methods in Natural Language Processing (EMNLP 2014).*

Jain, S., Kumar, A., & Mandal, S. (2013). B4: Experience with a globally-deployed software defined WAN. *Sigcomm,* 3–14. Retrieved May 15, 2015, from http://dl.acm.org/citation.cfm?id=2486019

Jarraya, Y., Madi, T., & Debbabi, M. (2014). A Survey and a Layered Taxonomy of Software-Defined Networking. *IEEE Communications Surveys and Tutorials*, *16*(4), 1955–1980. doi:10.1109/COMST.2014.2320094

Jelinek, F. (2005). Some of my best friends are linguists. *Language Resources and Evaluation*, *39*(1), 25–34. doi:10.1007/s10579-005-2693-4

Jewell, D., Barros, R. D., Diederichs, S., Duijvestijn, L. M., Hammersley, M., Hazra, A., & Plach, A. (2014). *Performance and Capacity Implications for Big Data*. IBM Redbooks.

Jhingran, A. (2006, September). Enterprise information mashups: integrating information, simply. In *Proceedings of the 32nd international conference on Very large data bases* (pp. 3-4). VLDB Endowment.

Johnston, W. M., Paul Hanna, J. R., & Millar, R. J. (2004). Advances in Dataflow Programming Languages. *ACM Computing Surveys*, *36*(1), 1–34. doi:10.1145/1013208.1013209

Jose, J., & Lal, P. S. (2012). An Indiscernibility Approach for preprocessing of Web Log Files. *International journal of Internet Computing, 1* (3), 58-61.

Józefowska, J., Ławrynowicz, A., & Łukaszewski, T. (2008). On Reducing Redundancy in Mining Relational Association Rules from the Semantic Web. In D. Calvanese & G. Lausen (Eds.), *Web Reasoning and Rule Systems* (Vol. 5341, pp. 205–213). New York: Springer Berlin Heidelberg. doi:10.1007/978-3-540-88737-9_16

Józefowska, J., Ławrynowicz, A., & Łukaszewski, T. (2010). The role of semantics in mining frequent patterns from knowledge bases in description logics with rules. *Theory and Practice of Logic Programming*, *10*(3), 251–289. doi:10.1017/S1471068410000098

Juels, A., & Oprea, A. (2013). New approaches to security and availability for cloud data. *Communications of the ACM*, *56*(2), 64. doi:10.1145/2408776.2408793

Juniper. (2013). *Integrating SDN into the Data Center*. White Paper. Retrieved May 15, 2015, from http://www.juniper.net/us/en/local/pdf/whitepapers/2000542-en.pdf

Jutla, D. N., Bodorik, P., & Ali, S. (2013). Engineering Privacy for Big Data Apps with the Unified Modeling Language. In *2013 IEEE International Congress on Big Data* (pp. 38–45). IEEE. doi:10.1109/BigData.Congress.2013.15

Kaisler, S., Armour, F., Espinosa, J. A., & Money, W. (2013). Big Data: Issues and Challenges Moving Forward. In *Proceedings of the 46th Hawaii International Conference on System Sciences*. Maui, HI: IEEE. doi:10.1109/HICSS.2013.645

Kakade, K. N., & Chavan, T. A. (2014). Improving Efficiency of GEO-Distributed Data Sets using Pact. *International Journal of Current Engineering and Technology*, *4*(3), 1284–1287.

Karniadakis, G. E., & Kirby, R. M. II. (2003). *Parallel scientific computing in C++ and MPI: a seamless approach to parallel algorithms and their implementation* (Vol. 1). Cambridge University Press. doi:10.1017/CBO9780511812583

Karypis, G., & Kumar, V. (1998). Multilevelk-way partitioning scheme for irregular graphs. *Journal of Parallel and Distributed Computing*, *48*(1), 96–129. doi:10.1006/jpdc.1997.1404

Kasprzyk, L., Nawrowski, R., & Tomczewski, A. (2002). Application of a parallel virtual machine for the analysis of a luminous field. In *Recent Advances in Parallel Virtual Machine and Message Passing Interface* (pp. 122–129). Springer Berlin Heidelberg.

Katal, A., Wazid, M., & Goudar, R. H. (2013). Big Data: Issues, Challenges, Tools and Good Practices. In *Proceedings of the Sixth International Conference on Contemporary Computing (IC3)*. Noicla, India. doi:10.1109/IC3.2013.6612229

Katina, M., & Miller, K. W. (2013). Big Data: New Opportunities and New Challenges. *Computer, 46*(6), 22-24.

Katz, R. L. (2009). 'The Economic and Social Impact of Telecommunications Output'. *Inter Economics*, *44*(1), 41–48. doi:10.1007/s10272-009-0276-0

Kaur, D., & Paul, A. (2014). Performance Analysis of Different Data mining Techniques over Heart Disease dataset. *International Journal of Current Engineering and Technology*, *4*(1), 220–224.

Kazemian, P., Change, M., & Zheng, H. (2013). Real Time Network Policy Checking Using Header Space Analysis. *USENIX Symposium on Networked Systems Design and Implementation*. Retrieved May 15, 2015, from http://yuba.stanford.edu/~peyman/docs/net_plumber-nsdi13.pdf

Keim, D. A., Hao, M. C., Ladisch, J., Hsu, M., & Dayal, U. (2001). *Pixel bar charts: A new technique for visualizing large multi-attribute data sets without aggregation*. Academic Press.

Keim, D. A., Hao, M. C., Dayal, U., & Lyons, M. (2007). Value-cell bar charts for visualizing large transaction data sets. Visualization and Computer Graphics. *IEEE Transactions on*, *13*(4), 822–833.

Khwaja, A. A., & Urban, J. E. (2008a). RealSpec: An Executable Specification Language for Prototyping Concurrent Systems. In *Proceedings of the 19th IEEE/IFIP International Symposium on Rapid System Prototyping*. Monterey, CA: IEEE. doi:10.1109/RSP.2008.9

Khwaja, A. A., & Urban, J. E. (2008b). RealSpec: An Executable Specification Language for Modeling Resources. In *Proceedings of the 20th International Conference on Software Engineering and Knowledge Engineering (SEKE 2008)*. San Francisco Bay, CA.

Khwaja, A. A., & Urban, J. E. (2008c). Timing, Precedence, and Resource Constraints in the RealSpec Real-Time Specification Language. In *Proceedings of the 2008 IASTED International Conference on Software Engineering and Applications*. Orlando, FL: IASTED.

Khwaja, A. A., & Urban, J. E. (2010). Preciseness for Predictability with the RealSpec Real-Time Executable Specification Language. In *Proceedings of the 2010 IEEE Aerospace Conference*. Big Sky, MT: IEEE. doi:10.1109/AERO.2010.5446788

Kim, C., Jin, M.-H., Kim, J., & Shin, N. (2012). User perception of the quality, value, and utility of user-generated content. *Journal of Electronic Commerce Research*, *13*(4), 305–319.

Kindervag, J., Balaouras, S., Hill, B., & Mak, K. (2012). *Control And Protect Sensitive Information In the Era of Big Data*. Academic Press.

Kindervag, J., Wang, C., Balaouras, S., & Coit, L. (2011). *Applying Zero Trust To The Extending Enterprise*. Academic Press.

Kirkman, G. (1999). *Its More Than Just Being Connected: A Discussion of Some Issues of Information Technology and International Development*. Paper presented at the Development E-Commerce Workshop. Retrieved from: http://cyber.law.harvard.edu/itg/libpubs/beingconnected.pdf

Kleene, S. C. (1976). The work of Kurt Gödel. *Journal of Symbolic Logic*, 761-778.

Klir, G. J., & Yuan, B. (Eds.). (1995). *Fuzzy sets and fuzzy logic: theory and applications*. New Jersey: Prentice Hall.

Koller, R., Verma, A., & Rangaswami, R. (2011). Estimating application cache requirement for provisioning caches in virtualized systems. In *IEEE International Workshop on Modeling, Analysis, and Simulation of Computer and Telecommunication Systems - Proceedings* (pp. 55–62). doi:10.1109/MASCOTS.2011.67

Koobface. (n.d.). Retrieved May, 10 from http://en.wikipedia.org/wiki/Koobface

Koponen, T., Amidon, K., Balland, P., Casado, M., Chanda, A., & Fulton, B. … Zhang, R. (2014). Network Virtualization in Multi-tenant Datacenters. In *Proceedings of the 11th USENIX Symposium on Networked Systems Design and Implementation (NSDI 14)* (pp. 203–216). USENIX. Retrieved May 15, 2015, from http://blogs.usenix.org/conference/nsdi14/technical-sessions/presentation/koponen

Koren, Y. (2010). *The Global Manufacturing Revolution: Product-Process-Business Integration and Reconfigurable Systems*. John Wiley & Sons Inc. doi:10.1002/9780470618813

Kosinski, P. R. (1978). A Straightforward Denotational Semantics for Non-determinate Data Flow Programs. In *Proceedings of the 5th ACM SIGACT-SIGPLAN Symposium on Principles of Programming Languages*. Tucson, AZ: ACM. doi:10.1145/512760.512783

Krause, E., Shokin, Y. I., Resch, M., & Shokina, N. (2011). *Computational Science and High Performance Computing IV*. Springer. doi:10.1007/978-3-642-17770-5

Kreutz, D., & Ramos, F. (2014). Software-Defined Networking: A Comprehensive Survey. *arXiv Preprint arXiv: …*, 49. Retrieved May 15, 2015, from http://arxiv.org/abs/1406.0440

Krishnamurthy, B., & Wills, C. E. (2008), *Characterizing Privacy in Online Social Networks*. WOSN '08 Proceedings of the first workshop on Online social networks. Retrieved from http://www2.research.att.com/~bala/papers/posn.pdf

Kumar, H., Gharakheili, H. H., & Sivaraman, V. (2013). User control of quality of experience in home networks using SDN. In *Advanced Networks and Telecommunications Systems (ANTS), 2013 IEEE International Conference on* (pp. 1–6). doi:10.1109/ANTS.2013.6802847

Lairson, T. D., & Skidmore, D. (2003). *International Political Economy: The Struggle for Power and Wealth*. Belmont: Thompson and Wadsworth.

Lamb, R., & Kling, R. (2003). 'Reconceptualising Users as Social Actors in Information Systems Research'. *Management Information Systems Quarterly*, *27*(2), 197–235.

Landin, P. J. (1966). The Next 700 Programming Languages. *Communications of the ACM*, *9*(3), 157–166. doi:10.1145/365230.365257

Laney, D. (2001). *3D Data Management: Controlling Data Volume, Velocity, and Variety*. Gartner Group. Retrieved from: http://blogs.gartner.com/doug-laney/files/2012/01/ad949-3D-Data-Management-Controlling-Data-Volume-Velocity-and-Variety.pdf

Laney, D. (2012). *Deja VVVu: Others Claiming Gartner's Construct for Big Data*. Gartner Group. Retrieved from: http://blogs.gartner.com/doug-laney/deja-vvvue-others-claiming-gartners-volume-velocity-variety-construct-for-big-data/

Lange, J. R., Pedretti, K., Dinda, P., Bridges, P. G., Bae, C., Soltero, P., & Merritt, A. (2011). *Minimal-overhead virtualization of a large scale supercomputer*. ACM SIGPLAN Notices. doi:10.1145/1952682.1952705

Langhnoja, S. G., Barot, M. P., & Mehta, D. B. (2013). Web Usage Mining to Discover Visitor Group with Common Behavior Using DBSCAN Clustering Algorithm. *International Journal of Engineering and Innovative Technology*, *2*(7), 169–173.

Laplante, P. A. (1993). Real-time systems design. *Analysis*.

Lara, A., Kolasani, A., & Ramamurthy, B. (2013). Network Innovation using OpenFlow: A Survey. *IEEE Communications Surveys & Tutorials*, (99), 1–20. Retrieved May 15, 2015, from http://ieeexplore.ieee.org/lpdocs/epic03/wrapper.htm?arnumber=6587999

Lattanzi, S., Panconesi A. & Sivakumar D. (2011). *Milgram-Routing in Social Networks*. The International World Wide Web, IW3C2.

LaValle, S., Lesser, E., Shockley, R., Hopkins, M. S., & Kruschwitz, N. (2013). Big data, analytics and the path from insights to value. *MIT Sloan Management Review, 21*.

Le Page, M. (2002, May 4th). 'Village-Life.com'. New Scientist, 44–45.

Learn the Latest Social Advertising Trend. (n.d.). Retrieved July 20, from http://resolutionmedia.com/us/white-papers/resolution-media-social-trends-report

Lee, C. Y. (1959). Representation of switching circuits by binary decision diagrams. *Bell System Technology, 1*(38), 985–999. doi:10.1002/j.1538-7305.1959.tb01585.x

Lee, C., Chen, C., Yang, X., Zoebir, B., Chaisiri, S., & Lee, B.-S. (2013). A Workflow Framework for Big Data Analytics: Event Recognition in a Building. In *Proceedings of the IEEE 9th World Congress on Services*. Santa Clara, CA: IEEE.

Lehmann, M., Büter, A., Frankenstein, B., Schubert, F., & Brunner, B. (2006). Monitoring System for Delamination Detection–Qualification of Structural Health Monitoring (SHM) Systems. In *Proceedings of the Conference on Damage in Composite Material (CDCM '06)*. Stuttgart.

Leitão, P. (2004). *An Agile and Adaptive Holonic Architecture for Manufacturing Control*. (PhD Thesis). University of Porto.

Levis, K. (2009). Winners and Losers: Creators and Casualties of the Age of the Internet. London: Atlantic Books Ltd.

Li, B., Ma, M., & Jin, Z. (2011). 'A VoIP Traffic Identification Scheme Based On Host and Flow Behavior Analysis'. Journal of Network and Systems Management, 19(1), 111–129. doi:10.1007/s10922-010-9184-7 doi:10.1007/s10922-010-9184-7

Li, R. E. Z., & Midkiff, S. P. (2005). *Languages and Compilers for High Performance Computing*. Academic Press.

Liang, H. (2005). Regression testing of classes based on TCOZ specifications. In *Proceedings of the 10th IEEE International Conference on Engineering of Complex Computer Systems (ICECCS'05)* (pp. 450 – 457). IEEE. doi:10.1109/ICECCS.2005.71

Liben-Nowell, D., & Kleinberg, J. (2007). The Link Prediction Problem for Social Networks. *Journal of the American Society for Information Science and Technology, 58*(7), 1019–1031. doi:10.1002/asi.20591

Li, D. Y., & Hu, B. Q. (2007). A kind of dynamic rough sets. In *Proceedings of the Fourth International Conference on Fuzzy Systems and Knowledge Discovery (FSKD)*, (pp. 79-85). doi:10.1109/FSKD.2007.51

Lim, C., Singh, N., & Yajnik, S. (2008). A log mining approach to failure analysis of enterprise telephony systems. In *Proceedings of the IEEE International Conference on Dependable Systems and Networks*, (pp. 398–403). IEEE.

Lindell, Y., & Pinkas, B. (2002). Privacy Preserving Data Mining. *Journal of Cryptology, 15*(3), 177–206. doi:10.1007/s00145-001-0019-2

Linden, G., Smith, B., & York, J. (2003). Amazon.com recommendations: Item-to-item collaborative filtering. *IEEE Internet Computing, 7*(1), 76–80. doi:10.1109/MIC.2003.1167344

Lind, P., & Alm, M. (2006). A database-centric virtual chemistry system. *Journal of Chemical Information and Modeling, 46*(3), 1034–1039. doi:10.1021/ci050360b PMID:16711722

Lin, J. H., & Haug, P. J. (2008). Exploiting missing clinical data in Bayesian network modeling for predicting medical problems. *Journal of Biomedical Informatics, New York, 41*(1), 1–14. doi:10.1016/j.jbi.2007.06.001 PMID:17625974

Little, R. J. A., & Rubin, D. B. (2002). *Statistical analysis with missing data* (2nd ed.). Wiley-Interscience. doi:10.1002/9781119013563

Liu, D. T., & Franklin, M. J. (2004, August). GridDB: a data-centric overlay for scientific grids. In *Proceedings of the Thirtieth international conference on Very large data bases-Volume 30* (pp. 600-611). VLDB Endowment. doi:10.1016/B978-012088469-8.50054-1

Liu, B. (2009). *Web Data Mining: Exploring Hyperlinks, Contents and Usage Data*. Springer.

Li, Y., & Wahi, N. J. (1999). An overview of regression testing. *Software Engineering Notes, 24*(1), 69–73. doi:10.1145/308769.308790

Lopez, J. J. P. J., Shon, S. S. Y. T., & Taniar, D. (n.d.). *Secure and Trust Computing, Data Management, and Applications*. Academic Press.

Lopez, D., & Van Slyke, W. J. (1977). Logic Tree Analysis for Decision Making. *Omega, The Int. Journal of Management Science, 5*, 5.

Lukasiewicz, T., & Straccia, U. (2009). Description logic programs under probabilistic uncertainty and fuzzy vagueness. *International Journal of Approximate Reasoning, 50*(6), 837–853. doi:10.1016/j.ijar.2009.03.004

Luo, H., Lin, Y., Zhang, H., & Zukerman, M. (2013). Preventing DDoS attacks by identifier/locator separation. *IEEE Network, 27*(6), 60–65. doi:10.1109/MNET.2013.6678928

Lu, R., Li, X., Liang, X., Shen, X., & Lin, X. (2011). GRS: The Green, Reliability, and Security of Emerging Machine to Machine Communications. *IEEE Communications Magazine, 49*(4), 28–35. doi:10.1109/MCOM.2011.5741143

Lusher, D., Koskinen, J., & Robins, G. (2013). *Exponential Random Graphs Models for Social Networks: Theory, Methods and Application*. Cambridge: Cambridge University press.

Lynch, N. A. (1996). *Distributed algorithms*. Morgan Kaufmann.

M, K., & Dixit, D. (2010). Mining Access Patterns Using Clustering. *International Journal of Computer Applications, 4* (11), 22-26.

MacDonald, N. (2012). *Information Security Is Becoming a Big Data Analytics Problem*. Gartner Report. Retrieved from https://www.gartner.com/doc/1960615/information-security-big-data-analytics

Madden, S. (2012). From Databases to Big Data. *IEEE Internet Computing, 16*(3), 4–6. doi:10.1109/MIC.2012.50

Mahjoub, M., Mdhaffar, A., Halima, R. B., & Jmaiel, M. (2011, November). A comparative study of the current Cloud Computing technologies and offers. In *Network Cloud Computing and Applications (NCCA), 2011 First International Symposium on* (pp. 131-134). IEEE. doi:10.1109/NCCA.2011.28

Main, L. (2001). 'The Global Information Infrastructure: Empowerment or Imperialism?'. Third World Quarterly, 22(1), 83–97. doi:10.1080/713701143 doi:10.1080/713701143

Mak, G., & Long, J. (2009). *Spring Enterprise Recipes: A Problem-solution Approach*. Apress.

Mak, G., Long, J., & Rubio, D. (2010). Spring AOP and AspectJ support. In *Spring Recipes* (pp. 117–158). Apress. doi:10.1007/978-1-4302-2500-3_3

Makhoul, J., Kubala, F., Schwartz, R., & Weischedel, R. (1999). *Performance measures for information extraction*. Paper presented at the DARPA Broadcast News Workshop.

Malawski, M., Meizner, J., Bubak, M., & Gepner, P. (2011). Component approach to computational applications on clouds. *Procedia Computer Science, 4*, 432–441. doi:10.1016/j.procs.2011.04.045

Mallo, C., & Merlo, J. (1995). *Control de gestión y control presupuestario*. McGraw-Hill.

Maltby, D. (2011). Big Data Analytics. *ASIST Conference*, New Orleans, LA.

Manyika, J., Chui, M., Brown, B., Bughin, J., Dobbs, R., Roxburgh, C., & Byers, A. H. (2011). Big data: The next frontier for innovation, competition, and productivity. McKinsey Global Institute.

Manyika, J., Chui, M., Brown, B., Bughin, J., Dobbs, R., Roxburgh, C., & Byers, A. H. (2011). *Big data: The next frontier for innovation, competition, and productivity*. The McKinsey Global Institute.

Map Reduce. (n.d.). Retrieved Aug 01, from http://docs.mongodb.org/manual/core/map-reduce/

Marques, J., & Serrão, C. (2013a). Improving Content Privacy on Social Networks Using Open Digital Rights Management Solutions. *Procedia Technology, 9*, 405–410. doi:10.1016/j.protcy.2013.12.045

Marques, J., & Serrão, C. (2013b). Improving user content privacy on social networks using rights management systems. *Annals of Telecommunications -. Annales des Télécommunications, 69*(1-2), 37–45. doi:10.1007/s12243-013-0388-1

Marre, B. & Blanc. (2005). *Test Selection Strategies for Lustre Descriptions in GATeL*. Laboratoire Sûreté des Logiciels, CEA/DRT/DTSI/SOL.

Martin, H., & Horcher, M. (1995). Improving software tests using Z specifications. In *Proceedings of the 9th International Conference of Z Users on The Z Formal Specification Notation* (pp. 152 – 166). Academic Press.

Martin, W. J. (1988). The Information Society. London: Aslib Press.

Marx, V. (2013). Biology: The big challenges of big data. *Nature, 498*(7453), 255–260. doi:10.1038/498255a PMID:23765498

Massa, A. J. (2003). *Embedded Software with eCos*. Prentice Hall.

McAfee, A., & Brynjolfsson, E. (2012). Big Data. The management revolution. *Harvard Business Review, 90*(10), 61–68. Retrieved May 15, 2015, from http://www.buyukverienstitusu.com/s/1870/i/Big_Data_2.pdf

McAfee, A., & Erik Brynjolfsson, E. (2012). Big Data: The Management revolution. *Harvard Business Review*, 59–68. PMID:23074865

McChesney, R. W., Wood, E. M., & Foster, J. B. (1998). Capitalism and the Information Age: The Political Economy of the Global Communication Revolution. New York: Monthly Review Press.

McKenzie, P. J., Burkell, J., Wong, L., Whippey, C., Trosow, S. E., & McNally, M. B. (2012, June 6). User-generated online content: overview, current state and context. *First Monday*. Retrieved from http://firstmonday.org/ojs/index.php/fm/article/view/3912/3266

Mehtaa, P., Parekh, B. P., Modi, K., & Solamki, P. (2012). Web personalization Using Web Mining: Concept and Research issue. *International Journal of information and Education Technology, 2* (5), 510-512.

Mell, P., & Grance, T. (2009). The NIST definition of cloud computing. *National Institute of Standards and Technology, 53*(6), 50.

Meudec, C. (1999/2000). *Automatic Test Data Generation from VDM-SL Specifications. Queen's University of Belfast.* Northern Ireland.

Mi, H., Wang, H., Zhou, Y., Lyu, M.R., & Cai, H. (2013). Toward Fine-Grained, Unsupervised, Scalable Performance Diagnosis for Production Cloud Computing Systems. *IEEE Transactions on Parallel and Distributed Systems, 24*(6), 1245-1255.

Michael, K., & Miller, K. W. (2013). Big Data: New Opportunities and New Challenges. IEEE Computer, 46(6), 22-24.

Michael, K., & Miller, K. W. (2013). Big Data: New Opportunities and New Challenges. *Computer, 46*(6), 22–24. doi:10.1109/MC.2013.196

Midkiff, S. P. (2005). *Languages and Compilers for High Performance Computing.* Academic Press.

Mika, P., & Greaves, M. (2012). Editorial: Semantic Web & Web 2.0. *Web Semantics: Science, Services, and Agents on the World Wide Web, 6*(1).

Milgram, S. (1967). The small world problem. *Psychology Today, 1,* 61.

Minelli, M., Chambers, M., & Dhiraj, A. (2012). *Big data, big analytics: emerging business intelligence and analytic trends for today's businesses.* Hoboken, NJ: John Wiley & Sons.

Minor, R. (2014). Retrieved from http://rapid-i.com/content/view/181/190/

Mislove, A., Marcon, M., Gummadi, K. P., Druschel, P., & Bhattacharjee, B. (2007). Measurement and Analysis of Online Social Networks. *5th ACM/USENIX Internet Measurement Conference, IMC'07,* San Diego, CA. doi:10.1145/1298306.1298311

MIT. (2014). *Big Data Privacy Workshop, Advancing the state of the art in Technology and Practice - Workshop summary report.* Retrieved from http://web.mit.edu/bigdata-priv/images/MITBigDataPrivacyWorkshop2014_final05142014.pdf

Mohanty, S., Jagadeesh, M., & Srivatsa, H. (2013). *Big Data Imperatives: Enterprise 'Big Data' Warehouse, 'BI' Implementations and Analytics.* Apress. doi:10.1007/978-1-4302-4873-6

Monsanto, C., Reich, J., Foster, N., Rexford, J., & Walker, D. (2013). Composing software-defined networks. *Proceedings of the 10th USENIX Conference on Networked Systems Design and Implementation,* 1–14. Retrieved from http://dl.acm.org/citation.cfm?id=2482626.2482629\nhttp://www.frenetic-lang.org/pyretic/

Moret, B. M. E. (1982). Decision trees and diagrams. Computing Surveys, 14(14), 593-623.

Mostéfaoui, S. K., & Hirsbrunner, B. (2003, July). A context-based services discovery and composition framework for wireless environments. In *Proceedings of the IASTED International Conference on Wireless and Optical Networks (WOC'03),* (pp. 637-642). IASTED.

Nadeem, A., & Jaffar, M. (2004). *A Framework for Automated Testing from VDM-SL Specifications.* Pakistan: Muhammad Ali Jinnah University Islamabad.

Nadeem, A., & Jaffar, M. (2005). *TESTAF: A Test Automation Framework for class testing using object-oriented formal specification, center for software dependability. Muhammad Ali Jinnah University Islamabad.*

Nah, F., Lau, J., & Kuang, J. (2001). Critical factors for successful implementation of enterprise systems. *Business Process Management Journal, 7*(3), 285–297. doi:10.1108/14637150110392782

Nakamura, T., Hochstein, L., & Basili, V. R. (2006, September). Identifying domain-specific defect classes using inspections and change history. In *Proceedings of the 2006 ACM/IEEE international symposium on Empirical software engineering* (pp. 346-355). ACM. doi:10.1145/1159733.1159785

Nassar, O. A., & Al Saiyd, N. A. (2013, March). The integrating between web usage mining and data mining techniques. In *Computer Science and Information Technology (CSIT), 2013 5th International Conference on* (pp. 243-247). IEEE. doi:10.1109/CSIT.2013.6588787

Nature. (2008). Community cleverness required. *Nature, 455*(7209), 1.

Naudts, B., Kind, M., Westphal, F. J., Verbrugge, S., Colle, D., & Pickavet, M. (2012). Techno-economic analysis of software defined networking as architecture for the virtualization of a mobile network. In *Proceedings - European Workshop on Software Defined Networks, EWSDN 2012* (pp. 67–72). doi:10.1109/EWSDN.2012.27

Nelson, T., Ferguson, A. D., Scheer, M. J. G., & Krishnamurthi, S. (2014). Tierless Programming and Reasoning for Software-Defined Networks. In *Proceedings of the 11th USENIX Symposium on Networked Systems Design and Implementation (NSDI 14)* (pp. 519–531). USENIX. Retrieved May 15, 2015, from http://blogs.usenix.org/conference/nsdi14/technical-sessions/presentation/nelson

Niranjan Mysore, R., Pamboris, A., Farrington, N., Huang, N., Miri, P., & Radhakrishnan, S. … Mysore, R. N. (2009). PortLand: a scalable fault-tolerant layer 2 data center network fabric. In *SIGCOMM '09 Proceedings of the ACM SIGCOMM 2009 Conference on Data Communication* (pp. 39–50). ACM. Retrieved May 15, 2015, from http://doi.acm.org/10.1145/1592568.1592575

NIST. (2013). *Glossary of Key Information Security Terms, NISTIR 7298, Revision 2*. Retrieved from: http://nvlpubs.nist.gov/nistpubs/ir/2013/NIST.IR.7298r2.pdf

NIST. (2014). *Framework for Improving Critical Infrastructure Cybersecurity*. Retrieved from http://www.nist.gov/cyberframework/upload/cybersecurity-framework-021214-final.pdf

NIST Cybersecurity Framework. (n.d.). Retrieved from http://www.nist.gov/cyberframework/

Noeth, M., Ratn, P., Mueller, F., Schulz, M., & de Supinski, B. R. (2009). ScalaTrace: Scalable compression and replay of communication traces for high-performance computing. *Journal of Parallel and Distributed Computing, 69*(8), 696–710. doi:10.1016/j.jpdc.2008.09.001

Noonan, W., & Dubrawsky, I. (2006). *Firewall fundamentals*. Pearson Education.

Norris, P. (2001). Digital Divide: Civic Engagement, Information Poverty and the Internet Worldwide. Cambridge: Cambridge University Press. doi:10.1017/CBO9781139164887 doi:10.1017/CBO9781139164887

NUA Internet Surveys. (2014). *How Many Online?* Retrieved from: http://www.nua.ie/surveys/how_many_online/

Nunes, B. A. A., Mendonca, M., Nguyen, X. N., Obraczka, K., & Turletti, T. (2014). A Survey of Software-Defined Networking: Past, Present, and Future of Programmable Networks. *IEEE Communications Surveys and Tutorials, 16*(3), 1617–1634. doi:10.1109/SURV.2014.012214.00180

NuSMV. (2014). *An overview of NuSMV*. Retrieved July 23, 2014, from http://nusmv.fbk.eu/NuSMV/

O'reilly, T. (2007). What is Web 2.0: Design patterns and business models for the next generation of software. *Communications & Stratégies*, (1), 17.

Odendaal, N. (2002). 'ICTs in Development – Who Benefits? Use of Geographic Information Systems on the Cato Manor Development Project, South Africa'. Journal of International Development, 4(1), 89–100. doi:10.1002/jid.867 doi:10.1002/jid.867

Ohlhorst, F. (2013). *Turning Big Data into Big Money*. Wiley & Sons, Inc.

Okhravi, H., Hobson, T., Bigelow, D., & Streilein, W. (2014). Finding Focus in the Blur of Moving-Target Techniques. *IEEE Security and Privacy, 12*(2), 16–26. doi:10.1109/MSP.2013.137

O'Leary, D. E. (2013). 'Big data', the 'internet of things' and the 'internet of signs. *Intelligent Systems in Accounting, Finance & Management, 20*(1), 53–65. doi:10.1002/isaf.1336

Olston, C., & Najork, M. (2010). Web crawling. *Foundations and Trends in Information Retrieval, 4*(3), 175–246. doi:10.1561/1500000017

Oracle®. (2013). *Big Data for the Enterprise*. Retrieved August 15, 2013, from http://www.oracle.com/us/products/database/big-data-for-enterprise-519135.pdf

Organisation for Economic Co-operation and Development. (2000). *Learning to Bridge the Digital Divide*. Paris: OECD Publications.

Osman, A., El-Refaey, M., & Elnaggar, A. (2013). Towards Real-Time Analytics in the Cloud. In *Proceedings of the 2013 IEEE 9th World Congress on Services*. Santa Clara, CA: IEEE. doi:10.1109/SERVICES.2013.36

Ostermann, S., Iosup, A., Yigitbasi, N., Prodan, R., Fahringer, T., & Epema, D. (2010). A performance analysis of EC2 cloud computing services for scientific computing. In *Cloud computing* (pp. 115–131). Springer Berlin Heidelberg. doi:10.1007/978-3-642-12636-9_9

OWASP. (2014). *OWASP Internet of Things Top Ten Project*. Retrieved August 05, 2014, from https://www.owasp.org/index.php/OWASP_Internet_of_Things_Top_Ten_Project

Pacheco, P. S. (1997). *Parallel programming with MPI*. Morgan Kaufmann.

Paine, T. (2011). *M2M in Manufacturing*. Retrieved June 15, 2014, from http://www.kepware.com/News/M2M_in_Manufacturing-by_Tony_Paine.pdf

Papadimitriou, C. H. (2003). *Computational complexity* (pp. 260–265). John Wiley and Sons Ltd.

Parise, S., Iyer, B., & Vesset, D. (2012). Four Strategies to Capture and Create Value from Big Data. *Ivey Business Journal, 76*(4), 1–5. Retrieved May 15, 2015, from http://search.ebscohost.com/login.aspx?direct=true&db=bth&AN=78946504&site=bsi-live

Patel, A., Seyfi, A., Tew, Y., & Jaradat, A. (2011). Comparative study and review of grid, cloud, utility computing and software as a service for use by libraries. *Library Hi Tech News, 28*(3), 25–32. doi:10.1108/07419051111145145

Patil, P. V., & Patil, D. (2012). Preprocessing Web Logs for Web Intrusion Detection. *International Journal of Applied Information Systems*, 11-15.

Patterson, C. A., Snir, M., & Graham, S. L. (Eds.). (2005). *Getting Up to Speed: The Future of Supercomputing*. National Academies Press.

Paulk, M. C., Weber, C. V., Curtis, B., & Chrissis, M. B. (1995). *The Capability Maturity Model: Guidelines for Improving the Software Process. SEI series in software engineering*. Reading, MA: Addison-Wesley.

Pavlik, M. (2013). *Mi is az a big data*. Retrieved from http://www.scribd.com/doc/181439274/1-Mi-is-az-a-big-data-ppt

Pawlak, Z. (1981). Information systems: Theoretical foundations. *Information Systems, 6*(3), 205–218. doi:10.1016/0306-4379(81)90023-5

Pawlak, Z. (1991). *Rough sets: Theoretical Aspects of Reasoning about Data*. The Netherlands: Kluwer Academic Publishers. doi:10.1007/978-94-011-3534-4

Pawlak, Z., & Skowron, A. (2007a). Rudiments of rough sets. *Information Sciences, 177*(1), 3–27. doi:10.1016/j.ins.2006.06.003

Pawlak, Z., & Skowron, A. (2007b). Rough sets: Some extensions. *Information Sciences, 177*(1), 28–40. doi:10.1016/j.ins.2006.06.006

Pawlak, Z., & Skowron, A. (2007c). Rough sets and Boolean reasoning. *Information Sciences, 177*(1), 41–73. doi:10.1016/j.ins.2006.06.007

Pedarsani, P. (2013). *Privacy and dynamics of social networks*. Ecole Polytechnique Federale de Lausanne.

Pentikousis, K., Wang, Y., & Hu, W. (2013). Mobileflow: Toward software-defined mobile networks. *IEEE Communications Magazine, 51*(7), 44–53. doi:10.1109/MCOM.2013.6553677

Pentland, A. (2014). *Social Physics: How Good Ideas Spread – The Lessons from A New Science*. New York: The Penguin Press.

Perrit, H. H. (1998). 'The Internet as a Threat to Sovereignty? Thoughts on the Internet's Role in Strengthening National and Global Governance'. *Indiana Journal of Global Legal Studies, 5*(2), 431–444.

Perry, J., Ousterhout, A., Balakrishnan, H., Shah, D., & Fugal, H. (2014). Fastpass: A Centralized "Zero-Queue" Datacenter Network. In Sigcomm (pp. 307-318). doi:10.1145/2619239.2626309

Pinar Pérez, J. M., García Márquez, F. P., Tobias, A., & Papaelias, M. (2013). Wind turbine reliability analysis. *Renewable & Sustainable Energy Reviews, 23*, 463–472. doi:10.1016/j.rser.2013.03.018

Poblet, M. (2011). *Mobile Technologies for Conflict Management: Online Dispute Resolution, Governance, Participation*. London: Springer Verlag. doi:10.1007/978-94-007-1384-0

Pollard, A., Mewhort, D. J., & Weaver, D. F. (2000). *High performance computing systems and applications*. Springer Science & Business Media.

Popa, R., & Redfield, C. (2011). Cryptdb: protecting confidentiality with encrypted query processing. *Proceedings of the ...*, 85–100. doi:10.1145/2043556.2043566

Popa, R., & Redfield, C. (2012). CryptDB: Processing queries on an encrypted database. *Communications, 55*, 103. doi:10.1145/2330667.2330691

Porter, M. A. (2012). *Small World Network*. Retrieved Apr 12, from http://www.scholarpedia.org/article/Small-world_network

Prakash, N. (2012). 'Empowering Women Using Environmentally Friendly Technology in Paper Recycling'. *Research in Political Sociology, 20*(1), 125–136. doi:10.1108/S0895-9935(2012)0000020009

Press, G. (2013). A Very Short History of Big Data. *Forbes Magazine*. Retrieved from: http://www.forbes.com/sites/gilpress/2013/05/09/a-very-short-history-of-big-data/

Press, G. (2013). A Very Short History Of Big Data. *Forbes*. Retrieved April 2, 2014, from http://www.forbes.com/sites/gilpress/2013/05/09/a-very-short-history-of-big-data/

Privacy and Information Security Law Blog. (n.d.). Retrieved from https://www.huntonprivacyblog.com/

Pyretic. (2014). *Pyretic Language*. Retrieved August 05, 2014, from https://github.com/frenetic-lang/pyretic/wiki/Language-Basics

Python. (2014). *Python Language*. Retrieved August 03, 2014, from https://www.python.org/

Rajkumar, R., Lee, I., Sha, L., & Stankovic, J. (2010). Cyber-Physical Systems: The Next Computing Revolution. In *Proceedings of the 47th Design Automation Conference* (pp. 731-736). New York: ACM Digital Library. Retrieved June 20, 2014, from http://dl.acm.org/citation.cfm?id=1837461

Ram, K., Cox, A., Chadha, M., & Rixner, S. (2013). Hyper-Switch: A Scalable Software Virtual Switching Architecture. In USENIX ATC 2013 (pp. 13–24).

Ramze Rezaee, M., Lelieveldt, B. P. F., & Reiber, J. H. C. (1998). A new cluster validity index for the fuzzy c-mean. *Pattern Recognition Letters*, *19*(3–4), 237–246. doi:10.1016/S0167-8655(97)00168-2

Rana, C. (2012). A Study of Web Usage Mining Research Tools. *Int. J. Advanced Networking and Applications*, *3*(6), 1422–1429.

Randles, M., Lamb, D., & Taleb-Bendiab, A. (2010, April). A comparative study into distributed load balancing algorithms for cloud computing. In *Advanced Information Networking and Applications Workshops (WAINA), 2010 IEEE 24th International Conference on* (pp. 551-556). IEEE. doi:10.1109/WAINA.2010.85

Raymer, M. L., Punch, W. F., Goodman, E. D., Kuhn, L. A., & Jain, A. K. (2000). Dimensionality reduction using genetic algorithms. *Evolutionary Computation. IEEE Transactions on*, *4*(2), 164–171.

Rego, V. J., & Sunderam, V. S. (1992). Experiments in concurrent stochastic simulation: The EcliPSe paradigm. *Journal of Parallel and Distributed Computing*, *14*(1), 66–84. doi:10.1016/0743-7315(92)90098-8

Rennard, J. P. (2000). Introduction to genetic algorithms a reference book. Academic Press.

Ren, T., & Xu, Y. (2014). Analysis of the New Features of OpenFlow 1.4. In *2nd International Conference on Information, Electronics and Computer* (pp. 73-77). doi:10.2991/icieac-14.2014.17

Research Report. (2013). *State of Social Media Span*. Retrieved July 12, from www.nexgate.com

Reynolds, P., Killian, C., Wiener, J. L., Mogul, J. C., Shah, M. A., & Vahdat, A. (2006). Pip: detecting the unexpected in distributed systems. In *Proceedings of the 3rd Symposium on Networked Systems Design and Implementation (NSDI)*, (pp. 1–14). NSDI.

Rimal, B. P., Choi, E., & Lumb, I. (2009, August). A taxonomy and survey of cloud computing systems. In *INC, IMS and IDC, 2009. NCM'09. Fifth International Joint Conference on* (pp. 44-51). Ieee. doi:10.1109/NCM.2009.218

Rivera, J., & van der Meulen, R. (2014). *Gartner Says the Internet of Things Will Transform the Data Center*. Retrieved August 05, 2014, from http://www.gartner.com/newsroom/id/2684915

Roberts, J. C. (2007, July). State of the art: Coordinated & multiple views in exploratory visualization. In *Coordinated and Multiple Views in Exploratory Visualization, 2007. CMV'07. Fifth International Conference on* (pp. 61-71). IEEE.

Robins, G. (2009). Social Networks, Exponential Random Graph (P*) Models for Computational Complexity: Theory, Techniques, and Applications. New York: Springer.

Robins, G., Pattison, P., Kalish, Y., & Lusher, D. (2007). An introduction to exponential random graph (p*) models for social networks. *Social Networks*, *29*(2), 173–191. doi:10.1016/j.socnet.2006.08.002

Robins, K. (1992). *Understanding Information: Business, Technology and Geography*. London: Belhaven Press.

Rocha, L. M. (2001). TalkMine: A soft computing approach to adaptive knowledge recommendation. In Soft Computing Agents: New Trends for Designing Autonomous Systems (pp. 89-116). Springer. doi:10.1007/978-3-7908-1815-4_4

Rodda, C. (2004). *'The Five Stages of Economic Growth'*. Retrieved from: http://www.cr1.dircon.co.uk/TB/5/fivestages.htm

Rodríguez, E., Rodríguez, V., Carreras, A., & Delgado, J. (2009). A Digital Rights Management approach to privacy in online social networks. In *Workshop on Privacy and Protection in Web-based Social Networks (within ICAIL'09), Barcelona*.

Ropo, M., Westerholm, J., & Dongarra, J. (Eds.). (2009). *Recent Advances in Parallel Virtual Machine and Message Passing Interface: 16th European PVM/MPI Users' Group Meeting, Espoo, Finland, September 7-10, 2009, Proceedings* (Vol. 5759). Springer.

Rose, E. A., Gelijns, A. C., Moskowitz, A. J., Heitjan, D. F., Stevenson, L. W., Dembitsky, W., & Meier, P. (2001). Long-term use of a left ventricular assist device for end-stage heart failure. *The New England Journal of Medicine*, *345*(20), 1435–1443. doi:10.1056/NEJMoa012175 PMID:11794191

Roseman, D. (2003). 'The Digital Divide and the Competitive Nature of ISPs: Part 1 – Issues and Arguments'. *Info: The Journal of Policy Regulation and Strategy for Telecommunications*, *5*(5), 25–37. doi:10.1108/14636690310500439

Ross, P. L., Huang, Y. N., Marchese, J. N., Williamson, B., Parker, K., Hattan, S., & Pappin, D. J. et al. (2004). Multiplexed protein quantitation in Saccharomyces cerevisiae using amine-reactive isobaric tagging reagents. *Molecular & Cellular Proteomics*, *3*(12), 1154–1169. doi:10.1074/mcp.M400129-MCP200 PMID:15385600

Ross, T. J. (2010). *Fuzzy Logic with Engineering Applications*. John Wiley & Sons, Ltd. doi:10.1002/9781119994374.index

Rothermel, G., & Harrold, M. J. (1994). A framework for evaluating regression test selection techniques. In *Proceedings of the 16th international conference on Software engineering* (pp. 201 – 210). Academic Press.

Rowe, N. (2012). *The Big Data Imperative: Why Information Governance Must be Addressed*. Aberdeen Group Research Report.

Rubin, D. B. (1976). Inference and missing data. *Biometrika*, *63*(3), 581–592. doi:10.1093/biomet/63.3.581

Rumbaugh, J., Jacobson, I., & Booch, G. (2005). *The Unified Modeling Language Reference Manual* (2nd Ed.). Pearson Education Inc. Retrieved August 10, 2013, from https://www.utdallas.edu/~chung/Fujitsu/UML_2.0/Rumbaugh--UML_2.0_Reference_CD.pdf

Rus, S., Rauchwerger, L., & Hoeflinger, J. (2003). Hybrid analysis: Static & dynamic memory reference analysis. *International Journal of Parallel Programming*, *31*(4), 251–283. doi:10.1023/A:1024597010150

Russell, S. J., Norvig, P., & Davis, E. (2010). *Artificial intelligence: a modern approach* (Vol. 2). Prentice Hall.

Russom, P. (2011). *Big Data Analytic, The Data Warehouse Institute (TDWI), Best Practices Report*. Fourth Quarter.

Rysavy, S. J., Bromley, D., & Daggett, V. (2014). DIVE: A graph-based visual-analytics framework for big data. *IEEE Computer Graphics and Applications*, *34*(2), 26–37. doi:10.1109/MCG.2014.27 PMID:24808197

S, Y., K, A., & J, S. (2011). Analysis of Web Mining Applications and Benefcial Areas. *IIUM Engineering Journal, 12*(2), 185-195.

Saenz, B., Artiba, A., & Pellerin, R. (2009). Manufacturing Execution System- A Literature Review. *Production Planning and Control*, *20*(6), 525–539. doi:10.1080/09537280902938613

Sagiroglu, S., & Sinanc, D. (2013). *Big data: A review.* Paper presented at the Collaboration Technologies and Systems (CTS), 2013 International Conference on.

Saleem, H. M., Hassan, M. F., & Asirvadam, V. S. (2011). P2P service discovery in clouds with message level intelligence. In *2011 National Postgraduate Conference - Energy and Sustainability: Exploring the Innovative Minds, NPC 2011.*

Samwald, M., Jentzsch, A., Bouton, C., Kallesøe, C. S., Willighagen, E., Hajagos, J., . . . Pichler, E. (2011). Linked open drug data for pharmaceutical research and development. *Journal of Cheminformatics, 3*(1), 19.

Santra, A. K., & Jayasudha, S. (2012). Classification of Web Log Data to Identify Interested UsersUsing Naïve Bayesian Classification. *International Journal of Computer Science Issues, 9*(1), 381–387.

Sasaki, Y. (2007). *The truth of the F-measure.* Teach Tutor mater. Retrieved from http://www.flowdx.com/F-measure-YS-26Oct07.pdf

Sathi, A. (2012). *Big Data Analytics. Disruptive Technologies for Changing the Game. MC Press Online.*

Savas, O., Sagduyu, Y., Deng, J., & Li, J. (2014). Tactical big data analytics: Challenges, use cases, and solutions. *Performance Evaluation Review, 41*(4), 86–89. doi:10.1145/2627534.2627561

Schlinker, B. (2014). *Mininext.* Retrieved May 13, 2015, from https://github.com/USC-NSL/miniNeXT

Schneider, C. M., Belik, V., Couronne, T., Smoreda, Z., & Gonzalez, M. C. (2013). Unraveling daily human mobility motifs. *Journal of the Royal Society, 10*(84), 1742–5662.

Schneider, R. D. (2012). *Hadoop for Dummies* (Special Edition). Canada: John Wiley&Sons.

Schwiegelshohn, U., Badia, R. M., Bubak, M., Danelutto, M., Dustdar, S., Gagliardi, F., & Von Voigt, G. et al. (2010). Perspectives on grid computing. *Future Generation Computer Systems, 26*(8), 1104–1115. doi:10.1016/j.future.2010.05.010

Scullarrd, G. T. (1998). Test Case Selection using VDM. *Lecture Notes in Computer Science, 328,* 178 – 186.

Seiler, L., Carmean, D., Sprangle, E., Forsyth, T., Abrash, M., Dubey, P., & Hanrahan, P. et al. (2008, August). Larrabee: A many-core x86 architecture for visual computing. *ACM Transactions on Graphics, 27*(3), 18. doi:10.1145/1360612.1360617

Selwyn, N. (2002). *'Defining the 'Digital Divide': Developing a Theoretical Understanding of Inequalities in the Information Age'.* Occasional Paper No. 49. Cardiff University.

Seref, S., & Duygu, S. (2013). *Big Data: A Review: Collaboration Technologies and Systems (CTS), 2013 International Conference.* IEEE.

Sergiy, A. V., & Bowen, J. P. (2001). Formalization of software testing criteria using the Z Notation. Computer Software and Applications Conference, (COMPSAC2001) 25th Annual International.

Serrão, C. (2008). *IDRM - Interoperable Digital Rights Management: Interoperability Mechanisms for Open Rights Management Platforms.* Universitat Politècnica de Catalunya. Retrieved from http://repositorio-iul.iscte.pt/handle/10071/1156

Serrão, C., Dias, M., & Delgado, J. (2005). *Using Web-Services to Manage and Control Access to Multimedia Content.* ISWS05-The 2005 International Symposium on Web Services and Applications, Las Vegas, NV.

Serrão, C., Neves, D., Barker, T., & Balestri, M. (2003). OpenSDRM -- An Open and Secure Digital Rights Management Solution. In *Proceedings of the IADIS International Conference e-Society.*

Serrão, C., Dias, J. M. S., & Kudumakis, P. (2005). From OPIMA to MPEG IPMP-X: A standard's history across R&D projects. *Signal Processing Image Communication, 20*(9), 972–994. doi:10.1016/j.image.2005.04.005

Serrão, C., Rodriguez, E., & Delgado, J. (2011). Approaching the rights management interoperability problem using intelligent brokerage mechanisms. *Computer Communications*, *34*(2), 129–139. doi:10.1016/j.comcom.2010.04.001

Shadbolt, N., & Berners-Lee, T. (2008). Web Science Emerges. *Scientific American*, *299*(4), 76–81. doi:10.1038/scientificamerican1008-76 PMID:18847088

Shah, A. (2004). *'Poverty Facts and Stats'*. Retrieved from: http://www.globalissues.org/TradeRelated/Facts.asp

Shang, W., Jiang, Z. M., Hemmati, H., Adams, B., Hassan, A. E., & Martin, P. (2013). Assisting Developers of Big Data Analytics Applications When Deploying on Hadoop Clouds. *35th International Conference on Software Engineering (ICSE 2013)*. doi:10.1109/ICSE.2013.6606586

Sharma, P., & Kumar, S. (2011). An Approach for Customer Behavior Analysis Using Web Mining. *International Journal of Internet Computing*, *1*(2), 1–6.

Shastri, A., Patil, D., & Wadhai, V. (2010). Constraint-based Web Log Mining for AnalyzingCustomers' Behaviour. *International Journal of Computers and Applications*, *11*(10), 7–11.

Sheetal, & Shailendra. (2012). Efficient Preprocessing technique using Web log mining. *International Journal of Advancements in Research & Technology*, *1* (6), 59-63.

Sheikh, N. (2013). *Implementing Analytics: A Blueprint for Design, Development, and Adoption*. Morgan Kaufmann.

Sherwood, R., Gibb, G., Yap, K. K.-K. K., Appenzeller, G., Casado, M., McKeown, N., & Parulkar, G. M. (2010). Can the Production Network Be the Testbed? In R. H. Arpaci-Dusseau & B. Chen (Eds.), *9th USENIX Symposium on Operating Systems Design and Implementation, OSDI 2010, October 4-6, 2010, Vancouver, BC, Canada, Proceedings* (Vol. M, pp. 365–378). USENIX Association. Retrieved May 15, 2015, from http://static.usenix.org/legacy/events/osdi10/tech/full_papers/Sherwood.pdf

Sheshadri, H. S., & Kandaswamy, A. (2007). Experimental investigation on breast tissue classification based on statistical feature extraction of mammograms. *Computerized Medical Imaging and Graphics: The Official Journal of the Computerized Medical Imaging Society*, *31*(1), 46-48.

Shi, W., & Liu, M. (2011). *Tactics of handling data in internet of things*. Paper presented at the 2011 IEEE International Conference on Cloud Computing and Intelligence Systems (CCIS). doi:10.1109/CCIS.2011.6045121

Shmueli, G., & Koppius, O. R. (2011). Predictive Analytics in Information Systems Research. *Management Information Systems Quarterly*, *35*(3), 553–572.

Shroff, G. (2013). *The intelligent web: search, smart algorithms, and big data*. Oxford, UK: Oxford University Press.

Shukla, R., Silakari, S., & Chande, P. K. (2013). Web Personalization Systems and Web Usage Mining: A Review. *International Journal of Computers and Applications*, *72*(21), 6–13. doi:10.5120/10468-5189

Sigelman, B.H., Barroso, L.A., Burrows, M., Stephenson, P., Plakal, M., Beaver, D., Jaspan, S., & Shanbhag, C. (2010). *Dapper, a large-scale distributed systems tracing infrastructure*. Google Technical Report dapper-2010-1.

Silva, F., Dutra, I., & Costa, V. S. (Eds.). (2014). *Euro-Par 2014: Parallel Processing:20th International Conference, Porto, Portugal, August 25-29, 2014, Proceedings* (Vol. 8632). Springer.

Silverstone, R., & Haddon, L. (1996). Design and Domestication of Information and Communication Technologies: Technical Change and Everyday Life. In R. Mansell & R. Silverstone (Eds.), *Communication by Design: The Politics of Information and Communication Technologies* (pp. 16–44). Oxford: Oxford University Press.

Singh, H. & Sadegh. (1997). *Test Case Design based on Z and Classification Tree Method*. First IEEE International Conference on Formal Engineering Methods System technology research Berlin Germany.

Singh, S., & Singh, N. (2012). Big Data Analytics. In *Proceedings ofInternational Conference on Communication, Information & Computing Technology*, (pp. 1-4). Mumbai India: IEEE Conference Publications.

Sklair, L. (2002). *Globalisation: Capitalism and its Alternatives*. Oxford: Oxford University Press.

Skolnikoff, E. B. (1993). *The Elusive Transformation: Science, Technology and the Evolution of International Politics*. Princeton: Princeton University Press.

Slowinski, R., & Vanderpooten, D. (2000). A generalized definition of rough approximations based on similarity. *IEEE Transactions on Knowledge and Data Engineering*, *12*(2), 331–336. doi:10.1109/69.842271

Socher, R., & Lin, C. (2011). Parsing natural scenes and natural language with recursive neural networks. *Proceedings of the 28th International Conference on Machine Learning (ICML 2011)*, (pp. 129–136). http://nlp.stanford.edu/pubs/SocherLinNgManning_ICML2011.pdf

Socher, R., Karpathy, A., Le, Q. V., Manning, C. D., & Ng, A. Y. (2014). Grounded Compositional Semantics for Finding and Describing Images with Sentences. *Transactions of the Association for Computational Linguistics*, *2*(April), 207–218.

Social Media Update. (2013). Retrieved July 20, from http://www.pewinternet.org/2013/12/30/social-media-update-2013

Social Networks Modeling. (n.d.). Retrieved July 07, from http://columbiadatascience.com/2012/11/02/brief-introduction-to-social-network-modeling

Söker, H., Berg-Pollack, A., & Kensche, C. (2007). Rotor Blade Monitoring – The Technical Essentials. In *Proceedings of the German Wind Energy Conference (DEWEK '07)*. Bremen.

Sotto, L. J. (2013). *Privacy and Data Security Law Deskbook*. Frederick, MD: Aspen Publishers.

Sousa, T. B. (2012). Dataflow Programming Concept, Languages and Applications. In *Doctoral Symposium on Informatics Engineering*.

Soyata, T., Ba, H., Heinzelman, W., Kwon, M., & Shi, J. (2014). Accelerating Mobile-Cloud Computing. In Communication Infrastructures for Cloud Computing (pp. 175–197). doi:10.4018/978-1-4666-4522-6.ch008

Spence, R. (2001). *Information visualization* (Vol. 1). New York: Addison-Wesley.

Srivastava, J., Cooley, R., Deshpande, M., & Tan, P. N. (2000). Web usage mining: Discovery and applications of usage patterns from web data. *ACM SIGKDD Explorations Newsletter*, *1*(2), 12–23. doi:10.1145/846183.846188

Srivastava, J., Desikan, P., & Kumar, V. (2002). Web Mining Accomplishments& Future Directions.*National Science Foundation Workshop on Next Generation Data Mining (NGDM'02)*, (pp. 51-56).

Stankovic, J. A. (2014). Research Directions for the Internet of Things. *Internet of Things Journal, IEEE*, *1*(1), 3–9. doi:10.1109/JIOT.2014.2312291

Sterling, T. L. (2002). *Beowulf cluster computing with Linux*. MIT Press.

Stibel, J. M. (2009). *Wired for Thought: How the Brain is Shaping the Future of Internet* (pp. 105–115). Boston: Harvard Business Press.

Stiglitz, J. (1999). *'Scan Globally, Reinvent Locally: Knowledge Infrastructure and the Localisation of Knowledge'*. Keynote Address – First Global Development Network Conference, Bonn, Germany.

Stocks, P. A., & Carrington, D. A. (1993). A specification based testing framework. In *Proceedings of the 15th International Conference on Software Engineering.* Academic Press.

Stone, H. S. (1973). An efficient parallel algorithm for the solution of a tridiagonal linear system of equations. *Journal of the ACM, 20*(1), 27–38. doi:10.1145/321738.321741

Strover, S. (2003). 'Remapping the Digital Divide'. *The Information Society, 19*(4), 275–277. doi:10.1080/01972240309481

Stuckenschmidt, H., & Van Harmelen, F. (2004). *Information sharing on the semantic web.* Springer.

Sugumaran, V., & Gulla, J. A. (2012). *Applied semantic web technologies.* CRC Press.

Sujatha, M., & Punithavalli. (2011). A Study of Web Navigation Pattern Using Clustering Algorithm in Web Log Files. *International Journal of Scientific & Engineering Research, 2*(9), 1–5.

Sumathi, C. P., PadmajaValli, R., & Santhanam, T. (2011). An Overview of preprocessing of Web Log Files. *Journal of Theoretical and Applied Information Technology, 34*(2), 178–185.

Sundaresan, S., Teixeira, R., Tech, G., Feamster, N., Pescapè, A., & Crawford, S. (2011). Broadband Internet Performance : A View From the Gateway. *Computer Communication Review, 41*(4), 134–145. doi:10.1145/2043164.2018452

Sung-Hwan, K., Nam-Uk, K., & Tai-Myoung, C. (2013), *Attribute Relationship Evaluation Methodology for Big Data Security: IT Convergence and Security (ICITCS), 2013 International Conference.* ICITCS.

Su, Z., Ye, L., & Lu, Y. (2006). Guided Lamb waves for identification of damage in composite structures: A review. *Journal of Sound and Vibration, 295*(3), 753–780. doi:10.1016/j.jsv.2006.01.020

Tableau Software. (2006). Retrieved from http//www.tableausoftware.com

Tang, L., & Liu, H. (2010). *Communication Detection in Mining in Social Media for Data Mining and Knowledge Discovery.* Morgan & Claypool Publishers.

Taniar, D. (2009). *Progressive Methods in Data Warehousing and Business Intelligence: Concepts and Competitive Analytics.* Hershey, PA: IGI Global. doi:10.4018/978-1-60566-232-9

Tankard, C. (2012). Big Data Security. *Network Security Journal*, (7), 5–8.

Tankard, C. (2012). Big data security. *Network Security*, (7), 5–8. doi:10.1016/S1353-4858(12)70063-6

Tay, Y. P. (2012). *Getting Ready for Data Tsunami.* Kuala Lumpur: Nextwave Technology.

Tay, Y. P. (2013). *Nextwave Simplify Solution Description: Redefine the way we connect.* Kuala Lumpur: Nextwave Technology.

Technology, N. (2013). Mobile Connectivity Report 2013. Kuala Lumpur.

Telesca, L., Stanoevska-Slabeva, K., & Rakocevic, V. (2009). Digital Business. In *First International ICTS Conference, DigiBiz.*

Tellioglu, H., & Diesenreiter, S. (2013, October). Enterprise 2.0 in action: Potentials for improvement of awareness support in enterprises. In *Collaborative Computing: Networking, Applications and Worksharing (Collaboratecom), 2013 9th International Conference Conference on* (pp. 485-494). IEEE.

Tesler, L. G., & Enea, H. J. (1968). A Language Design for Concurrent Processes. In *Proceedings of AFIPS 1968 Spring Joint Computer Conference.* Atlantic City, NJ: AFIPS.

The 4V's of Big Data. (n.d.). Retrieved Apr 20, from http://www.ibmbigdatahub.com/infographic/four-vs-big-data

The Apache Software Foundation. (2014a). Apache Hadoop Project. *Hadoop*. Retrieved February 18, 2014, from http://hadoop.apache.org

The Apache Software Foundation. (2014b). Apache Mahout Project. *Mahout*. Retrieved July 18, 2014, from https://mahout.apache.org

The Apache Software Foundation. (2014c). Apache Cassandra Database. *Cassandra*. Retrieved February 18, 2014, from http://cassandra.apache.org/

The Big Data Landscape for Type of Application & Examples. (n.d.). Retrieved Apr, 15, from http://www.bigdatalandscape.com

The Open Networking Foundation. (2013). *OpenFlow Switch Specification, Version 1.4.0*. Retrieved April 10, 2014, from https://www.opennetworking.org/images/stories/downloads/sdn-resources/onf-specifications/openflow/openflow-spec-v1.4.0.pdf

Thereska, E., & Ganger, G. R. (2008). Ironmodel: Robust performance models in the wild. In *Proceedings of the 2008 ACM SIGMETRICS International Conference on Measurement and Modeling of Computer Systems*, (pp. 253–264). ACM.

Thomas, C., & Sheth, A. (2006). On the expressiveness of the languages for the semantic web — Making a case for 'a little more'. In S. Elie (Ed.), Capturing Intelligence (Vol. 1, pp. 3-20). Netherlands: Elsevier.

Thomas, S. A. (2000). SSL & TLS Essentials: Securing the Web (Pap/Cdr., p. 224). Wiley.

Toivonena, R., Kovanena, L., Kiveläa, M., Onnelab, J., Saramäkia, J., & Kaskia, K. (2009). A comparative study of social network models: Network evolution models and nodal attribute models. *Social Networks*, *31*(4), 240–254. doi:10.1016/j.socnet.2009.06.004

Toulouse, C., & Luke, T. W. (1998). *The Politics of Cyberspace*. New York, NY: Routledge.

Trending Topics. (2010). Retrieved Aug 13, from https://blog.twitter.com/2010/trend-or-not-trend

Tripathy, B. K., & Acharjya, D. P. (2010). Knowledge mining using ordering rules and rough sets on fuzzy approximation spaces. *International Journal of Advances in Science and Technology*, *1*(3), 41–50.

Tripathy, B. K., & Acharjya, D. P. (2011). Association rule granulation using rough sets on intuitionistic fuzzy approximation spaces and granular computing. *Annals Computer Science Series*, *9*(1), 125–144.

Tripathy, B. K., Acharjya, D. P., & Cynthya, V. (2011). A framework for intelligent medical diagnosis using rough set with formal concept analysis. *International Journal of Artificial Intelligence & Applications*, *2*(2), 45–66. doi:10.5121/ijaia.2011.2204

Trujillo, M. F. (2003). *'Does the Global Digital Divide Have Anything to do with Progress in Development?'*. Research Paper on Development Gateway: ICTs for Development (April 2003). Retrieved from: http://topics.developmentgateway.org/ict/rc/filedownload.do~itemId=307577

Truong, H. B., Duong, T. H., & Nguyen, N. T. (2013). A Hybrid Method For Fuzzy Ontology Integration. *Cybernetics and Systems*, *44*(2-3), 133–154. doi:10.1080/01969722.2013.762237

Tullsen, D. M., Eggers, S. J., & Levy, H. M. (1995, July). Simultaneous multithreading: Maximizing on-chip parallelism. In ACM SIGARCH Computer Architecture News (Vol. 23, No. 2, pp. 392-403). ACM.

Tveito, A., Langtangen, H. P., Nielsen, B. F., & Cai, X. (2010). *Elements of Scientific Computing* (Vol. 7). Springer Science & Business Media. doi:10.1007/978-3-642-11299-7

Ugander, J., Karrer, B., Backstrom, L., & Marlow, C. (2011). *The anatomy of the Facebook social graph.* Cornell University.

Uimonen, P. (1997). *'The Internet as a Tool for Social Development'.* Paper presented at the Annual Conference of the Internet Society. Retrieved from: http://www.i-connect.ch/uimonen/INET97.htm

Unger, H., Böhme, T., & Mikler, A. (Eds.). (2002). *Innovative Internet Computing Systems: Second International Workshop, IICS 2002: Proceedings.* Springer-Verlag.

United Nations Development Programme. (2001). *Human Development Report (1996-2001).* Retrieved from: http://hdr.undp.org/reports/view_reports.cfm?type=1

Vajteršic, M., Zinterhof, P., & Trobec, R. (2009). *Overview–Parallel Computing: Numerics, Applications, and Trends* (pp. 1–42). Springer London.

Valera, M., & Rathod, K. (2013). A novel approach of Mining Frequent Sequential Patterns from Customized Web Log Preprocessing. *International Journal of Engineering Research and Applications*, *3*(1), 369–380.

Van Dijk, M., Gentry, C., Halevi, S., & Vaikuntanathan, V. (2010). Fully homomorphic encryption over the integers. In Advances in Cryptology– EUROCRYPT '10 (pp. 24–43). doi:10.1007/978-3-642-13190-5_2

Van Heijenoort, J. (1977). *From Frege to Gödel: a source book in mathematical logic, 1879-1931* (Vol. 9). Harvard University Press.

Vandervalk, B. P., McCarthy, E. L., & Wilkinson, M. D. (2013). *SHARE: A Web Service Based Framework for Distributed Querying and Reasoning on the Semantic Web.* Retrieved from http://arxiv.org/abs/1305.4455

Vandervalk, B., McCarthy, E. L., & Wilkinson, M. (2009). SHARE: A Semantic Web Query Engine for Bioinformatics. In A. Gómez-Pérez, Y. Yu, & Y. Ding (Eds.), *The Semantic Web* (Vol. 5926, pp. 367–369). New York, NY: Springer Berlin Heidelberg. doi:10.1007/978-3-642-10871-6_27

Vavliakis, K. N., Symeonidis, A. L., Karagiannis, G. T., & Mitkas, P. A. (2011). An integrated framework for enhancing the semantic transformation, editing and querying of relational databases. *Expert Systems with Applications*, *38*(4), 3844–3856. doi:10.1016/j.eswa.2010.09.045

Venner, J. (2009). *Pro Hadoop.* Apress. doi:10.1007/978-1-4302-1943-9

Vera-Baquero, A., Colomo-Palacios, R., & Molloy, O. (2013). Business process analytics using a big data approach. *IT Professional*, *15*(6), 29–35. doi:10.1109/MITP.2013.60

Villars, R. L., Olofson, C. W., & Eastwood, M. (2011). *Big data: What it is and why you should care.* White Paper, IDC.

Vissicchio, S., Vanbever, L., & Bonaventure, O. (2014). Opportunities and research challenges of hybrid software defined networks. *Computer Communication Review*, *44*(2), 70–75. doi:10.1145/2602204.2602216

Von Laszewski, G. (2002, January). Grid computing: Enabling a vision for collaborative research. In *Applied Parallel Computing* (pp. 37–52). Springer Berlin Heidelberg. doi:10.1007/3-540-48051-X_4

Wade, R. H. (2002). 'Bridging the Digital Divide: New Route to Development or New Form of Dependency?'. *Global Governance*, *8*(4), 443–466.

Wadge, W. W., & Ashcroft, E. A. (1985). *Lucid – The Dataflow Programming Language.* London: Academic Press.

Waldrop, M. (2008). Big data: Wikiomics. *Nature*, *455*(7209), 22–25. doi:10.1038/455022a PMID:18769412

Wang, D., Pedreschi, D., Song, C., Giannotti, F., & Barabasi, A. (2011). Human mobility, social ties and link prediction. *KDD Conference*. doi:10.1145/2020408.2020581

Wang, H., Liu, W., & Soyata, T. (2014). Accessing Big Data in the Cloud Using Mobile Devices. In P. I. S. R. Hershey (Ed.), *Handbook of Research on Cloud Infrastructures for Big Data Analytics* (pp. 444–470). doi:10.4018/978-1-4666-5864-6.ch018

Ward, J. S., & Barker, A. (2013). *Undefined By Data: A Survey of Big Data Definitions*. Retrieved May 15, 2015, from http://arxiv.org/abs/1309.5821

Watts, D. J., & Strogatz, S. H. (1998). Collective dynamics of `small-world' networks. *Nature*, *393*(6684), 440–442. doi:10.1038/30918 PMID:9623998

Webster, F. (2002). *Theories of the Information Society* (2nd ed.). London: Routledge Press. doi:10.4324/9780203426265

Weka. (2013) Retrieved from http://www.cs.waikato.ac.nz/ml/weka/

White, T. (2012). *Hadoop: The definitive guide*. O'Reilly Media, Inc.

Williams, K., Li, L., Khabsa, M., Wu, J., Shih, P., & Giles, C. L. (2014). *A web service for scholarly big data information extraction*. In *Proceeding of the 2014 IEEE International Conference on Web Services (ICWS)*, (pp. 105 – 112). Anchorage, AK: IEEE. doi:10.1109/ICWS.2014.27

Wireless Broadband Alliance. (2011). *Industry Report: Global Developments in Public Wi-Fi*. Author.

Wookcock, J. & Davies. (1998). *Using Z, specification, refinement and proof*. Academic Press.

Woolgar, S. (2002). *Virtual Society? Technology, Cyberbole and Reality*. Oxford: Oxford University Press.

World Bank. (2002). *'The Networking Revolution: Opportunities and Challenges for Developing Countries'*. InfoDev Working Paper.

World Wind Energy Association. (2012). *World wind energy report*. Bonn: WWEA.

Xindong, W., Xingquan, Z., Gong-Qing, W., & Wei, D. (2014). Data mining with big data. *Knowledge and Data Engineering. IEEE Transactions on*, *26*(1), 97–107.

Xindong, W., Xingquan, Z., Gong-Qing, W., & Wei, D. (2014).Data Mining with Big Data. *IEEE Transactions on Knowledge and Data Engineering*, *26*(1), 97–107.

Xu, L., Dias, M., & Richardson, D. (2004). Generating regression tests via model checking. In *Proceedings of the 28th Annual International Computer Software and Applications Conference* (COMPSAC'04) (vol. 1, pp. 336 – 341). Academic Press.

Xu, W., Huang, L., Fox, A., Patterson, D., & Jordan, M. I. (2009). Detecting large-scale system problems by mining console logs. In *Proceedings of the ACM 22nd Symposium on Operating Systems Principles (SOSP'09)*, (pp. 117–132). ACM. doi:10.1145/1629575.1629587

Yang, Z., Yuan, N. J., Xie, X., Lian, D., Rui, Y., & Zhou, T. (2014). Indigenization of Urban Mobility. *arXiv preprint arXiv:1405.7769*.

Yang, L. T., & Guo, M. (2005). *High-performance computing: paradigm and infrastructure* (Vol. 44). John Wiley & Sons. doi:10.1002/0471732710

Yao, Y. Y. (2000). Information tables with neighborhood semantics. In Data Mining and Knowledge Discovery: Theory, Tools, and Technology (pp. 108-116). Society for Optical Engineering.

Yao, Y. Y., & Sai, Y. (2001). Mining ordering rules using rough set theory. *Bulletin of International Rough Set Society*, *5*, 99–106.

Yeo, S. S., Park, J. J. J. H., Yang, L. T., & Hsu, C. H. (Eds.). (2010). *Algorithms and Architectures for Parallel Processing: 10th International Conference, ICA3PP 2010, Busan, Korea, May 21-23, 2010. Proceedings* (Vol. 6081). Springer.

Yiakoumis, Y., Yap, K.-K., Katti, S., Parulkar, G., & McKeown, N. (2011). Slicing home networks. In *Proceedings of the 2nd ACM SIGCOMM workshop on Home networks - HomeNets '11* (pp. 1-6). doi:10.1145/2018567.2018569

York, J., & Pendharkar, P. C. (2004). Human–computer interaction issues for mobile computing in a variable work context. *International Journal of Human-Computer Studies*, *60*(5), 771–797. doi:10.1016/j.ijhcs.2003.07.004

Yu, S., Zhou, W., & Wu, Y. (2002, October). Research on network anycast. In *Algorithms and Architectures for Parallel Processing, 2002. Proceedings. Fifth International Conference on* (pp. 154-161). IEEE.

Yu, L. (2011). *A Developer's Guide to the Semantic Web*. New York, NY: Springer. doi:10.1007/978-3-642-15970-1

Zadeh, L. A. (1965). Fuzzy sets. *Information and Control*, *8*(3), 338–353. doi:10.1016/S0019-9958(65)90241-X

Zadeh, L. A. (2004). A Note on Web Intelligence, World Knowledge and Fuzzy Logic. *Data & Knowledge Engineering*, *50*(3), 291–304. doi:10.1016/j.datak.2004.04.001

Zafarani, R., Abbasi, M., & Liu, H. (2014). *Social Media Mining: An Introduction*. Cambridge: Cambridge University Press. doi:10.1017/CBO9781139088510

Zaharia, M., Chowdhury, M., Das, T., Dave, A., Ma, J., McCauley, M., . . . Stoica, I. (2012). *Resilient distributed datasets: a fault-tolerant abstraction for in-memory cluster computing*. Paper presented at the 9th USENIX conference on Networked Systems Design and Implementation, San Jose, CA.

Zhao, G., Rong, C., Jaatun, M. G., & Sandnes, F. E. (2010, June). Deployment models: Towards eliminating security concerns from cloud computing. In *High Performance Computing and Simulation (HPCS), 2010 International Conference on* (pp. 189-195). IEEE.

Zhao, J., & Boley, H. (2010). Knowledge Representation and Reasoning in Norm-Parameterized Fuzzy Description Logics. In *Canadian Semantic Web* (pp. 27–53). Springer. doi:10.1007/978-1-4419-7335-1_2

Zhao, J., Wang, L., Tao, J., Chen, J., Sun, W., Ranjan, R., & Georgakopoulos, D. et al. (2014). A security framework in G-Hadoop for big data computing across distributed Cloud data centres. *Journal of Computer and System Sciences*, *80*(5), 994–1007. doi:10.1016/j.jcss.2014.02.006

Zheng, W., Wang, B., & Wu, Y. (2010, July). Task partition comparison between multi-core system and GPU. In ChinaGrid Conference (ChinaGrid), 2010 Fifth Annual (pp. 175-182). IEEE. doi:10.1109/ChinaGrid.2010.17

Zhou, R., & Li, T. (2013). Leveraging Phase Change Memory to Achieve Efficient Virtual Machine Execution. In *International Conference on Virtual Execution Environments (VEE)* (pp. 179-190). doi:10.1145/2451512.2451547

Zhu, W., & Wang, F. Y. (2007). On three types of covering rough sets. *IEEE Transactions on Knowledge and Data Engineering*, *19*(8), 1131–1144. doi:10.1109/TKDE.2007.1044

Zibin, Z., Jieming, Z., & Michael, L. (2013), *Service-generated Big Data and Big Data-as-a-Service: An Overview: Big Data (Big Data Congress), 2013 IEEE International Congress*. IEEE Conference Publications.

Zikopoulos, P. C., Eaton, C., deRoos, D., Deutsch, T., & Lapis, C. (2012). *Understanding big data – Analytics for enterprise class Hadoop and streaming data*. New York, NY: McGraw Hill.

Zikopoulos, P., & Eaton, C. (2011). *Understanding big data: Analytics for enterprise class hadoop and streaming data.* New York: McGraw-Hill.

Zikopoulos, P., Parasuraman, K., Deutsch, T., Giles, J., & Corrigan, D. (2012). *Harness the Power of Big Data The IBM Big Data Platform.* McGraw Hill Professional.

Zin, A. N. M., & Yunos, Z. (2004). *'Computer Viruses: Future Cyber Weapons'.* National ICT Security and Emergency Response Center (NISER) Resource Paper. Retrieved from: http://www.niser.org.my/resources/computer_virus.pdf

Zoumas, C. E., Bakirtzis, A. G., Theocharis, J. B., & Petridis, V. (2004). A genetic algorithm solution approach to the hydrothermal coordination problem. *Power Systems. IEEE Transactions on, 19*(3), 1356–1364.

About the Contributors

Noor Zaman acquired his degree in Engineering in 1998, and Master's in Computer Science at the University of Agriculture at Faisalabad in 2000. His academic achievements further extended with a PhD in Information Technology at University Technology Malaysia (UTP). He has vast experience of 15 years in the field of teaching and research. He is currently working as a Faculty member at the College of Computer Science and Information Technology, King Faisal University, in Saudi Arabia. He has contributed well in King Faisal University for achieving ABET Accreditation by working as a member and Secretary for Accreditation and Quality cell for more than 7 years. He takes care of versatile operations including teaching, research activities, leading ERP projects, IT consultancy and IT management. He headed the department of IT, and administered the prometric center in the Institute of Business and Technology (BIZTEK), in Karachi Pakistan. He has worked as a consultant for Network and Server Management remotely in Apex Canada USA base Software house and call center. Dr. Noor Zaman has authored several research papers, and edited five international reputed Computer Science area books and has many publications to his credit. He is an associate Editor, Regional Editor and reviewer for reputed international journals and conferences around the world. He has completed several research grants and currently involved with funded projects in different courtiers. His areas of interest include Wireless Sensor Network (WSN), Network, Cloud Computing, Big Data, Mobile Computing, Software Engineering, Unix, and Linux.

Mohamed Elhassan Seliaman, Assistant Professor at the Department of Information Systems, College of Computer Science and Information Technology, King Faisal University, Saudi Arabia. He holds B.Sc. (First Class honors) in Mathematics and Computer Science from the Faculty of Mathematical Sciences, University of Khartoum, Sudan. He has taught at University of Khartoum in Sudan, King Fahd University of Petroleum & Minerals, and King Faisal University, Saudi Arabia. His research interests include Decisions Support Systems, Machine Learning, Computer simulation, supply chain management, operations and information management, operations research, information systems, applied statistics, and computer-human interaction. His research work is published in International Journal of Production Economics, Elsevier, Applied Mathematics and Computation, Elsevier, Transportation Research Part E: Logistics and Transportation Review, Elsevier, Journal of Quality Measurement and Analysis, Advanced Materials Research, and Advances in Decision Sciences.

Mohd Fadzil Hassan is currently the Dean of Centre for Graduate Studies, Universiti Teknologi Petronas (UTP), a private university fully owned by PETRONAS, the national Oil and Gas Company of Malaysia. His responsibilities include overseeing the development, management and quality assurance of all graduate level courses. Currently UTP offers 9 MSc (Coursework), 10 MSc (Research) and 10 PhD programs which has been accredited by the Malaysian Qualification Agency (MQA). Prior to the current appointment, he served as the Head for Computer and Information Sciences department from 2010- 2012. He joined UTP in 2001 and later promoted to the current position of Associate Professor in 2011. He has been responsible for the development of the Information and Communication Technology (ICT) & Business Information Systems (BIS) programs including curriculum design, facility development, quality assurance, student advisory, staff training & development, and R&D. He is an alumnus of the Malay College Kuala Kangsar (MCKK) and graduated in 1999 from the Colorado State University, USA with a BSc (*cum-laude*) in Computer Information Systems. He obtained his MSc in Artificial Intelligence in 2001 and PhD in Informatics in 2007 from the University of Edinburgh, UK. As a lecturer, he has taught many courses ranging from Structured Programming, System Analysis and Design, Software Engineering, Artificial Intelligence among others. His research interests are in the area of Artificial Intelligence, Multi-Agent Systems and Service Oriented Architecture (SOA). He is actively involved in research works focusing on these areas and has secured numerous research grants as a principal investigator namely FRGS, ERGS and Technofund from the Malaysian government. He is also actively involved with international collaborative research works particularly with universities from the Middle East and ASEAN region. He has involved in authoring more than 100 indexed publications.

Fausto Pedro García Márquez got the European Doctorate on Engineering at the School of Industrial Engineers (ETSII) of Ciudad Real, University of Castilla-La Mancha (UCLM), 2004. He received his Engineering Degree from University of Cartagena in Murcia, Spain in 1998 and Technical Engineer Degree from the Polytechnic University School at UCLM in 1995, and the degree in Business Administration and Management at the Faculty of Law and Social Sciences at UCLM 2006. He also holds the titles of Supper Technician in Labor Risks Prevention by UCLM 2000 and Transport Specialist at the Polytechnic University of Madrid, Spain, 2001. He is Senior Lecture (Full professor accredited) at UCLM, and Honorary Senior Research Fellow at Bimingham University UK. He has been Senior Manager in Accenture 2013/2014, Lecturer in Instituto Europeo de Postgrado since 2014 an Director of Ingenium Research Group.

* * *

Abubakr Gafar Abdalla holds B.Sc and master's degree in Computer Science from University of Khartoum, Sudan. He has been in the web development industry for more than five years. After four years of web developing, he went back to college to study towards master's degree in Computer Science where he got the opportunity to experience the web from a different perspective as a researcher. His notable interests include Web Engineering, Web Mining and Analytics, Web Usability and User Experience, and Big Data.

Faisal Abdullah is a student in his 8th semester of BS (Computer Science) in HIET, FEST, Hamdard University, Karachi. He has received Full funded ICT scholarship for BS program from ICTR&D Funds provided by the ministry of Pakistan. His fields of interest are Computer Science, programming tools and platforms, and Internet of Things.

D. P. Acharjya received his PhD in computer science from Berhampur University, India. He has been awarded with Gold Medal in M. Sc. from NIT, Rourkela. Currently he is working as a Professor in the School of Computing Science and Engineering, VIT University, Vellore, India. He has authored many national and international journal papers, and five books to his credit. In addition to this, he has also edited two books to his credit. Also, he has published many chapters in different books published by International publishers. He is reviewer of many international journals such as Fuzzy Sets and Systems, Knowledge Based Systems, and Applied Journal of Soft Computing. Dr. Acharjya is actively associated with many professional bodies like CSI, ISTE, IMS, AMTI, ISIAM, OITS, IACSIT, CSTA, IEEE and IAENG. He was founder secretary of OITS Rourkela chapter. His current research interests include rough sets, formal concept analysis, knowledge representation, data mining, granular computing and business intelligence.

Afrand Agah, in addition to her work on security in wireless sensor networks, Dr. Agah's scholarly interests include economical modeling of security protocols; security and trust in pervasive computing. She is PI for a grant from National Science Foundation for a proposal on security in Wireless Sensor Networks and security in mobile ad-hoc networks. Dr. Agah is recipient of several grants from the West Chester University College of Arts and Sciences, Office of Multicultural Faculty, and Faculty Development Committee at West Chester University. She is also Co-PI for a grant from Hewlett Packard for "Active Collaborative Learning Community Using HP Tablet PCs". She also served as a reviewer for a number of journals such as the Journal of Mobile Communication, Computation and Information; the International Journal of Network Security. In past she has also contributed as a reviewer for handbook of information security, and the Internet Encyclopedia, by John Wiley and sons.

Farooq Ahmad did his PhD in Computer Science from Harbin Institute of Information Technology, P.R. China. He is currently working as an Associate Professor, COMSATS Institute of Information Technology, Lahore, Pakistan.

Khawaja Tehseen Ahmed is currently serving as lecturer at Computer Science department, Bahauddin Zakariya University Multan Pakistan. Currently he is pursuing his PhD degree from department of Information Technology, University of Central Punjab Pakistan. His research interests include image processing, computational intelligence and cloud computing.

Usman Akhtar received the B.S degree in Information Technology from Bahauddin Zakariya University Multan. Usman is currently enrolled in M.S. degree in Computer Science from Air University Multan Campus. His main research interests include big data, clustering in very large data. He also writes term papers during his course work and finalizing his thesis work in big data mining based on computational intelligence and fuzzy clustering.

Tarig Mohamed Ahmed Al Hassan, Assistant Professor at the Department of Management Information Systems, College of Business Administration Salaman bin Abdulaziz University, Saudi Arabia. He holds B.Sc. (Second Class Level 1 honors) in Computer Science from the Faculty of Mathematical Sciences, University of Khartoum, Sudan. He has taught at University of Khartoum in Sudan, and King Faisal University, Saudi Arabia. His research interests include Decisions Support Systems, Data Mining, Programming, Databases, Distributed Systems, and Cryptography.

Adeel Ansari is currently doing his PhD in Information Technology from Universiti Teknologi PETRONAS, Malaysia. He completed his MPhil. in Software Engineering in 2011 and MBA-MIS in 2008 from Pakistan Air Force - Karachi Institute of Economics & Technology (PAF-KIET). He received his degree in BSc (Hons) in Computing with a First Class Honors from Staffordshire University, United Kingdom in 2006. His work experience includes one year as a Trainee Engineer at Siemens Pakistan, three years in Credit Consumer Risk Banking Group, as an Assistant Manager II, in Habib Bank Limited, and one year as a Consulting Associate at A. F. Ferguson & Co., involved within the audits of the IT infrastructures of different clients. Currently, he is teaching undergrads at UTP and doing his PhD research. His area of expertise is in Software development, Information systems, expert systems, programming languages, data mining, and statistical signal processing. His research interest include Seabed Logging using ICA, PCA, INFOMAX and related algorithms.

Seema Ansari is a PhD researcher at University of Malaga, Spain. She did her MS-CS/Telecommunication from University of Missouri, KC, USA and B.E. Electronic Engineering from NED University of Engineering & Technology, Karachi, Pakistan. She is Head of Electrical Engineering Department and Assistant Professor at College of Engineering & Sciences, Institute of Business Management. She has published many research articles in renowned international journals, participated in international & national conferences. She also contributed a chapter in a book titled: "Wireless Sensor Networks and Energy Efficiency: Protocols, Routing and Management" published by IGI GLOBAL, USA in Jan. 2011. She has over 27 years of experience in teaching, research and management positions at institutions of high repute. Her area of research interests are Underwater Communications, MAC and Routing Protocols, Seabed logging, and Wireless Sensor Networks for underwater communications.

Mehran Asadi obtained his Ph.D. degree in Computer Science from the University of Texas at Arlington. Dr. Asadi's scholarly interests include Machine Learning, in particular hierarchical reinforcement learning and security in mobile ad-hoc networks. Dr. Asadi has presented his research at several national and international conferences. Dr. Asadi is recipient of several grants from college of Arts and Sciences and office of multicultural faculty at West Chester University of Pennsylvania. He is also PI for a grant from Hewlett Packard for "Active Collaborative Learning Community Using HP Tablet PCs" and Co-PI for a grant from National Science Foundation in Wireless Sensor Networks and security in mobile ad-hoc networks. Dr. Asadi has been program committee member of several national and international conferences. He has been reviewer for the journal of information science and in addition, he has contributed as a reviewer for handbook of computer networks by John Wiley and sons.

Fernando Batista is a teaching assistant at the Lisbon University Institute (ISCTE-IUL) and researcher at the Spoken Language Systems Lab (L2F) of INESC-ID. He graduated (1997) in Mathematics and Computer Sciences from UBI, Portugal, received the Mestre degree (2003) in Electrical and Computer Engineering from Instituto Superior Técnico (IST), Lisbon, Portugal, and received his PhD (2011) in Computer Science and Engineering also from IST. He has been lecturer in Computer Science at ISCTE-IUL since 2000. From 1996 to 2000 he was a researcher at the Natural Language Processing Group of INESC, and in 2001 he became a member of the Spoken Language Systems Lab (L^{2}F) of INESC-ID. He is currently participating in several National and European projects. His current research covers spoken language processing, machine learning approaches, integration of different fields of natural language processing, and social network content analysis. He is member of IEEE and ISCA.

Elsa Cardoso is Assistant Professor, Director of the Master in Business Intelligence at ISCTE – University Institute of Lisbon, Portugal, and leader of the Business Intelligence Task Force of EUNIS (European University Information Systems organization). She is also a researcher at the Information Systems Group of INESC-ID Lisboa. She has a PhD in Information Science and Technology, with a specialization in Business Intelligence. Her research interests include business intelligence and data warehousing, big data analytics, performance management, balanced scorecard, business process management, applied to Higher Education, IT service management, and Healthcare.

Kamaluddeen Usman Danyaro is currently a PhD student and graduate assistant at the Department of Computer and Information Sciences, Universiti Teknologi PETRONAS (UTP), Malaysia. He obtained his MSc in Business IT from Northumbria University, UK. He received his BSc. in Mathematical Science from Bayero University, Kano. He started his PhD research in 2010. His research focuses on the development of Semantic Web in oil and gas sector. Danyaro's research interests include: Knowledge Representation, Semantic Web, Linked Data, Big Data, Web Intelligence, Computing Intelligence, Web 2.0, Fuzzy Logic Systems, Description Logics, Web Development and Knowledge Engineering. He is a reviewer in many conferences and Journals. He is also involved in many Web and software development projects.

Carlos Quiterio Gómez completed his studies in technical industrial engineer specializing in industrial electronics in the University of Castilla-La Mancha, in Toledo (Spain). Thereafter he realized the Industrial Engineering Master Degree, where he conducted a final year project which was related to the creation of an ultrasound system for research into new techniques for structural health monitoring and it was awarded by the Repsol company. He subsequently completed a Master in Engineering in Ciudad Real (Spain). Currently he is conducting his doctoral thesis in the area of signal processing of ultrasonic signals from structural health monitoring. During his Ph.D. he has also made a stay of five months in Cambridge, working with Brunel Innovation Center in several European projects.

Norman Gwangwava is a lecturer at the National University of Science and Technology (NUST), department of Industrial and Manufacturing Engineering. He submitted a PhD thesis in 2014 titled "Design of Novel Bending Press Tools Using Reconfigurable Manufacturing Principles" based on his research at Tshwane University of Technology (TUT), South Africa. He graduated with a first class in MEng Manufacturing Systems and Operations Management in 2011, and BEng honors in Industrial and Manufacturing Engineering in 2008 both from NUST. He has presented and published over 15 research papers at conferences and refereed journals. His research interests are in; Reconfigurable Manufacturing Systems (RMS), Cybe-Physical Production Systems (CPS), Collaborative Product Design and Closed Loop Life-Cycle Systems, Manufacturing Information and Database Systems.

Mehdi Hassan received his M.S. degree in Computer System Engineering from GIK Institute, Topi, Pakistan, in 2010 and he is currently continuing his Ph.D. studies at PIEAS, Islamabad, Pakistan. He is serving as a lecturer at Air University Multan Campus. His research interests are Image Processing, Data Mining and Machine Learning, Biomedical imaging and Classification.

Fiaz Hussain was awarded a PhD in the area of Computer Graphics from Brunel University. He has an MSc from the University of Nottingham and a BSc (Honours) from the Hatfield Polytechnic (now called University of Hertfordshire). Fiaz joined the Department of Computer Science & Technology in September 2001 and has led the creative technologies aspect of curriculum, as well being the Academic Director for over 30 undergraduate courses. In addition, Fiaz has been both BSc and MSc project co-ordinator for the department. He divides his professional time between teaching, research, employer links & opportunities and international work. Fiaz is currently Faculty Sub Dean and managing all aspects of international business for the Faculty of Creative Arts, Technologies and Science, including student recruitment and international partnerships.

Jafreezal Jaafar is the Assoc. Prof. and Head of Computer and Information Sciences Department at Universiti Teknologi PETRONAS, Malaysia. He is also active researcher at the university, in which his research areas include computational intelligence and human- computer interaction. He holds a Degree in Computer Science from Universiti Teknologi Malaysia (graduated in 1998) and Master of Applied Science in Information Technology from RMIT University, Australia (graduated in 2002). He obtained his PhD (Artificial Intelligence) degree from University of Edinburgh, United Kingdom in 2009. By extending his research interest in Fuzzy logic and Artificial Intelligence (AI) areas, he managed to secure a number of research grants.

Wajid Khan completed his master degree from University of Bedfordshire in 2007. Same year received research grant from EEDA and worked with University of Bedfordshire and Premier Connections on system automation in travel and transport industry, received further grant for a Phd in 2010 working on web 2.0 mash-up system for data analysis and information visualisation. Business analytic tool was extremely successful and helped commercial partner in boosting the revenue from £1mn to well over £4mn within two years. Currently Wajid Khan working as research and development consultant with various organizations based in London.

Amir Khwaja received his PhD degree in 2009 in Computer Science from Arizona State University, Arizona, USA. He received his MS degree in 1993 in Computer Science from Arizona State University and BE degree in Computer Engineering in 1989 from N.E.D. University of Science and Technology, Karachi, Pakistan. Dr. Khwaja worked in industry for 21 years. He was with Intel Corporation from 1993 to 2012 primarily working on CAD tools for chip package design and validation of XScale and Atom based SoCs for mobile products. He held various roles at Intel Corporation from senior software engineer to validation architect to senior engineering manager. He worked at Qualcomm from 2013 to 2014 as a validation architect and manager. Dr. Khwaja is currently working as an assistant professor in the College of Computer Science and Information Technology at King Faisal University, Al-Ahsa, Kingdom of Saudi Arabia. Dr. Khwaja also worked as a faculty associate at Arizona State University in 1998 and adjunct faculty at University of Phoenix from 1996 to 1997. Dr. Khwaja has served on the program committees and as session chairs in various conferences such as SEKE, IEEE COMPSAC, IEEE ISADS, Intel Software Development Conference, and Intel Design and Test Technology Conference (DTTC).

Lam Hong Lee received a Bachelor of Computer Science degree from Universiti Putra Malaysia in 2004, and a Ph.D. degree in Computer Science from the University of Nottingham in 2009. He joined Universiti Tunku Abdul Rahman, Malaysia since March 2009 as an Assistant Professor. He is currently an Associate Professor at Quest International University Perak, Malaysia since September 2013. His current research interest lies in improving text categorization using AI techniques, specifically Support Vector Machines. Besides this, he is also investigating on the implementation of data mining, pattern recognition and machine learning techniques in various kinds of intelligent systems.

M. S. Liew is a registered professional engineer. Shahir has spent more than 20 years in the engineering consulting industry as well as in engineering research prior to his engagement in the academia. He is one of the founding members of the UTP – PETRONAS Carigali Skill Group 11 Steering Committee, setting new directions for offshore research consultancies and academia-industry collaboration. He is also responsible for the management and leadership of the Offshore Engineering Centre's academic development, commercial growth and fostering of industrial collaborations. Initially centred on the core expertise of metocean and structural dynamics, he has developed the center into a multi-faceted research centre providing research and consultancies in the area of structural integrity, seismic, decommissioning, pipelines, geomatics, geotechnical and floating structures. Shahir's industrial initiatives span a wide spectrum from serving as the current Chairman of MOGSC Competency and Training Working Group, entrusted with the aim to develop core competencies of local oil and gas industry. He also acts as the Hon. Sec. of MOGSC and the Vice President of Malaysia Structural Steel Association (MSSA). On the technical side, he was formerly the Chairman of the Wind Engineering Development and National Standard for CIDB (MS1553) and is the Deputy Chairman of the current Technical Committee at SIRIM to develop the MS standards for Offshore Structures.

Alberto Pliego Marugan was born in Toledo (Spain) in 1988. He is Engineering from the University of Castilla-La Manacha, Ciudad Real, Spain, (June 2012) and Technical Engineer from the University of Castilla-La Mancha, Toledo, Spain, (June 2009). He worked as a consultor assistant in Everis Madrid S.L in 2012-2013. Nowadays he works as a researcher in the University of Castilla-La Mancha. His researching work is focused on Decision making, Fault detection and diagnosis, Fault tree analysis, Condition monitoring, and Wind energy. He has published papers in ISI journals, conference papers, and book chapters about these topics.

Samson Mhlanga is a Senior Lecturer and Chairman who holds a Masters Degree in Advance Manufacturing Systems from Brunel University, UK, and a B Eng in Industrial Engineering, NUST, Zimbabwe. Has edited 2 Conference Proceedings books, published over 18 journal papers (peer reviewed) and over 50 conference papers (peer reviewed) in regional and international conferences in the area of Manufacturing Systems focusing on Optimization.

Komal Mohanlal is currently pursuing her BBA degree from Institute of Business Administration. She plans to do her majors in Human Resource Management. Analyzing business trends in different fields interests her the most. Her research areas include application of data driven systems to workloads, understanding business intersection with data and applications of data in improving business strategies.

Radha Mohanlal is currently associated with the Institute of Business Management where she is faculty in the Electrical Engineering Department. She holds a B.E degree in Telecommunications from N.E.D University of Engineering and Technology. She is currently doing M.S (Telecommunications) from N.E.D University of Engineering and Technology. Her research projects include AODV Ad-Hoc Routing Protocols using remote access to a real test bed environment to perform real- time simulations and analysis. The simulations were performed using remote access to real test bed in NICTA (National ICT Australia). Her research interests are in the fields of Computer and Communication Networks, Networking Protocols, Information Theory as well as Wireless and Mobile Communications.

José André R. S. Moura received the BsC for Electronics and Telecommunications from Universidade de Aveiro, Portugal in 1989. From 1989 to 2000, he worked as a project manager at EFACEC Sistemas Electrónica. He holds a MsC since 2001 in computer networks from Universidade do Porto. Since 2001, he has been teaching in computer networks at Instituto Universitário de Lisboa (ISCTE-IUL), Lisboa. He is an assistant professor in the Department of Information Science and Technology at ISCTE-IUL. Jose holds since 2011 a PhD in managing the mobile access in heterogeneous wireless networks from Lancaster University, UK. His research interests include Wireless Networks, Game Theory, Software-Defined Networking, Virtualization, Cloud Computing and Big Data.

Khumbulani Mpofu is a specialist in Advanced Manufacturing, Expert Systems, Artificial Intelligence, Robotics and Mechatronics. He is continually endeavouring to acquire unequalled managerial acumen in both the technical and the business aspects of his engagements. Through the experience of independent research he has grown to have initiative, work with a team at a local institutional level, at the national consortium level and international level thus growing his interpersonal skills immensely. He has also established international collaborators. He describes himself as an effective player, self-starter, systematic thinker and worker, passionate about his responsibilities, a perseverant individual who is results oriented. In relating to a range of customers in his current position he is continuously perfecting the art of listening to the customer and with integrity and trustworthiness meeting their needs timeously.

Luís Miguel Martins Nunes received a PhD in Computer Engeneering from Faculdade de Engenharia da Universidade do Porto (FEUP), M.Sc in Electronics Engeneering and Computers, from Instituto Superior Técnico (IST) at Universidade Técnica de Lisboa (UTL), and graduated in Computer Science from Faculdade de Ciências da Universidade de Lisboa (FCUL). In 1997 he entered Instituto Universitário de Lisboa (ISCTE - IUL) where he coordinated and lectured several courses, mainly in the areas of Programming and Machine Learning. In the latest, he created in 2007 the Machine Learning course for the MSc in Computer Engineering, still under his coordination to this day. He is researcher at Instituto de Telecomunicações and ISTAR, having performed the same functions at INESC and ADETTI in the past. He has advised several trainingships and M.Sc. thesis, mostly in the areas lectured and he has participated in several national and international projects related to Machine Learning and Learning Agents.

Khine Khine Nyunt received her Bachelor of Science (Honors) Mathematics degree from University of Yangon, Myanmar in 1991, her Master in Computer Science from Institute of Computer Science & Technology, Yangon, Myanmar in 1995, and her second Master in Management of Technology from National University Singapore in 2008. She is currently holding a Lecturer (Part time) position at computer science and computing programs, University of Wollongong, Singapore Institute of Management Campus Singapore. Prior to that, she worked as a Lecturer at King Faisal University, Management Development Institute of Singapore, Curtin University of Technology, Multimedia University, Malaysia, and Institute of Computer Science and Technology, Myanmar with over ten years of teaching experience in course of Computer Science subjects. Her current research interests include Big Data, Knowledge Management, information retrieval, and data mining.

Youqin Pan received the BA in Management from Fudan University, Shanghai, China, in 1989. She received the PhD in Management Science from University of North Texas, Denton, TX, USA, in 2009. Currently, she is an Assistant Professor of operations and decision sciences at Salem State University. Her research interests include supply chain management, computer simulation, data mining, and financial forecasting.

Diego José Pedregal Tercero received his first degree in Economics from the Universidad Autónoma de Madrid (UAM, June 1991). IV M.A. in Public Finance and Economic Programming from the Institute of Fiscal Studies (June 1992). He completed his PhD in Economics in April 1995 from the UAM, from the Economic Analysis department. From September 1994 to October 1997 he held an Associate Research position at Lancaster University (UK) during a post doc. Ex-member of the Systems and Control Group of the Centre of Research on Environment and Statistics (CRES) at Lancaster University. He was assistant professor at the Universidad Autónoma de Madrid and Banco del Comercio staff (BBVA holding) from October 1997 until October 1999. He was professor in the Industrial Engineering Politecnic at the Castilla-La Mancha University since 2000, assistant professor since 2002, and full professor since 2009. His topics of interest include time series analysis, econometrics, state space modelling, dynamic system identification, and forecasting.

Javier Poncela received the M.Sc. degree in telecommunication engineering from the Polytechnic University of Madrid, Spain, in 1994 and the Ph.D. degree from the University of Málaga, Spain. He worked in Alcatel Spacio before joining the University of Málaga at the Communication Engineering Department. He has actively collaborated with multinational companies (Nokia, AT4wireless) on formal modeling and system testing in Bluetooth, UMTS and satellite systems. His actual research interests include methodologies for efficient development of complex communications systems, analysis of end-to-end QoS over heterogeneous networks and systems and models for the evaluation of QoE.

Vasaki Ponnusamy is an Assistant Professor at Quest International University Perak, Malaysia. She obtained her Bachelor of Computer Science and MSc (Computer Science) from Science University of Malaysia and her PhD in IT from Universiti Teknologi PETRONAS (UTP), Malaysia (2013). She is currently working on biologically-inspired computing, wireless sensor network and energy harvesting.

Edmond Prakash is an Academic, Author, Editor and Researcher. He was Professor in Computer Games Technology in the Department of Computer Science and Technology at University of Bedfordshire. As a visual computing expert, Edmond's research focus is on exploring the applications of visual computing across an unusually wide range of disciplines including engineering, business, science, medicine as well as in entertainment computing. He has worked on the design and implementation of walkthroughs of proposed structures, such as buildings, automobiles, and humans. In the process he has developed new algorithms for automatically generating object hierarchies, cinematic quality rendering, volume rendering, parallel computation, human modelling and animation for virtual environments. He has more than two hundred publications in academic journals, conferences and books and has worked extensively with companies including IBM, Microsoft, JP Morgan, and Silicon Graphics. He has also undertaken sponsored research funded by EPSRC and the industry. His first academic appointment was at the Supercomputer Centre at Indian Institute of Science as a Senior Scientific Officer. Subsequently, he was an Assistant Professor at Nanyang Technological University, Singapore, then as a Reader at Manchester Metropolitan University and now at University of Bedfordshire. He has an extensive international collaboration and has held visiting positions at NCSA, University of Illinois at Urbana Champaign, USA; CVC at State University of New York-Stony Brook, USA; Touch Lab, MIT, USA and Beijing Normal University, China.

Zahid Hussain Qaisar is currently working as Lecturer in the Department of Computer Science at King Faisal University, Alhassa, Saudi Arabia.

Raihan ur Rasool is currently serving at King Faisal University Saudi Arabia. He has been Associate Dean (Computing) at The National University of Sciences and Technology, School of EE & CS Pakistan. He earned PhD in Computer Engineering from Wuhan University of Technology China, under Cultural Exchange Scholarship and completed his Post doctorate at the University of Chicago, USA on prestigious Fulbright fellowship by the Department of State. He has numerous honors and awards to his credit, and best PhD student award is one of them. His research interests include computer architecture, virtualization technology, cluster and cloud computing, peer-to-peer computing, and network security. He has published in leading avenues of research like ISCA, HiPEC, CCGrid & ACM SIGARCH.

Aqeel-ur-Rehman received MS in Information Technology from Hamdrad University, Karachi, Pakistan in 2001 and BS in Electronic Engineering from Sir Syed University of Engineering and Technology, Karachi, Pakistan in 1998. He completed his Ph.D. degree in Computer Science from National University of Computer and Emerging Sciences, Karachi, Pakistan in 2012. He is associated with Faculty of Engineering Sciences and Technology, Hamdard University, Karachi, Pakistan as the Associate Professor and is the Chairman of Department of Computing. His current research interests include Sensor Networks, Ubiquitous Computing, Smart Agriculture, Context Modeling and Computer Networks.

V. Santhi received her B. Tech. (CSE), degree from Bharathidasan University in 1993, M. Tech. (CSE), degree from Pondicherry University in 2005 and Ph.D. (CSE), from VIT University in 2013. She has 16 years of experience in academic and 3 years of experience in Industry. She had served as Head of Department for more than eight years in Engineering colleges. She has received research award for publishing research papers in refereed Journals from VIT University 3 times consecutively. She has guided more than 80 graduate projects and more than 50 post graduate level projects. Her publications are indexed in IEEE Computer Society, SPIE Digital Library, NASA Astrophysics Data Systems and ACM Digital Library. She is a reviewer of IEEE Transaction on Multimedia Security, IEEE Transaction on Image Processing, IET – Image Processing, International Journal of Information and Computer Security. She is member of IEEE Signal Processing Society, Computer Society of India and senior member of IACSIT. She has published many papers in refereed Journals and in International Conferences. She took part in various administrative activities. She has Google citation H index as 4 and i10 index as 3. Currently she is holding a position of Programme and Division Chair in School of Computing Science and Engineering, VIT University.

Carlos Serrão is an assistant professor in the Department of Information Science and Technology at Instituto Universitário de Lisboa (ISCTE-IUL), Lisboa, Portugal. Carlos holds a PhD in Computer Architecture and Distributed Systems from Universitat Politecnica de Catalunya (UPC), Barcelona, Spain. His research interests include information security, public key infrastructures, secure access to multimedia content, access control, and rights management systems.

Arsalaan Ahmed Shaikh was born in Karachi, Pakistan, in 1985. He received a Bachelor's degree in computer science from the NED University, Karachi, Pakistan, in 2007, and master's degree in information technology from NUST, Islamabad, Pakistan, in 2014.

Manoj Kumar Singh is an Assistant Professor of Computer Science at Adama Science & Technology University, specializing in large-scale data management infrastructure and applications (these days called "Big Data"). Professor Singh works primarily in the Database (DB) and Data Mining and Networking Technology areas. He completed his PhD in Computer Science & Engineering in the field of Big Data and his research interests are in Big Data field. Dr. Singh's current work focuses on big data management and big data analytics. He wrote a number of books and is currently working on different research project ob big data platform.

Zaiyong Tang is an Associate Professor and Chairperson of the Department of Marketing and Decision Sciences at Salem State University. He obtained his Ph.D. in Management Information Systems from the University of Florida; an M.S. from Washington State University; an M.E. from Chengdu University of Science and Technology; and a B.E. from Chongqing University, P.R. China. Dr. Tang has over 40 refereed journal and conference publications. His work has appeared in INFORMS Journal on Computing, Information and Management, Simulation, Journal of Information Technology Theory and Application, Journal of Interactive Marketing, Neural Networks, Information Systems Management, and Computer and Information Science.

Yen Pei Tay has 13 years of industry experience at top Global Fortune 500 companies i.e. Motorola, Nokia and IBM. During his tenure, he gained valuable professional experience by holding various job roles in software development, systems integration, product management, pre-sales & consulting. With strong telecommunications background, he has in-depth knowledge in 3GPP standards development in 4G LTE and Access Network Discovery and Selection Function (ANDSF) technologies. Yen Pei received his Bachelor of Computer Science degree from Monash University in 2001 and Master of Business Administration from University of Manchester in 2013. With strong affection in continuing his post-graduate studies, his current research largely focuses on new disciplines of innovation namely Disruptive Innovation and Big Data. He is the founder of Nextwave Technology and also teaches Information Systems at Faculty of Business, Management and Social Sciences, Quest International University Perak, Malaysia.

Mazhar Ul Haq, Masters in IT from National University of Science and Technology and is currently working as Solution Architect at IBM GBS. He has recently published a Research Paper in the field of Information Extraction and Data retrieval and has 6 years of Industry Experience (Telco, Air Lines, and Image Processing).

Rafi Ullah was born in Khyber Agency FATA Pakistan on 30 July 1992. He has passed his metric and FSc. from his hometown Khyber Agency. He is a student in Hamdard institute of engineering and technology, FEST, Hamdard University, Karachi and is studying in 8th semester of BS computer science. He received Full funded ICT scholarship for BS program from ICT Ministry of Pakistan and is interested in computer programming and computer networks. He has 2 years of teaching experience.

Marco Villegas García received his MS in Computer Science from the Polytechnic University of Catalonia in 2013 after coming back from some years of data-mining jobs across industries. At present he works in OPTIMUS, a research project funded by the European Union's Seventh Framework Programme focused on the optimisation of operational reliability of large-scale industrial wind turbines.

Shefali Virkar, Department of Politics and International Relations, University of Oxford (UK). Shefali Virkar is a research student at the University of Oxford, UK and is currently reading for a D.Phil. in Politics. Her doctoral research seeks to explore the growing use of Information and Communication Technologies (ICTs) to promote better governance in the developing world, with special focus on the political and institutional impacts of ICTs on local public administration reform in India. Shefali holds an M.A. in Globalisation, Governance and Development from the University of Warwick, UK. Her Master's dissertation analysed the concept of the Digital Divide in a globalising world, its impact developing countries and the ensuing policy implications. At Oxford, Shefali is a member of Keble College.

Index

Information Resources Management Association

Become an IRMA Member

Members of the **Information Resources Management Association (IRMA)** understand the importance of community within their field of study. The Information Resources Management Association is an ideal venue through which professionals, students, and academicians can convene and share the latest industry innovations and scholarly research that is changing the field of information science and technology. Become a member today and enjoy the benefits of membership as well as the opportunity to collaborate and network with fellow experts in the field.

IRMA Membership Benefits:

- **One FREE Journal Subscription**

- **30% Off Additional Journal Subscriptions**

- **20% Off Book Purchases**

- Updates on the latest events and research on Information Resources Management through the IRMA-L listserv.

- Updates on new open access and downloadable content added to Research IRM.

- A copy of the Information Technology Management Newsletter twice a year.

- A certificate of membership.

IRMA Membership $195

Scan code to visit irma-international.org and begin by selecting your free journal subscription.

Membership is good for one full year.

www.irma-international.org

Printed in the United States
By Bookmasters